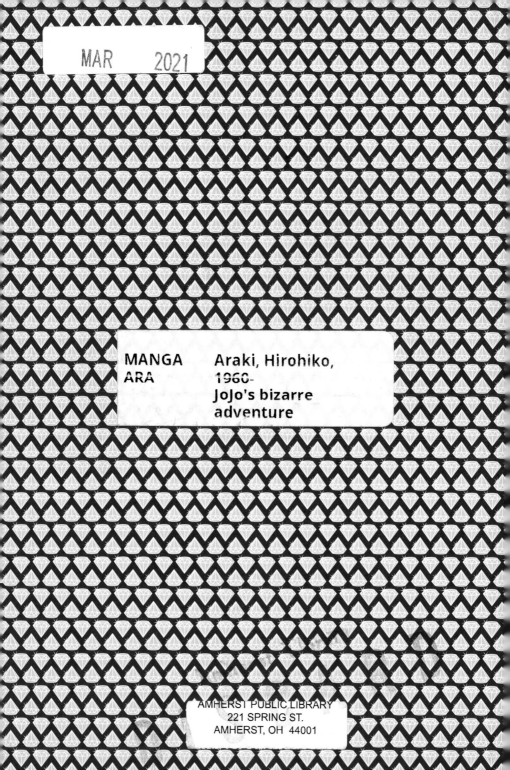

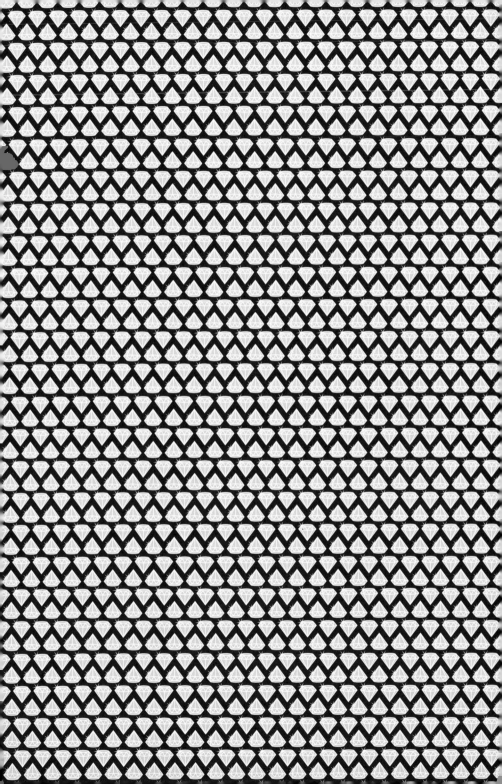

JoJo's BIZARRE ADVENTURE

HIROHIKO ARAKI

PART 4 ★ DIAMOND IS UNBREAKABLE

3

JoJo's

BIZARRE ADVENTURE

PART 4 ★ DIAMOND IS UNBREAKABLE

CONTENTS

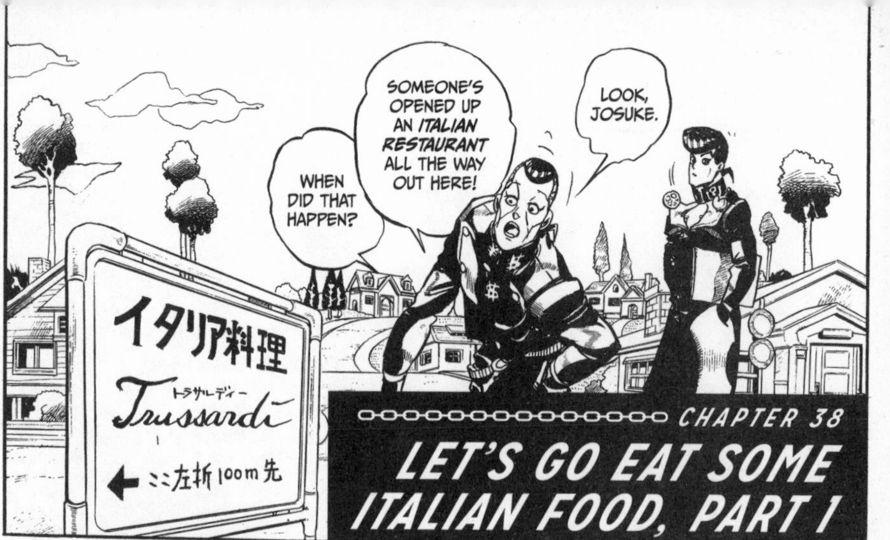
LOOK, JOSUKE.
SOMEONE'S OPENED UP AN *ITALIAN RESTAURANT* ALL THE WAY OUT HERE!
WHEN DID THAT HAPPEN?
イタリア料理
トラサルディー
Trussardi
ここ左折100m先
CHAPTER 38
LET'S GO EAT SOME ITALIAN FOOD, PART 1

SIGN: TRENDY'S ITALIAN RESTAURANT
← 100 METERS

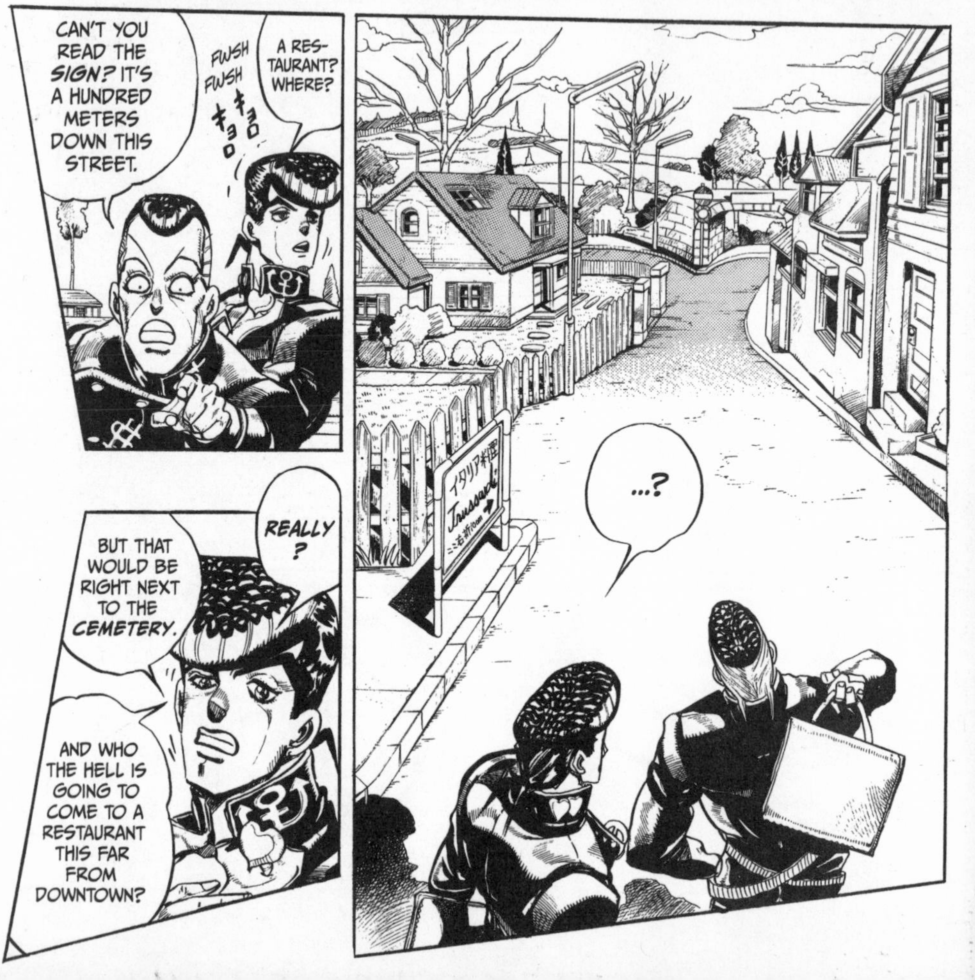
...?
A RES-TAURANT? WHERE?
FWSH FWSH
キョロ キョロ
CAN'T YOU READ THE *SIGN?* IT'S A HUNDRED METERS DOWN THIS STREET.
REALLY?
BUT THAT WOULD BE RIGHT NEXT TO THE *CEMETERY.*
AND WHO THE HELL IS GOING TO COME TO A RESTAURANT THIS FAR FROM DOWNTOWN?

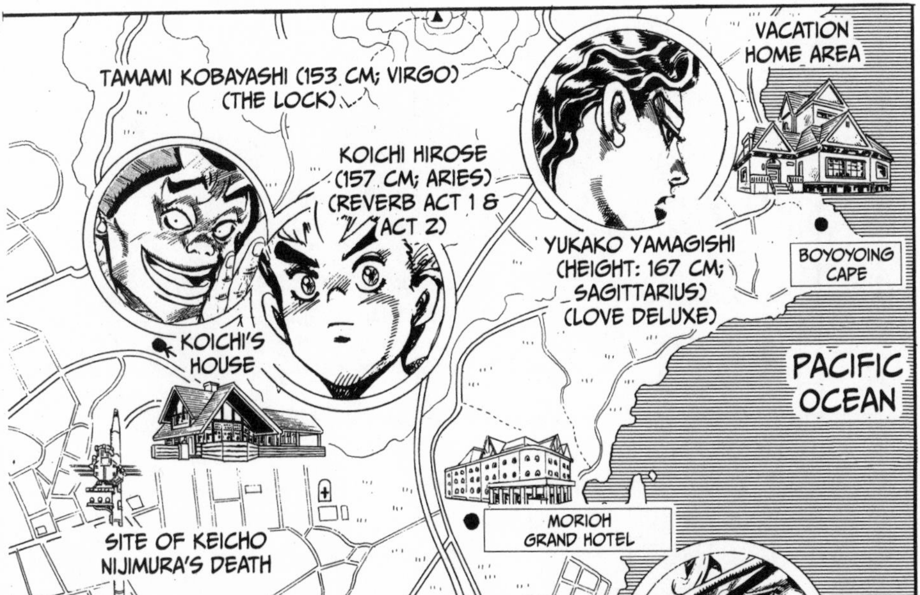
VACATION HOME AREA
TAMAMI KOBAYASHI (153 CM; VIRGO) (THE LOCK)
YUKAKO YAMAGISHI (HEIGHT: 167 CM; SAGITTARIUS) (LOVE DELUXE)
BOYOYOING CAPE
KOICHI HIROSE (157 CM; ARIES) (REVERB ACT 1 & ACT 2)
PACIFIC OCEAN
KOICHI'S HOUSE
MORIOH GRAND HOTEL
SITE OF KEICHO NIJIMURA'S DEATH
JOTARO KUJO (195 CM; AQUARIUS) (STAR PLATINUM)
ANGELO'S ROCK
JOSUKE'S HOUSE
OKUYASU NIJIMURA'S HOUSE

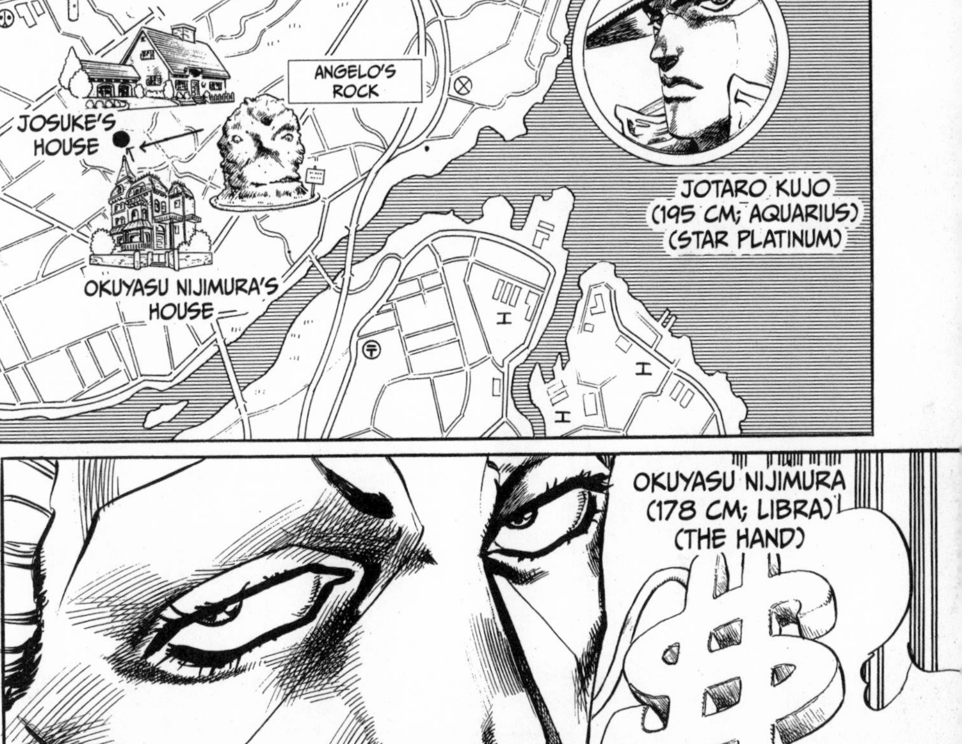
OKUYASU NIJIMURA (178 CM; LIBRA) (THE HAND)

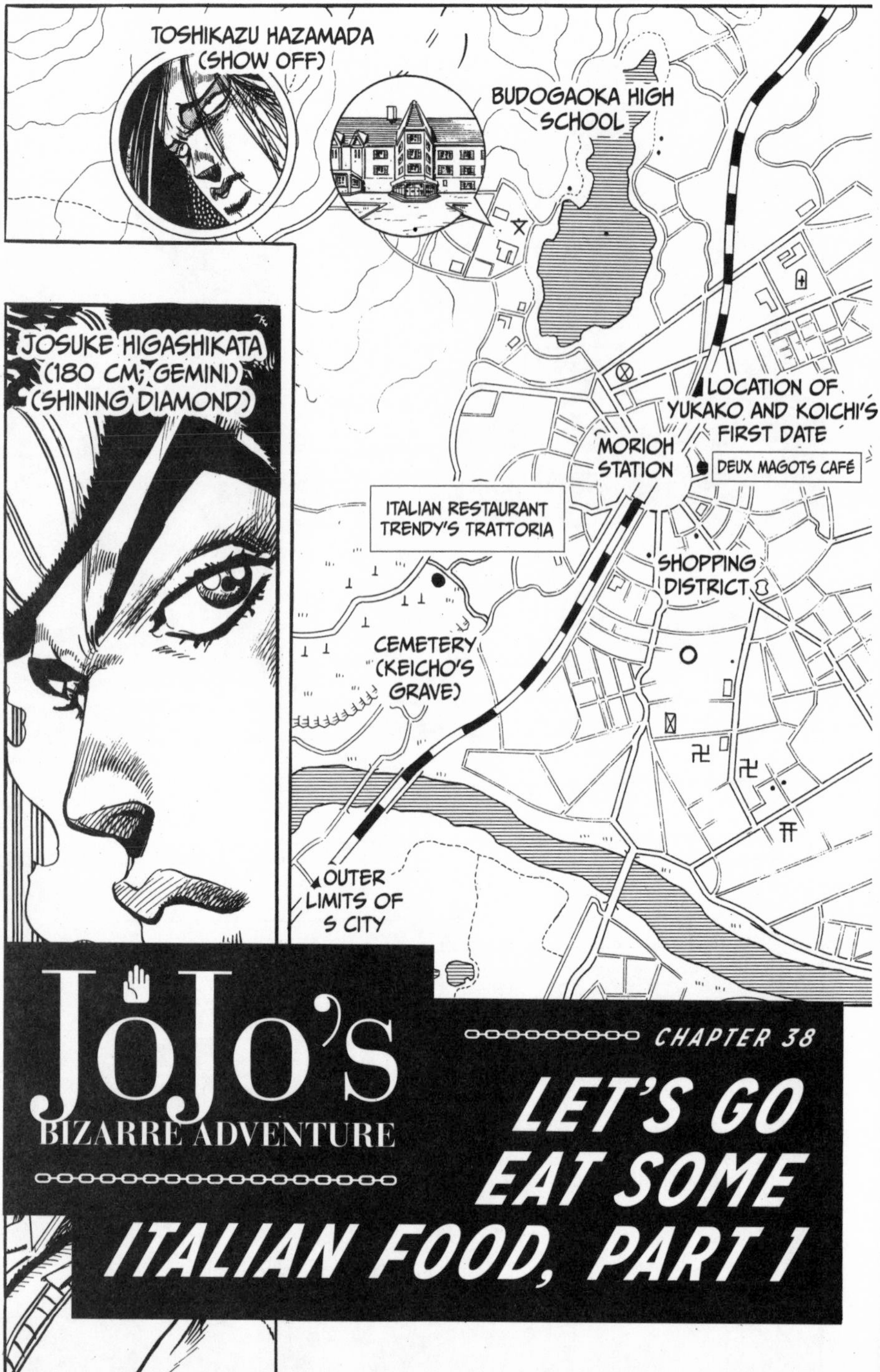
TOSHIKAZU HAZAMADA
(SHOW OFF)
BUDOGAOKA HIGH SCHOOL
LOCATION OF YUKAKO AND KOICHI'S FIRST DATE
MORIOH STATION
DEUX MAGOTS CAFÉ
ITALIAN RESTAURANT TRENDY'S TRATTORIA
SHOPPING DISTRICT
CEMETERY (KEICHO'S GRAVE)
OUTER LIMITS OF S CITY
JOSUKE HIGASHIKATA
(180 CM; GEMINI)
(SHINING DIAMOND)
JoJo's
BIZARRE ADVENTURE
CHAPTER 38
LET'S GO EAT SOME ITALIAN FOOD, PART 1

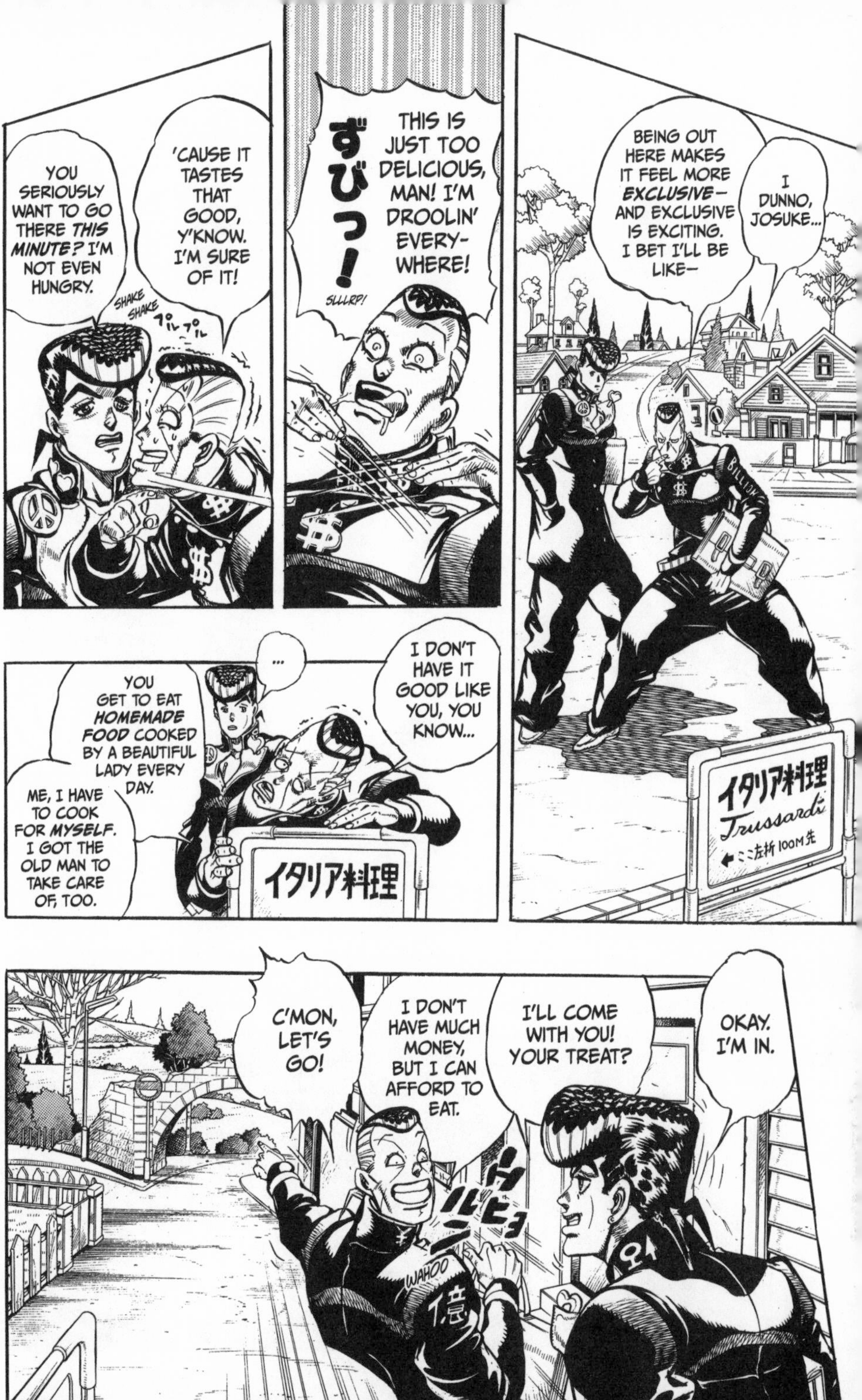
I DUNNO, JOSUKE...
BEING OUT HERE MAKES IT FEEL MORE EXCLUSIVE— AND EXCLUSIVE IS EXCITING. I BET I'LL BE LIKE—
イタリア料理
Trussardi
← ここ左折 100M先
ずびっ!
THIS IS JUST TOO DELICIOUS, MAN! I'M DROOLIN' EVERY-WHERE!
SLLLRP!
'CAUSE IT TASTES THAT GOOD, Y'KNOW. I'M SURE OF IT!
YOU SERIOUSLY WANT TO GO THERE THIS MINUTE? I'M NOT EVEN HUNGRY.
SHAKE SHAKE
I DON'T HAVE IT GOOD LIKE YOU, YOU KNOW...
...
YOU GET TO EAT HOMEMADE FOOD COOKED BY A BEAUTIFUL LADY EVERY DAY.
ME, I HAVE TO COOK FOR MYSELF. I GOT THE OLD MAN TO TAKE CARE OF, TOO.
イタリア料理
OKAY. I'M IN.
I'LL COME WITH YOU! YOUR TREAT?
I DON'T HAVE MUCH MONEY, BUT I CAN AFFORD TO EAT.
C'MON, LET'S GO!
WAHOO

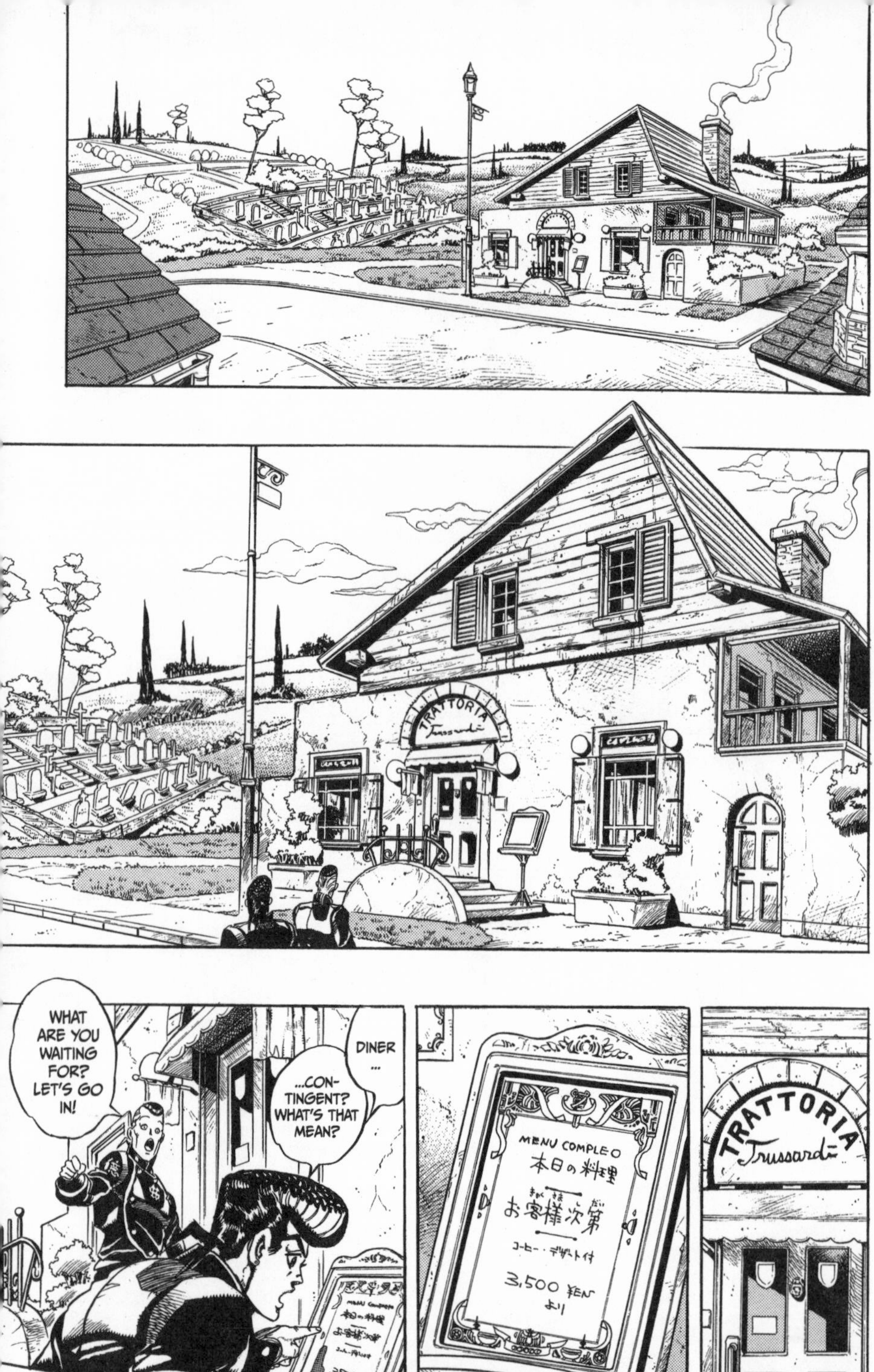
TRATTORIA
Trussardi
TRATTORIA
Trussardi
MENU COMPLEO
本日の料理
お客様次第
コーヒー・デザート付
3,500 YEN
より
DINER ...
...CONTINGENT? WHAT'S THAT MEAN?
WHAT ARE YOU WAITING FOR? LET'S GO IN!

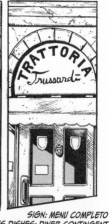

SIGN: MENU COMPLETO
TODAY'S DISHES: DINER CONTINGENT
COFFEE AND DESSERT INCLUDED - STARTING AT 3,500 YEN

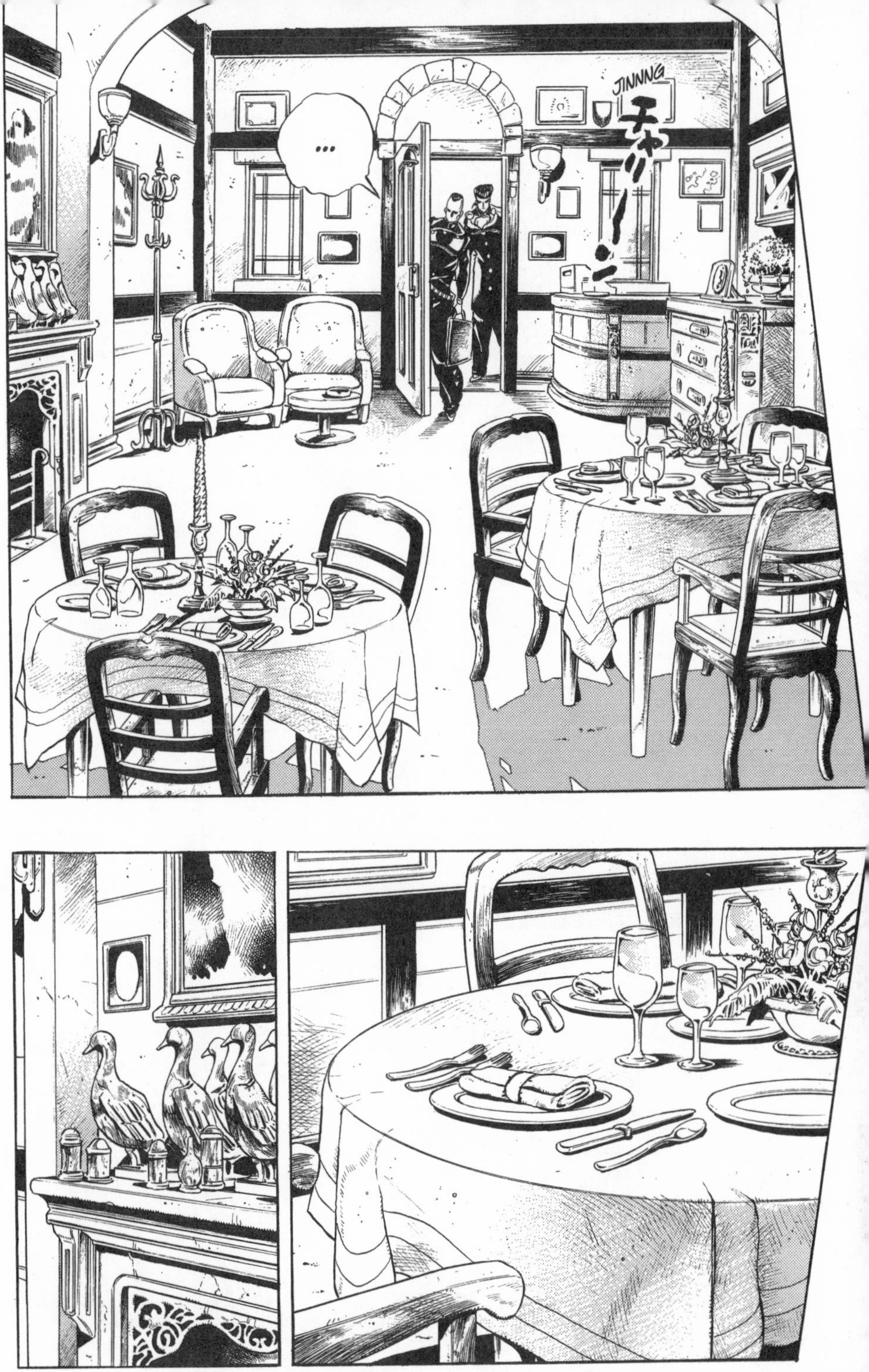
JINNNG
チャリーン
...

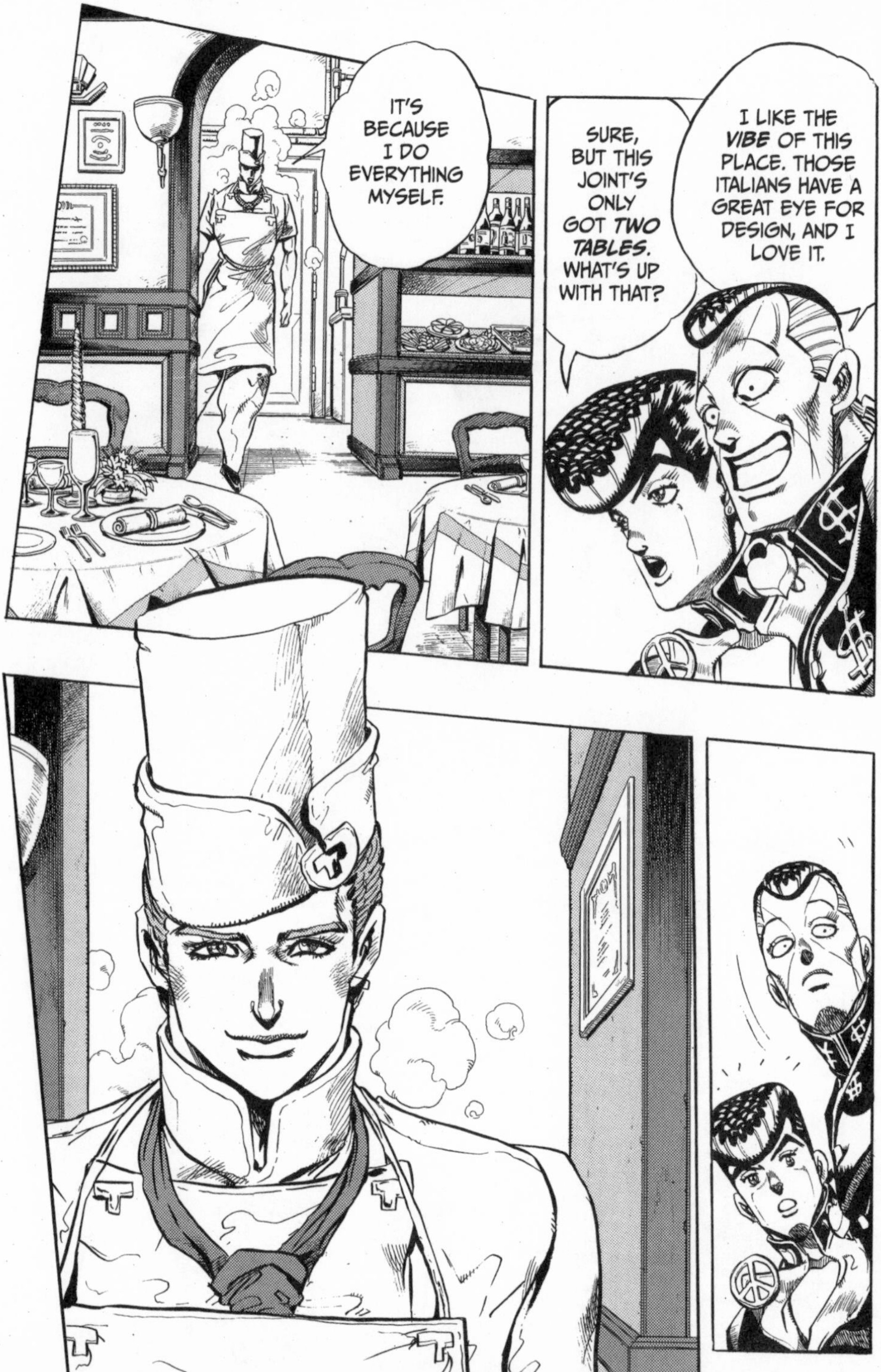
I LIKE THE *VIBE* OF THIS PLACE. THOSE ITALIANS HAVE A GREAT EYE FOR DESIGN, AND I LOVE IT.
SURE, BUT THIS JOINT'S ONLY GOT *TWO TABLES*. WHAT'S UP WITH THAT?
IT'S BECAUSE I DO EVERYTHING MYSELF.

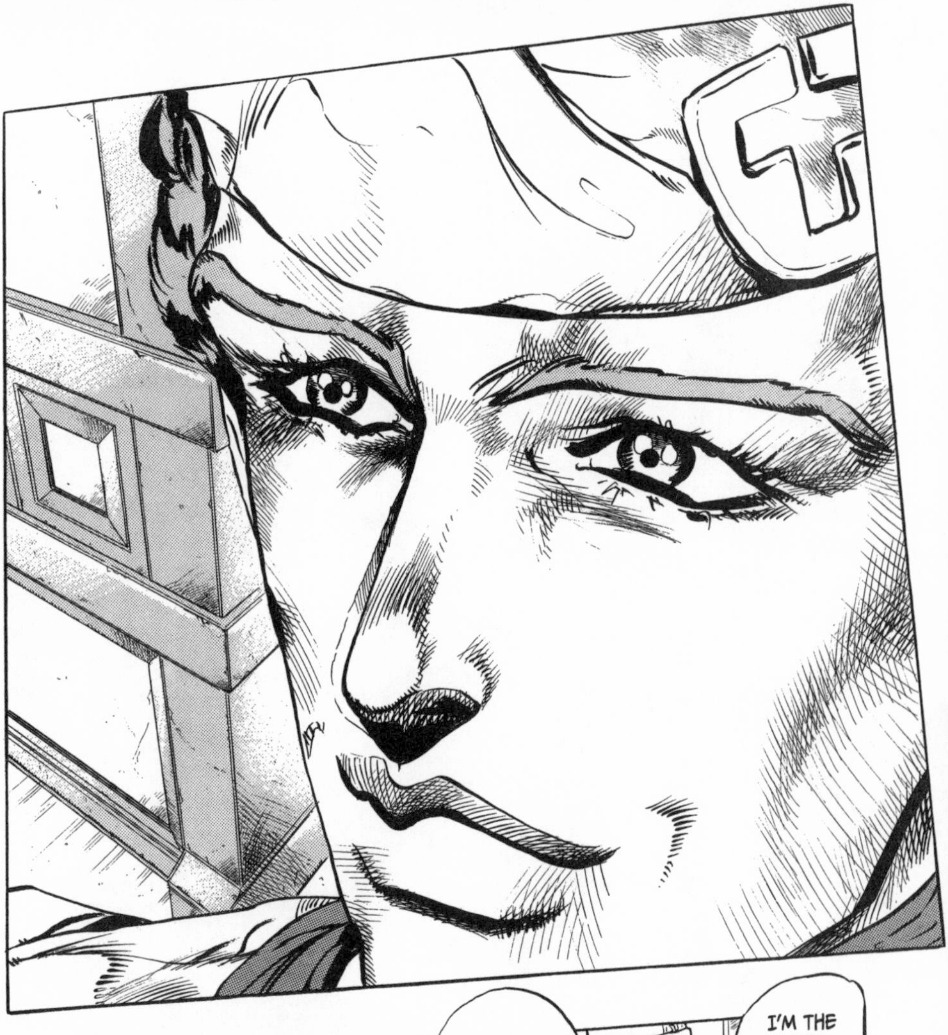

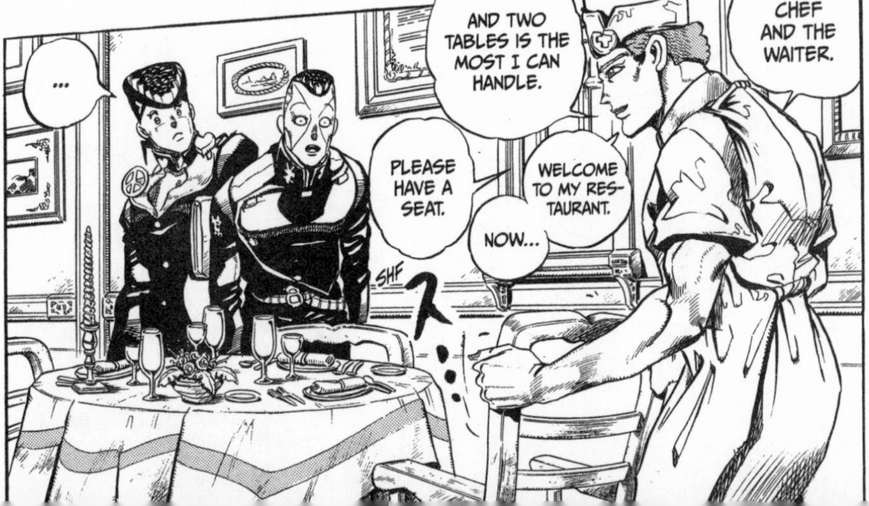
I'M THE CHEF AND THE WAITER.
AND TWO TABLES IS THE MOST I CAN HANDLE.
WELCOME TO MY RES-TAURANT.
NOW...
PLEASE HAVE A SEAT.
SHF
...

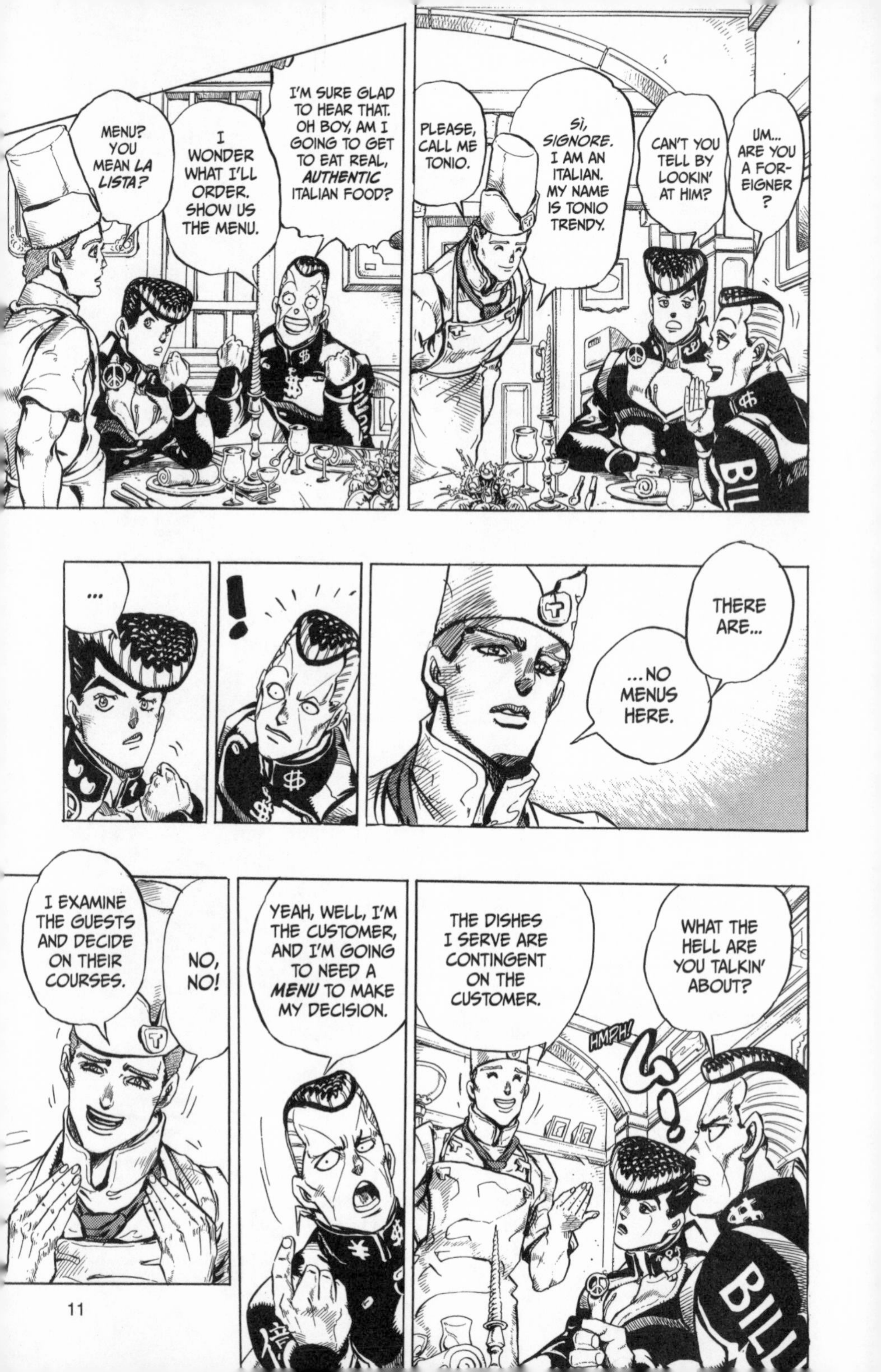
UM... ARE YOU A FOR-EIGNER?
CAN'T YOU TELL BY LOOKIN' AT HIM?
Sì, *SIGNORE.* I AM AN ITALIAN. MY NAME IS TONIO TRENDY.
PLEASE, CALL ME TONIO.
I'M SURE GLAD TO HEAR THAT. OH BOY, AM I GOING TO GET TO EAT REAL, ***AUTHENTIC*** ITALIAN FOOD?
I WONDER WHAT I'LL ORDER. SHOW US THE MENU.
MENU? YOU MEAN *LA LISTA?*
THERE ARE...
...NO MENUS HERE.
!
...
WHAT THE HELL ARE YOU TALKIN' ABOUT?
HMPH!
THE DISHES I SERVE ARE CONTINGENT ON THE CUSTOMER.
YEAH, WELL, I'M THE CUSTOMER, AND I'M GOING TO NEED A ***MENU*** TO MAKE MY DECISION.
NO, NO!
I EXAMINE THE GUESTS AND DECIDE ON THEIR COURSES.

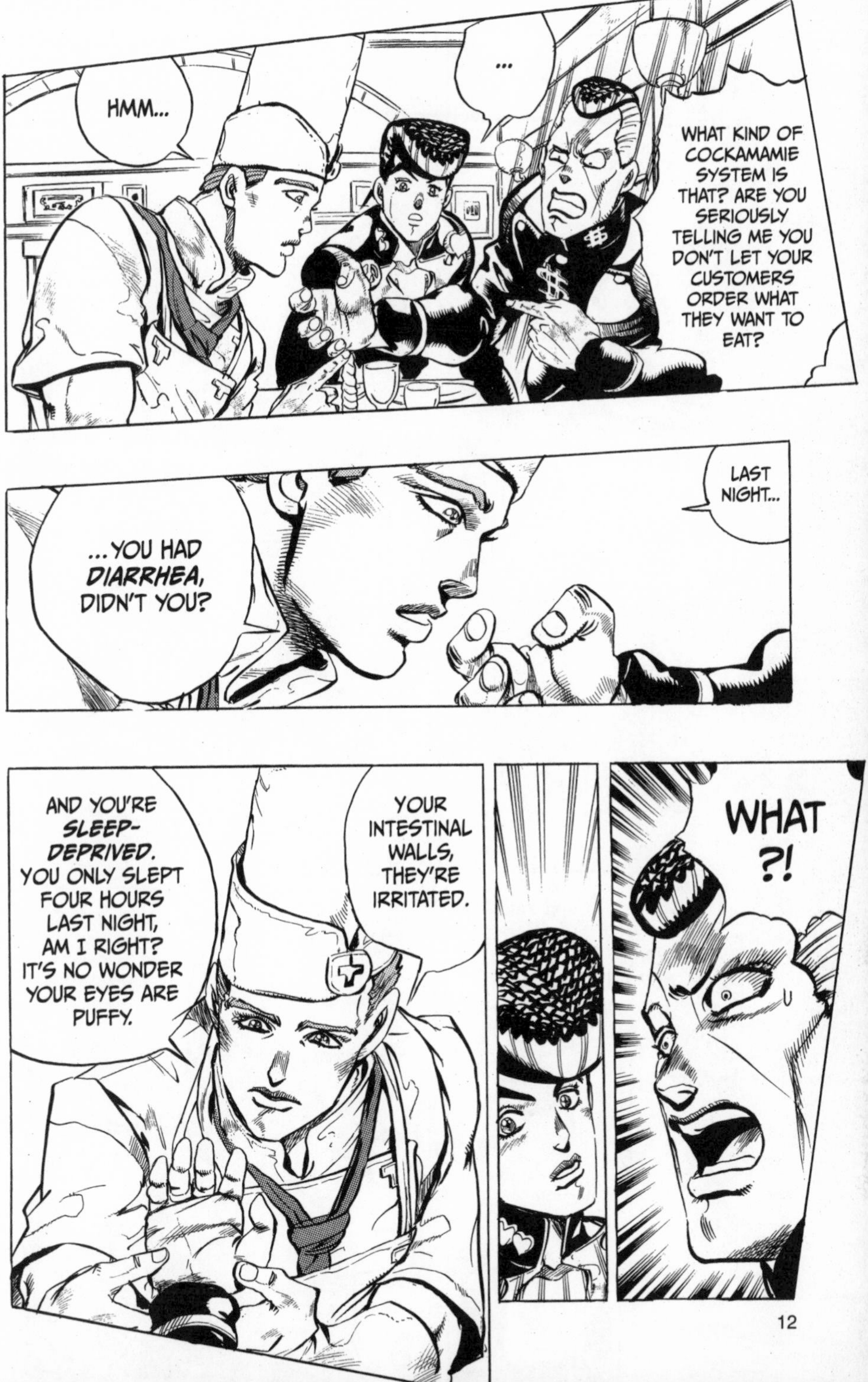
WHAT KIND OF COCKAMAMIE SYSTEM IS THAT? ARE YOU SERIOUSLY TELLING ME YOU DON'T LET YOUR CUSTOMERS ORDER WHAT THEY WANT TO EAT?
...
HMM...
LAST NIGHT...
...YOU HAD *DIARRHEA,* DIDN'T YOU?
WHAT ?!
YOUR INTESTINAL WALLS, THEY'RE IRRITATED.
AND YOU'RE *SLEEP-DEPRIVED.* YOU ONLY SLEPT FOUR HOURS LAST NIGHT, AM I RIGHT? IT'S NO WONDER YOUR EYES ARE PUFFY.

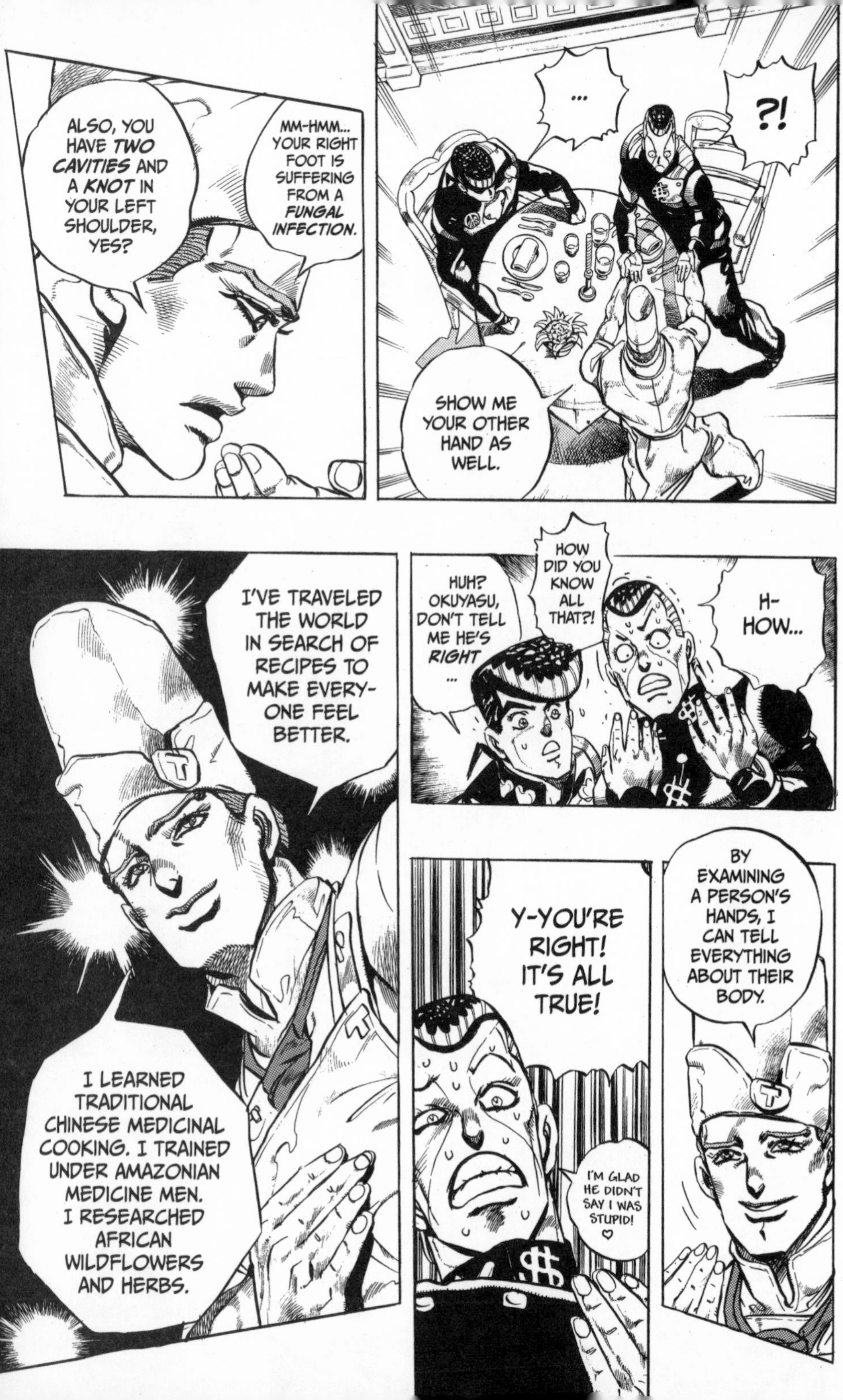
?!
...
SHOW ME YOUR OTHER HAND AS WELL.
MM-HMM... YOUR RIGHT FOOT IS SUFFERING FROM A *FUNGAL INFECTION*.
ALSO, YOU HAVE *TWO CAVITIES* AND A *KNOT* IN YOUR LEFT SHOULDER, YES?
H- HOW...
HOW DID YOU KNOW ALL THAT?!
HUH? OKUYASU, DON'T TELL ME HE'S *RIGHT* ...
BY EXAMINING A PERSON'S HANDS, I CAN TELL EVERYTHING ABOUT THEIR BODY.
Y-YOU'RE RIGHT! IT'S ALL TRUE!
I'M GLAD HE DIDN'T SAY I WAS STUPID! ♡
I'VE TRAVELED THE WORLD IN SEARCH OF RECIPES TO MAKE EVERY-ONE FEEL BETTER.
I LEARNED TRADITIONAL CHINESE MEDICINAL COOKING. I TRAINED UNDER AMAZONIAN MEDICINE MEN. I RESEARCHED AFRICAN WILDFLOWERS AND HERBS.

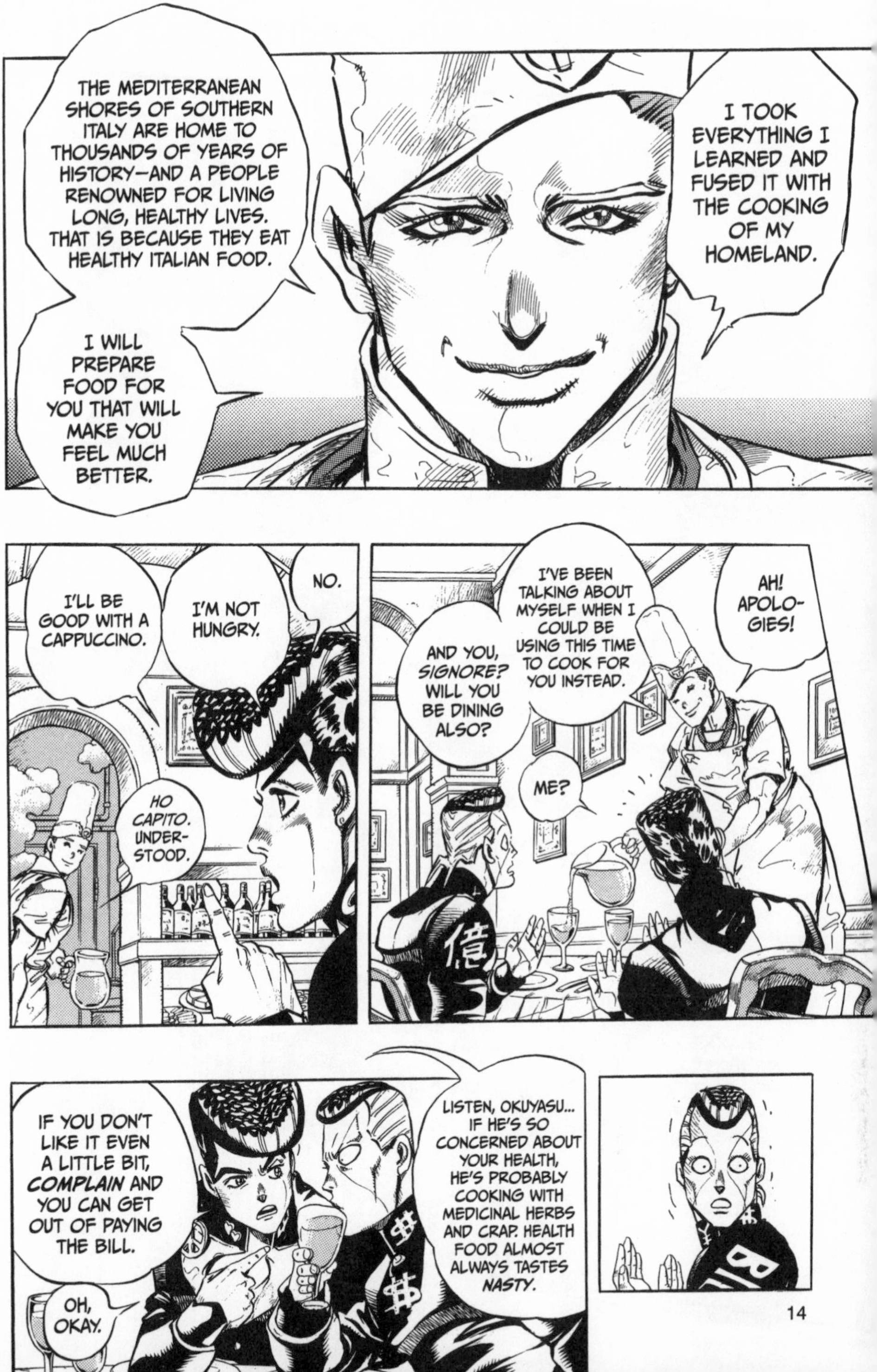
I TOOK EVERYTHING I LEARNED AND FUSED IT WITH THE COOKING OF MY HOMELAND.
THE MEDITERRANEAN SHORES OF SOUTHERN ITALY ARE HOME TO THOUSANDS OF YEARS OF HISTORY—AND A PEOPLE RENOWNED FOR LIVING LONG, HEALTHY LIVES. THAT IS BECAUSE THEY EAT HEALTHY ITALIAN FOOD.
I WILL PREPARE FOOD FOR YOU THAT WILL MAKE YOU FEEL MUCH BETTER.
AH! APOLOGIES!
I'VE BEEN TALKING ABOUT MYSELF WHEN I COULD BE USING THIS TIME TO COOK FOR YOU INSTEAD.
AND YOU, *SIGNORE?* WILL YOU BE DINING ALSO?
ME?
NO.
I'M NOT HUNGRY.
I'LL BE GOOD WITH A CAPPUCCINO.
HO CAPITO. UNDERSTOOD.
LISTEN, OKUYASU... IF HE'S SO CONCERNED ABOUT YOUR HEALTH, HE'S PROBABLY COOKING WITH MEDICINAL HERBS AND CRAP. HEALTH FOOD ALMOST ALWAYS TASTES ***NASTY***.
IF YOU DON'T LIKE IT EVEN A LITTLE BIT, ***COMPLAIN*** AND YOU CAN GET OUT OF PAYING THE BILL.
OH, OKAY.

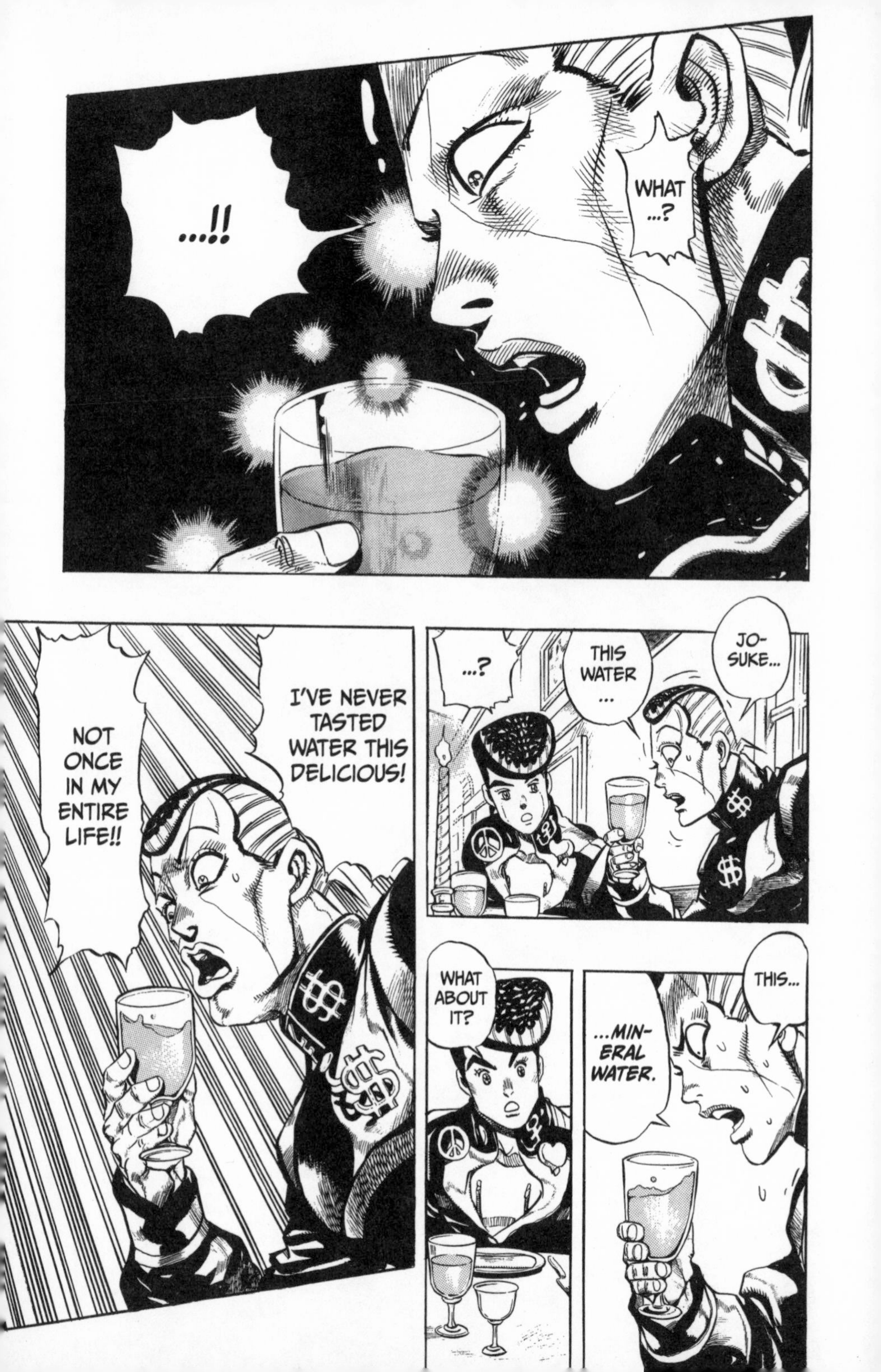
WHAT ...?
...!!
JO-SUKE...
THIS WATER ...
...?
THIS...
...MIN-ERAL WATER.
WHAT ABOUT IT?
I'VE NEVER TASTED WATER THIS DELICIOUS!
NOT ONCE IN MY ENTIRE LIFE!!

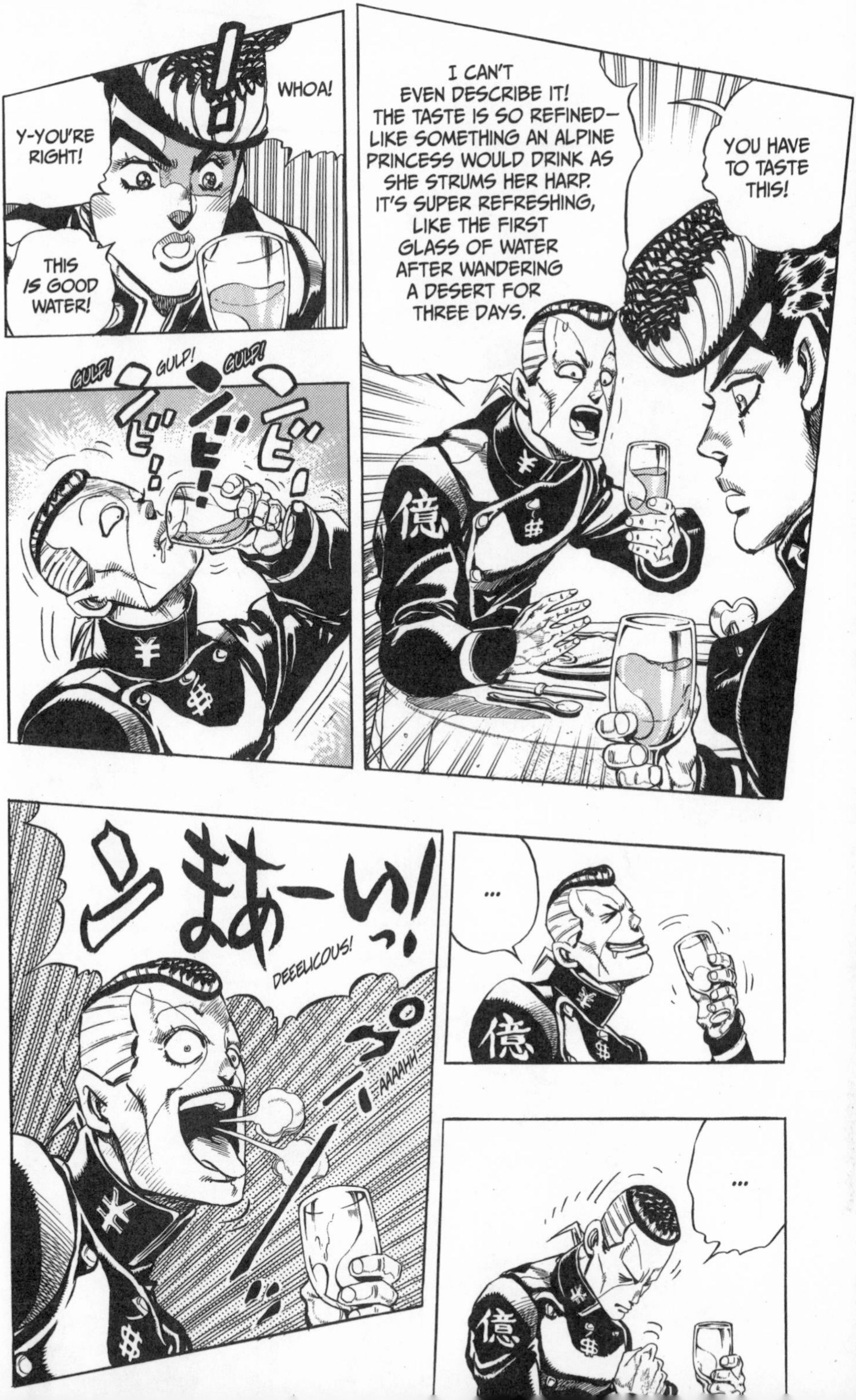

YOU HAVE TO TASTE THIS!
I CAN'T EVEN DESCRIBE IT! THE TASTE IS SO REFINED—LIKE SOMETHING AN ALPINE PRINCESS WOULD DRINK AS SHE STRUMS HER HARP. IT'S SUPER REFRESHING, LIKE THE FIRST GLASS OF WATER AFTER WANDERING A DESERT FOR THREE DAYS.
WHOA!
Y-YOU'RE RIGHT!
THIS IS GOOD WATER!
GULP!
GULP!
GULP!
...
...
DEEELICOUS!
AAAAHH

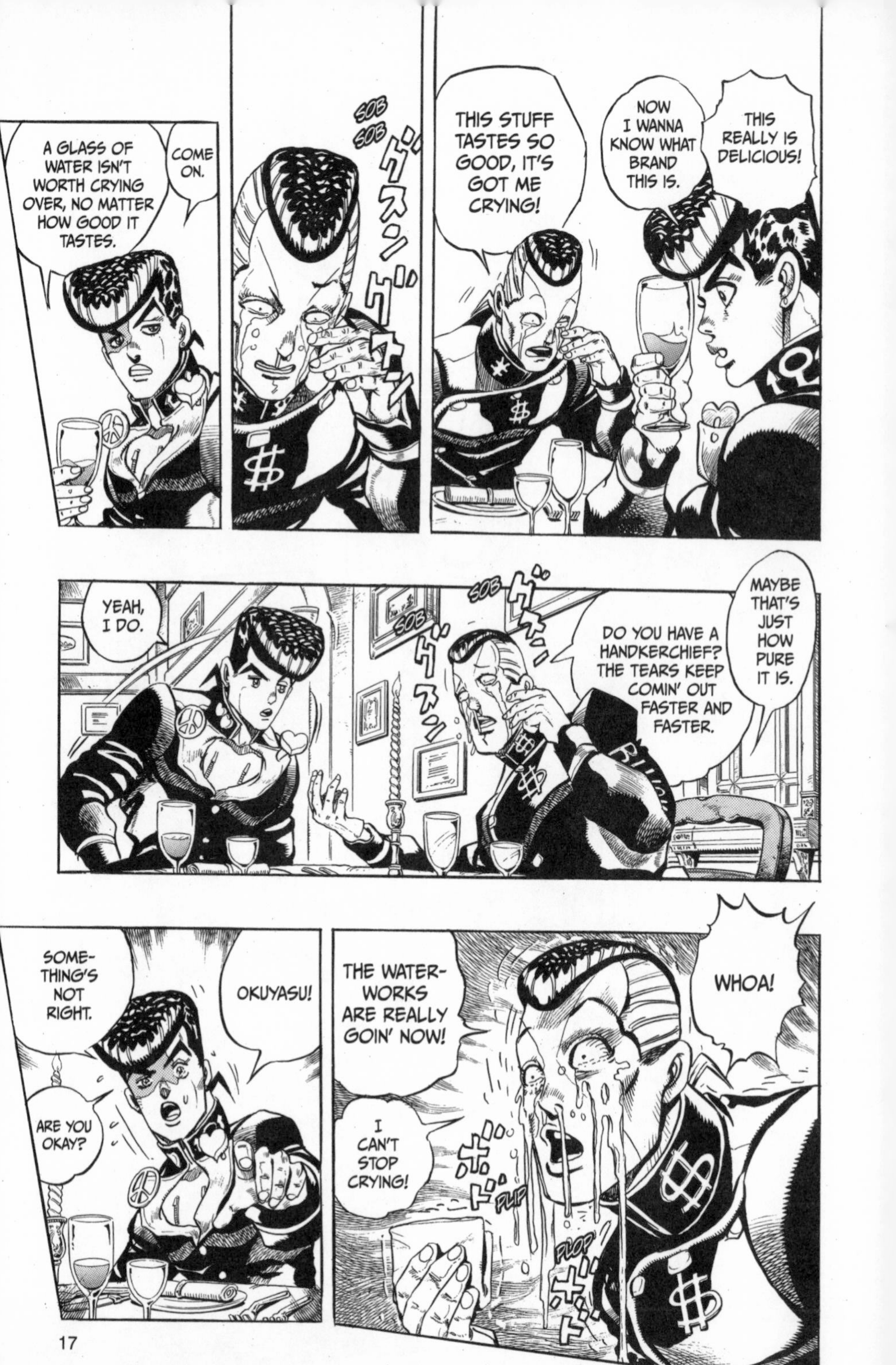
THIS REALLY IS DELICIOUS!
NOW I WANNA KNOW WHAT BRAND THIS IS.
THIS STUFF TASTES SO GOOD, IT'S GOT ME CRYING!
SOB SOB
COME ON.
A GLASS OF WATER ISN'T WORTH CRYING OVER, NO MATTER HOW GOOD IT TASTES.
MAYBE THAT'S JUST HOW PURE IT IS.
DO YOU HAVE A HANDKERCHIEF? THE TEARS KEEP COMIN' OUT FASTER AND FASTER.
SOB
SOB
YEAH, I DO.
WHOA!
THE WATER-WORKS ARE REALLY GOIN' NOW!
I CAN'T STOP CRYING!
PLIP
PLOP
OKUYASU!
SOME-THING'S NOT RIGHT.
ARE YOU OKAY?

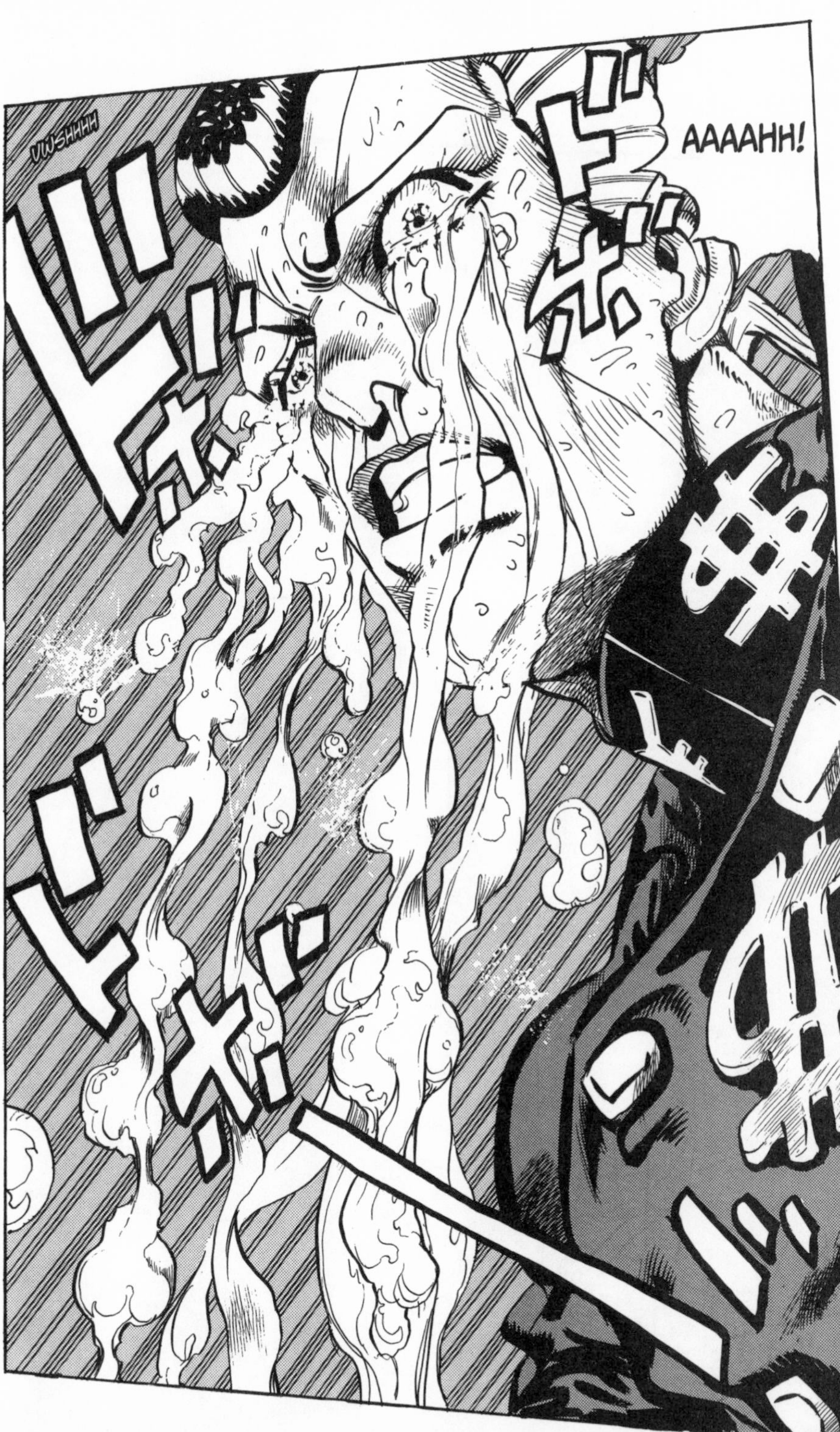
AAAAHH!
VWSHHHH

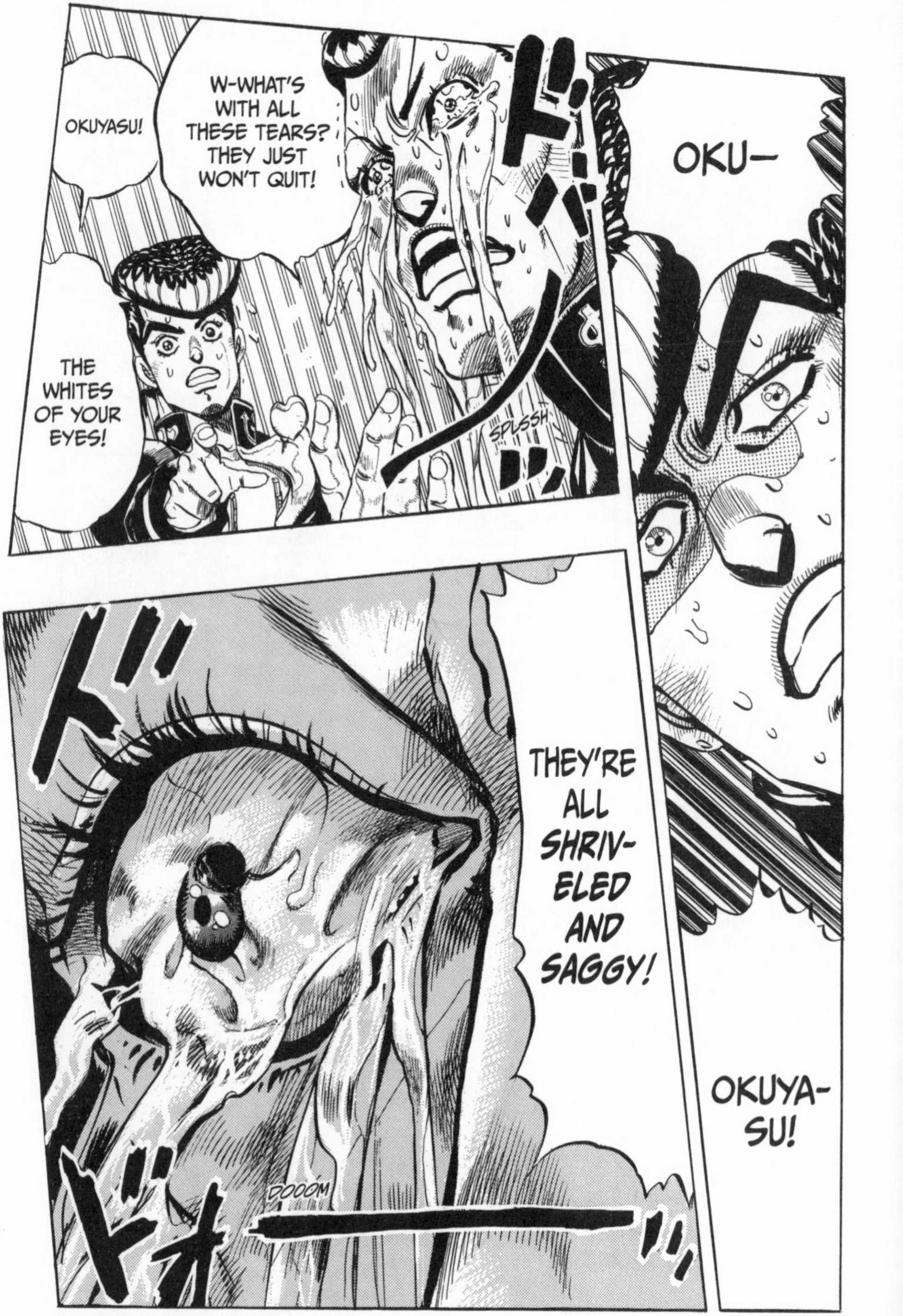
OKU—
OKUYA-SU!
W-WHAT'S WITH ALL THESE TEARS? THEY JUST WON'T QUIT!
SPLSSH
OKUYASU!
THE WHITES OF YOUR EYES!
THEY'RE ALL SHRIV-ELED AND SAGGY!
DOOOM

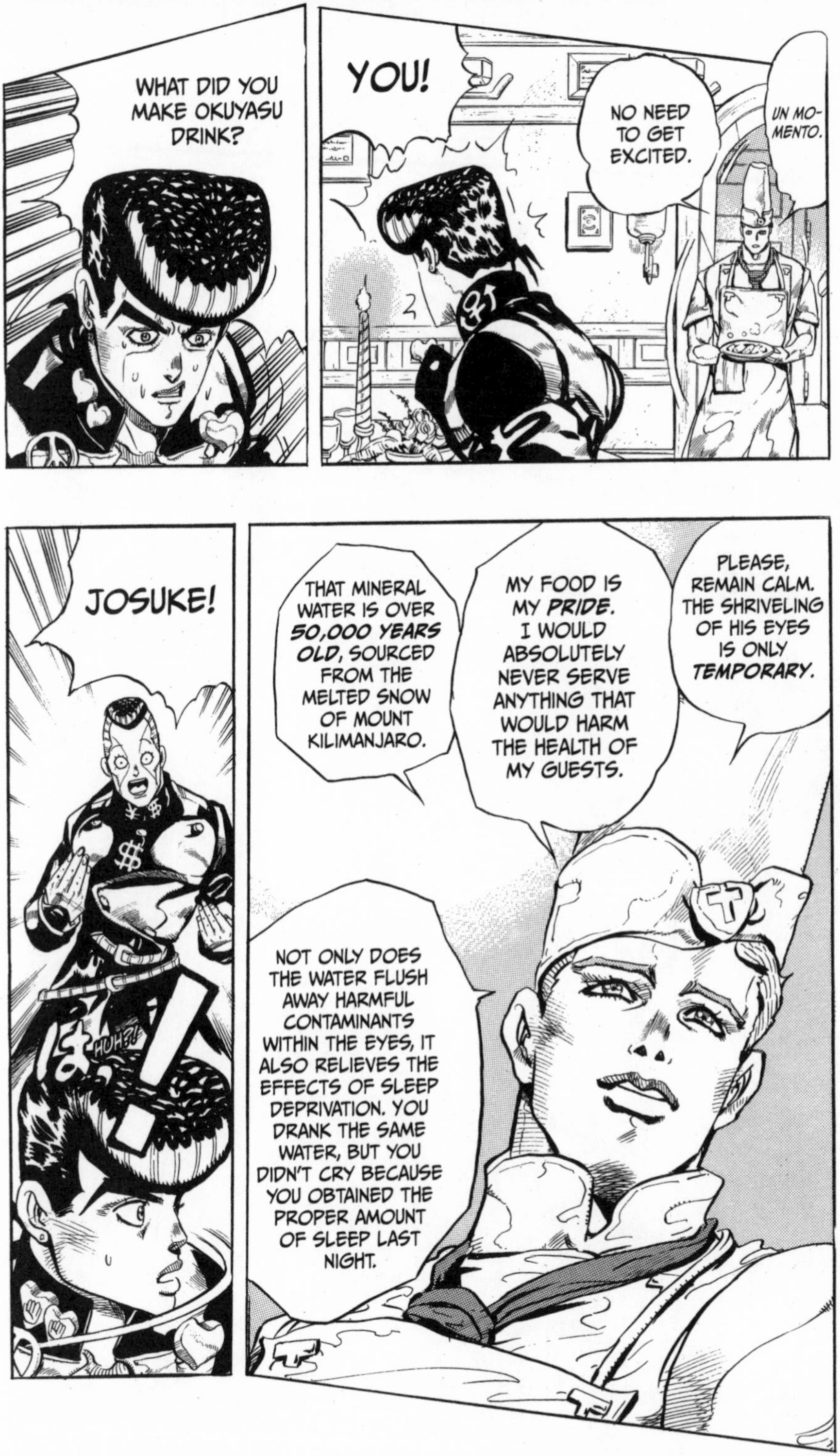
UN MOMENTO.
NO NEED TO GET EXCITED.
YOU!
WHAT DID YOU MAKE OKUYASU DRINK?
PLEASE, REMAIN CALM. THE SHRIVELING OF HIS EYES IS ONLY *TEMPORARY*.
MY FOOD IS MY *PRIDE*. I WOULD ABSOLUTELY NEVER SERVE ANYTHING THAT WOULD HARM THE HEALTH OF MY GUESTS.
THAT MINERAL WATER IS OVER *50,000 YEARS OLD*, SOURCED FROM THE MELTED SNOW OF MOUNT KILIMANJARO.
NOT ONLY DOES THE WATER FLUSH AWAY HARMFUL CONTAMINANTS WITHIN THE EYES, IT ALSO RELIEVES THE EFFECTS OF SLEEP DEPRIVATION. YOU DRANK THE SAME WATER, BUT YOU DIDN'T CRY BECAUSE YOU OBTAINED THE PROPER AMOUNT OF SLEEP LAST NIGHT.
JOSUKE!
HUH?!

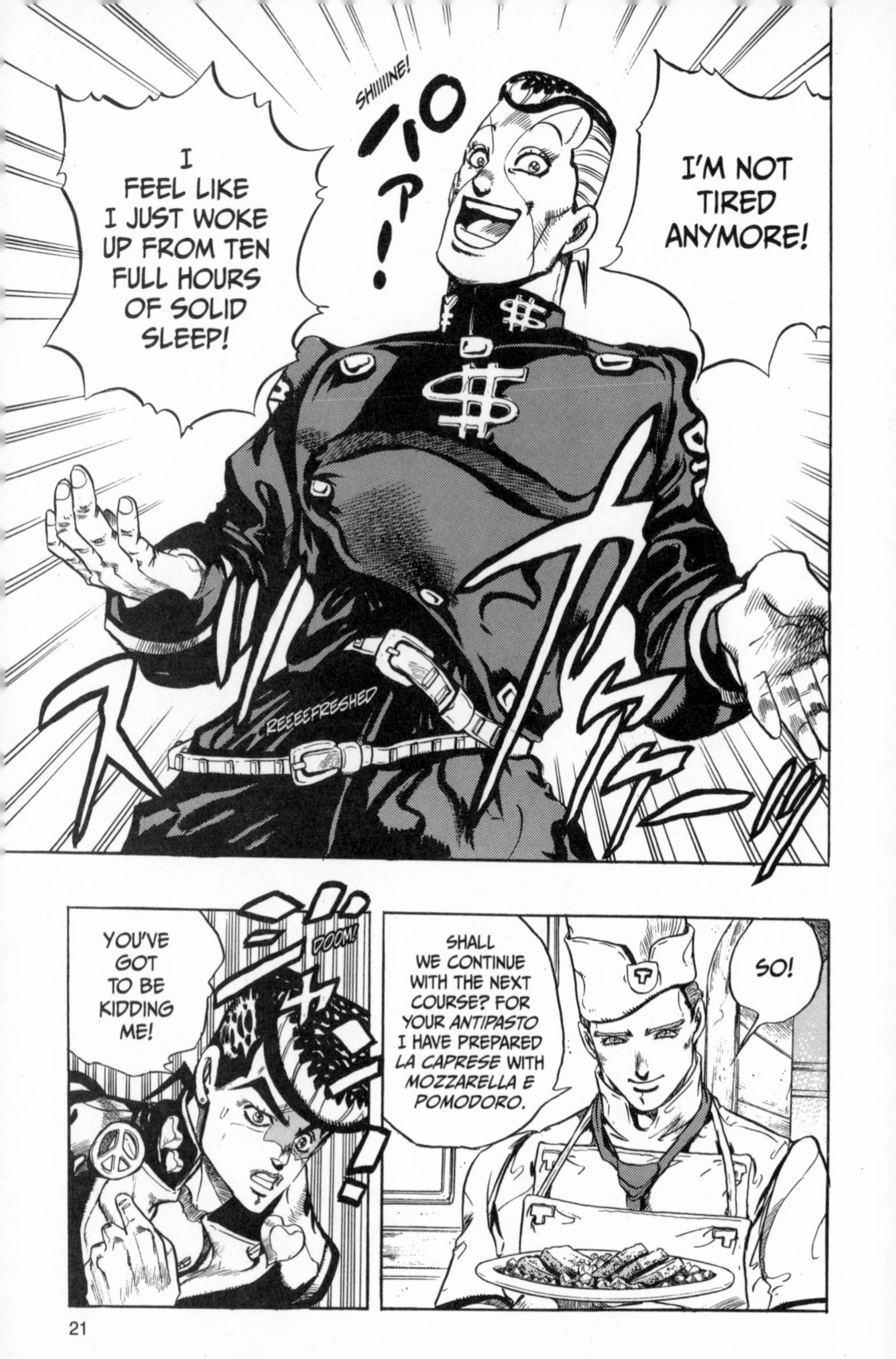
I'M NOT TIRED ANYMORE!
SHIIIIINE!
I FEEL LIKE I JUST WOKE UP FROM TEN FULL HOURS OF SOLID SLEEP!
REEEEFRESHED
SO!
SHALL WE CONTINUE WITH THE NEXT COURSE? FOR YOUR *ANTIPASTO* I HAVE PREPARED *LA CAPRESE* WITH *MOZZARELLA E POMODORO*.
DOOM!
YOU'VE GOT TO BE KIDDING ME!

T-
TRUSSARDI

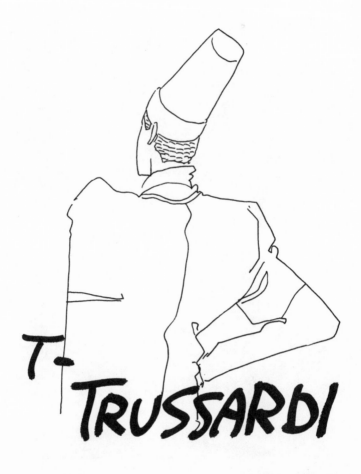

CHAPTER 39

LET'S GO EAT SOME ITALIAN FOOD, PART 2

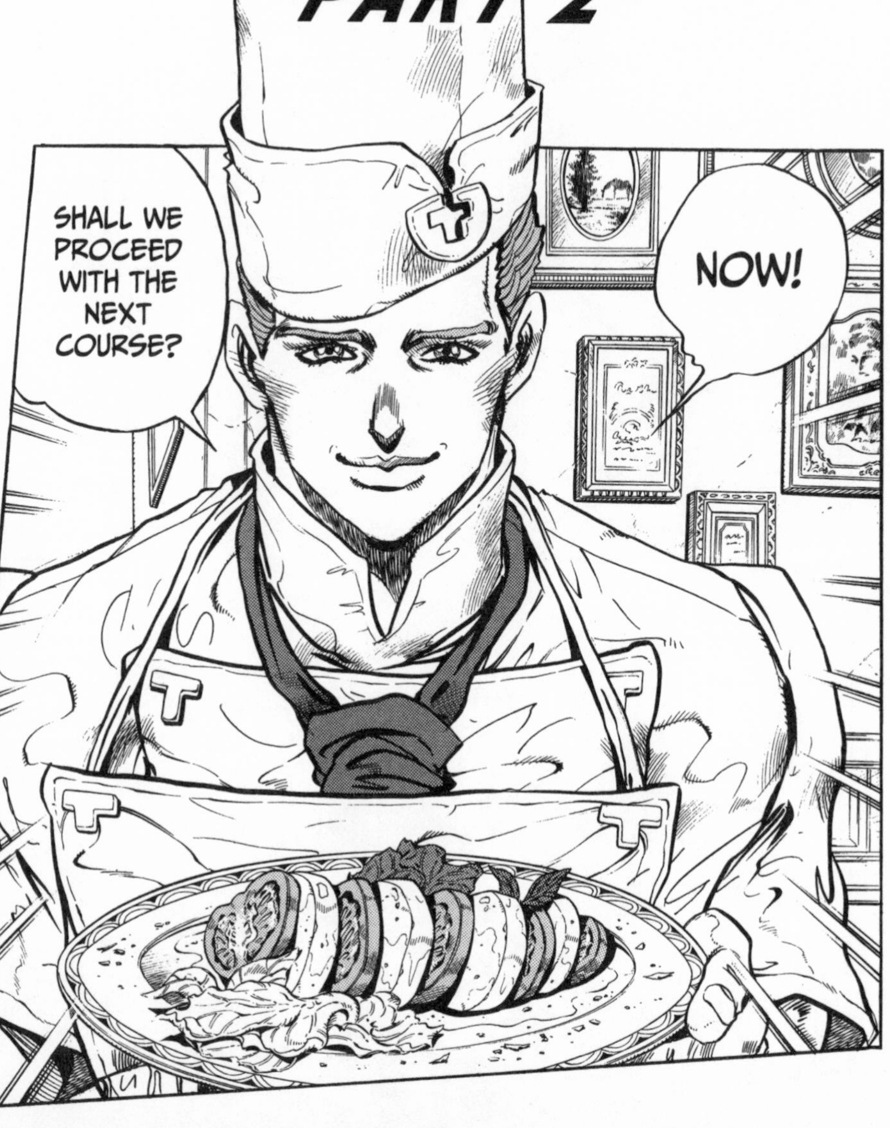
NOW!
SHALL WE PROCEED WITH THE NEXT COURSE?

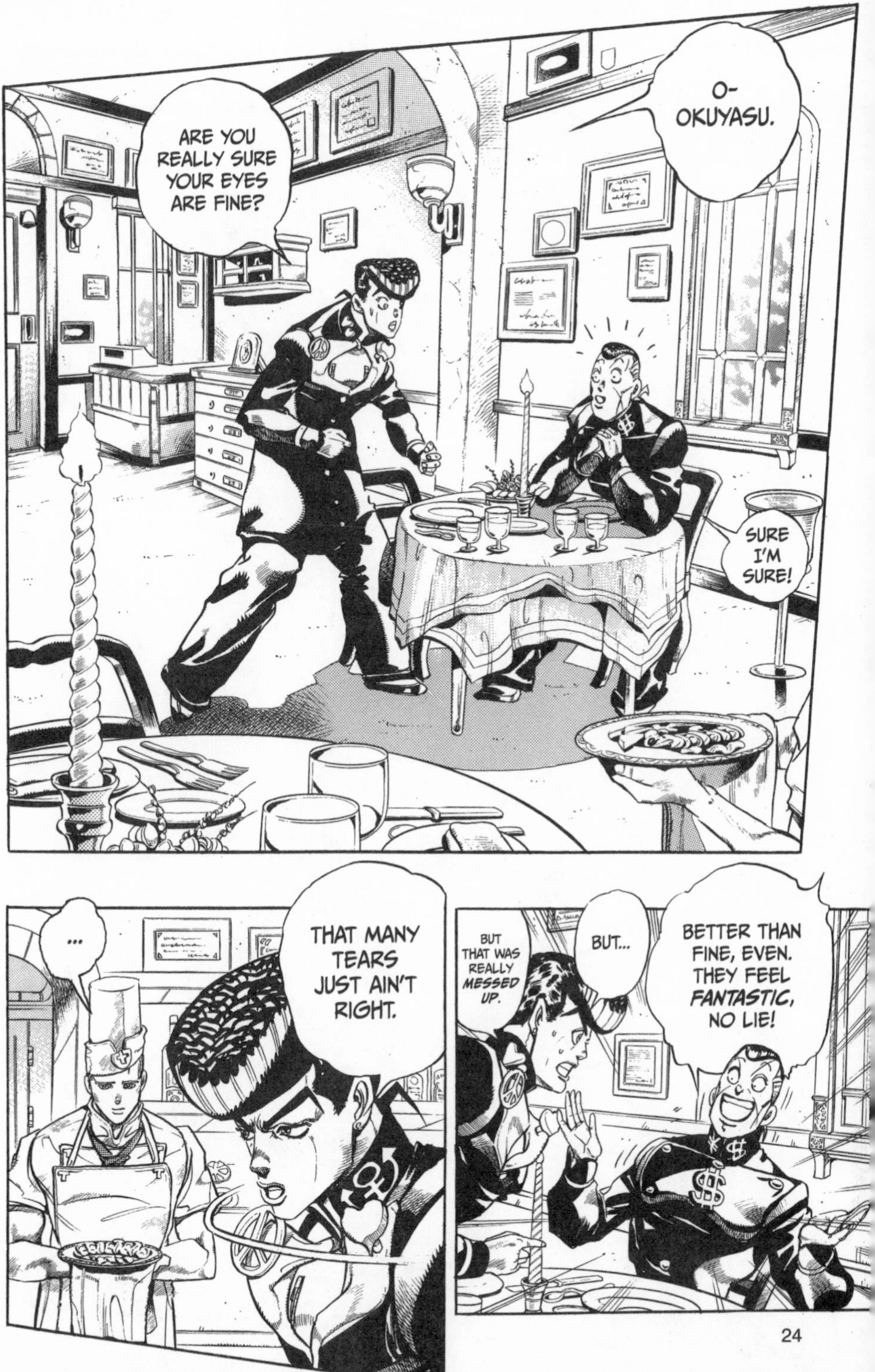
O- OKUYASU.
ARE YOU REALLY SURE YOUR EYES ARE FINE?
SURE I'M SURE!
BETTER THAN FINE, EVEN. THEY FEEL *FANTASTIC*, NO LIE!
BUT...
BUT THAT WAS REALLY *MESSED* UP.
THAT MANY TEARS JUST AIN'T RIGHT.
...

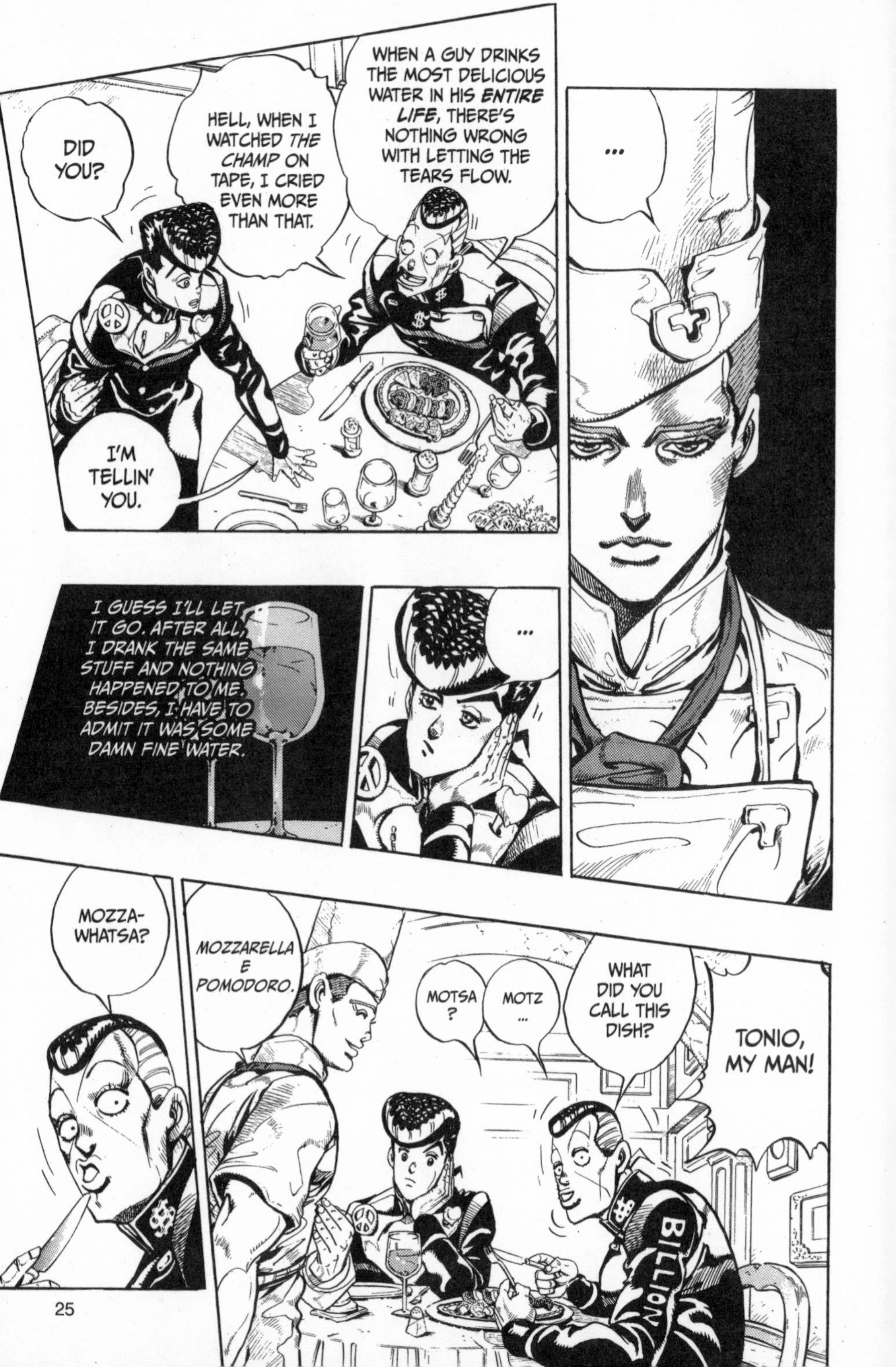
...
WHEN A GUY DRINKS THE MOST DELICIOUS WATER IN HIS *ENTIRE LIFE*, THERE'S NOTHING WRONG WITH LETTING THE TEARS FLOW.
HELL, WHEN I WATCHED *THE CHAMP* ON TAPE, I CRIED EVEN MORE THAN THAT.
DID YOU?
I'M TELLIN' YOU.
...
I GUESS I'LL LET IT GO. AFTER ALL, I DRANK THE SAME STUFF AND NOTHING HAPPENED TO ME. BESIDES, I HAVE TO ADMIT IT WAS SOME DAMN FINE WATER.
TONIO, MY MAN!
WHAT DID YOU CALL THIS DISH?
MOTZ ...
MOTSA ?
MOZZARELLA E POMODORO.
MOZZA-WHATSA?
BILLION

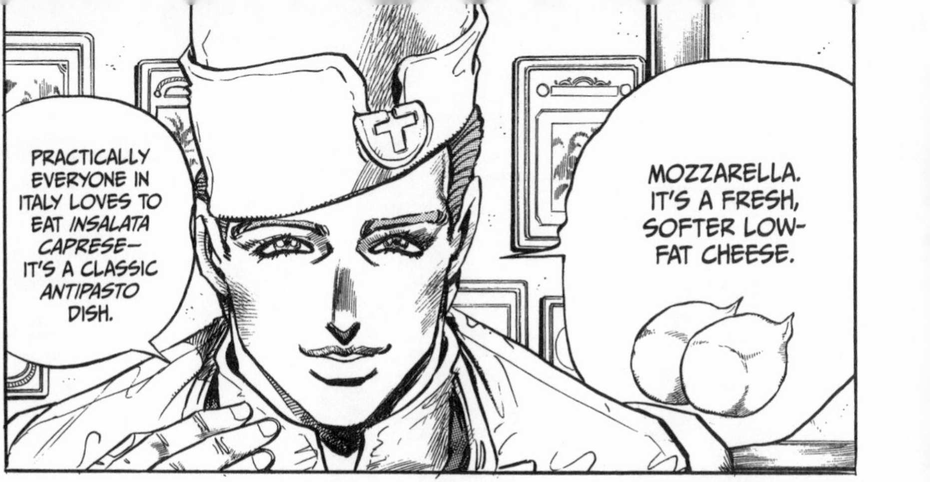
MOZZARELLA. IT'S A FRESH, SOFTER LOW-FAT CHEESE.
PRACTICALLY EVERYONE IN ITALY LOVES TO EAT *INSALATA CAPRESE*— IT'S A CLASSIC *ANTIPASTO* DISH.

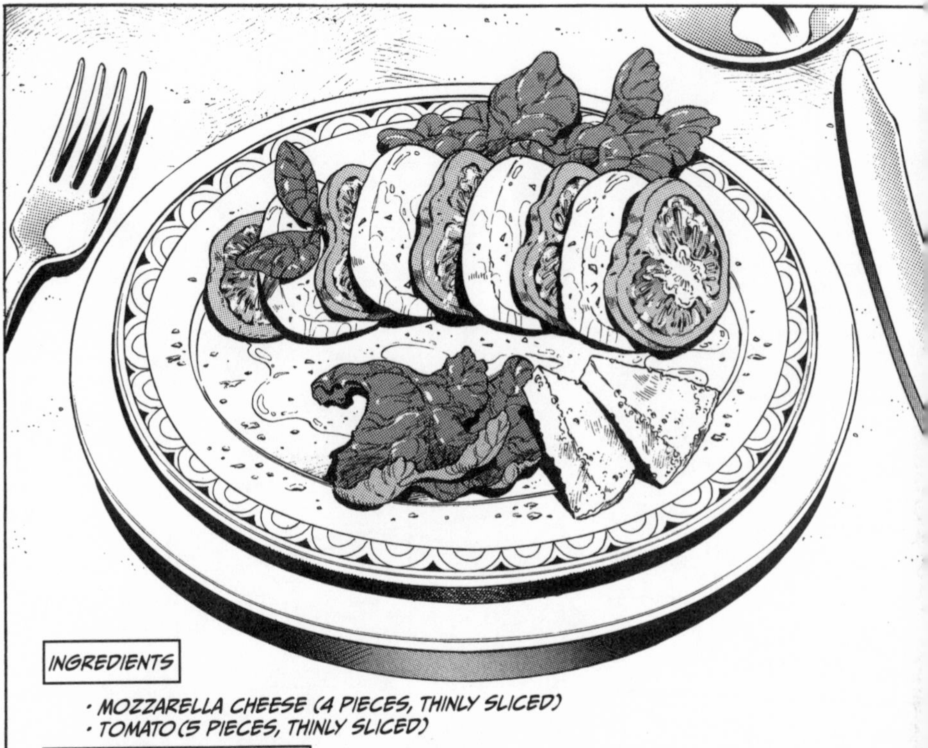
INGREDIENTS
· MOZZARELLA CHEESE (4 PIECES, THINLY SLICED)
· TOMATO (5 PIECES, THINLY SLICED)
TONIO'S HOUSE DRESSING
· ANCHOVY FILLET (1) · WAKAME · OLIVE OIL
· WHITE WINE VINEGAR · LEMON JUICE · SALT · PEPPER · SPICES
· BASIL (LIGHTLY SPRINKLED)
· TOASTED BREAD · LETTUCE (AS GARNISH)
(BEST EATEN WITHIN 15 MINUTES)

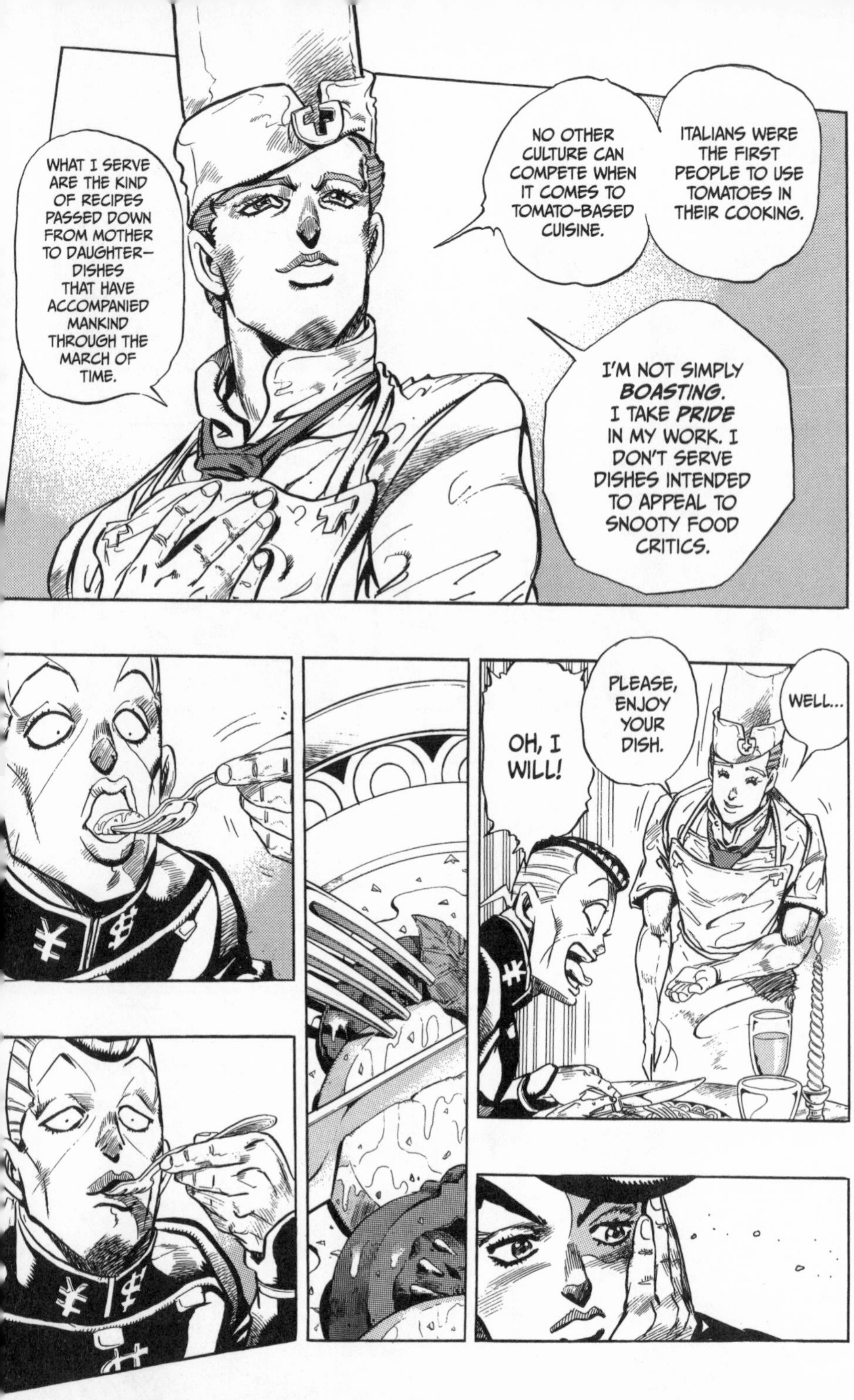
ITALIANS WERE THE FIRST PEOPLE TO USE TOMATOES IN THEIR COOKING.
NO OTHER CULTURE CAN COMPETE WHEN IT COMES TO TOMATO-BASED CUISINE.
WHAT I SERVE ARE THE KIND OF RECIPES PASSED DOWN FROM MOTHER TO DAUGHTER— DISHES THAT HAVE ACCOMPANIED MANKIND THROUGH THE MARCH OF TIME.
I'M NOT SIMPLY *BOASTING*. I TAKE *PRIDE* IN MY WORK. I DON'T SERVE DISHES INTENDED TO APPEAL TO SNOOTY FOOD CRITICS.
WELL...
PLEASE, ENJOY YOUR DISH.
OH, I WILL!

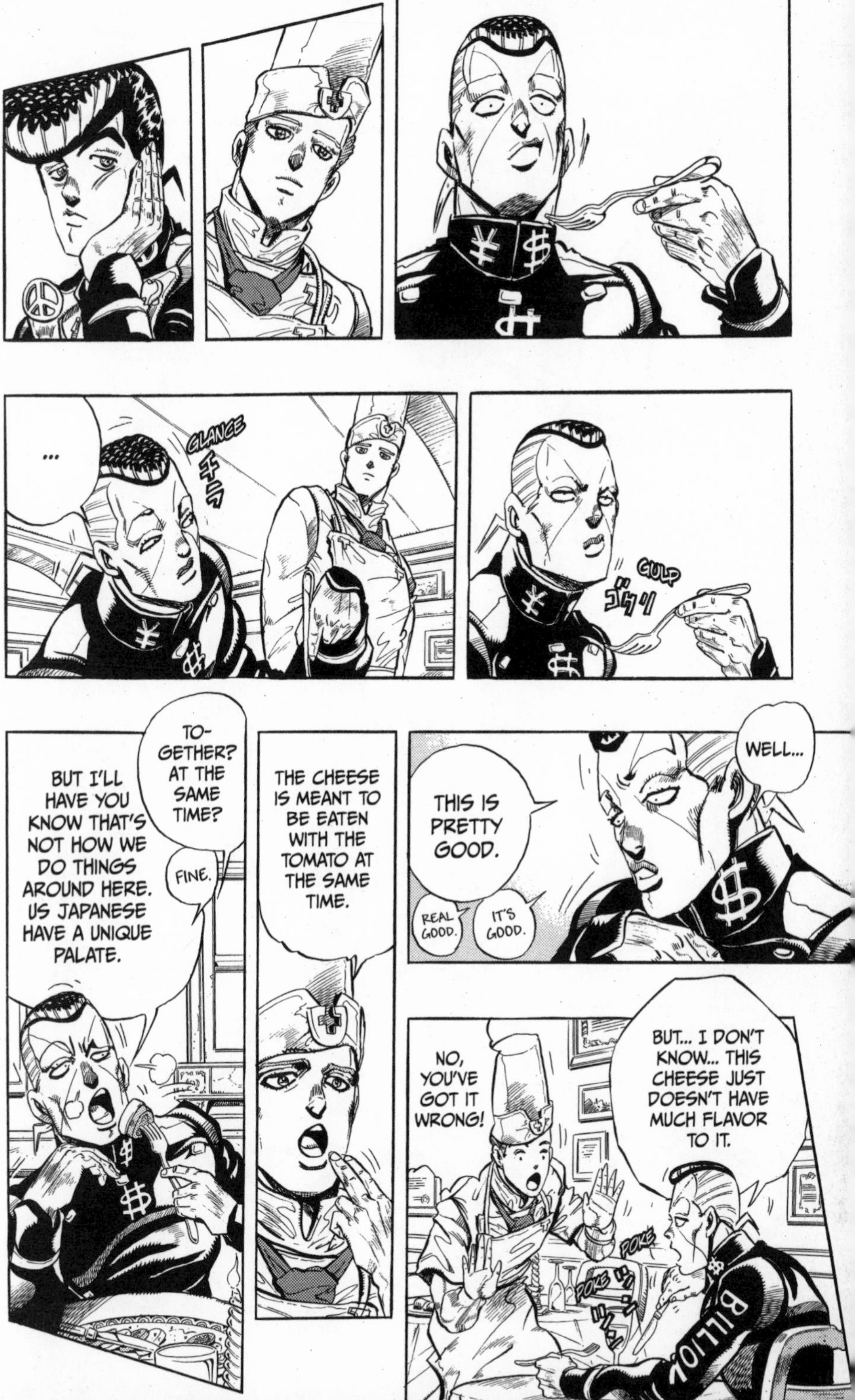
GULP
ゴクリ
GLANCE
チラ
...
WELL...
THIS IS PRETTY GOOD.
IT'S GOOD.
REAL GOOD.
BUT... I DON'T KNOW... THIS CHEESE JUST DOESN'T HAVE MUCH FLAVOR TO IT.
NO, YOU'VE GOT IT WRONG!
POKE
POKE
THE CHEESE IS MEANT TO BE EATEN WITH THE TOMATO AT THE SAME TIME.
TO-GETHER? AT THE SAME TIME?
FINE.
BUT I'LL HAVE YOU KNOW THAT'S NOT HOW WE DO THINGS AROUND HERE. US JAPANESE HAVE A UNIQUE PALATE.

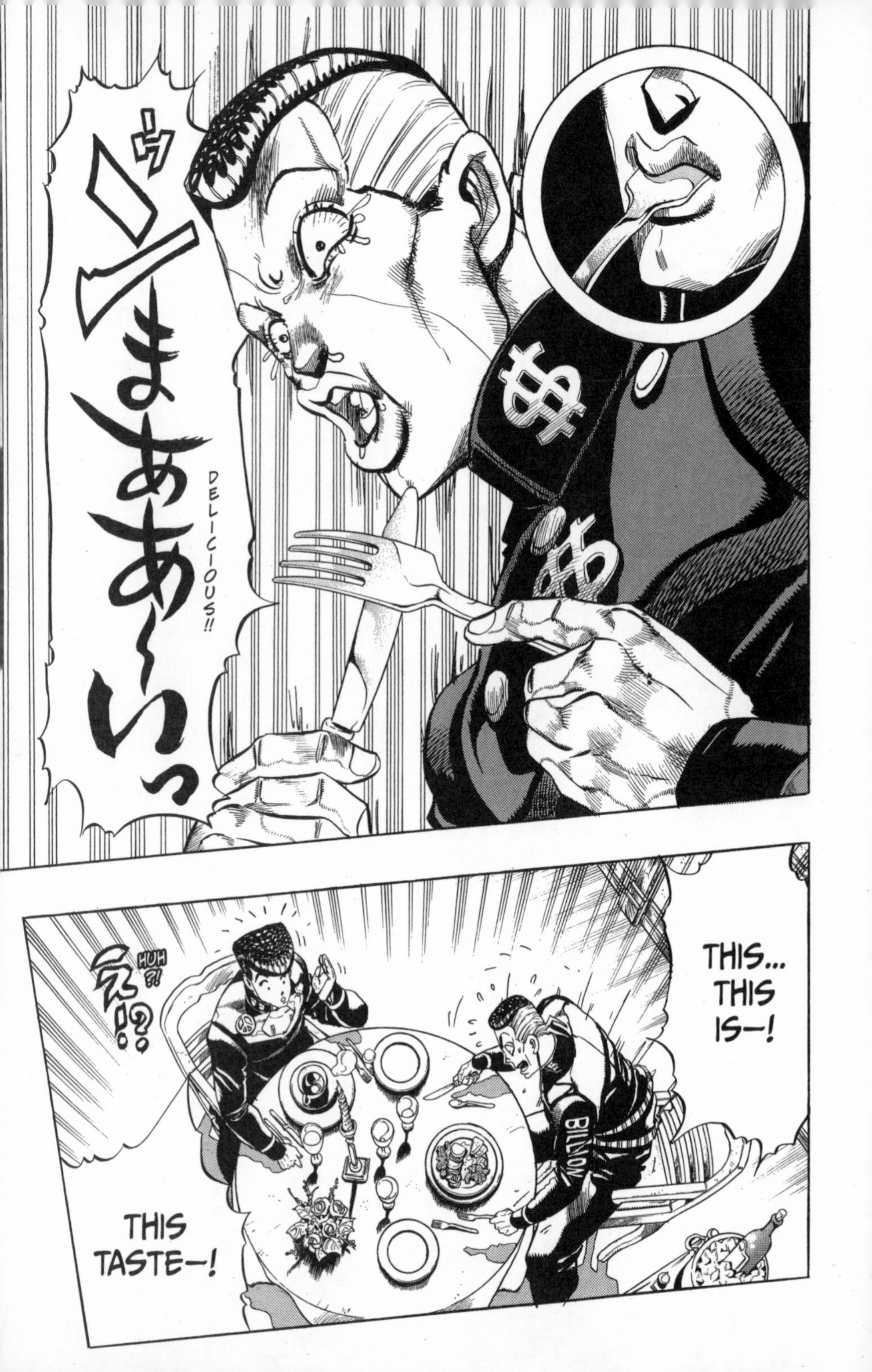
ウンまああ～いっ
DELICIOUS!!
THIS... THIS IS—!
え!?
HUH?!
THIS TASTE—!

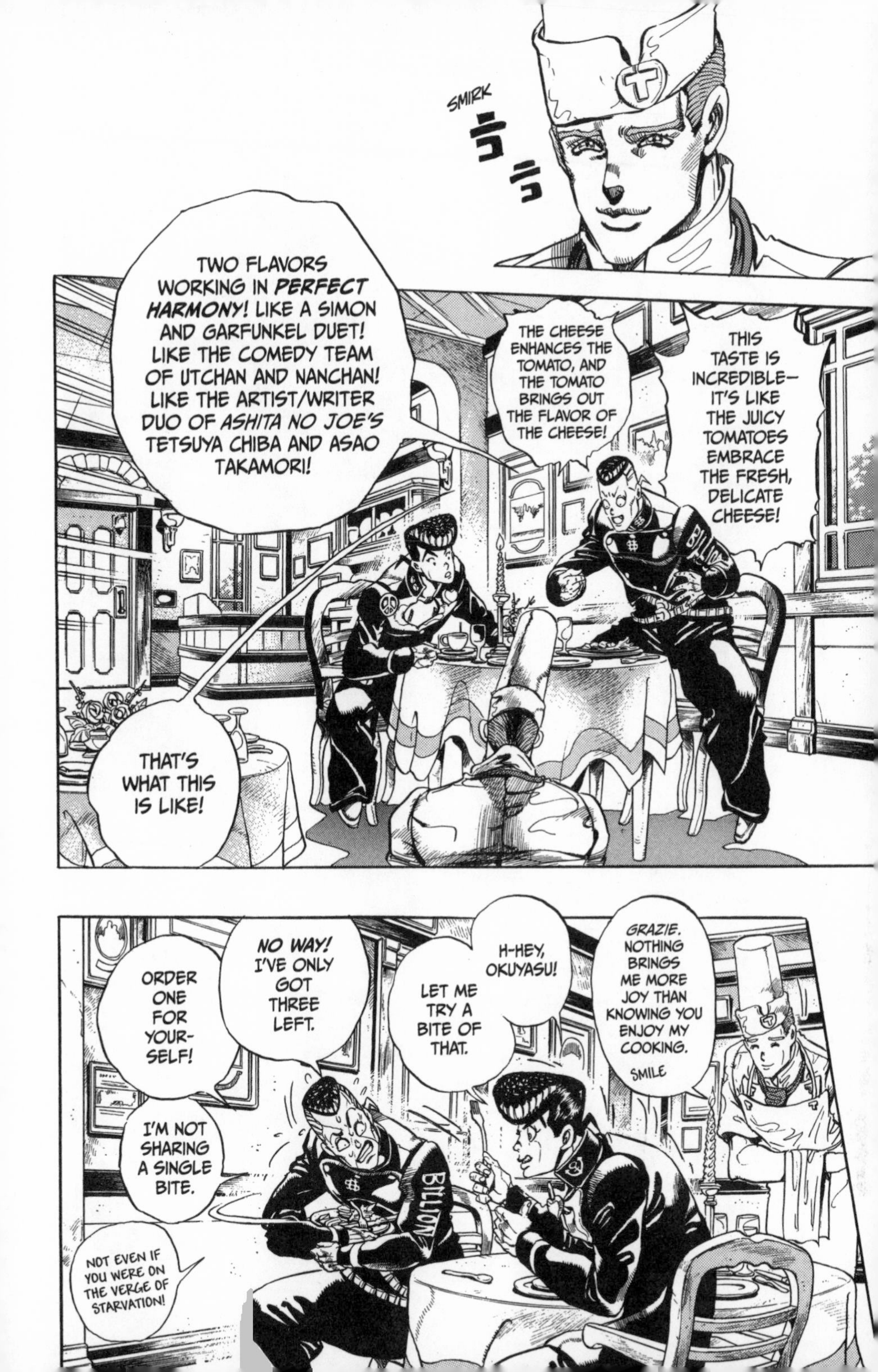
SMIRK
THIS TASTE IS INCREDIBLE—IT'S LIKE THE JUICY TOMATOES EMBRACE THE FRESH, DELICATE CHEESE!
THE CHEESE ENHANCES THE TOMATO, AND THE TOMATO BRINGS OUT THE FLAVOR OF THE CHEESE!
TWO FLAVORS WORKING IN *PERFECT HARMONY*! LIKE A SIMON AND GARFUNKEL DUET! LIKE THE COMEDY TEAM OF UTCHAN AND NANCHAN! LIKE THE ARTIST/WRITER DUO OF *ASHITA NO JOE'S* TETSUYA CHIBA AND ASAO TAKAMORI!
THAT'S WHAT THIS IS LIKE!
GRAZIE. NOTHING BRINGS ME MORE JOY THAN KNOWING YOU ENJOY MY COOKING.
SMILE
H-HEY, OKUYASU!
LET ME TRY A BITE OF THAT.
NO WAY! I'VE ONLY GOT THREE LEFT.
ORDER ONE FOR YOUR-SELF!
I'M NOT SHARING A SINGLE BITE.
NOT EVEN IF YOU WERE ON THE VERGE OF STARVATION!

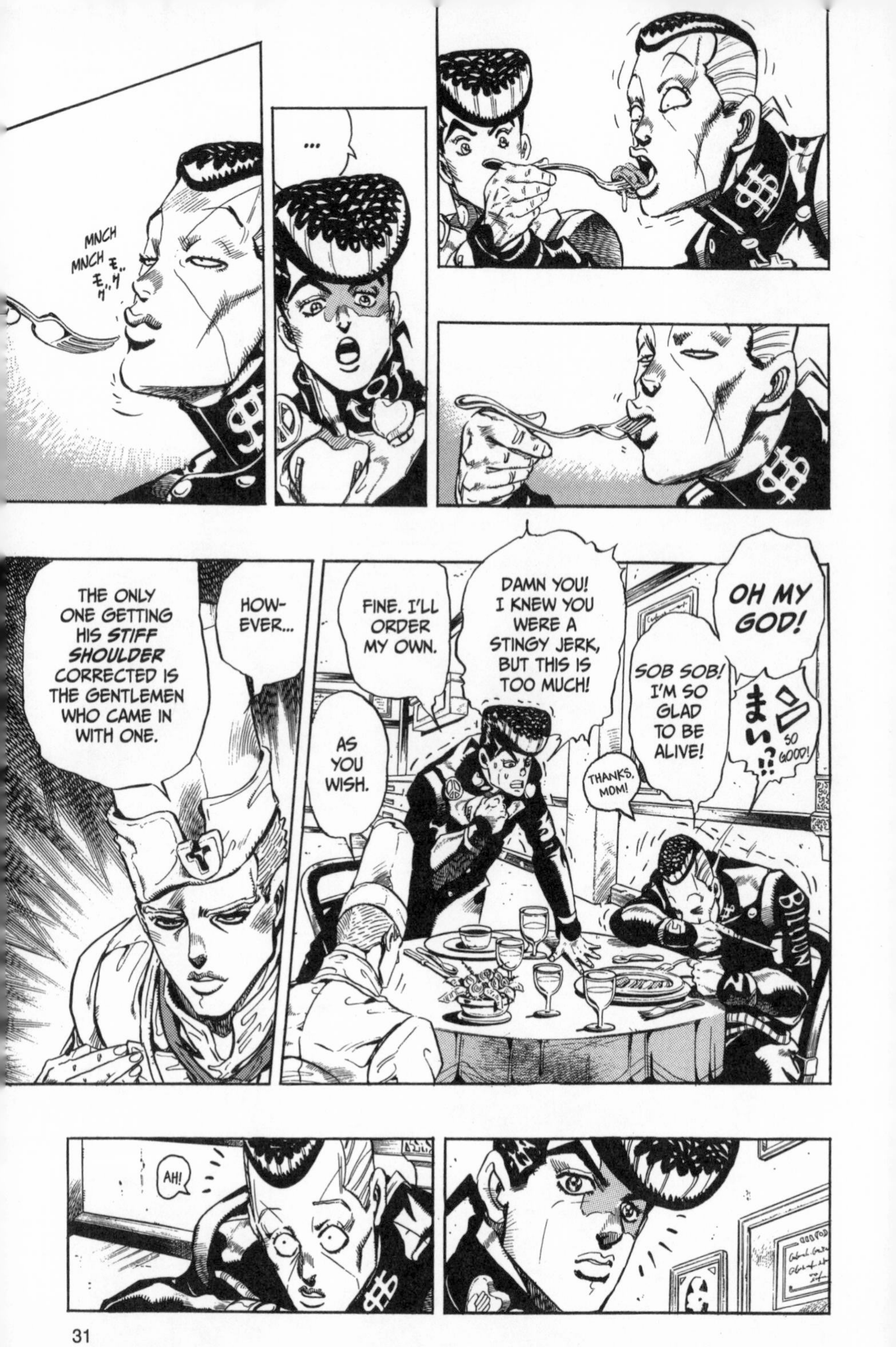
...
MNCH MNCH
OH MY GOD!
SO GOOD!
SOB SOB! I'M SO GLAD TO BE ALIVE!
THANKS, MOM!
DAMN YOU! I KNEW YOU WERE A STINGY JERK, BUT THIS IS TOO MUCH!
FINE. I'LL ORDER MY OWN.
AS YOU WISH.
HOW-EVER...
THE ONLY ONE GETTING HIS *STIFF SHOULDER* CORRECTED IS THE GENTLEMEN WHO CAME IN WITH ONE.
AH!

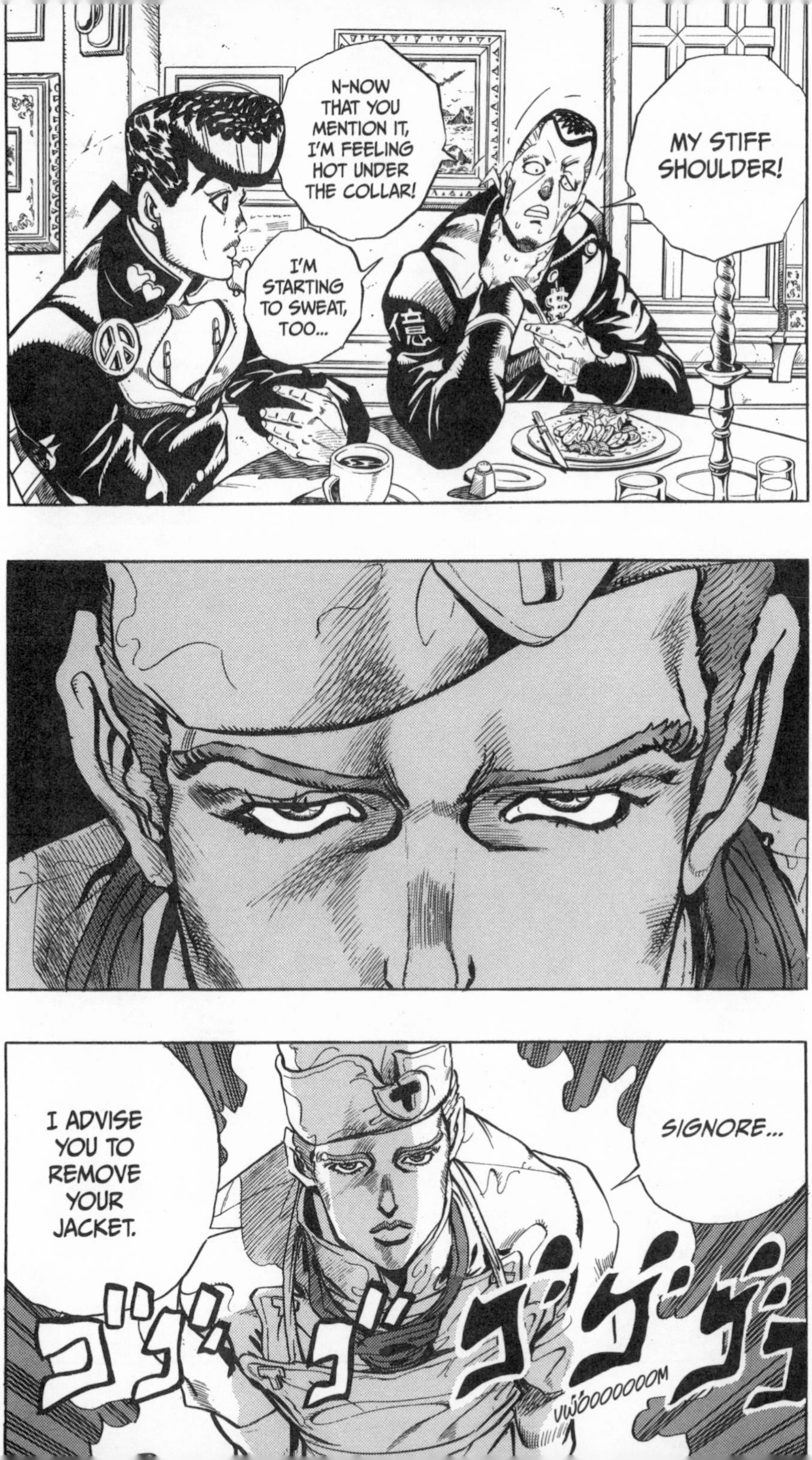
MY STIFF SHOULDER!
N-NOW THAT YOU MENTION IT, I'M FEELING HOT UNDER THE COLLAR!
I'M STARTING TO SWEAT, TOO...
SIGNORE...
I ADVISE YOU TO REMOVE YOUR JACKET.
VWOOOOOOOM

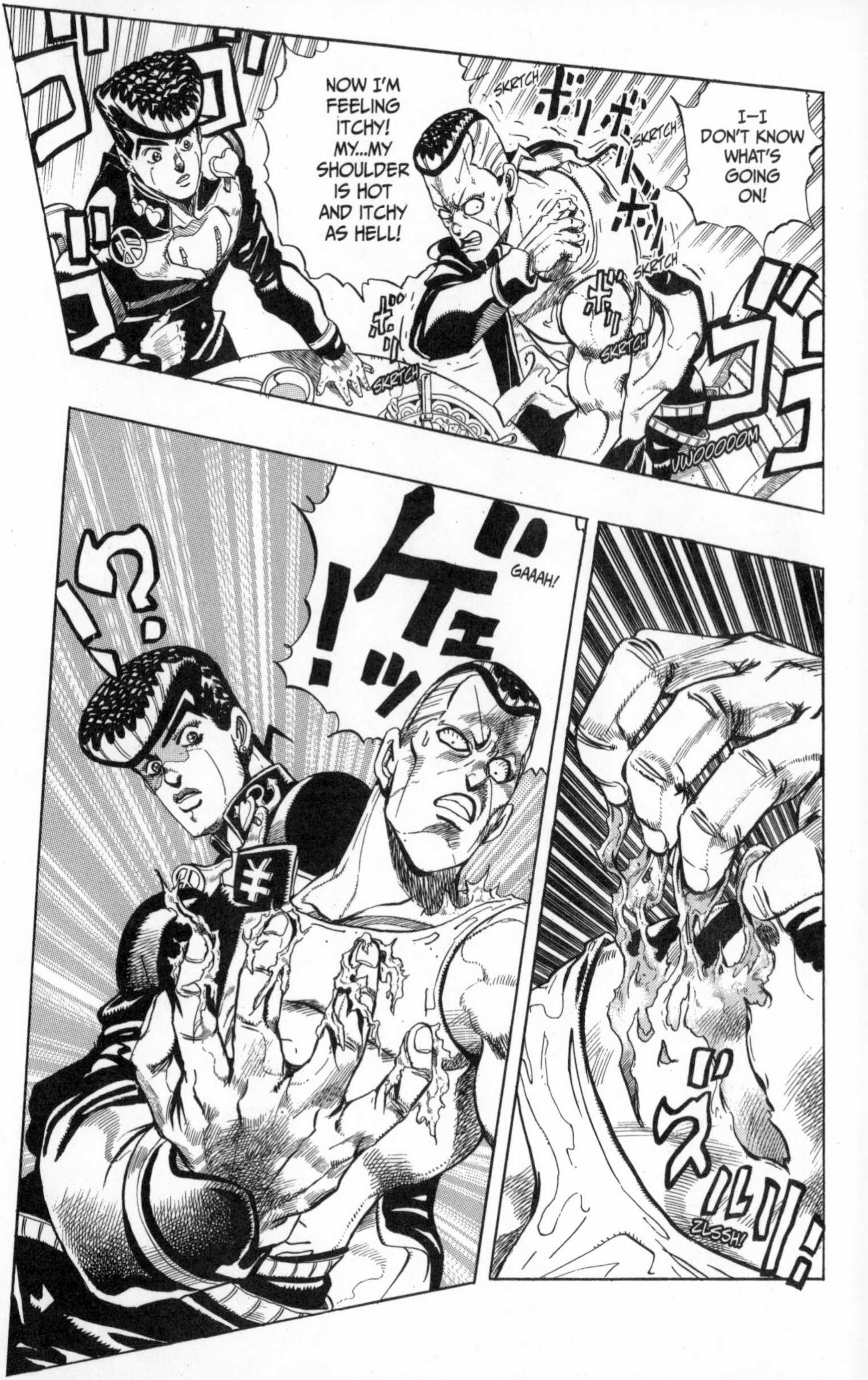
I—I DON'T KNOW WHAT'S GOING ON!
SKRTCH
SKRTCH
NOW I'M FEELING ITCHY! MY...MY SHOULDER IS HOT AND ITCHY AS HELL!
SKRTCH
SKRTCH
SKRTCH
VWOOOOOM
ZLSSH!
GAAAH!

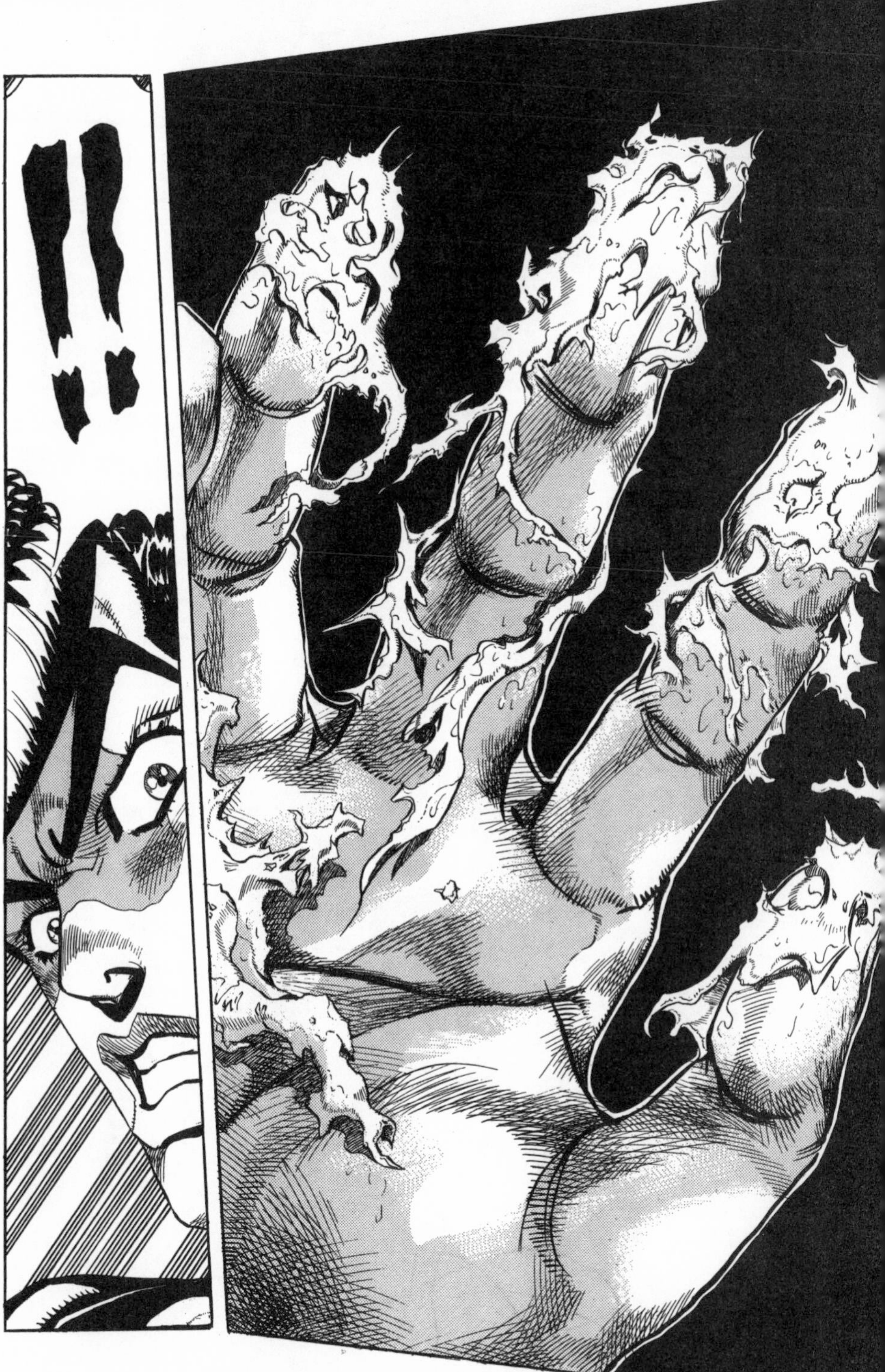
!!

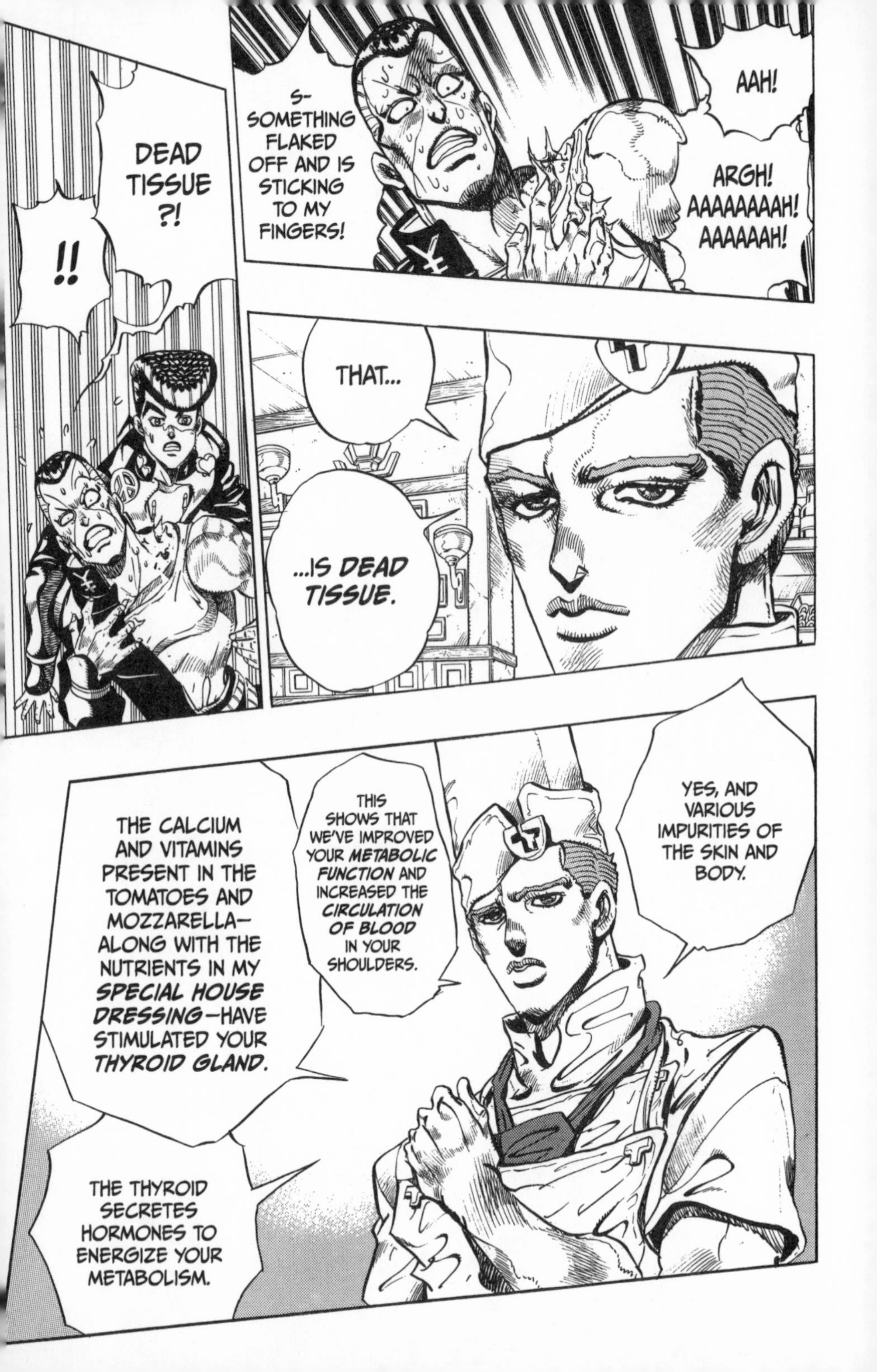
AAH!
ARGH! AAAAAAAAH! AAAAAAH!
S-SOMETHING FLAKED OFF AND IS STICKING TO MY FINGERS!
THAT...
...IS *DEAD TISSUE.*
DEAD TISSUE ?!
!!
YES, AND VARIOUS IMPURITIES OF THE SKIN AND BODY.
THIS SHOWS THAT WE'VE IMPROVED YOUR *METABOLIC FUNCTION* AND INCREASED THE *CIRCULATION OF BLOOD* IN YOUR SHOULDERS.
THE CALCIUM AND VITAMINS PRESENT IN THE TOMATOES AND MOZZARELLA—ALONG WITH THE NUTRIENTS IN MY *SPECIAL HOUSE DRESSING*—HAVE STIMULATED YOUR *THYROID GLAND*.
THE THYROID SECRETES HORMONES TO ENERGIZE YOUR METABOLISM.

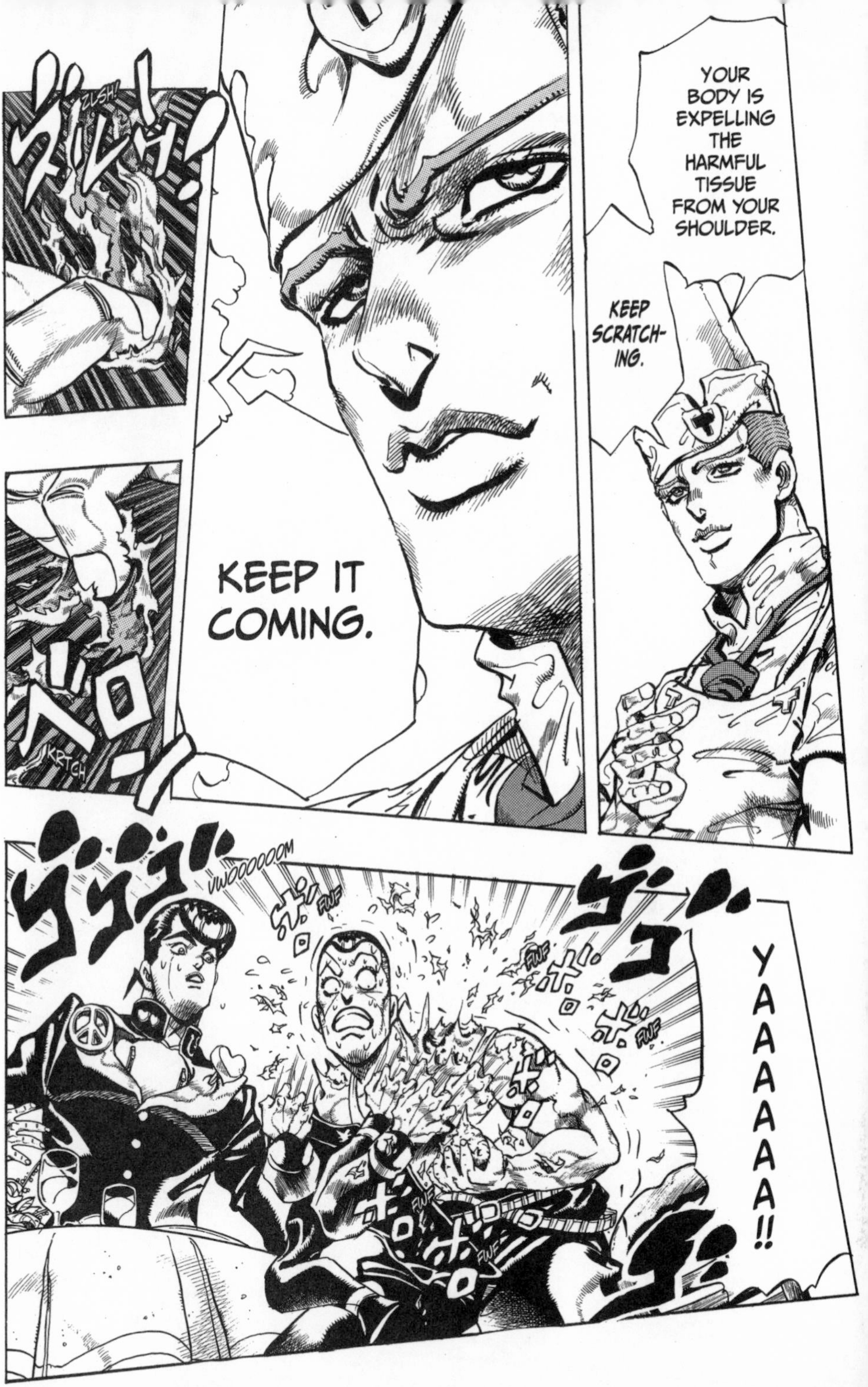
YOUR BODY IS EXPELLING THE HARMFUL TISSUE FROM YOUR SHOULDER.
KEEP SCRATCHING.
KEEP IT COMING.
ZLSH!
KRTCH
YAAAAAAA!!
FWF
FWF
FWF
VWOOOOOOM
FWF
FWF

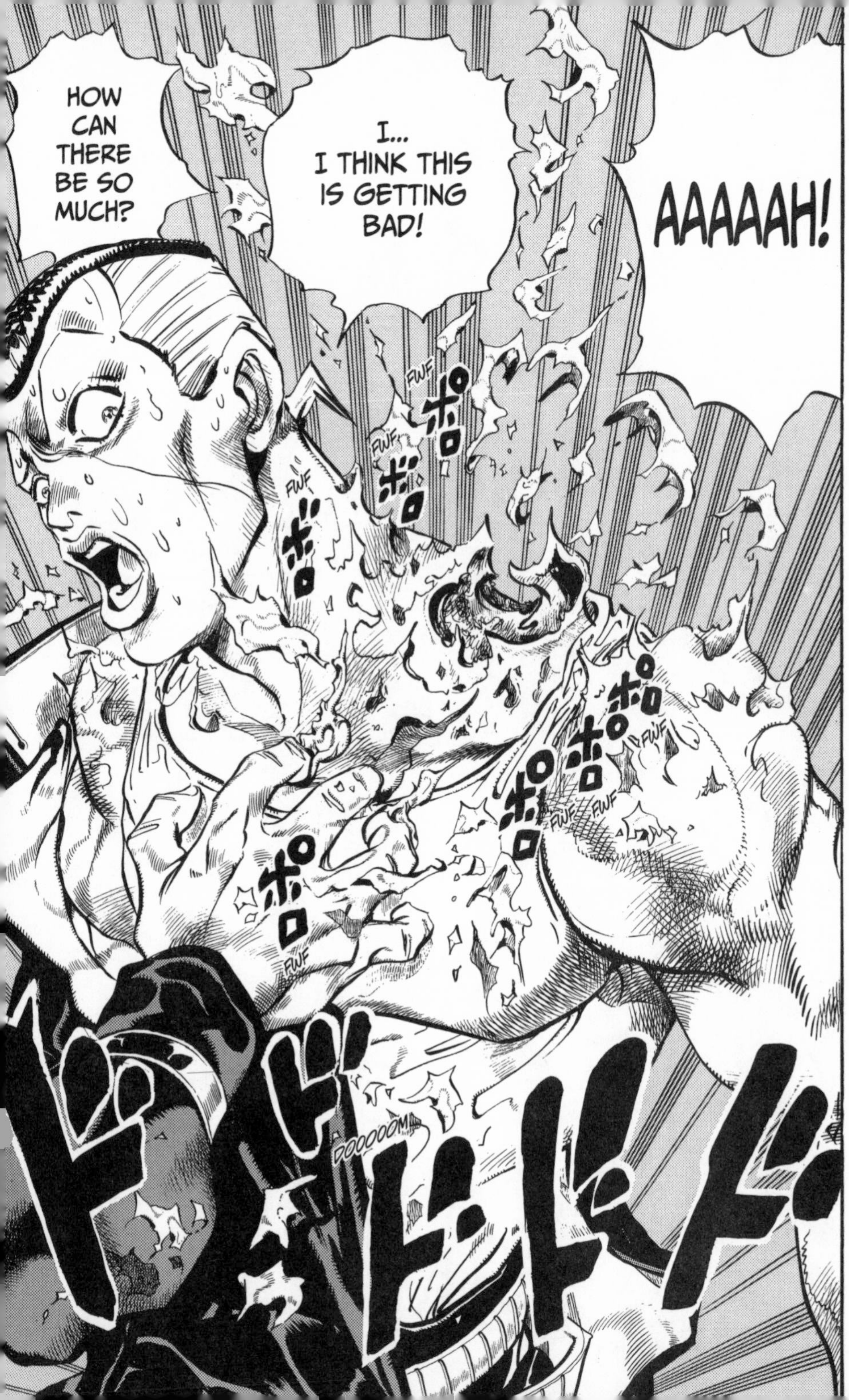
AAAAAH!
I... I THINK THIS IS GETTING BAD!
HOW CAN THERE BE SO MUCH?
FWF
FWF
FWF
FWF
FWF
FWF
FWF
DOOOOOM

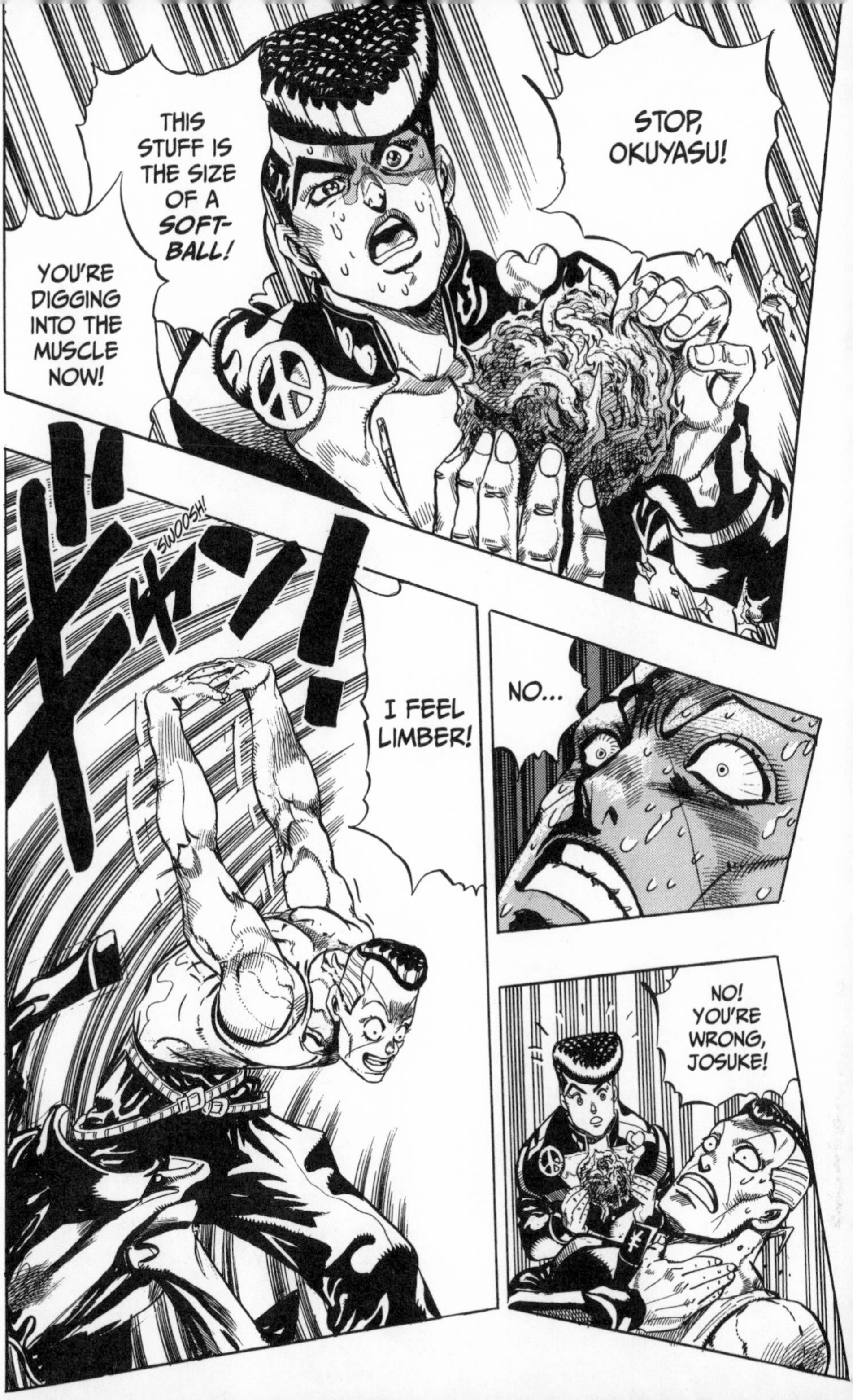
STOP, OKUYASU!
THIS STUFF IS THE SIZE OF A SOFT-BALL!
YOU'RE DIGGING INTO THE MUSCLE NOW!
NO...
NO! YOU'RE WRONG, JOSUKE!
SWOOSH!
I FEEL LIMBER!

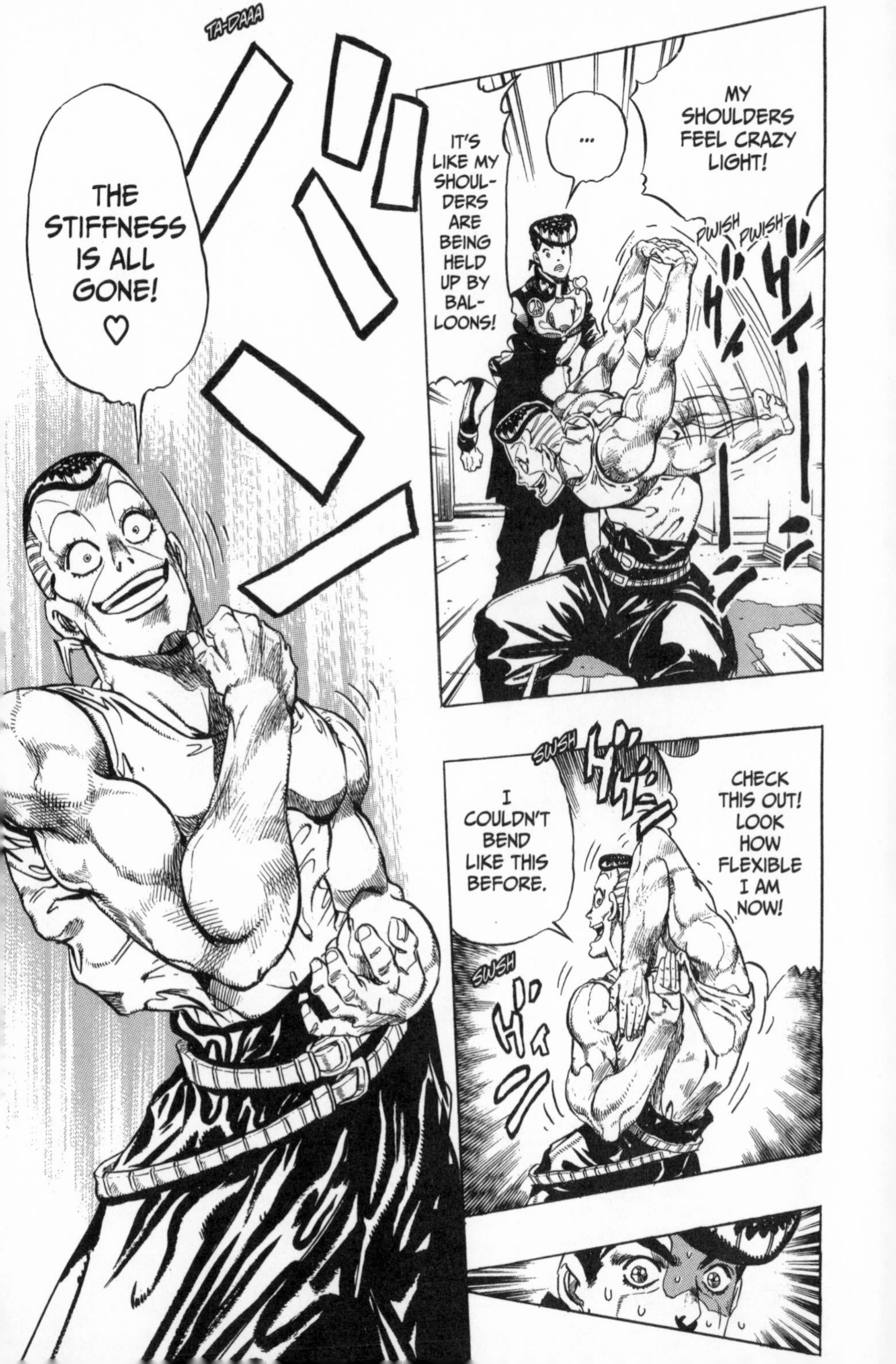
MY SHOULDERS FEEL CRAZY LIGHT!
...
IT'S LIKE MY SHOUL-DERS ARE BEING HELD UP BY BAL-LOONS!
PWISH
PWISH
SWSH
CHECK THIS OUT! LOOK HOW FLEXIBLE I AM NOW!
I COULDN'T BEND LIKE THIS BEFORE.
SWSH
TA-DAAA
THE STIFFNESS IS ALL GONE! ♡

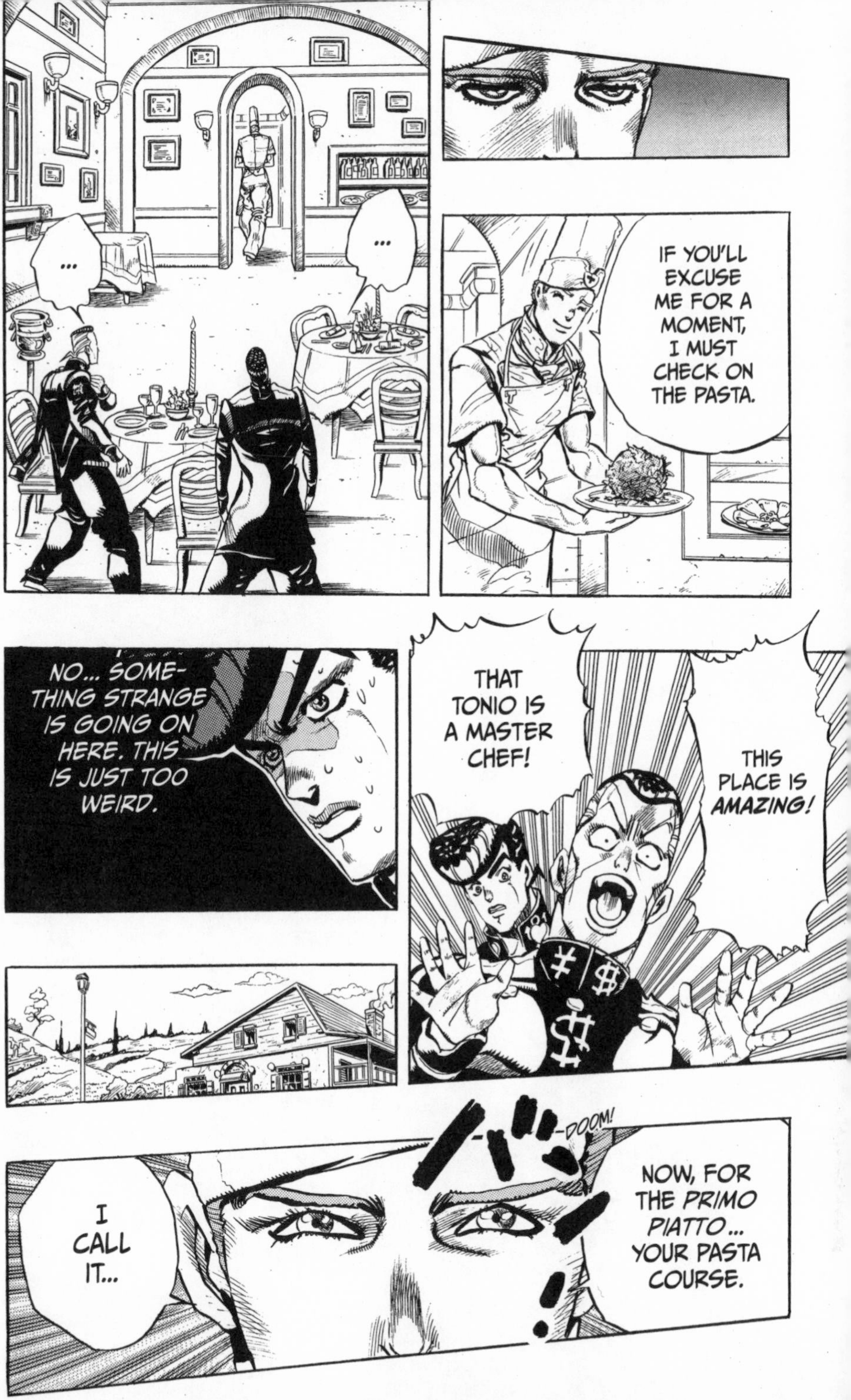
IF YOU'LL EXCUSE ME FOR A MOMENT, I MUST CHECK ON THE PASTA.
...
...
THAT TONIO IS A MASTER CHEF!
THIS PLACE IS *AMAZING!*
NO... SOME-THING STRANGE IS GOING ON HERE. THIS IS JUST TOO WEIRD.
-DOOM!
NOW, FOR THE *PRIMO PIATTO*... YOUR PASTA COURSE.
I CALL IT...

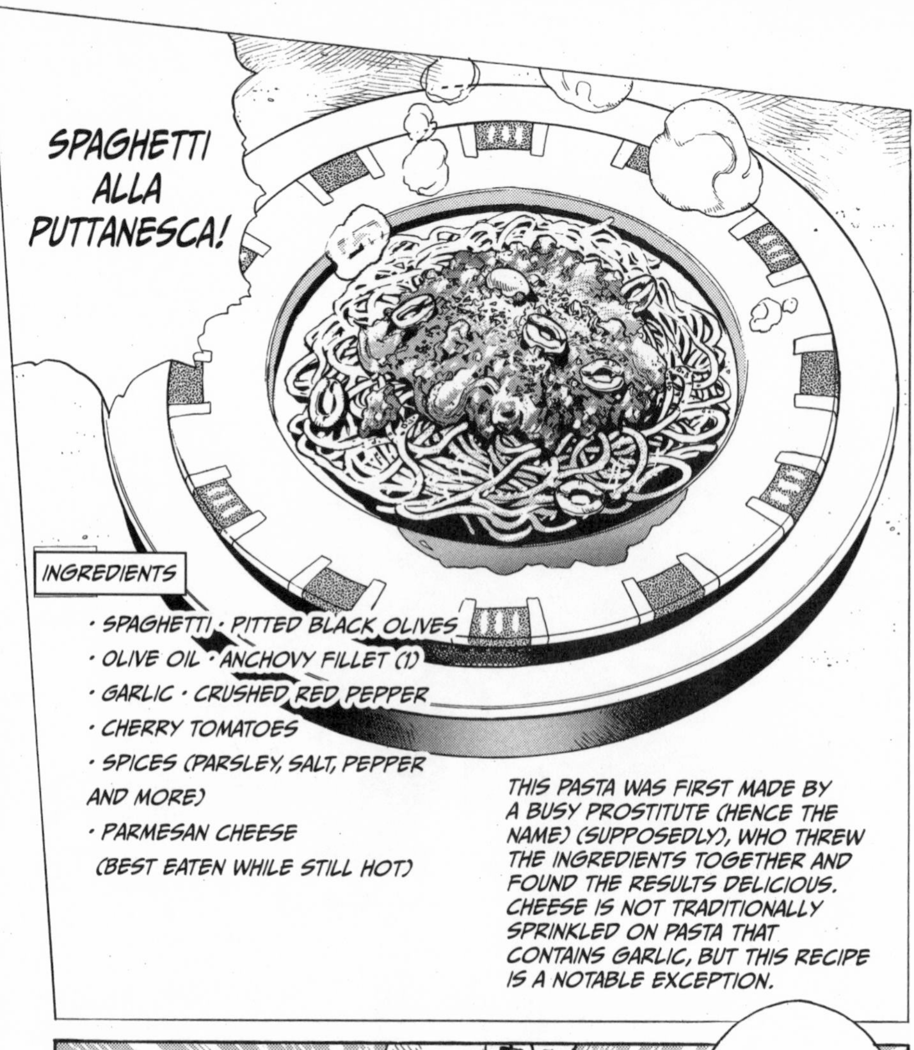
SPAGHETTI ALLA PUTTANESCA!
INGREDIENTS
· SPAGHETTI · PITTED BLACK OLIVES
· OLIVE OIL · ANCHOVY FILLET (1)
· GARLIC · CRUSHED RED PEPPER
· CHERRY TOMATOES
· SPICES (PARSLEY, SALT, PEPPER AND MORE)
· PARMESAN CHEESE
(BEST EATEN WHILE STILL HOT)
THIS PASTA WAS FIRST MADE BY A BUSY PROSTITUTE (HENCE THE NAME) (SUPPOSEDLY), WHO THREW THE INGREDIENTS TOGETHER AND FOUND THE RESULTS DELICIOUS. CHEESE IS NOT TRADITIONALLY SPRINKLED ON PASTA THAT CONTAINS GARLIC, BUT THIS RECIPE IS A NOTABLE EXCEPTION.
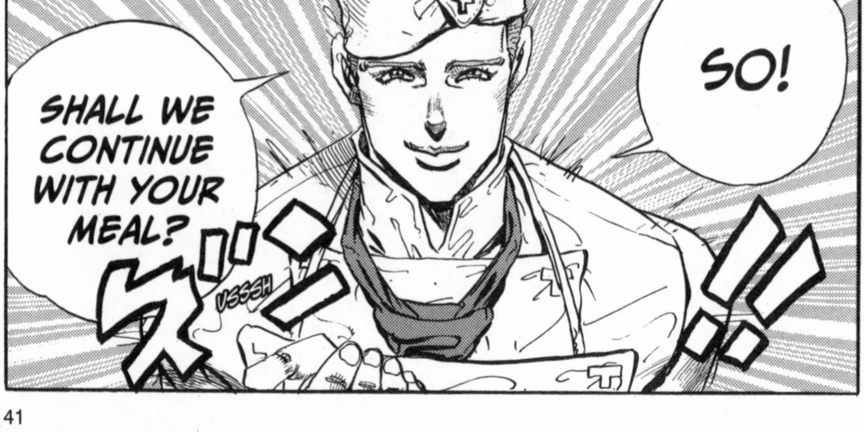
SO!
SHALL WE CONTINUE WITH YOUR MEAL?
USSSH

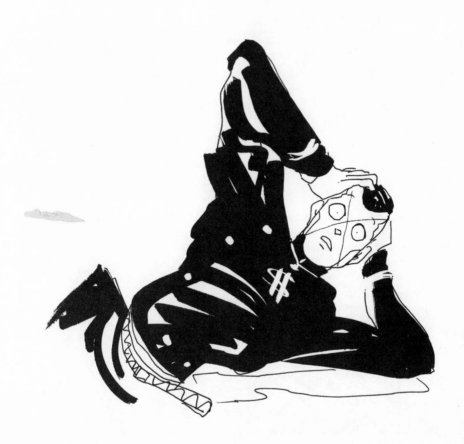

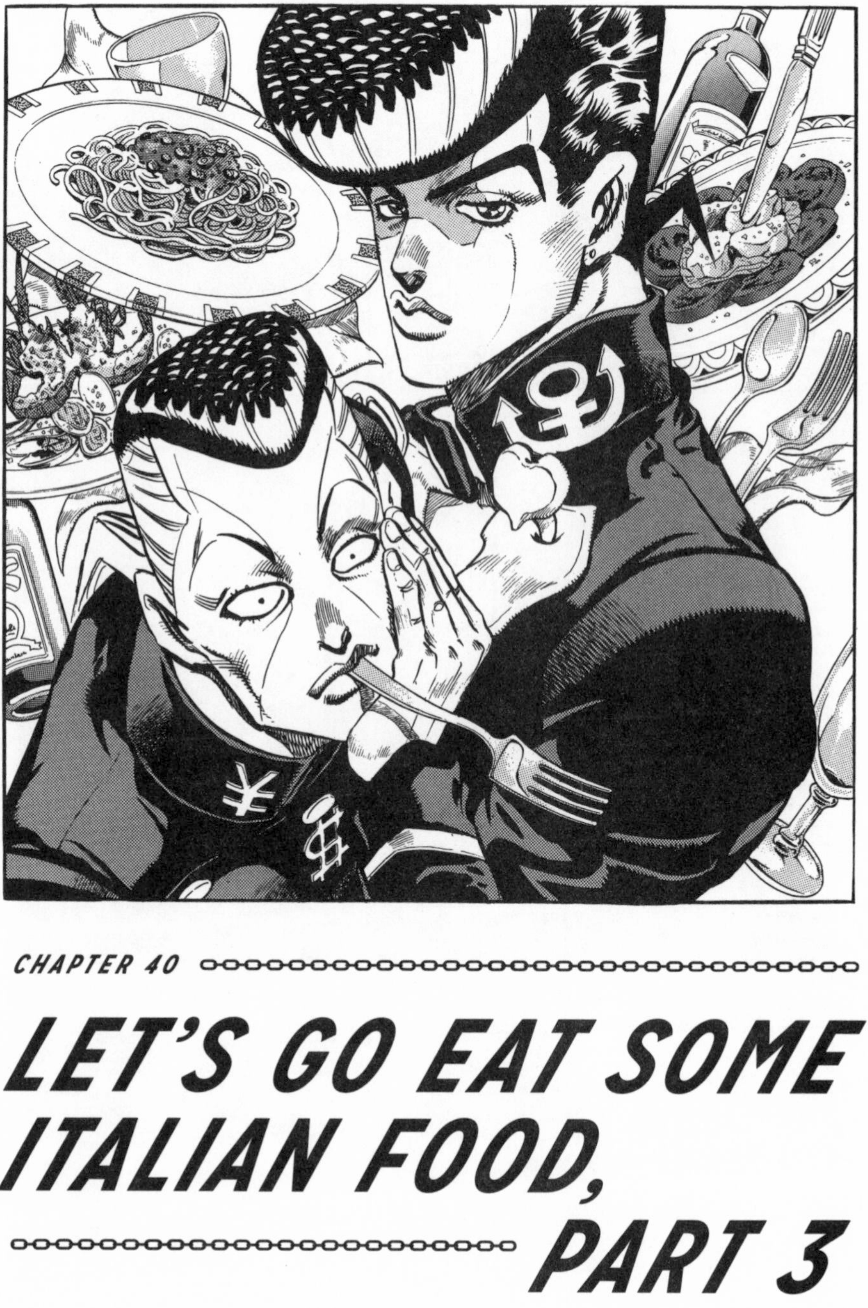

CHAPTER 40

LET'S GO EAT SOME ITALIAN FOOD, PART 3

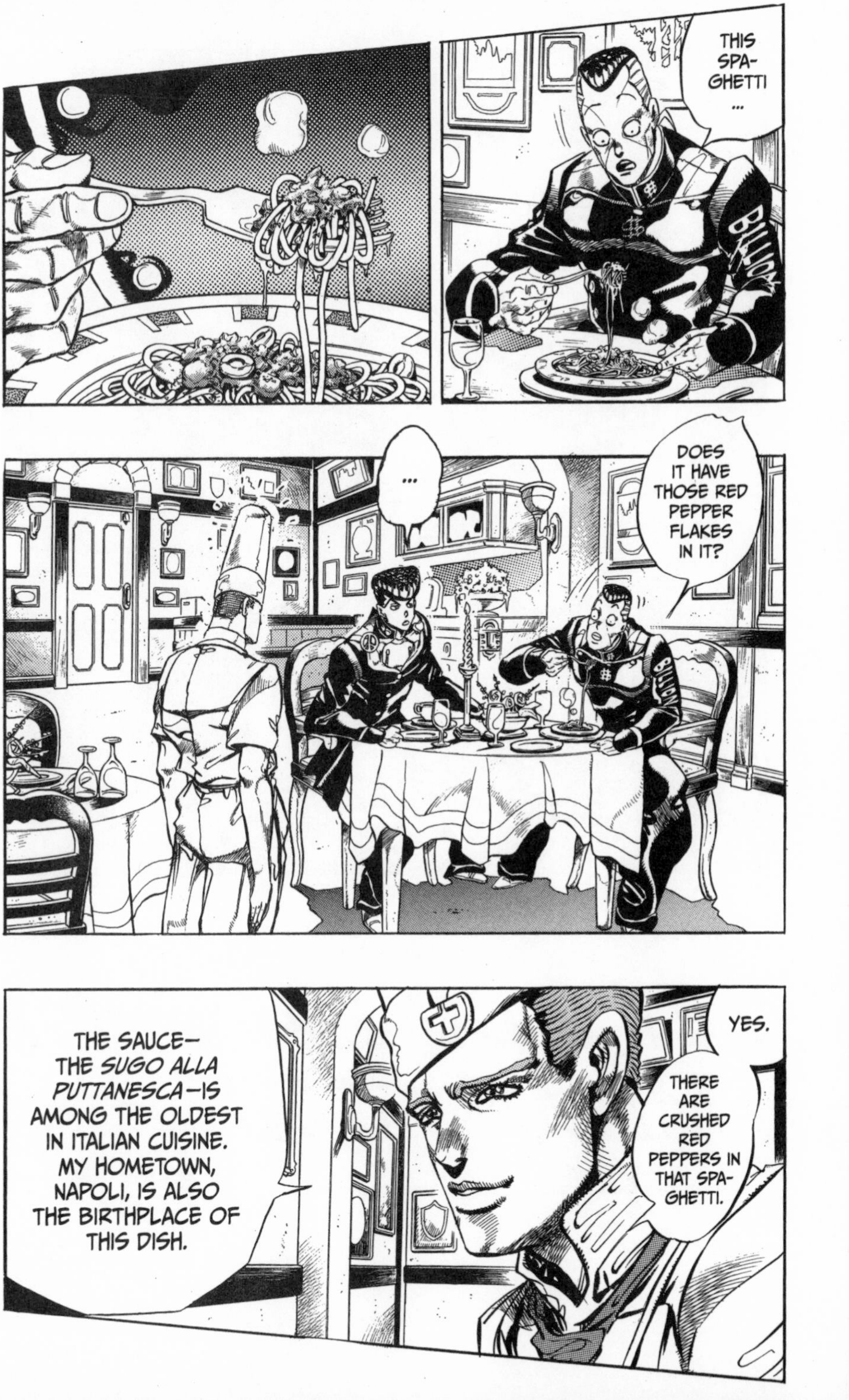
THIS SPA-GHETTI ...
DOES IT HAVE THOSE RED PEPPER FLAKES IN IT?
...
YES.
THERE ARE CRUSHED RED PEPPERS IN THAT SPA-GHETTI.
THE SAUCE—THE *SUGO ALLA PUTTANESCA*—IS AMONG THE OLDEST IN ITALIAN CUISINE. MY HOMETOWN, NAPOLI, IS ALSO THE BIRTHPLACE OF THIS DISH.

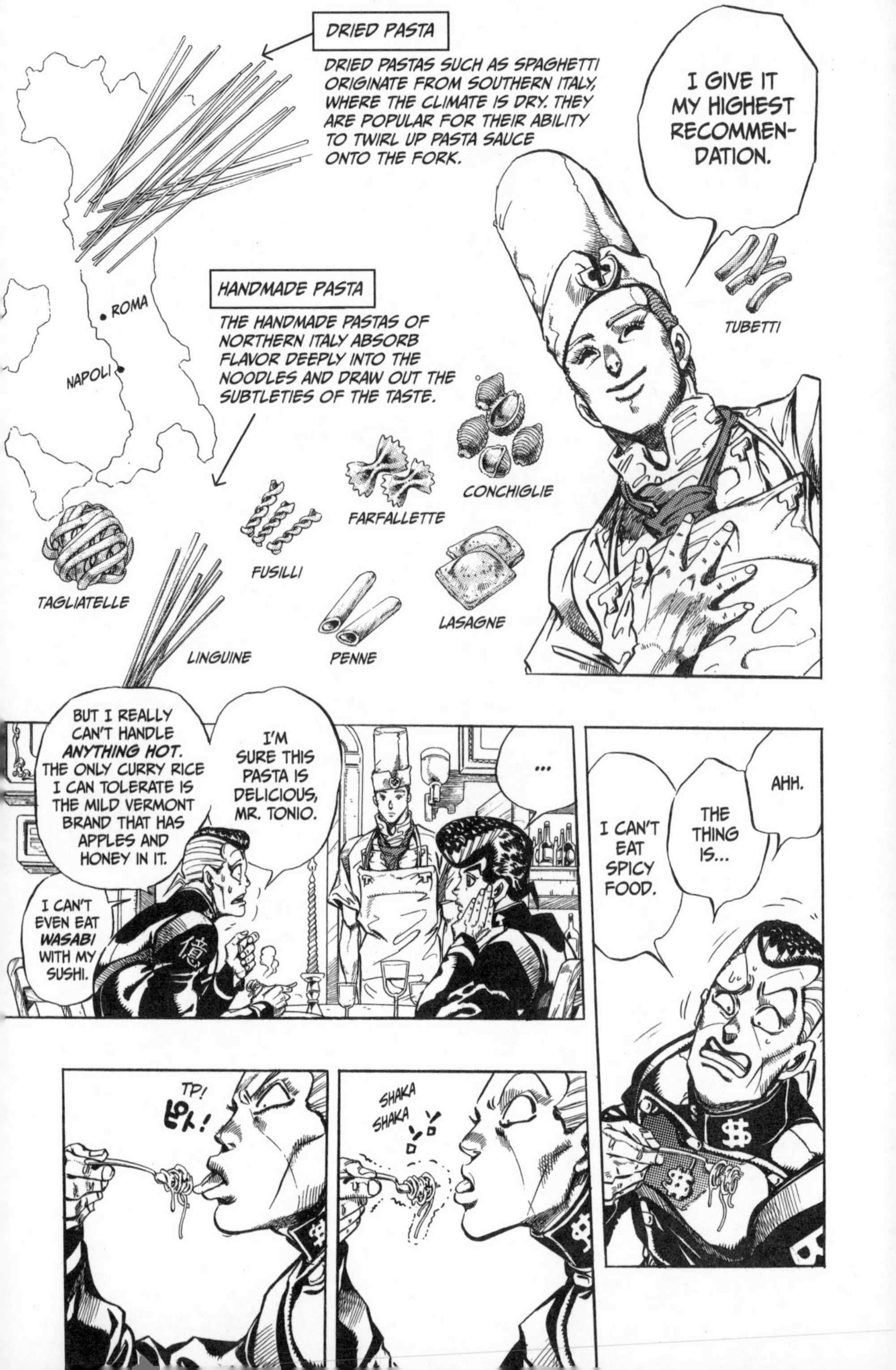
I GIVE IT MY HIGHEST RECOMMENDATION.
TUBETTI
DRIED PASTA
DRIED PASTAS SUCH AS SPAGHETTI ORIGINATE FROM SOUTHERN ITALY, WHERE THE CLIMATE IS DRY. THEY ARE POPULAR FOR THEIR ABILITY TO TWIRL UP PASTA SAUCE ONTO THE FORK.
ROMA
NAPOLI
HANDMADE PASTA
THE HANDMADE PASTAS OF NORTHERN ITALY ABSORB FLAVOR DEEPLY INTO THE NOODLES AND DRAW OUT THE SUBTLETIES OF THE TASTE.
CONCHIGLIE
FARFALLETTE
FUSILLI
TAGLIATELLE
LASAGNE
LINGUINE
PENNE
AHH.
THE THING IS...
I CAN'T EAT SPICY FOOD.
...
I'M SURE THIS PASTA IS DELICIOUS, MR. TONIO.
BUT I REALLY CAN'T HANDLE **ANYTHING HOT.** THE ONLY CURRY RICE I CAN TOLERATE IS THE MILD VERMONT BRAND THAT HAS APPLES AND HONEY IN IT.
I CAN'T EVEN EAT **WASABI** WITH MY SUSHI.
SHAKA SHAKA
TP!

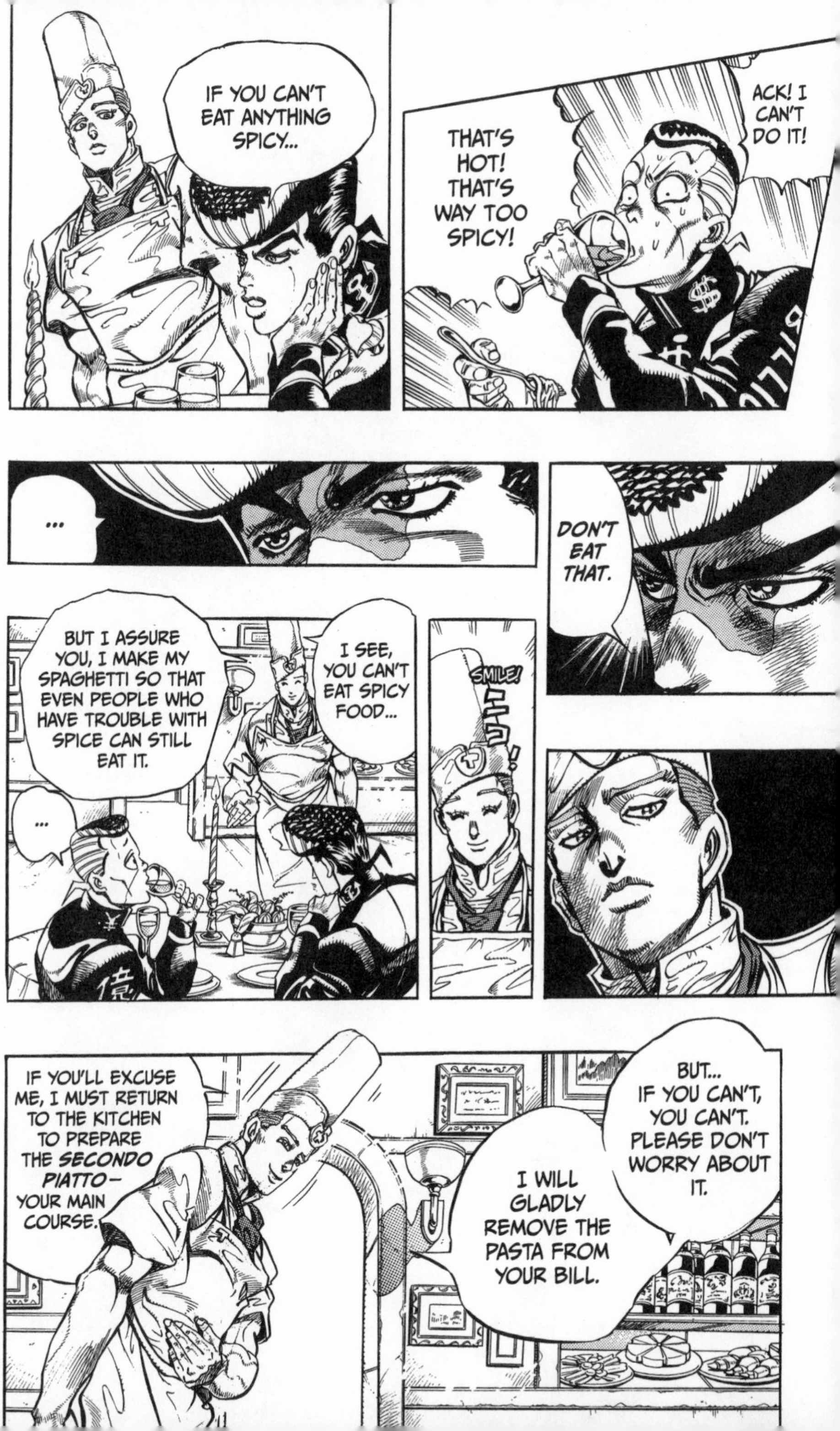

ACK! I CAN'T DO IT!
THAT'S HOT! THAT'S WAY TOO SPICY!
IF YOU CAN'T EAT ANYTHING SPICY...
DON'T EAT THAT.
...
SMILE!
I SEE, YOU CAN'T EAT SPICY FOOD...
BUT I ASSURE YOU, I MAKE MY SPAGHETTI SO THAT EVEN PEOPLE WHO HAVE TROUBLE WITH SPICE CAN STILL EAT IT.
...
BUT... IF YOU CAN'T, YOU CAN'T. PLEASE DON'T WORRY ABOUT IT.
I WILL GLADLY REMOVE THE PASTA FROM YOUR BILL.
IF YOU'LL EXCUSE ME, I MUST RETURN TO THE KITCHEN TO PREPARE THE *SECONDO PIATTO*— YOUR MAIN COURSE.

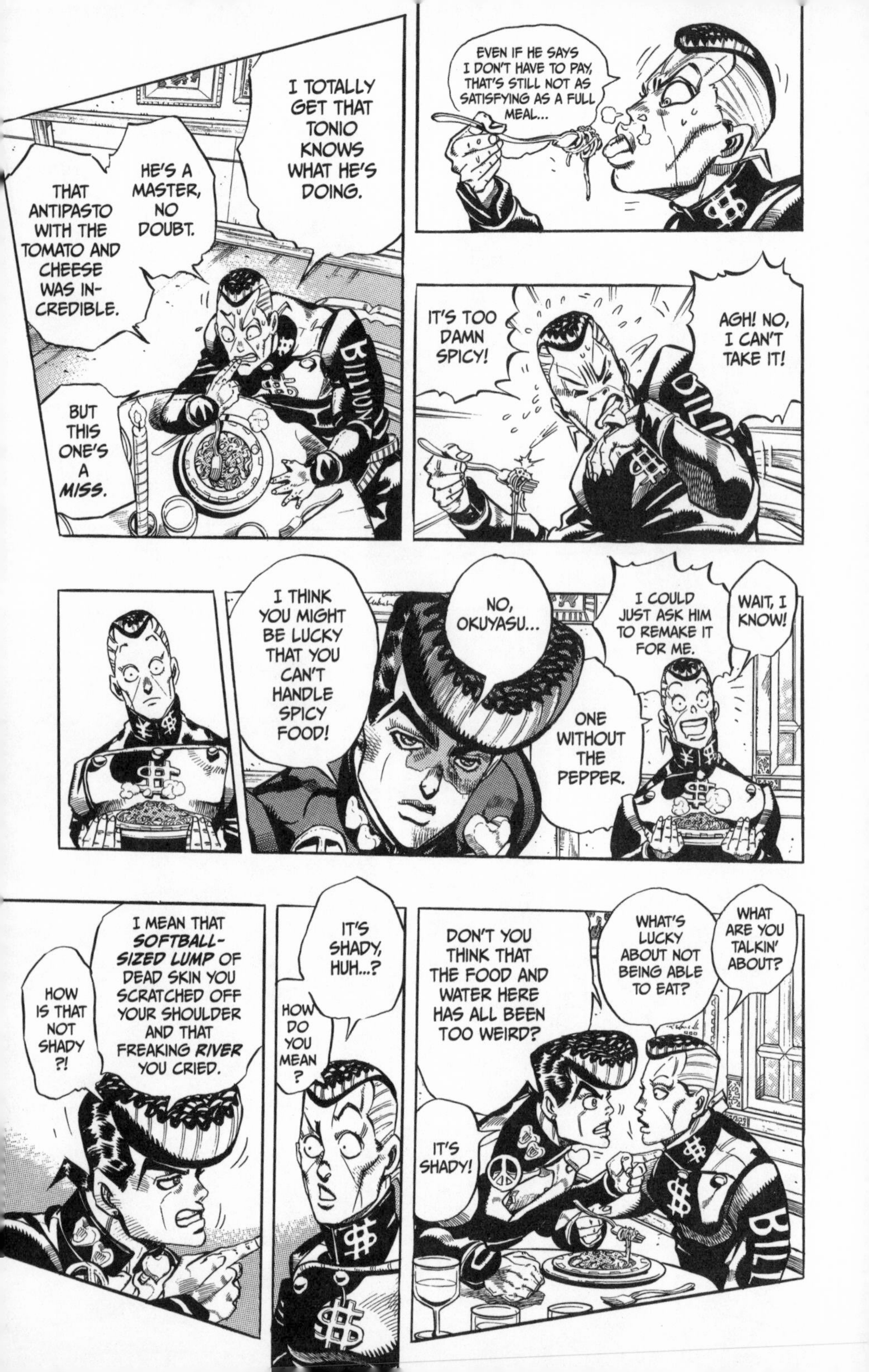
EVEN IF HE SAYS I DON'T HAVE TO PAY, THAT'S STILL NOT AS SATISFYING AS A FULL MEAL...
AGH! NO, I CAN'T TAKE IT!
IT'S TOO DAMN SPICY!
I TOTALLY GET THAT TONIO KNOWS WHAT HE'S DOING.
HE'S A MASTER, NO DOUBT.
THAT ANTIPASTO WITH THE TOMATO AND CHEESE WAS IN-CREDIBLE.
BUT THIS ONE'S A *MISS*.
WAIT, I KNOW!
I COULD JUST ASK HIM TO REMAKE IT FOR ME.
ONE WITHOUT THE PEPPER.
NO, OKUYASU...
I THINK YOU MIGHT BE LUCKY THAT YOU CAN'T HANDLE SPICY FOOD!
WHAT ARE YOU TALKIN' ABOUT?
WHAT'S LUCKY ABOUT NOT BEING ABLE TO EAT?
DON'T YOU THINK THAT THE FOOD AND WATER HERE HAS ALL BEEN TOO WEIRD?
IT'S SHADY!
IT'S SHADY, HUH...?
HOW DO YOU MEAN?
I MEAN THAT *SOFTBALL-SIZED LUMP* OF DEAD SKIN YOU SCRATCHED OFF YOUR SHOULDER AND THAT FREAKING *RIVER* YOU CRIED.
HOW IS THAT NOT SHADY?!

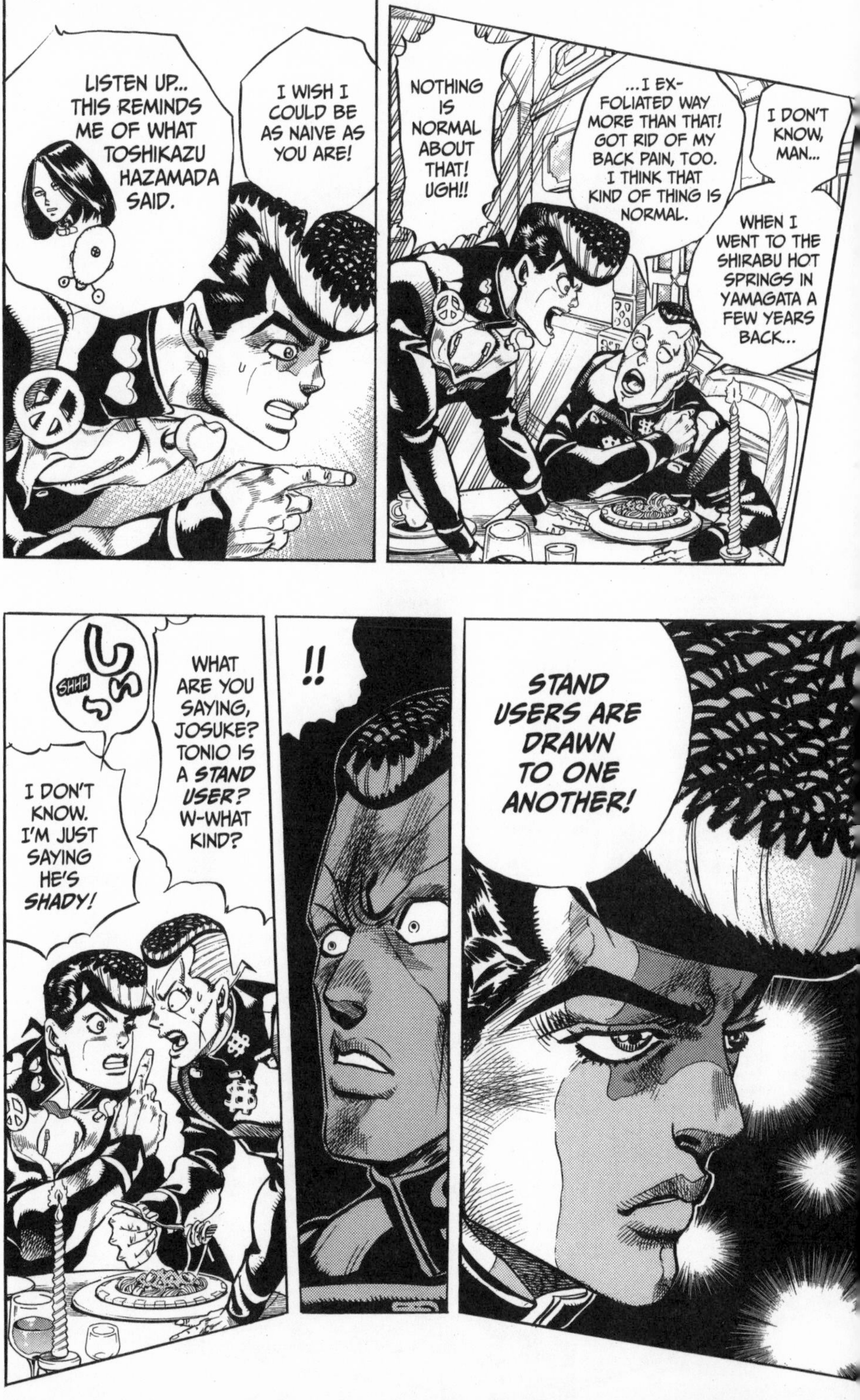
I DON'T KNOW, MAN...
WHEN I WENT TO THE SHIRABU HOT SPRINGS IN YAMAGATA A FEW YEARS BACK...
...I EXFOLIATED WAY MORE THAN THAT! GOT RID OF MY BACK PAIN, TOO. I THINK THAT KIND OF THING IS NORMAL.
NOTHING IS NORMAL ABOUT THAT! UGH!!
I WISH I COULD BE AS NAIVE AS YOU ARE!
LISTEN UP... THIS REMINDS ME OF WHAT TOSHIKAZU HAZAMADA SAID.
STAND USERS ARE DRAWN TO ONE ANOTHER!
!!
WHAT ARE YOU SAYING, JOSUKE? TONIO IS A *STAND USER?* W-WHAT KIND?
SHHH
I DON'T KNOW. I'M JUST SAYING HE'S *SHADY!*

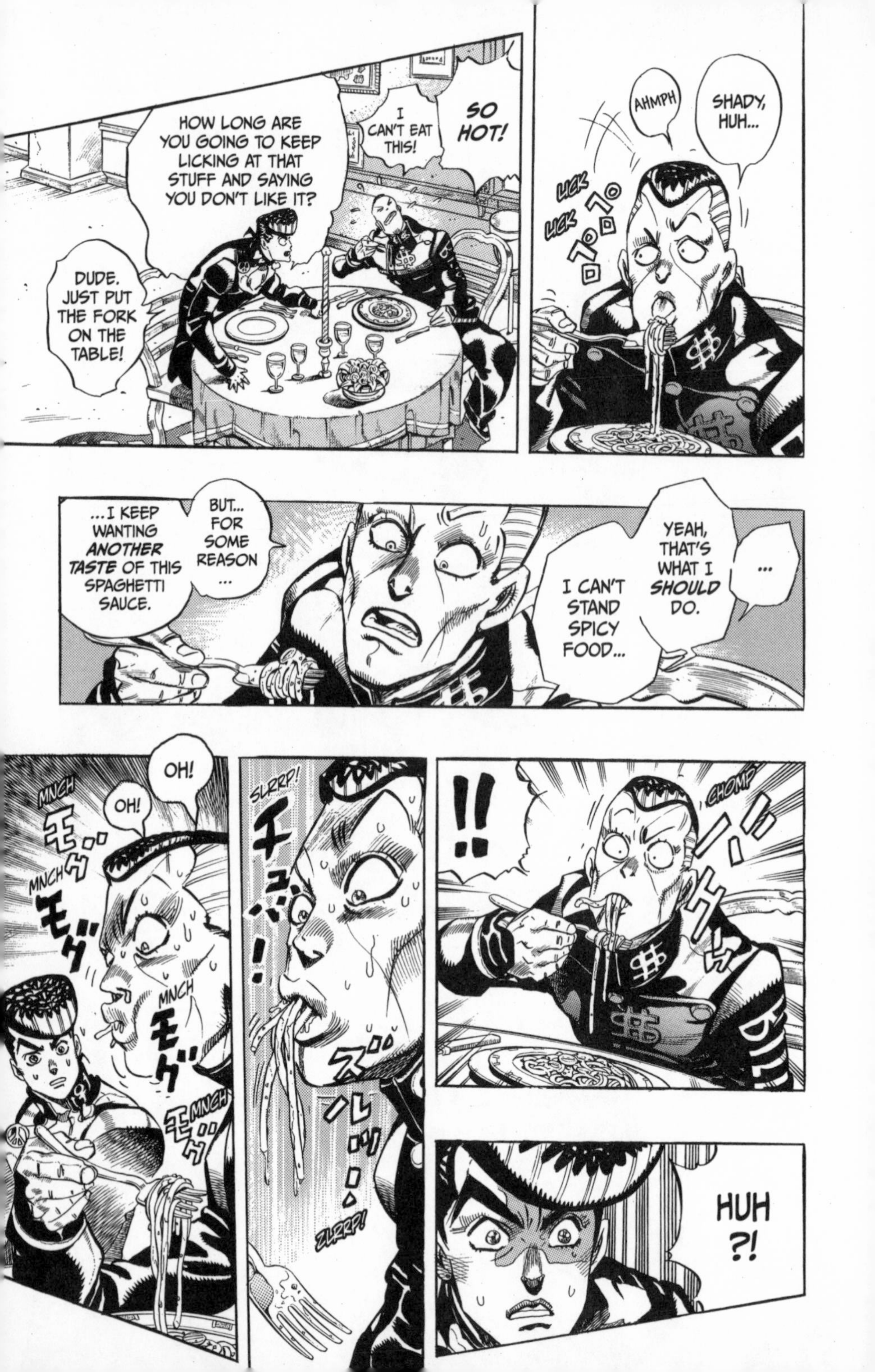

SHADY, HUH...
AHMPH
LICK
LICK
SO HOT!
I CAN'T EAT THIS!
HOW LONG ARE YOU GOING TO KEEP LICKING AT THAT STUFF AND SAYING YOU DON'T LIKE IT?
DUDE. JUST PUT THE FORK ON THE TABLE!
...
YEAH, THAT'S WHAT I SHOULD DO.
I CAN'T STAND SPICY FOOD...
BUT... FOR SOME REASON ...
...I KEEP WANTING ANOTHER TASTE OF THIS SPAGHETTI SAUCE.
CHOMP
!!
HUH ?!
SLRRP!
ZLRRP!
OH!
OH!
MNCH
MNCH
MNCH
MNCH

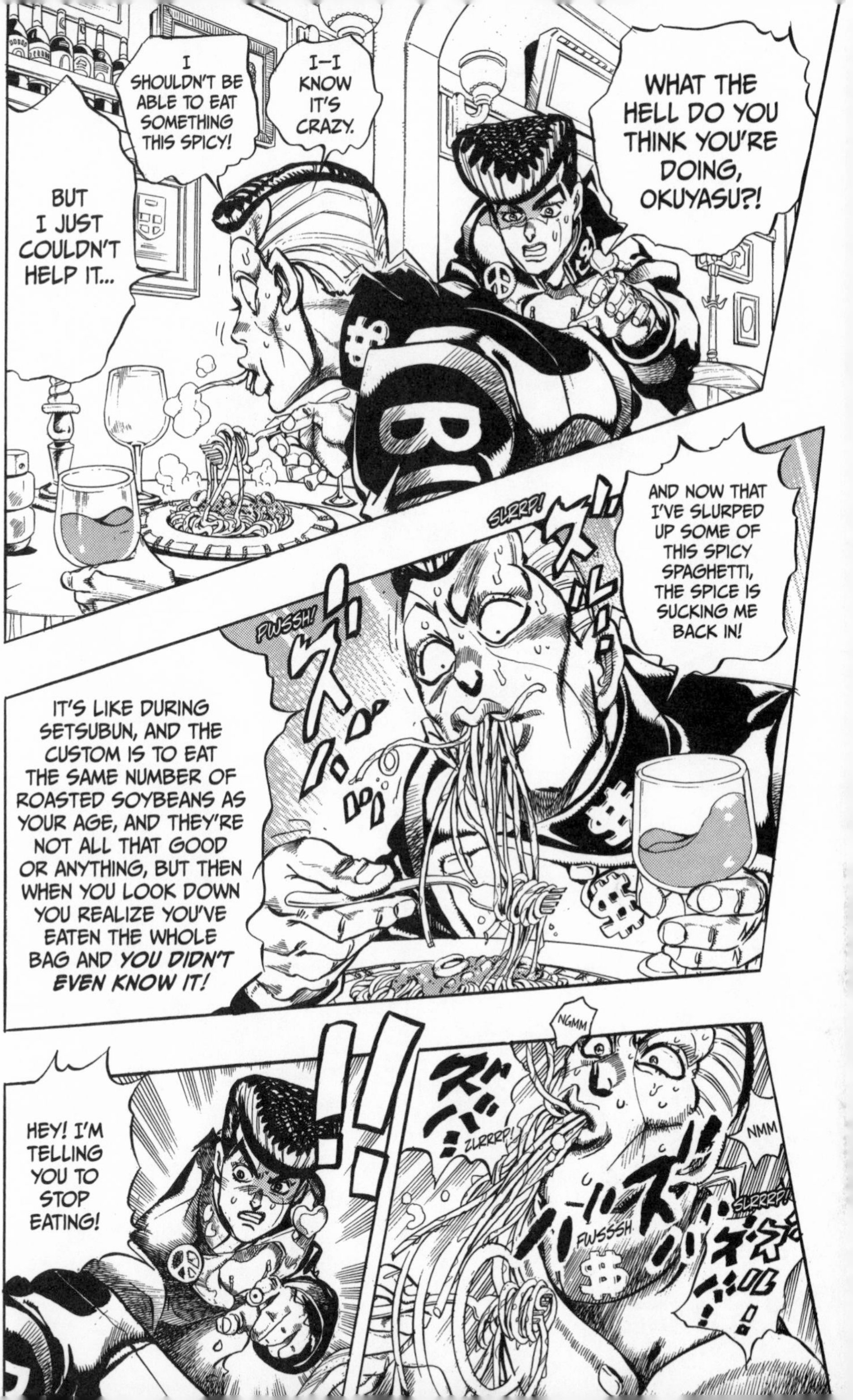
WHAT THE HELL DO YOU THINK YOU'RE DOING, OKUYASU?!
I—I KNOW IT'S CRAZY.
I SHOULDN'T BE ABLE TO EAT SOMETHING THIS SPICY!
BUT I JUST COULDN'T HELP IT...
AND NOW THAT I'VE SLURPED UP SOME OF THIS SPICY SPAGHETTI, THE SPICE IS SUCKING ME BACK IN!
SLURRP!
PWUSSH!
IT'S LIKE DURING SETSUBUN, AND THE CUSTOM IS TO EAT THE SAME NUMBER OF ROASTED SOYBEANS AS YOUR AGE, AND THEY'RE NOT ALL THAT GOOD OR ANYTHING, BUT THEN WHEN YOU LOOK DOWN YOU REALIZE YOU'VE EATEN THE WHOLE BAG AND *YOU DIDN'T EVEN KNOW IT!*
NGMM
NMM
SLURRRP!
FWSSSH
ZLURRRP!
HEY! I'M TELLING YOU TO STOP EATING!

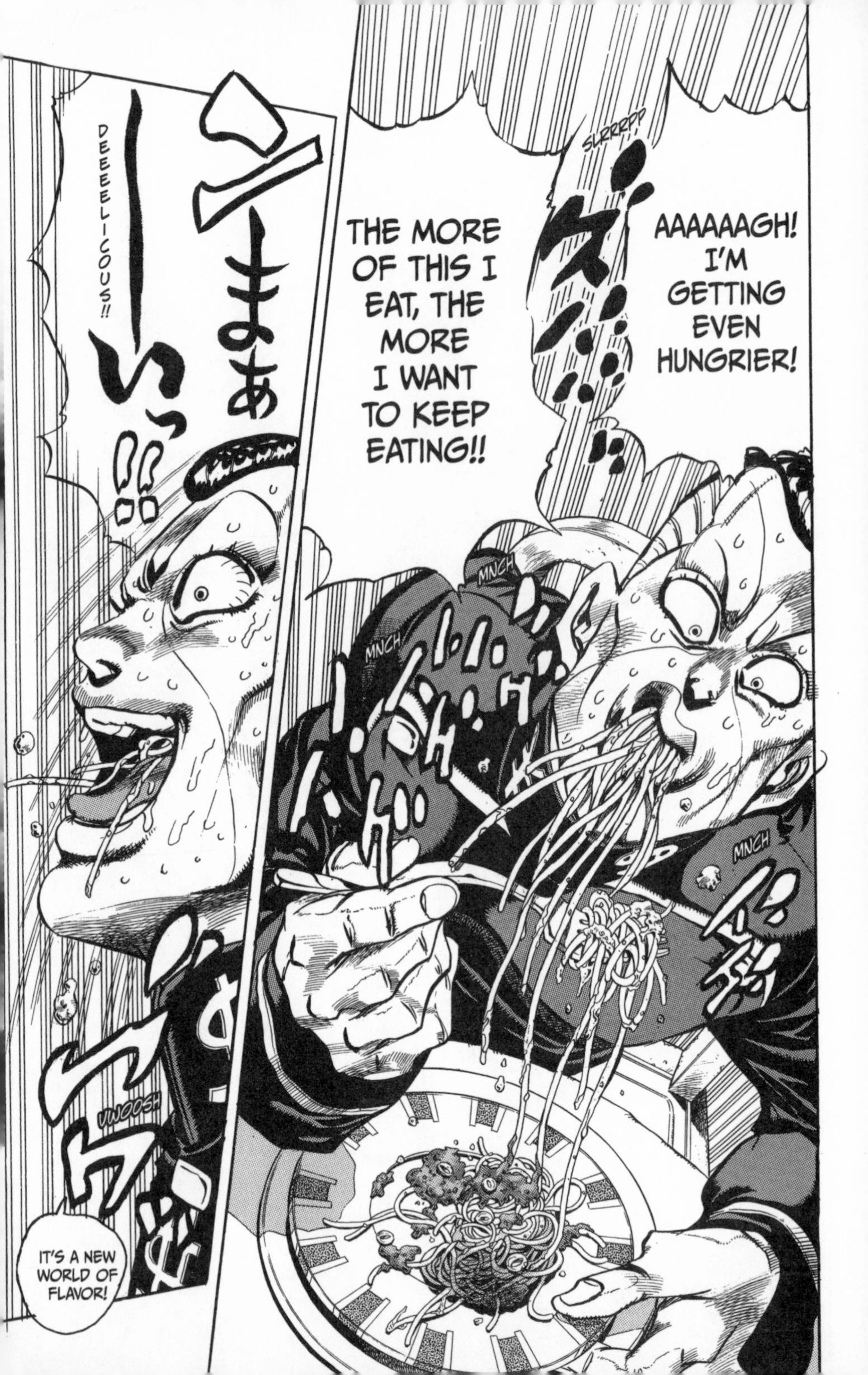
SLRRRPP
AAAAAAGH! I'M GETTING EVEN HUNGRIER!
THE MORE OF THIS I EAT, THE MORE I WANT TO KEEP EATING!!
MNCH
MNCH
MNCH
DEEEELICOUS!!
UWOOSH
IT'S A NEW WORLD OF FLAVOR!

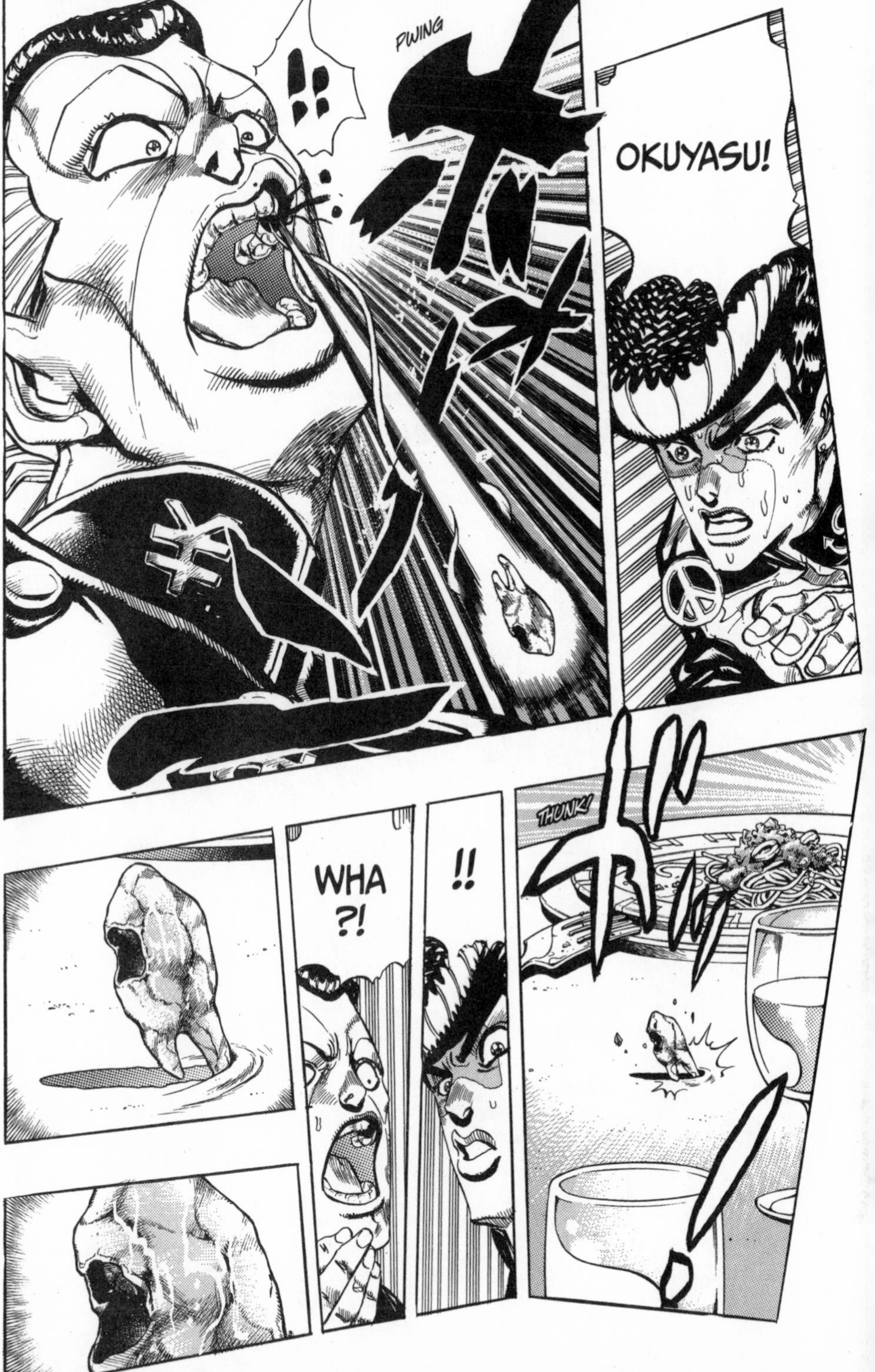
OKUYASU!
PWING
!!
THUNK!
!!
WHA ?!

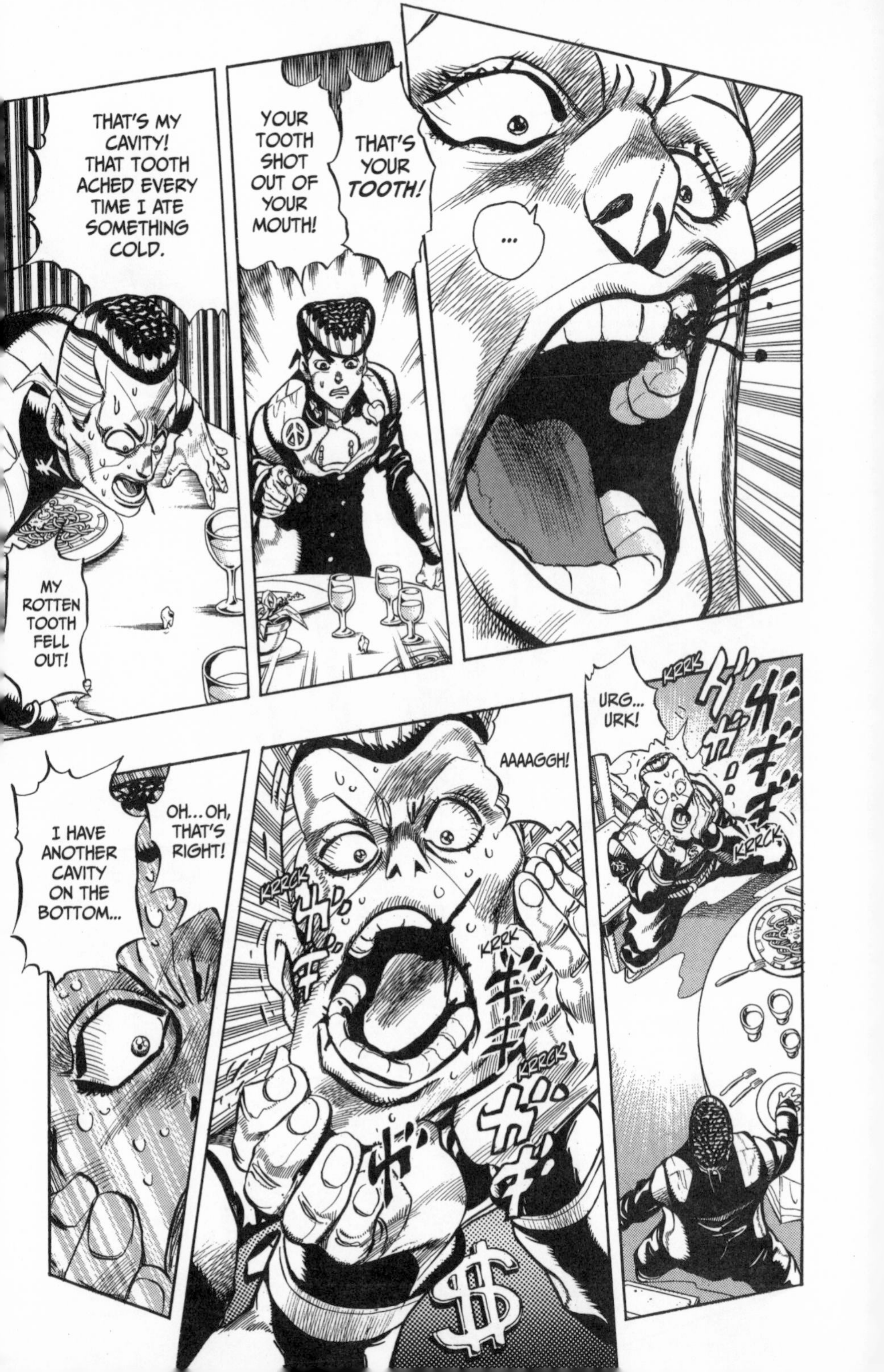
...
THAT'S YOUR TOOTH!
YOUR TOOTH SHOT OUT OF YOUR MOUTH!
THAT'S MY CAVITY! THAT TOOTH ACHED EVERY TIME I ATE SOMETHING COLD.
MY ROTTEN TOOTH FELL OUT!
KRRK
URG... URK!
KRRCK
AAAAGGH!
KRRCK
KRRK
KRRCK
OH...OH, THAT'S RIGHT!
I HAVE ANOTHER CAVITY ON THE BOTTOM...

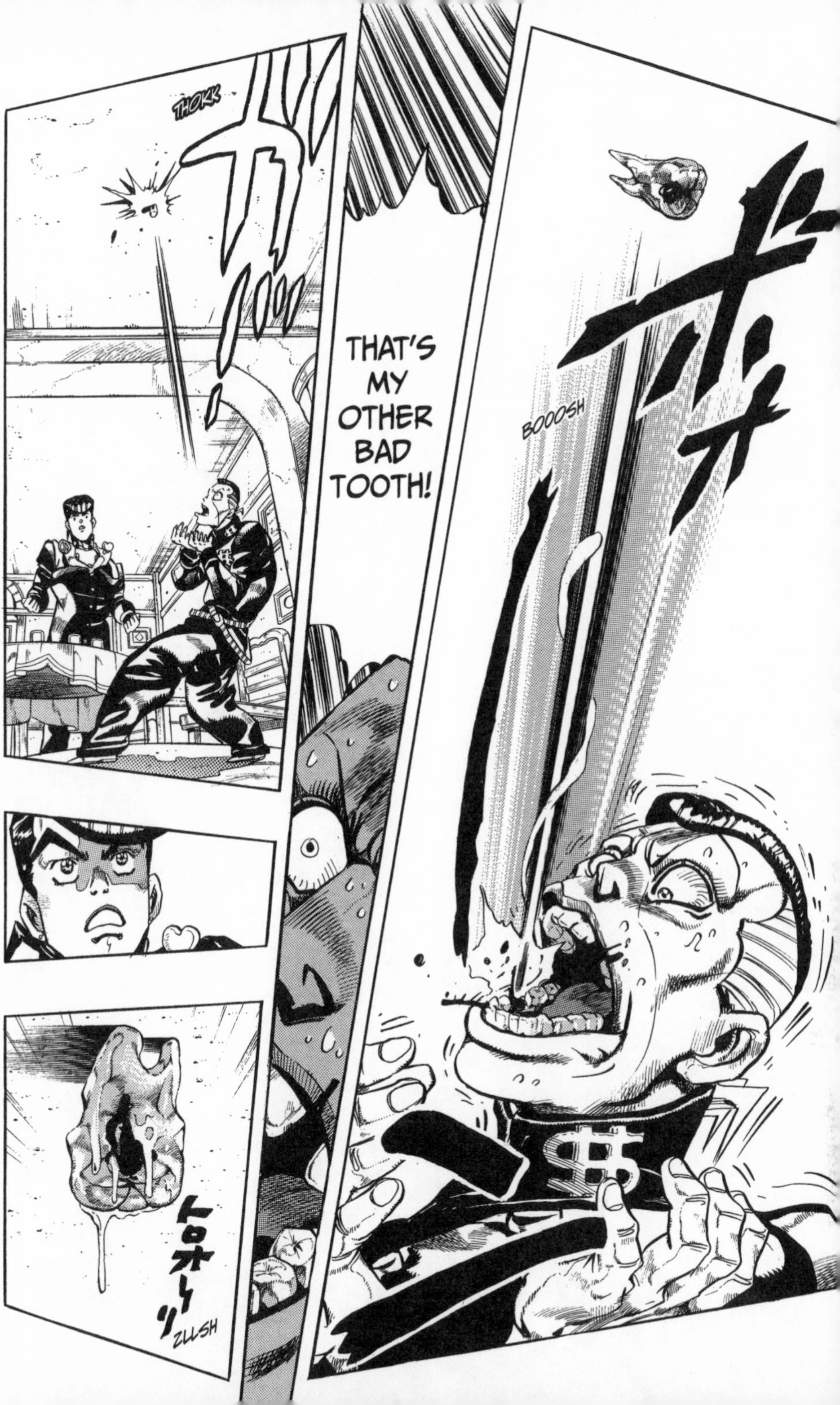
BOOOSH
THAT'S MY OTHER BAD TOOTH!
THOKK
ZULLSH

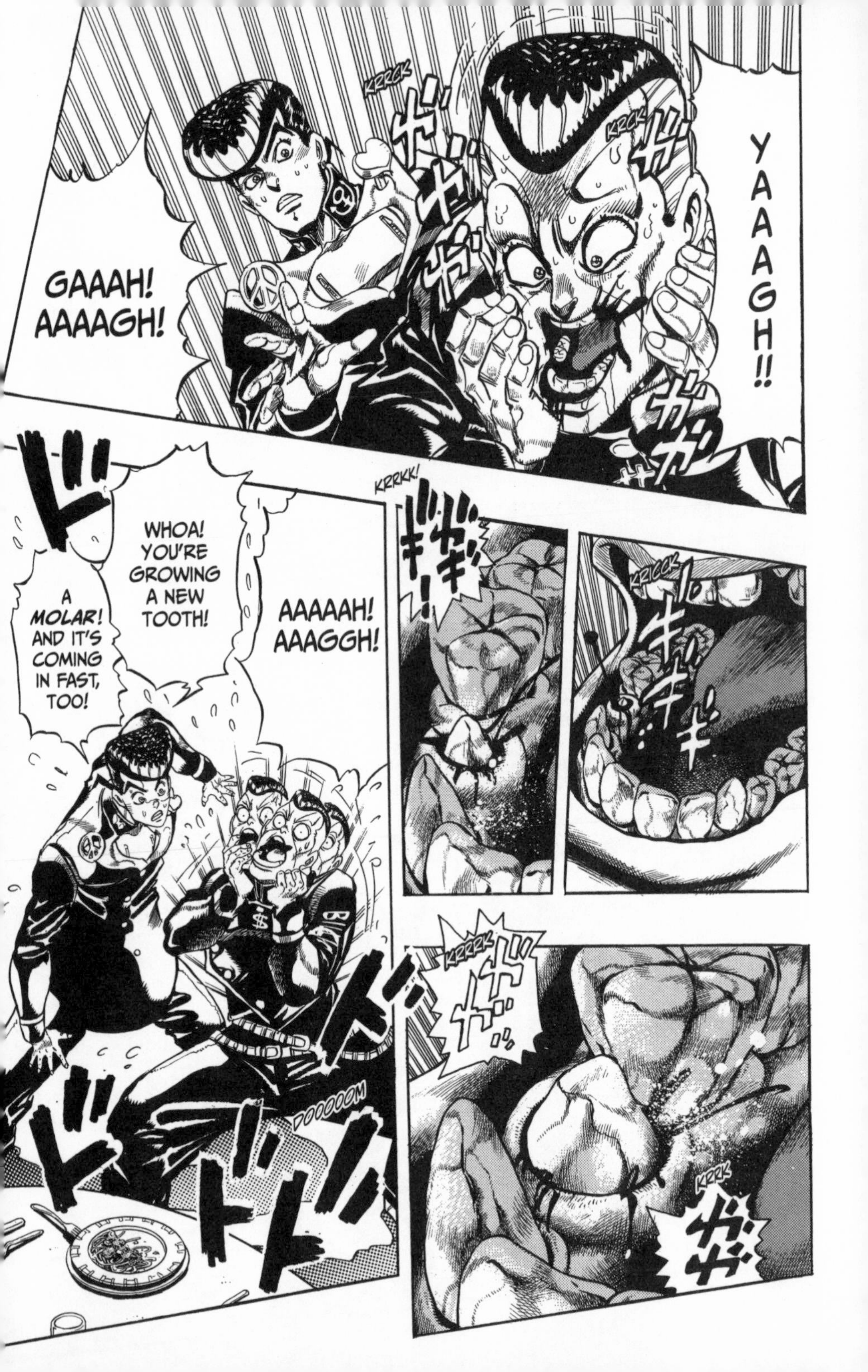
YAAAAGH!!
KRRCK
KRRCK
GAAAH! AAAAGH!
KRICCK
KRRKK!
KRRRK
KRRK
AAAAAH! AAAGGH!
WHOA! YOU'RE GROWING A NEW TOOTH!
A *MOLAR!* AND IT'S COMING IN FAST, TOO!
DOOOOOM

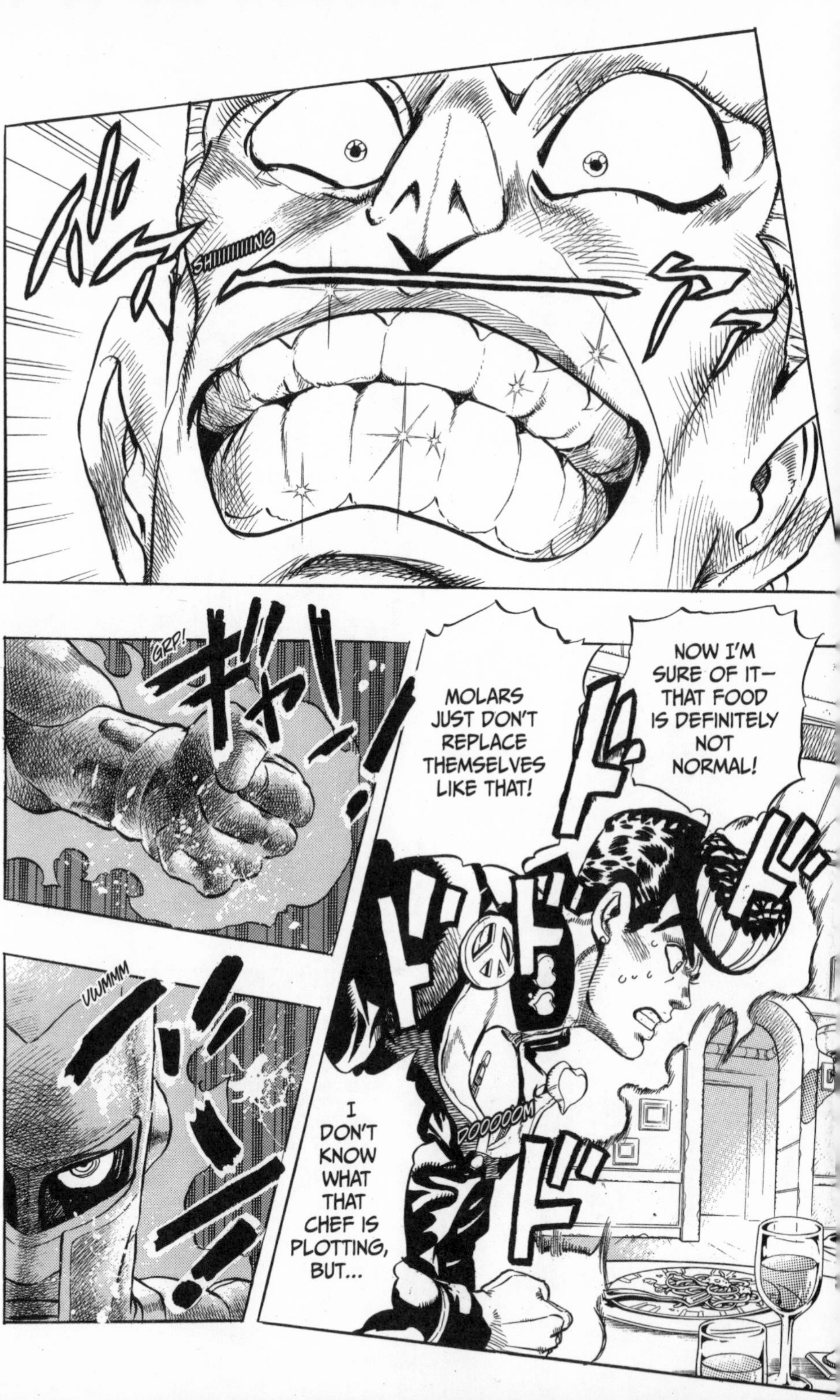
SHIIIIIIING
NOW I'M SURE OF IT—THAT FOOD IS DEFINITELY NOT NORMAL!
MOLARS JUST DON'T REPLACE THEMSELVES LIKE THAT!
DOOOOOM
I DON'T KNOW WHAT THAT CHEF IS PLOTTING, BUT...
GRP!
VWMMM

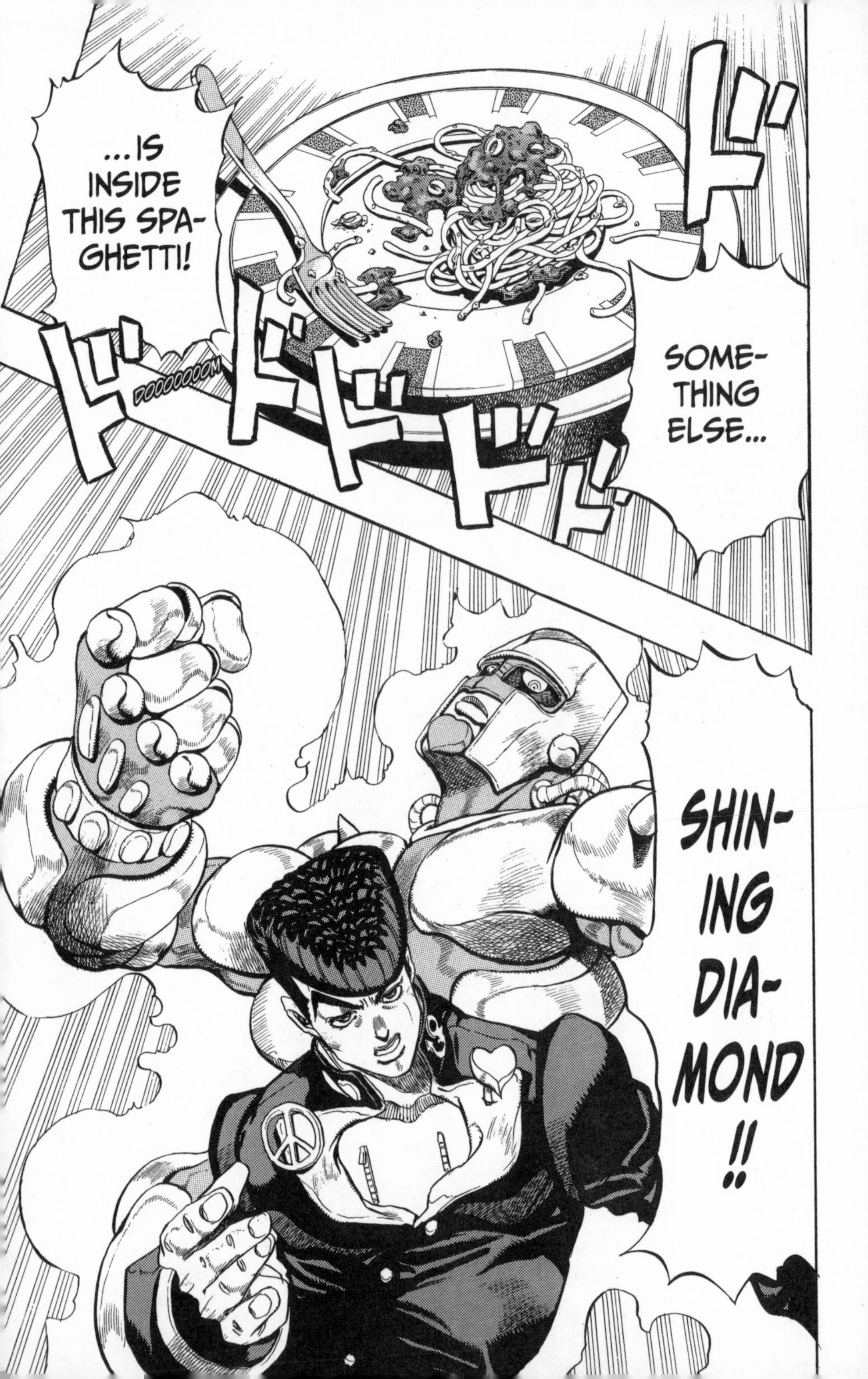
SOME-
THING
ELSE...
...IS
INSIDE
THIS SPA-
GHETTI!
ドドドドドドドド
DOOOOOOOM
SHIN-
ING
DIA-
MOND
!!

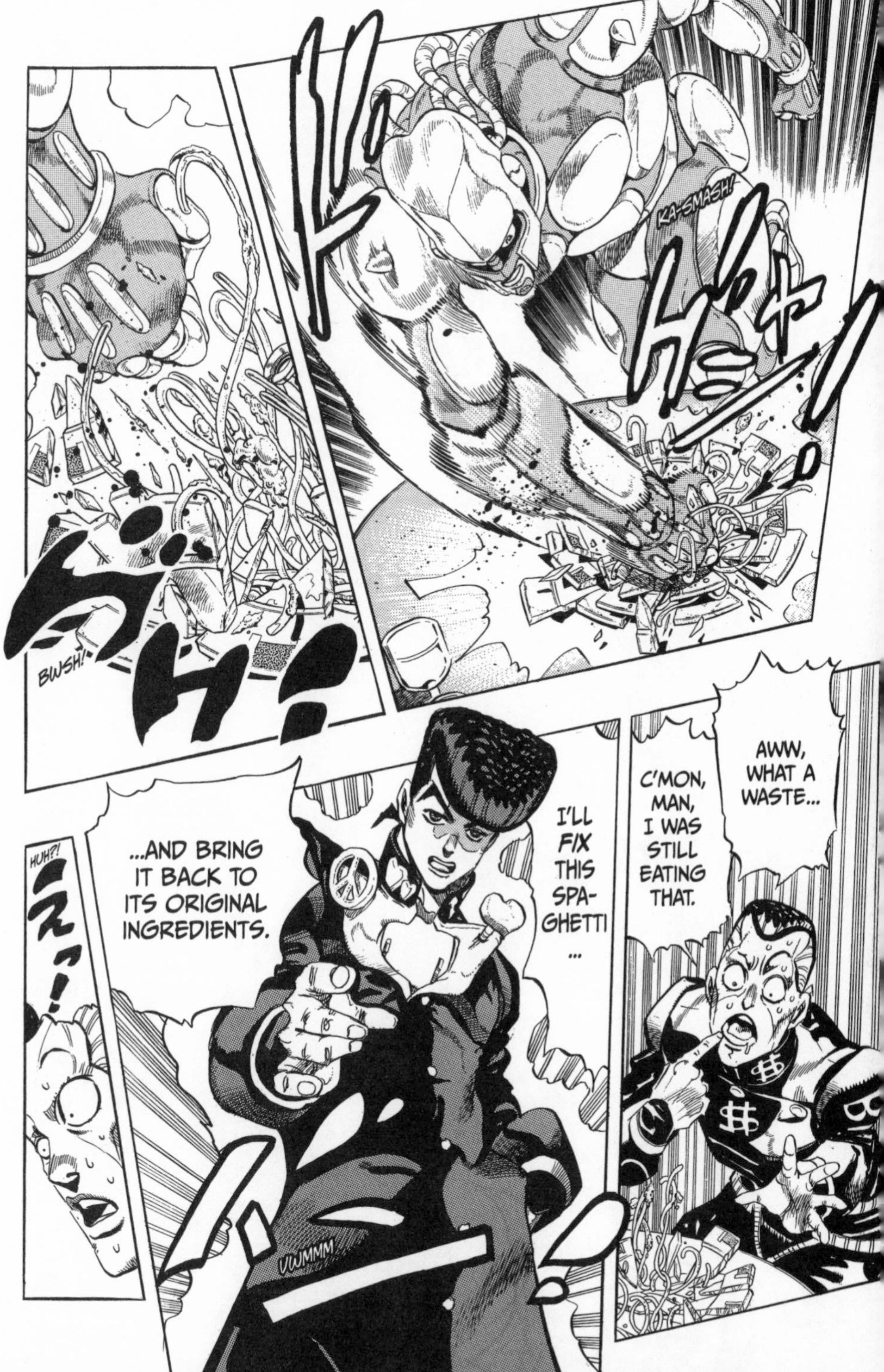
KA-SMASH!
BWSH!
AWW, WHAT A WASTE...
C'MON, MAN, I WAS STILL EATING THAT.
I'LL FIX THIS SPA-GHETTI ...
...AND BRING IT BACK TO ITS ORIGINAL INGREDIENTS.
VWMMM
HUH?!

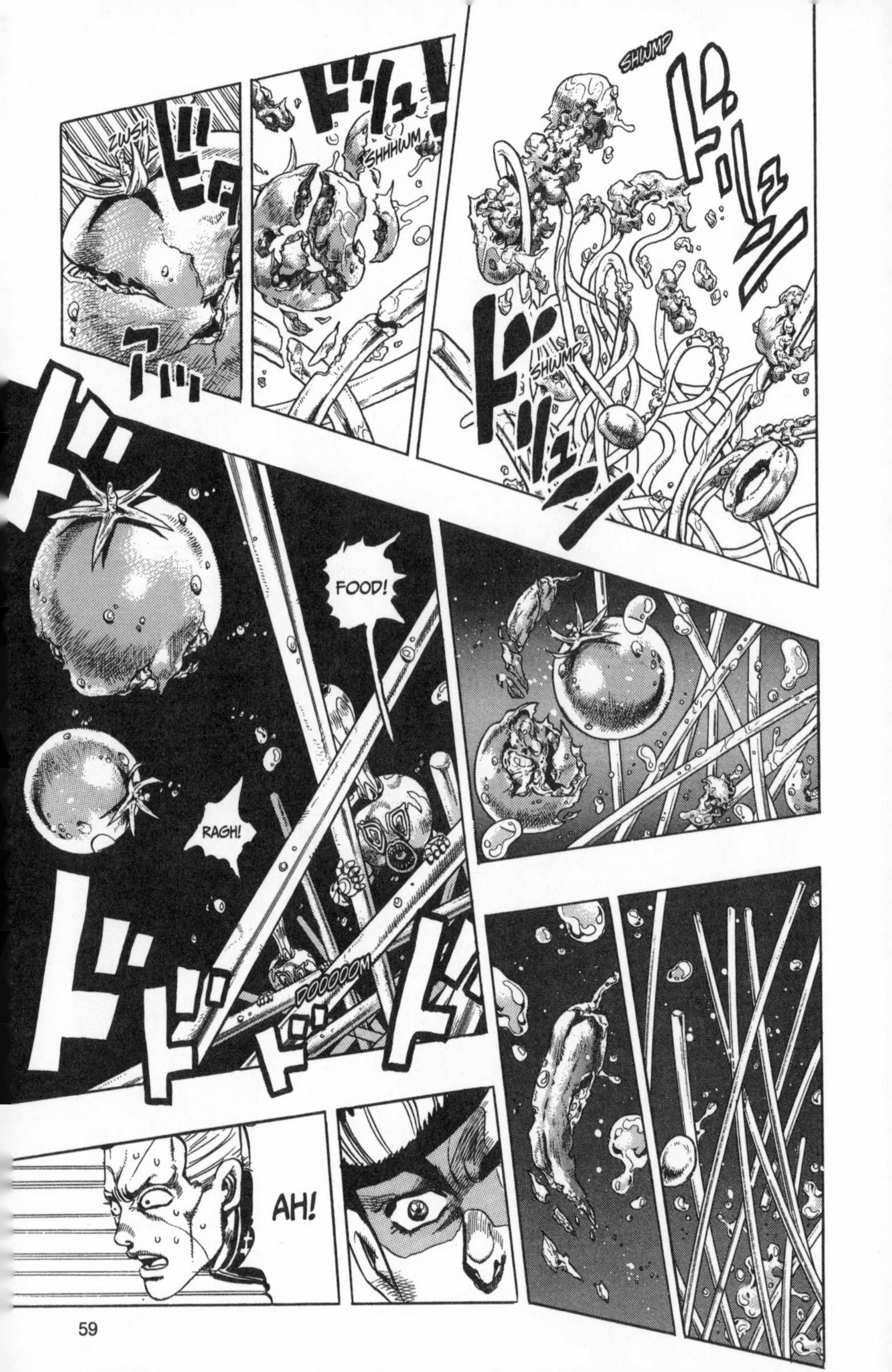
SHWUMP
SHWUMP
SHHHWUM
ZWSH
FOOD!
RAGH!
DOOOOOM
AH!

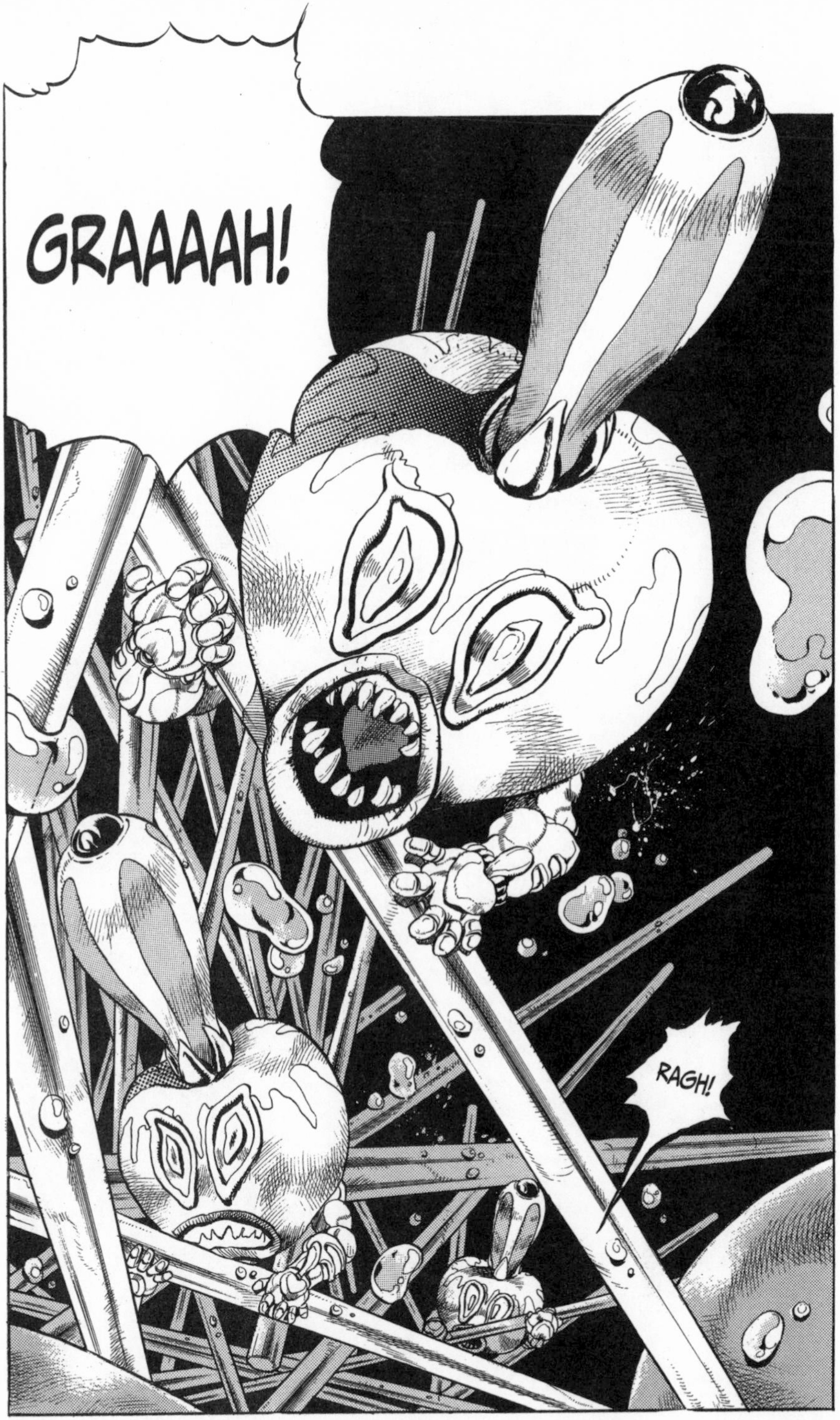
GRAAAAH!
RAGH!

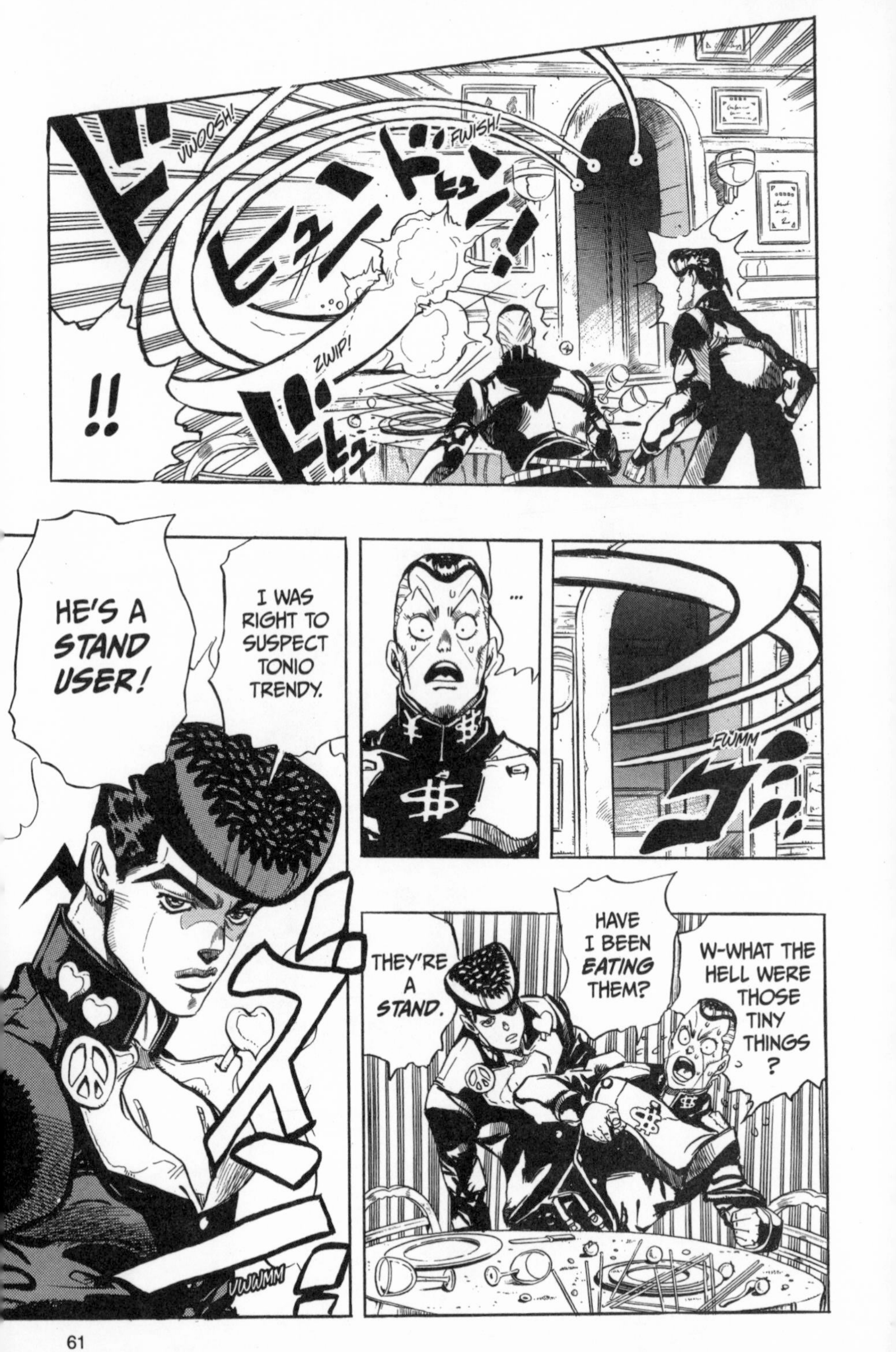
FWISH!
VWOOSH!
ZWIP!
!!
FWMM
...
W-WHAT THE HELL WERE THOSE TINY THINGS?
HAVE I BEEN EATING THEM?
THEY'RE A STAND.
I WAS RIGHT TO SUSPECT TONIO TRENDY.
HE'S A STAND USER!
VWWMM

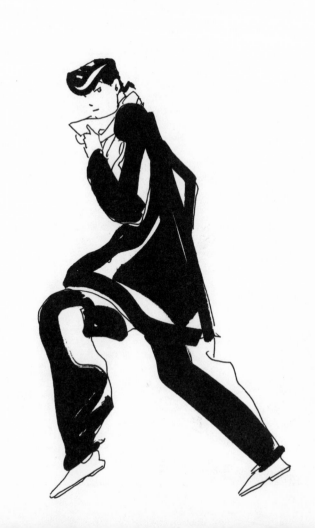

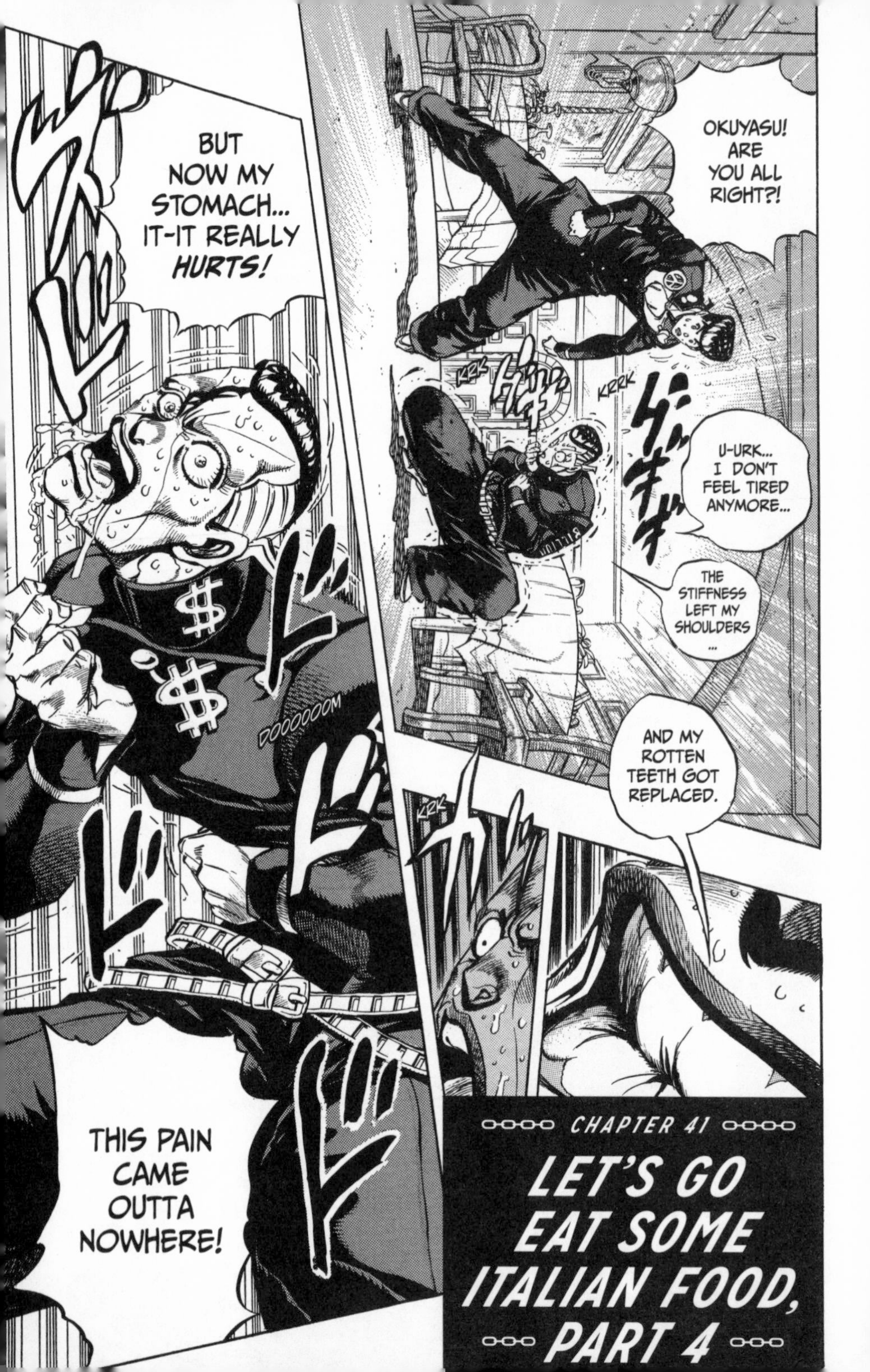

OKUYASU! ARE YOU ALL RIGHT?!
KRK
KRRK
U-URK... I DON'T FEEL TIRED ANYMORE...
THE STIFFNESS LEFT MY SHOULDERS ...
AND MY ROTTEN TEETH GOT REPLACED.
KRK
CHAPTER 41
LET'S GO EAT SOME ITALIAN FOOD, PART 4
BUT NOW MY STOMACH... IT-IT REALLY *HURTS!*
DOOOOOOM
THIS PAIN CAME OUTTA NOWHERE!

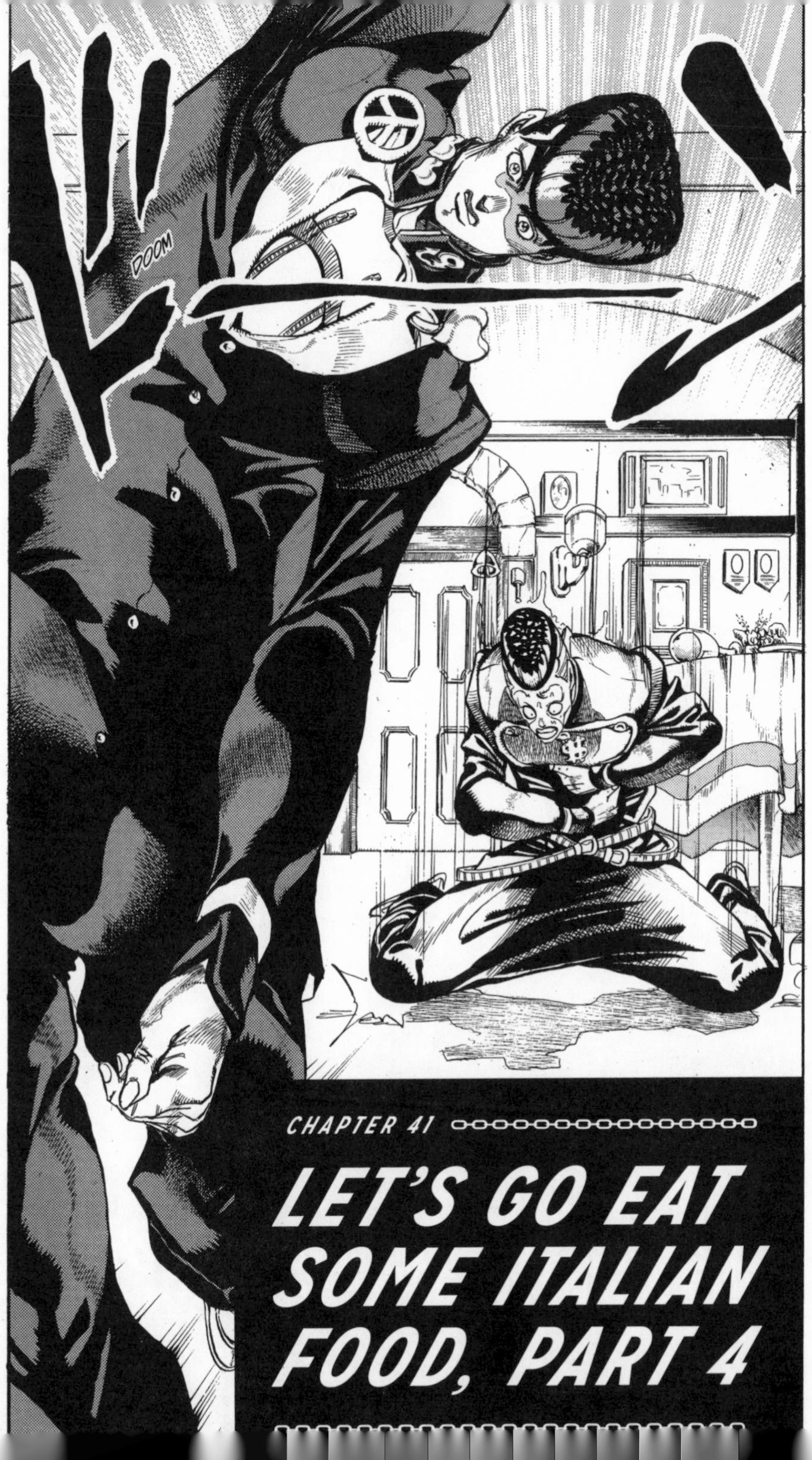
DOOM

CHAPTER 41

LET'S GO EAT SOME ITALIAN FOOD, PART 4

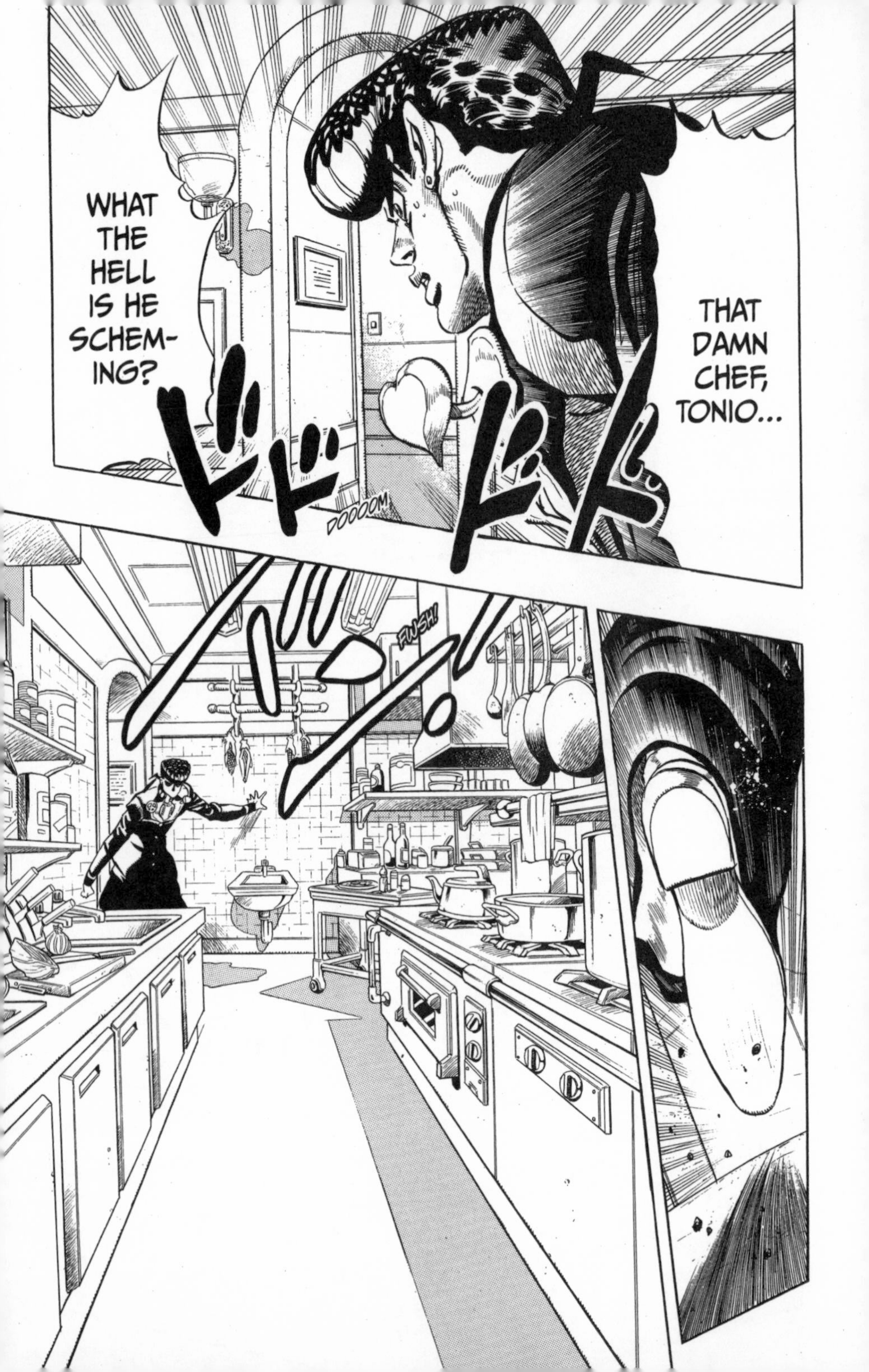
THAT DAMN CHEF, TONIO...
WHAT THE HELL IS HE SCHEM-ING?
DOOOOM
FWSH!

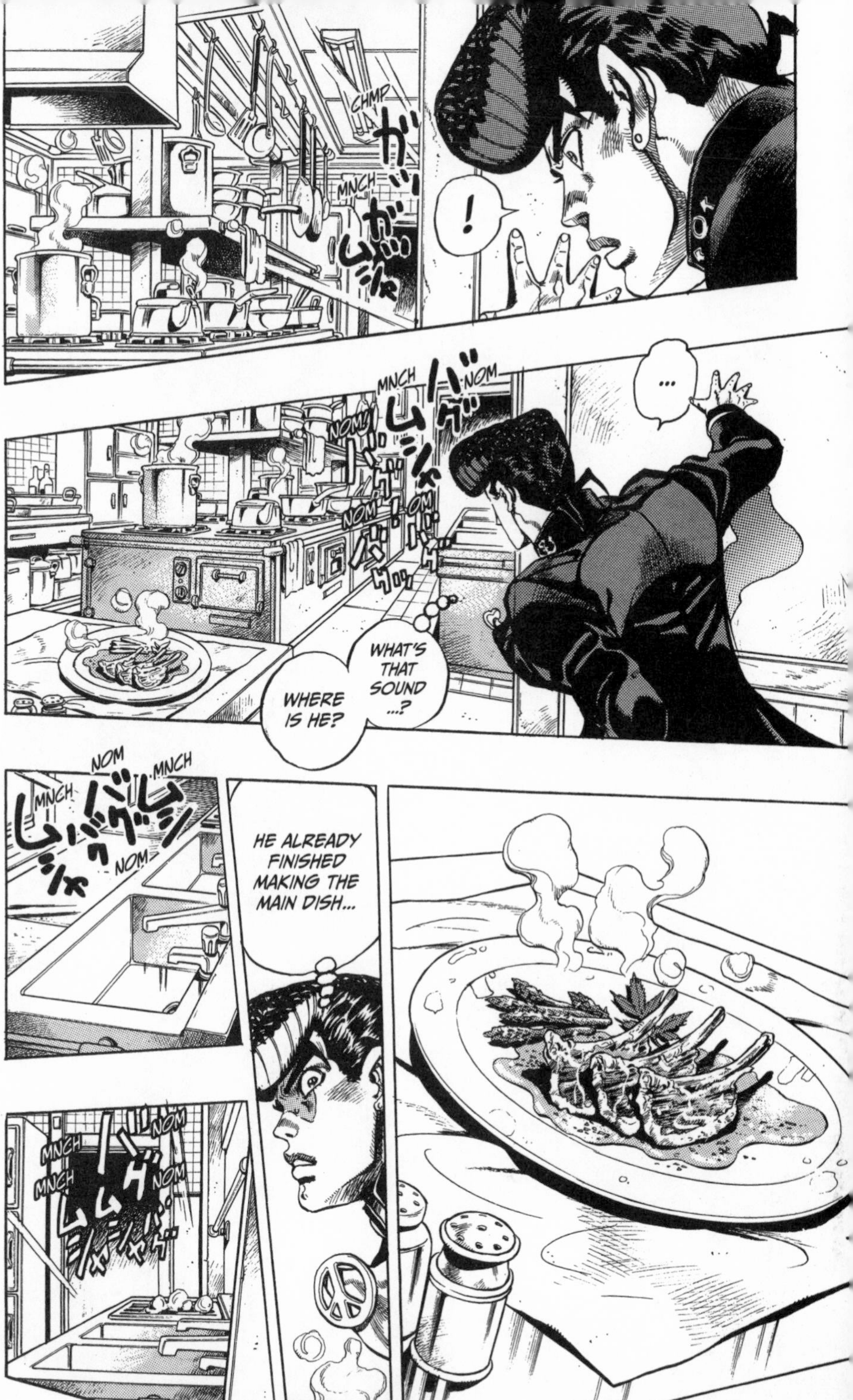
!
CHMP
MNCH
...
NOM
MNCH
NOM
NOM
NOM
WHAT'S THAT SOUND ...?
WHERE IS HE?
HE ALREADY FINISHED MAKING THE MAIN DISH...
MNCH
NOM
MNCH
NOM
MNCH
MNCH
NOM
NOM

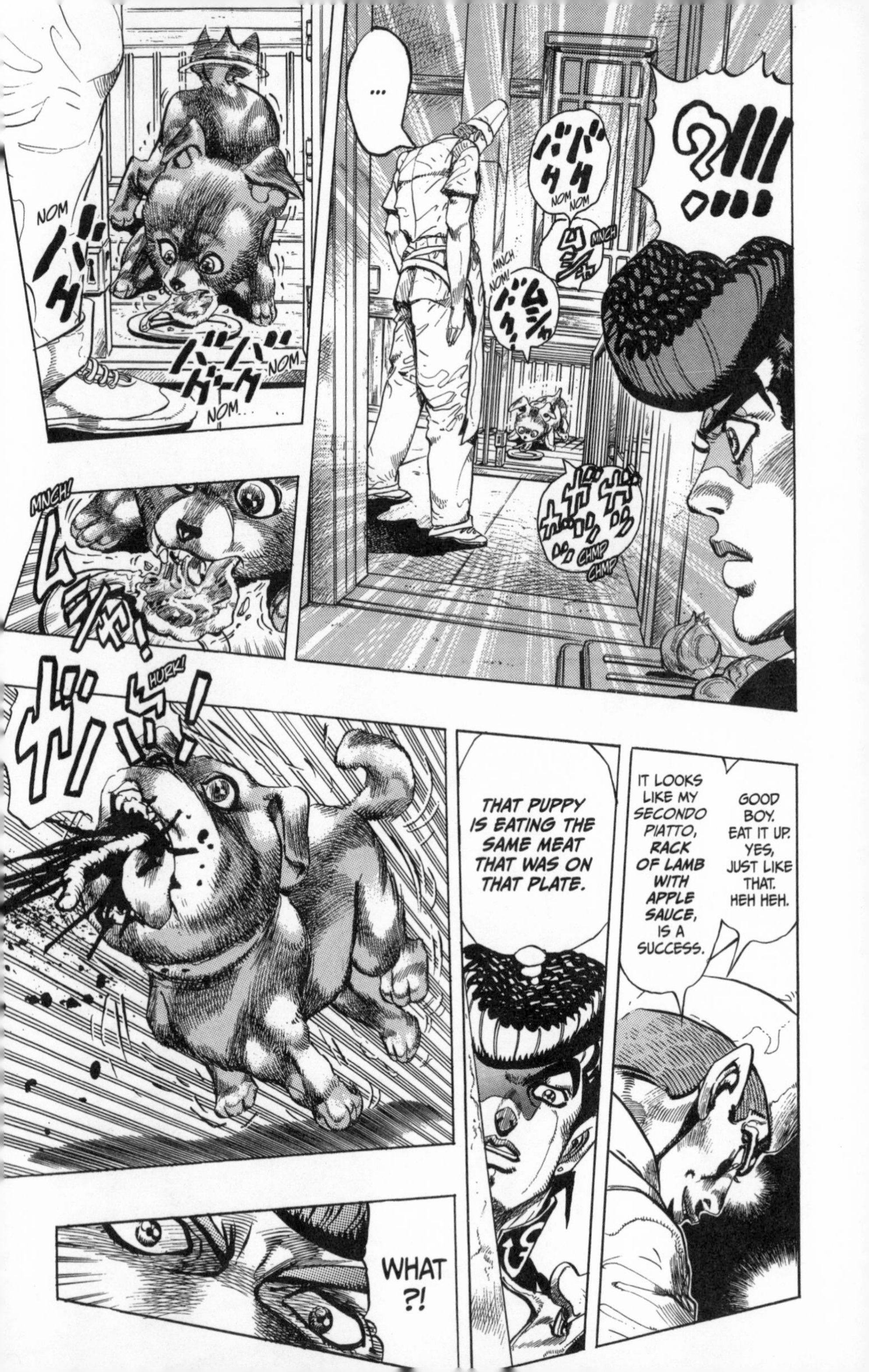
?!!!
...
...
NOM NOM
MNCH
MNCH NOM!
CHMP CHMP
NOM
NOM NOM
MNCH!
HURK!
GOOD BOY. EAT IT UP. YES, JUST LIKE THAT. HEH HEH.
IT LOOKS LIKE MY SECONDO PIATTO, RACK OF LAMB WITH APPLE SAUCE, IS A SUCCESS.
THAT PUPPY IS EATING THE SAME MEAT THAT WAS ON THAT PLATE.
WHAT ?!

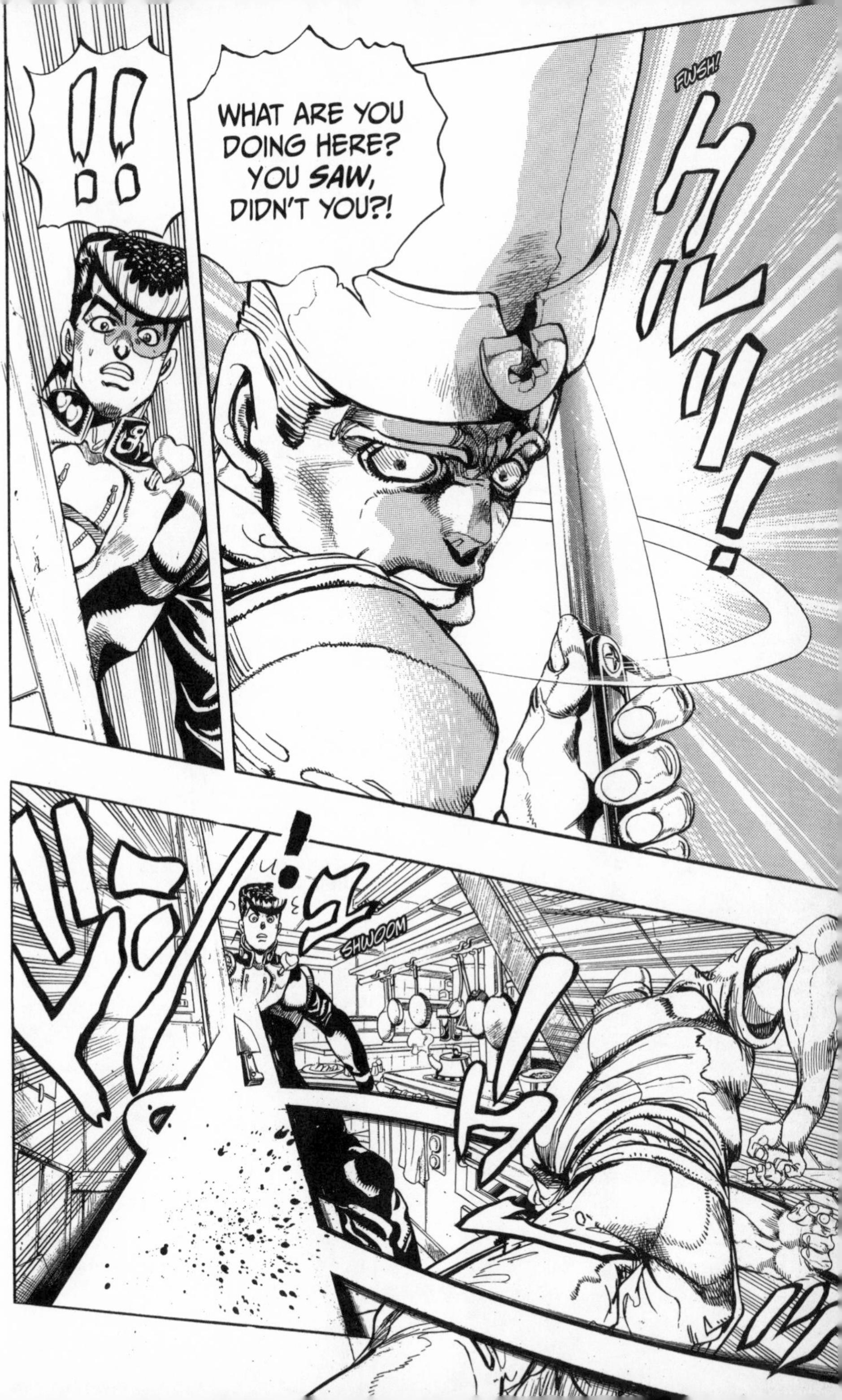
FWSH!
WHAT ARE YOU DOING HERE? YOU SAW, DIDN'T YOU?!
!!
SHWOOM

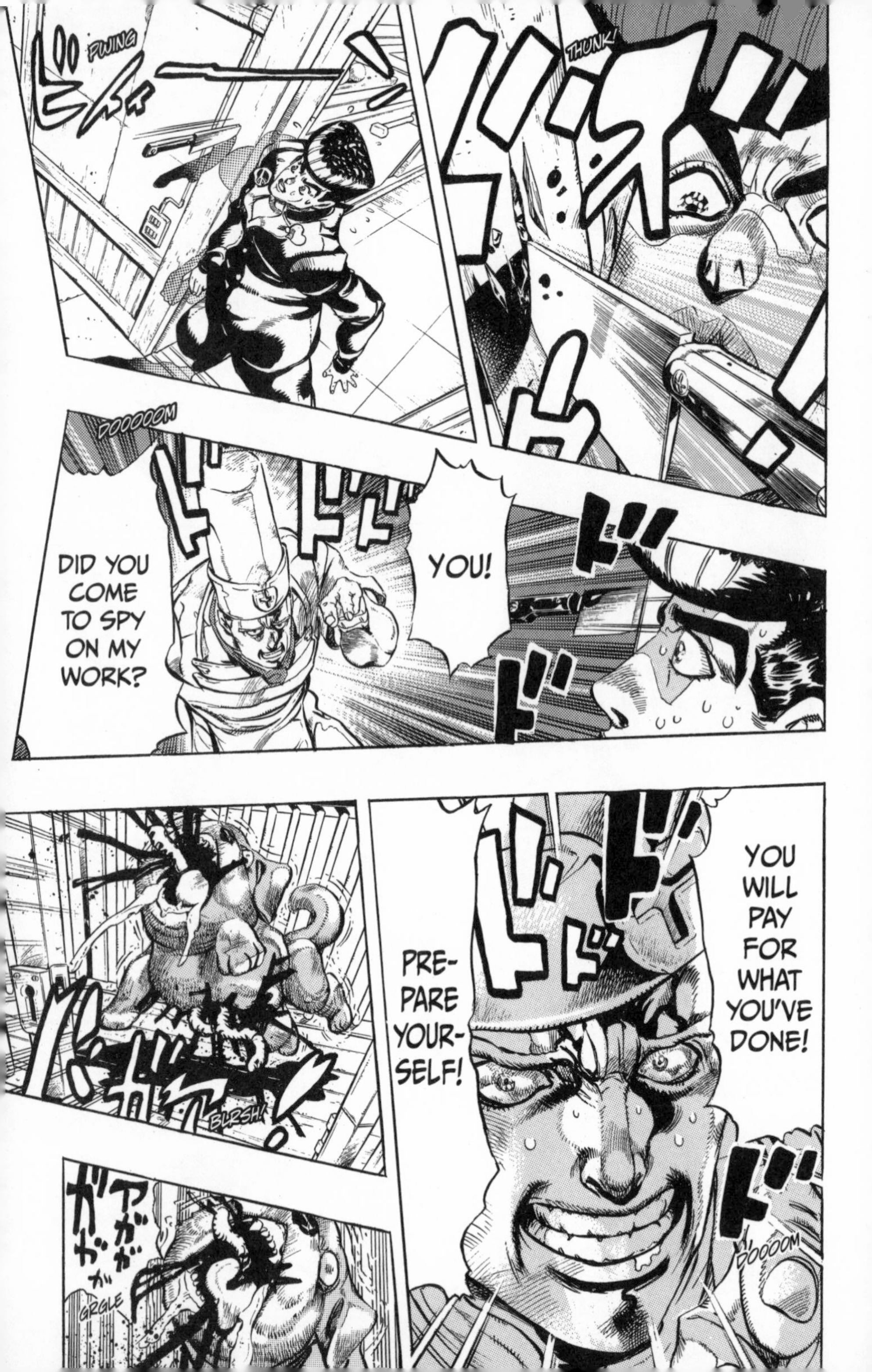
THUNK!
PWING
YOU!
DOOOOOM
DID YOU COME TO SPY ON MY WORK?
YOU WILL PAY FOR WHAT YOU'VE DONE!
PRE-PARE YOUR-SELF!
DOOOOM
BLRSH!
GRGLE

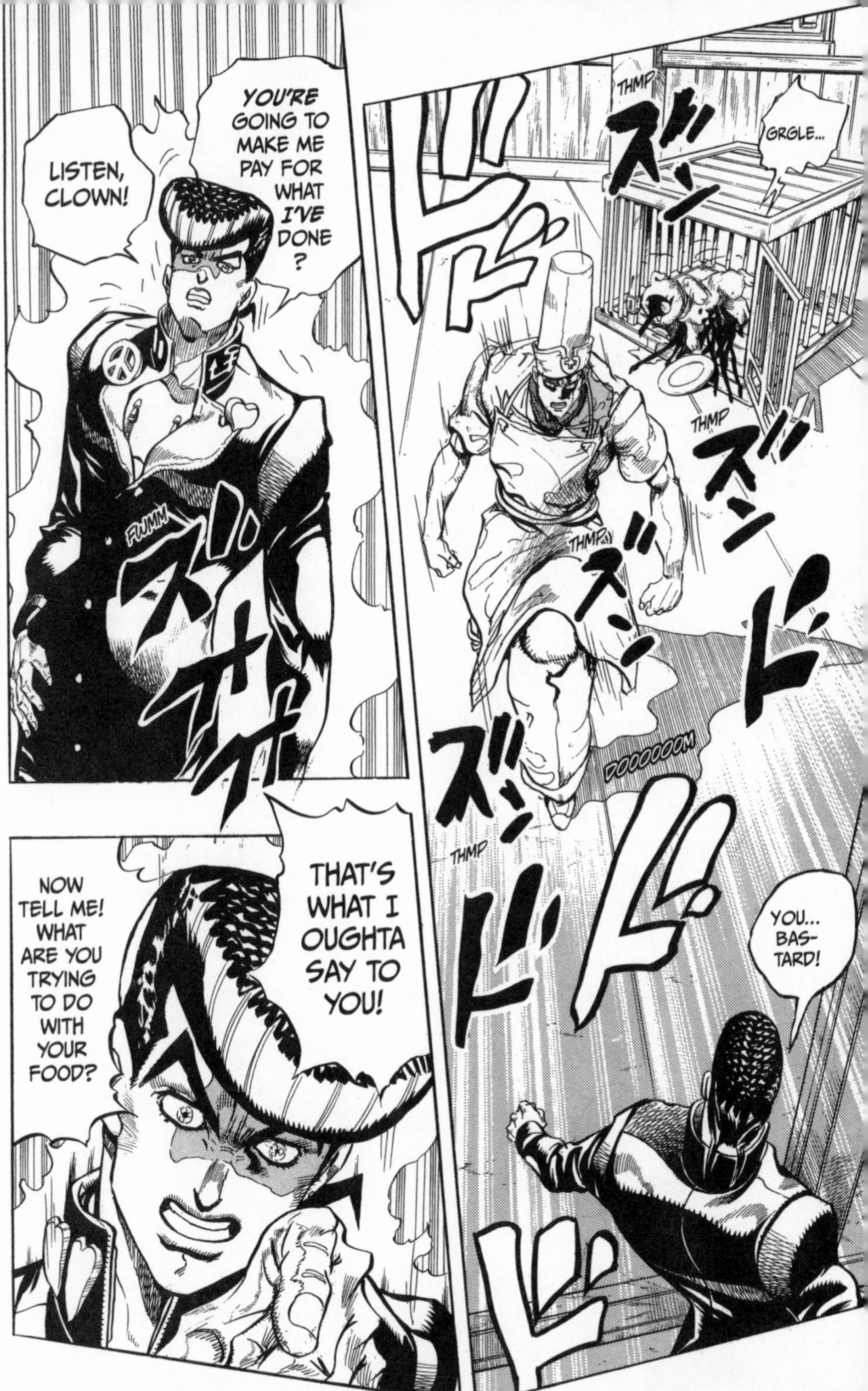
THMP
GRGLE...
THMP
THMP
DOOOOOOM
THMP
YOU... BAS-TARD!
YOU'RE GOING TO MAKE ME PAY FOR WHAT I'VE DONE?
LISTEN, CLOWN!
FWMM
THAT'S WHAT I OUGHTA SAY TO YOU!
NOW TELL ME! WHAT ARE YOU TRYING TO DO WITH YOUR FOOD?

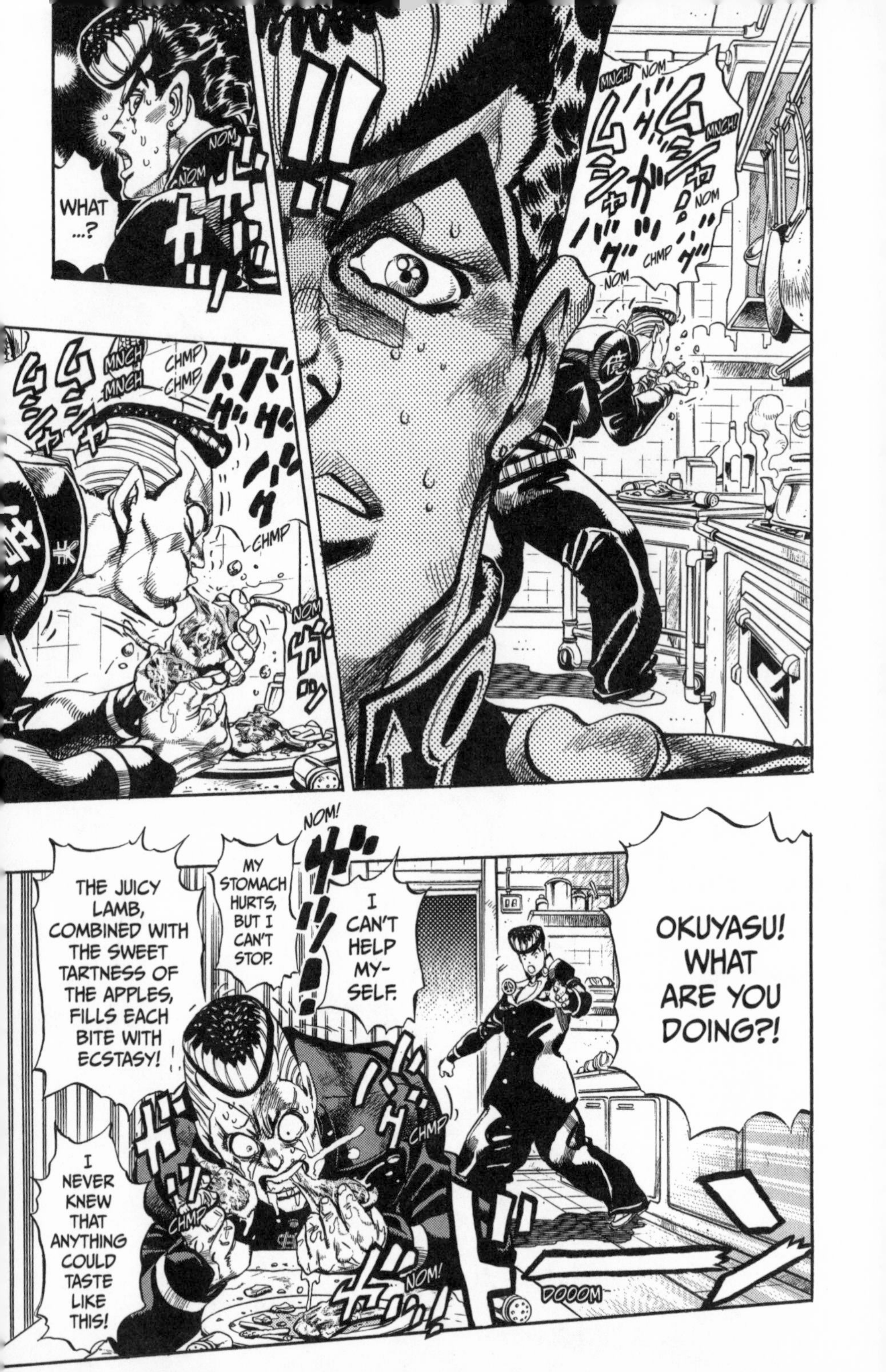
MNCH! NOM
MNCH!
NOM
CHMP
NOM
NOM
NOM
WHAT ...?
MNCH MNCH
CHMP CHMP
CHMP
NOM
OKUYASU! WHAT ARE YOU DOING?!
I CAN'T HELP MY-SELF.
MY STOMACH HURTS, BUT I CAN'T STOP.
NOM!
THE JUICY LAMB, COMBINED WITH THE SWEET TARTNESS OF THE APPLES, FILLS EACH BITE WITH ECSTASY!
CHMP
I NEVER KNEW THAT ANYTHING COULD TASTE LIKE THIS!
CHMP
NOM!
DOOOM

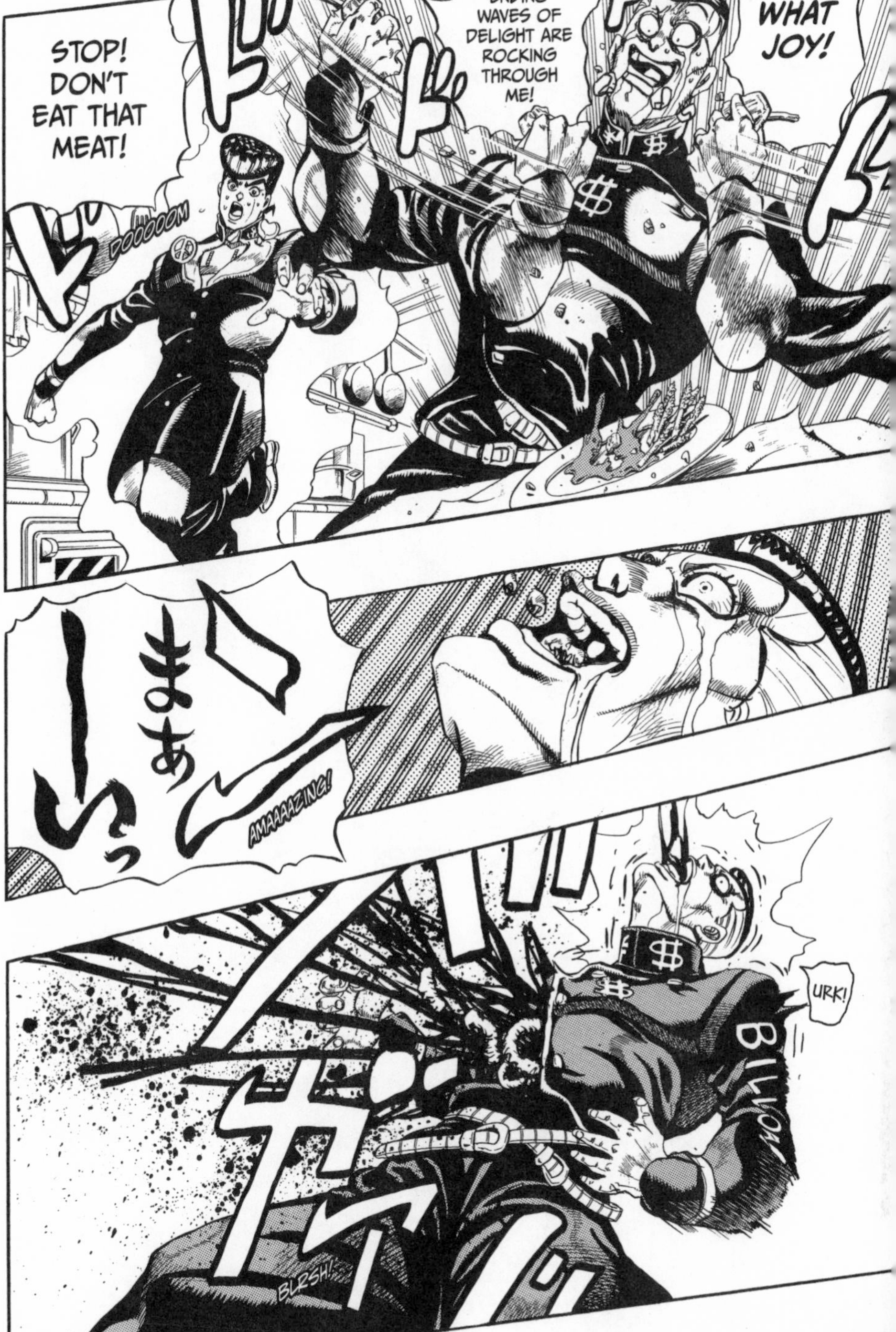
WHAT JOY!
NEVER-ENDING WAVES OF DELIGHT ARE ROCKING THROUGH ME!
STOP! DON'T EAT THAT MEAT!
DOOOOOOM
うまあーいっ
AMAAAAZING!
URK!
BILLOW
BLRSH!

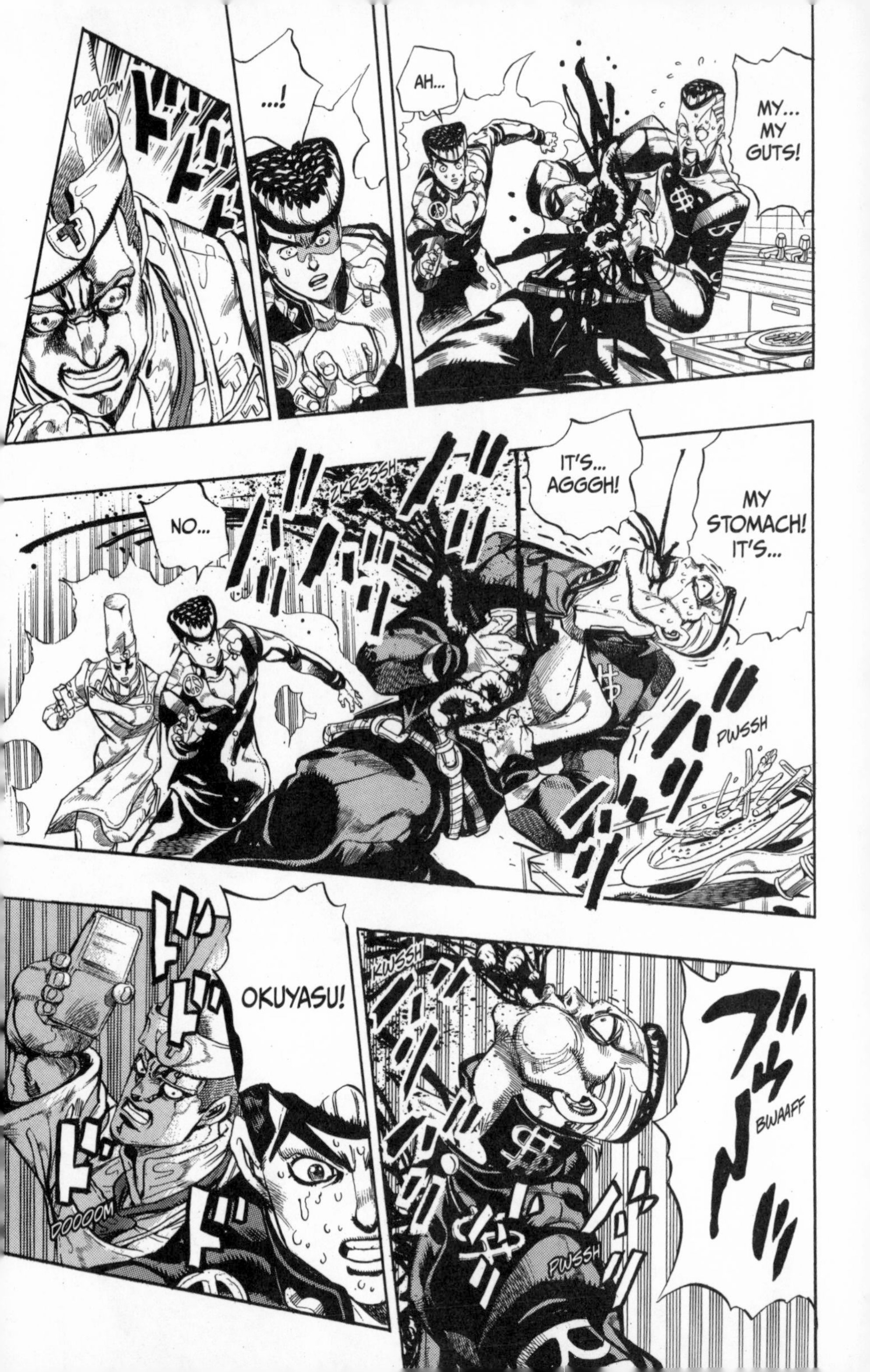
MY... MY GUTS!
AH...
...!
DOOOOM
MY STOMACH! IT'S...
IT'S... AGGGH!
ZKRSSSH
NO...
PWSSH
BWAAFF
KWSSH
PWSSH
OKUYASU!
DOOOOM

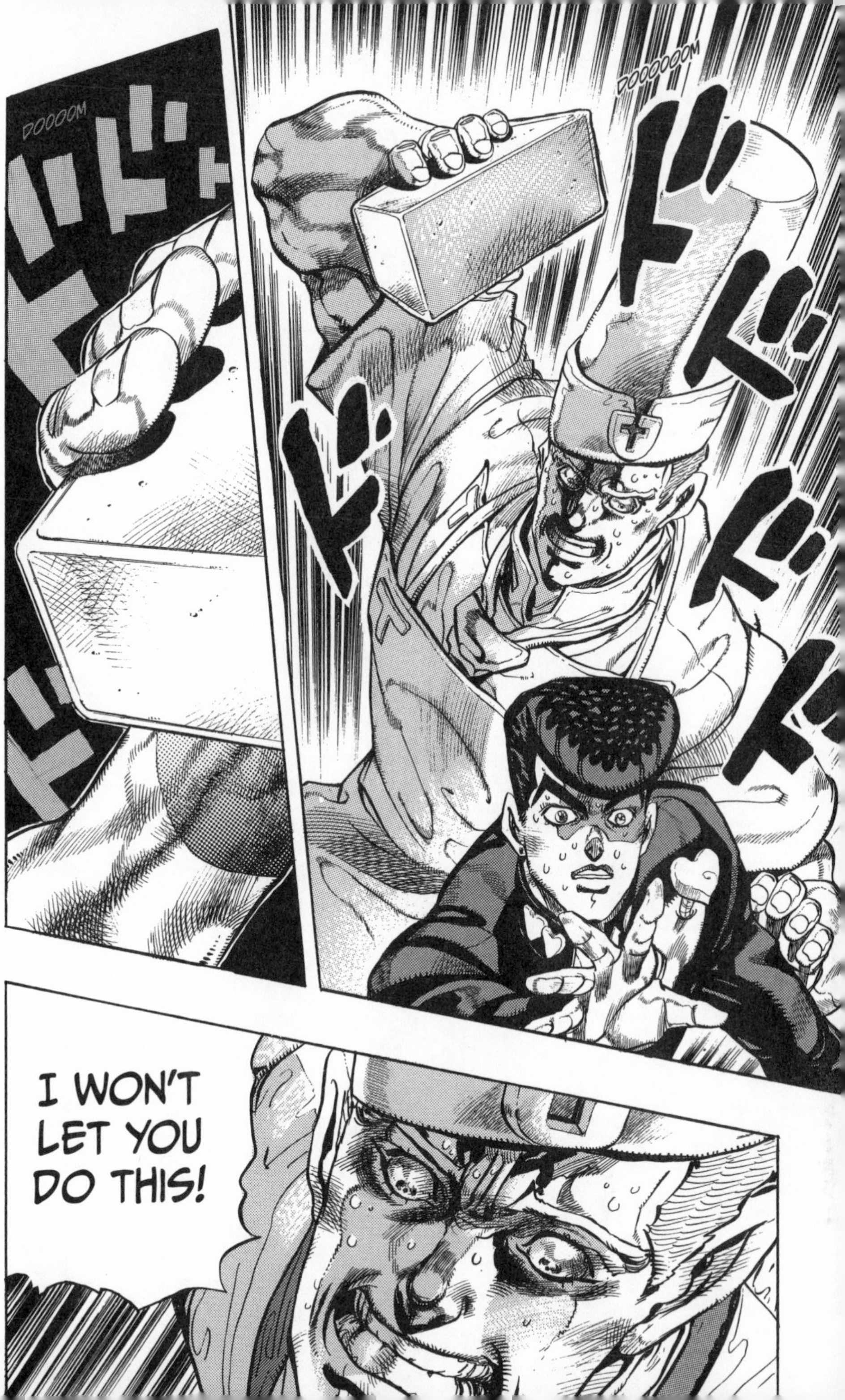
DOOOOOOM
DOOOOM
I WON'T LET YOU DO THIS!

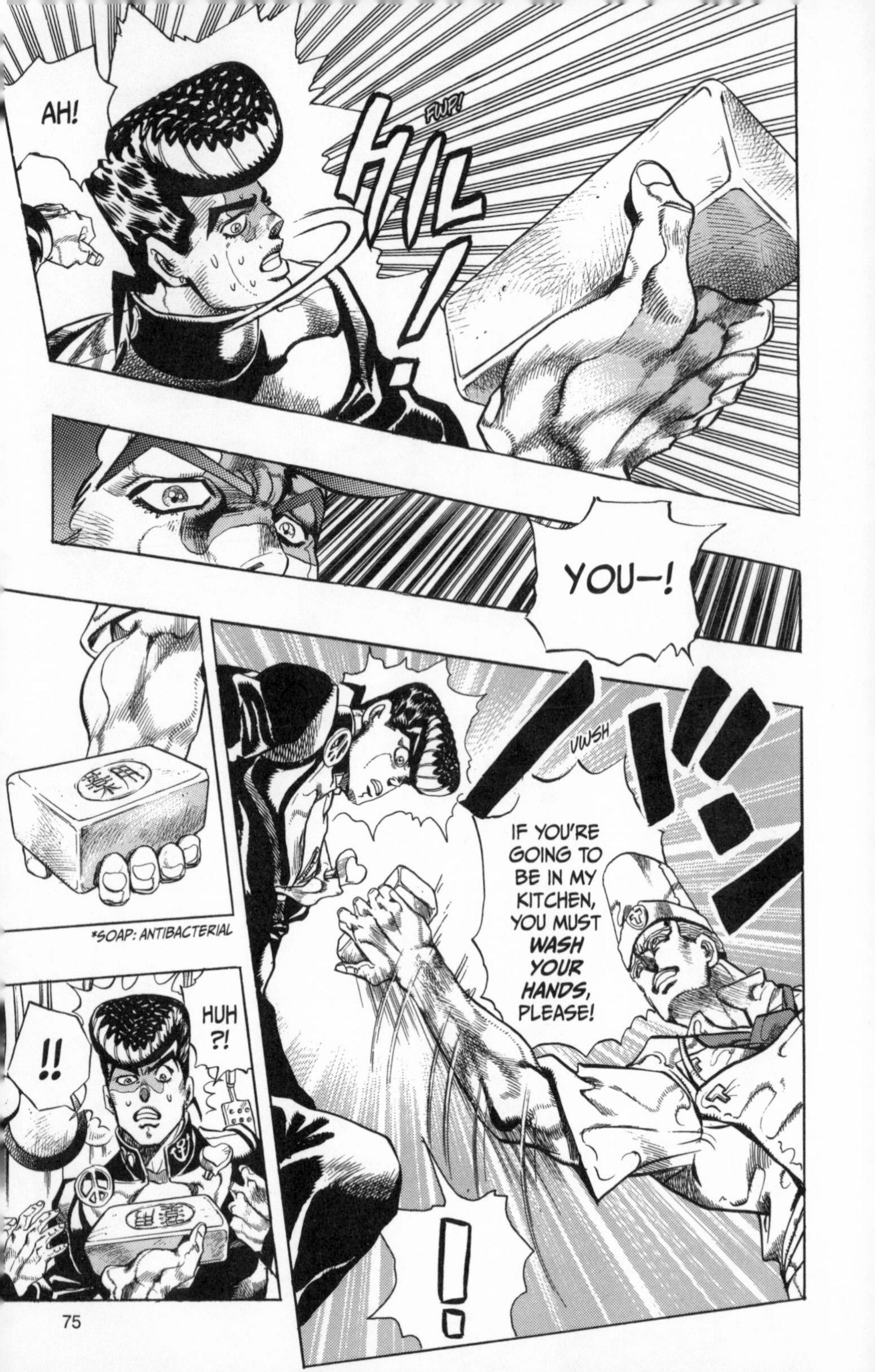
FWP!
AH!
YOU—!
UWSH
IF YOU'RE GOING TO BE IN MY KITCHEN, YOU MUST WASH YOUR HANDS, PLEASE!
!
*SOAP: ANTIBACTERIAL
HUH ?!
!!

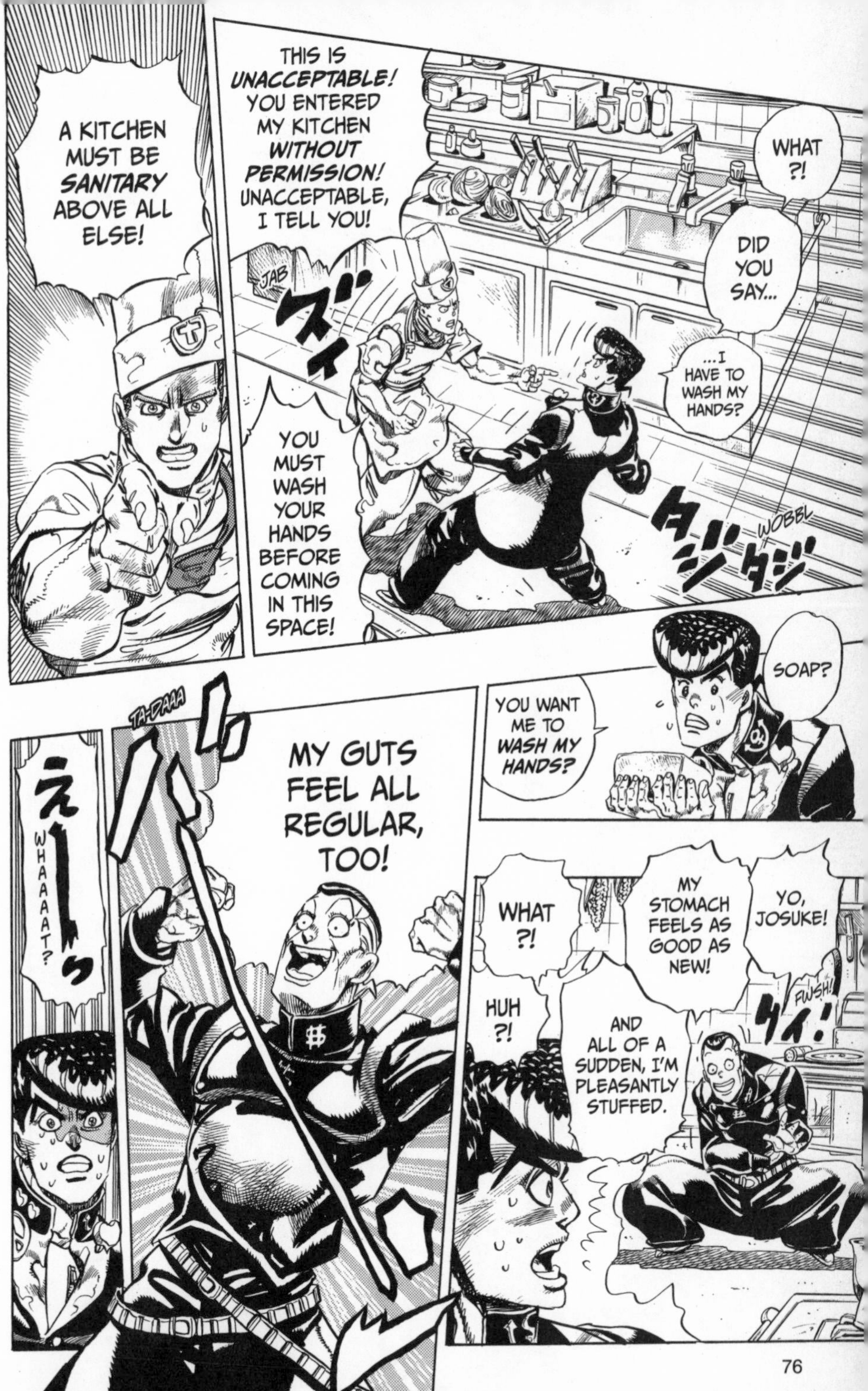
WHAT ?!
DID YOU SAY...
THIS IS UNACCEPTABLE! YOU ENTERED MY KITCHEN WITHOUT PERMISSION! UNACCEPTABLE, I TELL YOU!
...I HAVE TO WASH MY HANDS?
JAB
YOU MUST WASH YOUR HANDS BEFORE COMING IN THIS SPACE!
WOBBL
A KITCHEN MUST BE SANITARY ABOVE ALL ELSE!
SOAP?
YOU WANT ME TO WASH MY HANDS?
YO, JOSUKE!
FWSH!
MY STOMACH FEELS AS GOOD AS NEW!
WHAT ?!
AND ALL OF A SUDDEN, I'M PLEASANTLY STUFFED.
HUH ?!
TA-DAAA
MY GUTS FEEL ALL REGULAR, TOO!
WHAAAAAT?

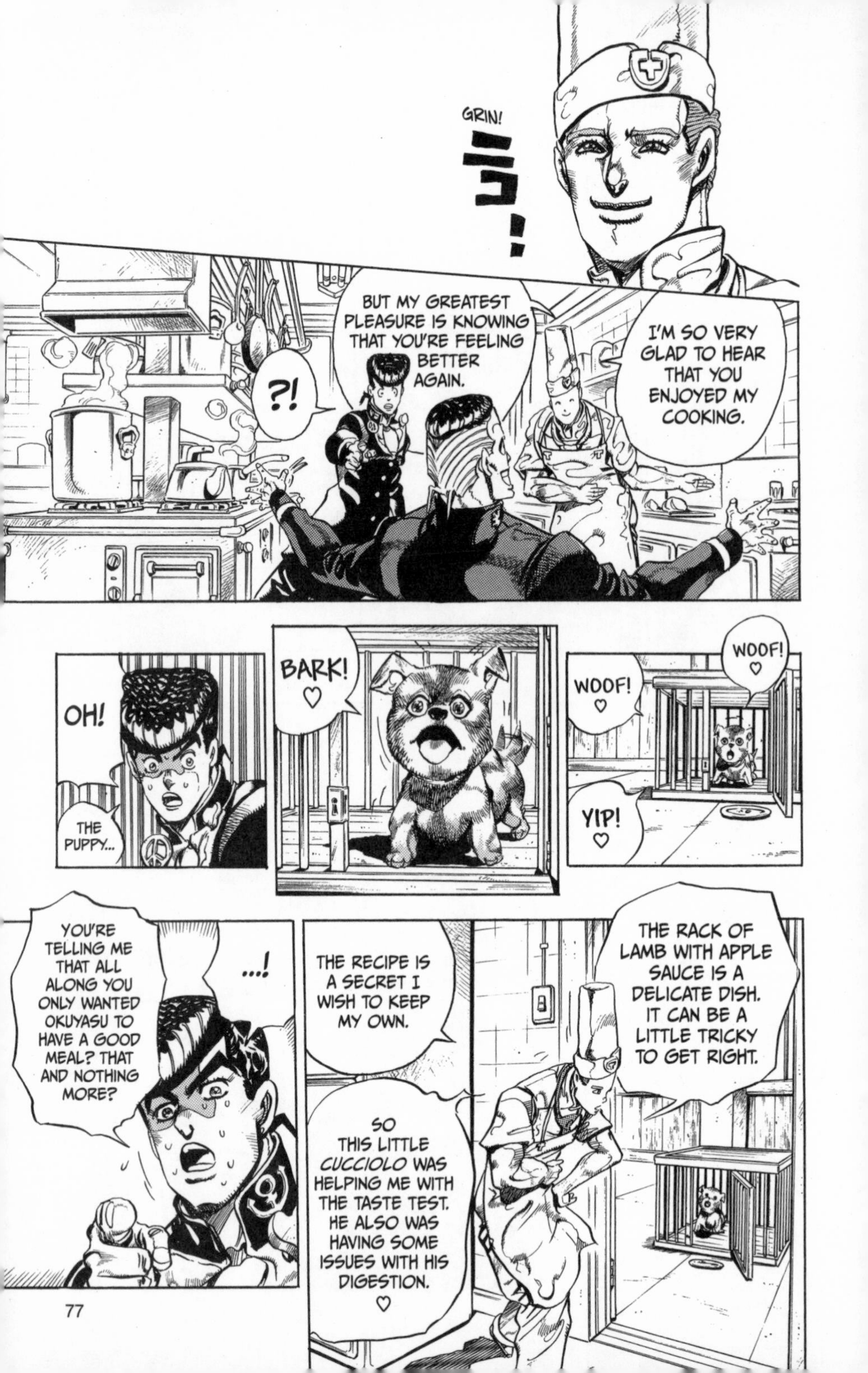
GRIN!
ニコ!
I'M SO VERY GLAD TO HEAR THAT YOU ENJOYED MY COOKING.
BUT MY GREATEST PLEASURE IS KNOWING THAT YOU'RE FEELING BETTER AGAIN.
?!
WOOF! ♡
WOOF! ♡
YIP! ♡
BARK! ♡
OH!
THE PUPPY...
THE RACK OF LAMB WITH APPLE SAUCE IS A DELICATE DISH. IT CAN BE A LITTLE TRICKY TO GET RIGHT.
THE RECIPE IS A SECRET I WISH TO KEEP MY OWN.
SO THIS LITTLE *CUCCIOLO* WAS HELPING ME WITH THE TASTE TEST. HE ALSO WAS HAVING SOME ISSUES WITH HIS DIGESTION. ♡
...!
YOU'RE TELLING ME THAT ALL ALONG YOU ONLY WANTED OKUYASU TO HAVE A GOOD MEAL? THAT AND NOTHING MORE?

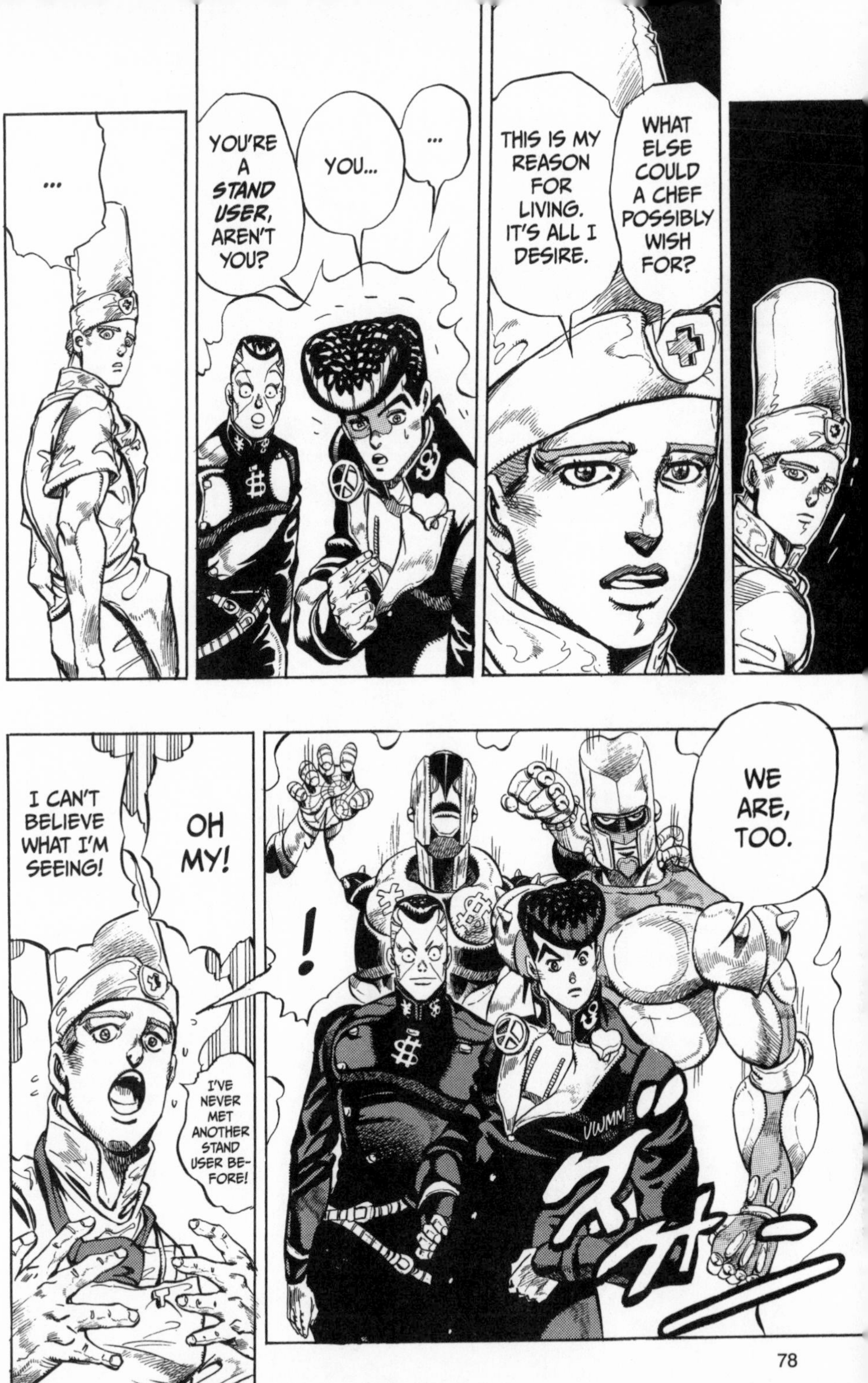
WHAT ELSE COULD A CHEF POSSIBLY WISH FOR?
THIS IS MY REASON FOR LIVING. IT'S ALL I DESIRE.
...
YOU...
YOU'RE A STAND USER, AREN'T YOU?
...
WE ARE, TOO.
!
VWMM
OH MY!
I CAN'T BELIEVE WHAT I'M SEEING!
I'VE NEVER MET ANOTHER STAND USER BEFORE!

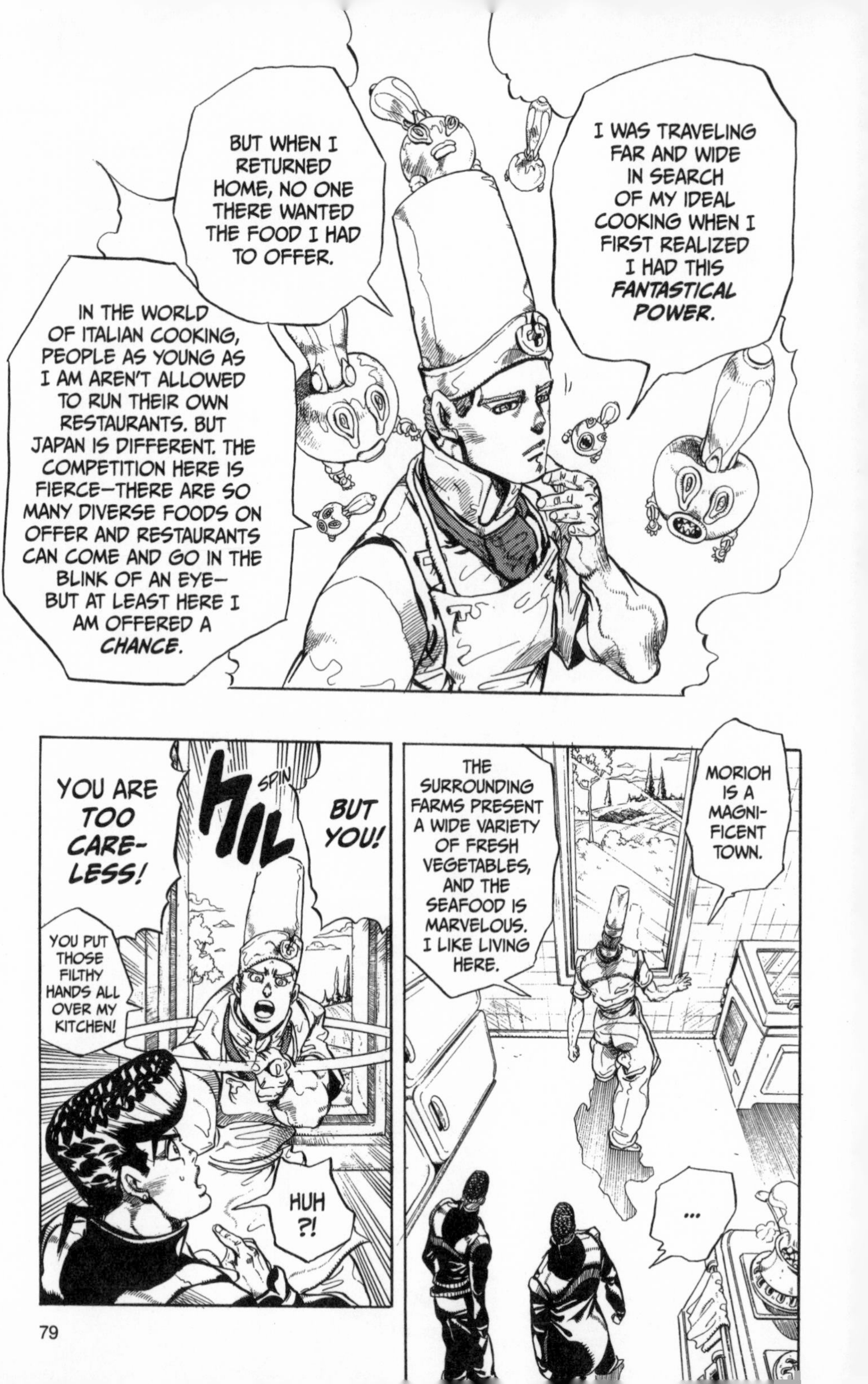
I WAS TRAVELING FAR AND WIDE IN SEARCH OF MY IDEAL COOKING WHEN I FIRST REALIZED I HAD THIS FANTASTICAL POWER.
BUT WHEN I RETURNED HOME, NO ONE THERE WANTED THE FOOD I HAD TO OFFER.
IN THE WORLD OF ITALIAN COOKING, PEOPLE AS YOUNG AS I AM AREN'T ALLOWED TO RUN THEIR OWN RESTAURANTS. BUT JAPAN IS DIFFERENT. THE COMPETITION HERE IS FIERCE—THERE ARE SO MANY DIVERSE FOODS ON OFFER AND RESTAURANTS CAN COME AND GO IN THE BLINK OF AN EYE—BUT AT LEAST HERE I AM OFFERED A CHANCE.
MORIOH IS A MAGNIFICENT TOWN.
THE SURROUNDING FARMS PRESENT A WIDE VARIETY OF FRESH VEGETABLES, AND THE SEAFOOD IS MARVELOUS. I LIKE LIVING HERE.
...
BUT YOU!
SPIN
YOU ARE TOO CARELESS!
YOU PUT THOSE FILTHY HANDS ALL OVER MY KITCHEN!
HUH?!

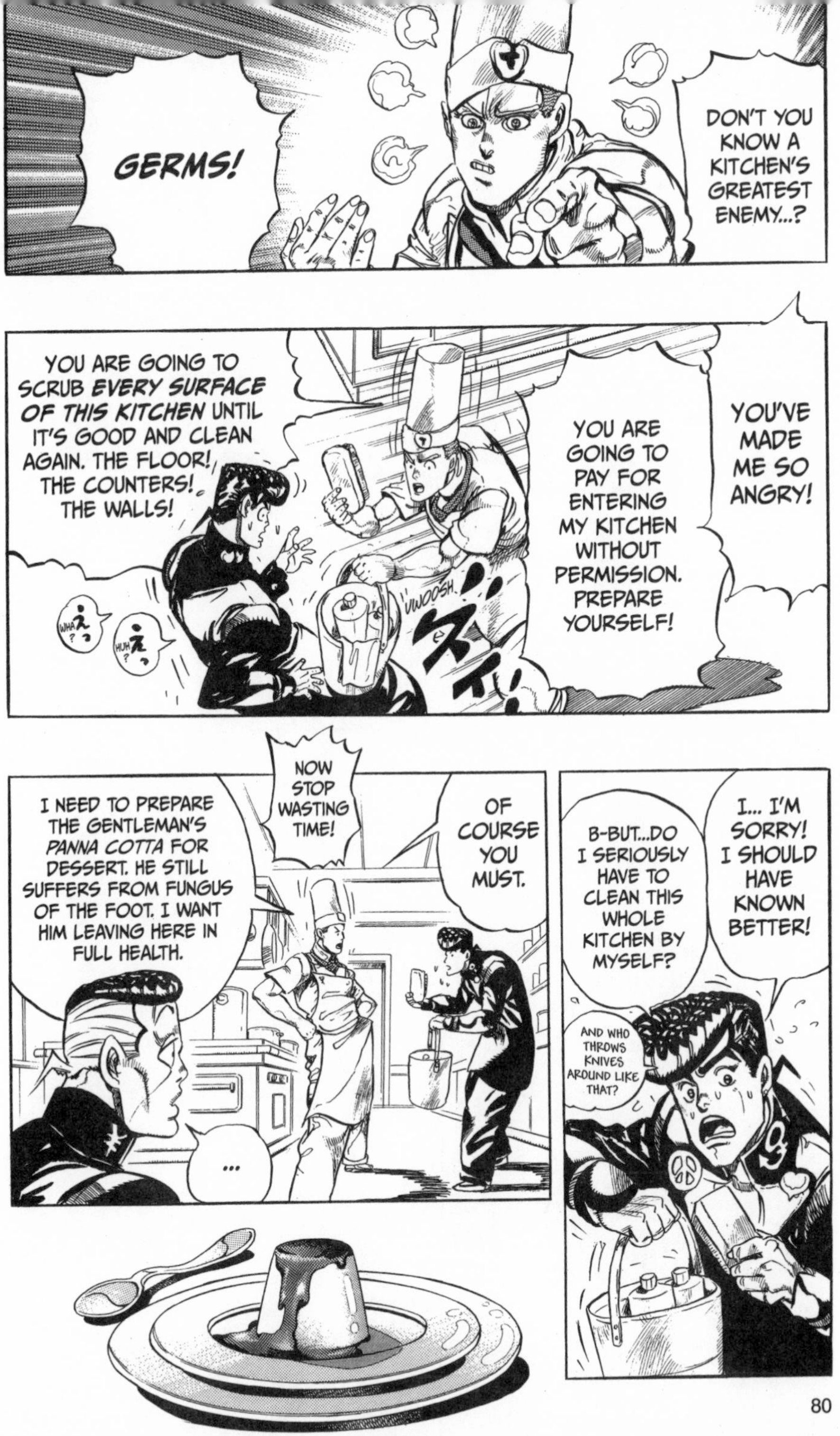
DON'T YOU KNOW A KITCHEN'S GREATEST ENEMY...?
GERMS!
YOU'VE MADE ME SO ANGRY!
YOU ARE GOING TO PAY FOR ENTERING MY KITCHEN WITHOUT PERMISSION. PREPARE YOURSELF!
YOU ARE GOING TO SCRUB *EVERY SURFACE OF THIS KITCHEN* UNTIL IT'S GOOD AND CLEAN AGAIN. THE FLOOR! THE COUNTERS! THE WALLS!
VWOOSH
HUH?
WHA?
I... I'M SORRY! I SHOULD HAVE KNOWN BETTER!
B-BUT...DO I SERIOUSLY HAVE TO CLEAN THIS WHOLE KITCHEN BY MYSELF?
AND WHO THROWS KNIVES AROUND LIKE THAT?
OF COURSE YOU MUST.
NOW STOP WASTING TIME!
I NEED TO PREPARE THE GENTLEMAN'S *PANNA COTTA* FOR DESSERT. HE STILL SUFFERS FROM FUNGUS OF THE FOOT. I WANT HIM LEAVING HERE IN FULL HEALTH.
...

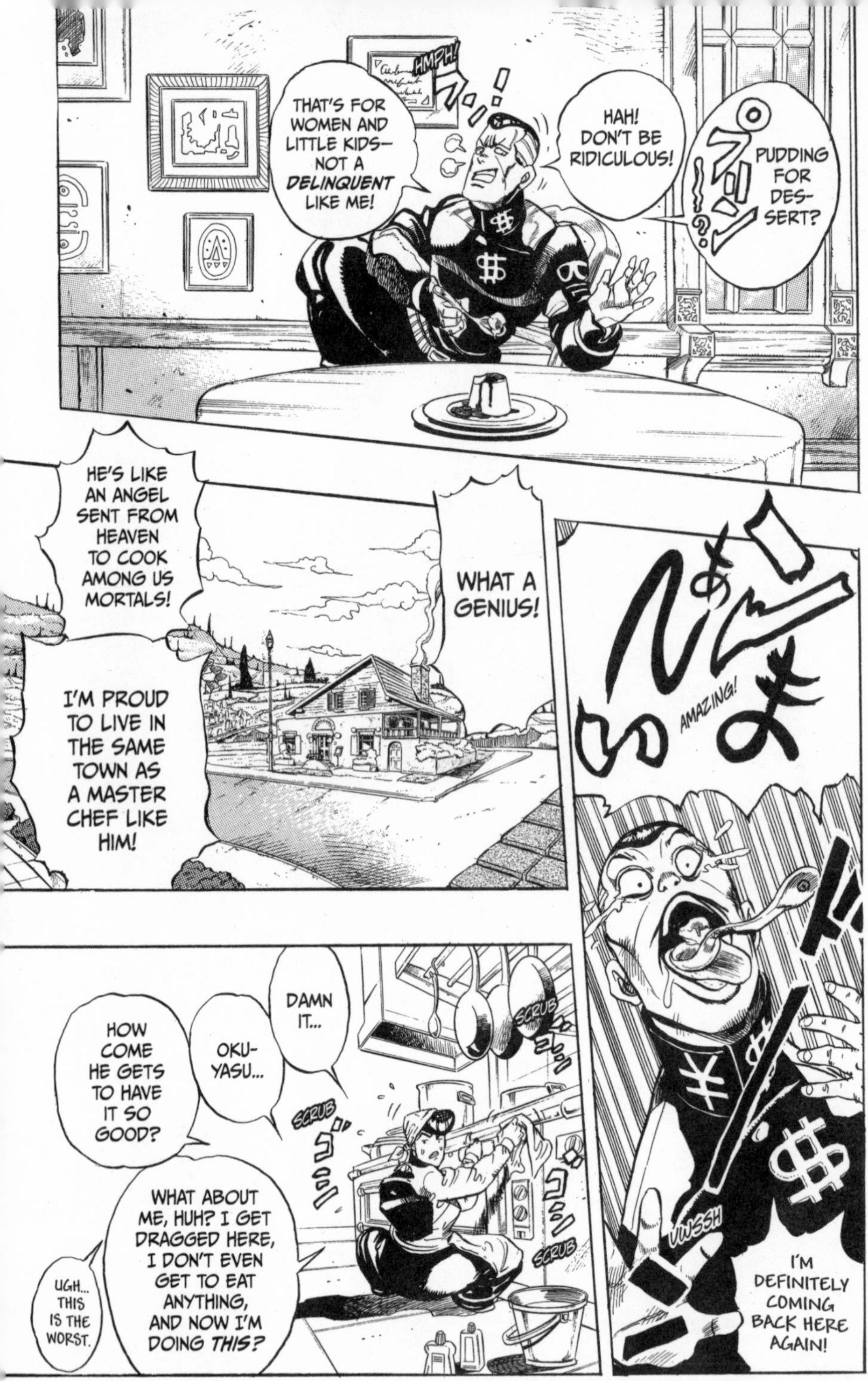
PUDDING FOR DES-SERT?
HAH! DON'T BE RIDICULOUS!
HMPH!
THAT'S FOR WOMEN AND LITTLE KIDS—NOT A *DELINQUENT* LIKE ME!
AMAZING!
VWSSH
I'M DEFINITELY COMING BACK HERE AGAIN!
WHAT A GENIUS!
HE'S LIKE AN ANGEL SENT FROM HEAVEN TO COOK AMONG US MORTALS!
I'M PROUD TO LIVE IN THE SAME TOWN AS A MASTER CHEF LIKE HIM!
DAMN IT...
OKU-YASU...
HOW COME HE GETS TO HAVE IT SO GOOD?
SCRUB
SCRUB
SCRUB
WHAT ABOUT ME, HUH? I GET DRAGGED HERE, I DON'T EVEN GET TO EAT ANYTHING, AND NOW I'M DOING *THIS*?
UGH... THIS IS THE WORST.

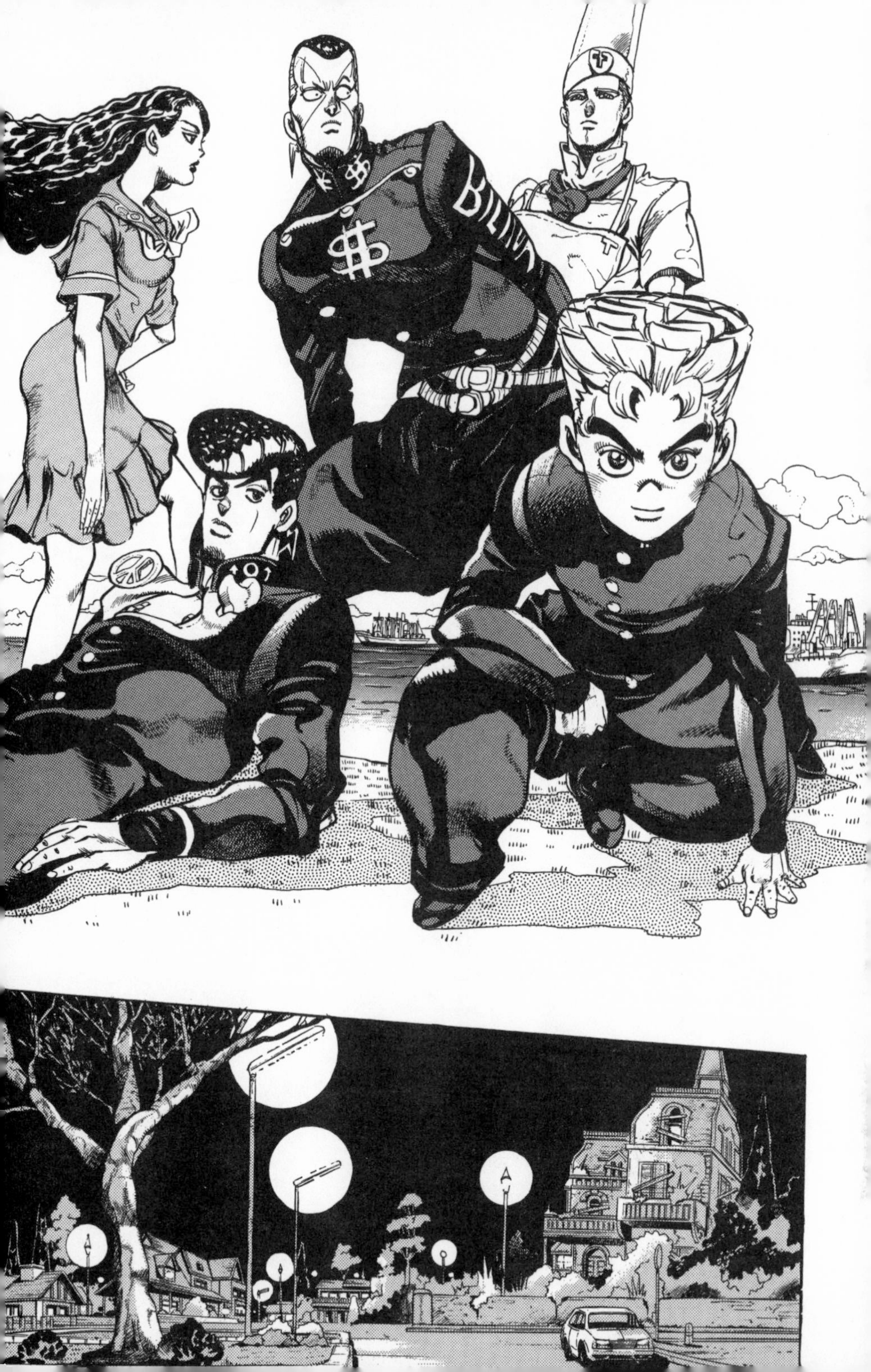

CHAPTER 42

CHILI PEPPER, PART 1

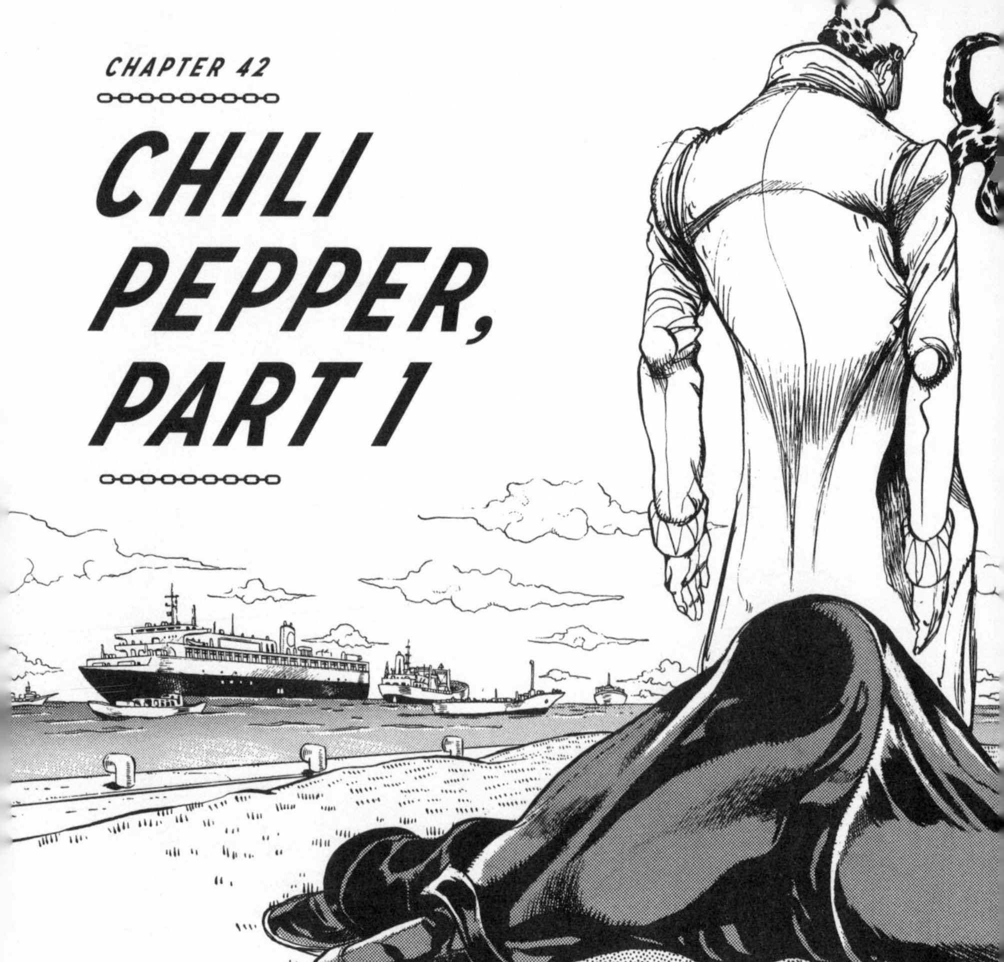

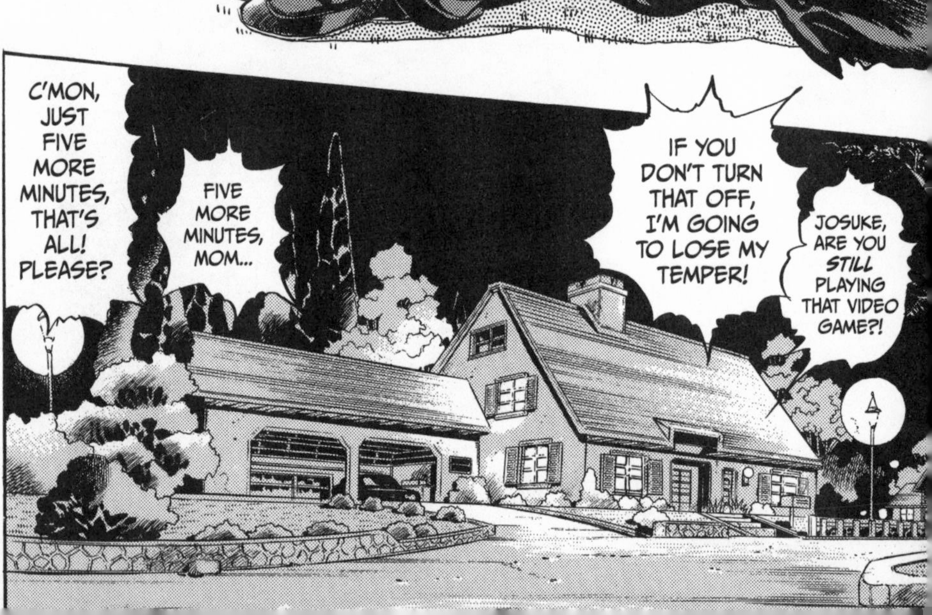
JOSUKE, ARE YOU *STILL* PLAYING THAT VIDEO GAME?!
IF YOU DON'T TURN THAT OFF, I'M GOING TO LOSE MY TEMPER!
FIVE MORE MINUTES, MOM...
C'MON, JUST FIVE MORE MINUTES, THAT'S ALL! PLEASE?

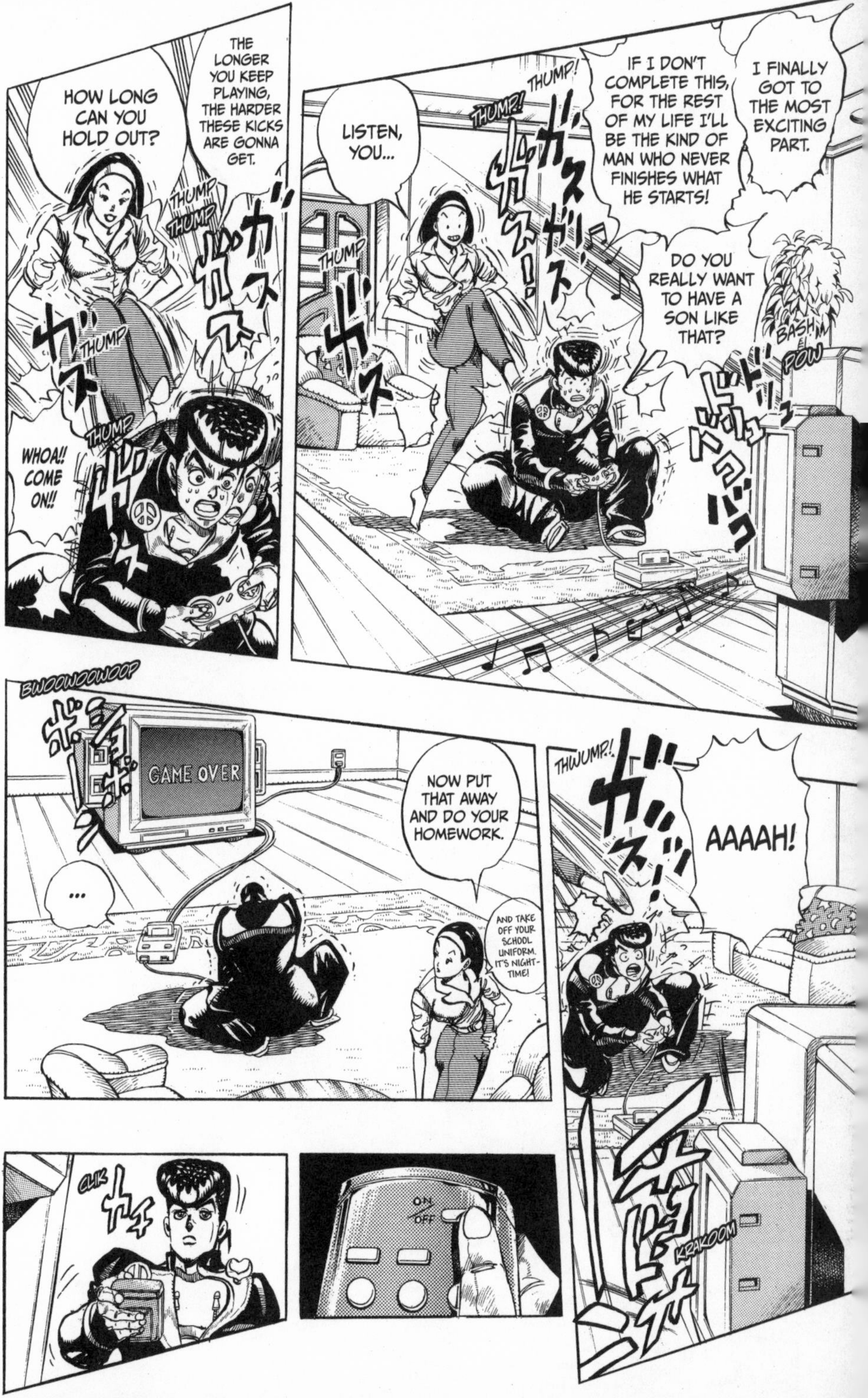
I FINALLY GOT TO THE MOST EXCITING PART.
IF I DON'T COMPLETE THIS, FOR THE REST OF MY LIFE I'LL BE THE KIND OF MAN WHO NEVER FINISHES WHAT HE STARTS!
THUMP!
THUMP!
LISTEN, YOU...
THUMP
DO YOU REALLY WANT TO HAVE A SON LIKE THAT?
BASH
POW
THE LONGER YOU KEEP PLAYING, THE HARDER THESE KICKS ARE GONNA GET.
HOW LONG CAN YOU HOLD OUT?
THUMP
THUMP
THUMP
THUMP
WHOA!! COME ON!!
THWUMP!
AAAAH!
KRAKOOM
BWOOWOOWOOP
GAME OVER
NOW PUT THAT AWAY AND DO YOUR HOMEWORK.
AND TAKE OFF YOUR SCHOOL UNIFORM. IT'S NIGHT-TIME!
...
ON
OFF
CLIK

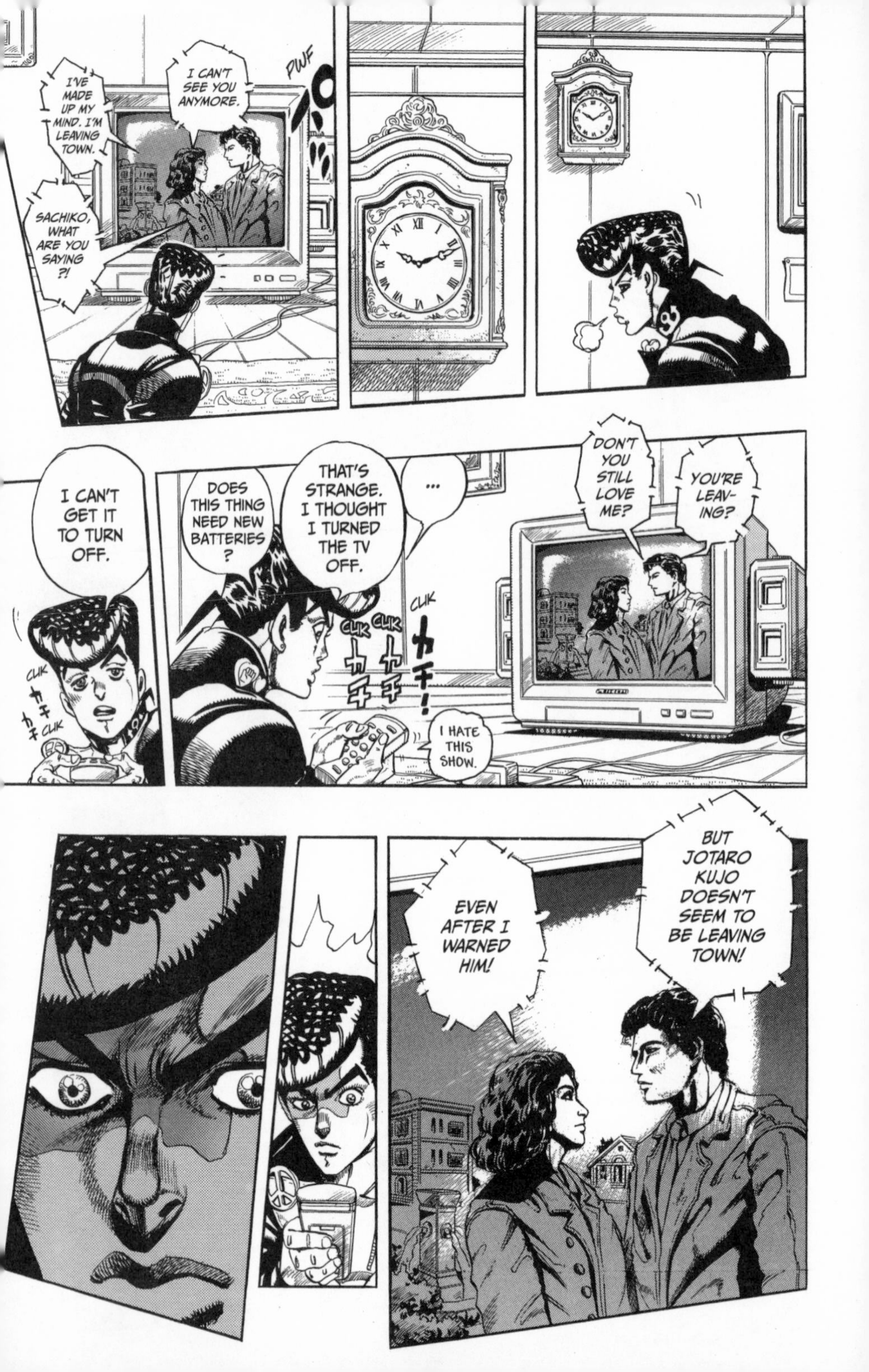
PWF
I CAN'T SEE YOU ANYMORE.
I'VE MADE UP MY MIND. I'M LEAVING TOWN.
SACHIKO, WHAT ARE YOU SAYING ?!
YOU'RE LEAV-ING?
DON'T YOU STILL LOVE ME?
...
THAT'S STRANGE. I THOUGHT I TURNED THE TV OFF.
DOES THIS THING NEED NEW BATTERIES ?
CLIK カチ!
CLIK カチ
CLIK カチ
I HATE THIS SHOW.
I CAN'T GET IT TO TURN OFF.
CLIK カチ
カチ CLIK
BUT JOTARO KUJO DOESN'T SEEM TO BE LEAVING TOWN!
EVEN AFTER I WARNED HIM!

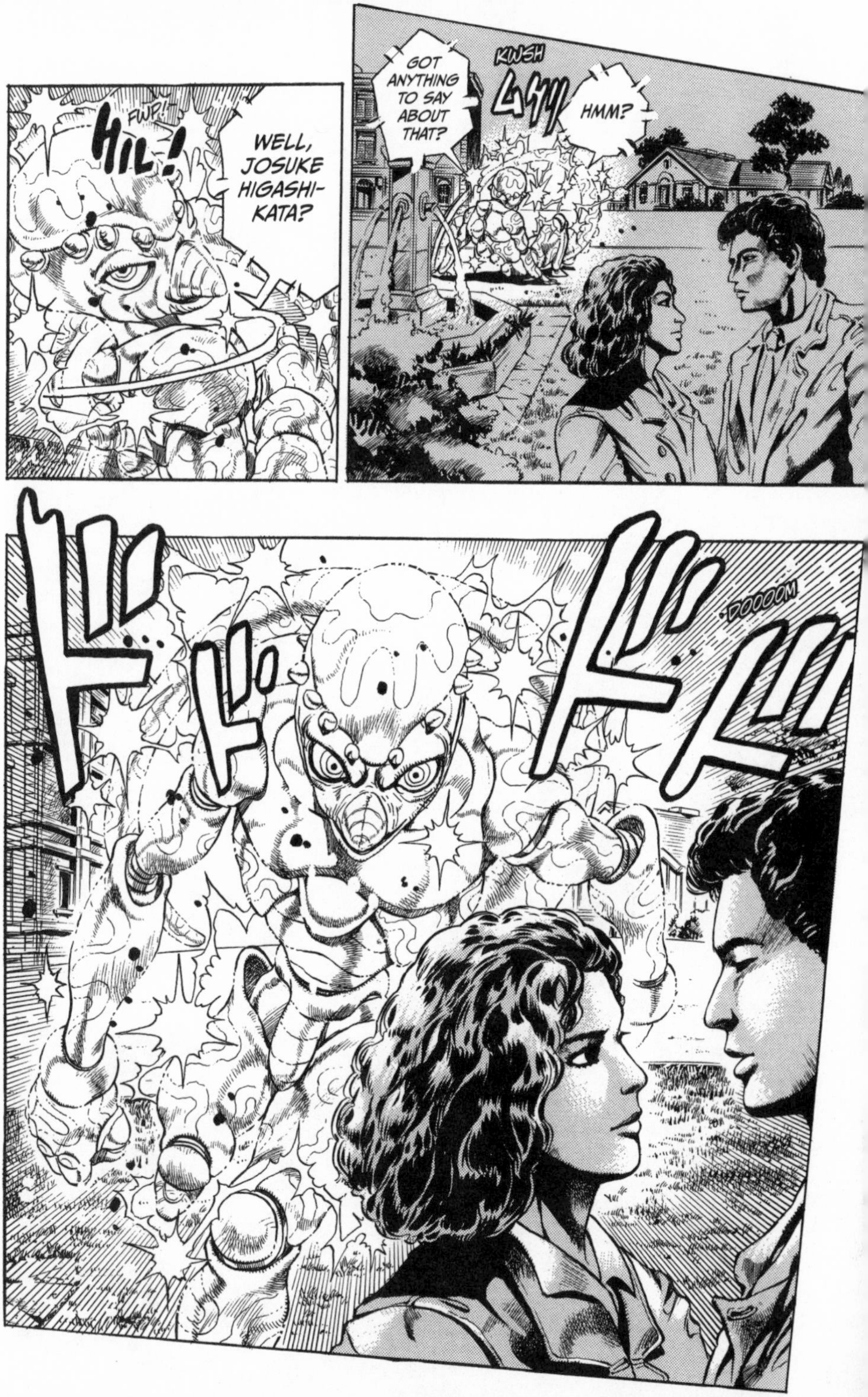
GOT ANYTHING TO SAY ABOUT THAT?
KWSH
HMM?
FWP!
WELL, JOSUKE HIGASHI-KATA?
DOOOOM

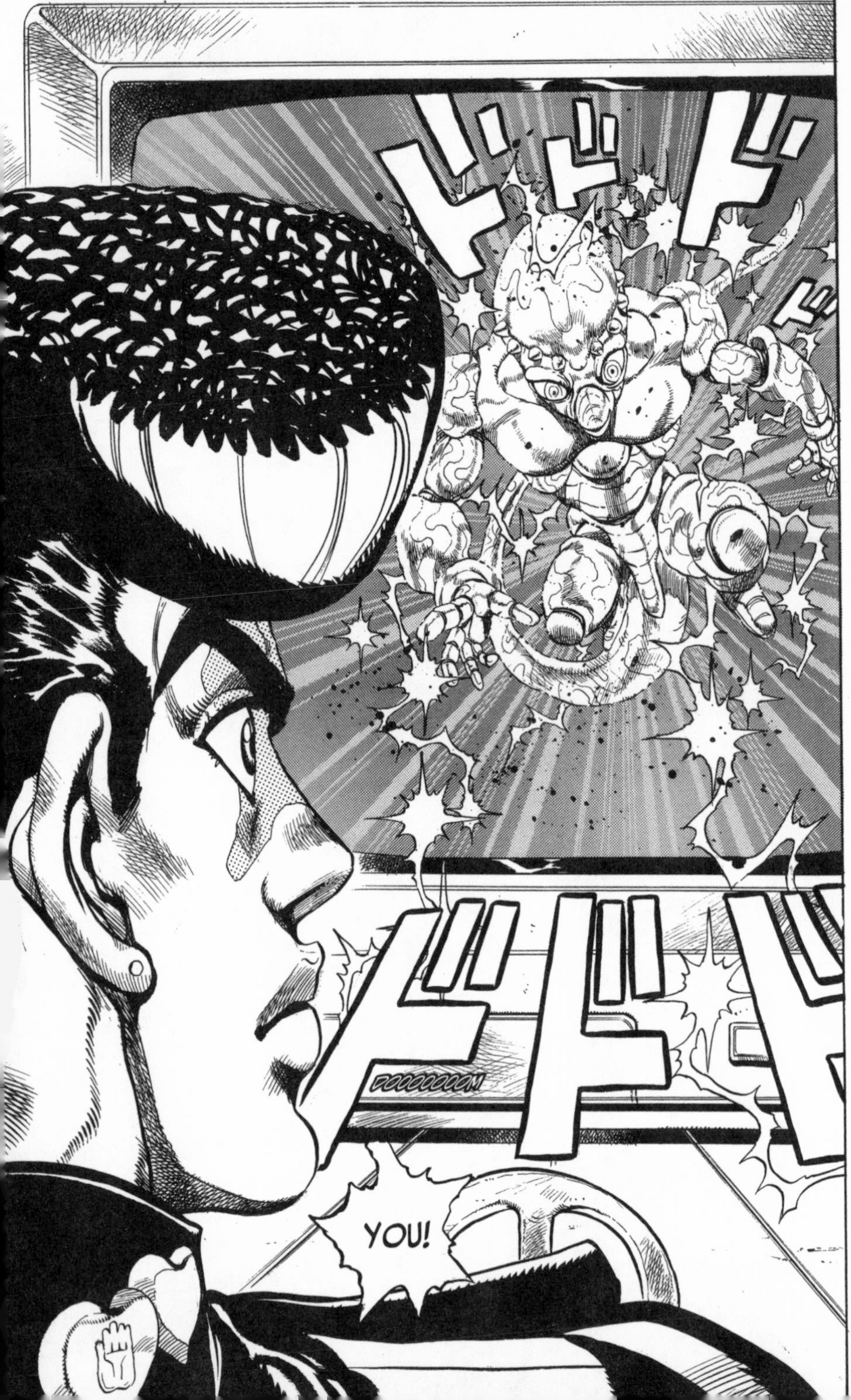
ドドドドド
ドドド
DOOOOOOOM
YOU!

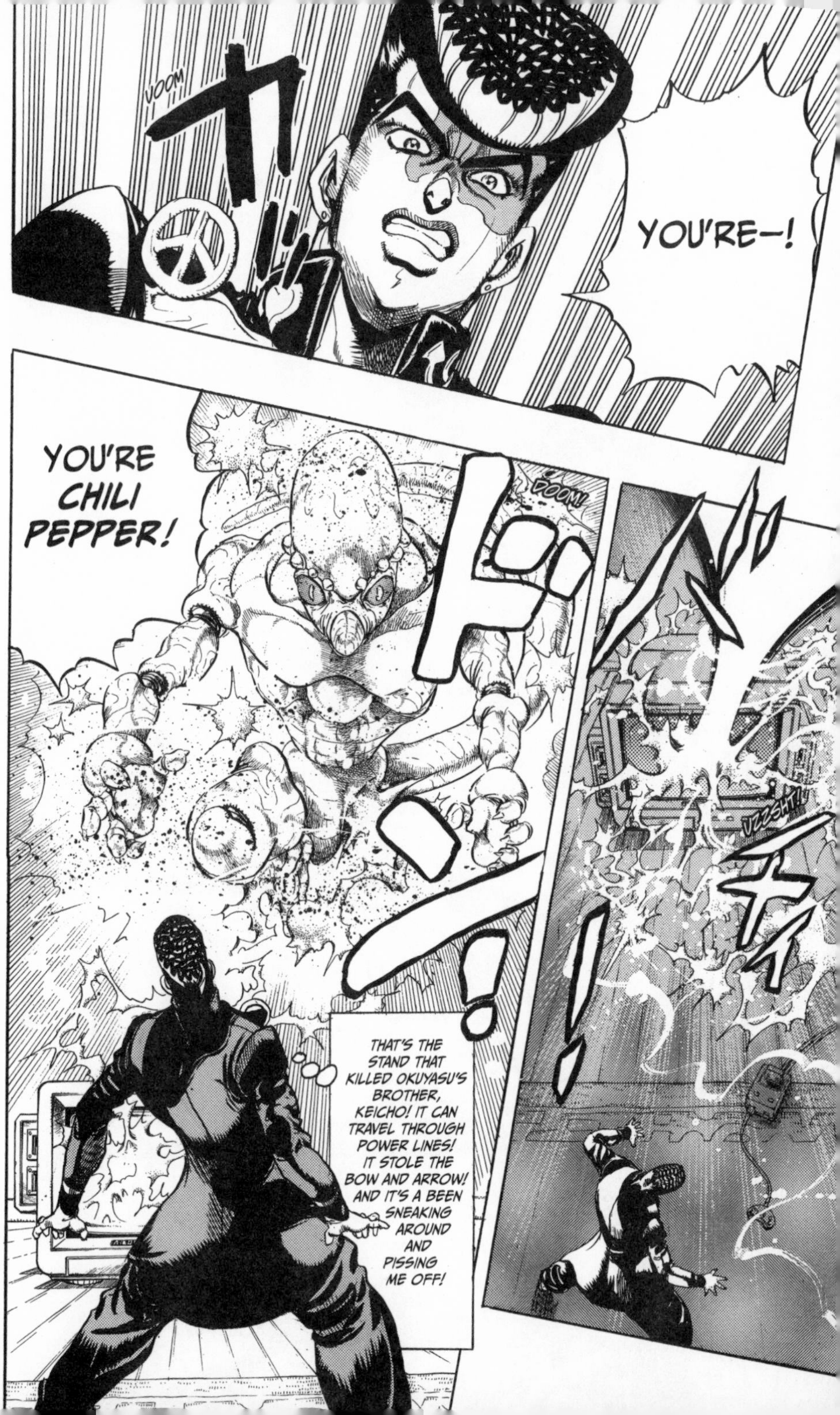
VOOM
YOU'RE—!
VZZSHT!!
YOU'RE CHILI PEPPER!
DOOM!
THAT'S THE STAND THAT KILLED OKUYASU'S BROTHER, KEICHO! IT CAN TRAVEL THROUGH POWER LINES! IT STOLE THE BOW AND ARROW! AND IT'S A BEEN SNEAKING AROUND AND PISSING ME OFF!

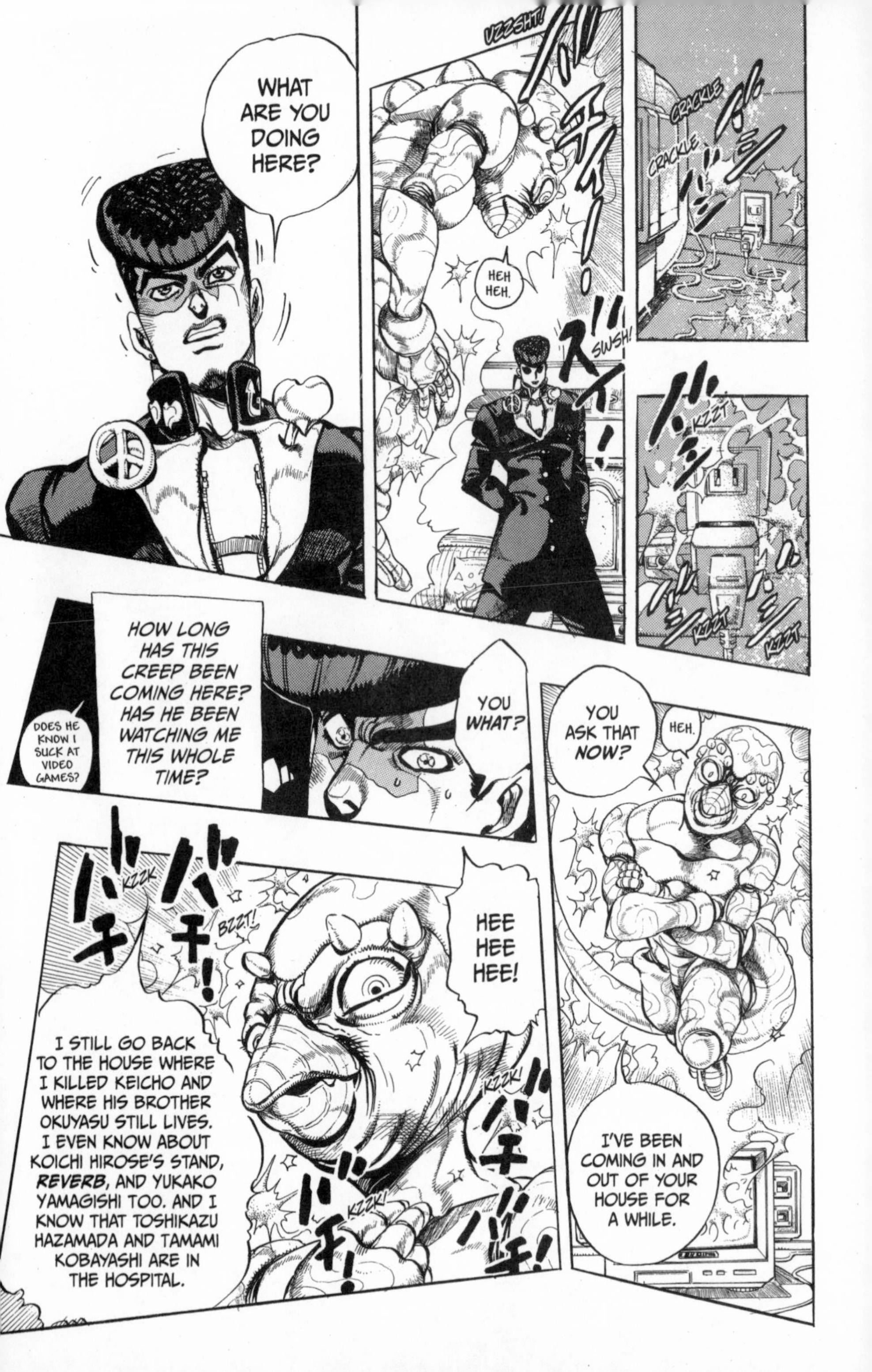
CRACKLE
CRACKLE
KZZT
KZZT
KZZT
UZZSHT!
HEH HEH.
SWSH!
WHAT ARE YOU DOING HERE?
YOU ASK THAT NOW?
HEH.
I'VE BEEN COMING IN AND OUT OF YOUR HOUSE FOR A WHILE.
YOU WHAT?
HOW LONG HAS THIS CREEP BEEN COMING HERE? HAS HE BEEN WATCHING ME THIS WHOLE TIME?
DOES HE KNOW I SUCK AT VIDEO GAMES?
HEE HEE HEE!
KZZK
BZZT!
I STILL GO BACK TO THE HOUSE WHERE I KILLED KEICHO AND WHERE HIS BROTHER OKUYASU STILL LIVES. I EVEN KNOW ABOUT KOICHI HIROSE'S STAND, **REVERB**, AND YUKAKO YAMAGISHI TOO. AND I KNOW THAT TOSHIKAZU HAZAMADA AND TAMAMI KOBAYASHI ARE IN THE HOSPITAL.
KZZK!
KZZK!

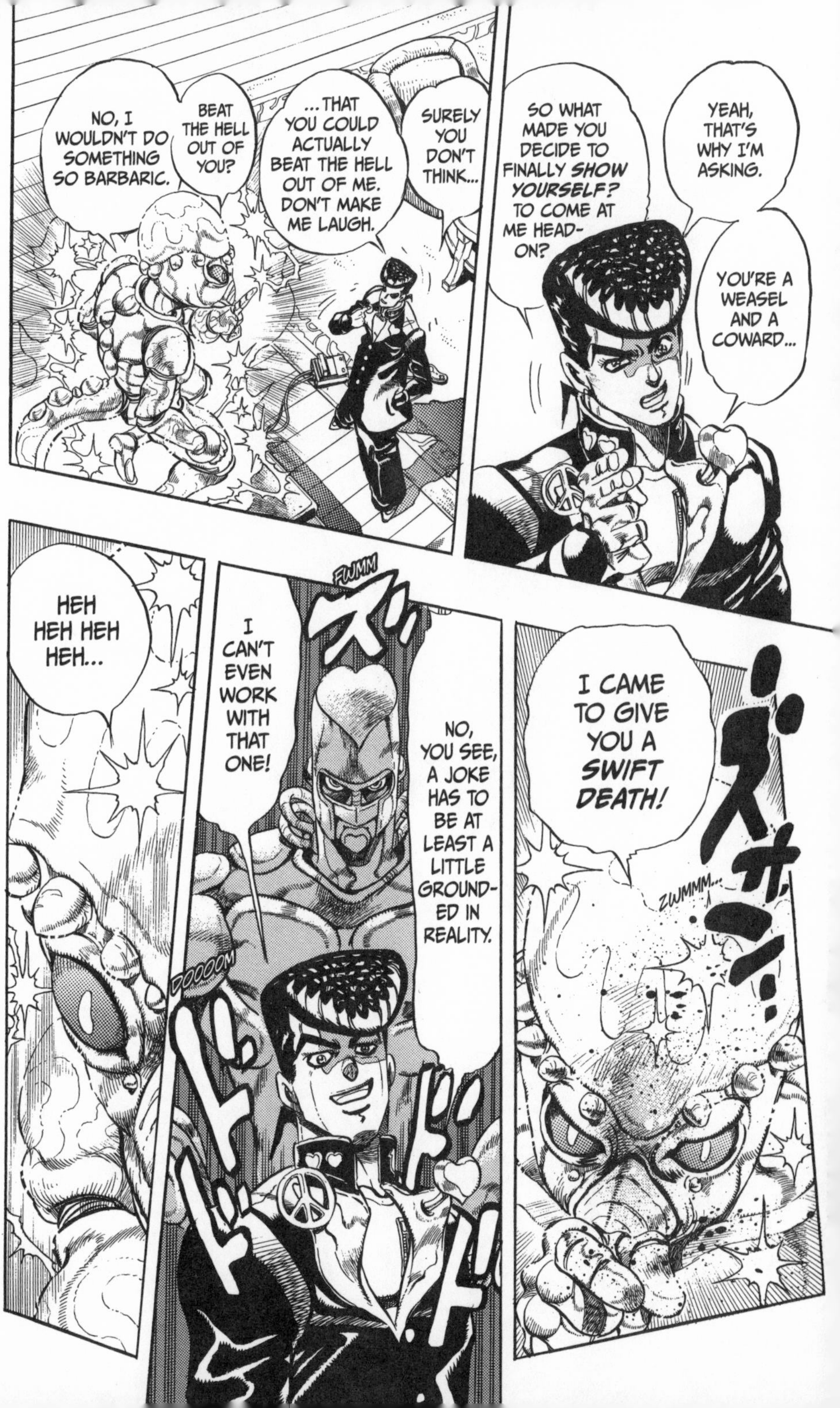
YEAH, THAT'S WHY I'M ASKING.
SO WHAT MADE YOU DECIDE TO FINALLY *SHOW YOURSELF?* TO COME AT ME HEAD-ON?
YOU'RE A WEASEL AND A COWARD...
SURELY YOU DON'T THINK...
...THAT YOU COULD ACTUALLY BEAT THE HELL OUT OF ME. DON'T MAKE ME LAUGH.
BEAT THE HELL OUT OF YOU?
NO, I WOULDN'T DO SOMETHING SO BARBARIC.
I CAME TO GIVE YOU A *SWIFT DEATH!*
ZWMMM...
FWMM
NO, YOU SEE, A JOKE HAS TO BE AT LEAST A LITTLE GROUND-ED IN REALITY.
I CAN'T EVEN WORK WITH THAT ONE!
DOOOOM
HEH HEH HEH HEH...

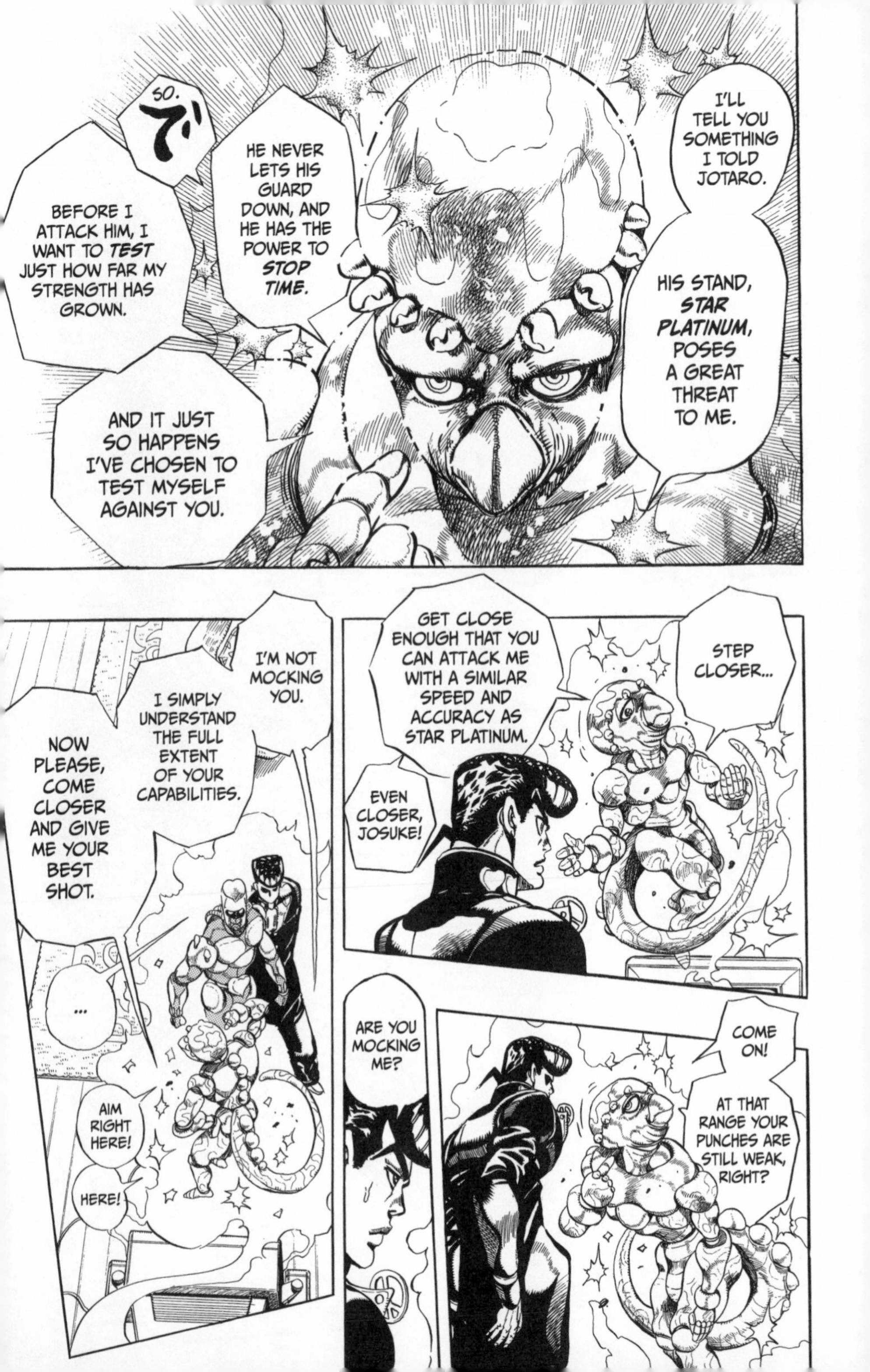

I'LL TELL YOU SOMETHING I TOLD JOTARO.
HIS STAND, STAR PLATINUM, POSES A GREAT THREAT TO ME.
HE NEVER LETS HIS GUARD DOWN, AND HE HAS THE POWER TO STOP TIME.
SO.
で
BEFORE I ATTACK HIM, I WANT TO TEST JUST HOW FAR MY STRENGTH HAS GROWN.
AND IT JUST SO HAPPENS I'VE CHOSEN TO TEST MYSELF AGAINST YOU.
STEP CLOSER...
GET CLOSE ENOUGH THAT YOU CAN ATTACK ME WITH A SIMILAR SPEED AND ACCURACY AS STAR PLATINUM.
EVEN CLOSER, JOSUKE!
COME ON!
AT THAT RANGE YOUR PUNCHES ARE STILL WEAK, RIGHT?
ARE YOU MOCKING ME?
I'M NOT MOCKING YOU.
I SIMPLY UNDERSTAND THE FULL EXTENT OF YOUR CAPABILITIES.
NOW PLEASE, COME CLOSER AND GIVE ME YOUR BEST SHOT.
...
AIM RIGHT HERE!
HERE!

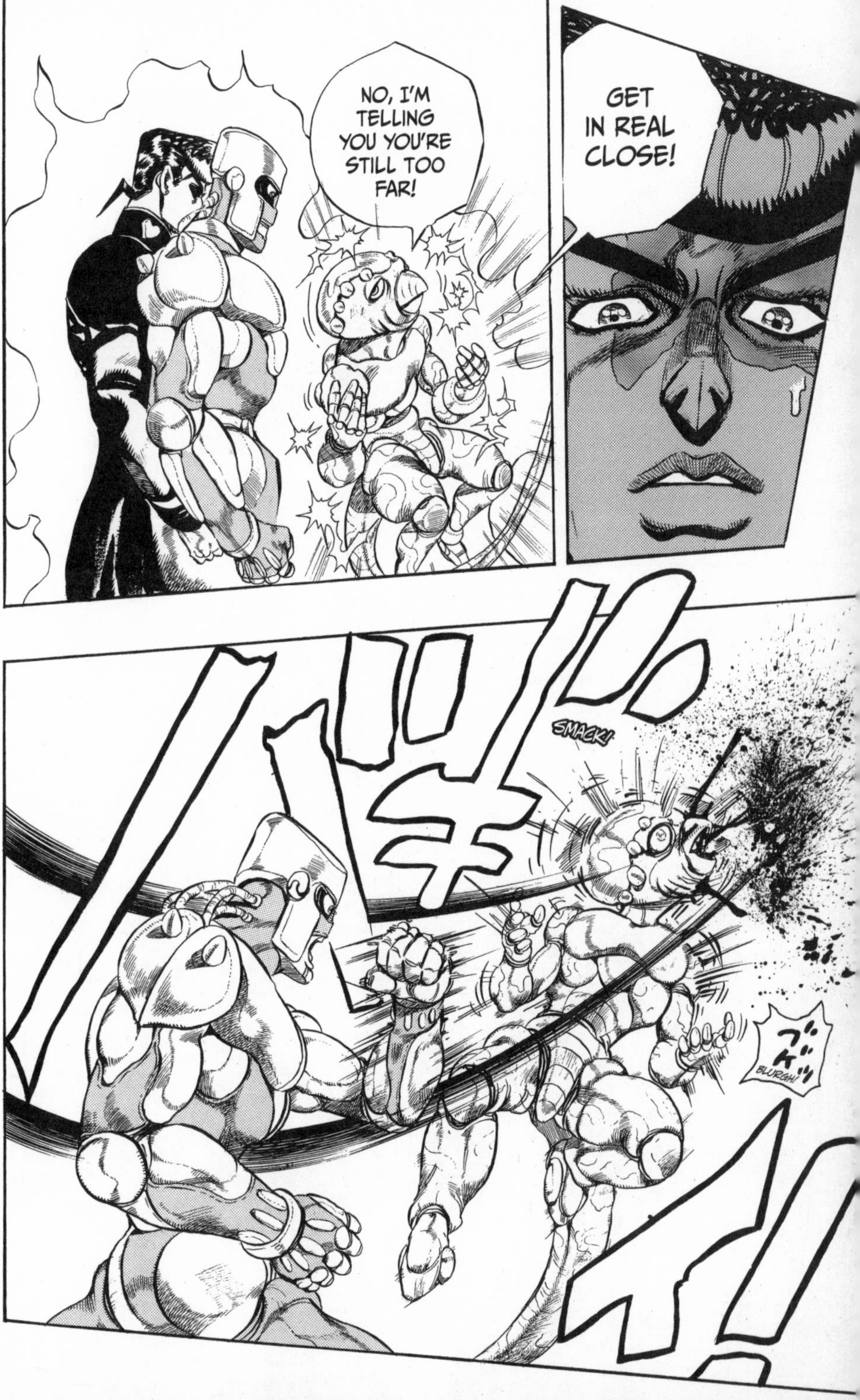
GET IN REAL CLOSE!
NO, I'M TELLING YOU YOU'RE STILL TOO FAR!
SMACK!
BLURGH!

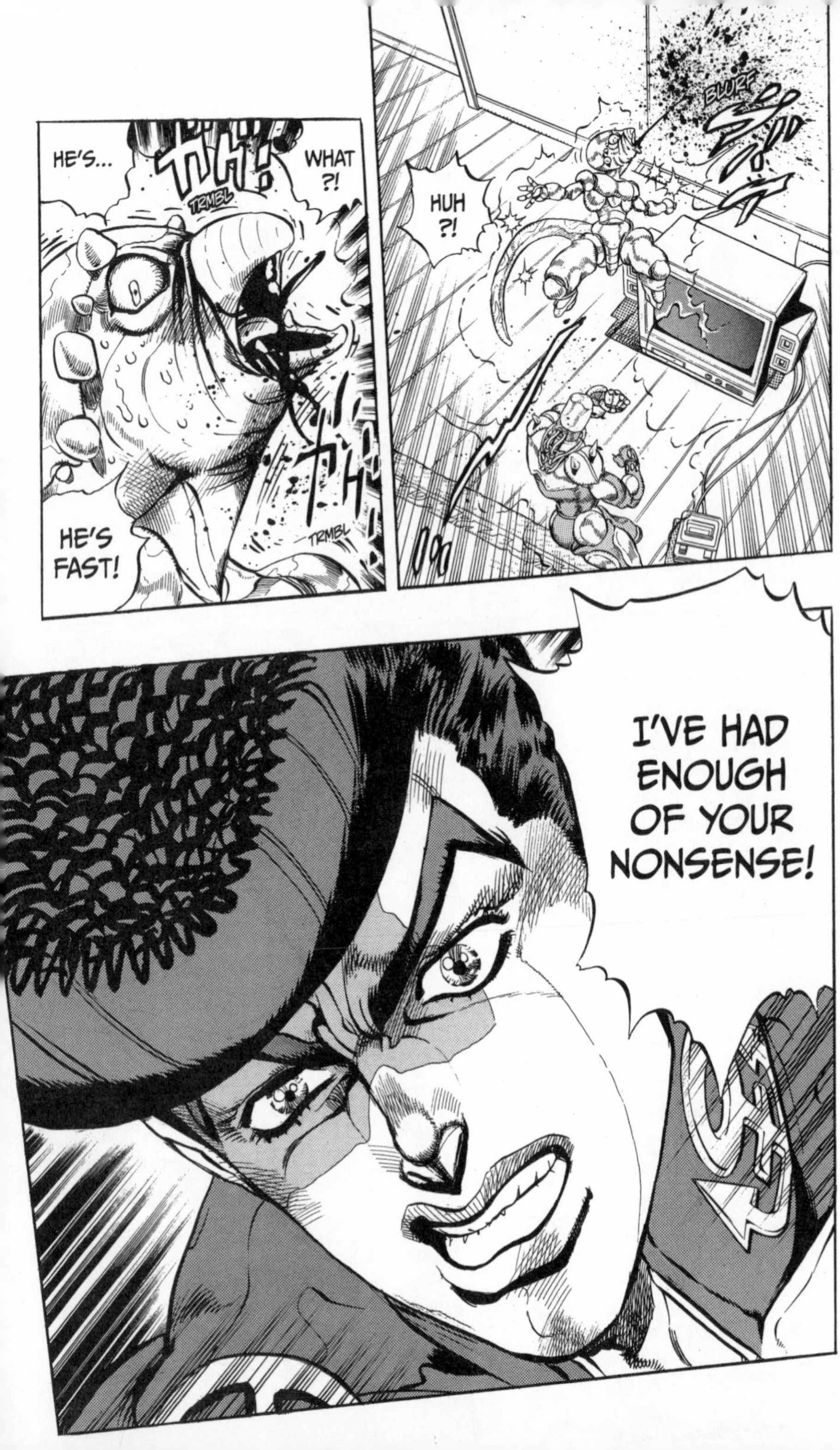
BLURF
HUH ?!
WHAT ?!
HE'S...
TRMBL
TRMBL
HE'S FAST!
I'VE HAD ENOUGH OF YOUR NONSENSE!

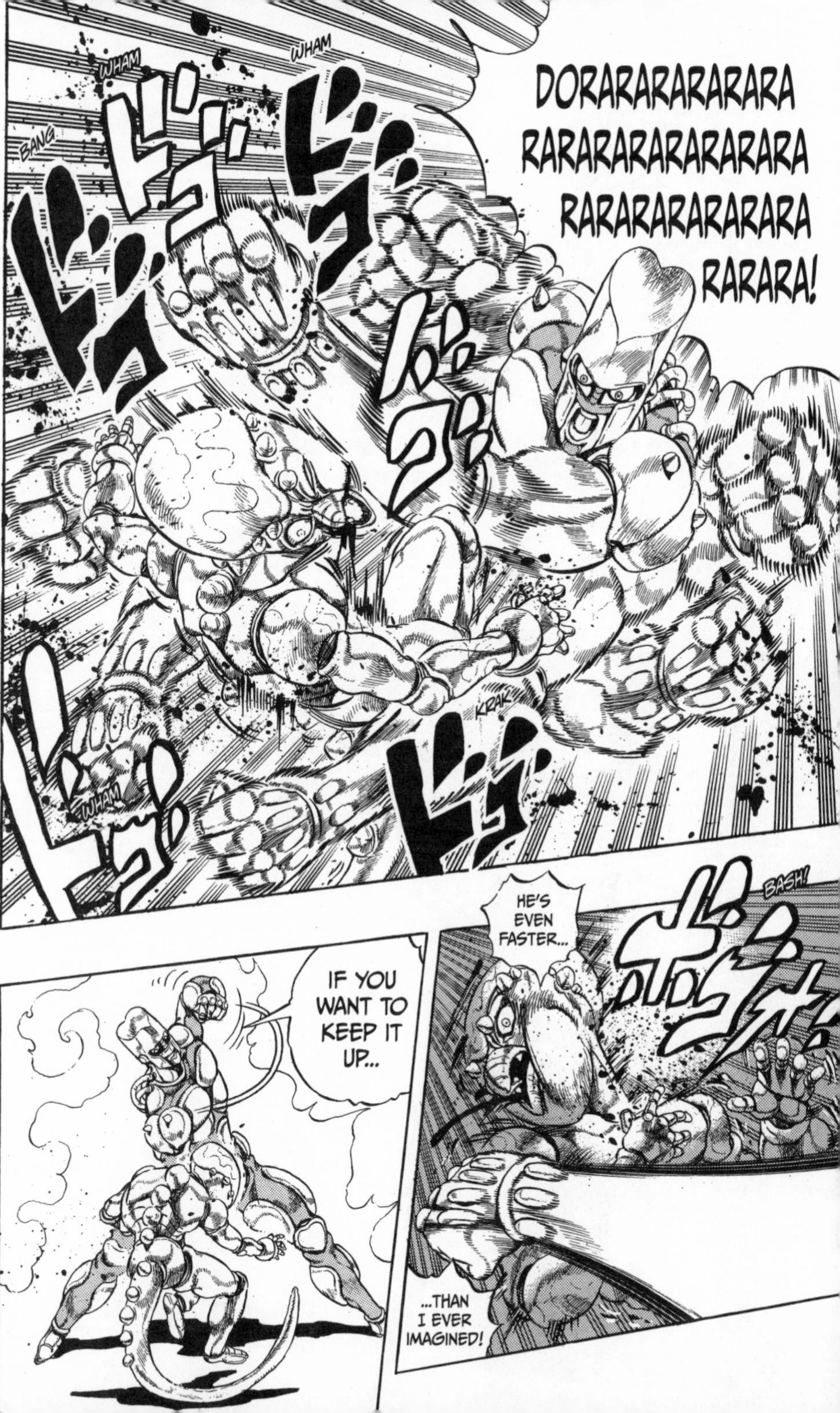
DORARARARARARA
RARARARARARARARA
RARARARARARARA
RARARA!
WHAM
WHAM
BANG
KRAK
WHAM
BASH!
HE'S EVEN FASTER...
DUD
...THAN I EVER IMAGINED!
IF YOU WANT TO KEEP IT UP...

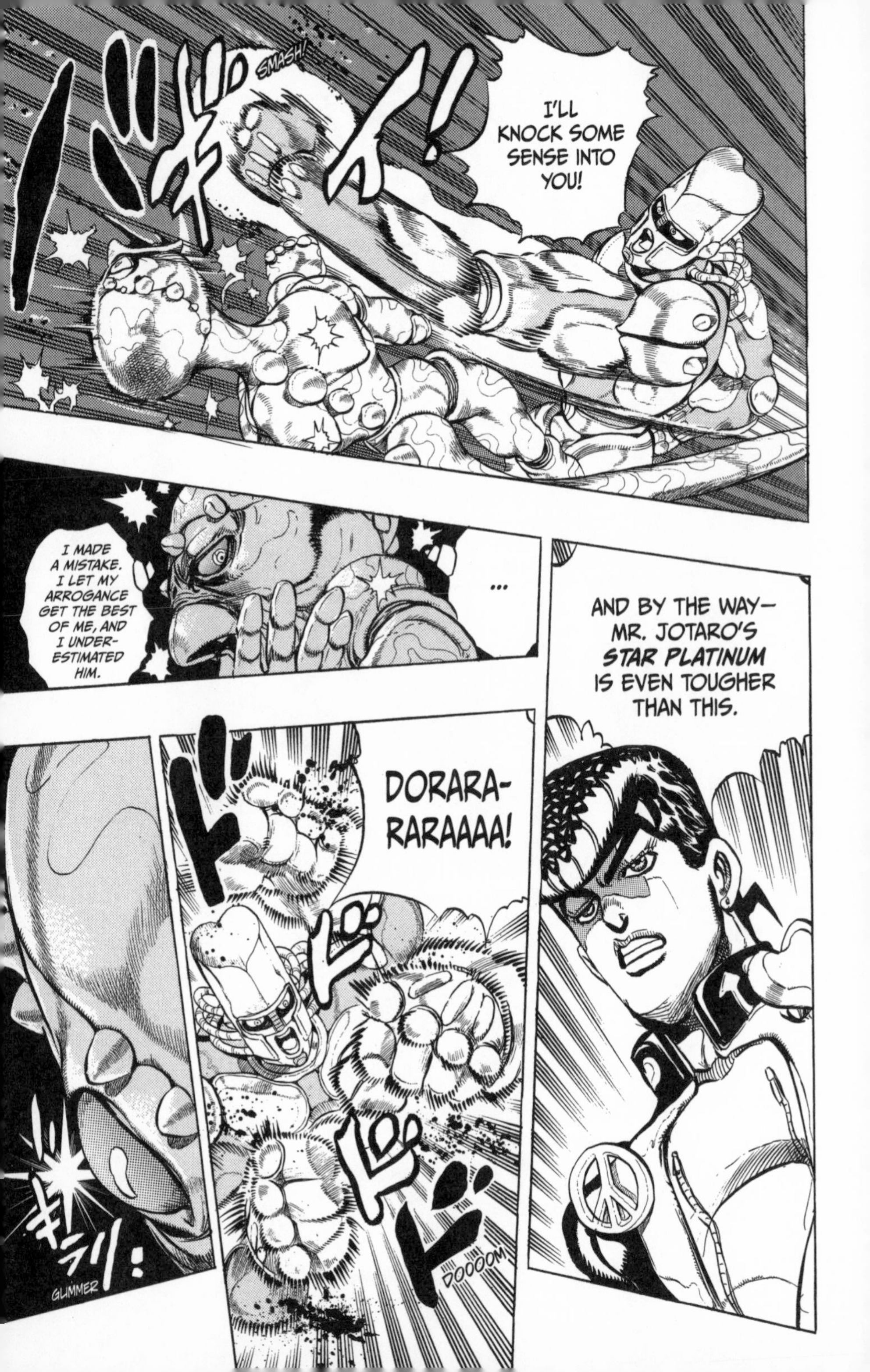
I'LL KNOCK SOME SENSE INTO YOU!
SMASH!
AND BY THE WAY— MR. JOTARO'S STAR PLATINUM IS EVEN TOUGHER THAN THIS.
...
I MADE A MISTAKE. I LET MY ARROGANCE GET THE BEST OF ME, AND I UNDER-ESTIMATED HIM.
DORARA-RARAAAA!
DOOOOM
GLIMMER

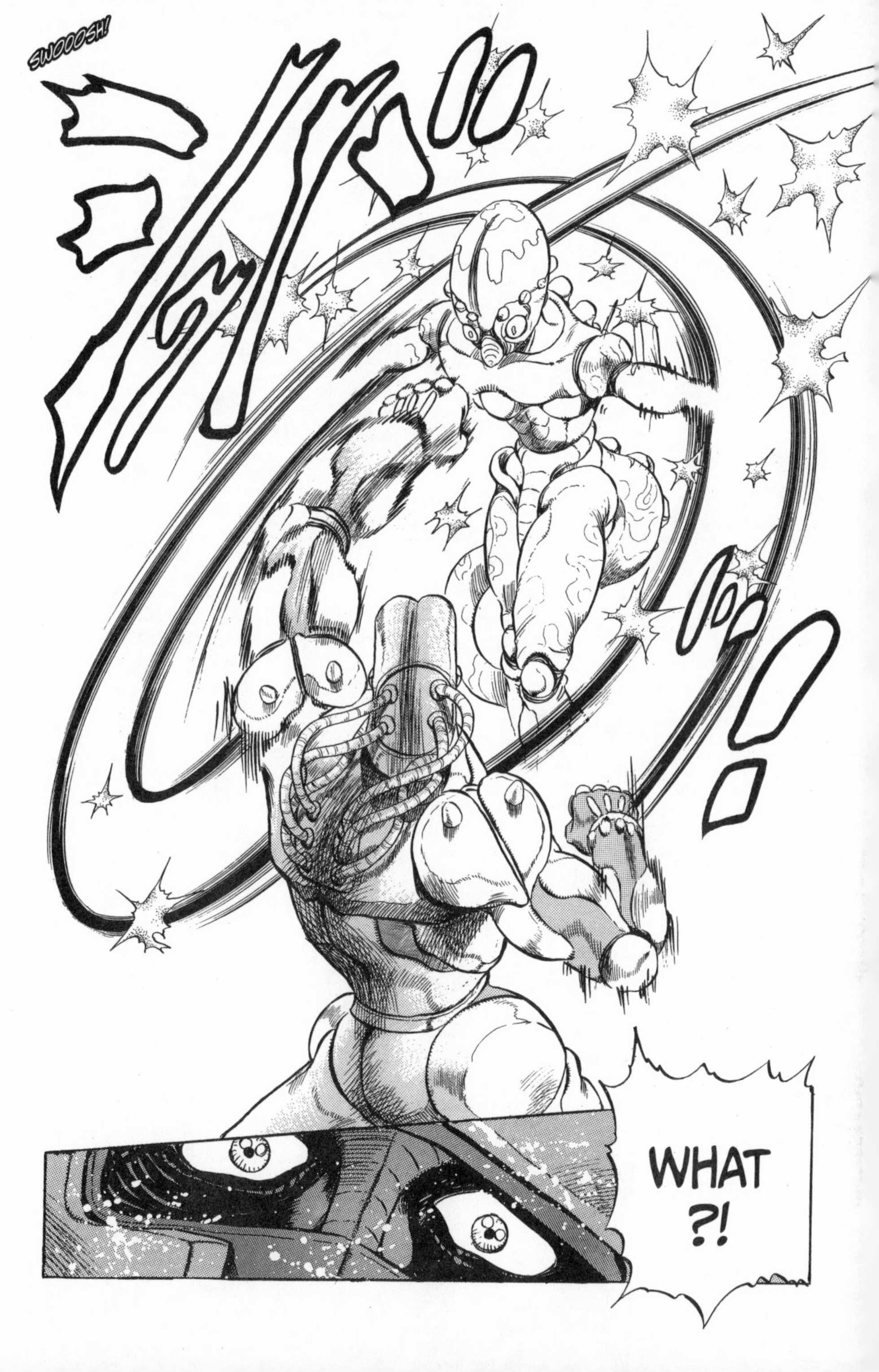
SWOOOSH!
WHAT ?!

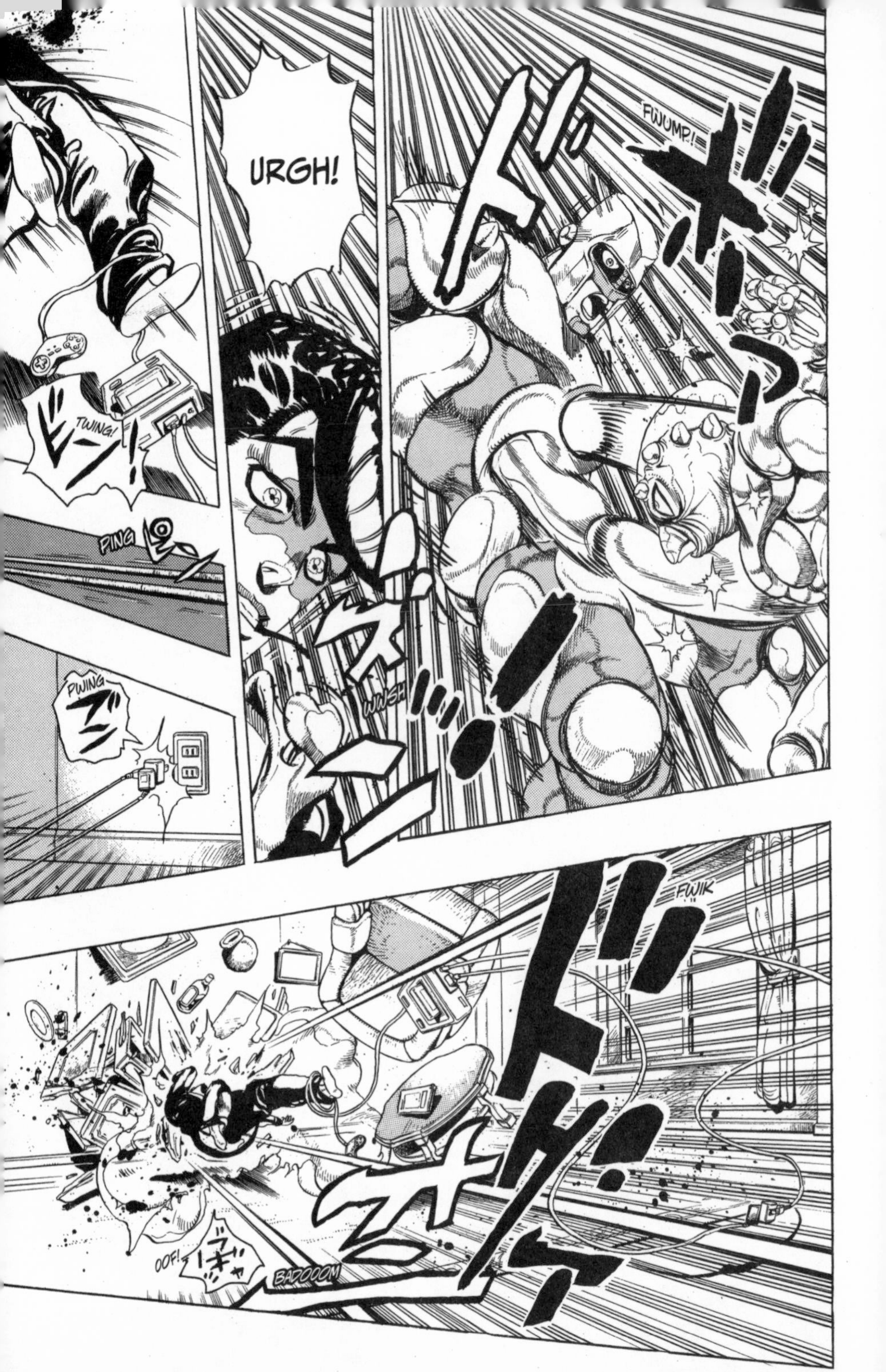
FWUMP!
WWSH
URGH!
TWING!
PING
PWING
FWIK
BADOOOM
OOF!

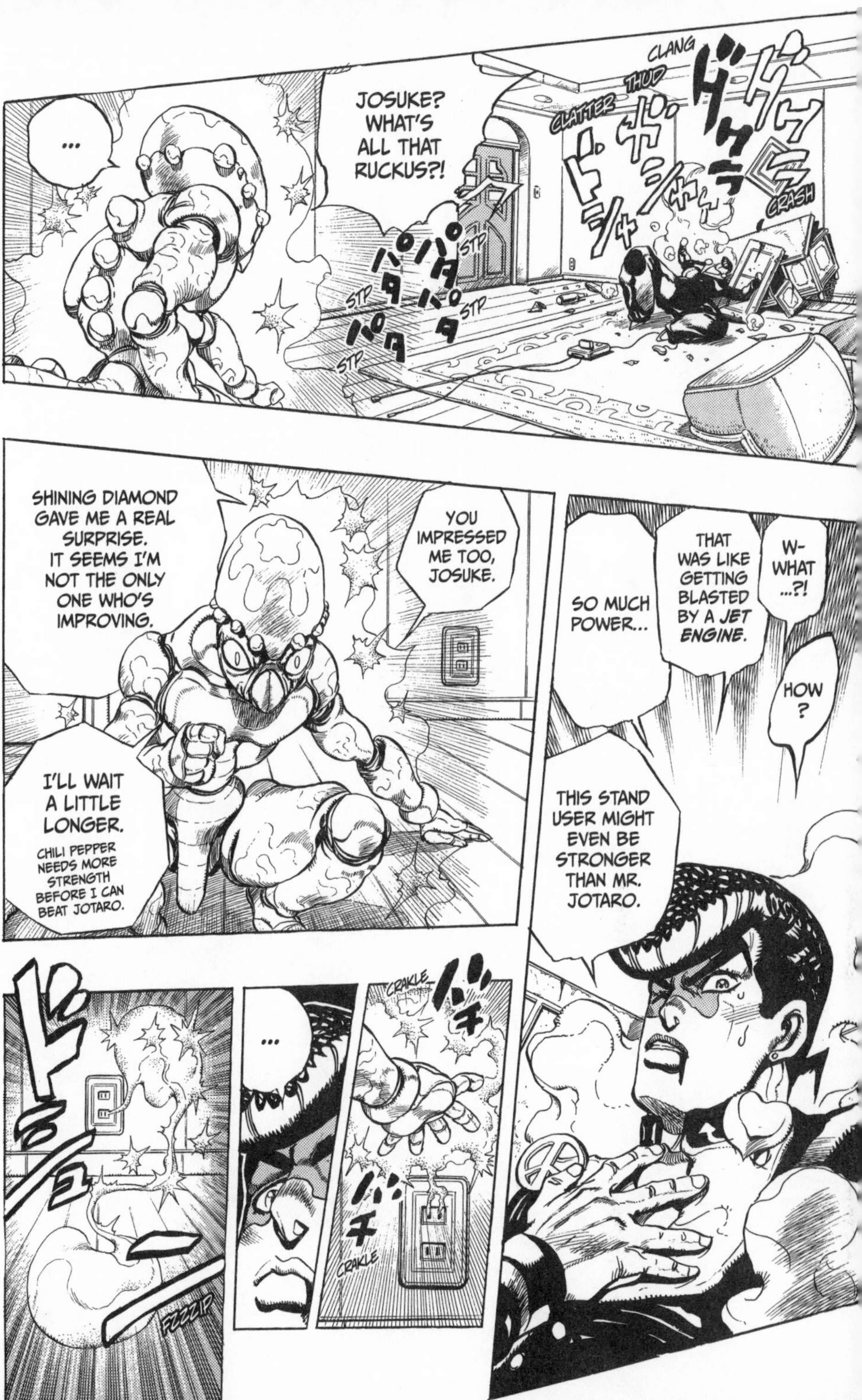
CLANG
CRASH
THUD
CLATTER
JOSUKE? WHAT'S ALL THAT RUCKUS?!
STP
STP
STP
STP
...
W- WHAT ...?!
THAT WAS LIKE GETTING BLASTED BY A *JET ENGINE*.
SO MUCH POWER...
HOW ?
THIS STAND USER MIGHT EVEN BE STRONGER THAN MR. JOTARO.
YOU IMPRESSED ME TOO, JOSUKE.
SHINING DIAMOND GAVE ME A REAL SURPRISE. IT SEEMS I'M NOT THE ONLY ONE WHO'S IMPROVING.
I'LL WAIT A LITTLE LONGER.
CHILI PEPPER NEEDS MORE STRENGTH BEFORE I CAN BEAT JOTARO.
CRAKLE
CRAKLE
...
FZZZIP

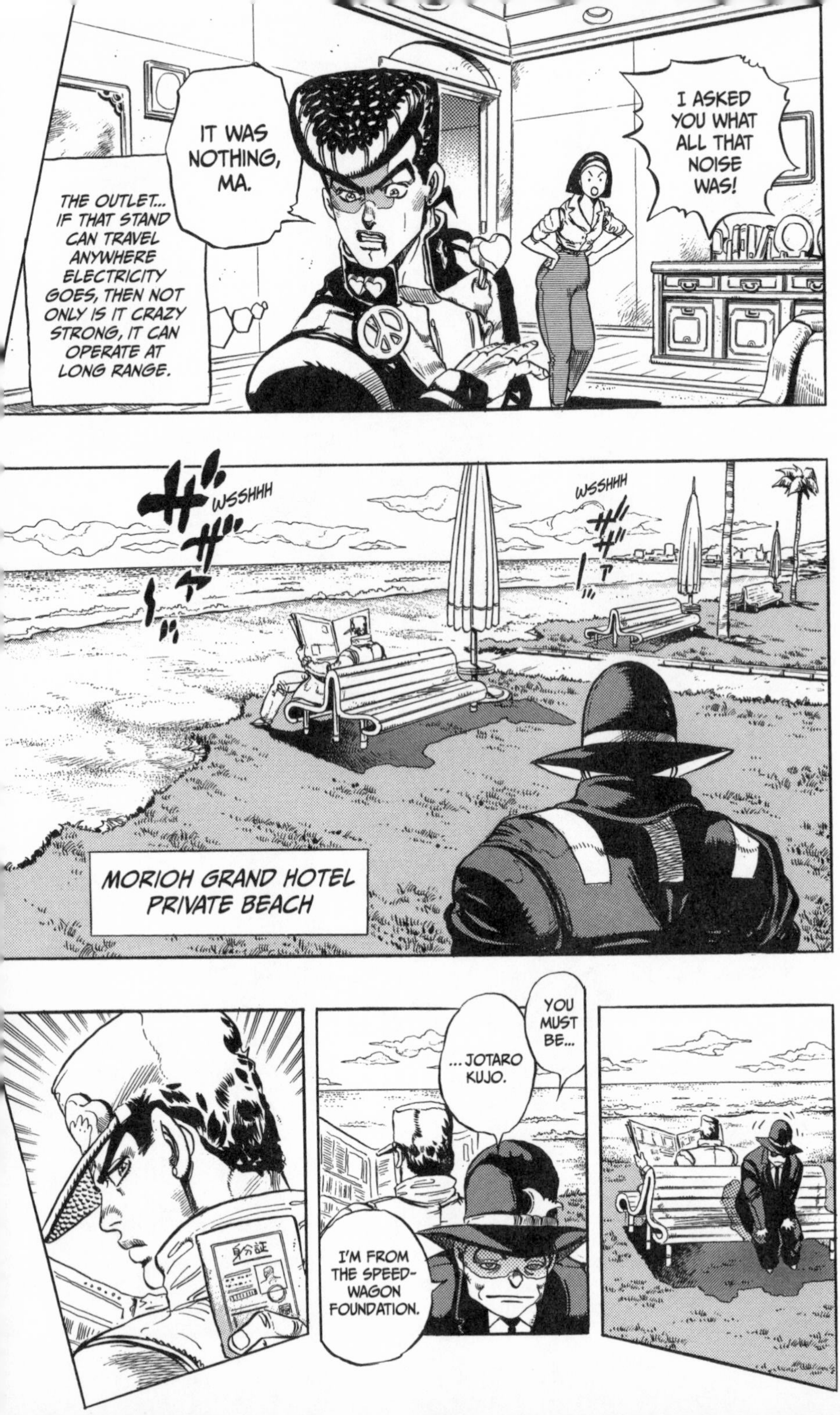
I ASKED YOU WHAT ALL THAT NOISE WAS!
IT WAS NOTHING, MA.
THE OUTLET... IF THAT STAND CAN TRAVEL ANYWHERE ELECTRICITY GOES, THEN NOT ONLY IS IT CRAZY STRONG, IT CAN OPERATE AT LONG RANGE.
WSSHHH
WSSHHH
MORIOH GRAND HOTEL PRIVATE BEACH
YOU MUST BE...
...JOTARO KUJO.
I'M FROM THE SPEED-WAGON FOUNDATION.
身分証

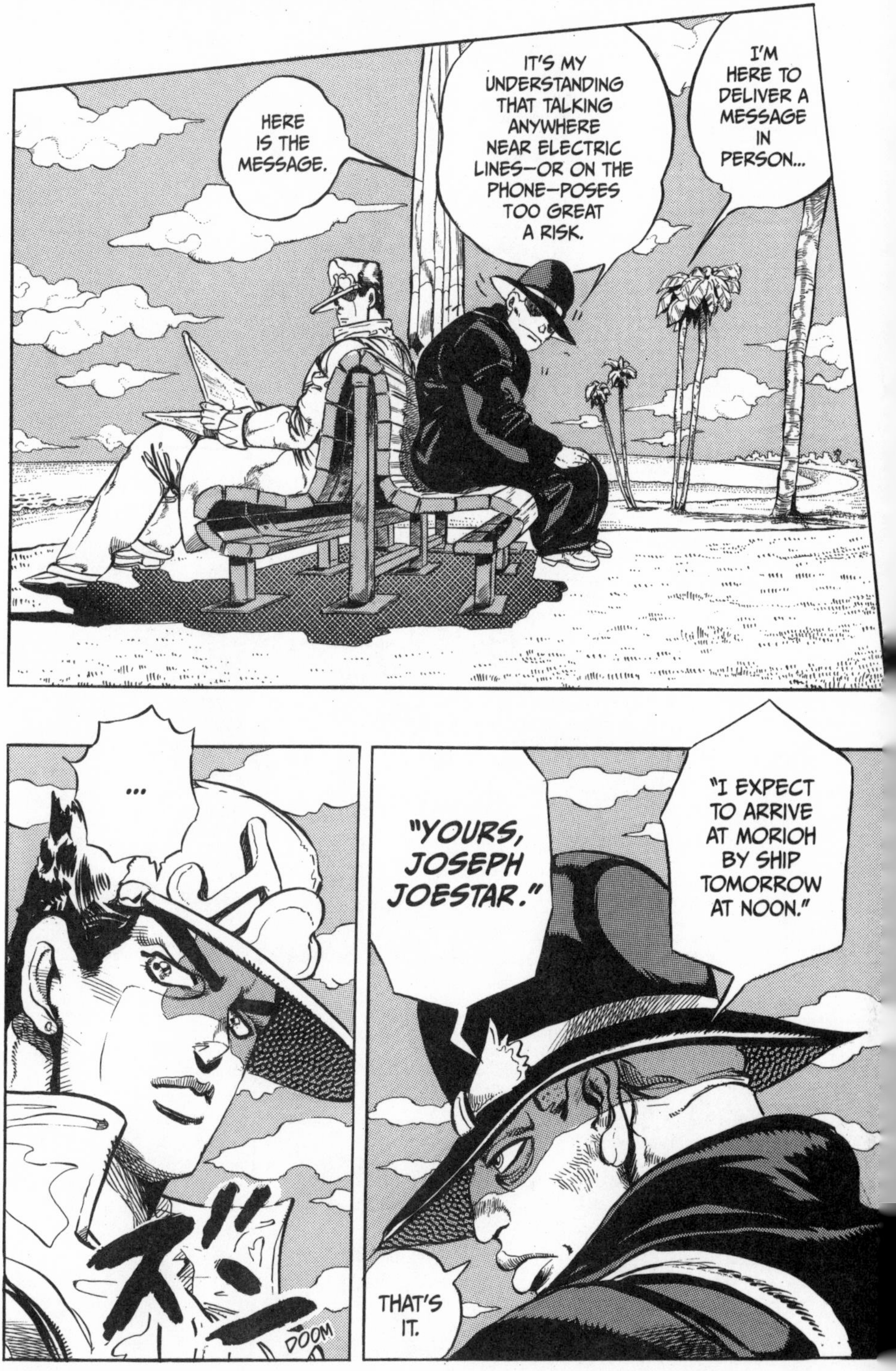
I'M HERE TO DELIVER A MESSAGE IN PERSON...
IT'S MY UNDERSTANDING THAT TALKING ANYWHERE NEAR ELECTRIC LINES—OR ON THE PHONE—POSES TOO GREAT A RISK.
HERE IS THE MESSAGE.
"I EXPECT TO ARRIVE AT MORIOH BY SHIP TOMORROW AT NOON."
"YOURS, JOSEPH JOESTAR."
THAT'S IT.
...
DOOM

CHAPTER 43

CHILI PEPPER, PART 2

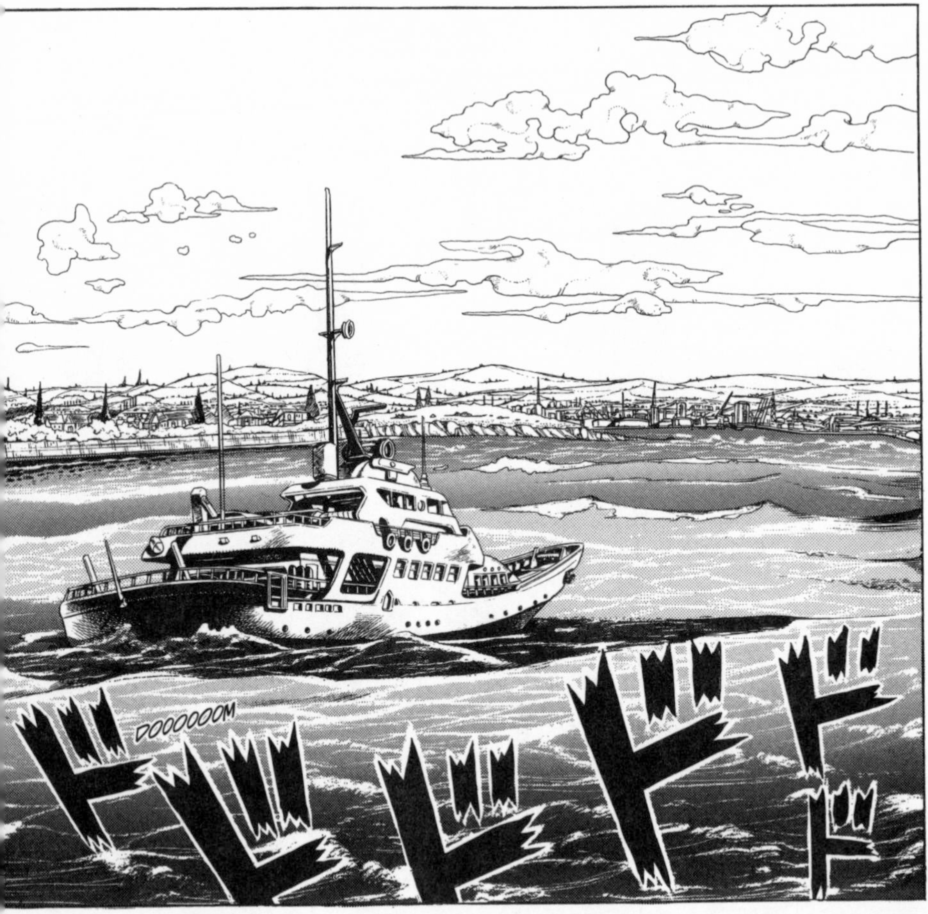
DOOOOOOM

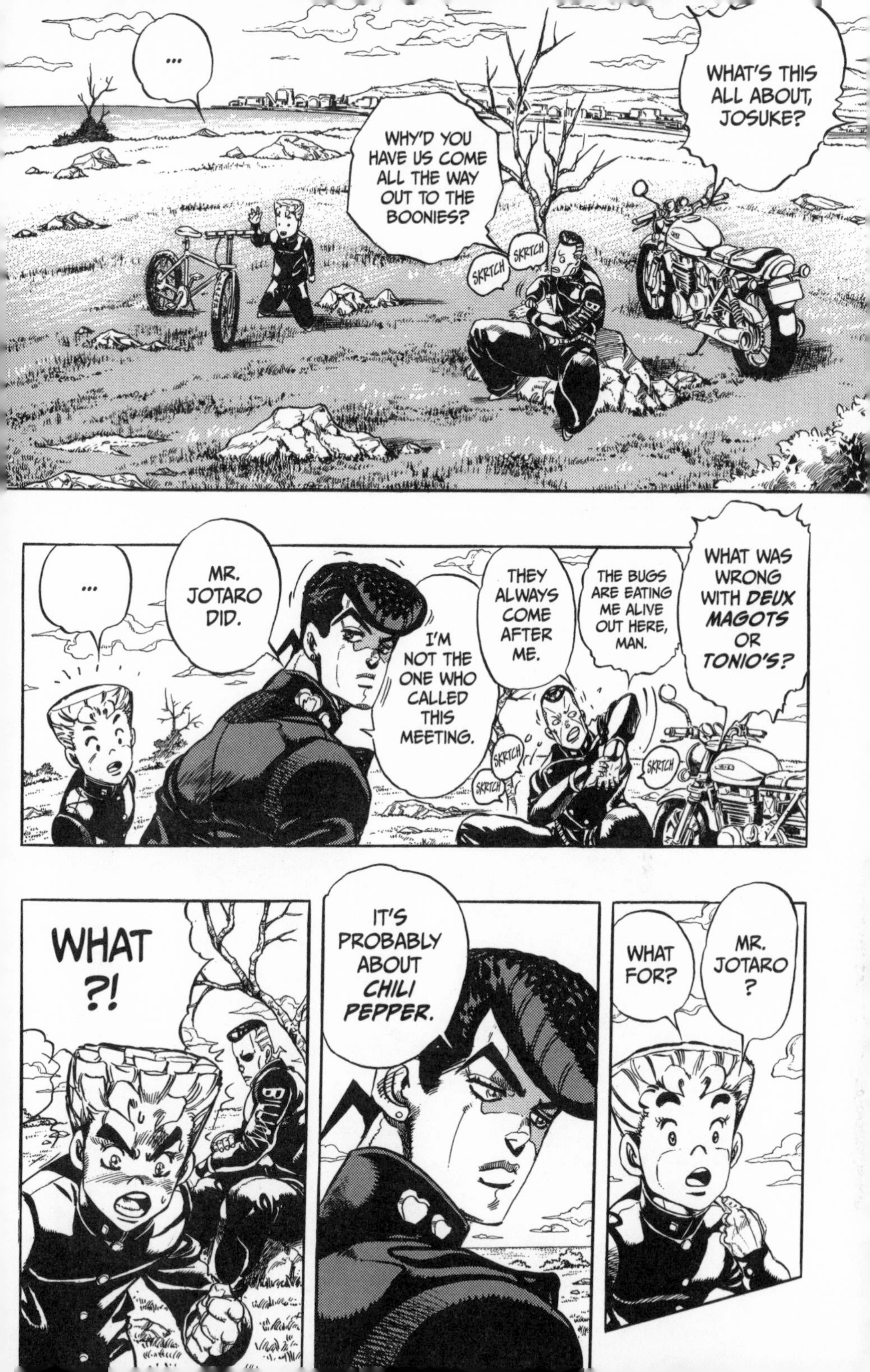
WHAT'S THIS ALL ABOUT, JOSUKE?
WHY'D YOU HAVE US COME ALL THE WAY OUT TO THE BOONIES?
SKRTCH
SKRTCH
...
WHAT WAS WRONG WITH *DEUX MAGOTS* OR *TONIO'S?*
THE BUGS ARE EATING ME ALIVE OUT HERE, MAN.
SKRTCH
SKRTCH
SKRTCH
THEY ALWAYS COME AFTER ME.
I'M NOT THE ONE WHO CALLED THIS MEETING.
MR. JOTARO DID.
...
MR. JOTARO?
WHAT FOR?
IT'S PROBABLY ABOUT *CHILI PEPPER*.
WHAT?!

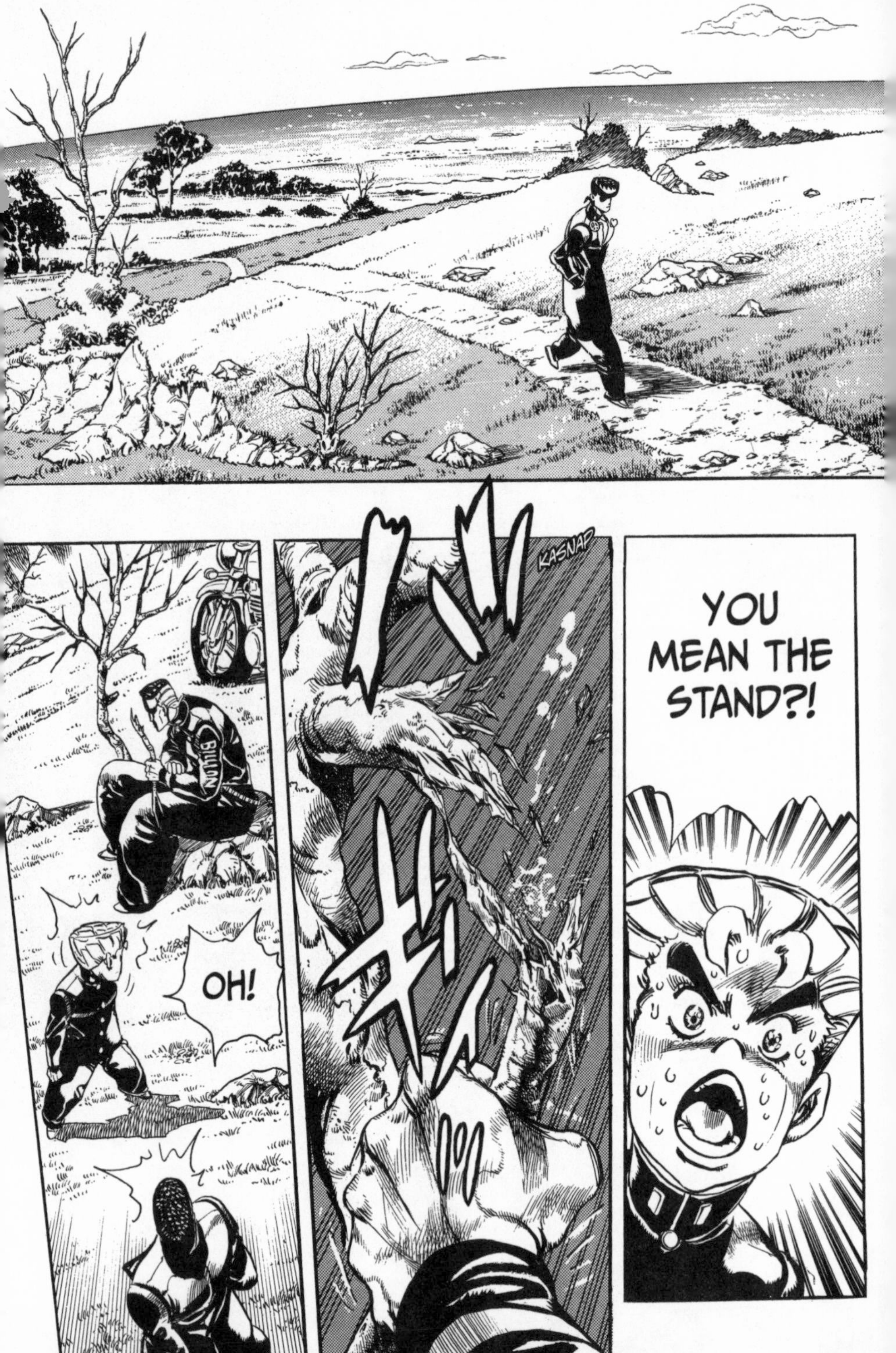
YOU MEAN THE STAND?!
KASNAP
OH!

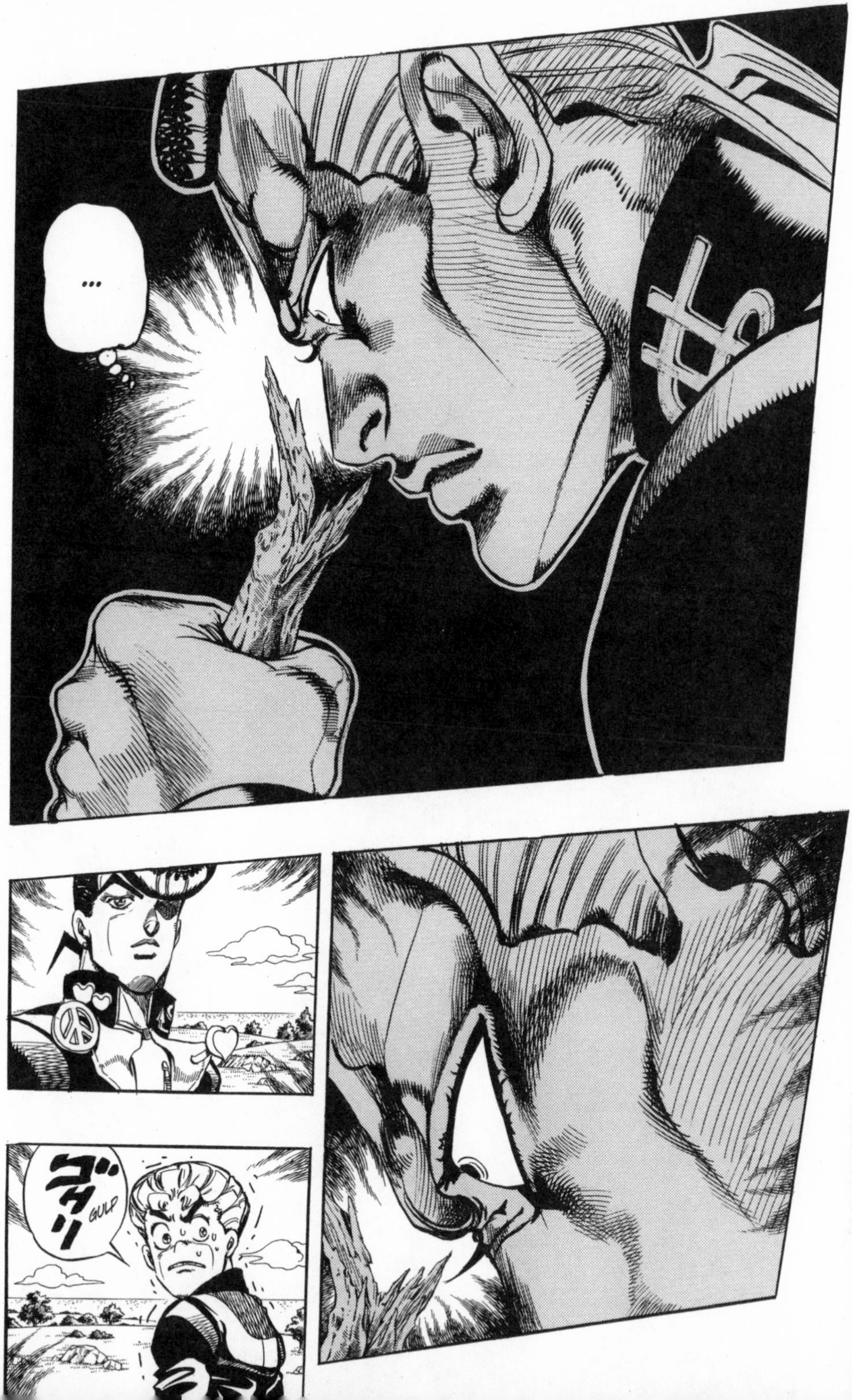
...
ゴクリ
GULP

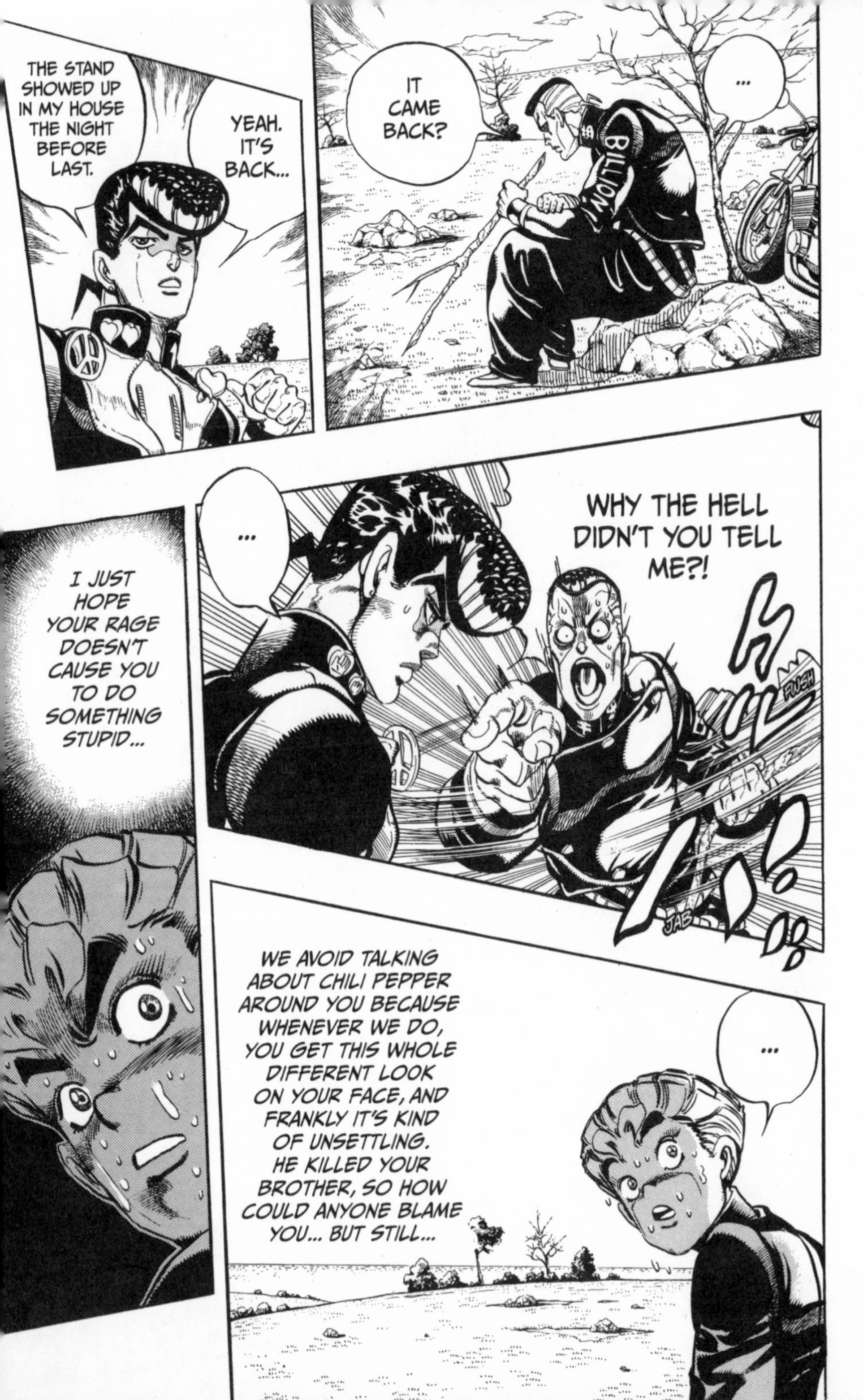
...
IT CAME BACK?
YEAH. IT'S BACK...
THE STAND SHOWED UP IN MY HOUSE THE NIGHT BEFORE LAST.
WHY THE HELL DIDN'T YOU TELL ME?!
...
FWSH
JAB
...
WE AVOID TALKING ABOUT CHILI PEPPER AROUND YOU BECAUSE WHENEVER WE DO, YOU GET THIS WHOLE DIFFERENT LOOK ON YOUR FACE, AND FRANKLY IT'S KIND OF UNSETTLING. HE KILLED YOUR BROTHER, SO HOW COULD ANYONE BLAME YOU... BUT STILL...
I JUST HOPE YOUR RAGE DOESN'T CAUSE YOU TO DO SOMETHING STUPID...

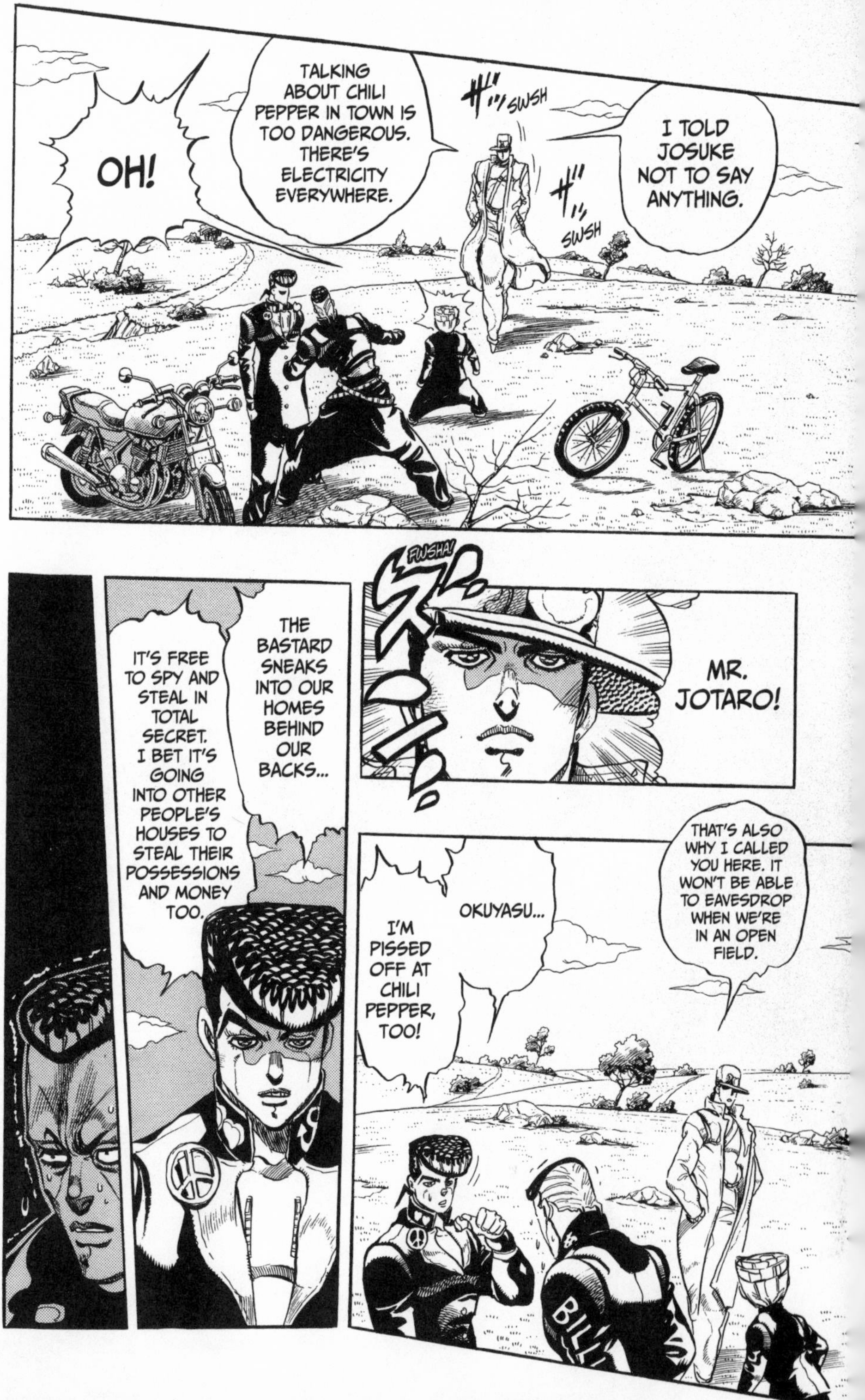
I TOLD JOSUKE NOT TO SAY ANYTHING.
SWSH
SWSH
TALKING ABOUT CHILI PEPPER IN TOWN IS TOO DANGEROUS. THERE'S ELECTRICITY EVERYWHERE.
OH!
FWSHA!
MR. JOTARO!
THAT'S ALSO WHY I CALLED YOU HERE. IT WON'T BE ABLE TO EAVESDROP WHEN WE'RE IN AN OPEN FIELD.
OKUYASU...
I'M PISSED OFF AT CHILI PEPPER, TOO!
THE BASTARD SNEAKS INTO OUR HOMES BEHIND OUR BACKS...
IT'S FREE TO SPY AND STEAL IN TOTAL SECRET. I BET IT'S GOING INTO OTHER PEOPLE'S HOUSES TO STEAL THEIR POSSESSIONS AND MONEY TOO.

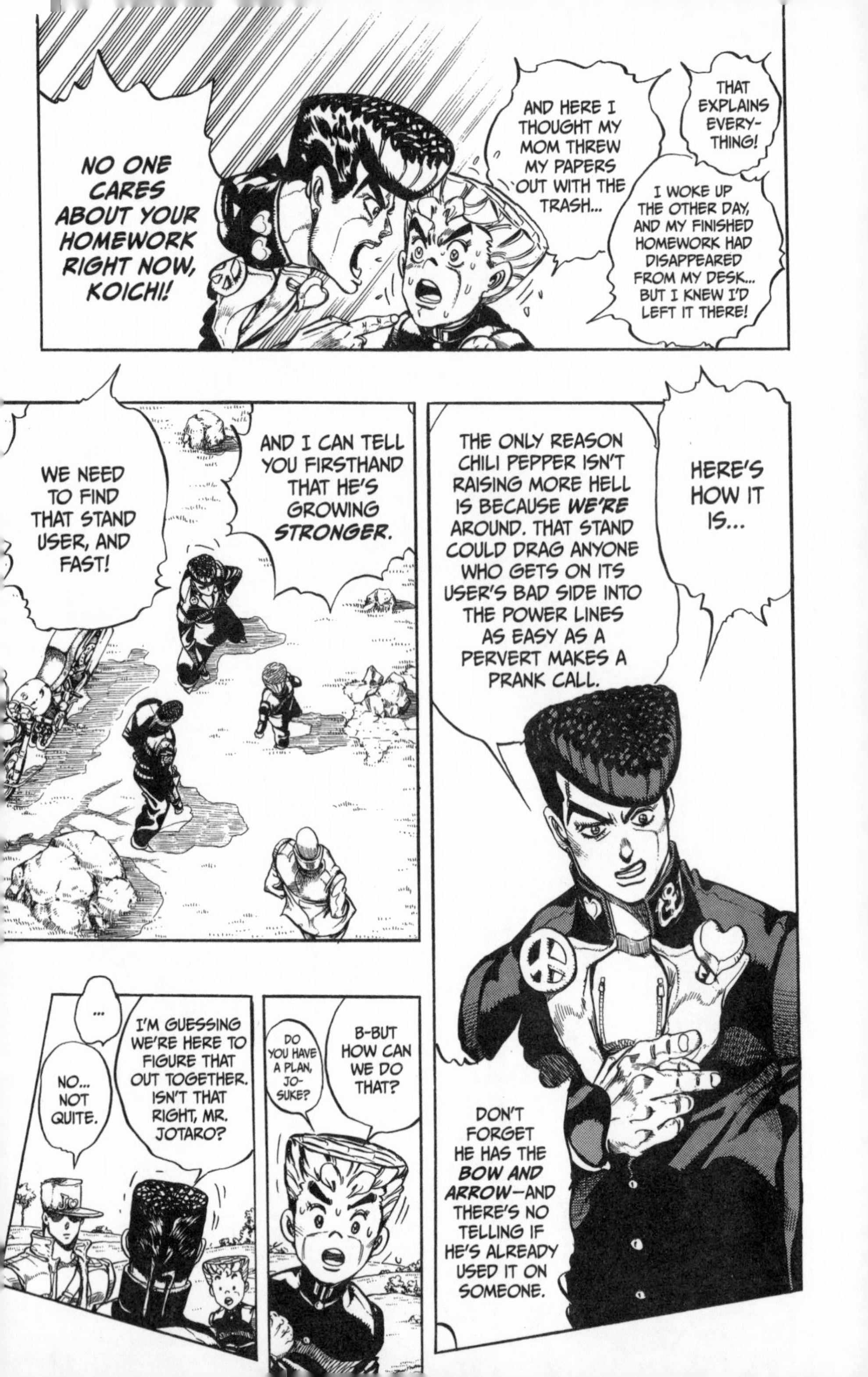

THAT EXPLAINS EVERY-THING!
AND HERE I THOUGHT MY MOM THREW MY PAPERS OUT WITH THE TRASH...
I WOKE UP THE OTHER DAY, AND MY FINISHED HOMEWORK HAD DISAPPEARED FROM MY DESK... BUT I KNEW I'D LEFT IT THERE!
NO ONE CARES ABOUT YOUR HOMEWORK RIGHT NOW, KOICHI!
HERE'S HOW IT IS...
THE ONLY REASON CHILI PEPPER ISN'T RAISING MORE HELL IS BECAUSE WE'RE AROUND. THAT STAND COULD DRAG ANYONE WHO GETS ON ITS USER'S BAD SIDE INTO THE POWER LINES AS EASY AS A PERVERT MAKES A PRANK CALL.
DON'T FORGET HE HAS THE BOW AND ARROW—AND THERE'S NO TELLING IF HE'S ALREADY USED IT ON SOMEONE.
AND I CAN TELL YOU FIRSTHAND THAT HE'S GROWING STRONGER.
WE NEED TO FIND THAT STAND USER, AND FAST!
B-BUT HOW CAN WE DO THAT?
DO YOU HAVE A PLAN, JO-SUKE?
...
I'M GUESSING WE'RE HERE TO FIGURE THAT OUT TOGETHER. ISN'T THAT RIGHT, MR. JOTARO?
NO... NOT QUITE.

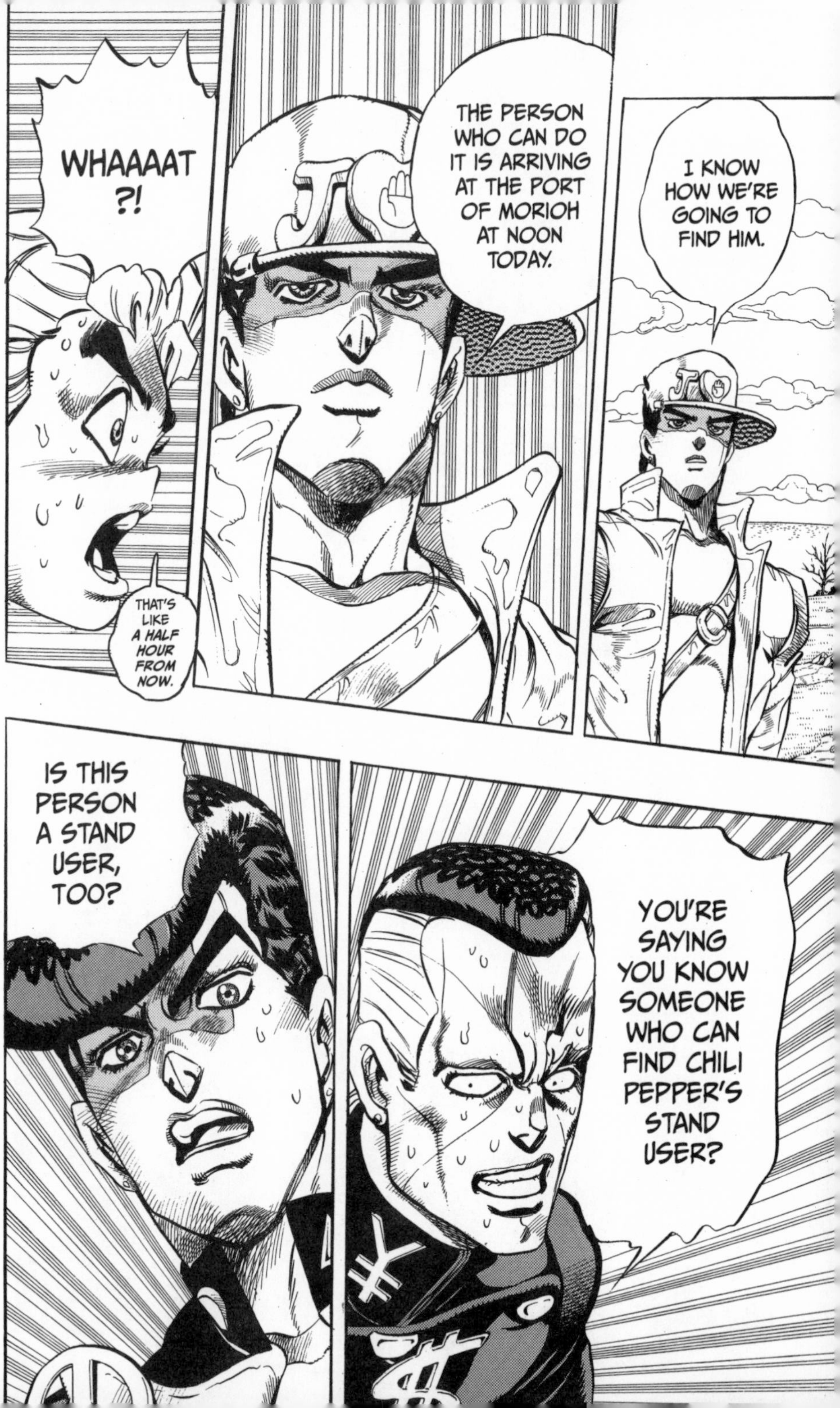
I KNOW HOW WE'RE GOING TO FIND HIM.
THE PERSON WHO CAN DO IT IS ARRIVING AT THE PORT OF MORIOH AT NOON TODAY.
WHAAAAT ?!
THAT'S LIKE A HALF HOUR FROM NOW.
YOU'RE SAYING YOU KNOW SOMEONE WHO CAN FIND CHILI PEPPER'S STAND USER?
IS THIS PERSON A STAND USER, TOO?

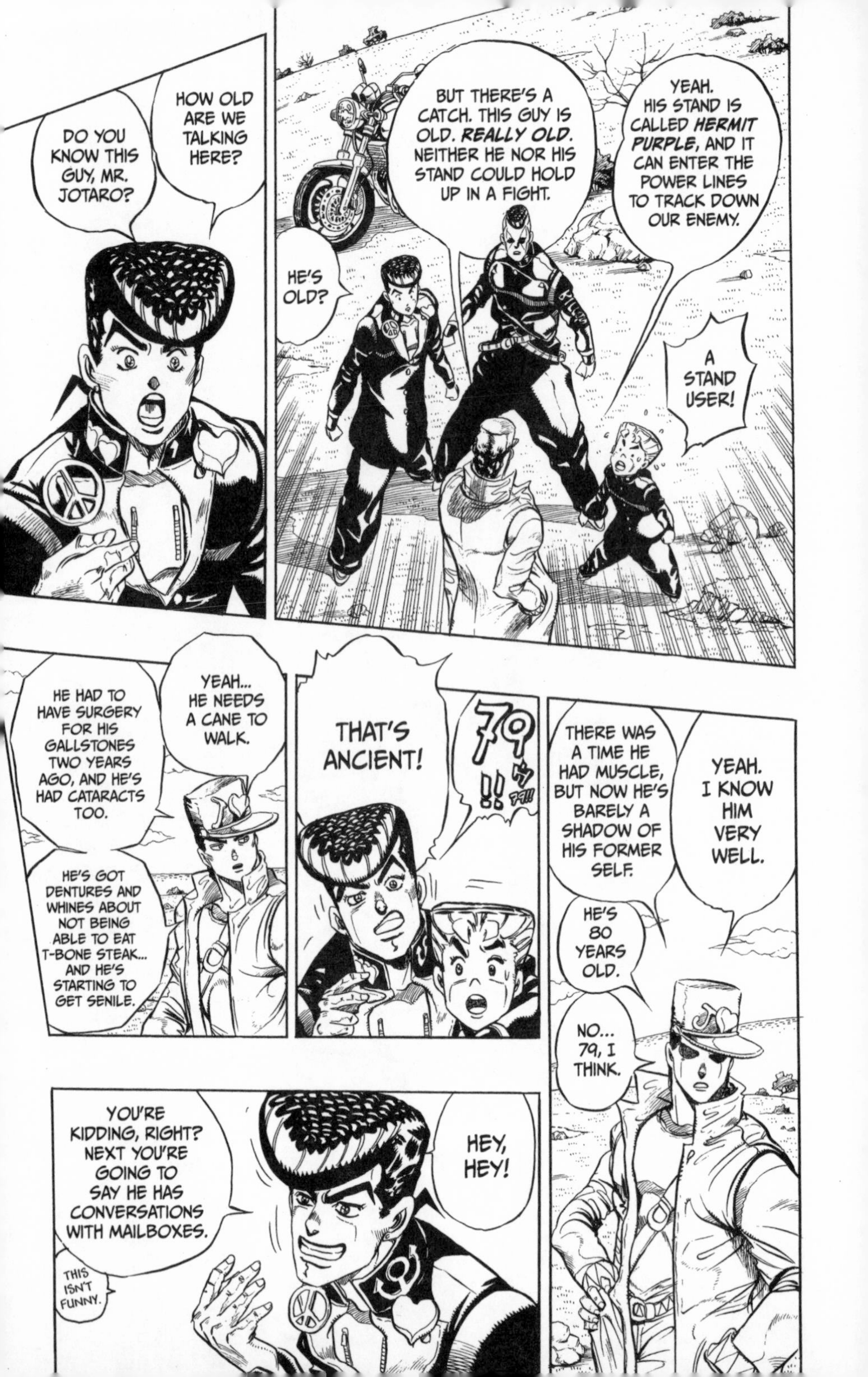
YEAH. HIS STAND IS CALLED *HERMIT PURPLE*, AND IT CAN ENTER THE POWER LINES TO TRACK DOWN OUR ENEMY.
BUT THERE'S A CATCH. THIS GUY IS OLD. *REALLY OLD*. NEITHER HE NOR HIS STAND COULD HOLD UP IN A FIGHT.
A STAND USER!
HE'S OLD?
HOW OLD ARE WE TALKING HERE?
DO YOU KNOW THIS GUY, MR. JOTARO?
YEAH. I KNOW HIM VERY WELL.
THERE WAS A TIME HE HAD MUSCLE, BUT NOW HE'S BARELY A SHADOW OF HIS FORMER SELF.
HE'S 80 YEARS OLD.
NO... 79, I THINK.
79!!
THAT'S ANCIENT!
YEAH... HE NEEDS A CANE TO WALK.
HE HAD TO HAVE SURGERY FOR HIS GALLSTONES TWO YEARS AGO, AND HE'S HAD CATARACTS TOO.
HE'S GOT DENTURES AND WHINES ABOUT NOT BEING ABLE TO EAT T-BONE STEAK... AND HE'S STARTING TO GET SENILE.
HEY, HEY!
YOU'RE KIDDING, RIGHT? NEXT YOU'RE GOING TO SAY HE HAS CONVERSATIONS WITH MAILBOXES.
THIS ISN'T FUNNY.

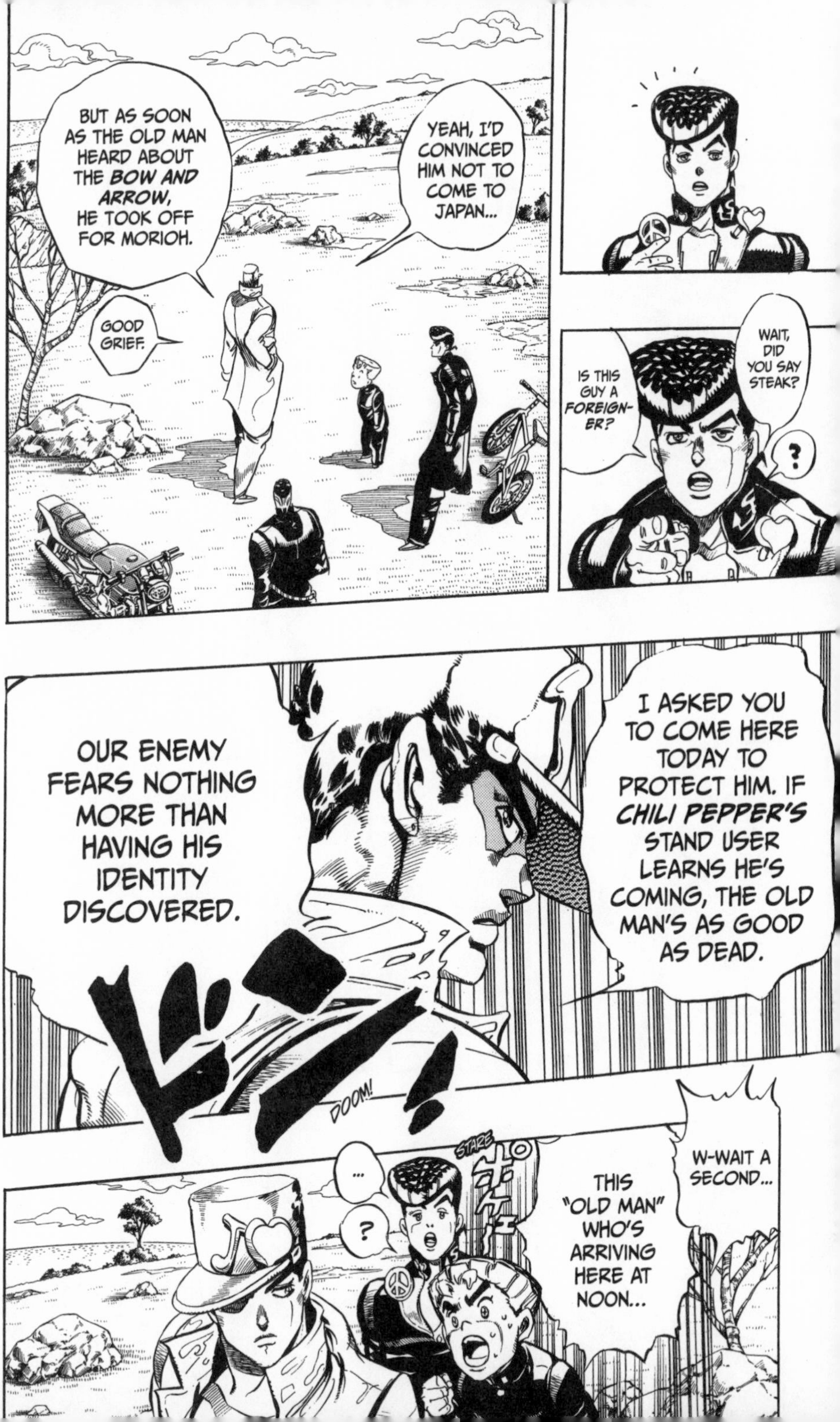
WAIT, DID YOU SAY STEAK?
IS THIS GUY A FOREIGNER?
?
YEAH, I'D CONVINCED HIM NOT TO COME TO JAPAN...
BUT AS SOON AS THE OLD MAN HEARD ABOUT THE *BOW AND ARROW*, HE TOOK OFF FOR MORIOH.
GOOD GRIEF.
I ASKED YOU TO COME HERE TODAY TO PROTECT HIM. IF *CHILI PEPPER'S* STAND USER LEARNS HE'S COMING, THE OLD MAN'S AS GOOD AS DEAD.
OUR ENEMY FEARS NOTHING MORE THAN HAVING HIS IDENTITY DISCOVERED.
DOOM!
W-WAIT A SECOND...
THIS "OLD MAN" WHO'S ARRIVING HERE AT NOON...
STARE
?
...

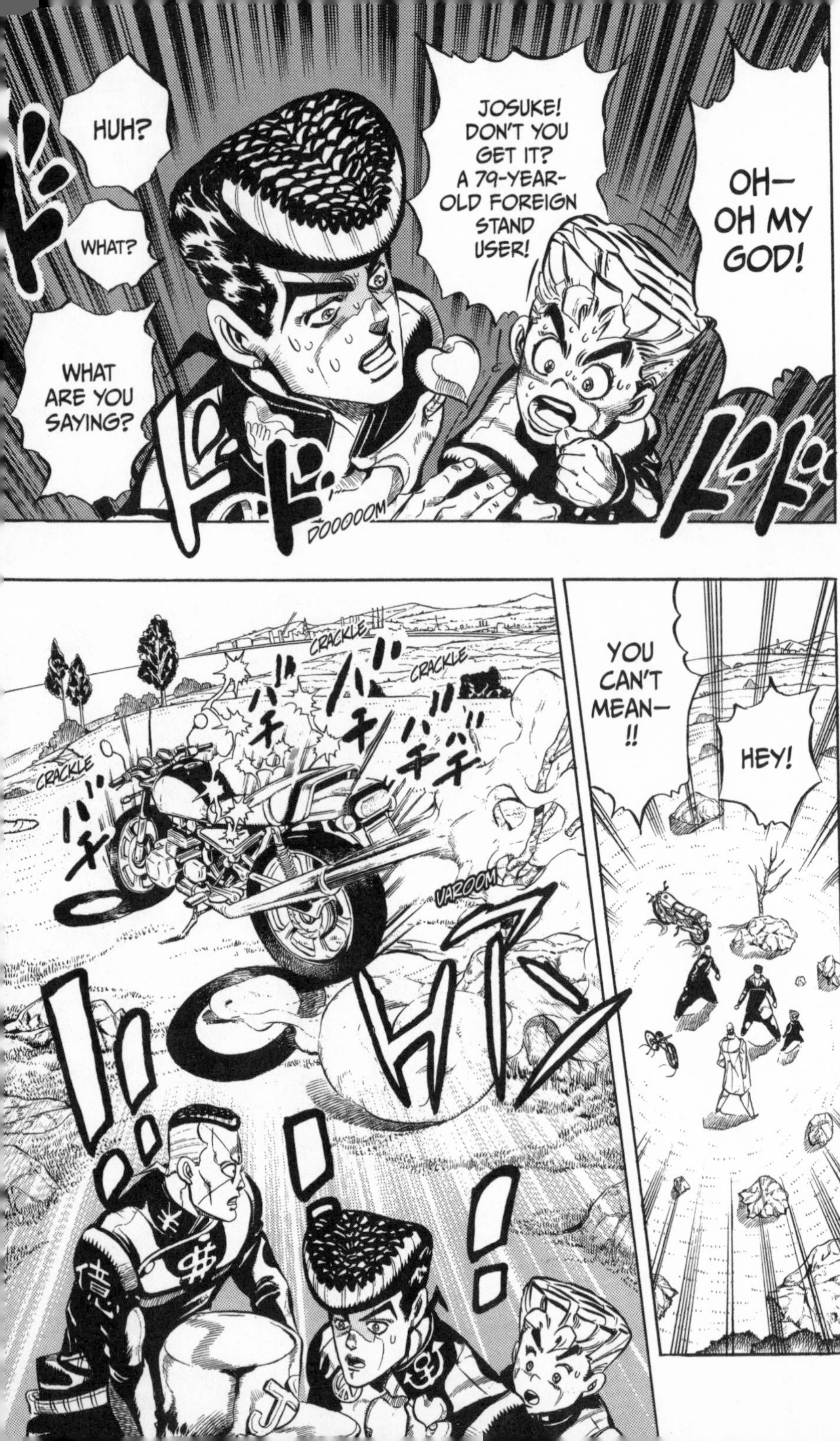
OH— OH MY GOD!
JOSUKE! DON'T YOU GET IT? A 79-YEAR-OLD FOREIGN STAND USER!
HUH?
WHAT?
WHAT ARE YOU SAYING?
DOOOOOM
YOU CAN'T MEAN— !!
HEY!
CRACKLE
CRACKLE
CRACKLE
VAROOM

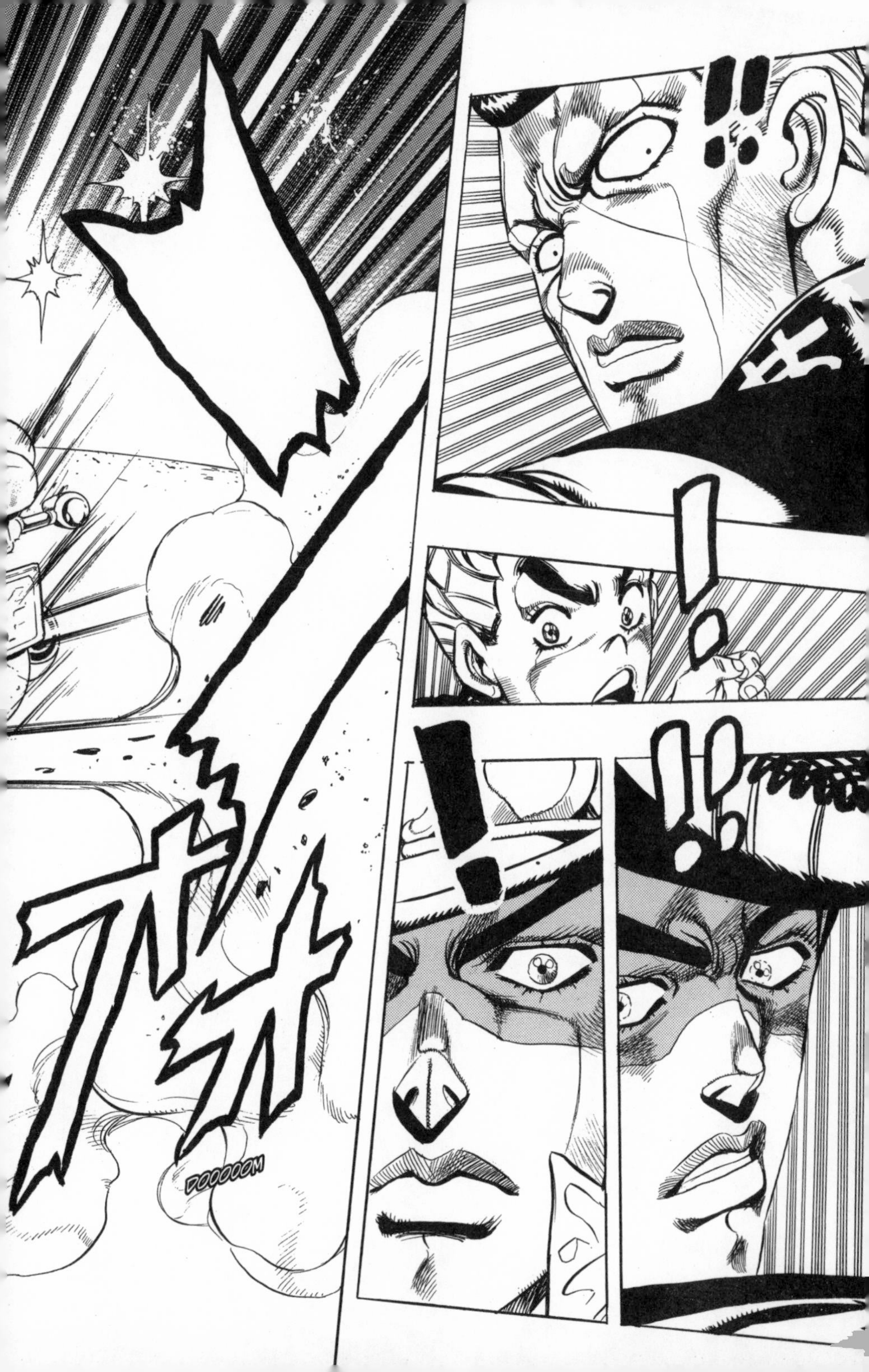
DOOOOOM

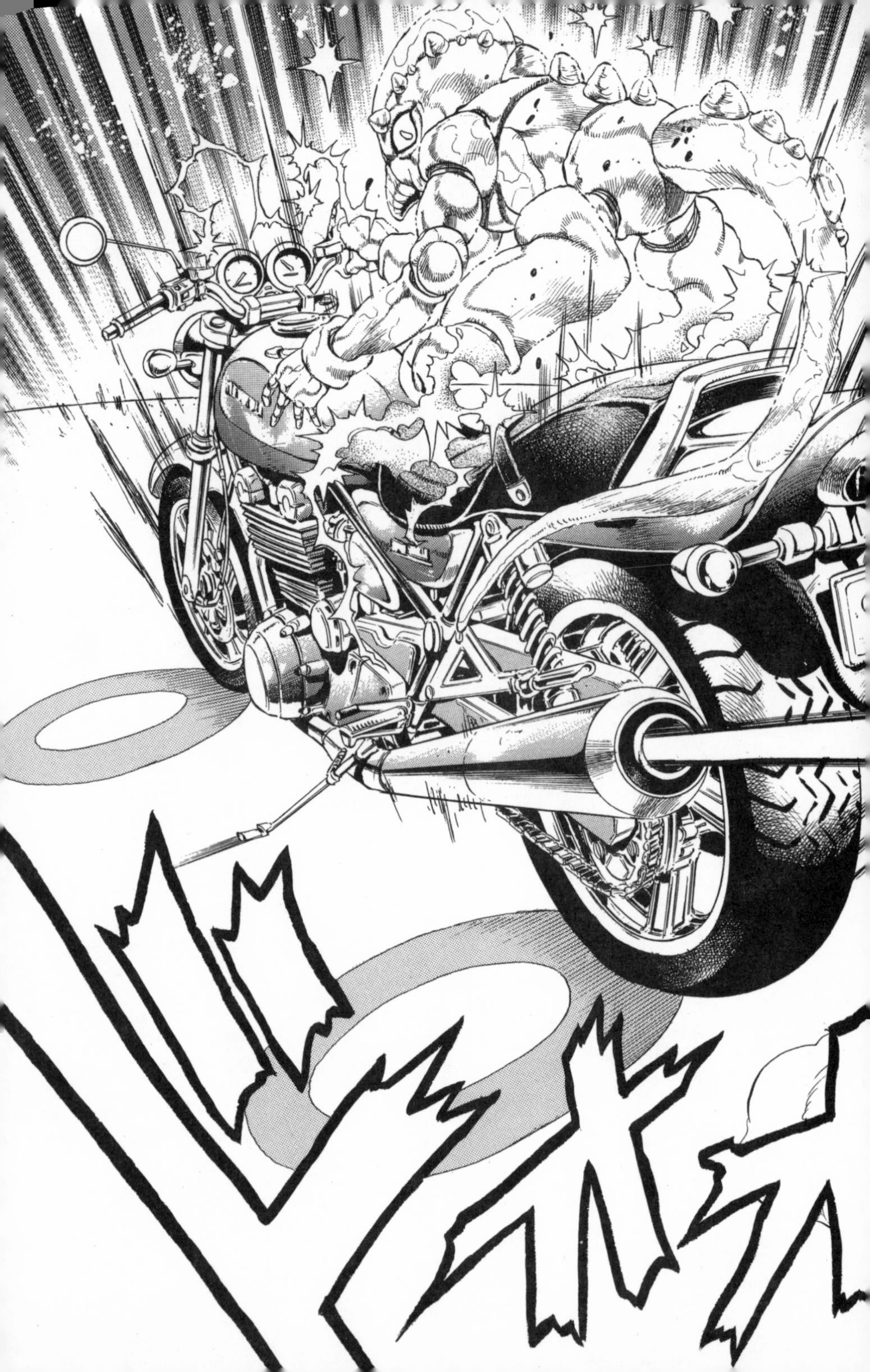

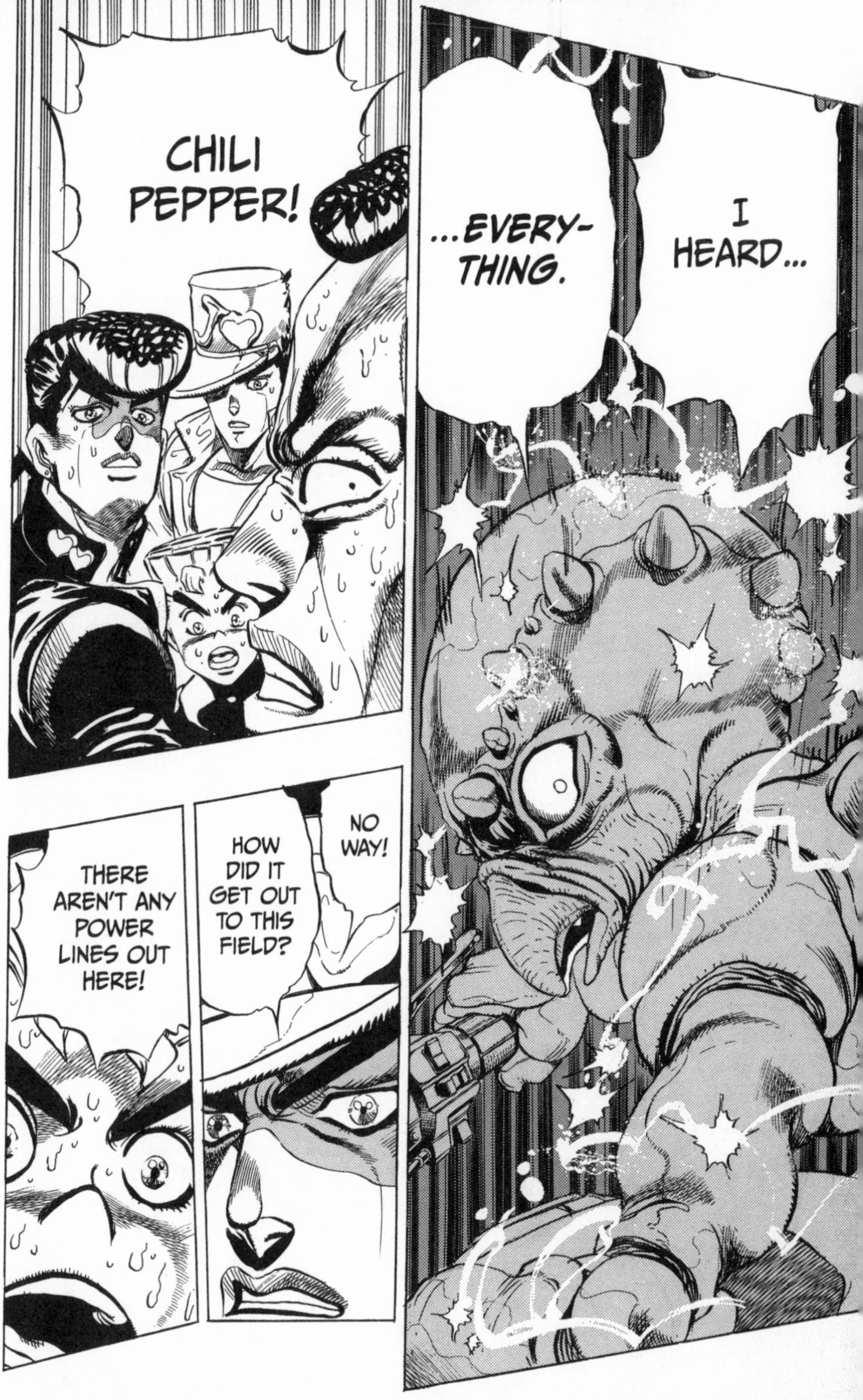
I HEARD...
...EVERY-THING.
CHILI PEPPER!
NO WAY!
HOW DID IT GET OUT TO THIS FIELD?
THERE AREN'T ANY POWER LINES OUT HERE!

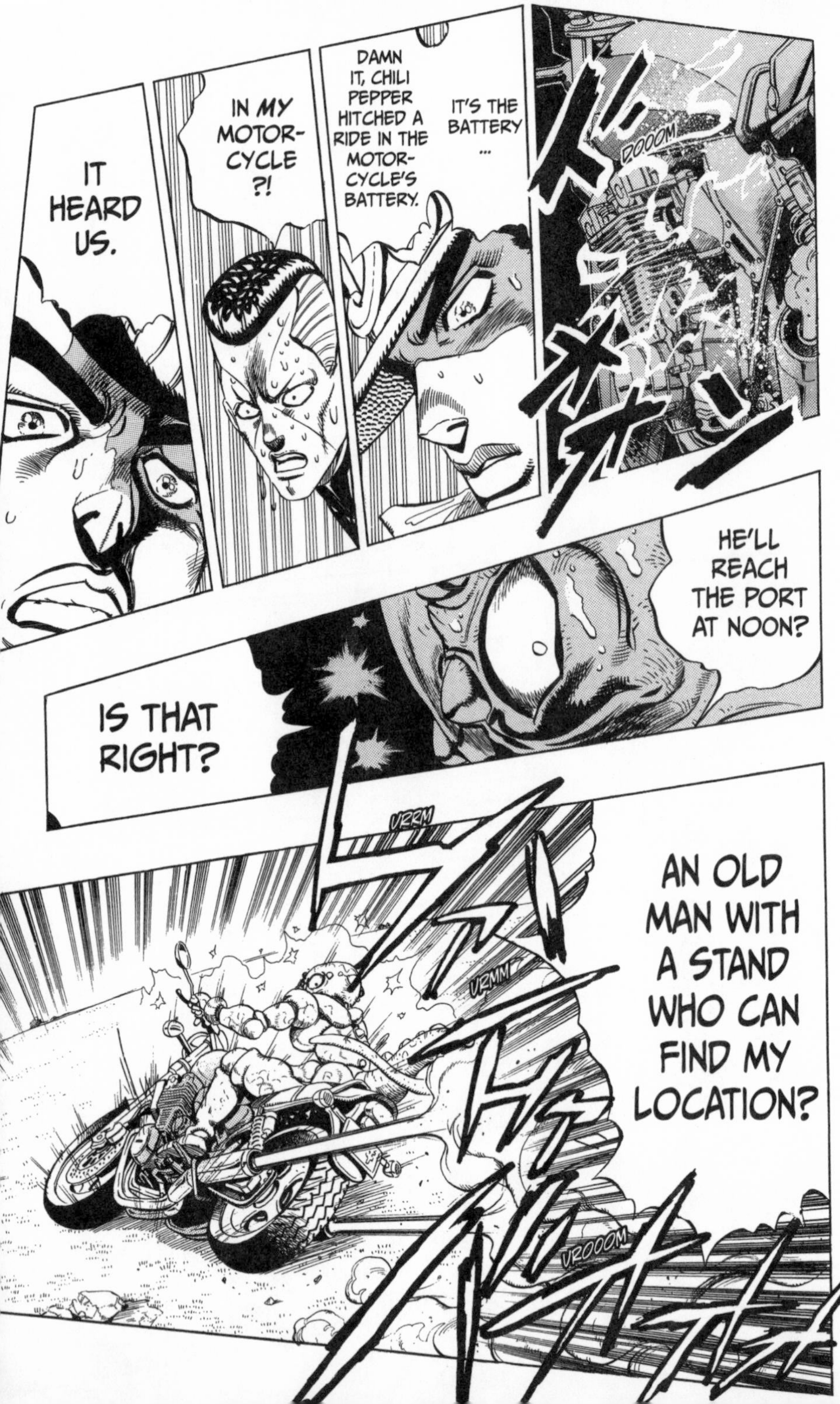
DOOOM
IT'S THE BATTERY ...
DAMN IT, CHILI PEPPER HITCHED A RIDE IN THE MOTORCYCLE'S BATTERY.
IN MY MOTORCYCLE ?!
IT HEARD US.
HE'LL REACH THE PORT AT NOON?
IS THAT RIGHT?
URRM
URMM
AN OLD MAN WITH A STAND WHO CAN FIND MY LOCATION?
VROOOM

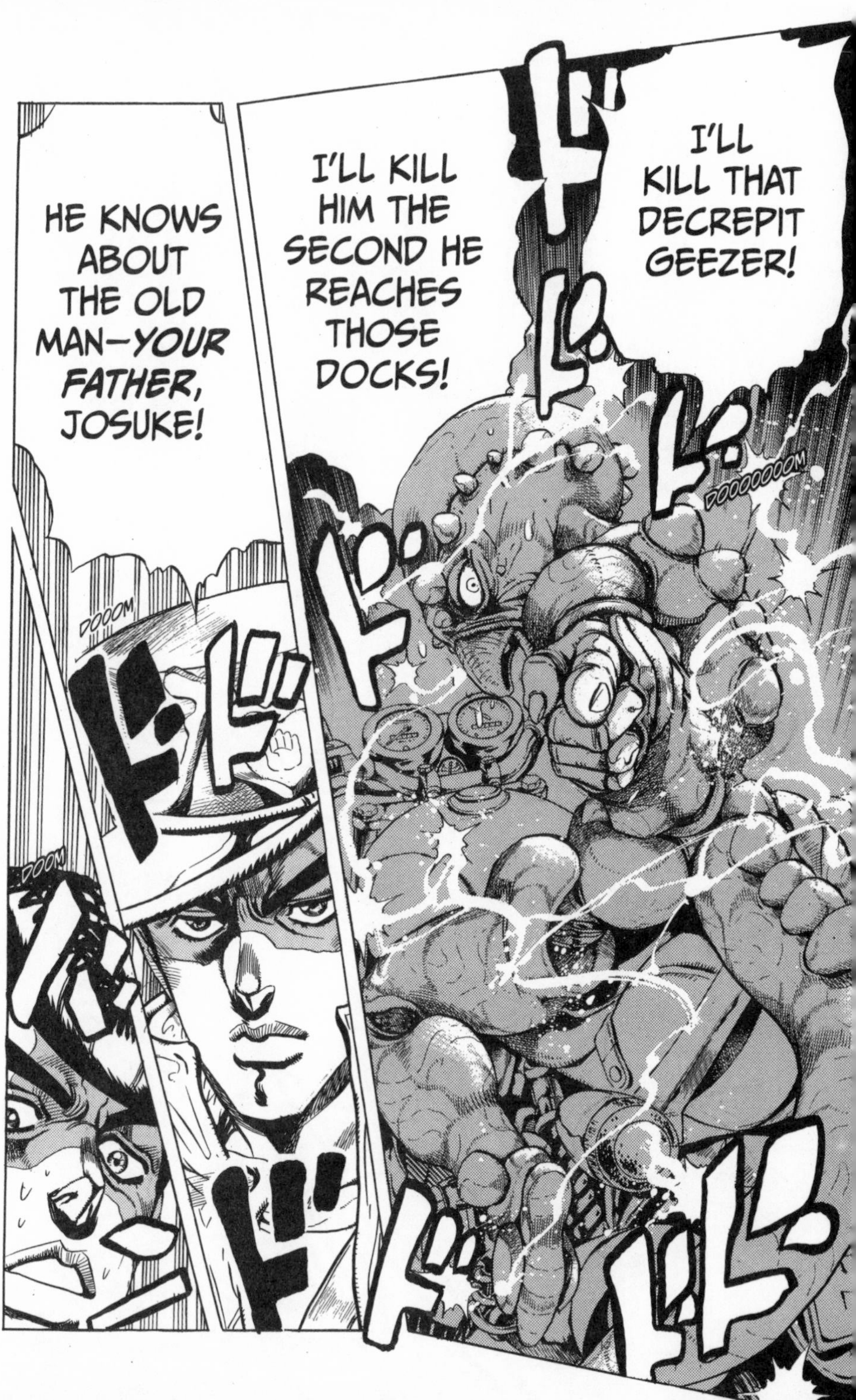
I'LL KILL THAT DECREPIT GEEZER!
I'LL KILL HIM THE SECOND HE REACHES THOSE DOCKS!
DOOOOOOOOM
HE KNOWS ABOUT THE OLD MAN—*YOUR FATHER*, JOSUKE!
DOOOM
DOOM

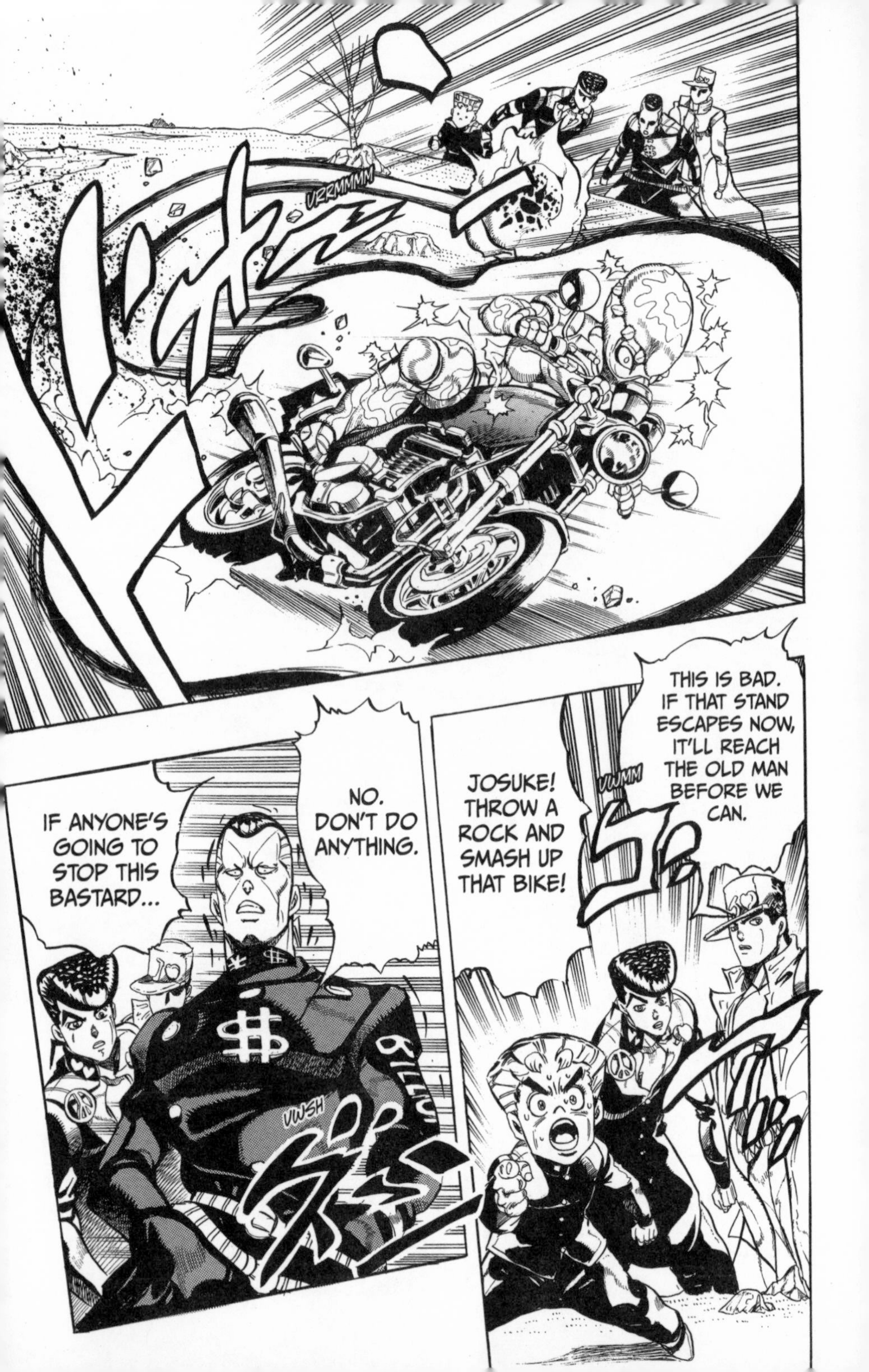
URRMMMM
THIS IS BAD. IF THAT STAND ESCAPES NOW, IT'LL REACH THE OLD MAN BEFORE WE CAN.
UWMM
JOSUKE! THROW A ROCK AND SMASH UP THAT BIKE!
NO. DON'T DO ANYTHING.
IF ANYONE'S GOING TO STOP THIS BASTARD...
VWSH

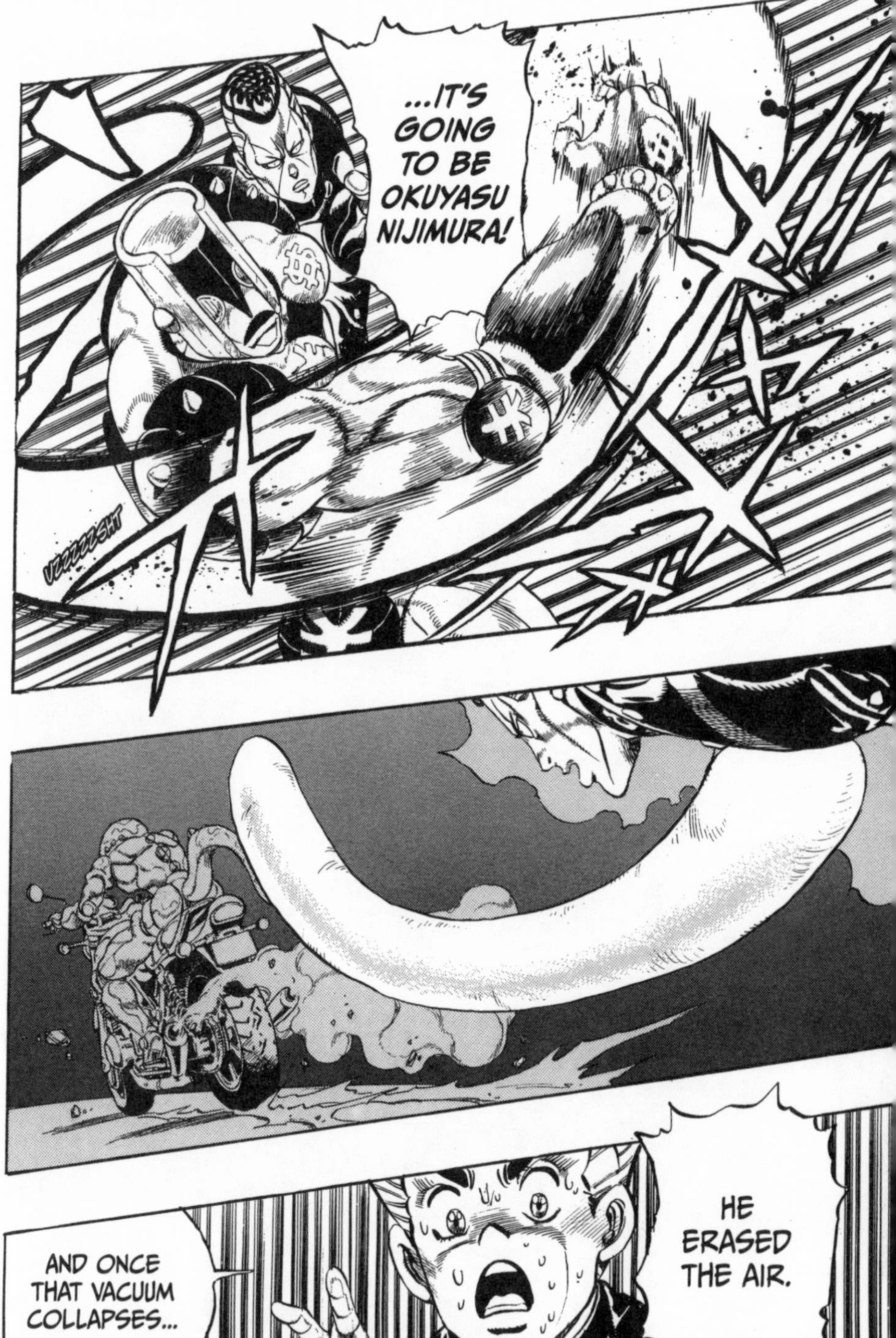
...IT'S GOING TO BE OKUYASU NIJIMURA!
VZZZZZSHT
HE ERASED THE AIR.
AND ONCE THAT VACUUM COLLAPSES...

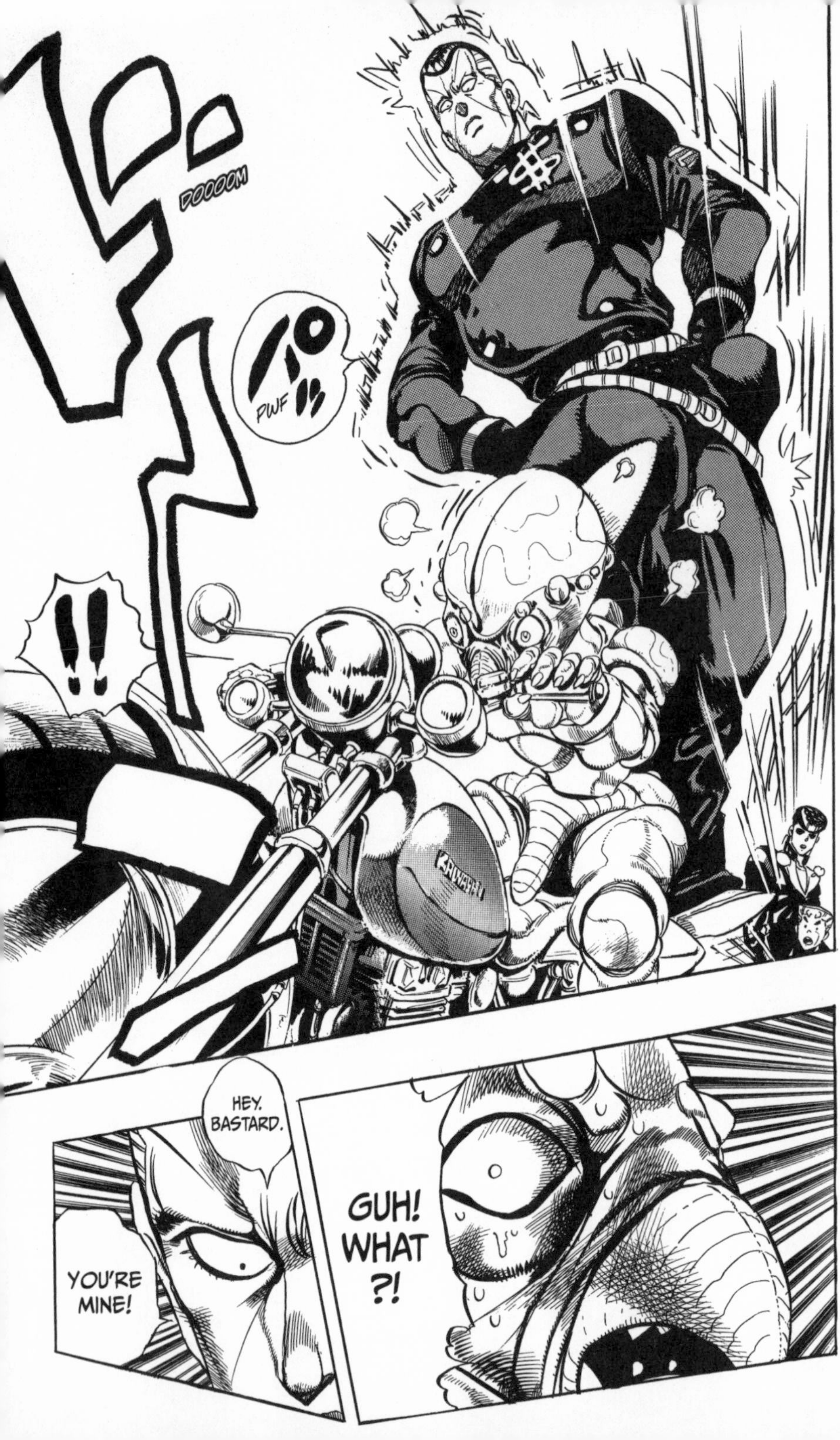
DOOOOM
PWF
!!
GUH! WHAT ?!
HEY. BASTARD.
YOU'RE MINE!

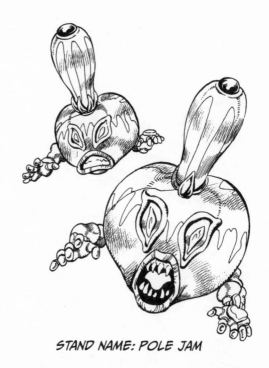

STAND NAME: POLE JAM

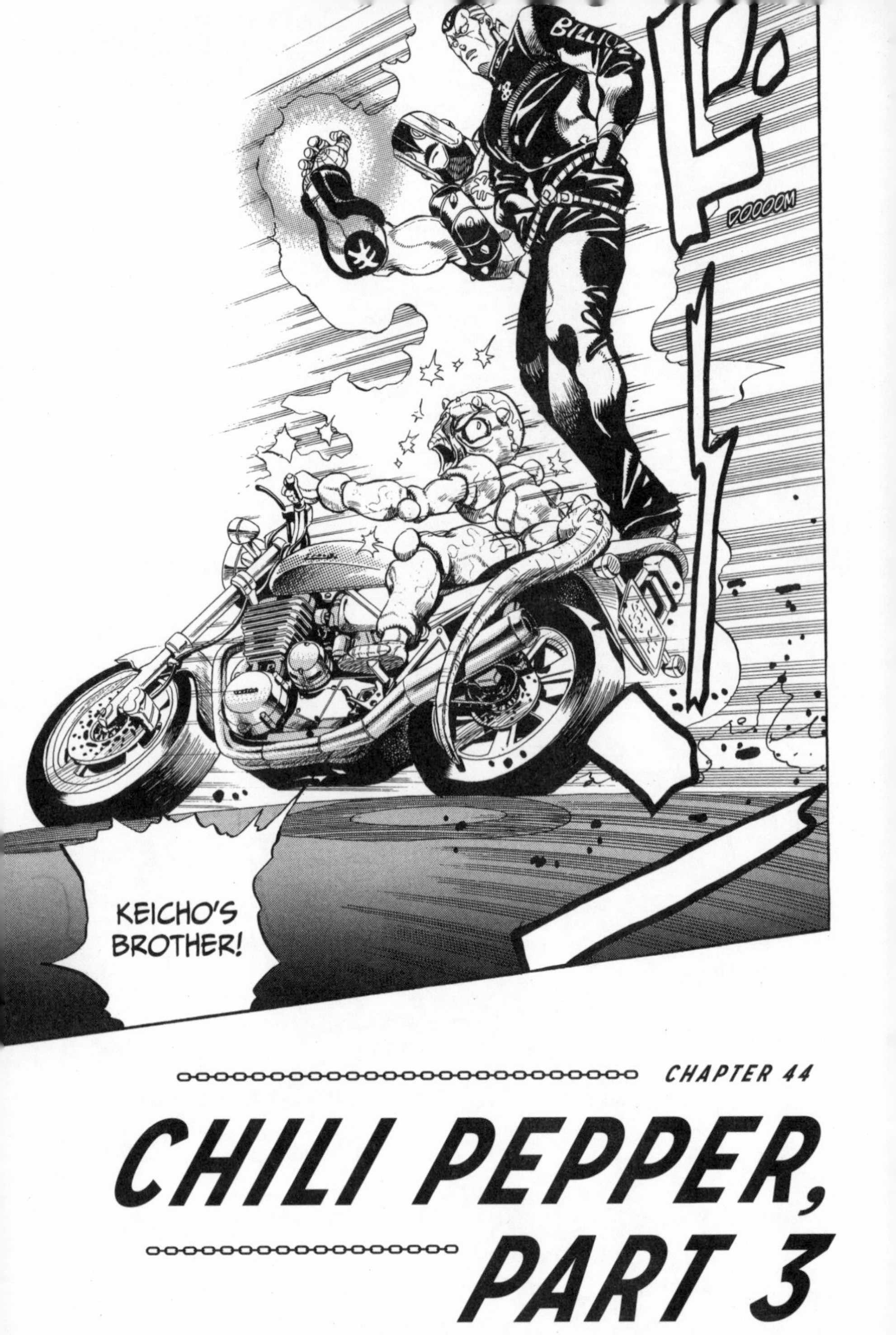
DOOOOM
KEICHO'S BROTHER!

CHAPTER 44

CHILI PEPPER, PART 3

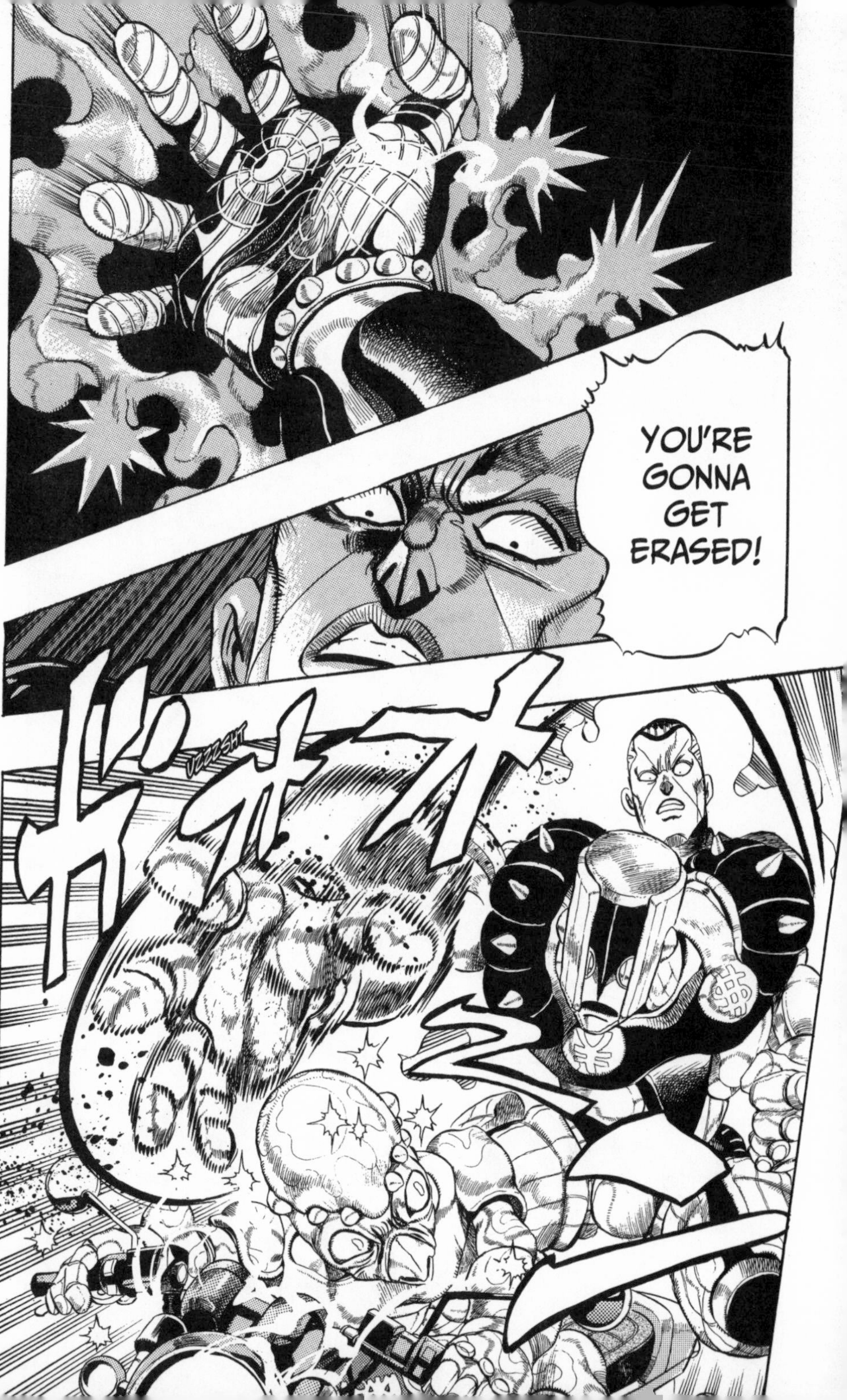
YOU'RE GONNA GET ERASED!
VZZZSHT

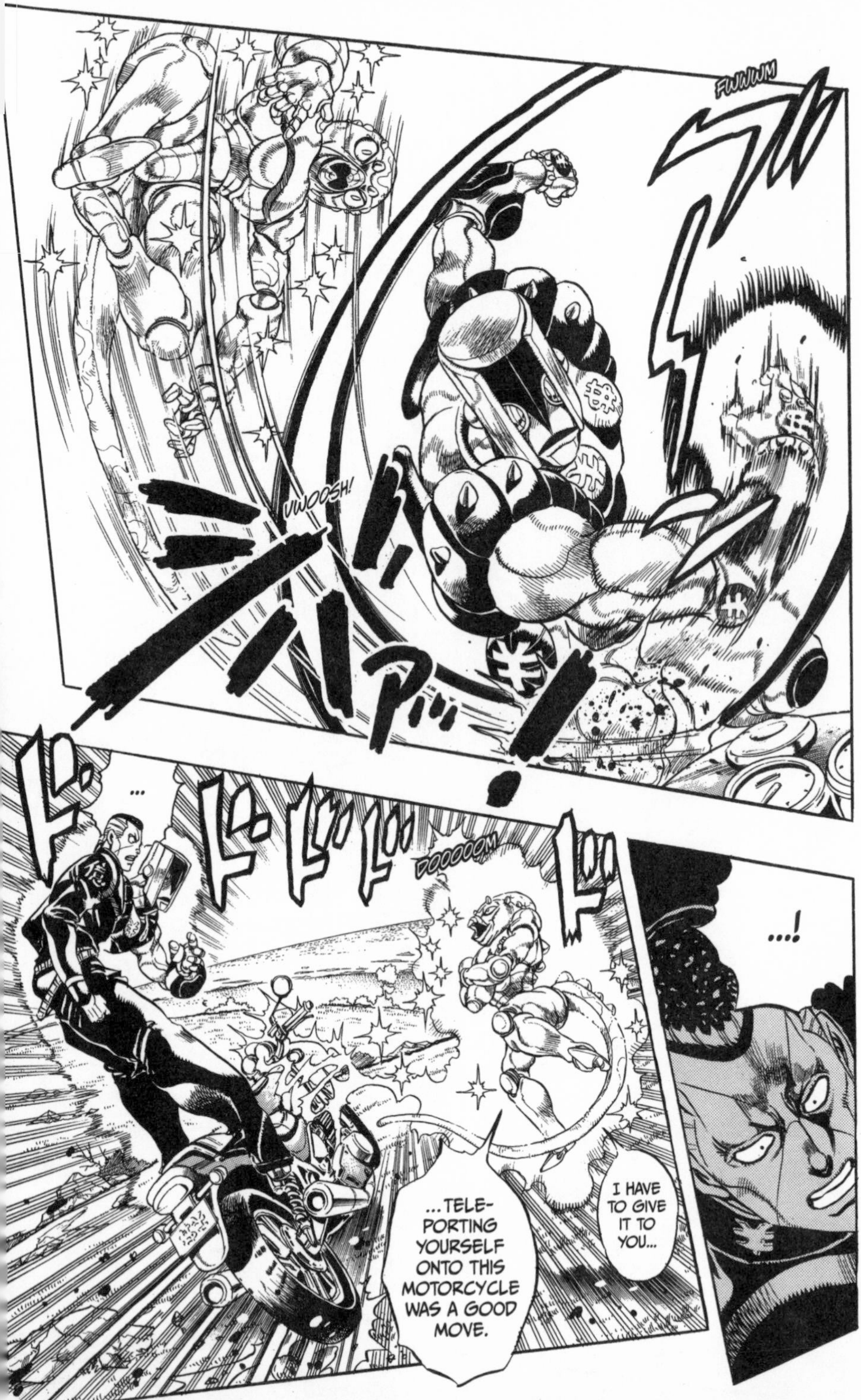
FWWWM
VWOOSH!
...!
DOOOOOM
...
I HAVE TO GIVE IT TO YOU...
...TELE-PORTING YOURSELF ONTO THIS MOTORCYCLE WAS A GOOD MOVE.

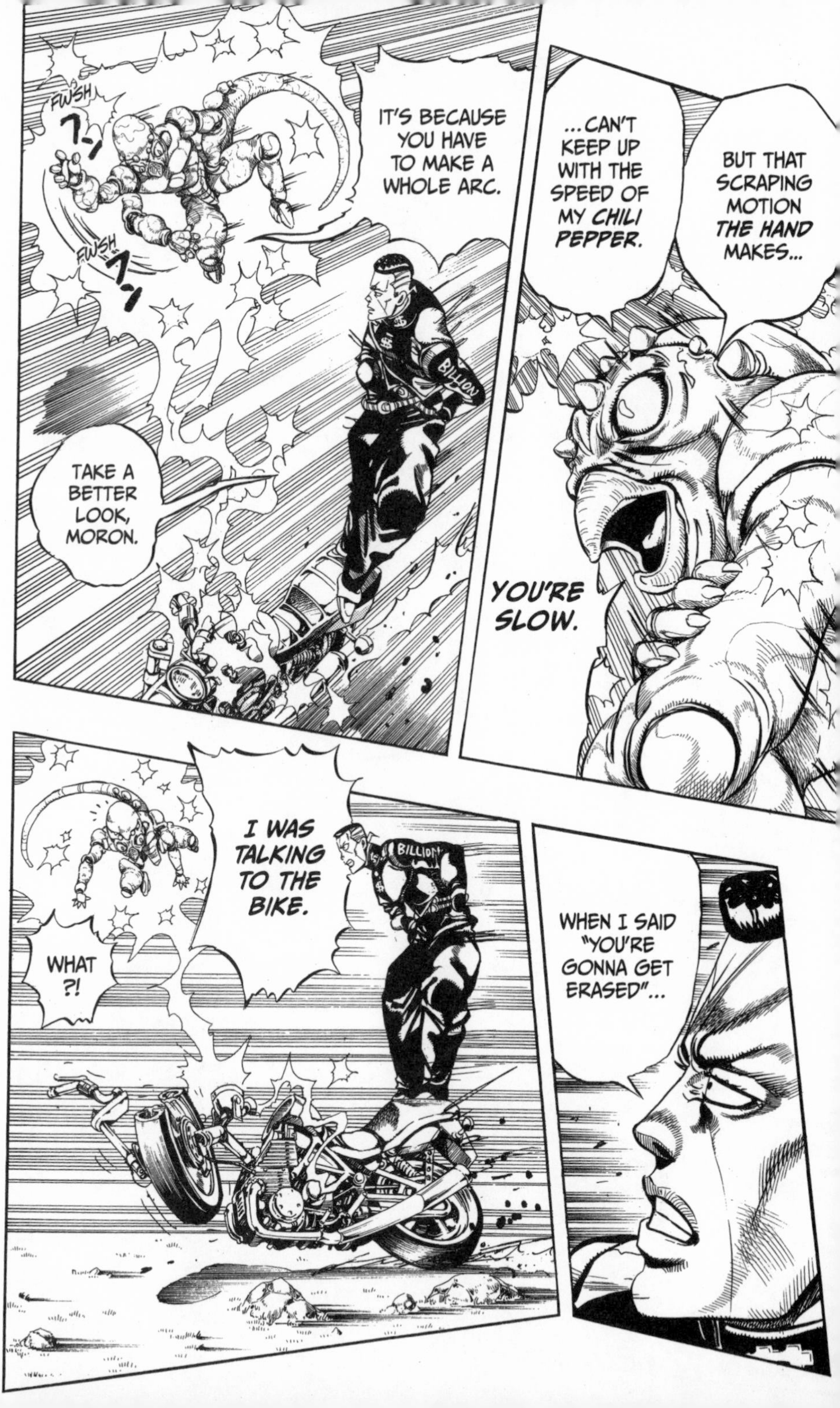
BUT THAT SCRAPING MOTION *THE HAND* MAKES...
...CAN'T KEEP UP WITH THE SPEED OF MY *CHILI PEPPER.*
YOU'RE SLOW.
IT'S BECAUSE YOU HAVE TO MAKE A WHOLE ARC.
FWSH
FWSH
TAKE A BETTER LOOK, MORON.
WHEN I SAID "YOU'RE GONNA GET ERASED"...
I WAS TALKING TO THE BIKE.
WHAT?!
BILLION

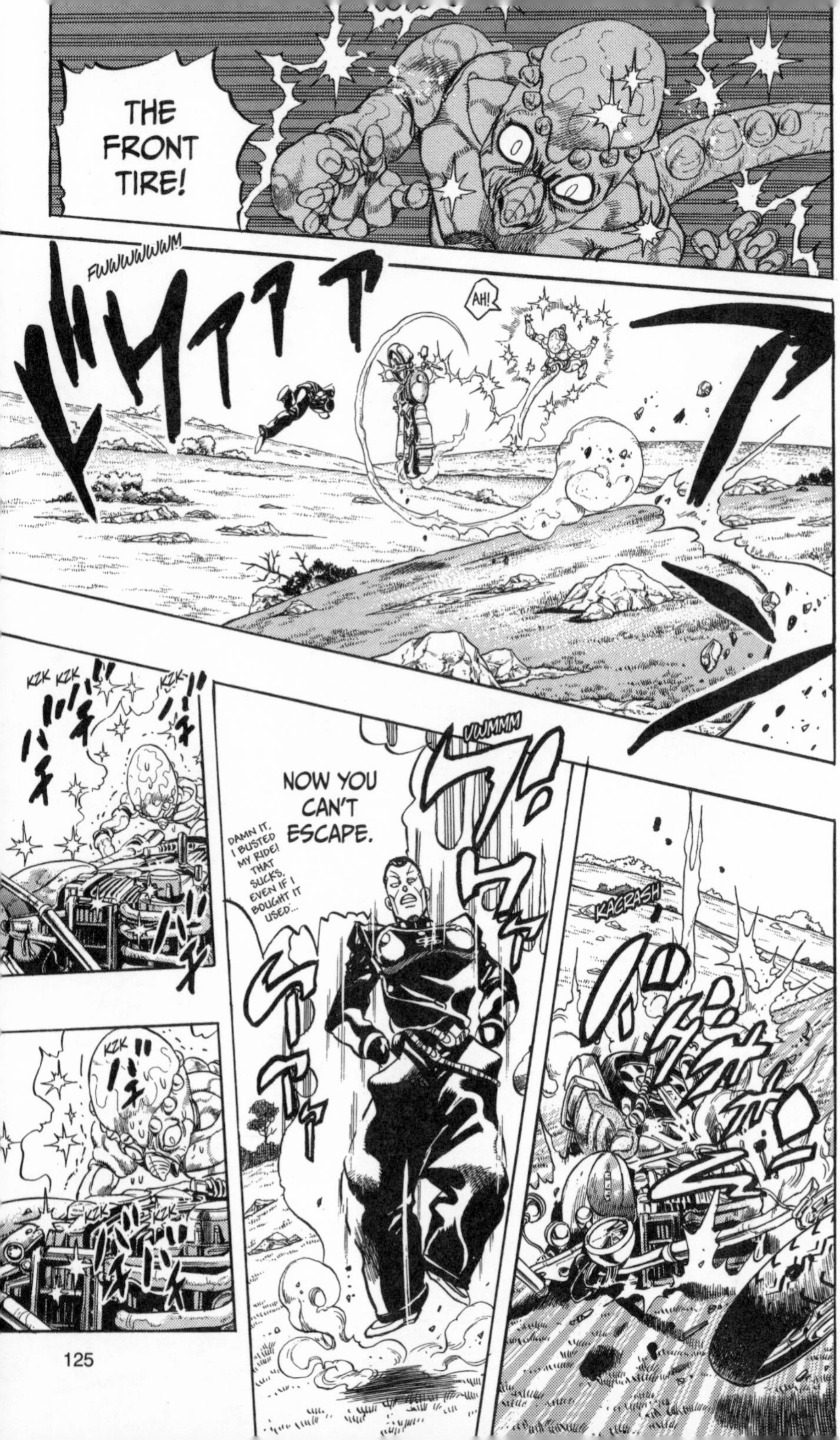
THE FRONT TIRE!
FWWWWWWM
AH!
KACRASH
VWMMM
NOW YOU CAN'T ESCAPE.
DAMN IT, I BUSTED MY RIDE! THAT SUCKS, EVEN IF I BOUGHT IT USED...
KZK KZK
KZK
KZK
KZK KZK

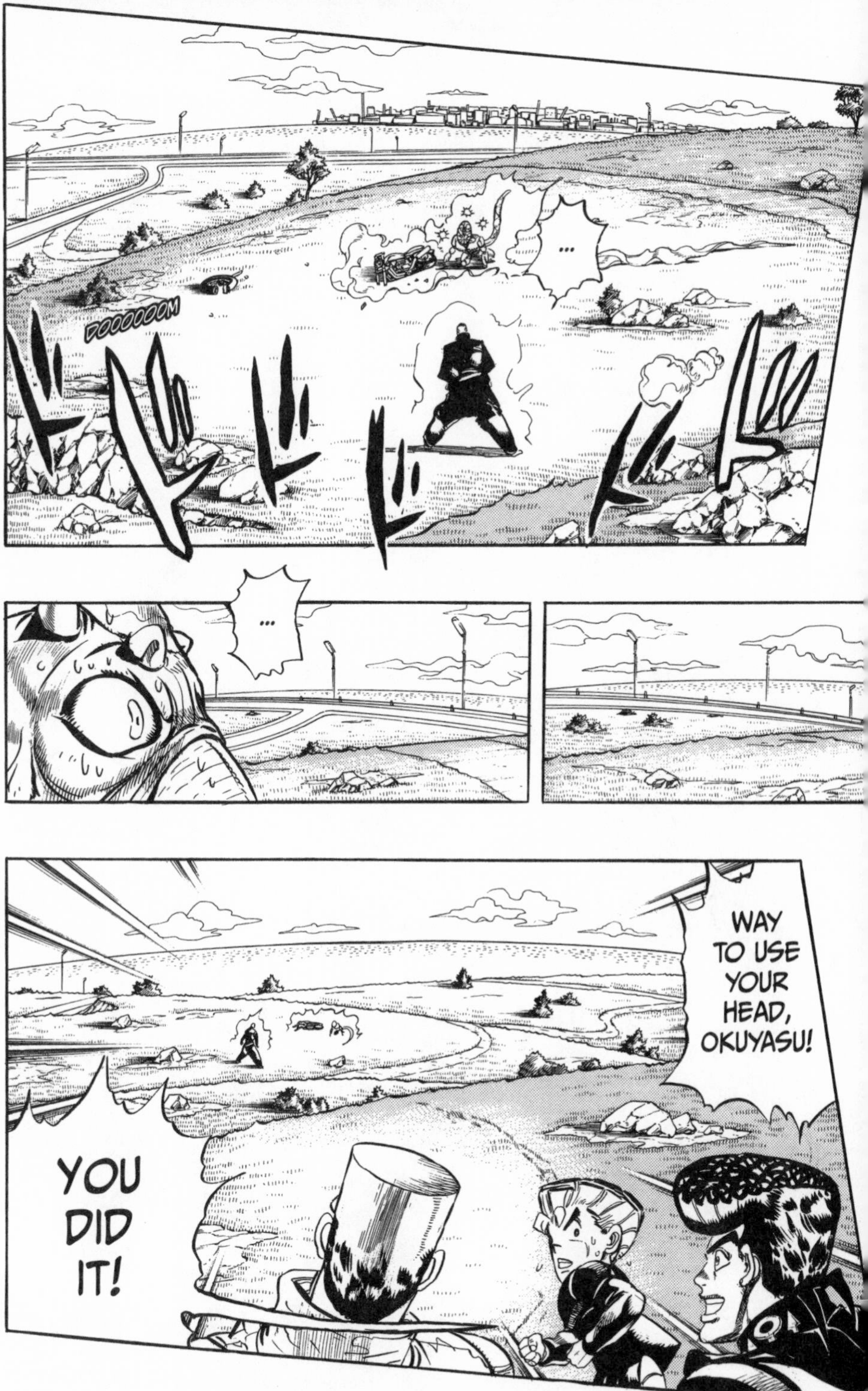
...
DOOOOOOOM
...
WAY TO USE YOUR HEAD, OKUYASU!
YOU DID IT!

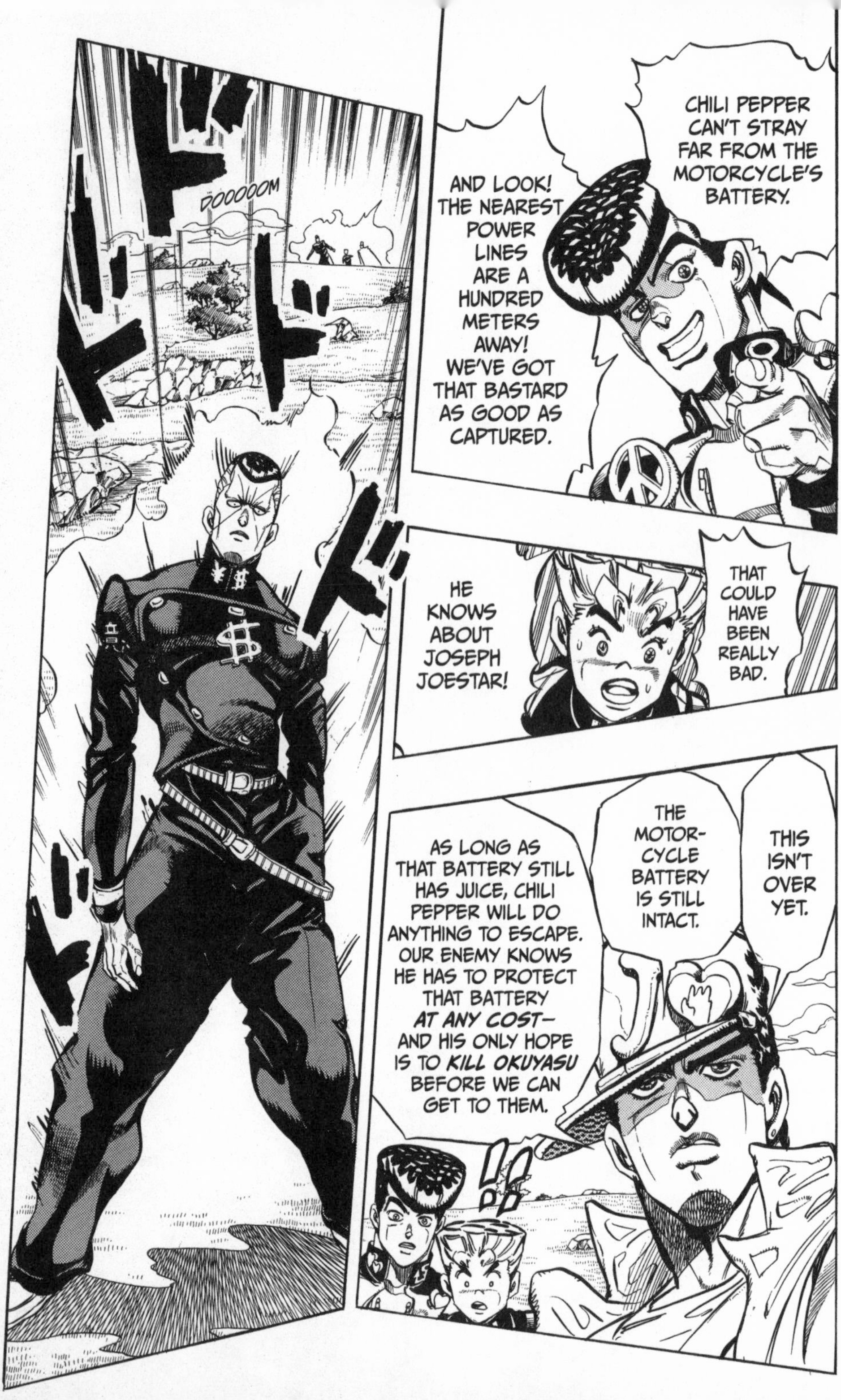
CHILI PEPPER CAN'T STRAY FAR FROM THE MOTORCYCLE'S BATTERY.
AND LOOK! THE NEAREST POWER LINES ARE A HUNDRED METERS AWAY! WE'VE GOT THAT BASTARD AS GOOD AS CAPTURED.
THAT COULD HAVE BEEN REALLY BAD.
HE KNOWS ABOUT JOSEPH JOESTAR!
THIS ISN'T OVER YET.
THE MOTOR-CYCLE BATTERY IS STILL INTACT.
AS LONG AS THAT BATTERY STILL HAS JUICE, CHILI PEPPER WILL DO ANYTHING TO ESCAPE. OUR ENEMY KNOWS HE HAS TO PROTECT THAT BATTERY *AT ANY COST*— AND HIS ONLY HOPE IS TO *KILL OKUYASU* BEFORE WE CAN GET TO THEM.
DOOOOOM

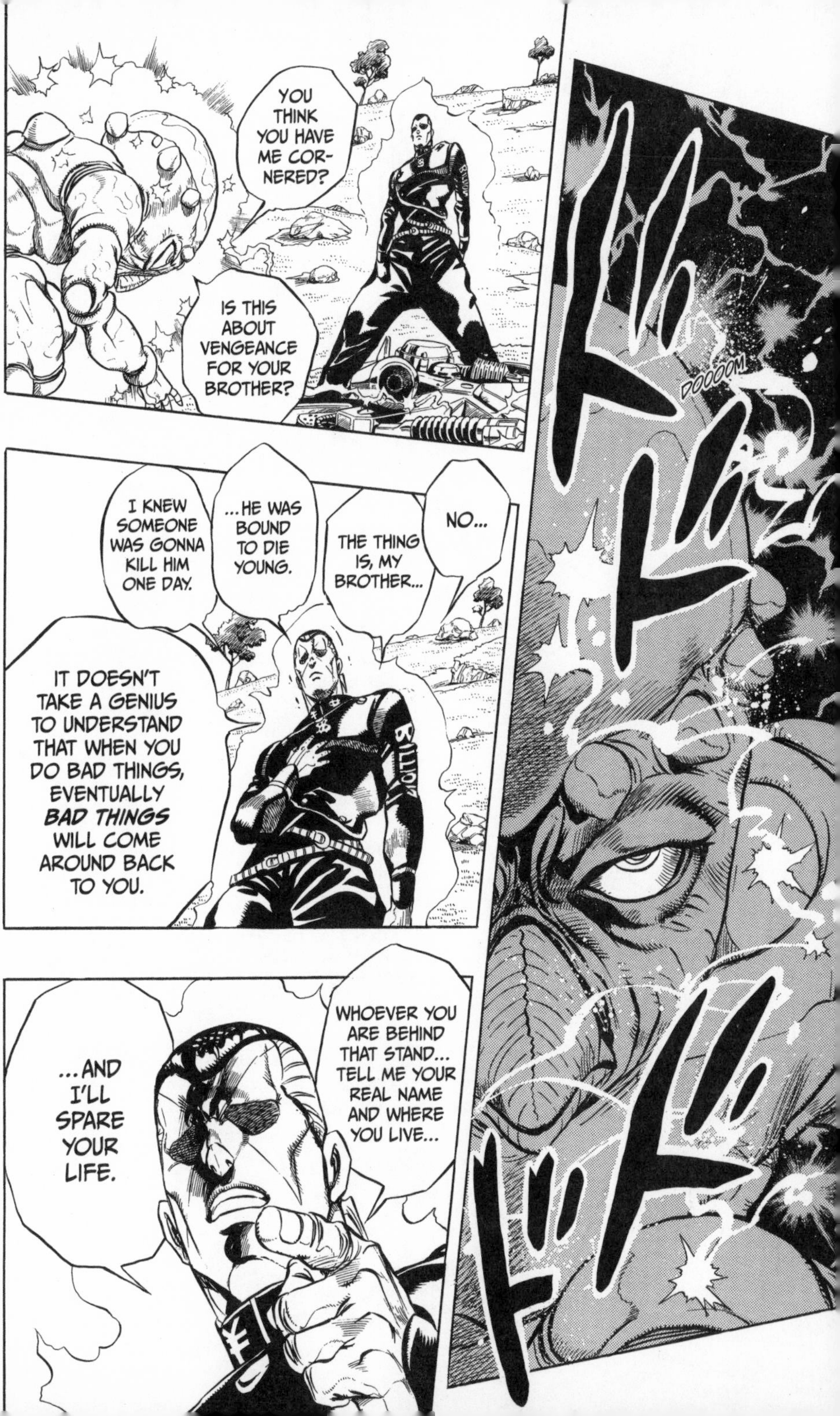
DOOOOM
YOU THINK YOU HAVE ME CORNERED?
IS THIS ABOUT VENGEANCE FOR YOUR BROTHER?
NO...
THE THING IS, MY BROTHER...
...HE WAS BOUND TO DIE YOUNG.
I KNEW SOMEONE WAS GONNA KILL HIM ONE DAY.
IT DOESN'T TAKE A GENIUS TO UNDERSTAND THAT WHEN YOU DO BAD THINGS, EVENTUALLY *BAD THINGS* WILL COME AROUND BACK TO YOU.
WHOEVER YOU ARE BEHIND THAT STAND... TELL ME YOUR REAL NAME AND WHERE YOU LIVE...
...AND I'LL SPARE YOUR LIFE.

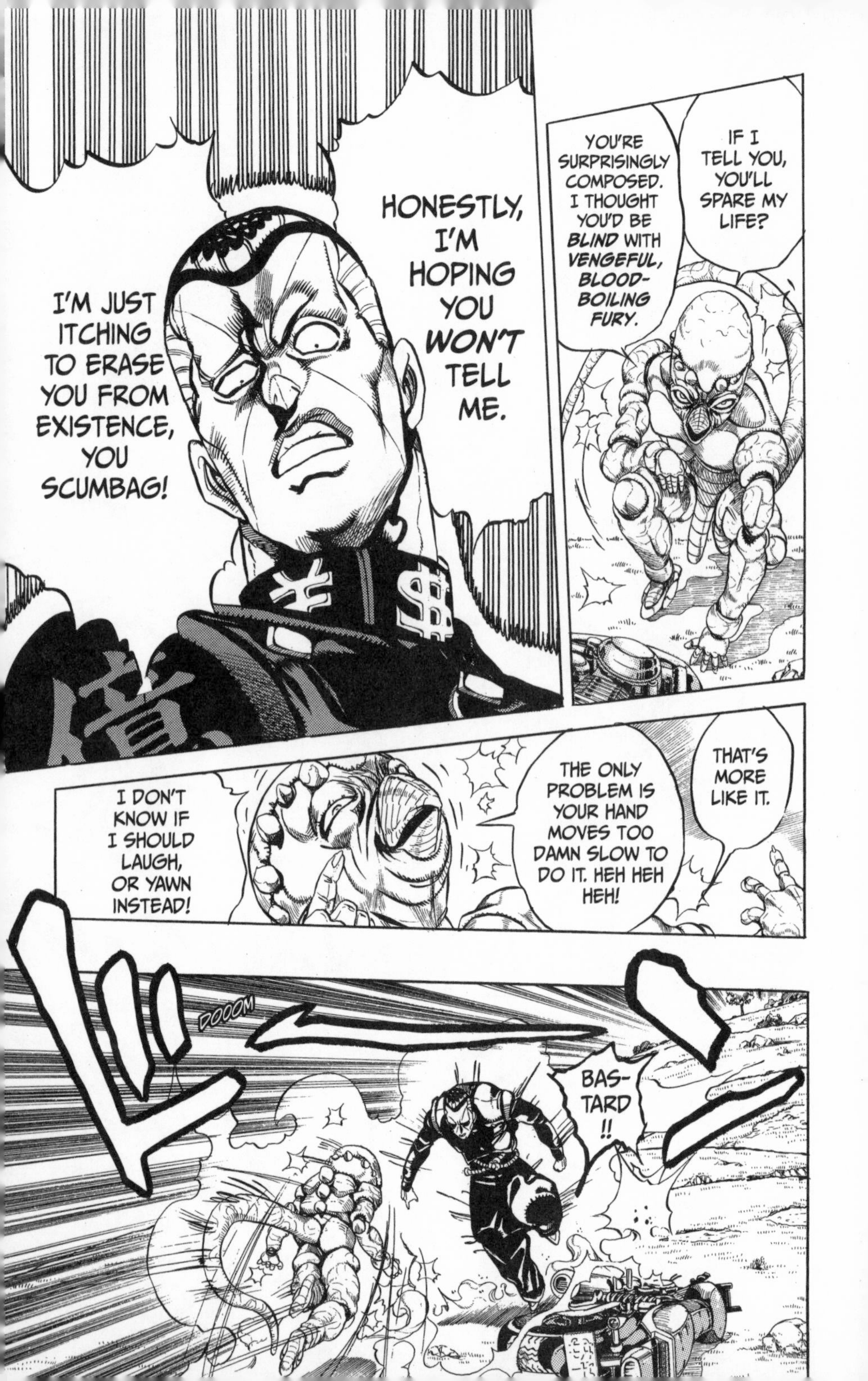
IF I TELL YOU, YOU'LL SPARE MY LIFE?
YOU'RE SURPRISINGLY COMPOSED. I THOUGHT YOU'D BE *BLIND* WITH *VENGEFUL, BLOOD-BOILING FURY.*
HONESTLY, I'M HOPING YOU *WON'T* TELL ME.
I'M JUST ITCHING TO ERASE YOU FROM EXISTENCE, YOU SCUMBAG!
THAT'S MORE LIKE IT.
THE ONLY PROBLEM IS YOUR HAND MOVES TOO DAMN SLOW TO DO IT. HEH HEH HEH!
I DON'T KNOW IF I SHOULD LAUGH, OR YAWN INSTEAD!
BAS-TARD!!
DOOOM

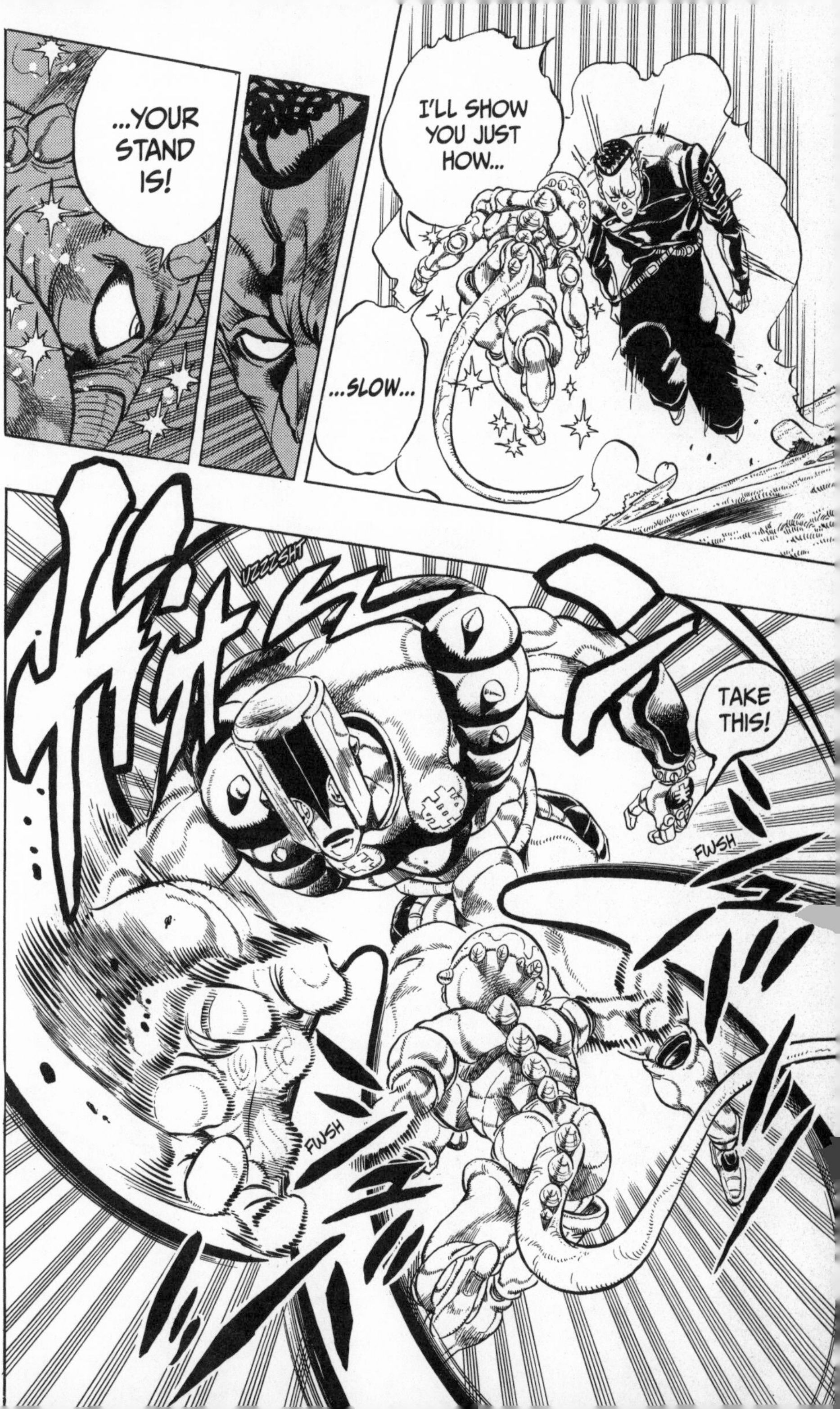
I'LL SHOW YOU JUST HOW...
...SLOW...
...YOUR STAND IS!
TAKE THIS!
UZZZSHT
FWSH
FWSH

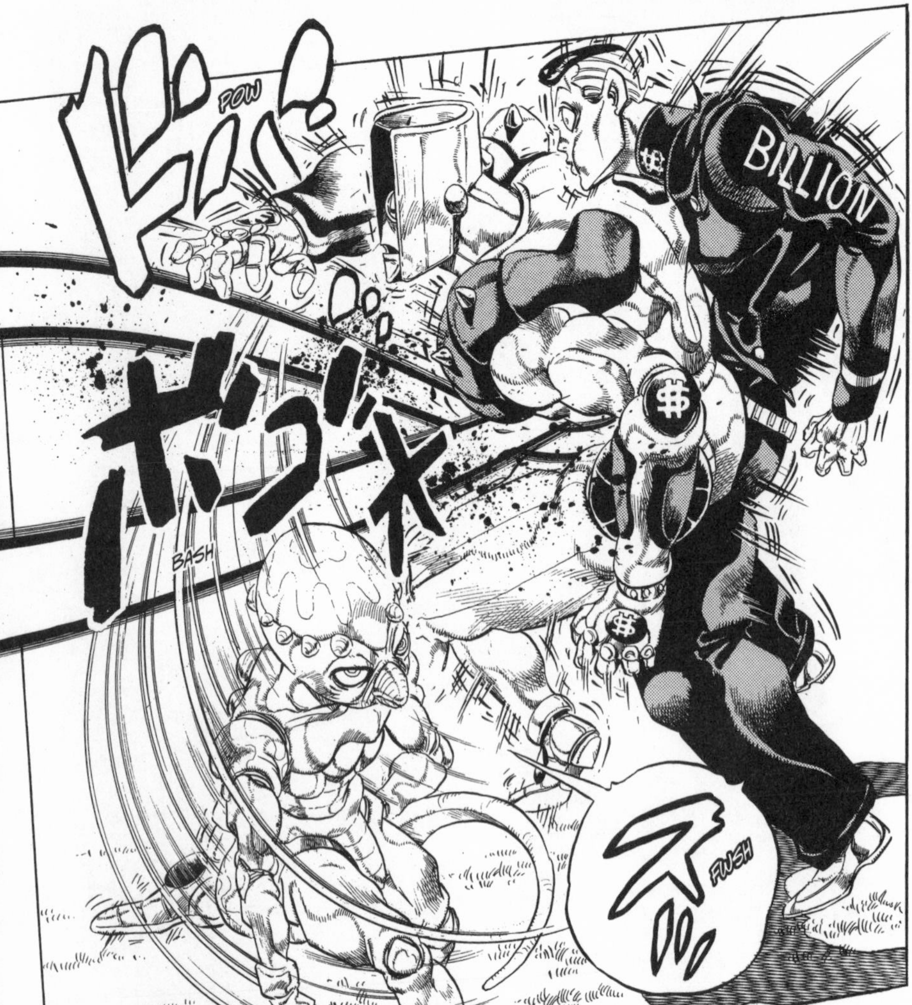
POW
BILLION
BASH
FWSH
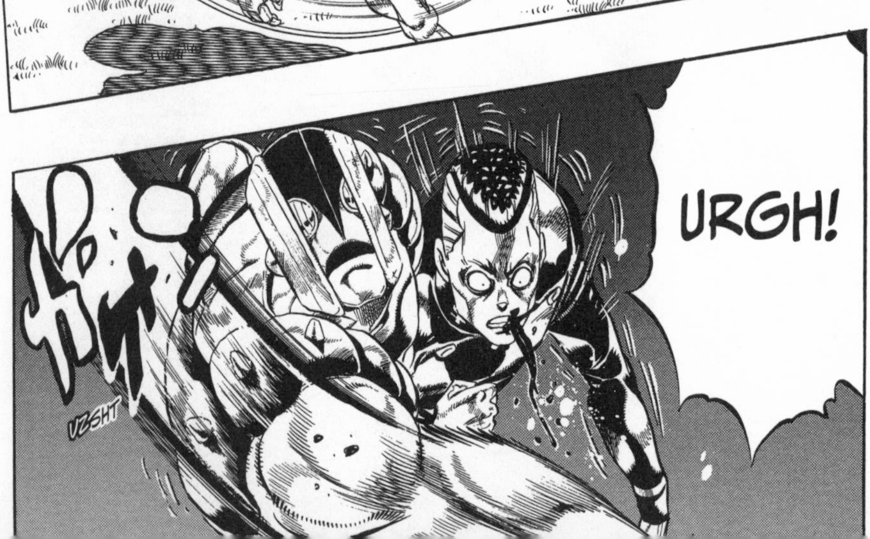
URGH!
VZSHT

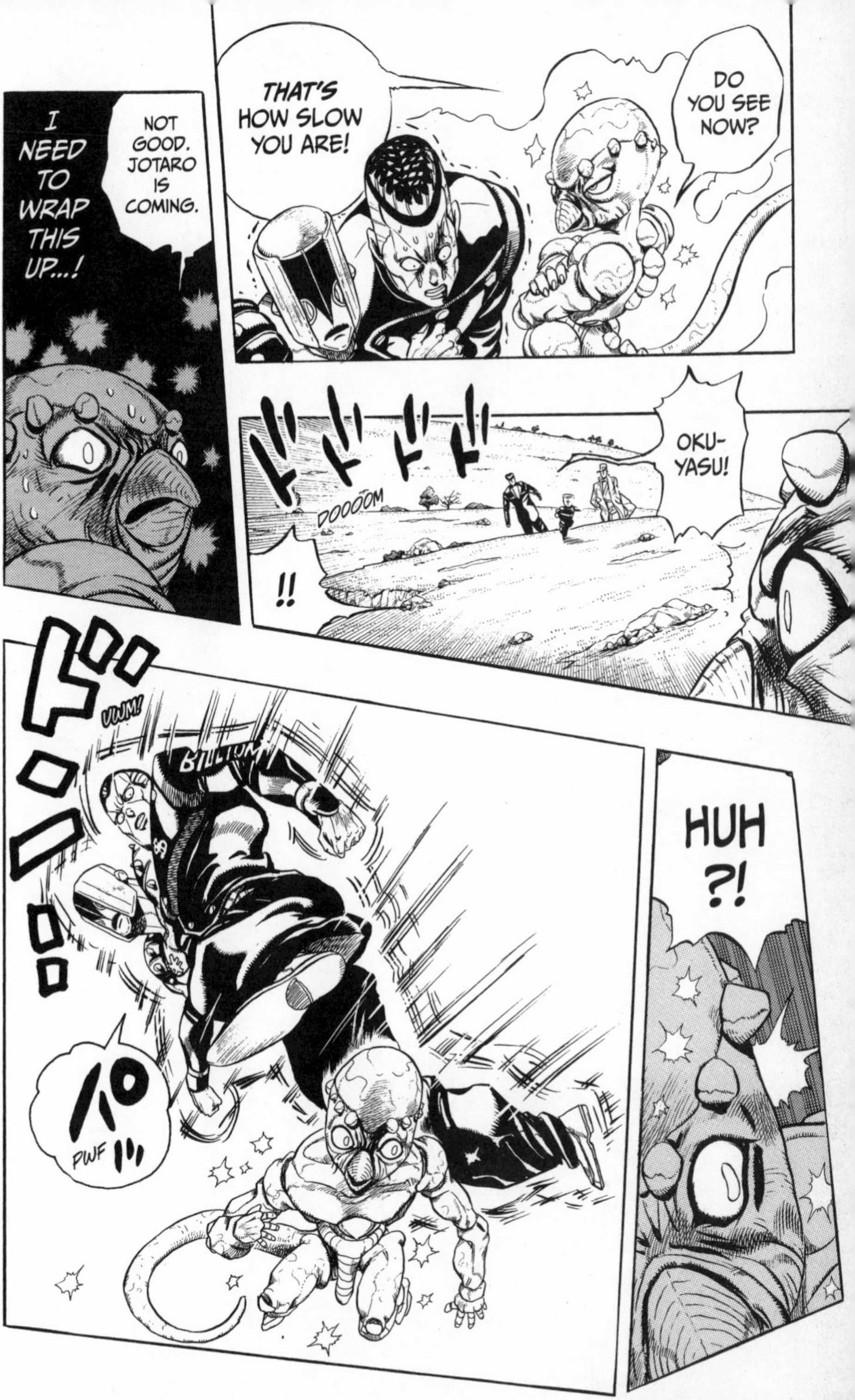
DO YOU SEE NOW?
THAT'S HOW SLOW YOU ARE!
OKU-YASU!
DOOOOM
!!
NOT GOOD. JOTARO IS COMING.
I NEED TO WRAP THIS UP...!
HUH ?!
UWM!
PWF

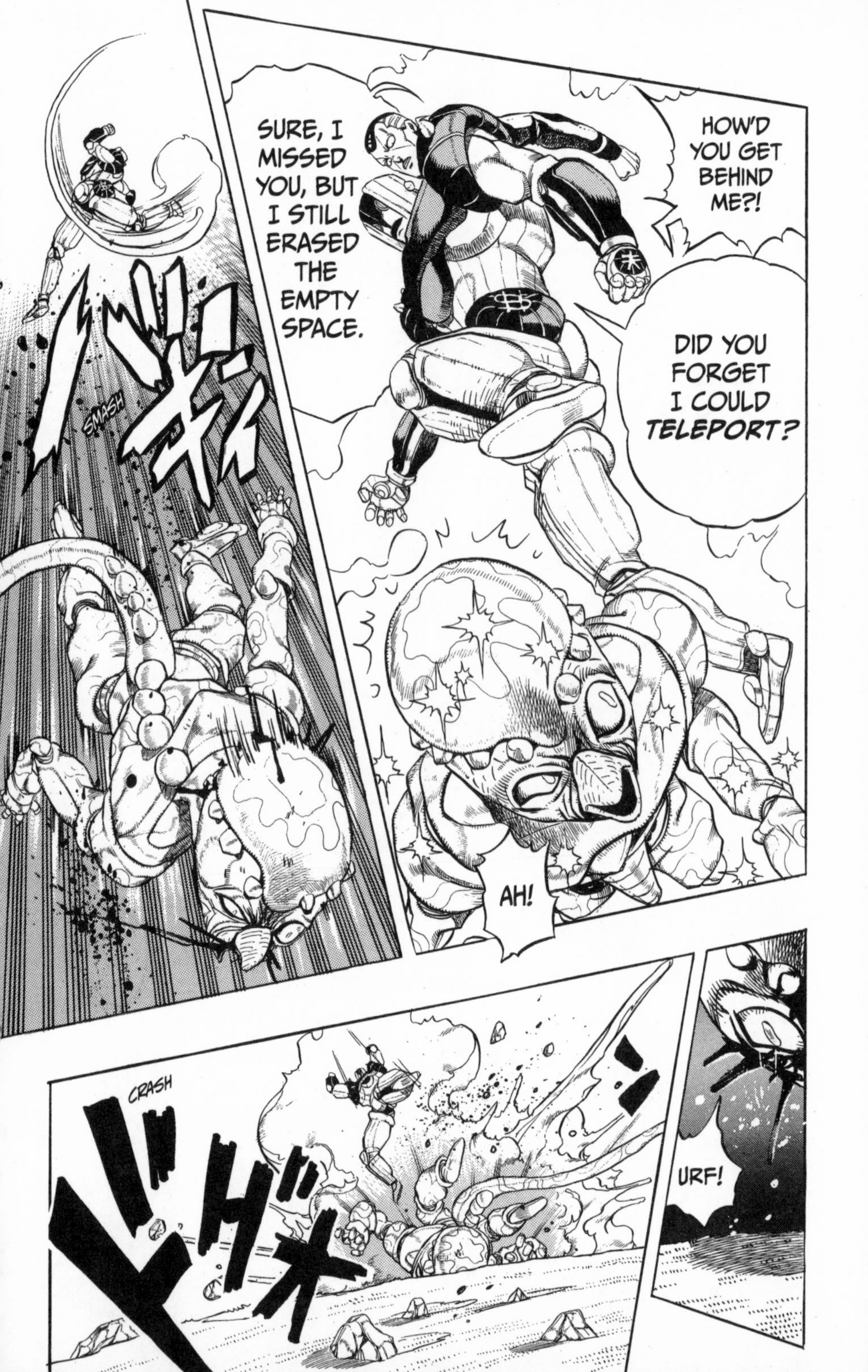
HOW'D YOU GET BEHIND ME?!
SURE, I MISSED YOU, BUT I STILL ERASED THE EMPTY SPACE.
DID YOU FORGET I COULD *TELEPORT*?
AH!
SMASH
URF!
CRASH

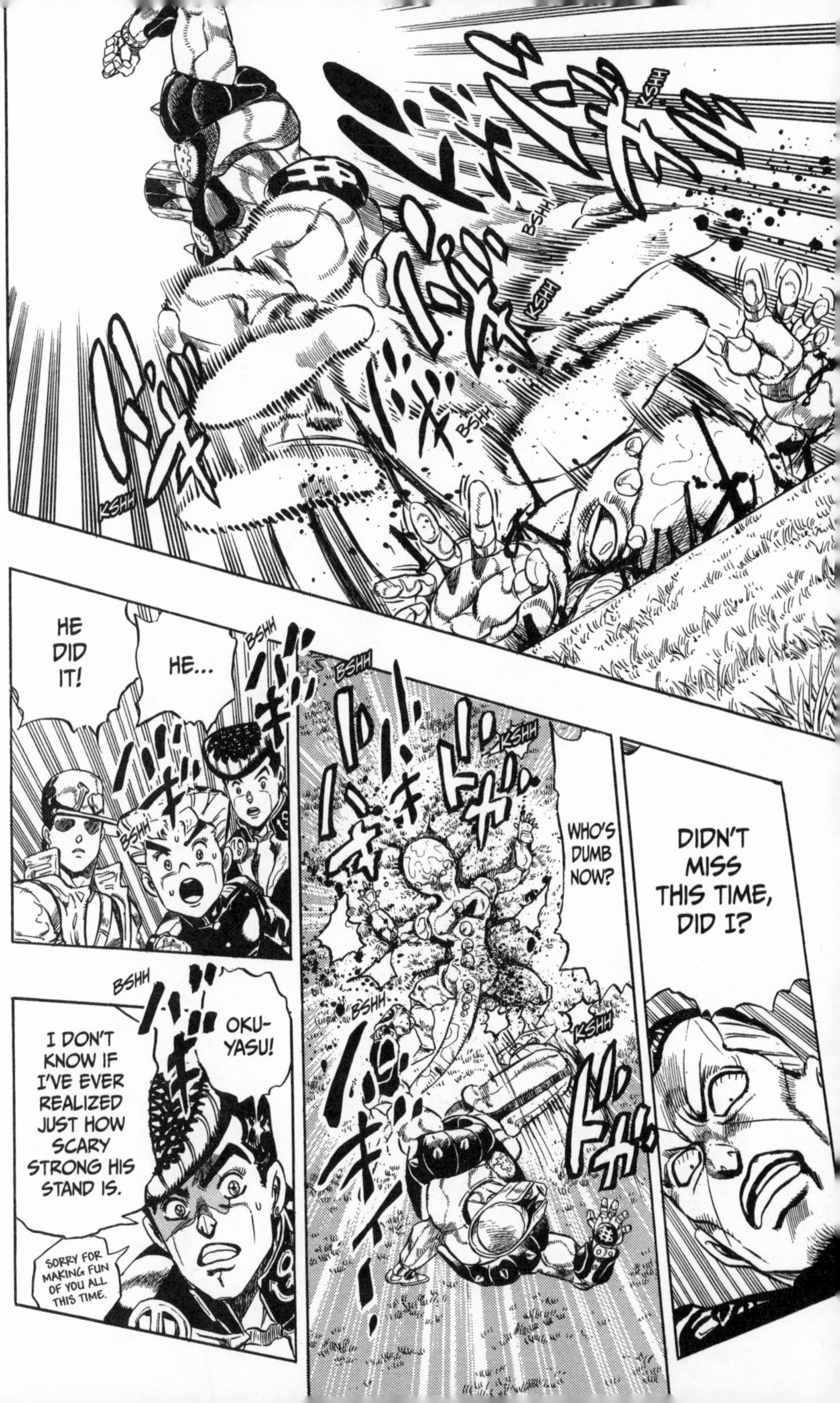
KSHH
BSHH
KSHH
BSHH
KSHH
DIDN'T MISS THIS TIME, DID I?
BSHH
KSHH
WHO'S DUMB NOW?
BSHH
KSHH
BSHH
HE...
HE DID IT!
BSHH
OKU-YASU!
BSHH
I DON'T KNOW IF I'VE EVER REALIZED JUST HOW SCARY STRONG HIS STAND IS.
SORRY FOR MAKING FUN OF YOU ALL THIS TIME.

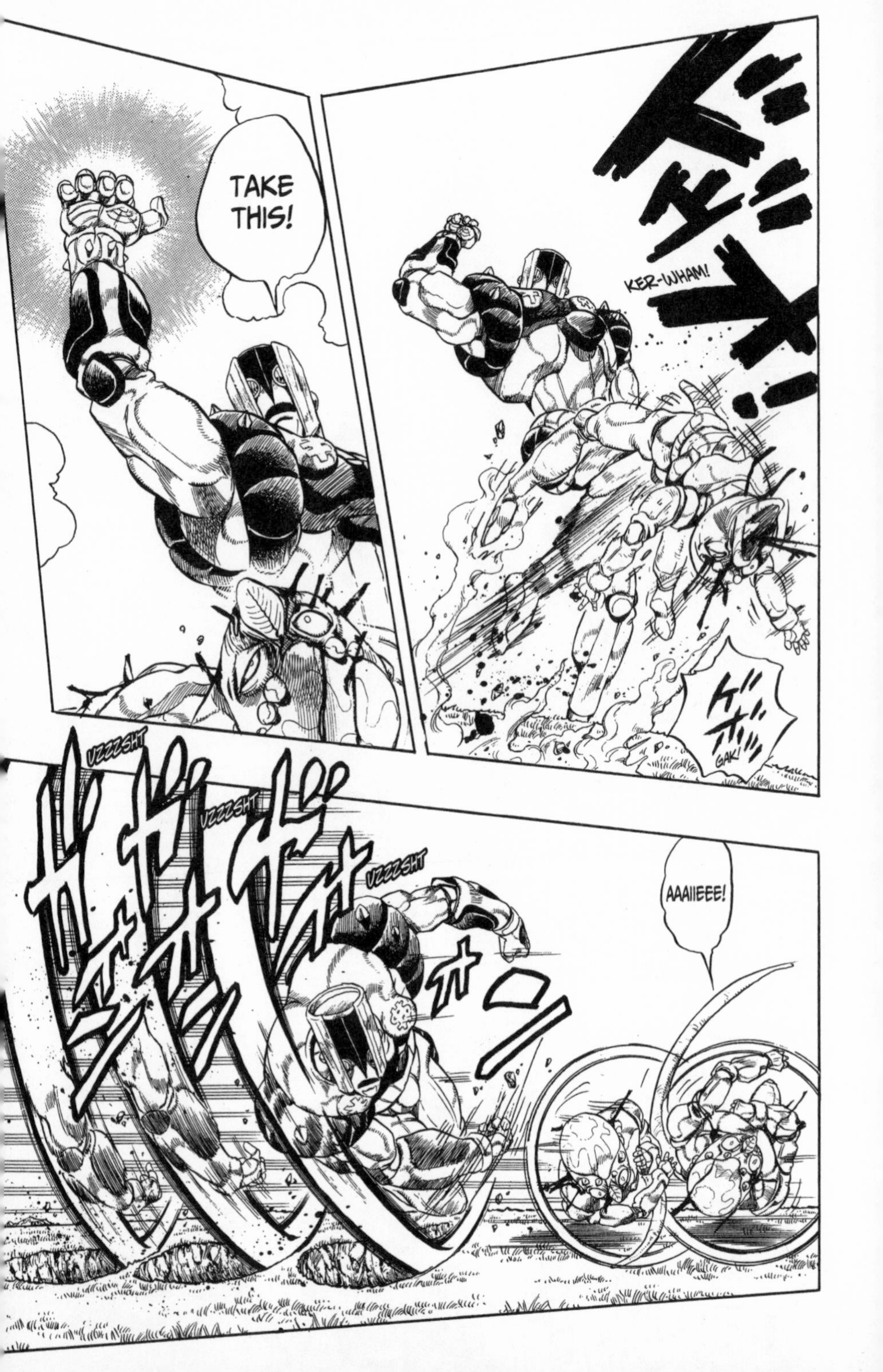
KER-WHAM!
GAK!
TAKE THIS!
AAAIIEEE!
UZZZSHT
UZZZSHT
UZZZSHT

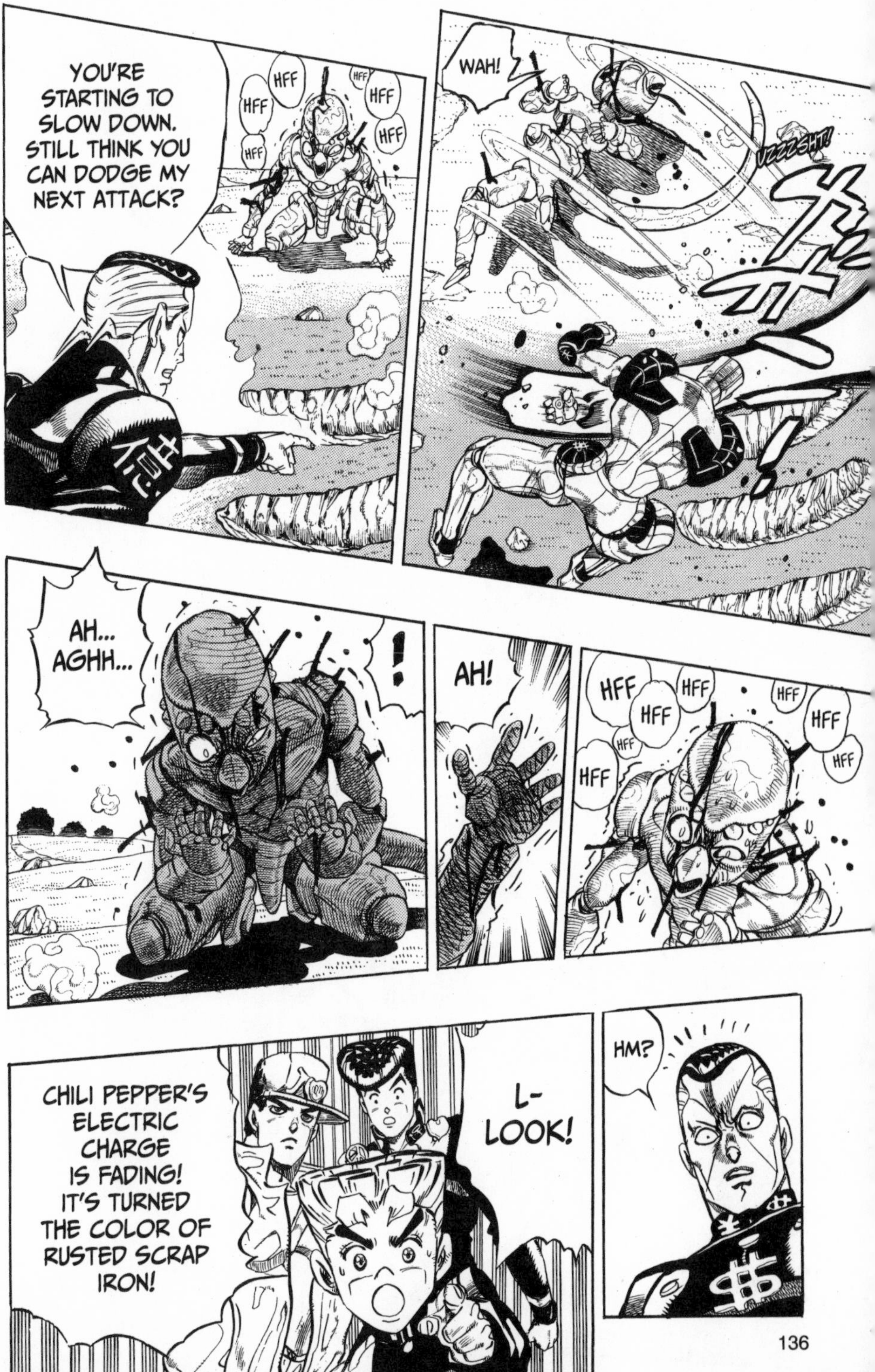
WAH!
VZZZSHT!
HFF
HFF
HFF
HFF
HFF
HFF
YOU'RE STARTING TO SLOW DOWN. STILL THINK YOU CAN DODGE MY NEXT ATTACK?
HFF
HFF
HFF
HFF
HFF
HFF
HFF
HFF
AH!
!
AH... AGHH...
HM?
L- LOOK!
CHILI PEPPER'S ELECTRIC CHARGE IS FADING! IT'S TURNED THE COLOR OF RUSTED SCRAP IRON!

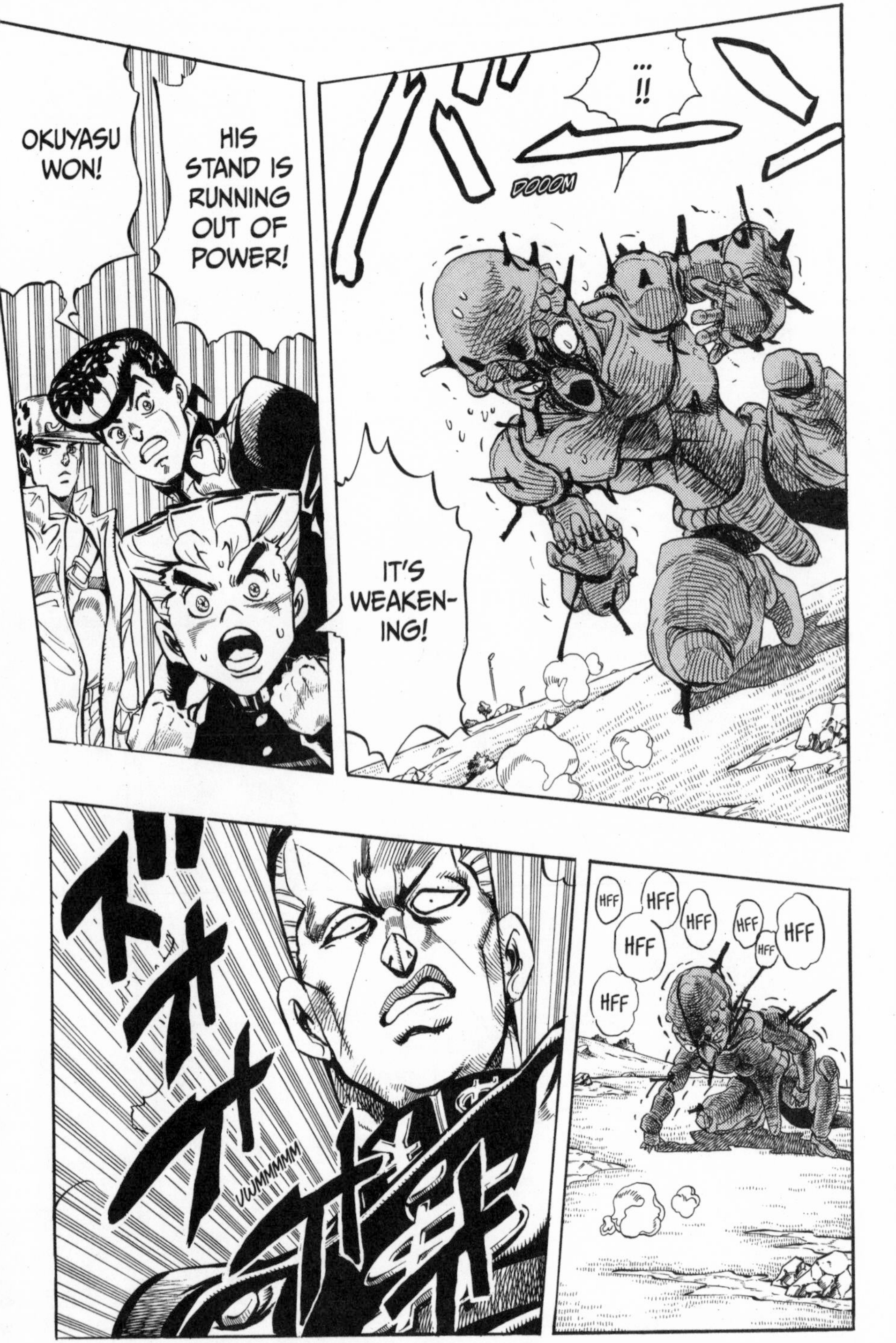
...!!
DOOOM
IT'S WEAKEN-ING!
HIS STAND IS RUNNING OUT OF POWER!
OKUYASU WON!
HFF
HFF
HFF
HFF
HFF
HFF
HFF
HFF
VWMMMMM

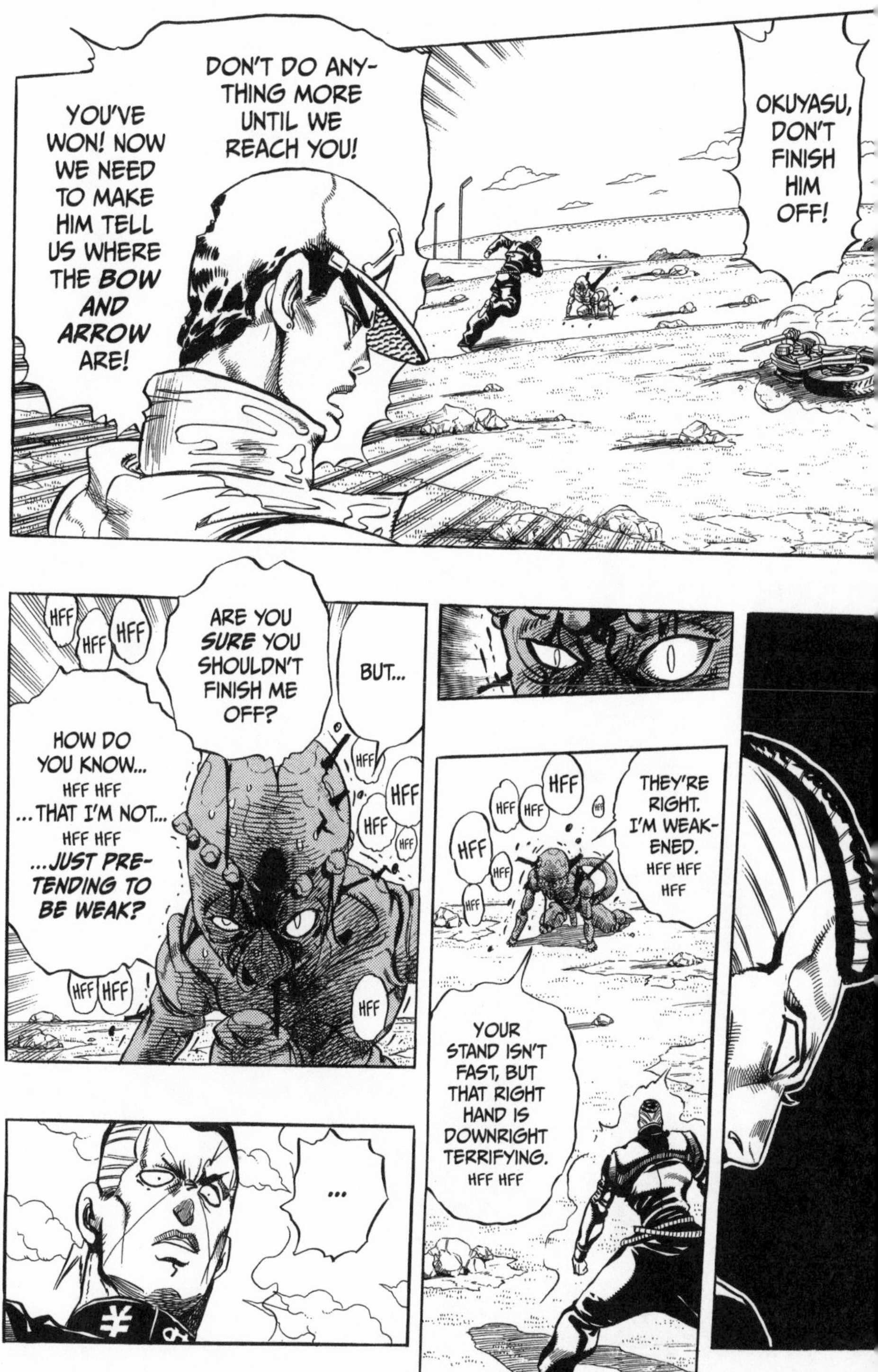
OKUYASU, DON'T FINISH HIM OFF!
DON'T DO ANY-THING MORE UNTIL WE REACH YOU!
YOU'VE WON! NOW WE NEED TO MAKE HIM TELL US WHERE THE *BOW AND ARROW* ARE!
HFF HFF HFF HFF HFF HFF
THEY'RE RIGHT. I'M WEAK-ENED. HFF HFF HFF
YOUR STAND ISN'T FAST, BUT THAT RIGHT HAND IS DOWNRIGHT TERRIFYING. HFF HFF
HFF HFF HFF HFF HFF
BUT...
ARE YOU *SURE* YOU SHOULDN'T FINISH ME OFF?
HFF HFF HFF
HOW DO YOU KNOW... HFF HFF ...THAT I'M NOT... HFF HFF ...*JUST PRE-TENDING TO BE WEAK?*
HFF HFF HFF
...

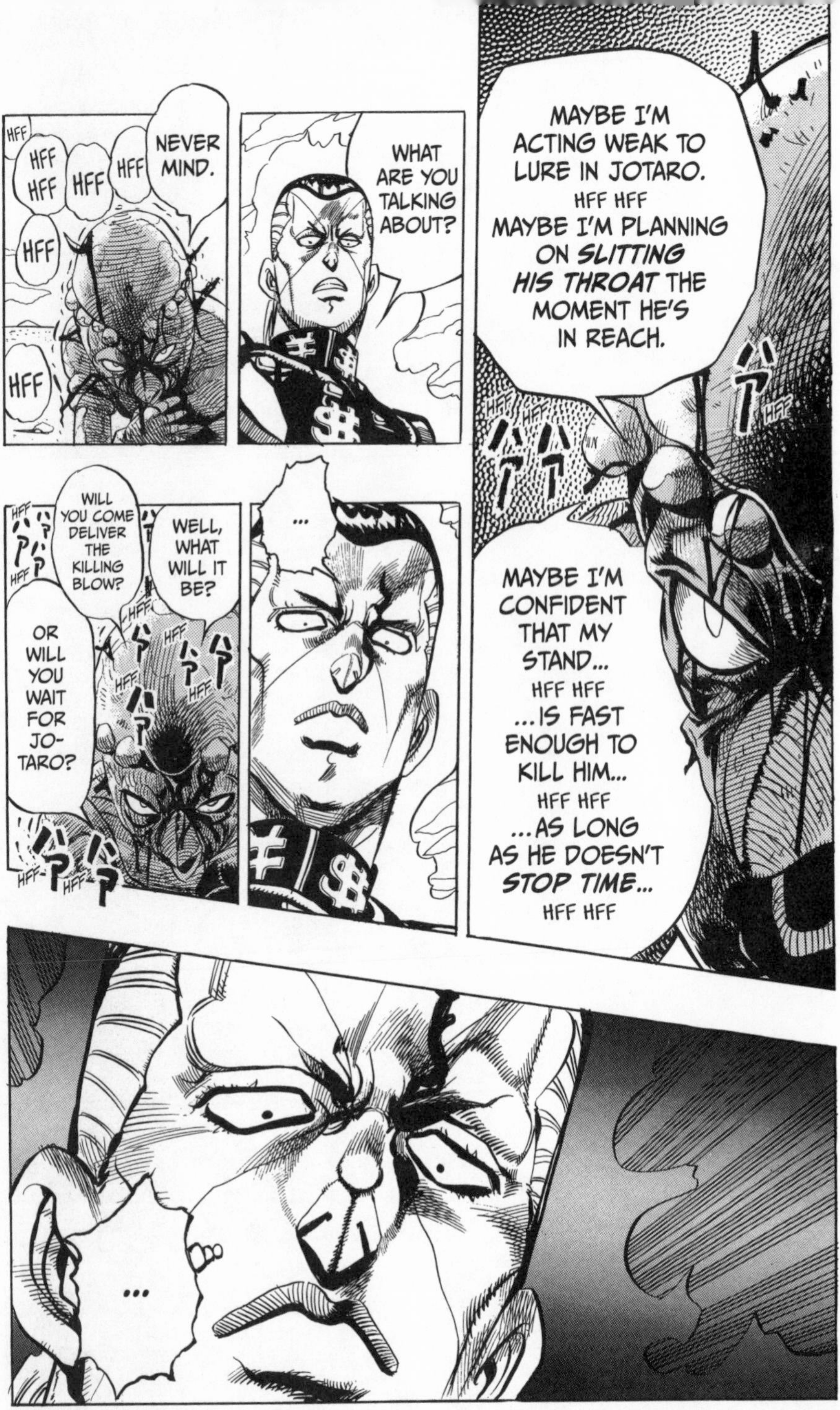
MAYBE I'M ACTING WEAK TO LURE IN JOTARO. HFF HFF MAYBE I'M PLANNING ON SLITTING HIS THROAT THE MOMENT HE'S IN REACH.
MAYBE I'M CONFIDENT THAT MY STAND... HFF HFF ...IS FAST ENOUGH TO KILL HIM... HFF HFF ...AS LONG AS HE DOESN'T STOP TIME... HFF HFF
WHAT ARE YOU TALKING ABOUT?
NEVER MIND.
HFF
HFF
HFF HFF
HFF
HFF
HFF
...
WELL, WHAT WILL IT BE?
WILL YOU COME DELIVER THE KILLING BLOW?
OR WILL YOU WAIT FOR JO-TARO?
...

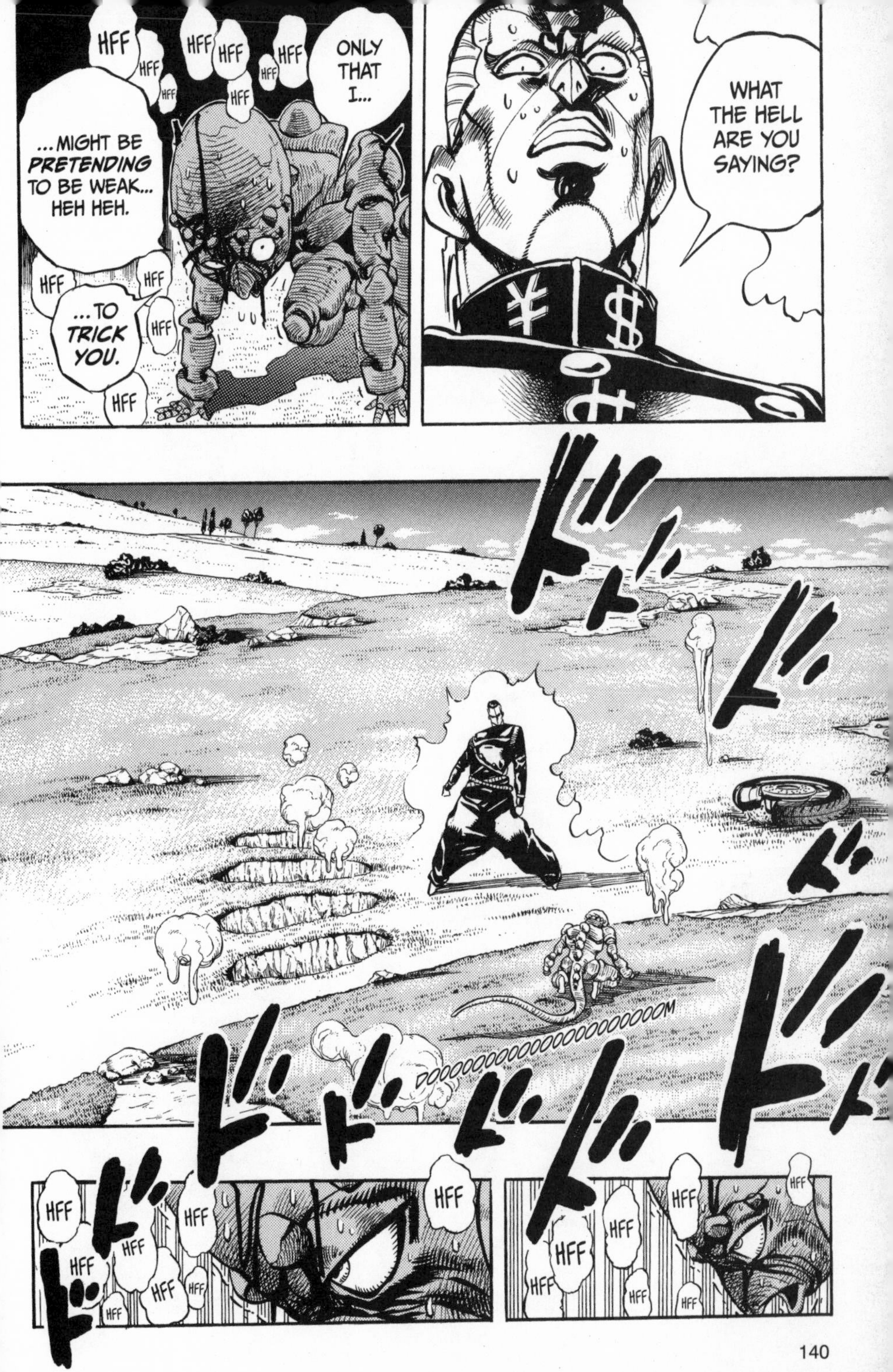
WHAT THE HELL ARE YOU SAYING?
HFF
HFF
HFF
HFF
ONLY THAT I...
...MIGHT BE *PRETENDING* TO BE WEAK... HEH HEH.
HFF
HFF
...TO *TRICK* YOU.
HFF
HFF
ドドドドドド
DOOOOOOOOOOOOOOOOOOOOOOOOOM
HFF
HFF
HFF
HFF
HFF
HFF
HFF
HFF
HFF
HFF
HFF
HFF

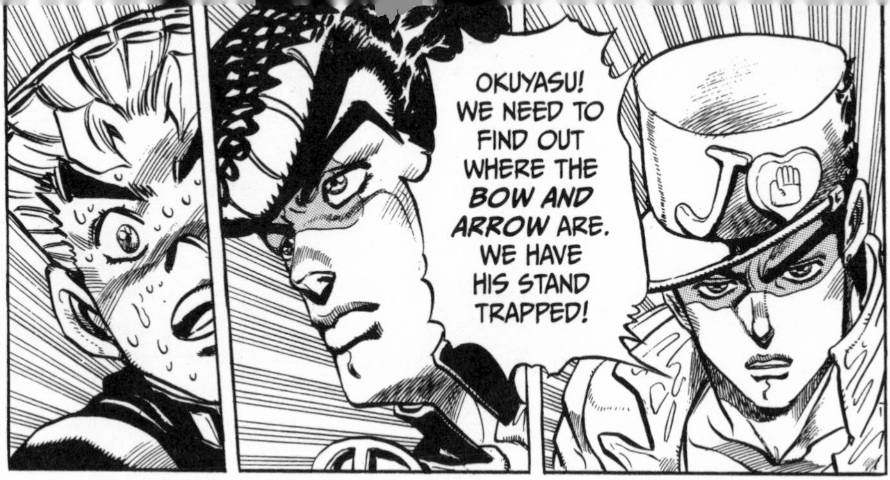
OKUYASU! WE NEED TO FIND OUT WHERE THE BOW AND ARROW ARE. WE HAVE HIS STAND TRAPPED!

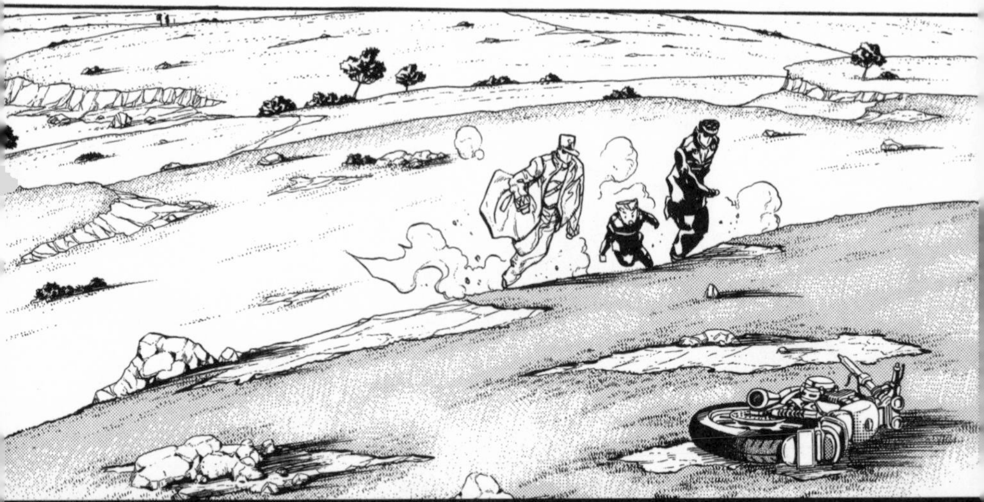

CHAPTER 45

CHILI PEPPER, PART 4

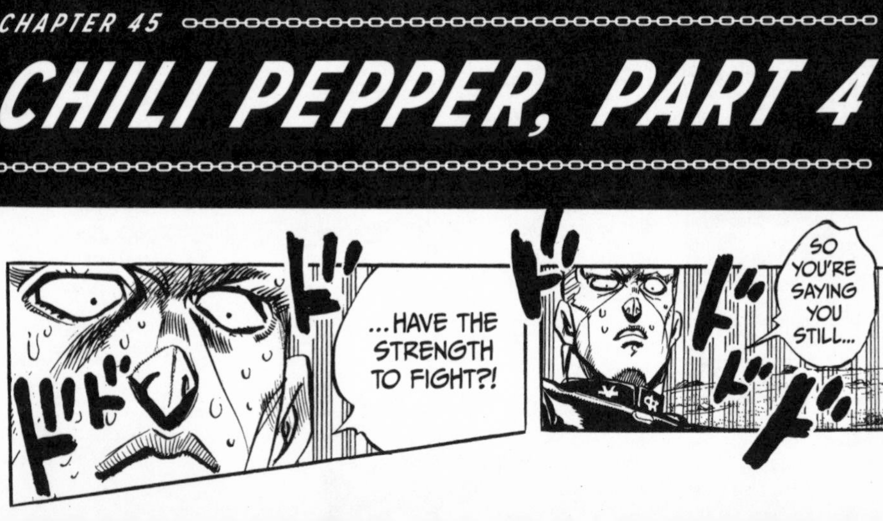
SO YOU'RE SAYING YOU STILL...
...HAVE THE STRENGTH TO FIGHT?!

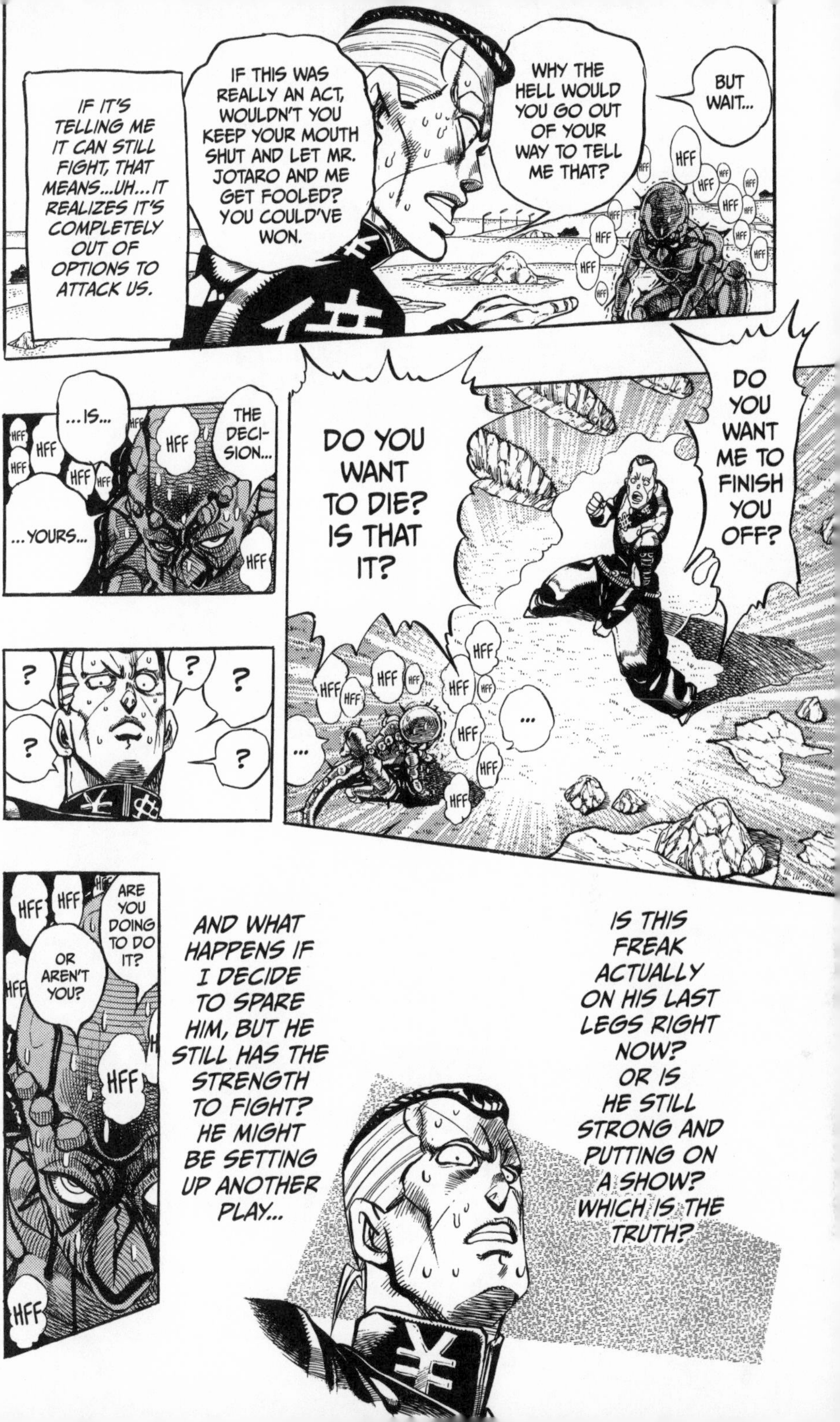
BUT WAIT...
WHY THE HELL WOULD YOU GO OUT OF YOUR WAY TO TELL ME THAT?
IF THIS WAS REALLY AN ACT, WOULDN'T YOU KEEP YOUR MOUTH SHUT AND LET MR. JOTARO AND ME GET FOOLED? YOU COULD'VE WON.
IF IT'S TELLING ME IT CAN STILL FIGHT, THAT MEANS...UH...IT REALIZES IT'S COMPLETELY OUT OF OPTIONS TO ATTACK US.
HFF HFF HFF HFF HFF
DO YOU WANT ME TO FINISH YOU OFF?
DO YOU WANT TO DIE? IS THAT IT?
HFF HFF HFF HFF HFF
...
...
THE DECI-SION...
HFF
...IS...
HFF HFF
...YOURS...
HFF
? ? ? ? ? ?
IS THIS FREAK ACTUALLY ON HIS LAST LEGS RIGHT NOW? OR IS HE STILL STRONG AND PUTTING ON A SHOW? WHICH IS THE TRUTH?
AND WHAT HAPPENS IF I DECIDE TO SPARE HIM, BUT HE STILL HAS THE STRENGTH TO FIGHT? HE MIGHT BE SETTING UP ANOTHER PLAY...
ARE YOU DOING TO DO IT?
HFF HFF
OR AREN'T YOU?
HFF
HFF

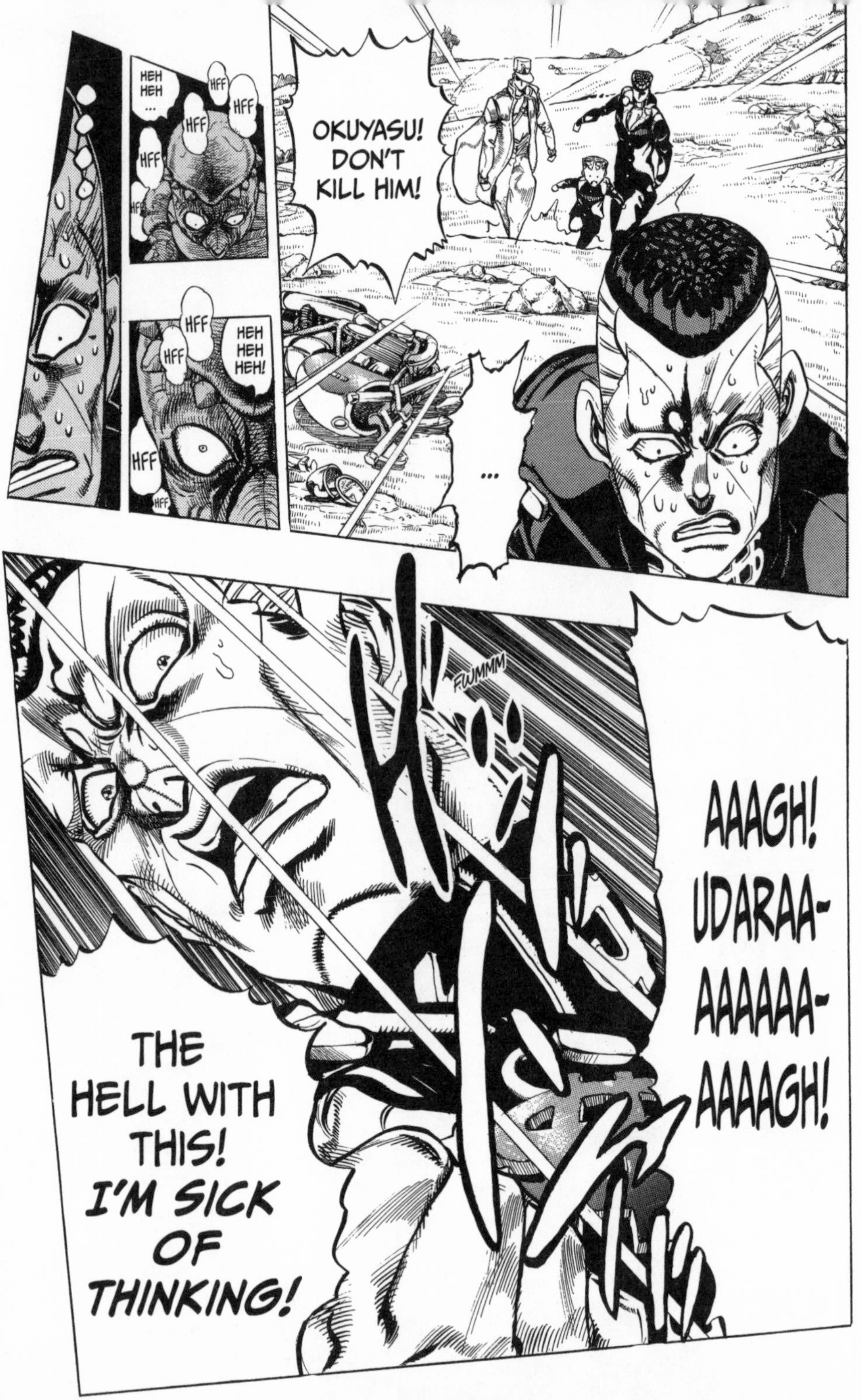
OKUYASU! DON'T KILL HIM!
...
HEH HEH ...
HFF
HFF
HFF
HFF
HFF
HFF
HEH HEH HEH!
HFF
HFF
HFF
HFF
AAAGH! UDARAA-AAAAAA-AAAAGH!
FWUMMM
THE HELL WITH THIS! I'M SICK OF THINKING!

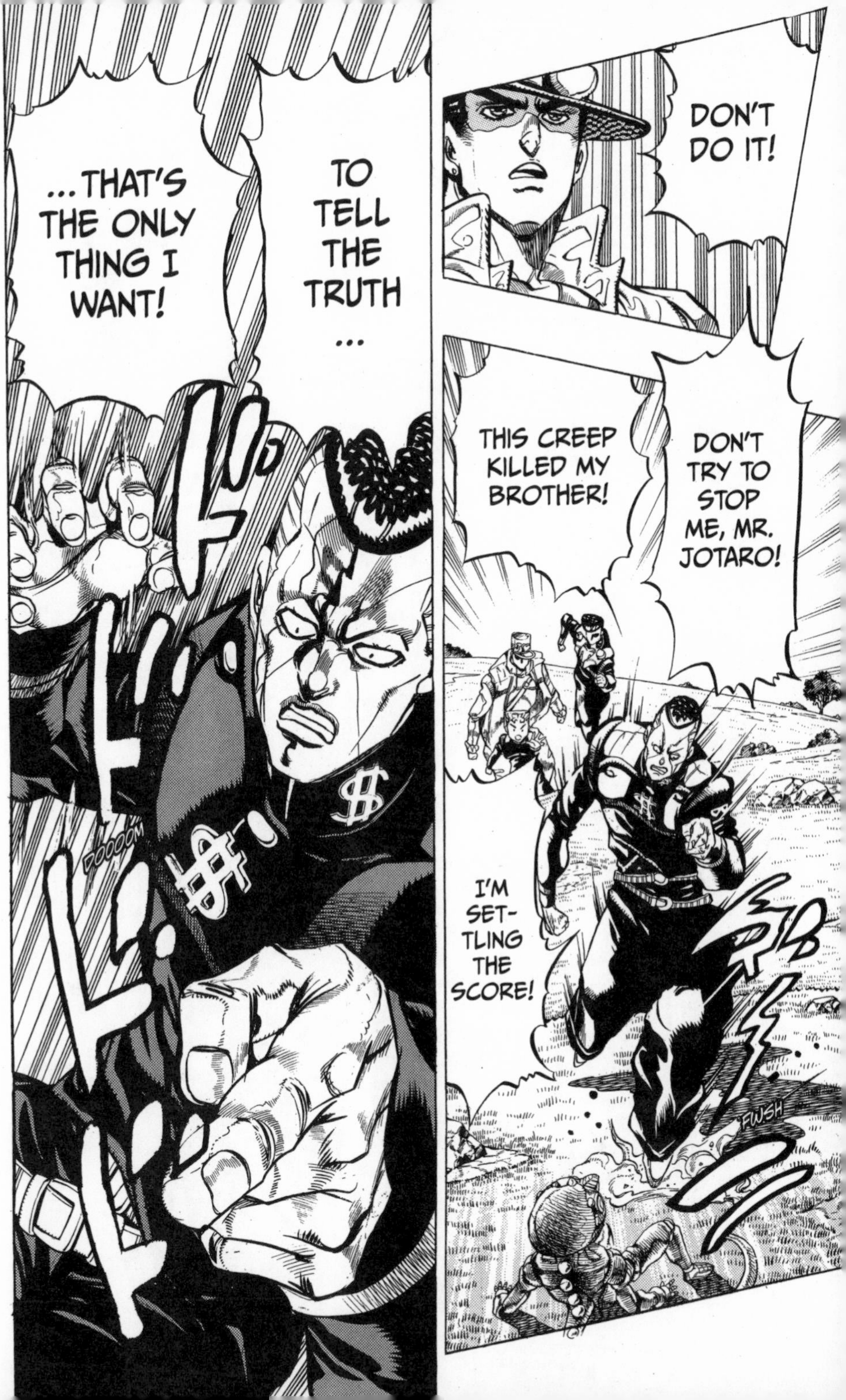
DON'T DO IT!
DON'T TRY TO STOP ME, MR. JOTARO!
THIS CREEP KILLED MY BROTHER!
I'M SET-TLING THE SCORE!
FWSH
TO TELL THE TRUTH ...
...THAT'S THE ONLY THING I WANT!
DOOOOM

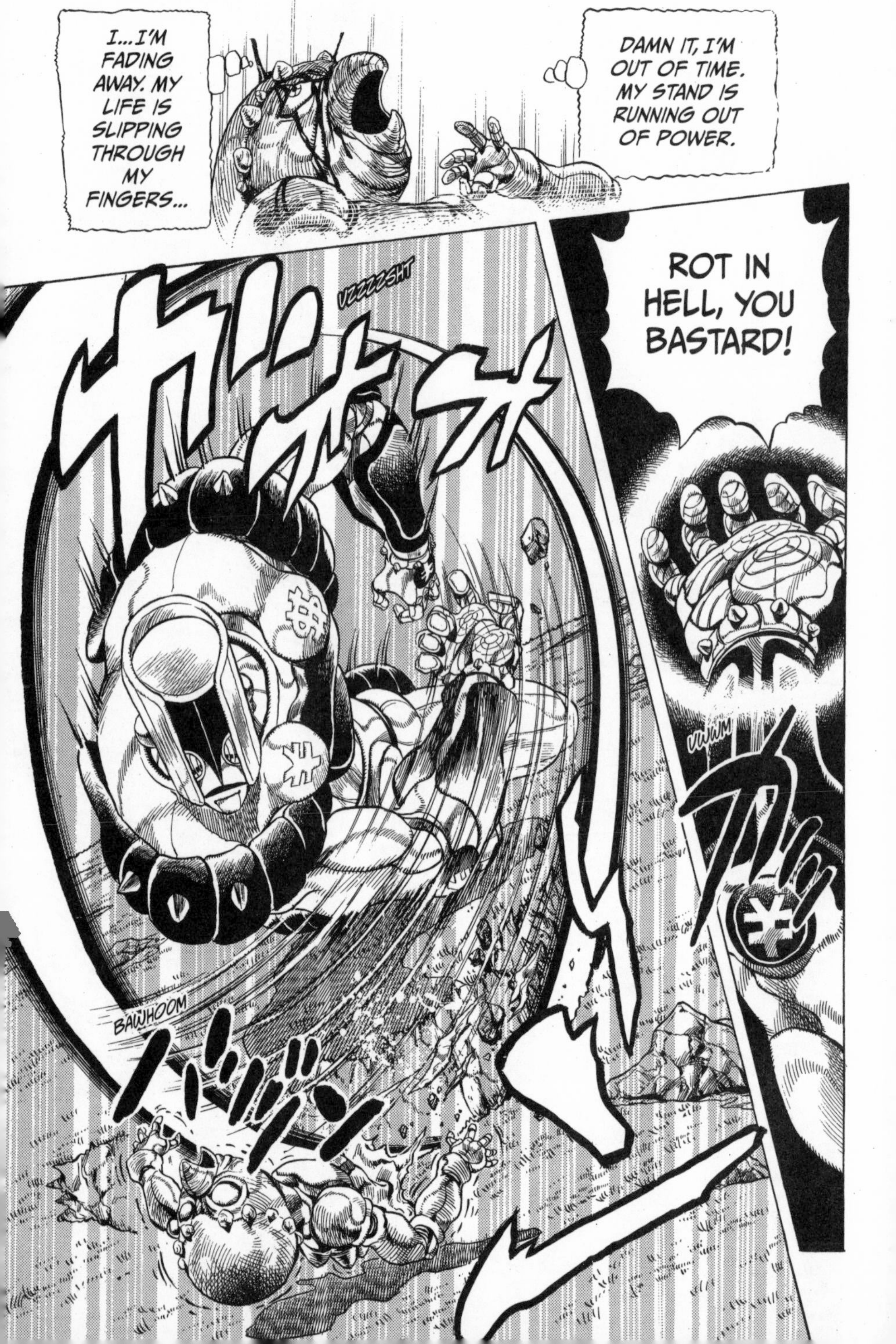
DAMN IT, I'M OUT OF TIME. MY STAND IS RUNNING OUT OF POWER.
I...I'M FADING AWAY. MY LIFE IS SLIPPING THROUGH MY FINGERS...
ROT IN HELL, YOU BASTARD!
VWWM
VZZZZSHT
BAWHOOM

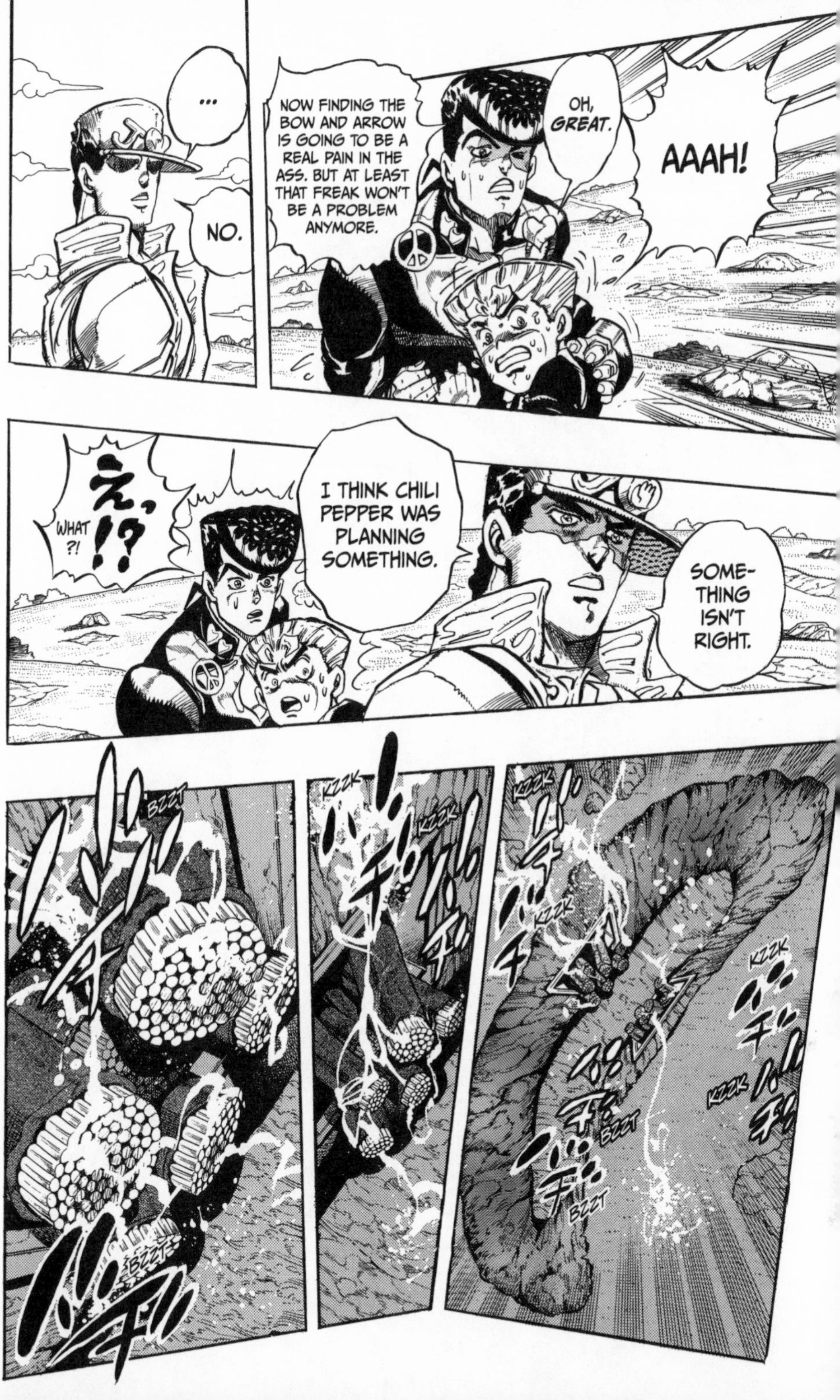
AAAH!
OH, GREAT.
NOW FINDING THE BOW AND ARROW IS GOING TO BE A REAL PAIN IN THE ASS. BUT AT LEAST THAT FREAK WON'T BE A PROBLEM ANYMORE.
...
NO.
SOME-THING ISN'T RIGHT.
I THINK CHILI PEPPER WAS PLANNING SOMETHING.
えっ!?
WHAT ?!
KZZK
KZZK
KZZK
KZZK
BZZT
BZZT
KZZK
KZZK
BZZT
BZZT

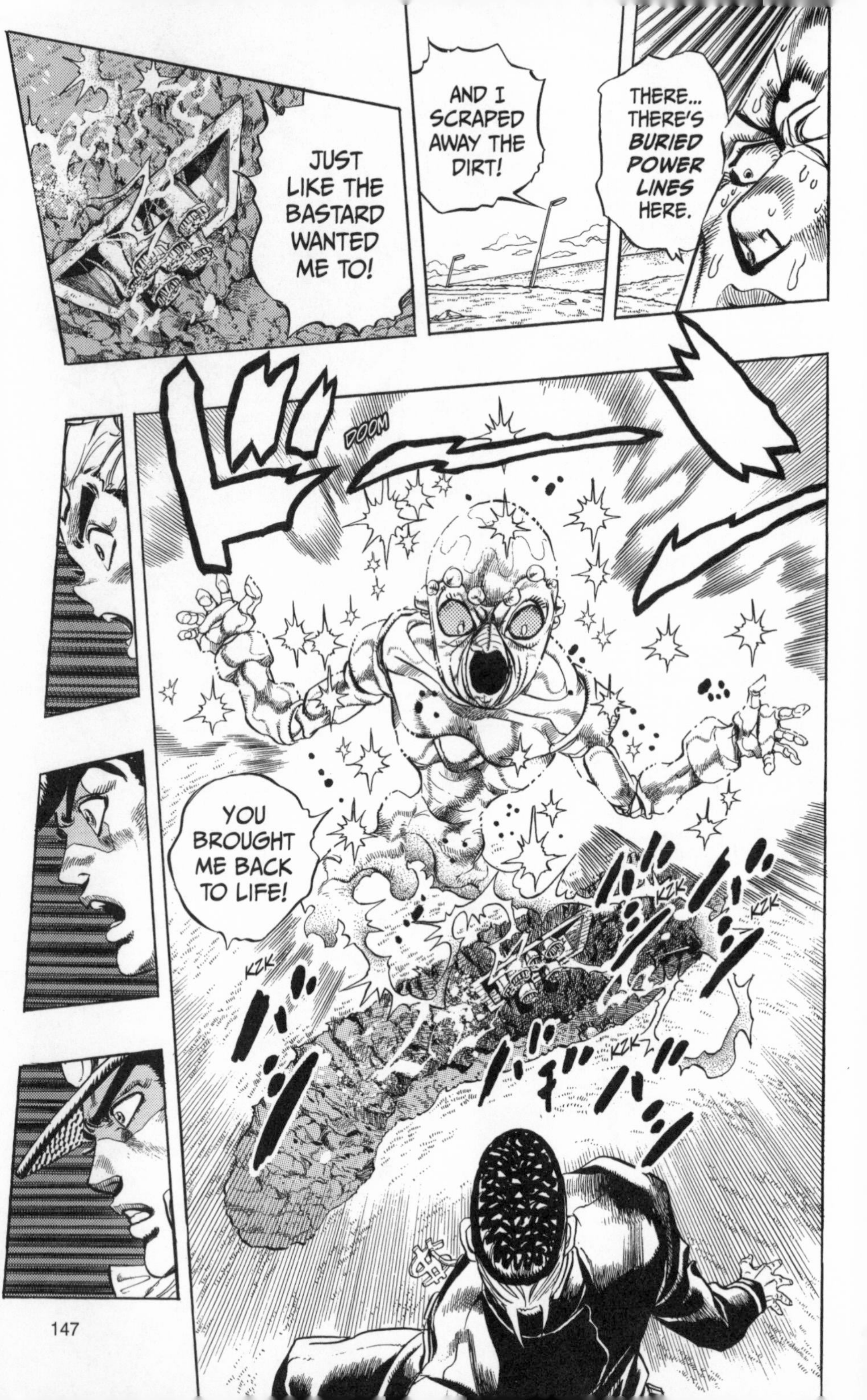
THERE... THERE'S BURIED POWER LINES HERE.
AND I SCRAPED AWAY THE DIRT!
JUST LIKE THE BASTARD WANTED ME TO!
DOOM
YOU BROUGHT ME BACK TO LIFE!
KZK
KZK
KZK
KZK

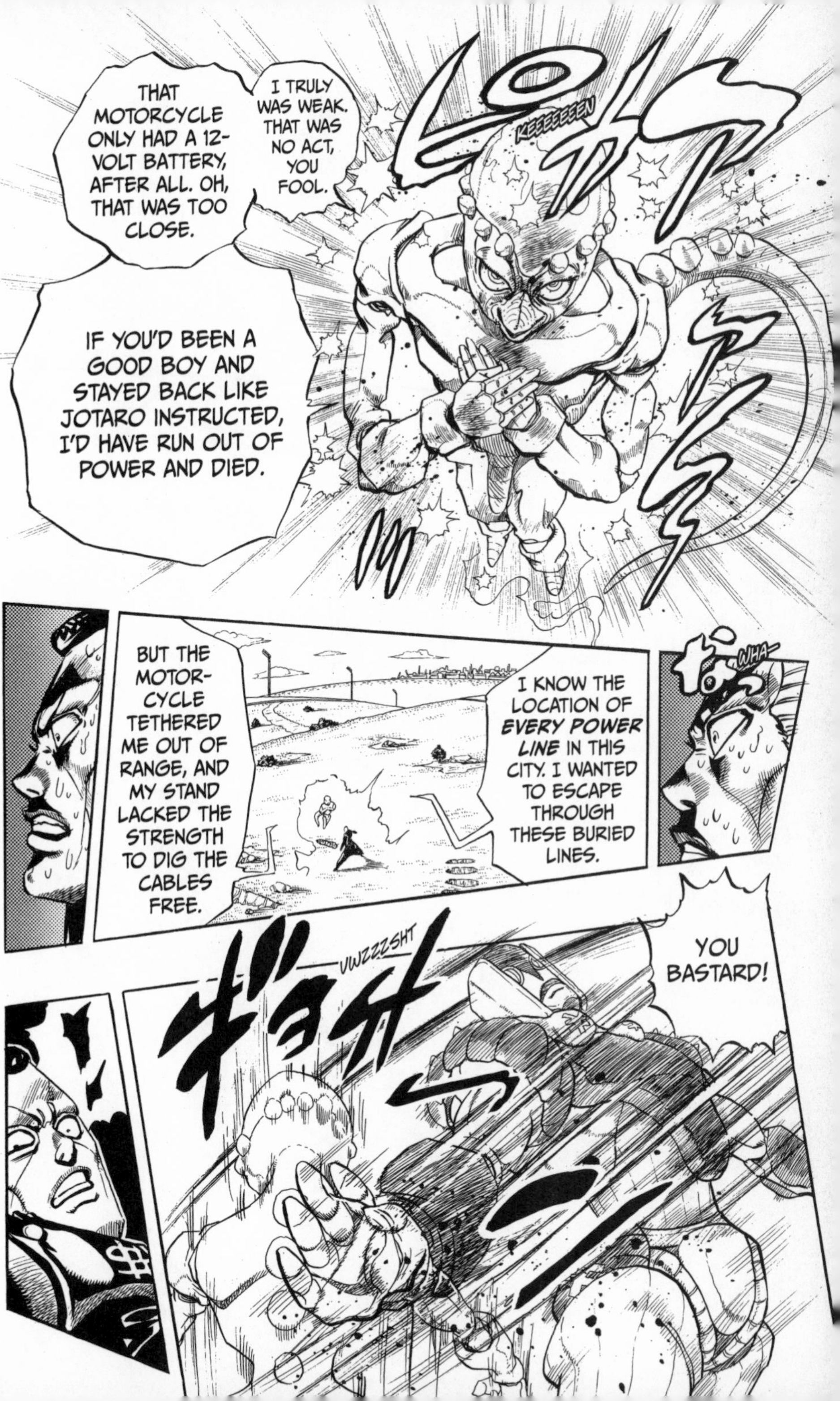
KEEEEEEEEN
I TRULY WAS WEAK. THAT WAS NO ACT, YOU FOOL.
THAT MOTORCYCLE ONLY HAD A 12-VOLT BATTERY, AFTER ALL. OH, THAT WAS TOO CLOSE.
IF YOU'D BEEN A GOOD BOY AND STAYED BACK LIKE JOTARO INSTRUCTED, I'D HAVE RUN OUT OF POWER AND DIED.
WHA—
I KNOW THE LOCATION OF *EVERY POWER LINE* IN THIS CITY. I WANTED TO ESCAPE THROUGH THESE BURIED LINES.
BUT THE MOTOR-CYCLE TETHERED ME OUT OF RANGE, AND MY STAND LACKED THE STRENGTH TO DIG THE CABLES FREE.
YOU BASTARD!
VWZZZSHT

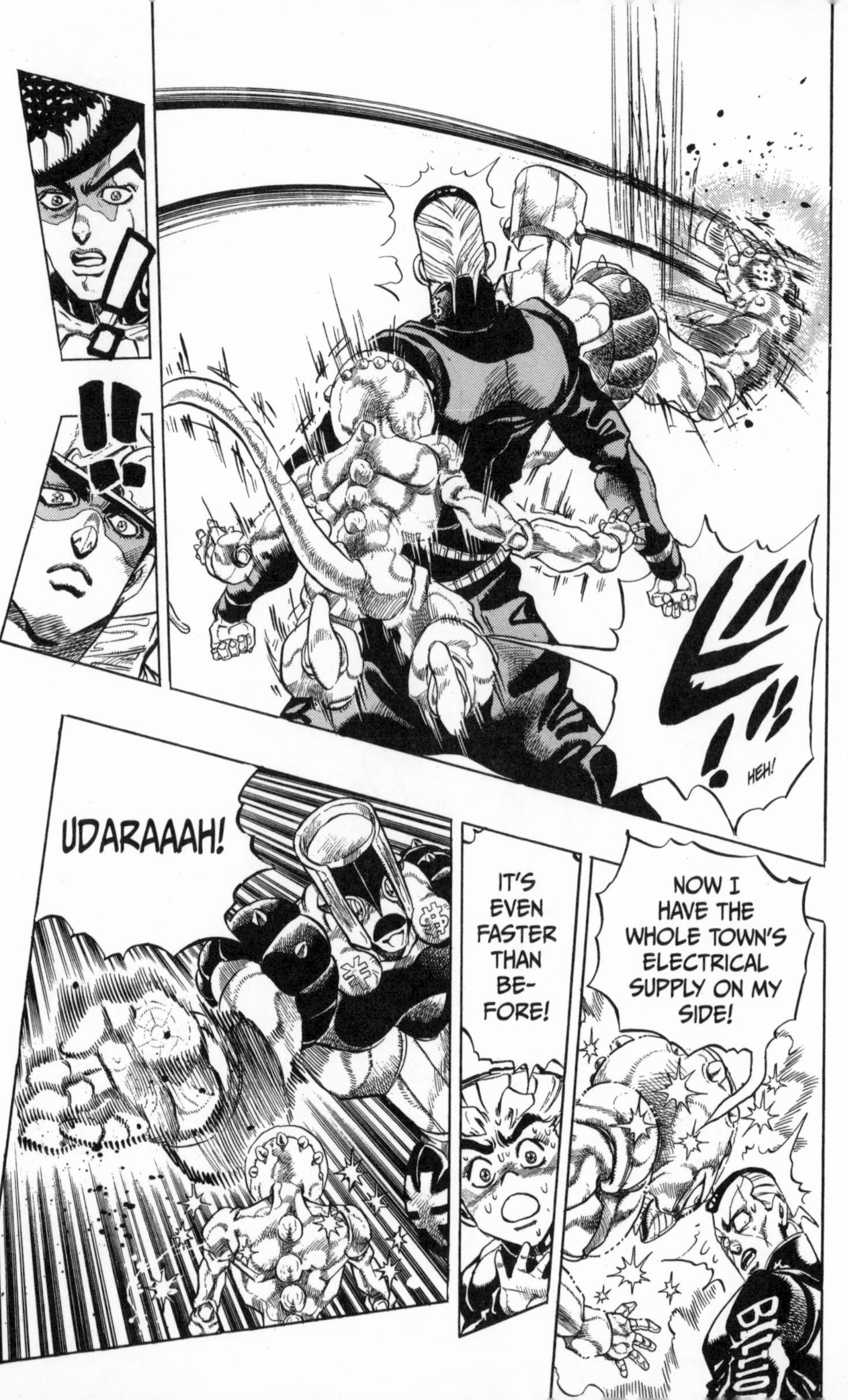
HEH!
NOW I HAVE THE WHOLE TOWN'S ELECTRICAL SUPPLY ON MY SIDE!
IT'S EVEN FASTER THAN BE-FORE!
UDARAAAH!

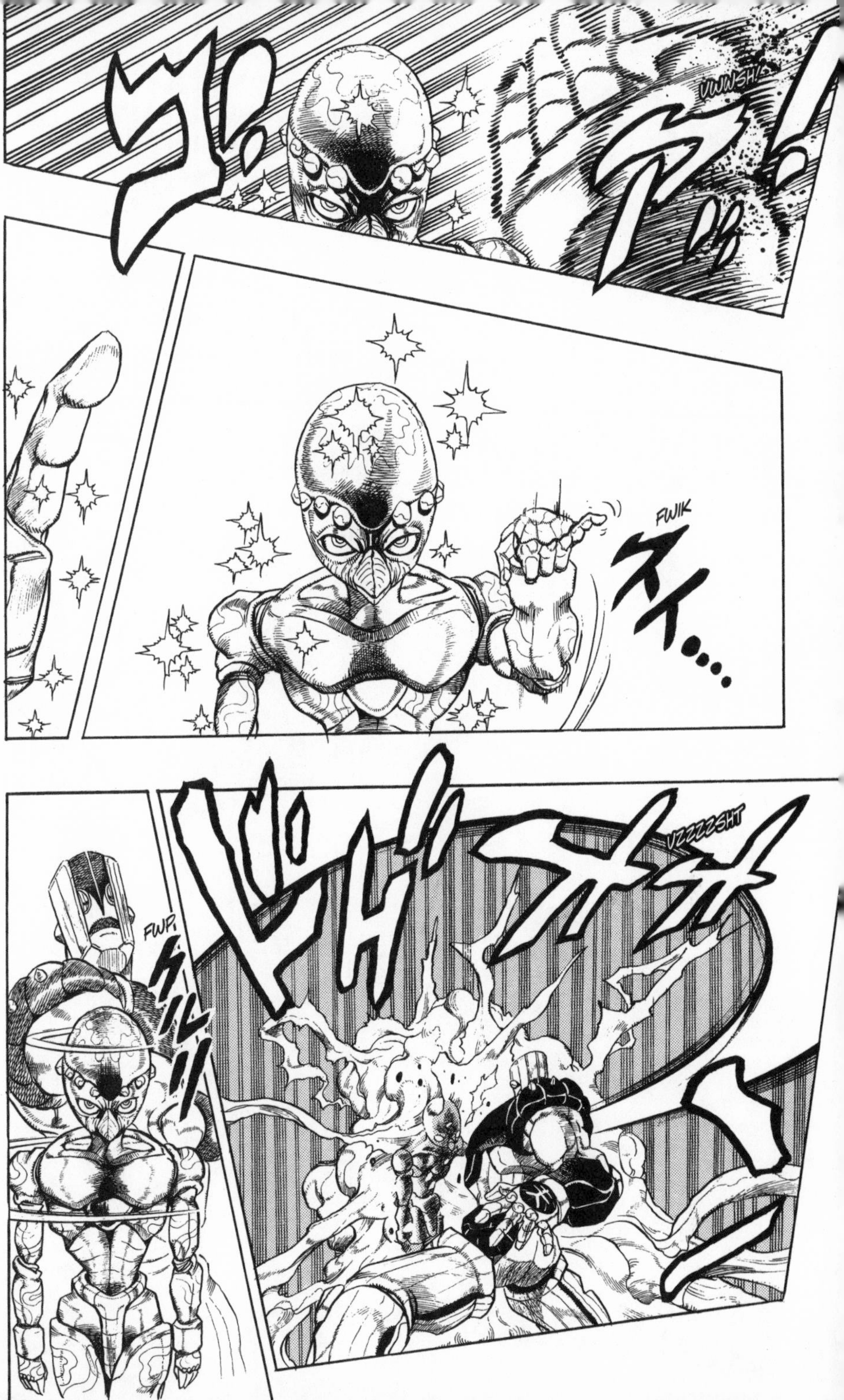
VWWSH!
FWIK
VZZZZSHT
FWP!

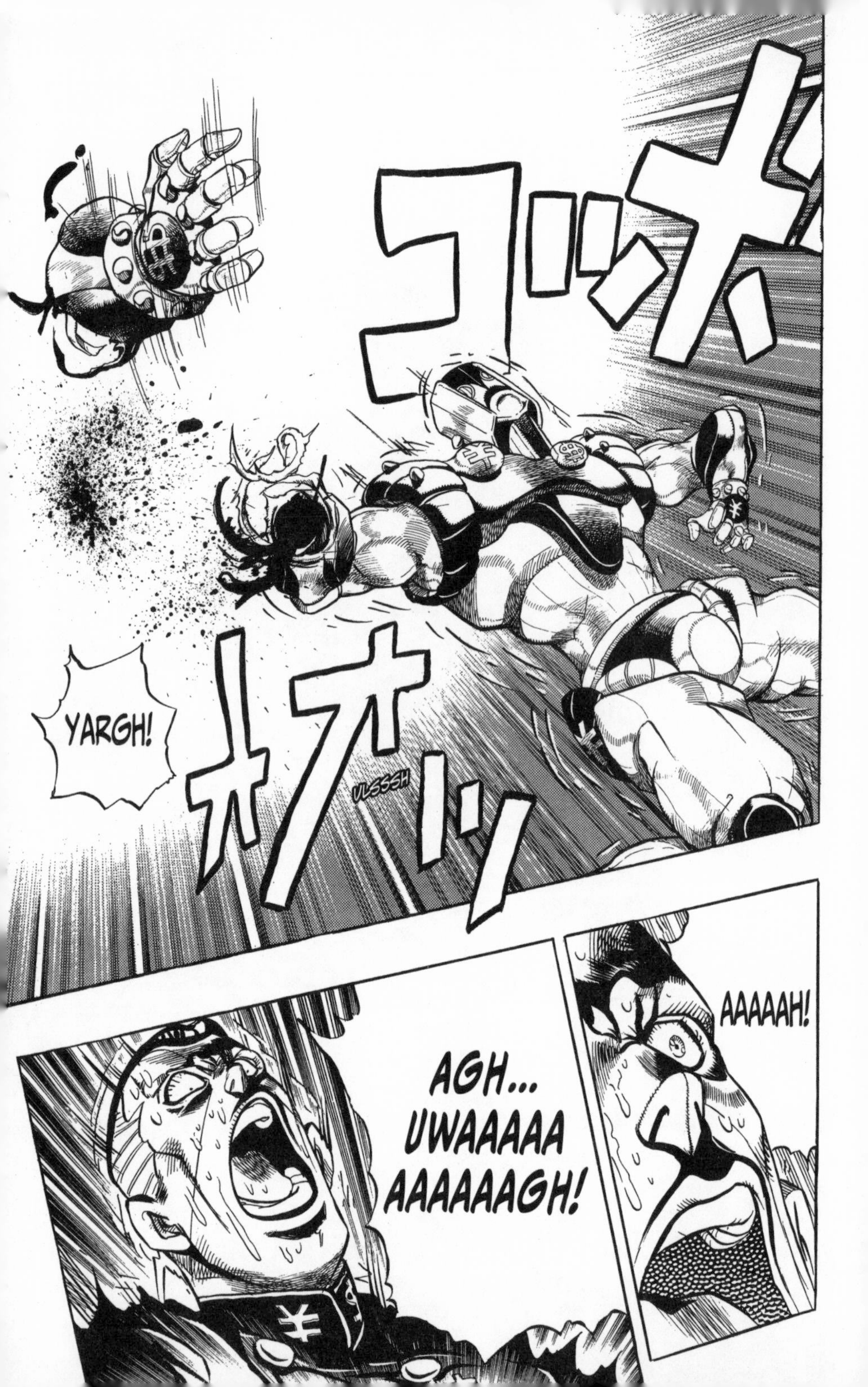
YARGH!
ULSSSH
AAAAAH!
AGH... UWAAAAA AAAAAAGH!

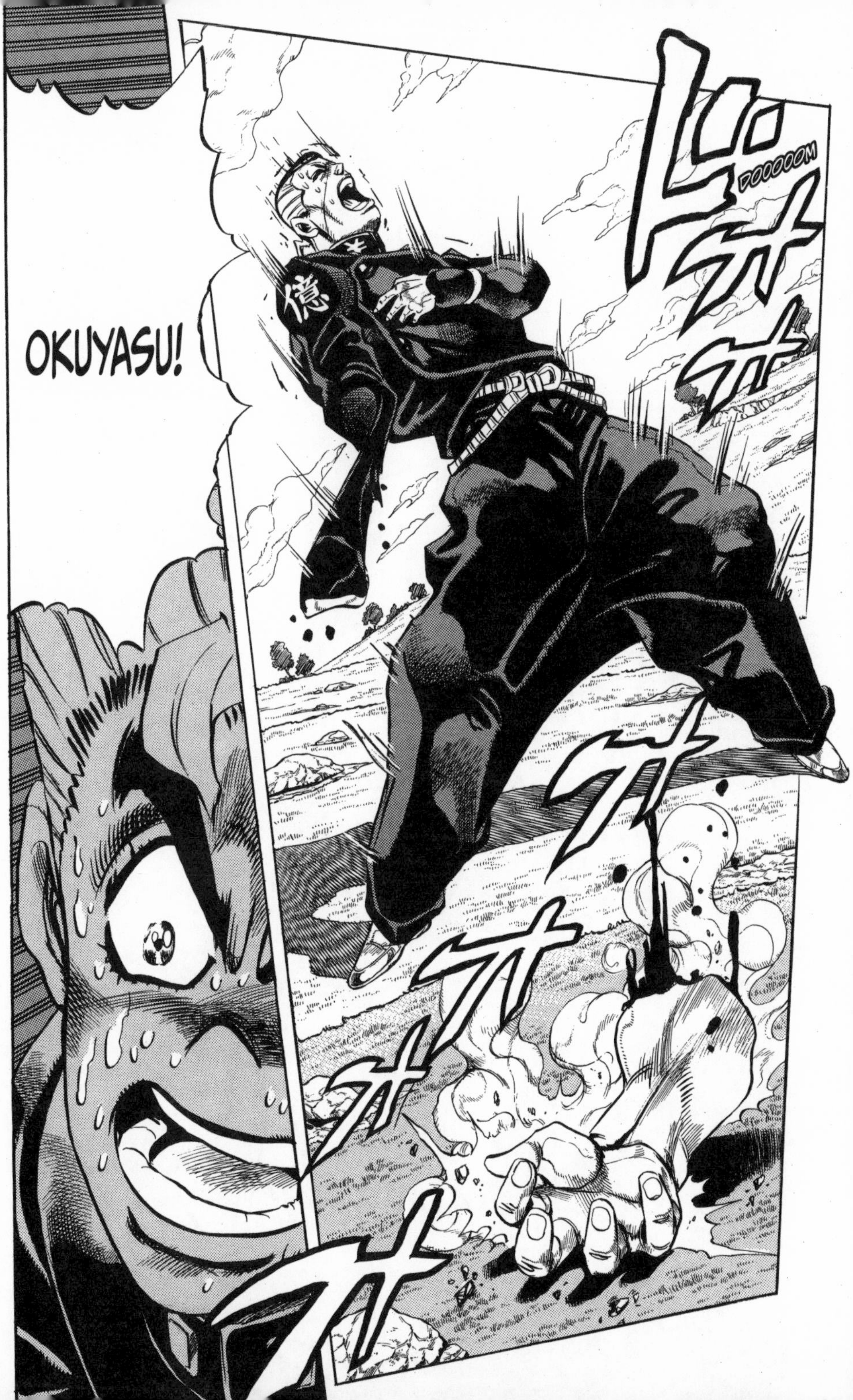
DOOOOOM
OKUYASU!

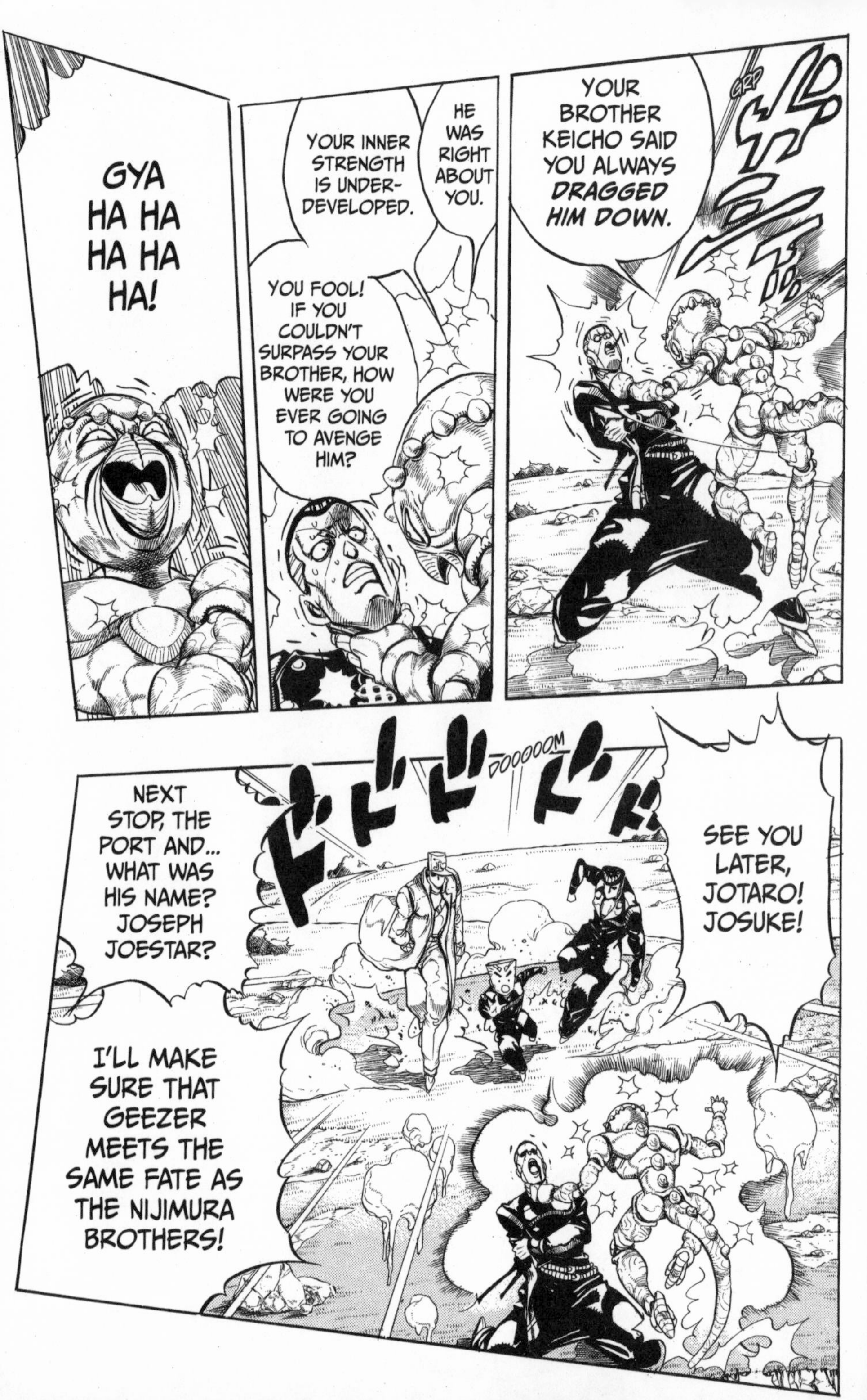
GRP
YOUR BROTHER KEICHO SAID YOU ALWAYS DRAGGED HIM DOWN.
HE WAS RIGHT ABOUT YOU.
YOUR INNER STRENGTH IS UNDER-DEVELOPED.
YOU FOOL! IF YOU COULDN'T SURPASS YOUR BROTHER, HOW WERE YOU EVER GOING TO AVENGE HIM?
GYA HA HA HA HA HA!
SEE YOU LATER, JOTARO! JOSUKE!
DOOOOOM
NEXT STOP, THE PORT AND... WHAT WAS HIS NAME? JOSEPH JOESTAR?
I'LL MAKE SURE THAT GEEZER MEETS THE SAME FATE AS THE NIJIMURA BROTHERS!

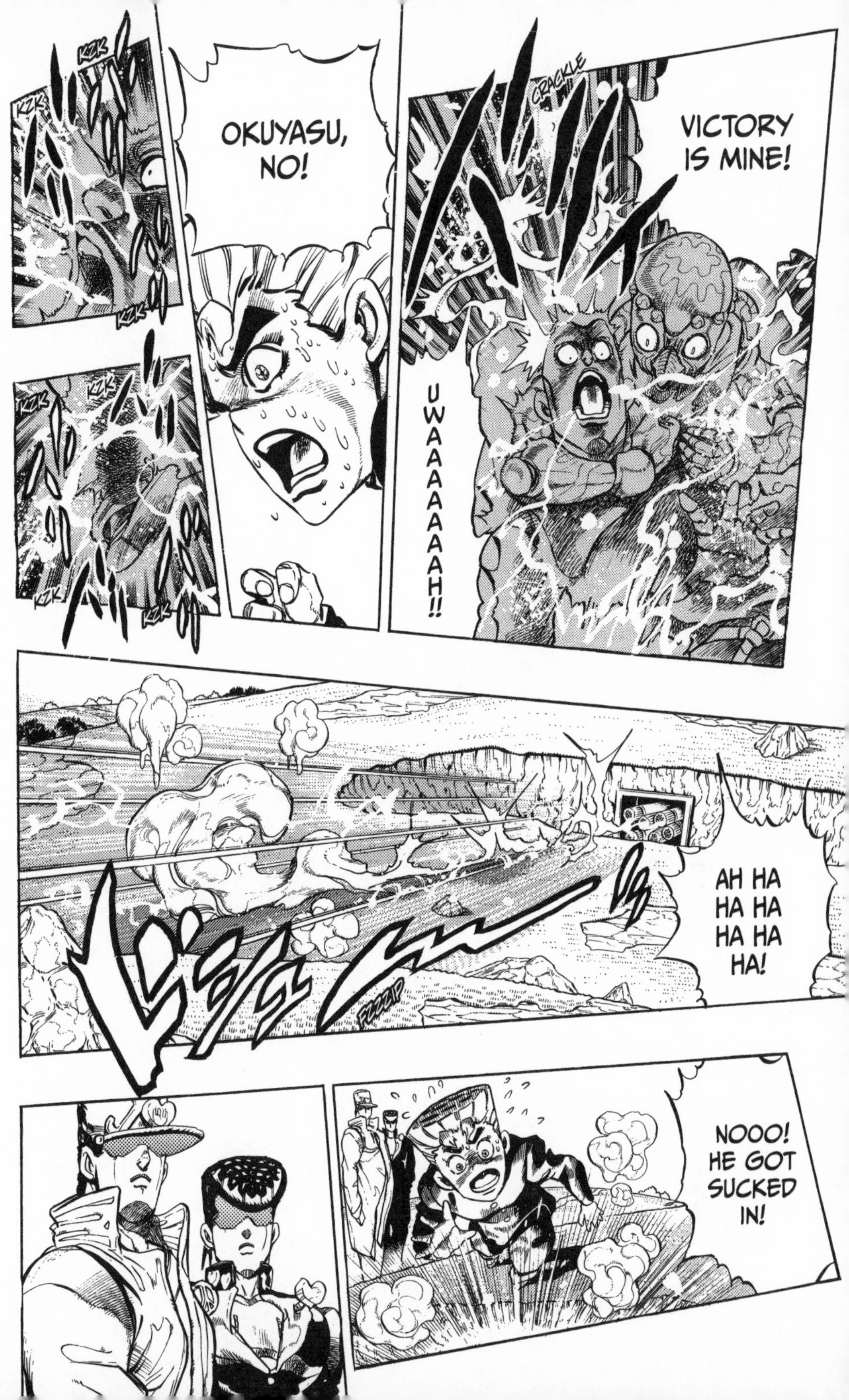
CRACKLE
VICTORY IS MINE!
UWAAAAAAAAAAH!!
OKUYASU, NO!
KZK
KZK
KZK
KZK
KZK
KZK
KZK
AH HA HA HA HA HA HA!
FZZZAP
NOOO! HE GOT SUCKED IN!

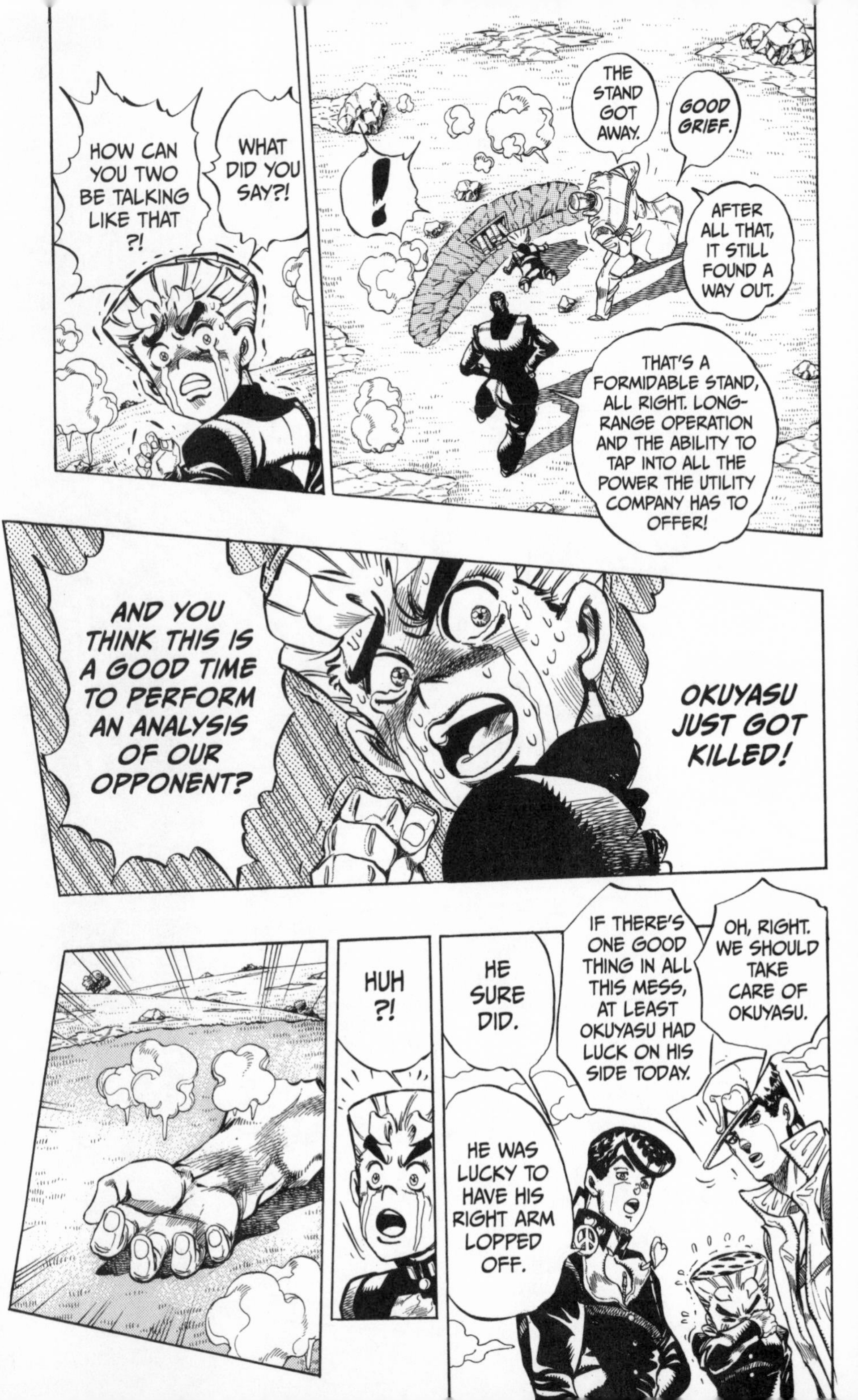
THE STAND GOT AWAY.
GOOD GRIEF.
!
AFTER ALL THAT, IT STILL FOUND A WAY OUT.
THAT'S A FORMIDABLE STAND, ALL RIGHT. LONG-RANGE OPERATION AND THE ABILITY TO TAP INTO ALL THE POWER THE UTILITY COMPANY HAS TO OFFER!
WHAT DID YOU SAY?!
HOW CAN YOU TWO BE TALKING LIKE THAT?!
OKUYASU JUST GOT KILLED!
AND YOU THINK THIS IS A GOOD TIME TO PERFORM AN ANALYSIS OF OUR OPPONENT?
OH, RIGHT. WE SHOULD TAKE CARE OF OKUYASU.
IF THERE'S ONE GOOD THING IN ALL THIS MESS, AT LEAST OKUYASU HAD LUCK ON HIS SIDE TODAY.
HE SURE DID.
HE WAS LUCKY TO HAVE HIS RIGHT ARM LOPPED OFF.
HUH?!

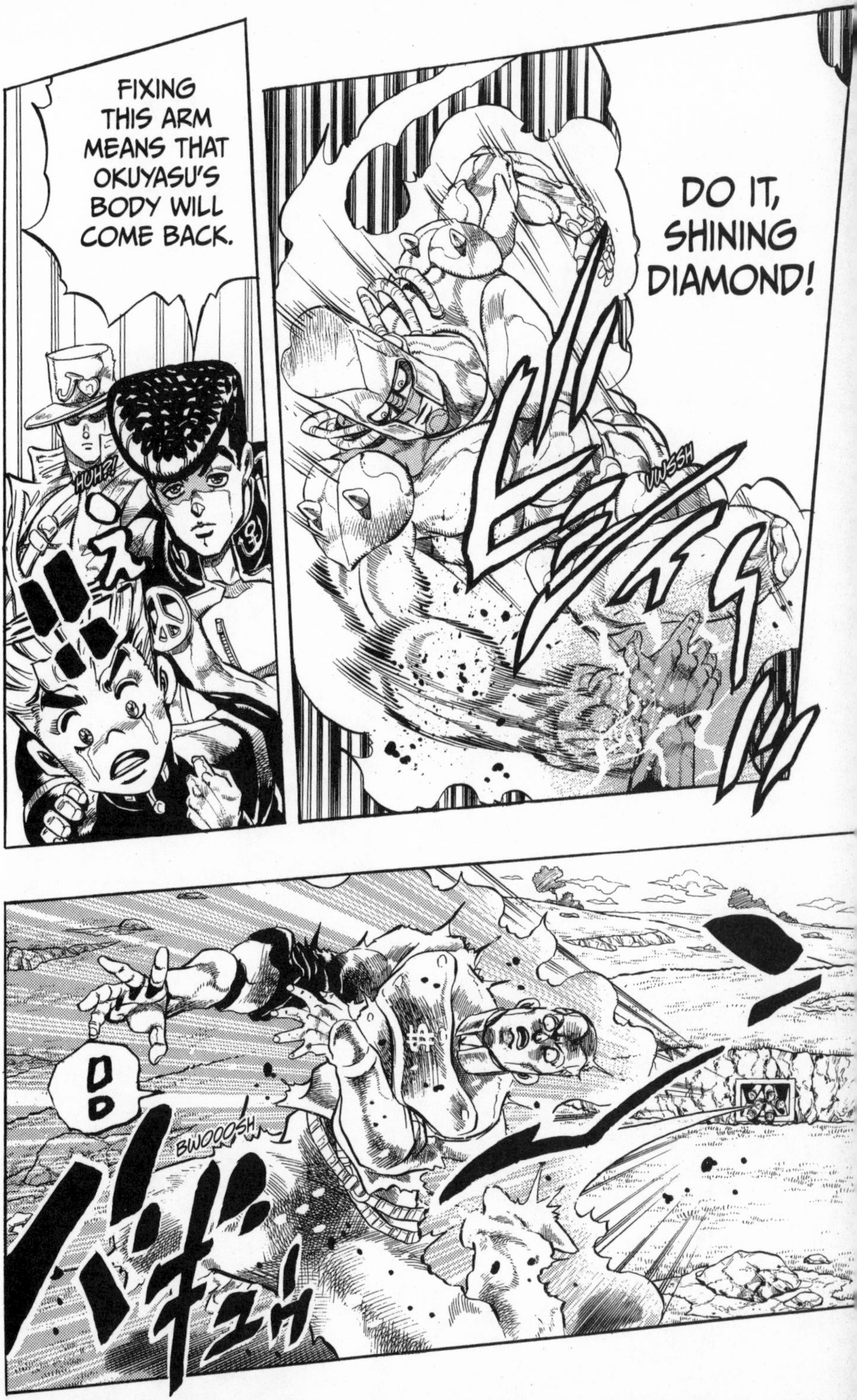
DO IT, SHINING DIAMOND!
VWSSH
FIXING THIS ARM MEANS THAT OKUYASU'S BODY WILL COME BACK.
HUH?!
BWOOOSH

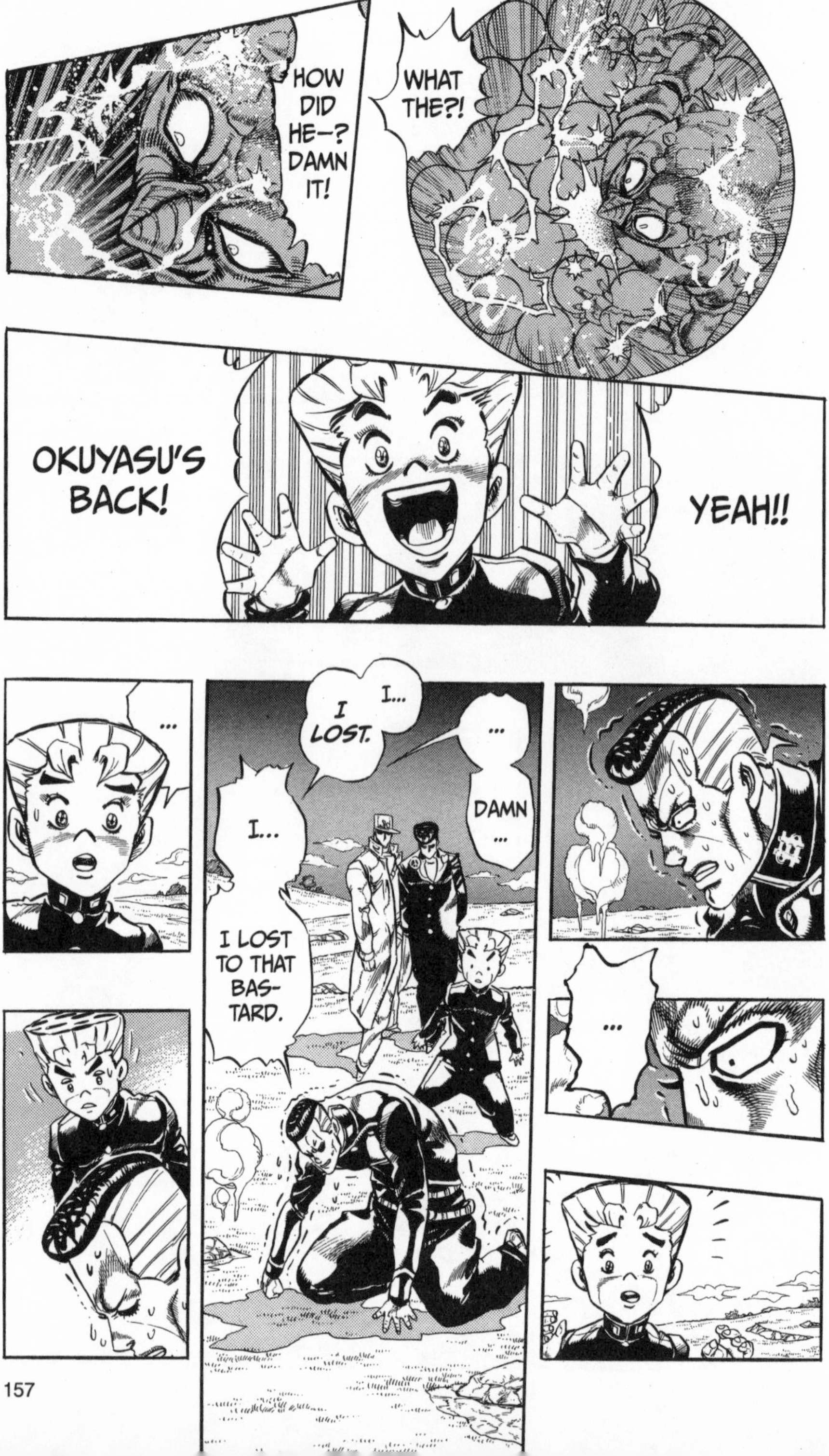
WHAT THE?!
HOW DID HE—? DAMN IT!
OKUYASU'S BACK!
YEAH!!
...
I... I LOST.
... DAMN ...
I... I LOST TO THAT BAS-TARD.
...

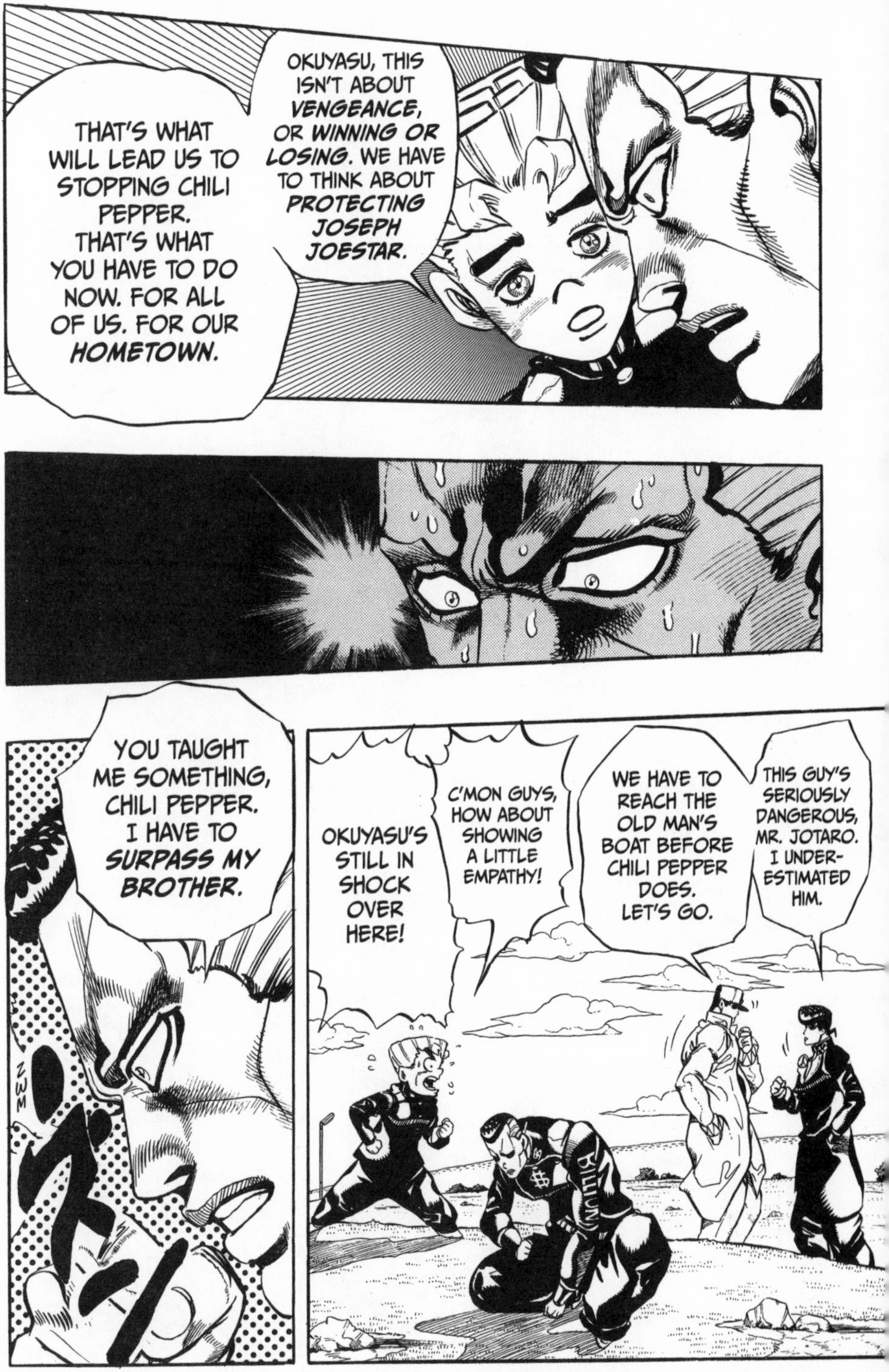
OKUYASU, THIS ISN'T ABOUT VENGEANCE, OR WINNING OR LOSING. WE HAVE TO THINK ABOUT PROTECTING JOSEPH JOESTAR.
THAT'S WHAT WILL LEAD US TO STOPPING CHILI PEPPER. THAT'S WHAT YOU HAVE TO DO NOW. FOR ALL OF US. FOR OUR HOMETOWN.
THIS GUY'S SERIOUSLY DANGEROUS, MR. JOTARO. I UNDER-ESTIMATED HIM.
WE HAVE TO REACH THE OLD MAN'S BOAT BEFORE CHILI PEPPER DOES. LET'S GO.
C'MON GUYS, HOW ABOUT SHOWING A LITTLE EMPATHY!
OKUYASU'S STILL IN SHOCK OVER HERE!
YOU TAUGHT ME SOMETHING, CHILI PEPPER. I HAVE TO SURPASS MY BROTHER.

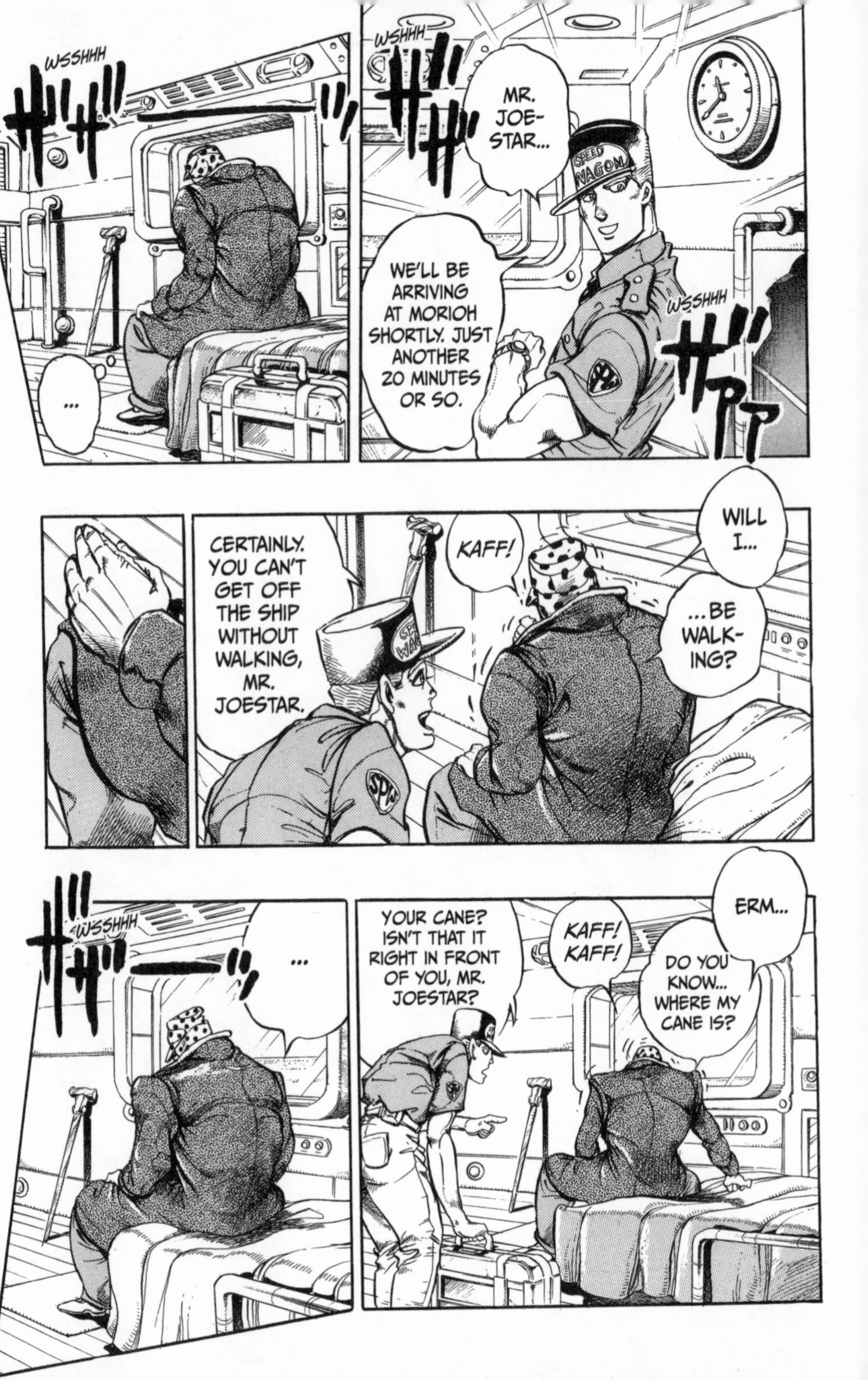
WSHHH
MR. JOE-STAR...
WE'LL BE ARRIVING AT MORIOH SHORTLY. JUST ANOTHER 20 MINUTES OR SO.
WSSHHH
WSSHHH
...
WILL I...
...BE WALKING?
KAFF!
CERTAINLY. YOU CAN'T GET OFF THE SHIP WITHOUT WALKING, MR. JOESTAR.
ERM...
DO YOU KNOW... WHERE MY CANE IS?
KAFF! KAFF!
YOUR CANE? ISN'T THAT IT RIGHT IN FRONT OF YOU, MR. JOESTAR?
WSSHHH
...

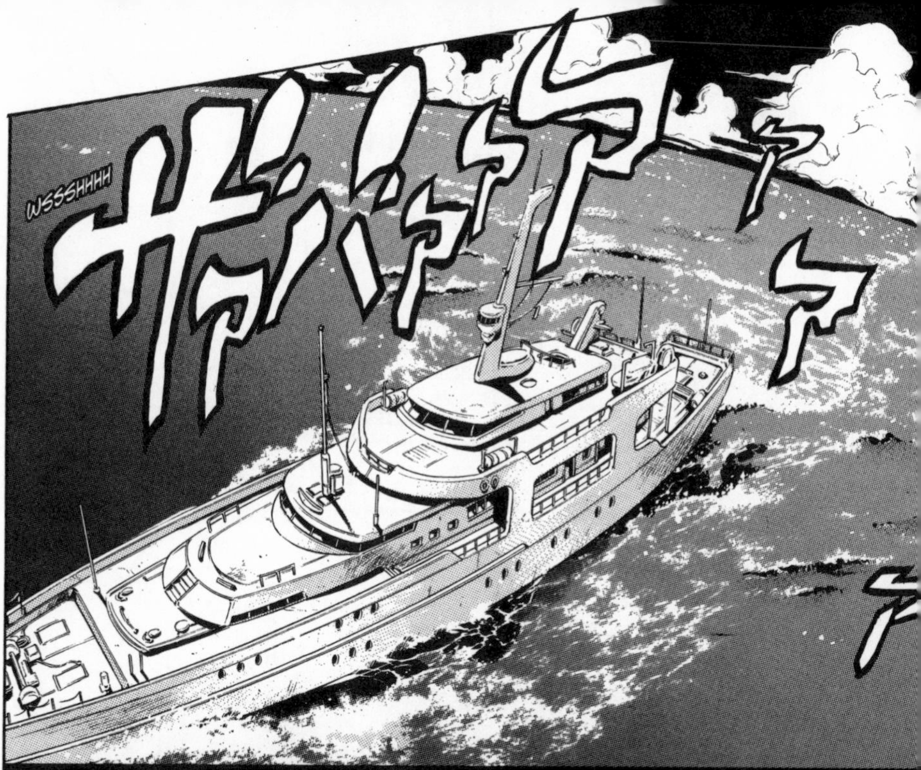
WSSSHHHH

CHAPTER 46

CHILI PEPPER, PART 5

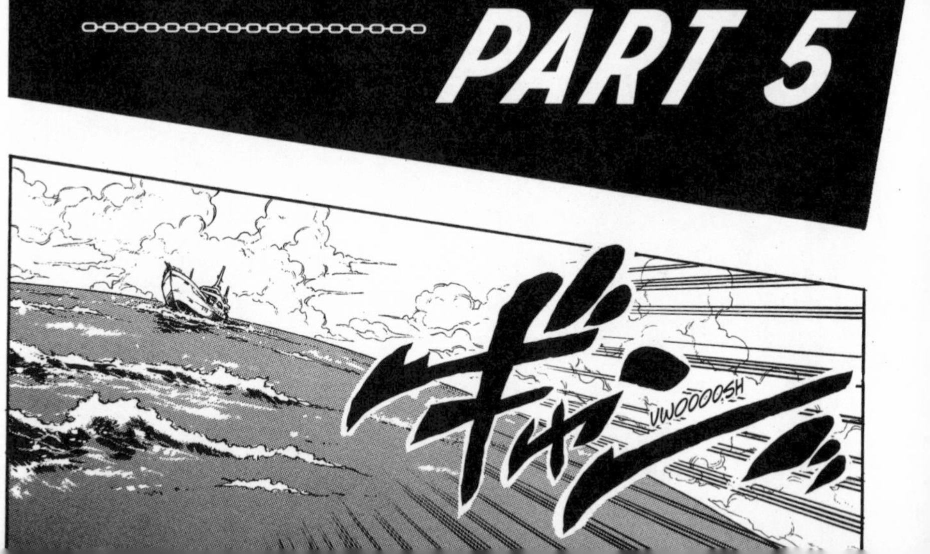
VWOOOOSH

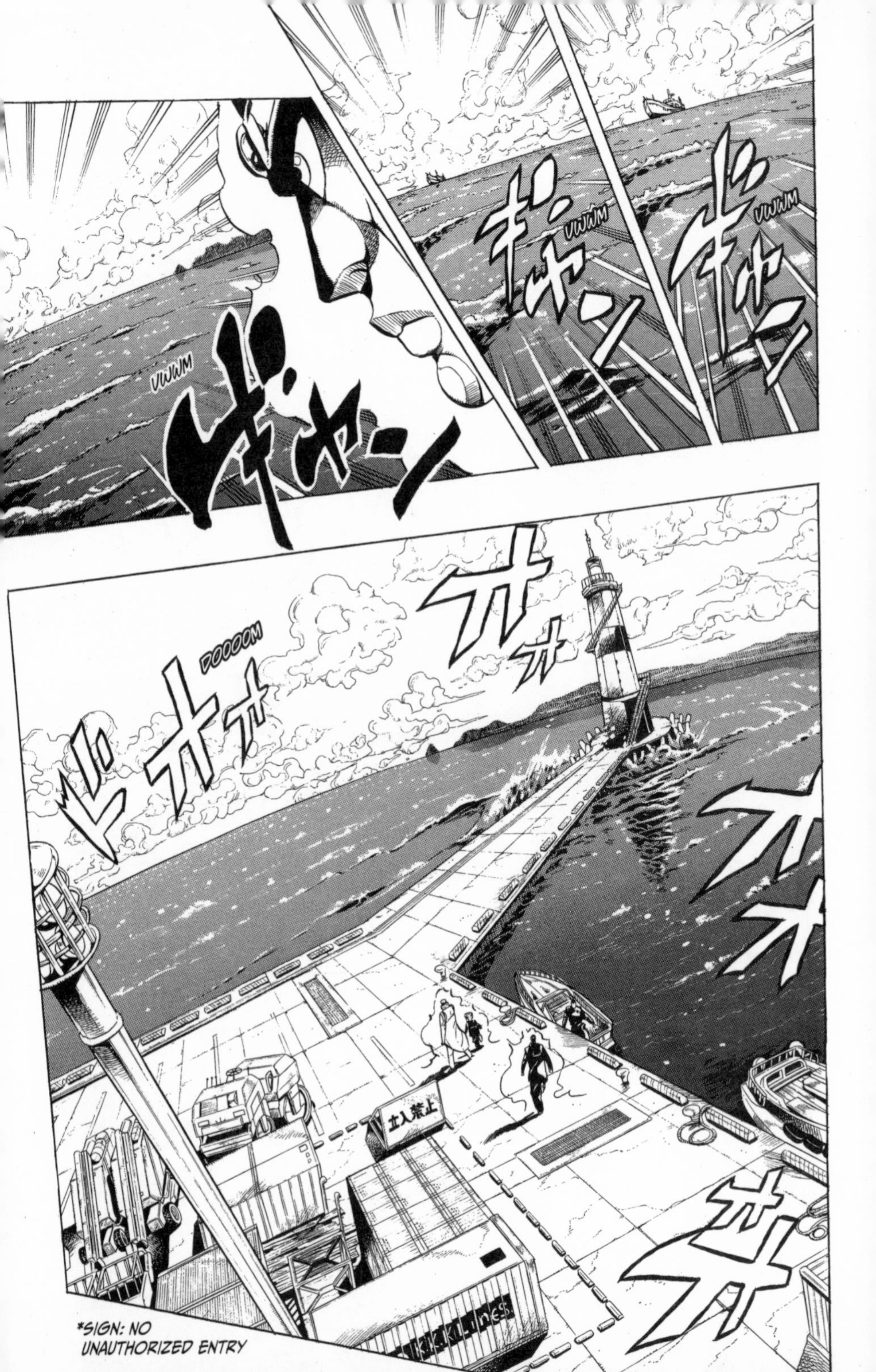
VWWM
VWWM
VWWM
DOOOOM
立入禁止

*SIGN: NO UNAUTHORIZED ENTRY

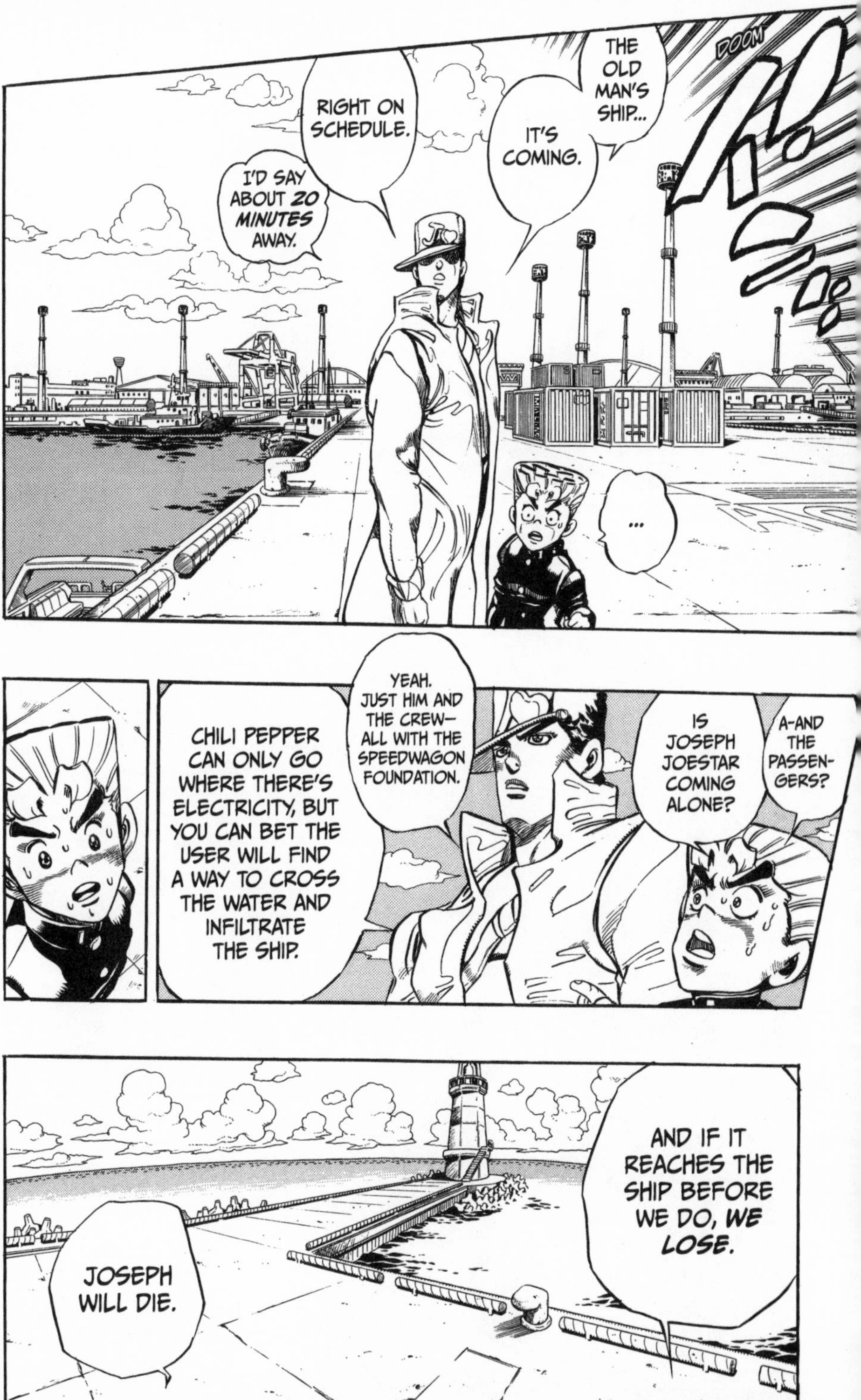
DOOM
THE OLD MAN'S SHIP...
IT'S COMING.
RIGHT ON SCHEDULE.
I'D SAY ABOUT 20 MINUTES AWAY.
...
A-AND THE PASSENGERS?
IS JOSEPH JOESTAR COMING ALONE?
YEAH. JUST HIM AND THE CREW— ALL WITH THE SPEEDWAGON FOUNDATION.
CHILI PEPPER CAN ONLY GO WHERE THERE'S ELECTRICITY, BUT YOU CAN BET THE USER WILL FIND A WAY TO CROSS THE WATER AND INFILTRATE THE SHIP.
AND IF IT REACHES THE SHIP BEFORE WE DO, WE LOSE.
JOSEPH WILL DIE.

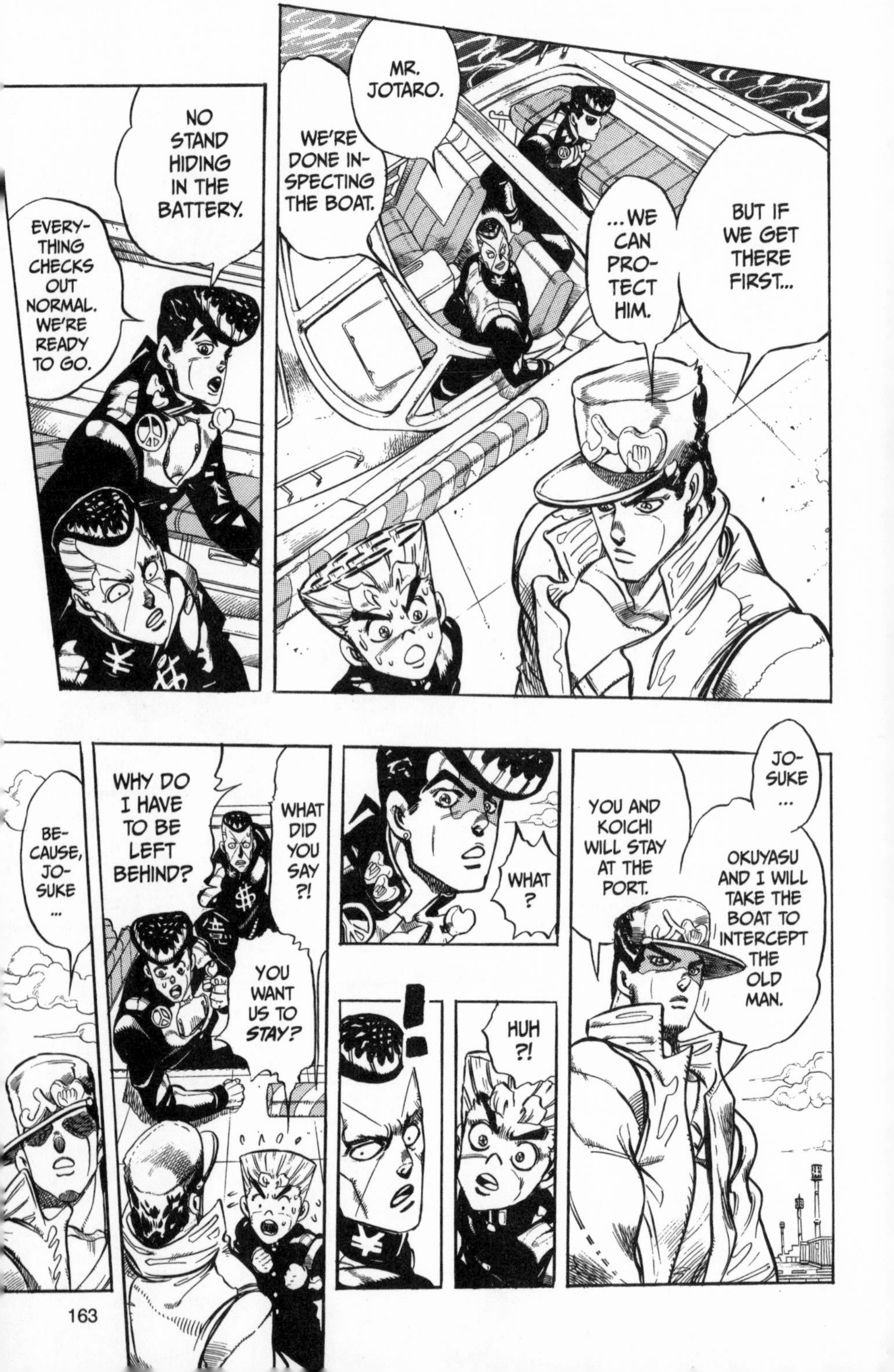
BUT IF WE GET THERE FIRST...
...WE CAN PROTECT HIM.
MR. JOTARO.
WE'RE DONE IN-SPECTING THE BOAT.
NO STAND HIDING IN THE BATTERY.
EVERY-THING CHECKS OUT NORMAL. WE'RE READY TO GO.
JO-SUKE ...
OKUYASU AND I WILL TAKE THE BOAT TO INTERCEPT THE OLD MAN.
YOU AND KOICHI WILL STAY AT THE PORT.
WHAT ?
HUH ?!
!!
WHAT DID YOU SAY ?!
WHY DO I HAVE TO BE LEFT BEHIND?
YOU WANT US TO *STAY?*
BE-CAUSE, JO-SUKE ...

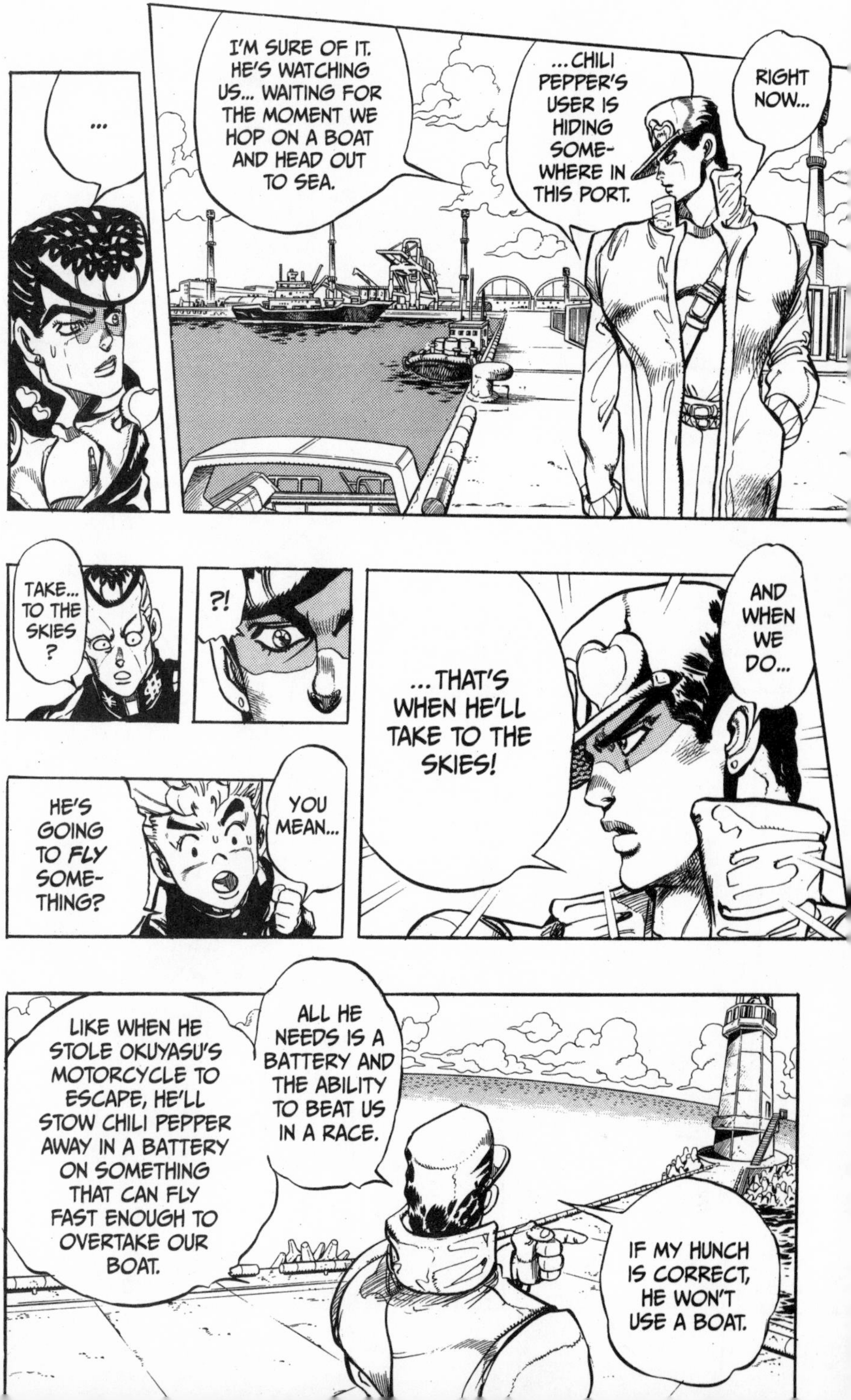
RIGHT NOW...
...CHILI PEPPER'S USER IS HIDING SOME-WHERE IN THIS PORT.
I'M SURE OF IT. HE'S WATCHING US... WAITING FOR THE MOMENT WE HOP ON A BOAT AND HEAD OUT TO SEA.
...
AND WHEN WE DO...
...THAT'S WHEN HE'LL TAKE TO THE SKIES!
?!
TAKE... TO THE SKIES ?
YOU MEAN...
HE'S GOING TO *FLY* SOME-THING?
IF MY HUNCH IS CORRECT, HE WON'T USE A BOAT.
LIKE WHEN HE STOLE OKUYASU'S MOTORCYCLE TO ESCAPE, HE'LL STOW CHILI PEPPER AWAY IN A BATTERY ON SOMETHING THAT CAN FLY FAST ENOUGH TO OVERTAKE OUR BOAT.
ALL HE NEEDS IS A BATTERY AND THE ABILITY TO BEAT US IN A RACE.

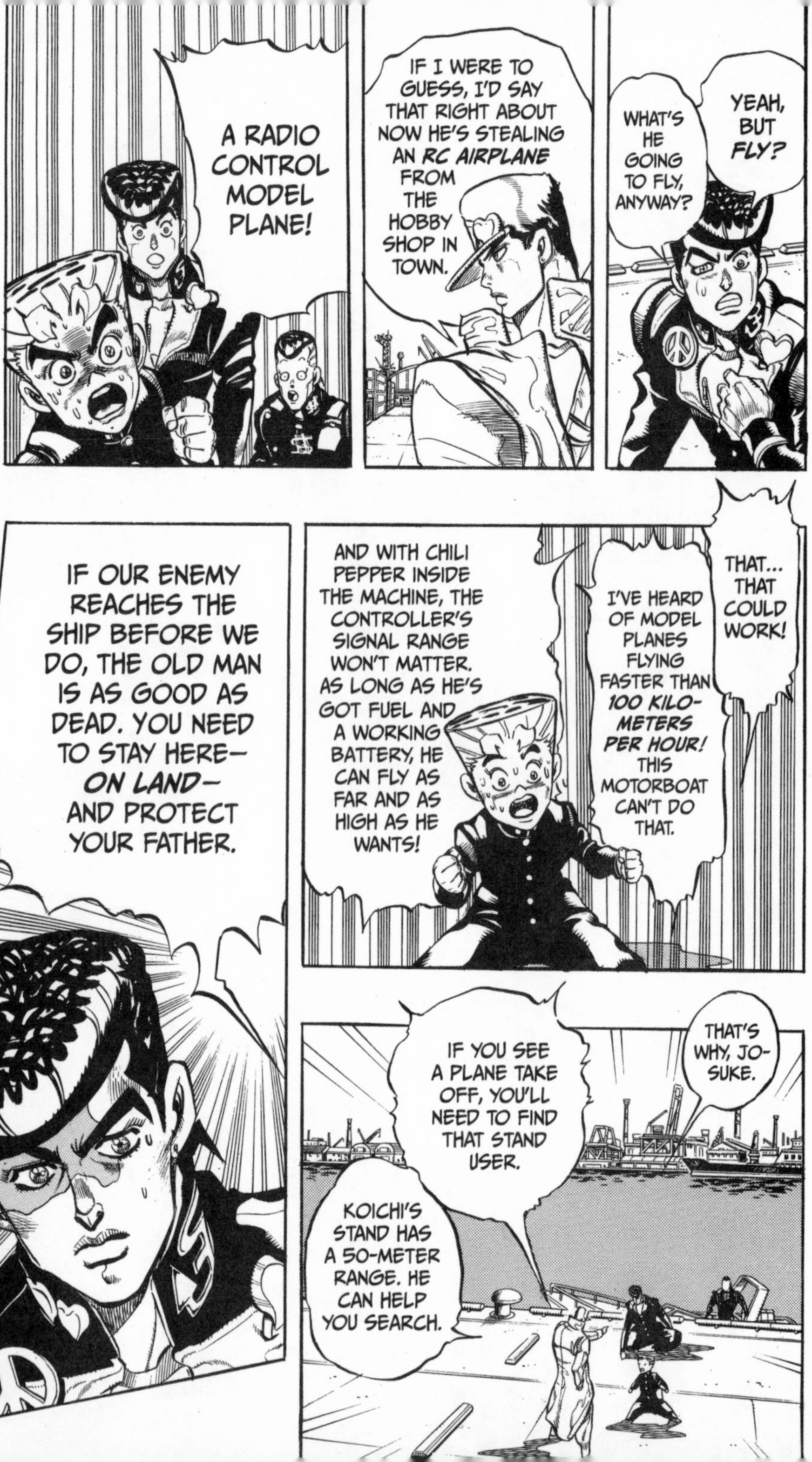
YEAH, BUT FLY?
WHAT'S HE GOING TO FLY, ANYWAY?
IF I WERE TO GUESS, I'D SAY THAT RIGHT ABOUT NOW HE'S STEALING AN RC AIRPLANE FROM THE HOBBY SHOP IN TOWN.
A RADIO CONTROL MODEL PLANE!
THAT... THAT COULD WORK!
I'VE HEARD OF MODEL PLANES FLYING FASTER THAN 100 KILOMETERS PER HOUR! THIS MOTORBOAT CAN'T DO THAT.
AND WITH CHILI PEPPER INSIDE THE MACHINE, THE CONTROLLER'S SIGNAL RANGE WON'T MATTER. AS LONG AS HE'S GOT FUEL AND A WORKING BATTERY, HE CAN FLY AS FAR AND AS HIGH AS HE WANTS!
THAT'S WHY, JO-SUKE.
IF YOU SEE A PLANE TAKE OFF, YOU'LL NEED TO FIND THAT STAND USER.
KOICHI'S STAND HAS A 50-METER RANGE. HE CAN HELP YOU SEARCH.
IF OUR ENEMY REACHES THE SHIP BEFORE WE DO, THE OLD MAN IS AS GOOD AS DEAD. YOU NEED TO STAY HERE—ON LAND—AND PROTECT YOUR FATHER.

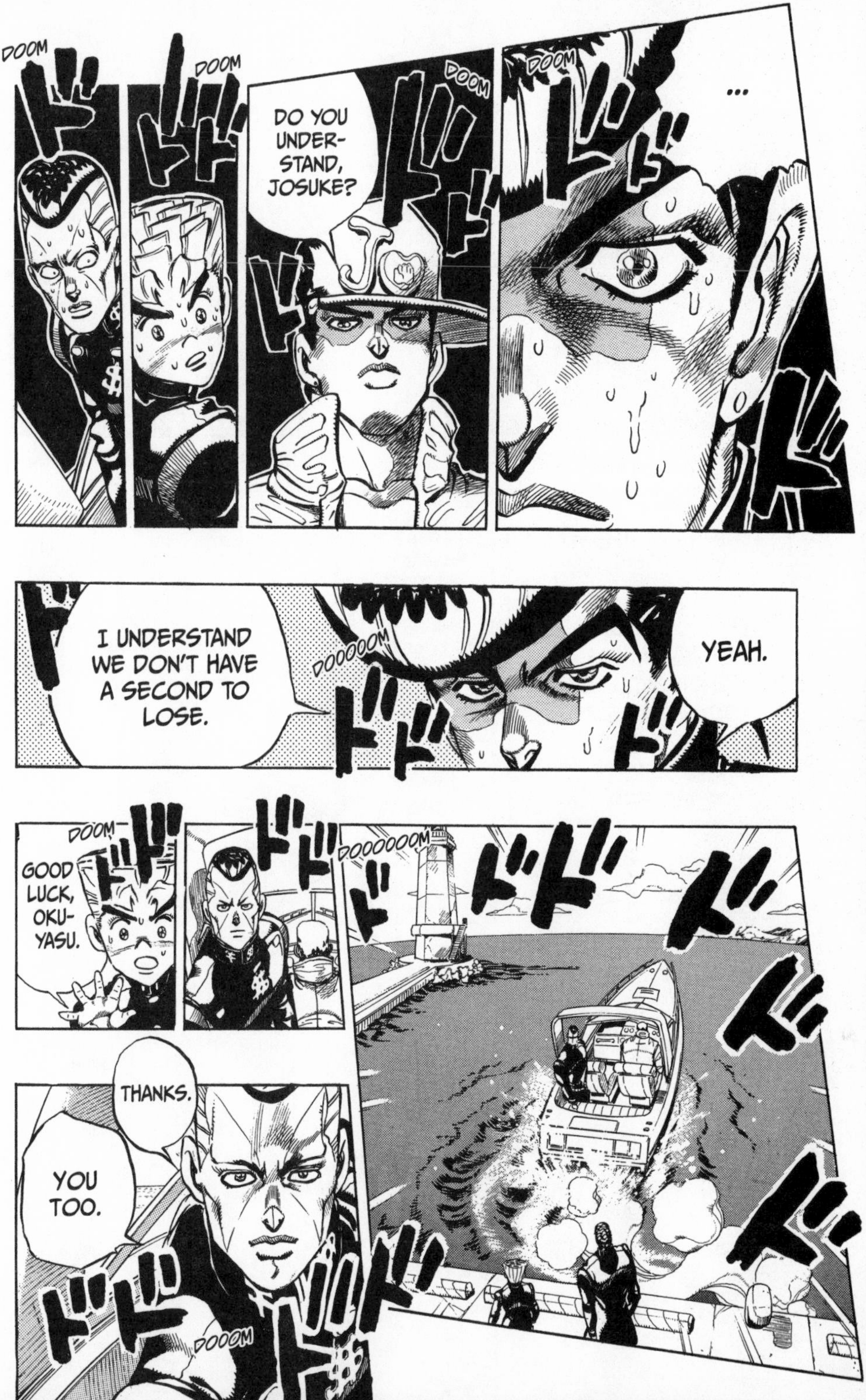
DOOM
...
DOOM
DO YOU UNDER-STAND, JOSUKE?
DOOM
DOOM
YEAH.
DOOOOOM
I UNDERSTAND WE DON'T HAVE A SECOND TO LOSE.
DOOOOOOM
DOOM
GOOD LUCK, OKU-YASU.
THANKS.
YOU TOO.
DOOOM

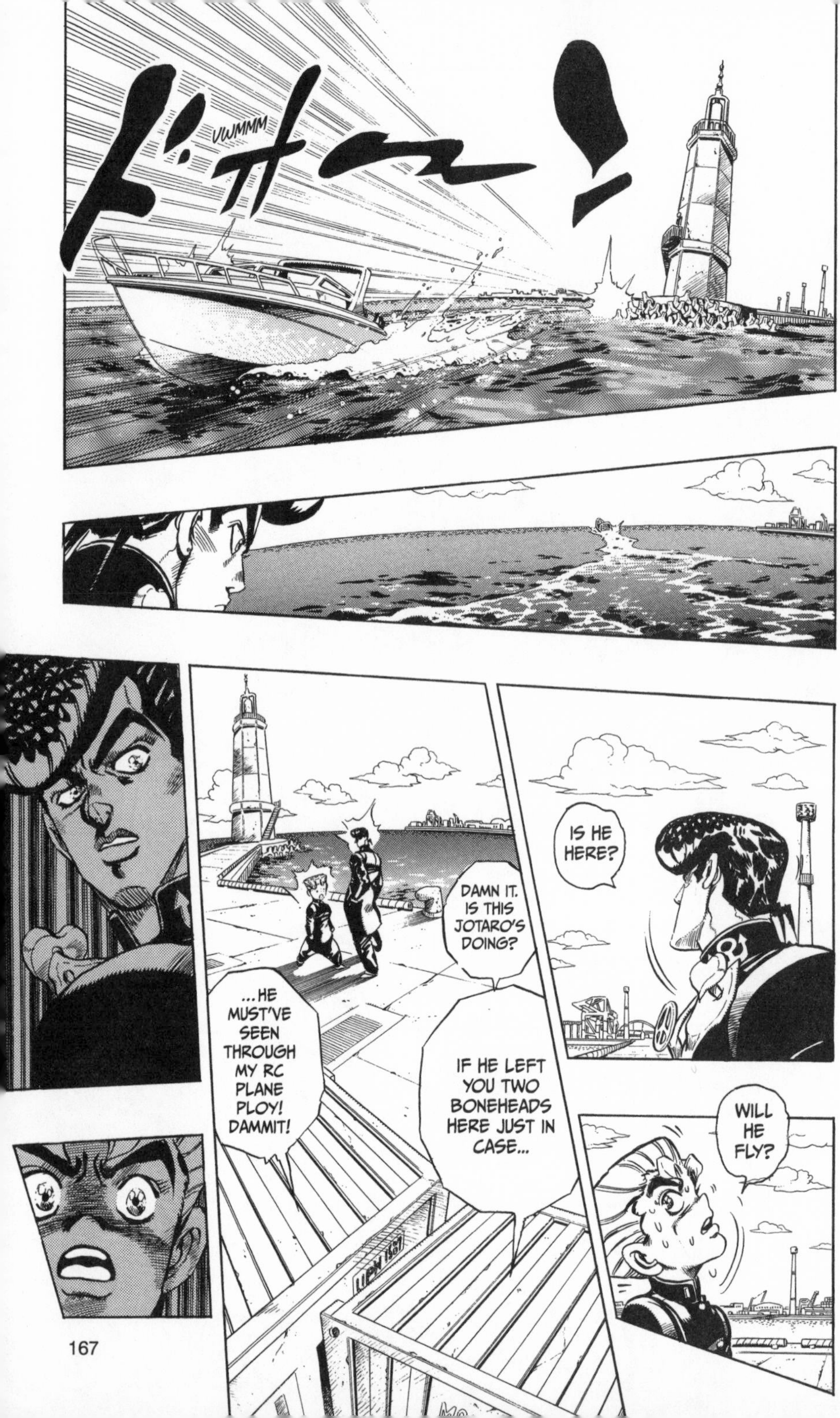
VWMMM
IS HE HERE?
WILL HE FLY?
DAMN IT. IS THIS JOTARO'S DOING?
IF HE LEFT YOU TWO BONEHEADS HERE JUST IN CASE...
...HE MUST'VE SEEN THROUGH MY RC PLANE PLOY! DAMMIT!

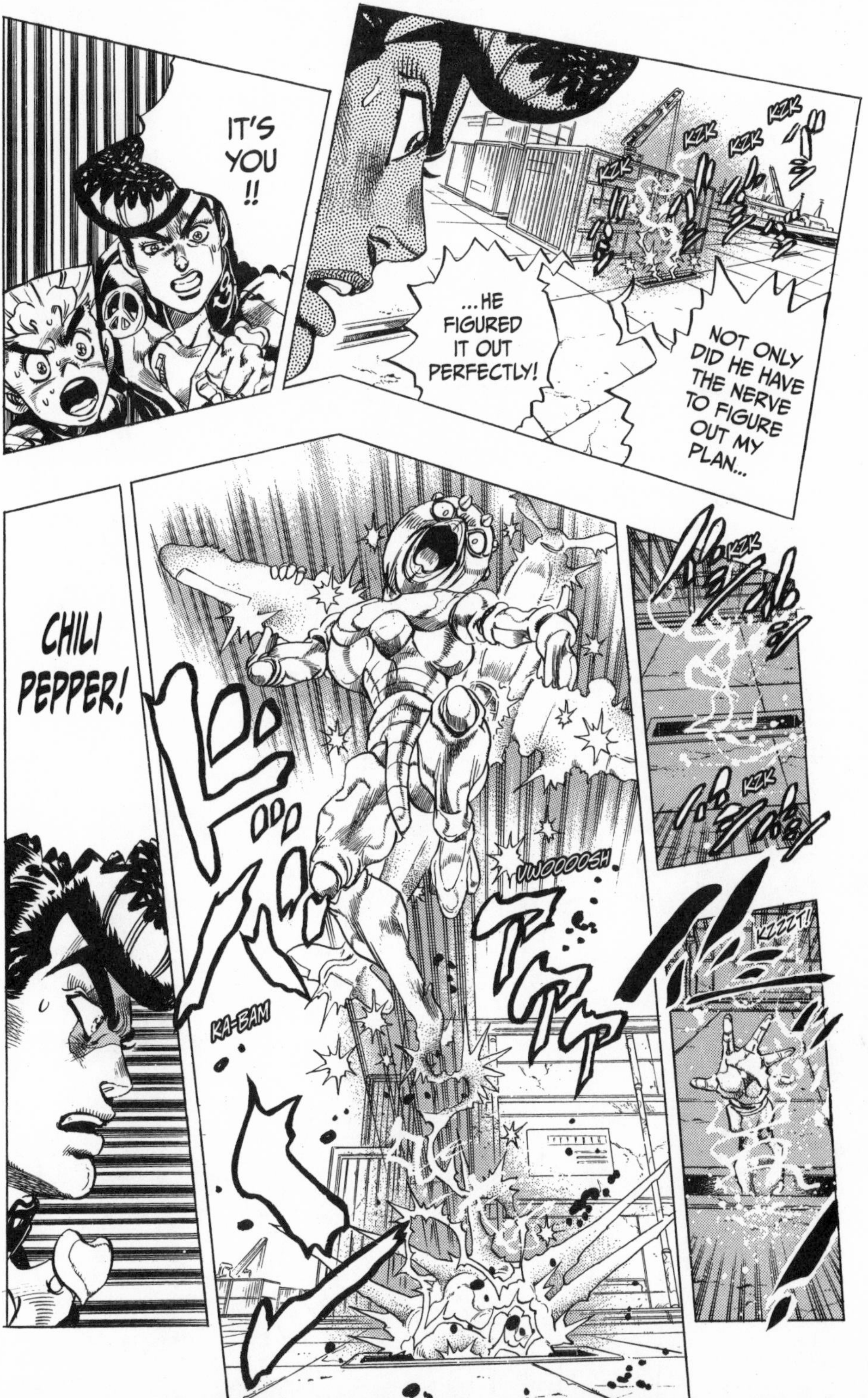
KZK
KZK
KZK
KZK
NOT ONLY DID HE HAVE THE NERVE TO FIGURE OUT MY PLAN...
...HE FIGURED IT OUT PERFECTLY!
IT'S YOU!!
KZK
KZK
KZZZT!
UWOOOOSH
KA-BAM
CHILI PEPPER!

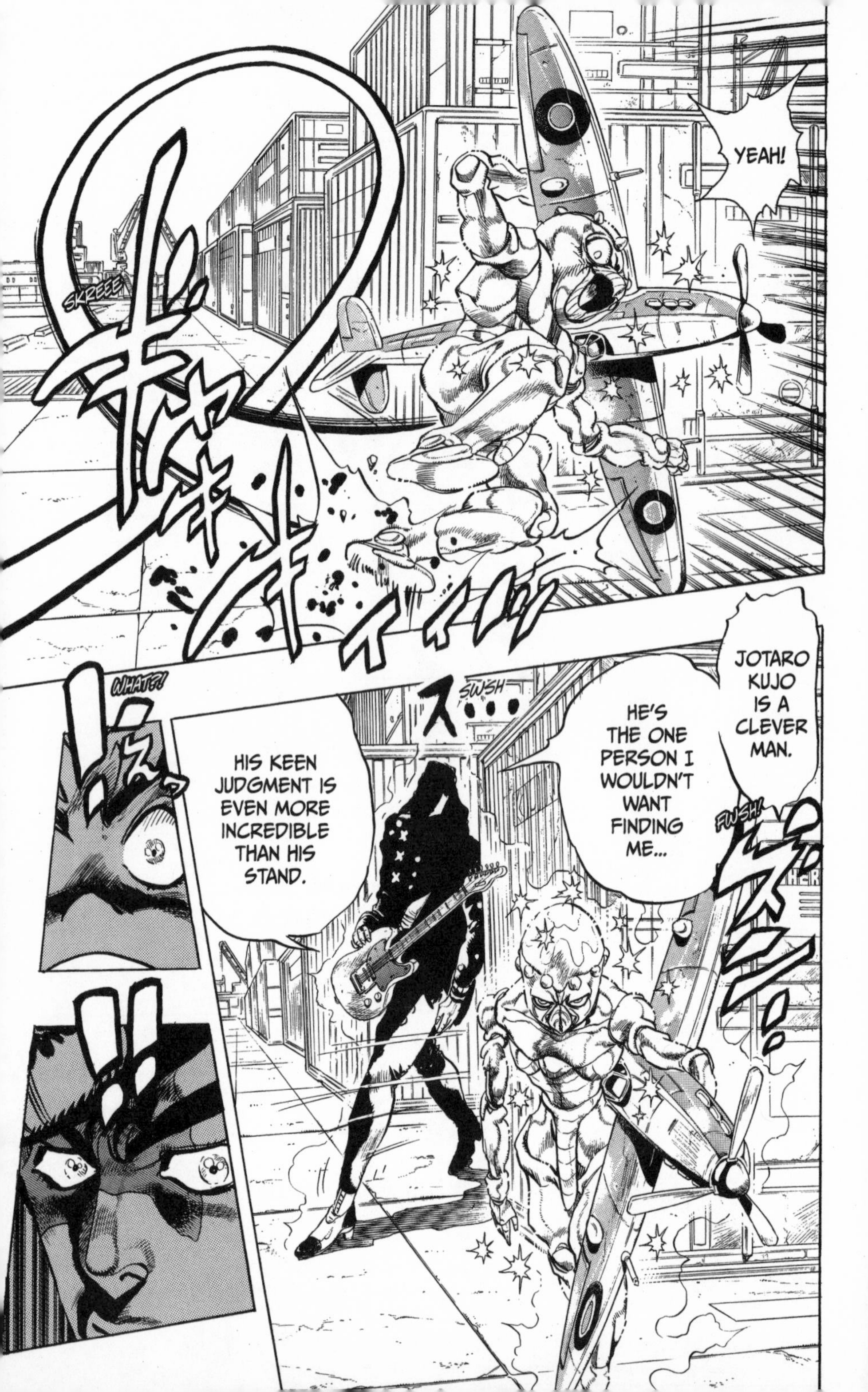
YEAH!
SKREEE
JOTARO KUJO IS A CLEVER MAN.
HE'S THE ONE PERSON I WOULDN'T WANT FINDING ME...
SWSH
HIS KEEN JUDGMENT IS EVEN MORE INCREDIBLE THAN HIS STAND.
FWSH!
WHAT?!

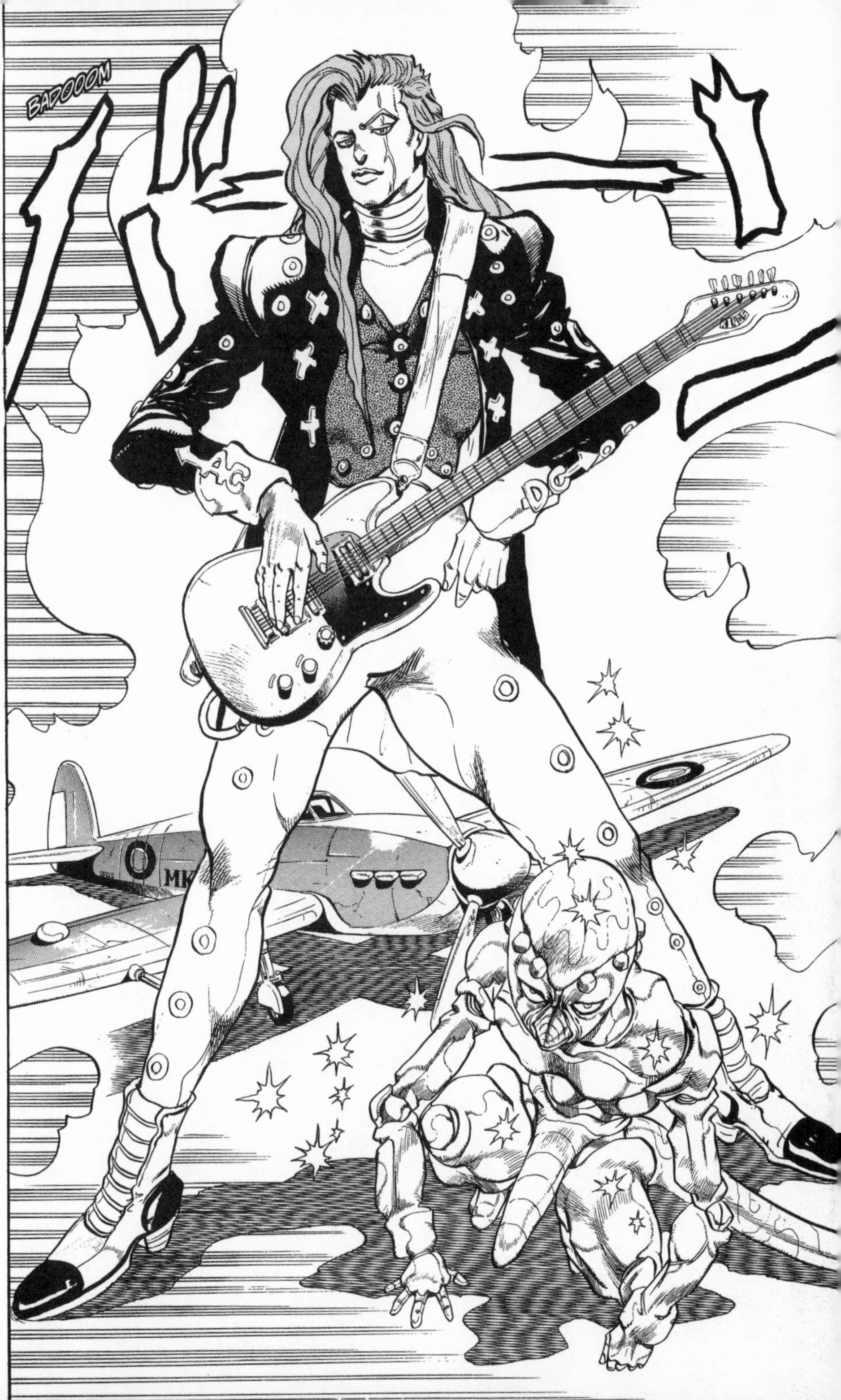
BADOOOM
AC
MK

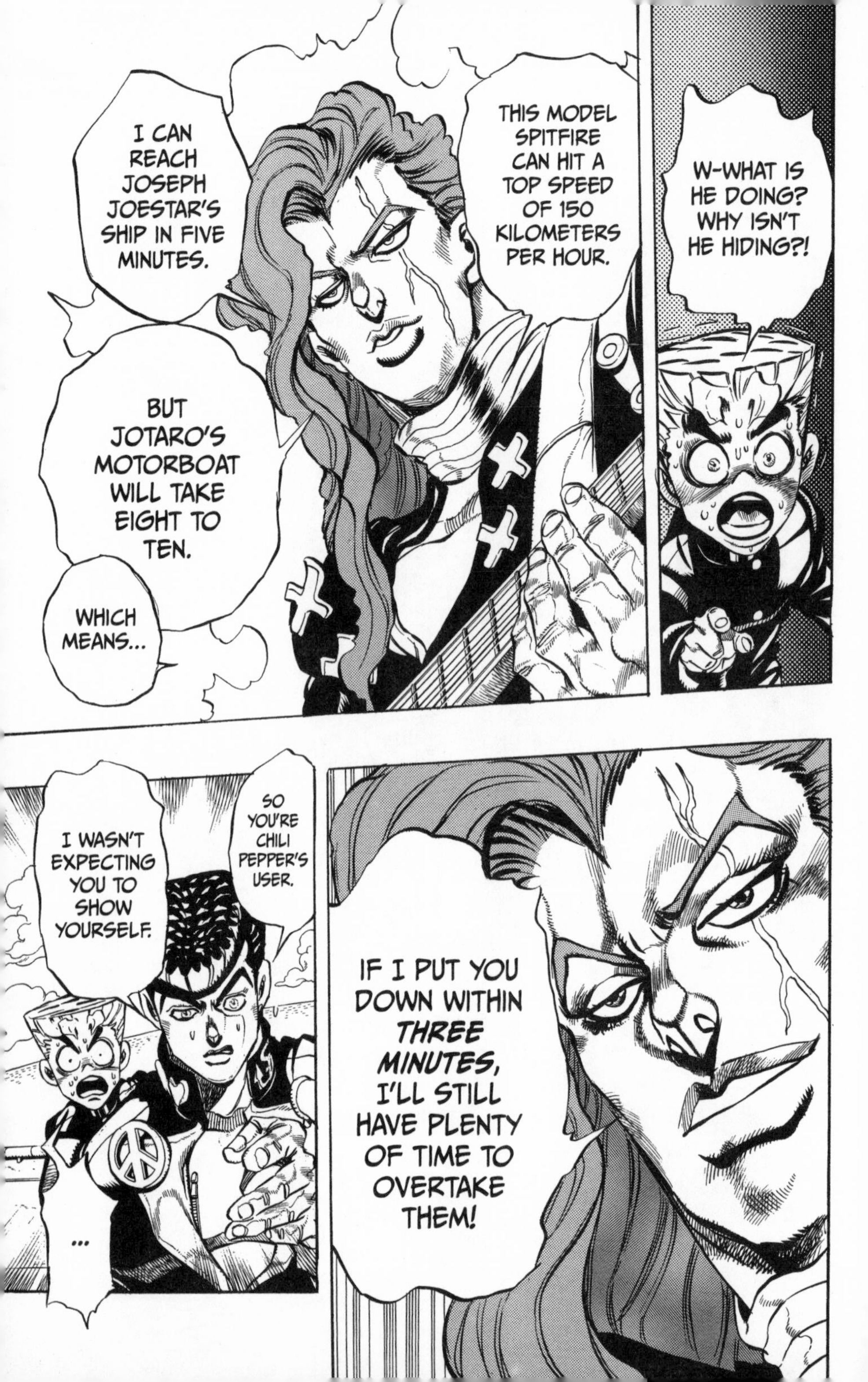
W-WHAT IS HE DOING? WHY ISN'T HE HIDING?!
THIS MODEL SPITFIRE CAN HIT A TOP SPEED OF 150 KILOMETERS PER HOUR.
I CAN REACH JOSEPH JOESTAR'S SHIP IN FIVE MINUTES.
BUT JOTARO'S MOTORBOAT WILL TAKE EIGHT TO TEN.
WHICH MEANS...
IF I PUT YOU DOWN WITHIN *THREE MINUTES*, I'LL STILL HAVE PLENTY OF TIME TO OVERTAKE THEM!
SO YOU'RE CHILI PEPPER'S USER.
I WASN'T EXPECTING YOU TO SHOW YOURSELF.
...

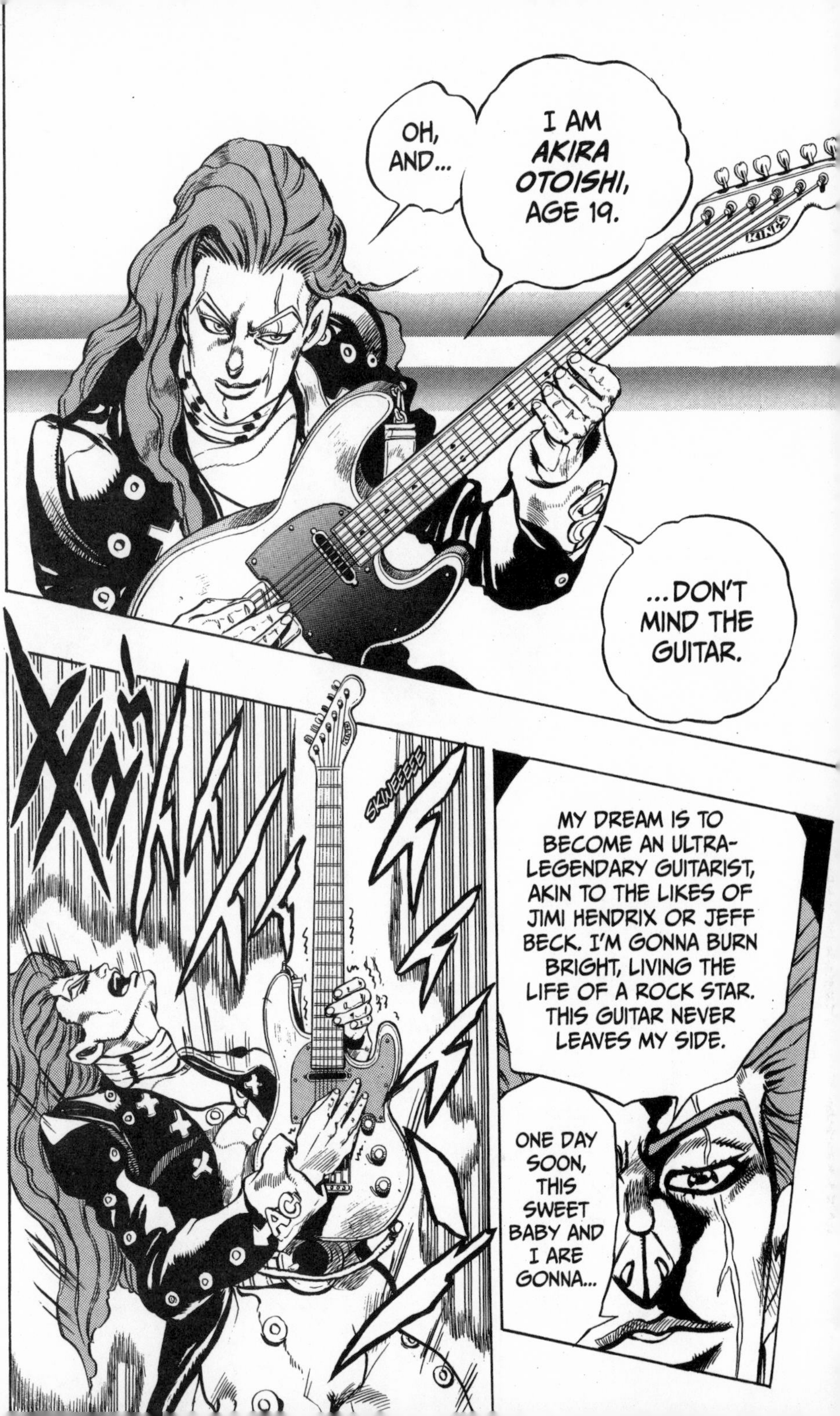
I AM AKIRA OTOISHI, AGE 19.
OH, AND...
...DON'T MIND THE GUITAR.
MY DREAM IS TO BECOME AN ULTRA-LEGENDARY GUITARIST, AKIN TO THE LIKES OF JIMI HENDRIX OR JEFF BECK. I'M GONNA BURN BRIGHT, LIVING THE LIFE OF A ROCK STAR. THIS GUITAR NEVER LEAVES MY SIDE.
ONE DAY SOON, THIS SWEET BABY AND I ARE GONNA...
SKWEEEEE

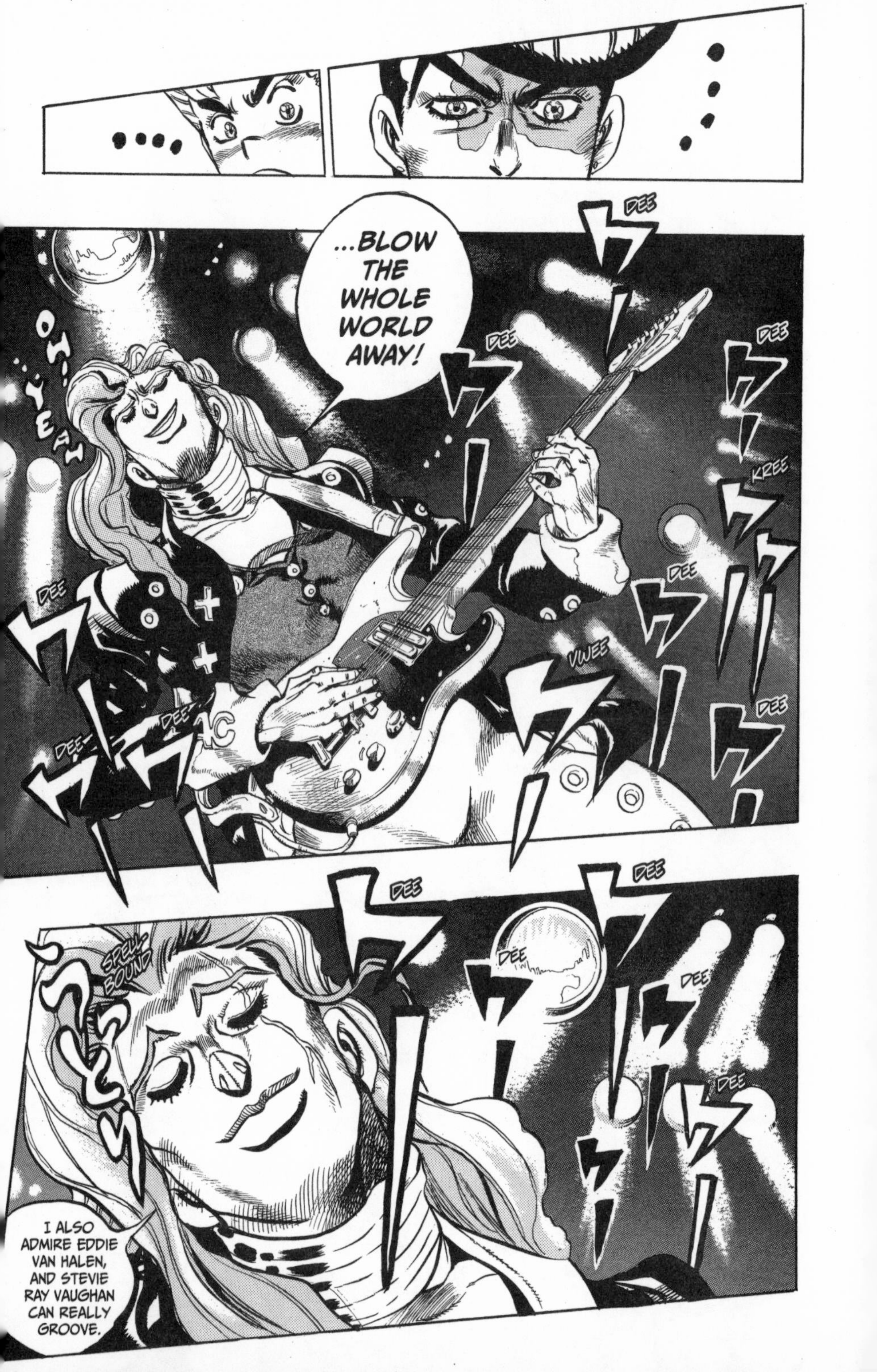
....
....
DEE
DEE
...BLOW THE WHOLE WORLD AWAY!
DEE
KREE
DEE
DEE
VWEE
OH... YEAH
DEE
DEE
DEE
DEE
DEE
DEE
DEE
DEE
SPELLBOUND
I ALSO ADMIRE EDDIE VAN HALEN, AND STEVIE RAY VAUGHAN CAN REALLY GROOVE.

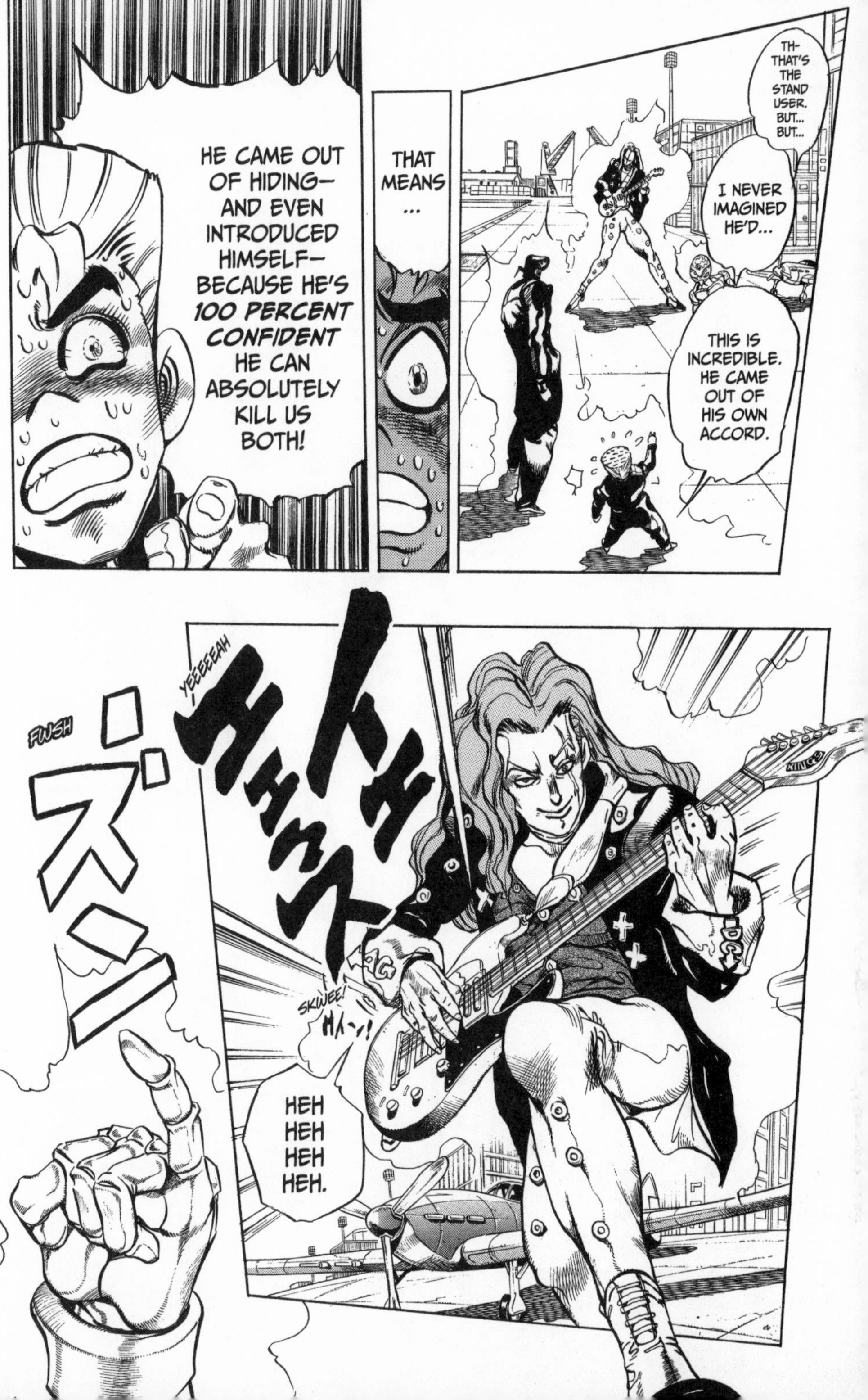
TH- THAT'S THE STAND USER. BUT... BUT...
I NEVER IMAGINED HE'D...
THIS IS INCREDIBLE. HE CAME OUT OF HIS OWN ACCORD.
THAT MEANS ...
HE CAME OUT OF HIDING— AND EVEN INTRODUCED HIMSELF— BECAUSE HE'S *100 PERCENT CONFIDENT* HE CAN ABSOLUTELY KILL US BOTH!
YEEEEEEAH
FWSH
SKWEE!
HEH HEH HEH HEH.

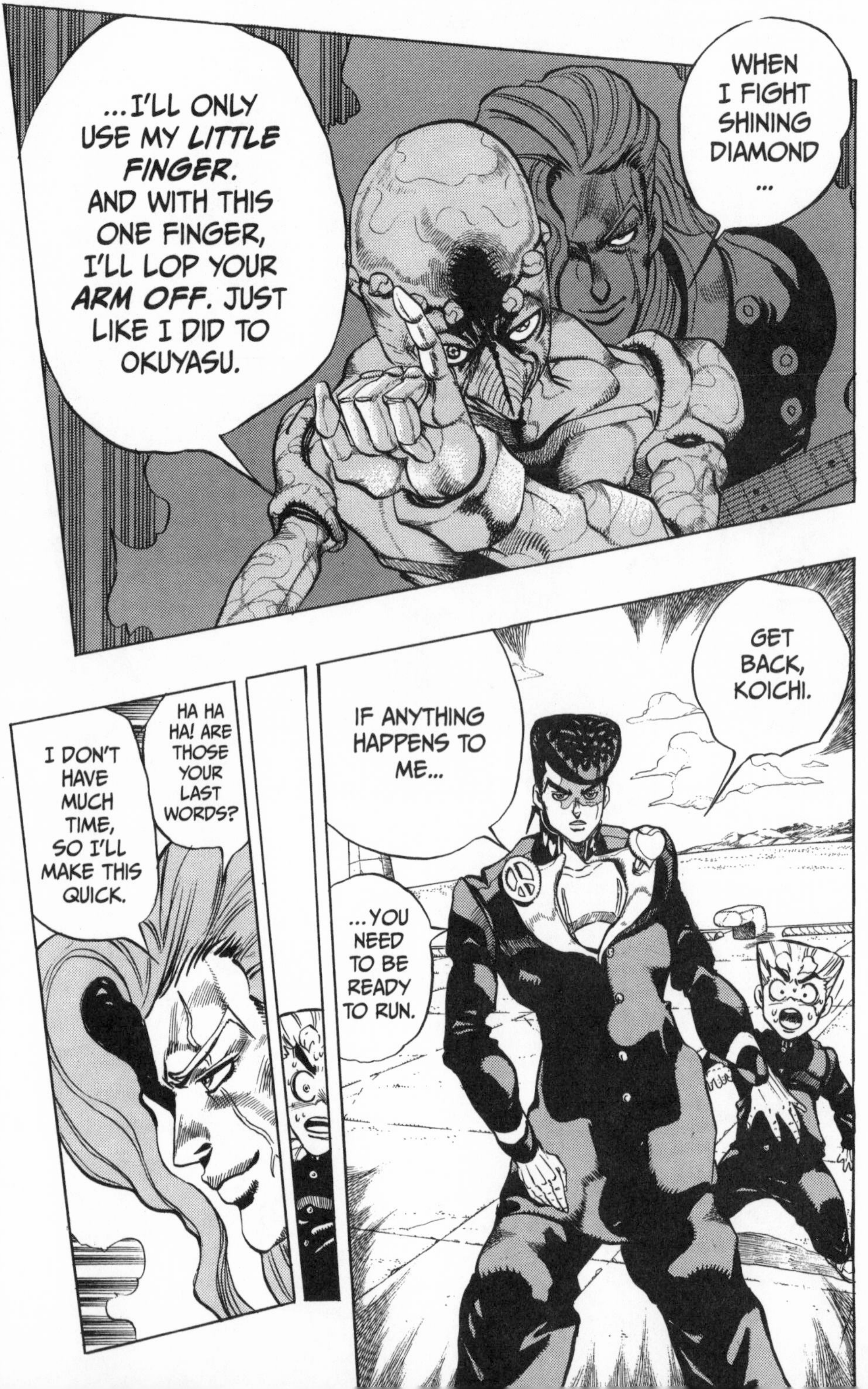
WHEN I FIGHT SHINING DIAMOND ...
...I'LL ONLY USE MY LITTLE FINGER. AND WITH THIS ONE FINGER, I'LL LOP YOUR ARM OFF. JUST LIKE I DID TO OKUYASU.
GET BACK, KOICHI.
IF ANYTHING HAPPENS TO ME...
...YOU NEED TO BE READY TO RUN.
HA HA HA! ARE THOSE YOUR LAST WORDS?
I DON'T HAVE MUCH TIME, SO I'LL MAKE THIS QUICK.

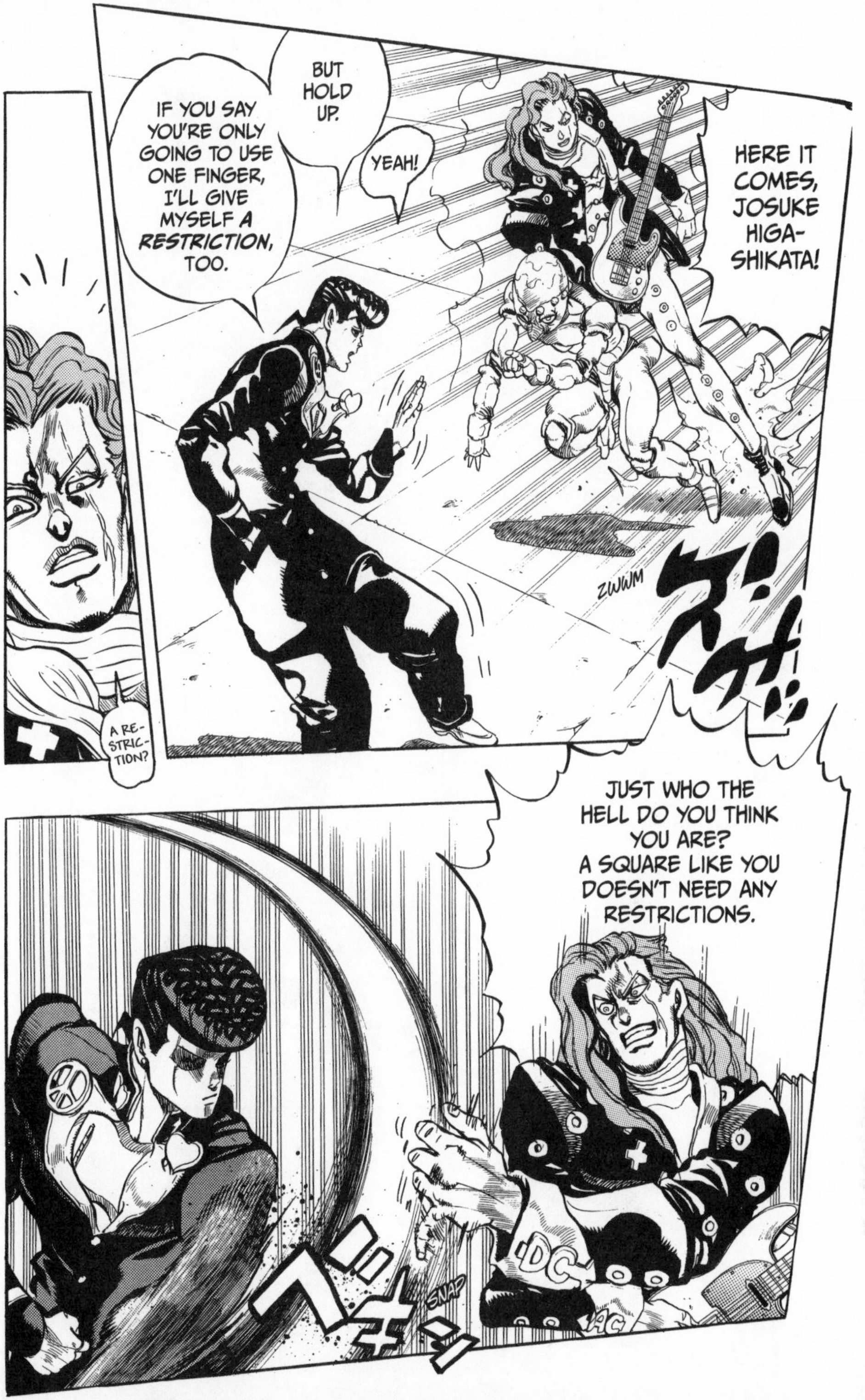
HERE IT COMES, JOSUKE HIGA-SHIKATA!
YEAH!
BUT HOLD UP.
IF YOU SAY YOU'RE ONLY GOING TO USE ONE FINGER, I'LL GIVE MYSELF A *RESTRICTION*, TOO.
ZWWM
A RE-STRIC-TION?
JUST WHO THE HELL DO YOU THINK YOU ARE? A SQUARE LIKE YOU DOESN'T NEED ANY RESTRICTIONS.
SNAP

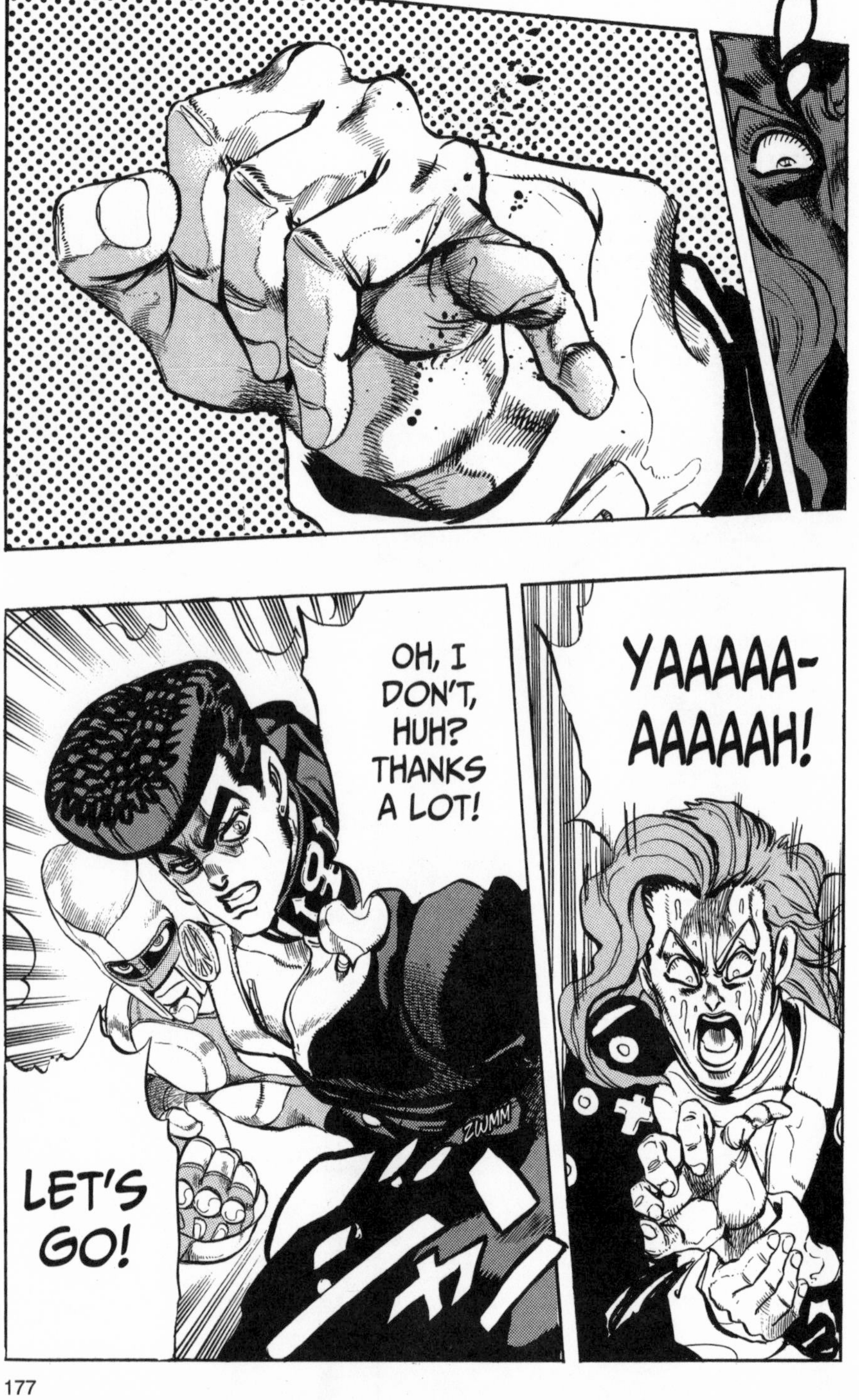
YAAAAA-
AAAAAH!
OH, I DON'T, HUH? THANKS A LOT!
ZWMM
LET'S GO!

THE SPEEDWAGON FOUNDATION

ROBERT E.O. SPEEDWAGON (1863–1939) WAS A SOLITARY ENGLISHMAN WHO CROSSED THE ATLANTIC OCEAN TO AMERICA, WHERE HE STRUCK OIL AND BECAME ONE OF THE RICHEST MEN IN THE WORLD. HE DEVOTED THE ENTIRETY OF HIS VAST RICHES TO THE ADVANCEMENT OF MEDICAL RESEARCH AND ECOLOGICAL PRESERVATION. TO THAT PURPOSE, HE CREATED THE SPEEDWAGON FOUNDATION, WHICH CONTINUES ITS MISSION TO THIS DAY.

WITHIN THE FOUNDATION, SPEEDWAGON ESTABLISHED A DEPARTMENT SPECIALIZING IN SUPERNATURAL PHENOMENA. THAT DEPARTMENT CURRENTLY SUPPLIES JOSEPH AND JOTARO WITH INFORMATION, SUPPLIES AND MANPOWER, IN ACCORDANCE WITH THE LATE FOUNDER'S INSTRUCTIONS.

THE SPEEDWAGON FOUNDATION IS HEADQUARTERED IN DALLAS, TEXAS, BUT A BRANCH OFFICE IS LOCATED IN TOKYO'S MEGURO WARD.

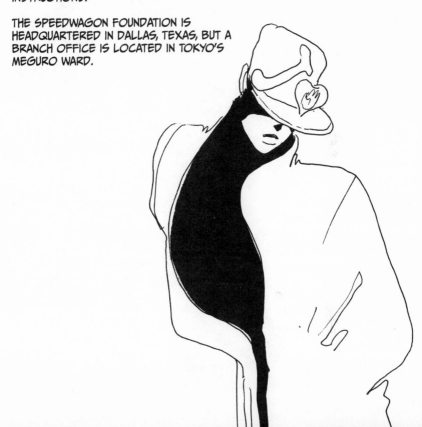

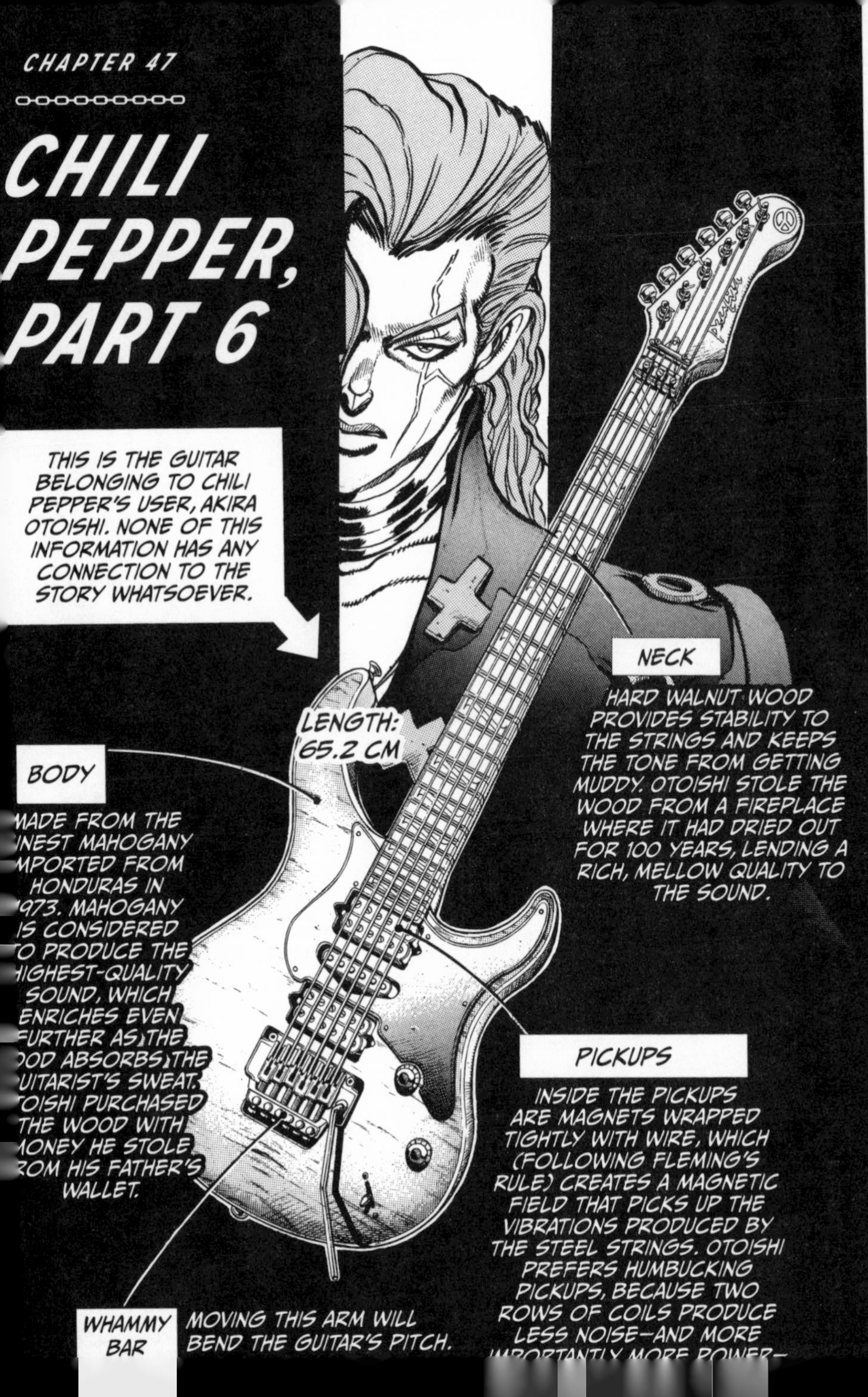
CHAPTER 47
CHILI PEPPER, PART 6
THIS IS THE GUITAR BELONGING TO CHILI PEPPER'S USER, AKIRA OTOISHI. NONE OF THIS INFORMATION HAS ANY CONNECTION TO THE STORY WHATSOEVER.
NECK
HARD WALNUT WOOD PROVIDES STABILITY TO THE STRINGS AND KEEPS THE TONE FROM GETTING MUDDY. OTOISHI STOLE THE WOOD FROM A FIREPLACE WHERE IT HAD DRIED OUT FOR 100 YEARS, LENDING A RICH, MELLOW QUALITY TO THE SOUND.
LENGTH: 65.2 CM
BODY
MADE FROM THE INEST MAHOGANY MPORTED FROM HONDURAS IN 973. MAHOGANY IS CONSIDERED O PRODUCE THE IGHEST-QUALITY SOUND, WHICH ENRICHES EVEN URTHER AS THE OOD ABSORBS THE UITARIST'S SWEAT. TOISHI PURCHASED THE WOOD WITH MONEY HE STOLE ROM HIS FATHER'S WALLET.
PICKUPS
INSIDE THE PICKUPS ARE MAGNETS WRAPPED TIGHTLY WITH WIRE, WHICH (FOLLOWING FLEMING'S RULE) CREATES A MAGNETIC FIELD THAT PICKS UP THE VIBRATIONS PRODUCED BY THE STEEL STRINGS. OTOISHI PREFERS HUMBUCKING PICKUPS, BECAUSE TWO ROWS OF COILS PRODUCE LESS NOISE—AND MORE IMPORTANTLY MORE POWER—
WHAMMY BAR
MOVING THIS ARM WILL BEND THE GUITAR'S PITCH.

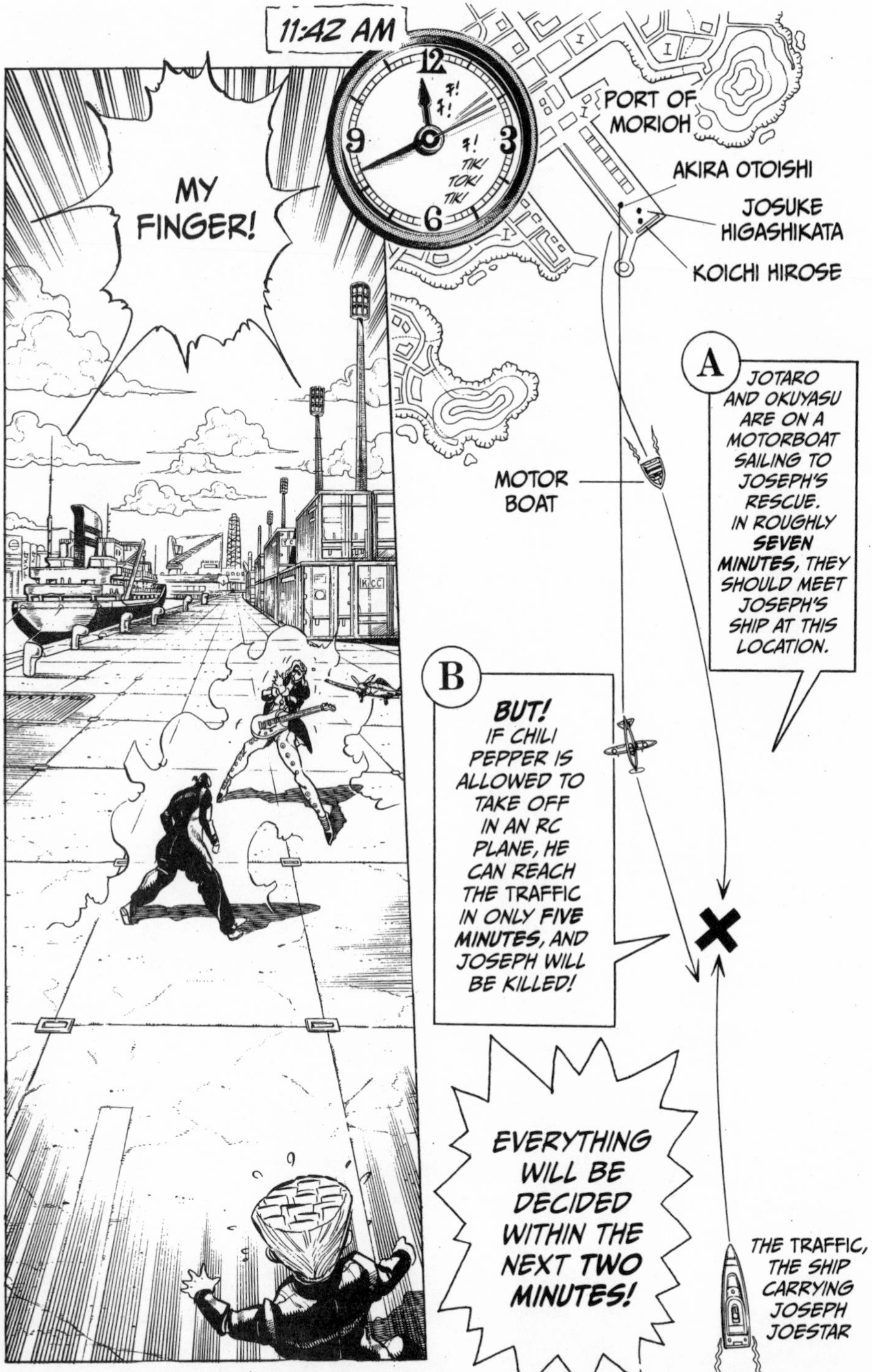
11:42 AM
TIK! TOK! TIK!
PORT OF MORIOH
AKIRA OTOISHI
JOSUKE HIGASHIKATA
KOICHI HIROSE
MOTOR BOAT
A
JOTARO AND OKUYASU ARE ON A MOTORBOAT SAILING TO JOSEPH'S RESCUE. IN ROUGHLY SEVEN MINUTES, THEY SHOULD MEET JOSEPH'S SHIP AT THIS LOCATION.
B
BUT! IF CHILI PEPPER IS ALLOWED TO TAKE OFF IN AN RC PLANE, HE CAN REACH THE TRAFFIC IN ONLY FIVE MINUTES, AND JOSEPH WILL BE KILLED!
EVERYTHING WILL BE DECIDED WITHIN THE NEXT TWO MINUTES!
THE TRAFFIC, THE SHIP CARRYING JOSEPH JOESTAR
MY FINGER!

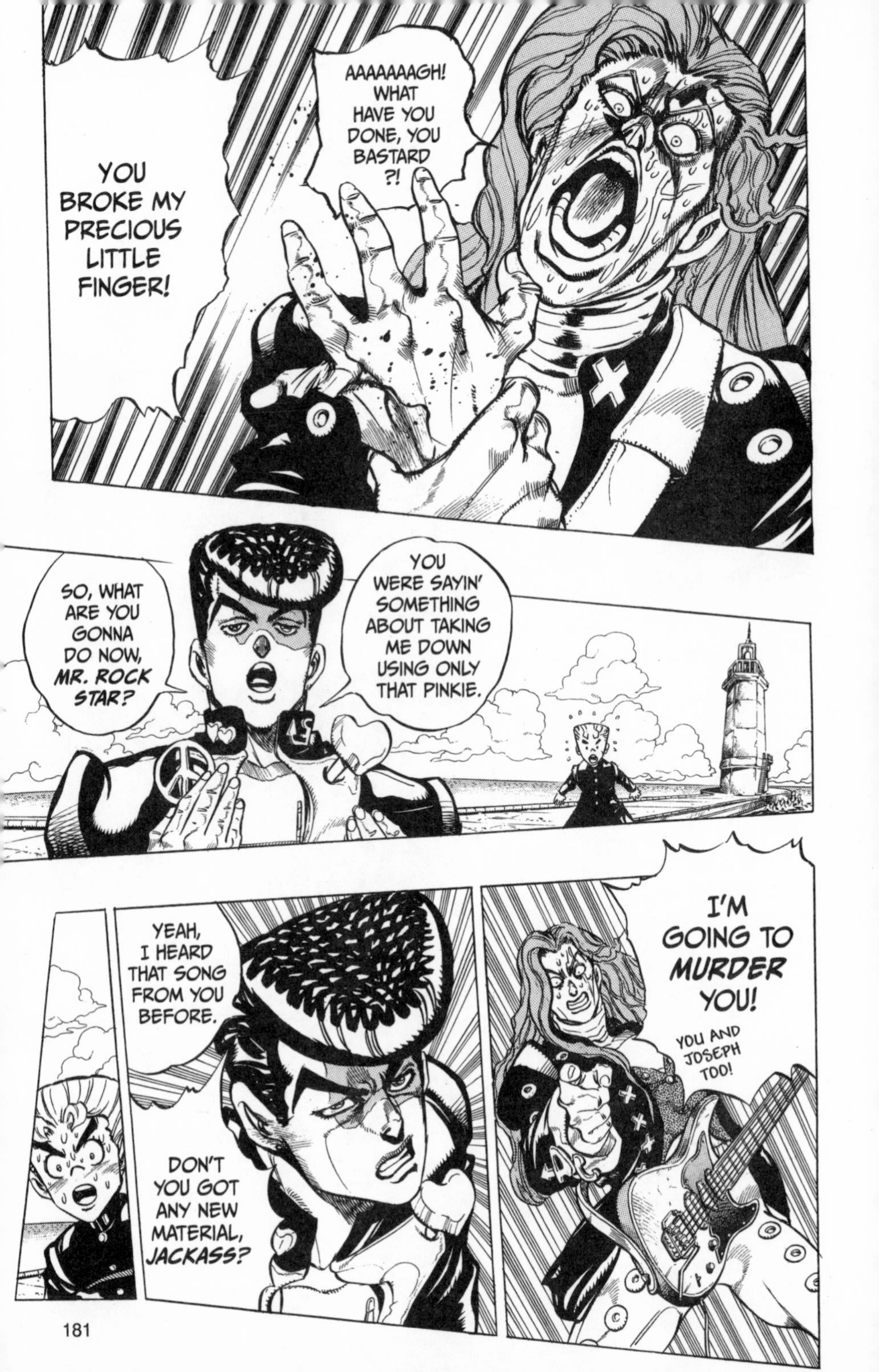
AAAAAAAGH! WHAT HAVE YOU DONE, YOU BASTARD ?!
YOU BROKE MY PRECIOUS LITTLE FINGER!
YOU WERE SAYIN' SOMETHING ABOUT TAKING ME DOWN USING ONLY THAT PINKIE.
SO, WHAT ARE YOU GONNA DO NOW, MR. ROCK STAR?
I'M GOING TO MURDER YOU!
YOU AND JOSEPH TOO!
YEAH, I HEARD THAT SONG FROM YOU BEFORE.
DON'T YOU GOT ANY NEW MATERIAL, JACKASS?

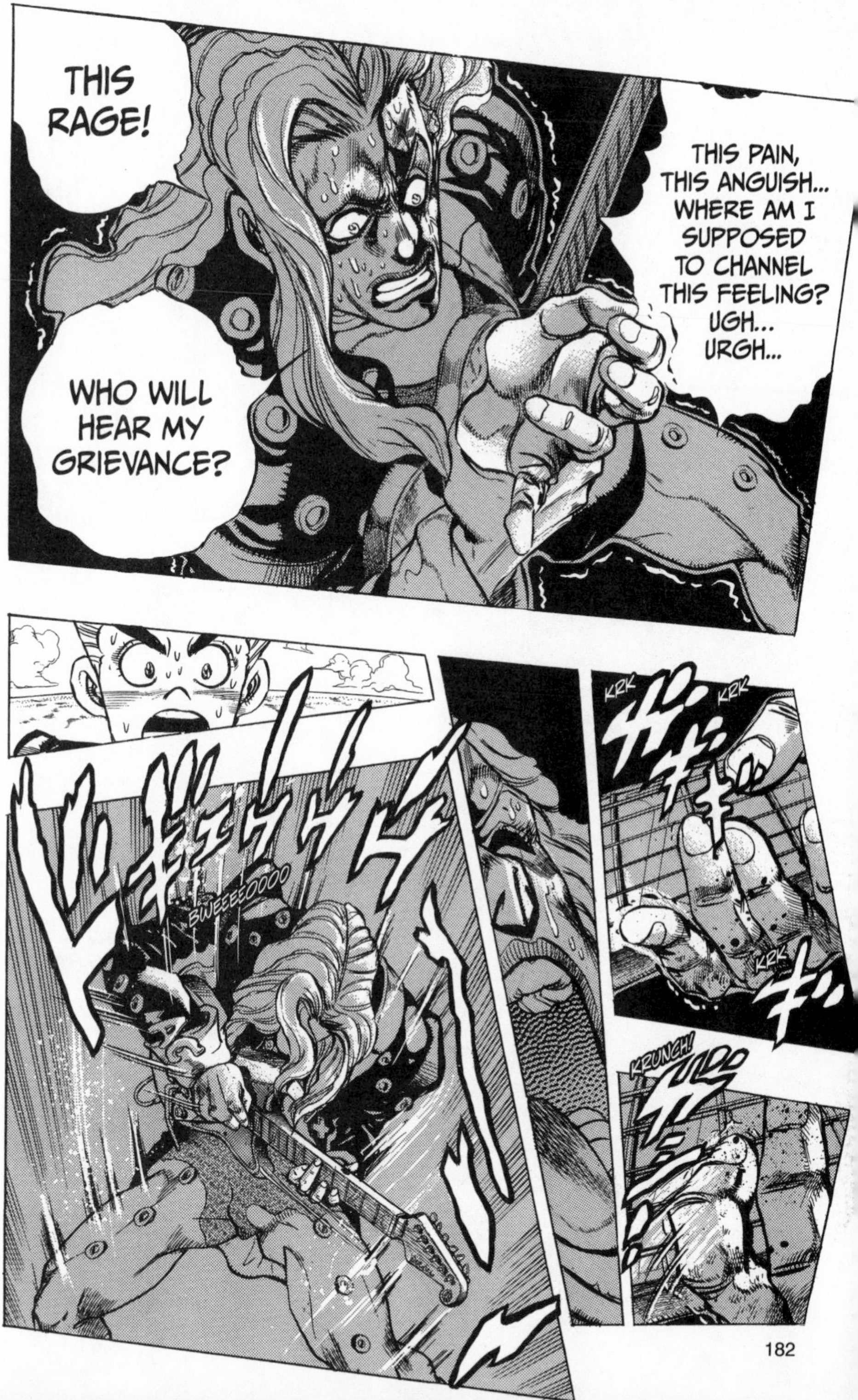

THIS RAGE!
THIS PAIN, THIS ANGUISH... WHERE AM I SUPPOSED TO CHANNEL THIS FEELING? UGH... URGH...
WHO WILL HEAR MY GRIEVANCE?
KRK KRK
KRK
KRUNCH!
BWEEEEOOOO

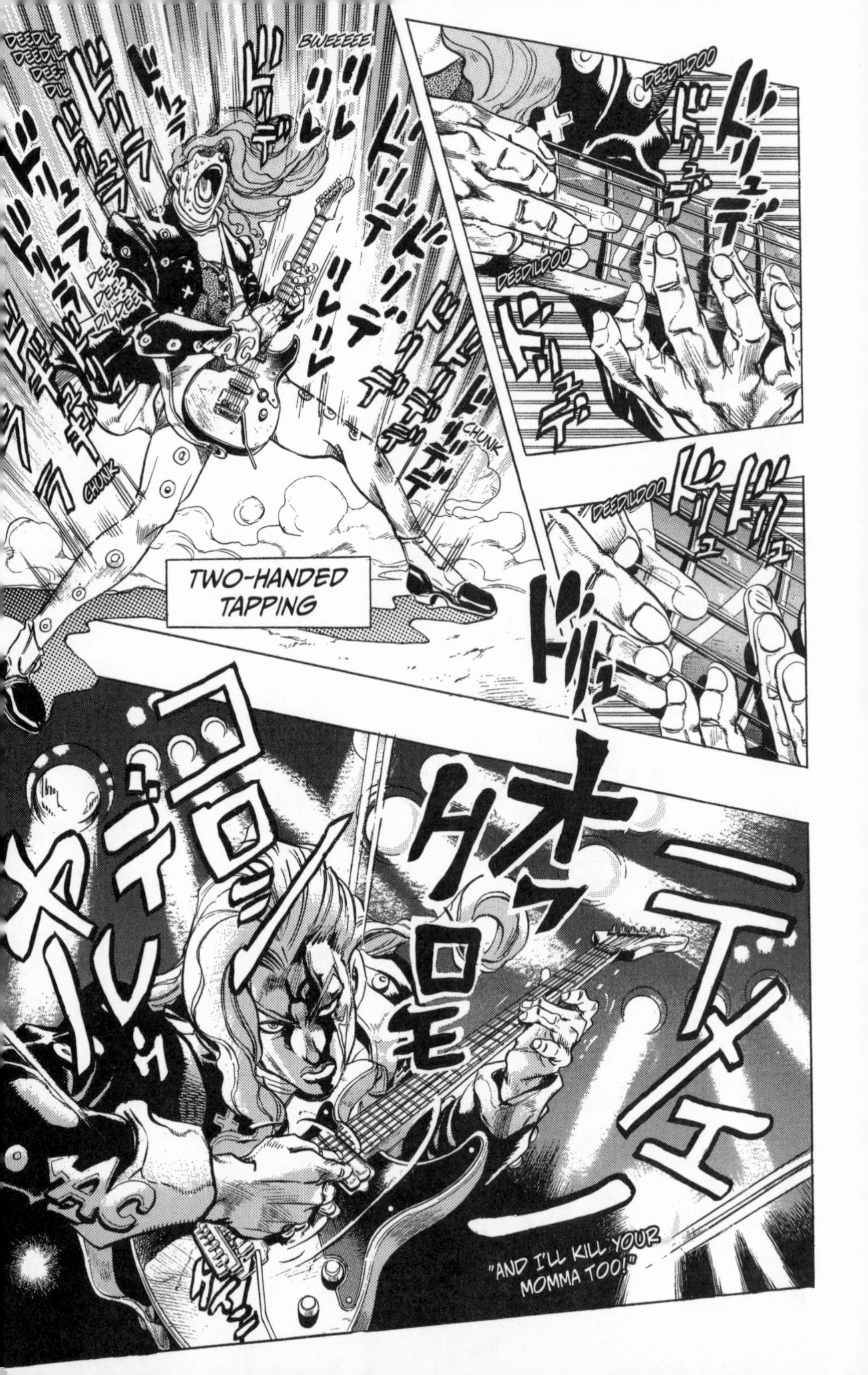
DEEDILDOO
DEEDILDOO
DEEDILDOO
BWEEEEE
DEEDIL-DEEDIL-DEE-DIL
DEE-DEE-DILDEE
CHUNK
CHUNK
TWO-HANDED TAPPING
"AND I'LL KILL YOUR MOMMA TOO!"

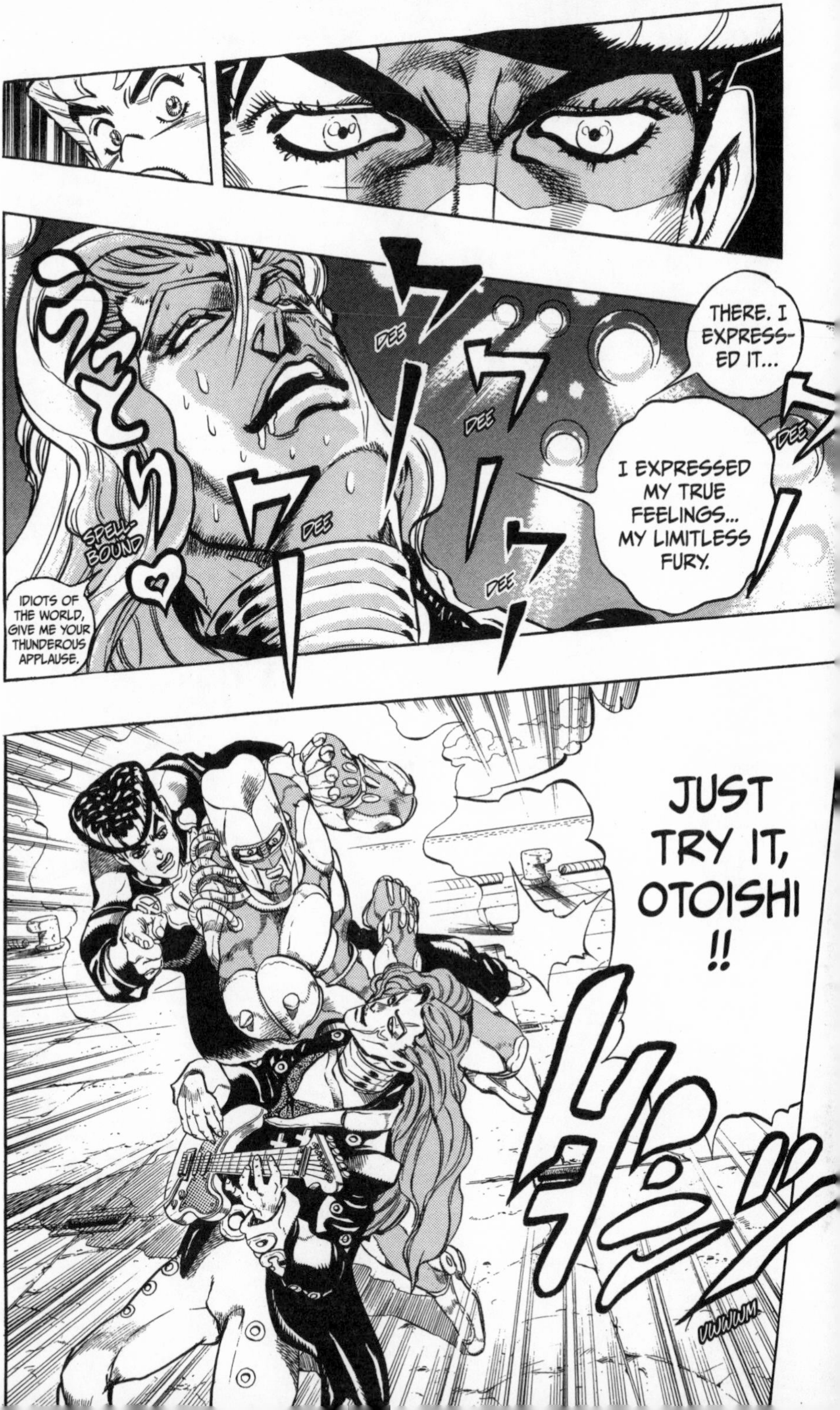
THERE. I EXPRESSED IT...
DEE
I EXPRESSED MY TRUE FEELINGS... MY LIMITLESS FURY.
DEE
DEE
DEE
DEE
SPELLBOUND
IDIOTS OF THE WORLD, GIVE ME YOUR THUNDEROUS APPLAUSE.
JUST TRY IT, OTOISHI !!
VWWWM

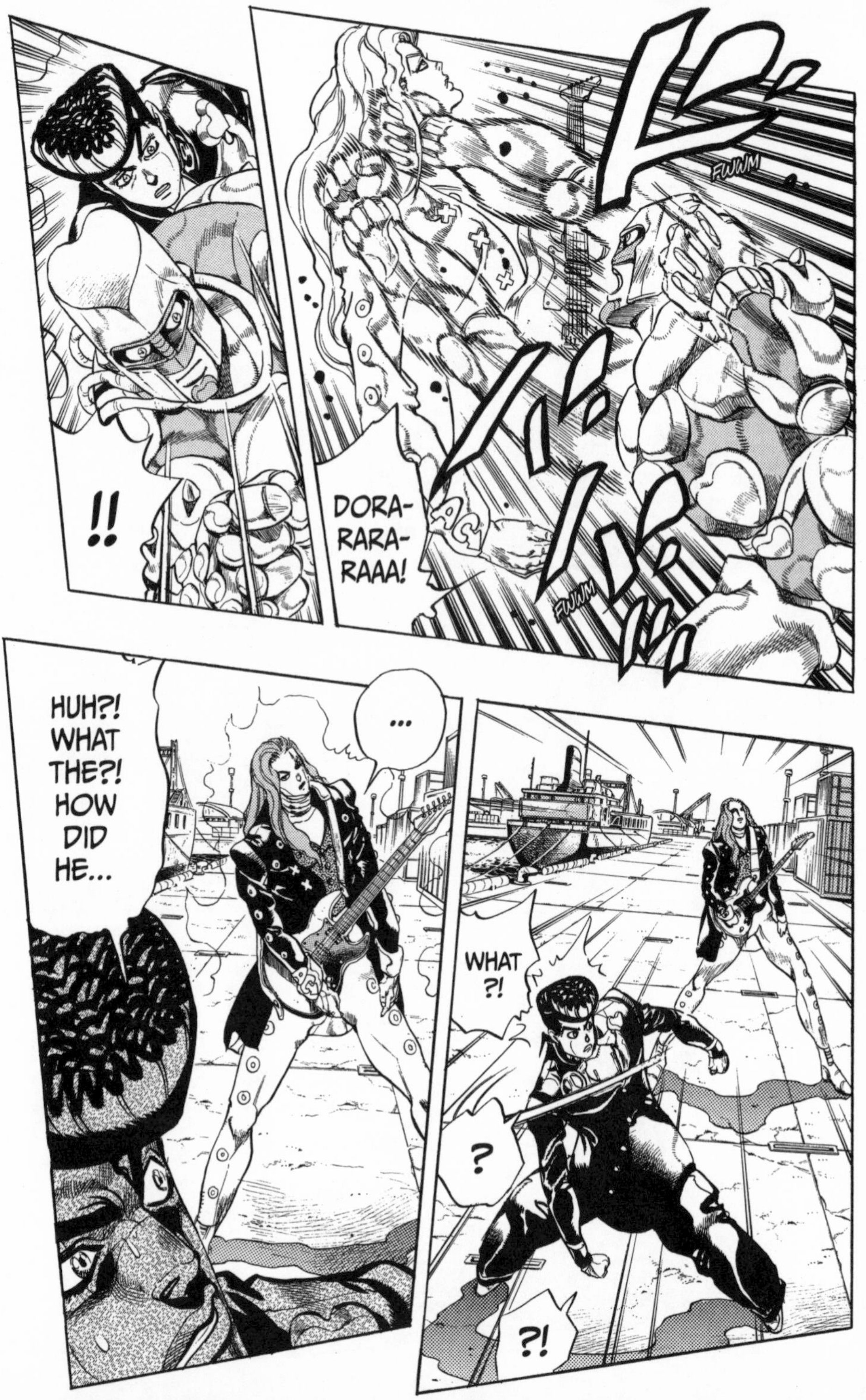
FWWM
DORA-RARA-RAAA!
FWWM
!!
WHAT ?!
?
?!
...
HUH?! WHAT THE?! HOW DID HE...

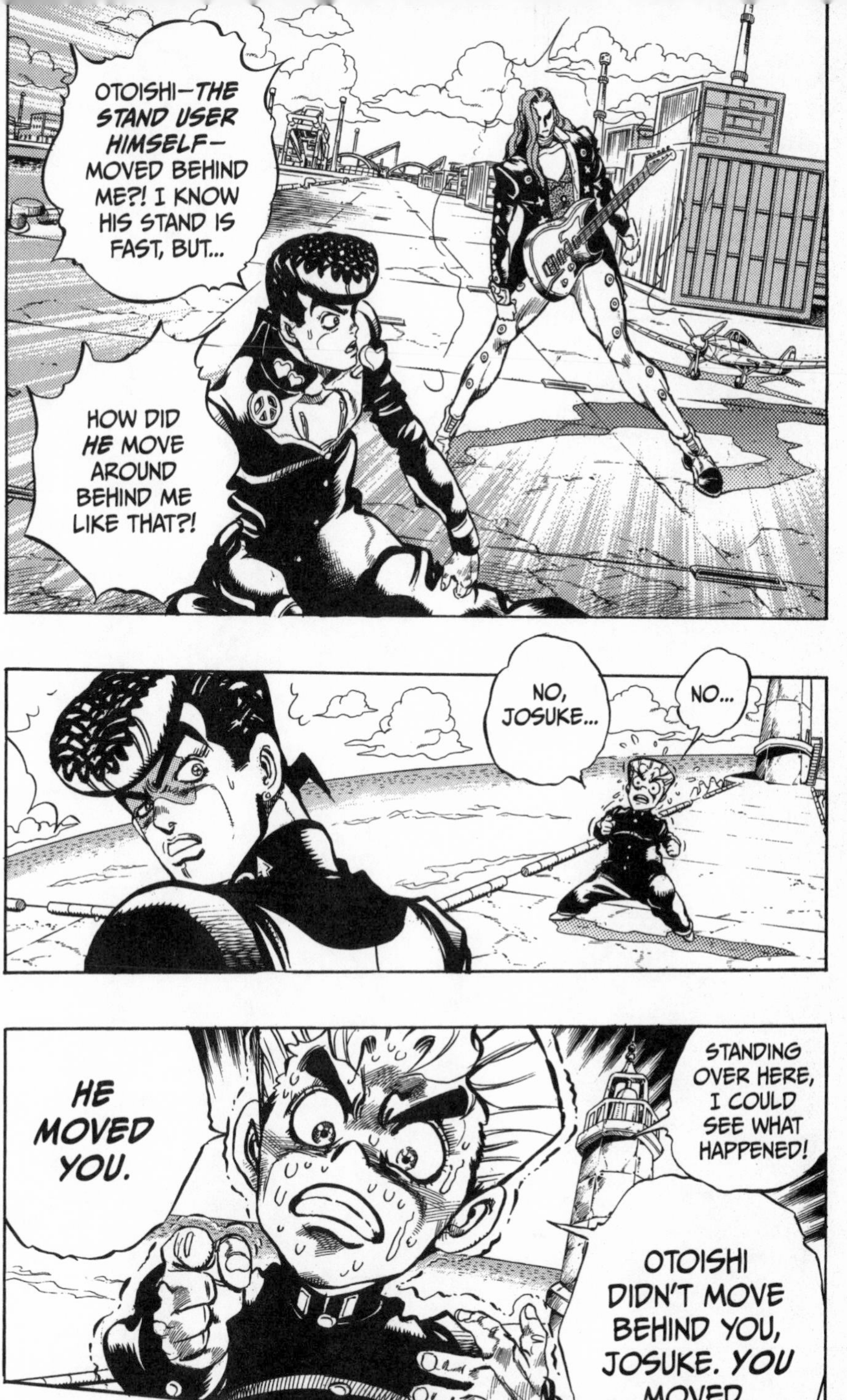
OTOISHI—THE STAND USER HIMSELF—MOVED BEHIND ME?! I KNOW HIS STAND IS FAST, BUT...
HOW DID HE MOVE AROUND BEHIND ME LIKE THAT?!
NO...
NO, JOSUKE...
STANDING OVER HERE, I COULD SEE WHAT HAPPENED!
OTOISHI DIDN'T MOVE BEHIND YOU, JOSUKE. YOU MOVED.
HE MOVED YOU.

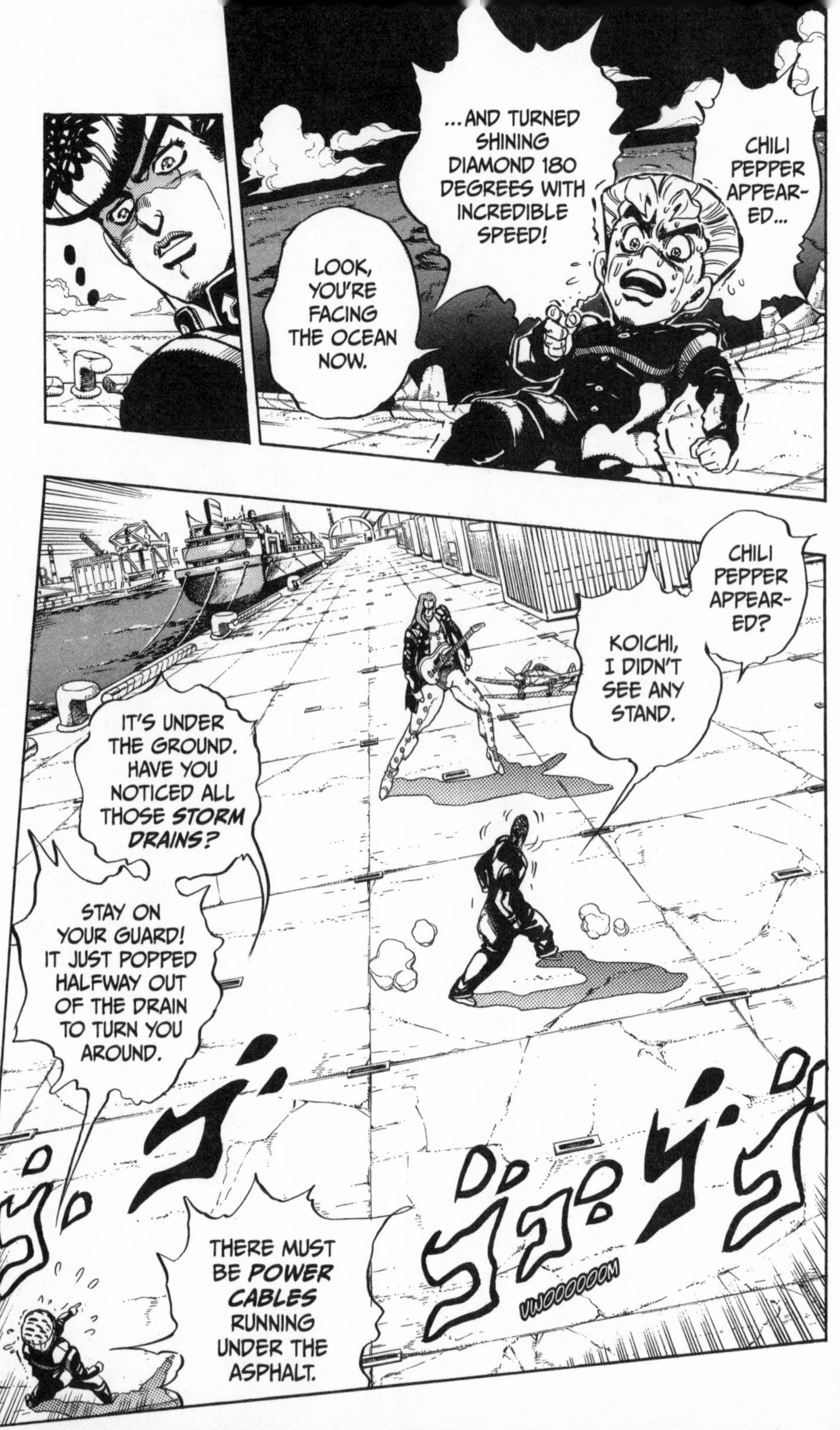
CHILI PEPPER APPEARED...
...AND TURNED SHINING DIAMOND 180 DEGREES WITH INCREDIBLE SPEED!
LOOK, YOU'RE FACING THE OCEAN NOW.
CHILI PEPPER APPEARED?
KOICHI, I DIDN'T SEE ANY STAND.
IT'S UNDER THE GROUND. HAVE YOU NOTICED ALL THOSE *STORM DRAINS?*
STAY ON YOUR GUARD! IT JUST POPPED HALFWAY OUT OF THE DRAIN TO TURN YOU AROUND.
VWOOOOOOM
THERE MUST BE *POWER CABLES* RUNNING UNDER THE ASPHALT.

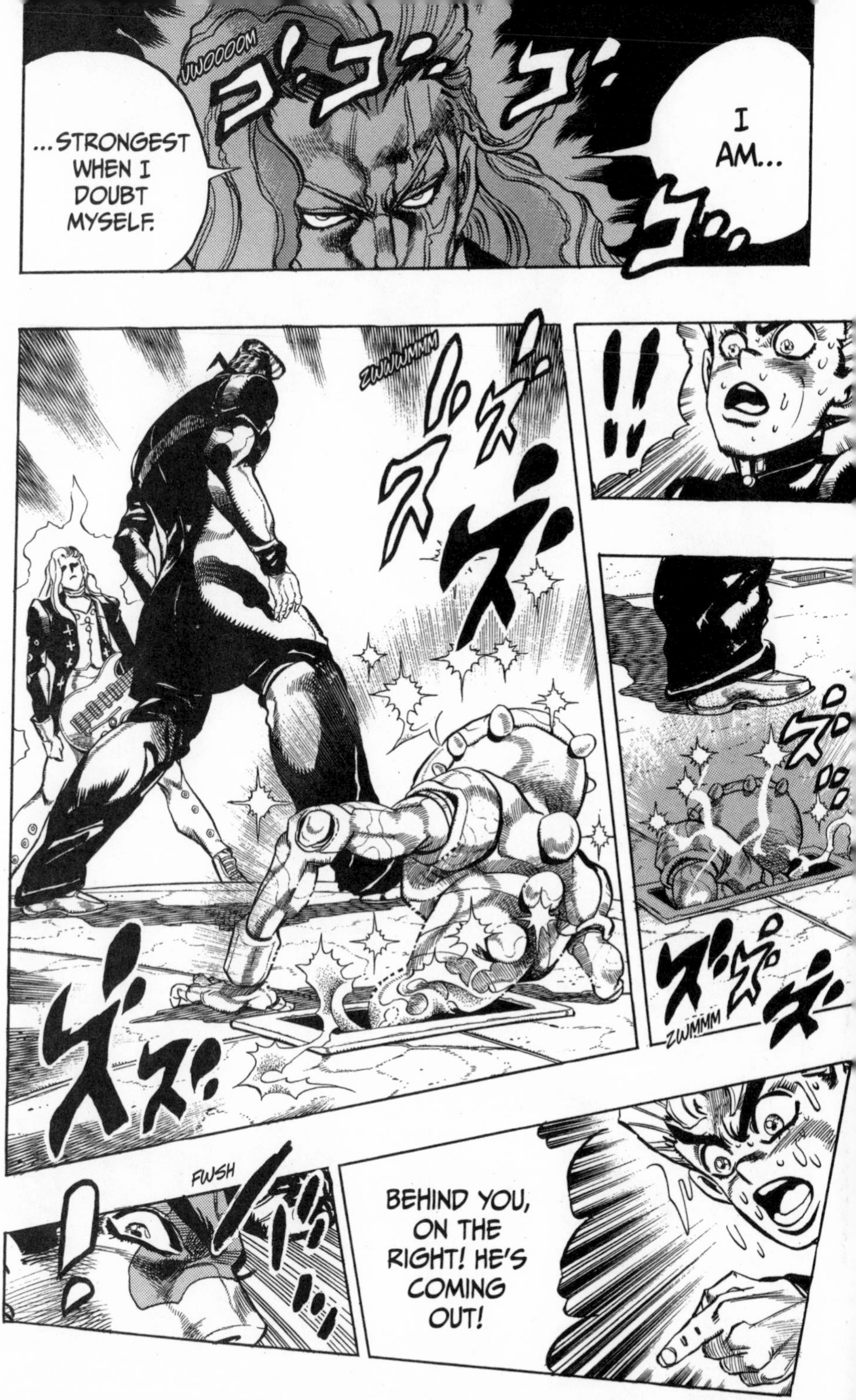
I AM...
VWOOOOM
...STRONGEST WHEN I DOUBT MYSELF.
ZWMMM
ZWWUMMM
BEHIND YOU, ON THE RIGHT! HE'S COMING OUT!
FWSH

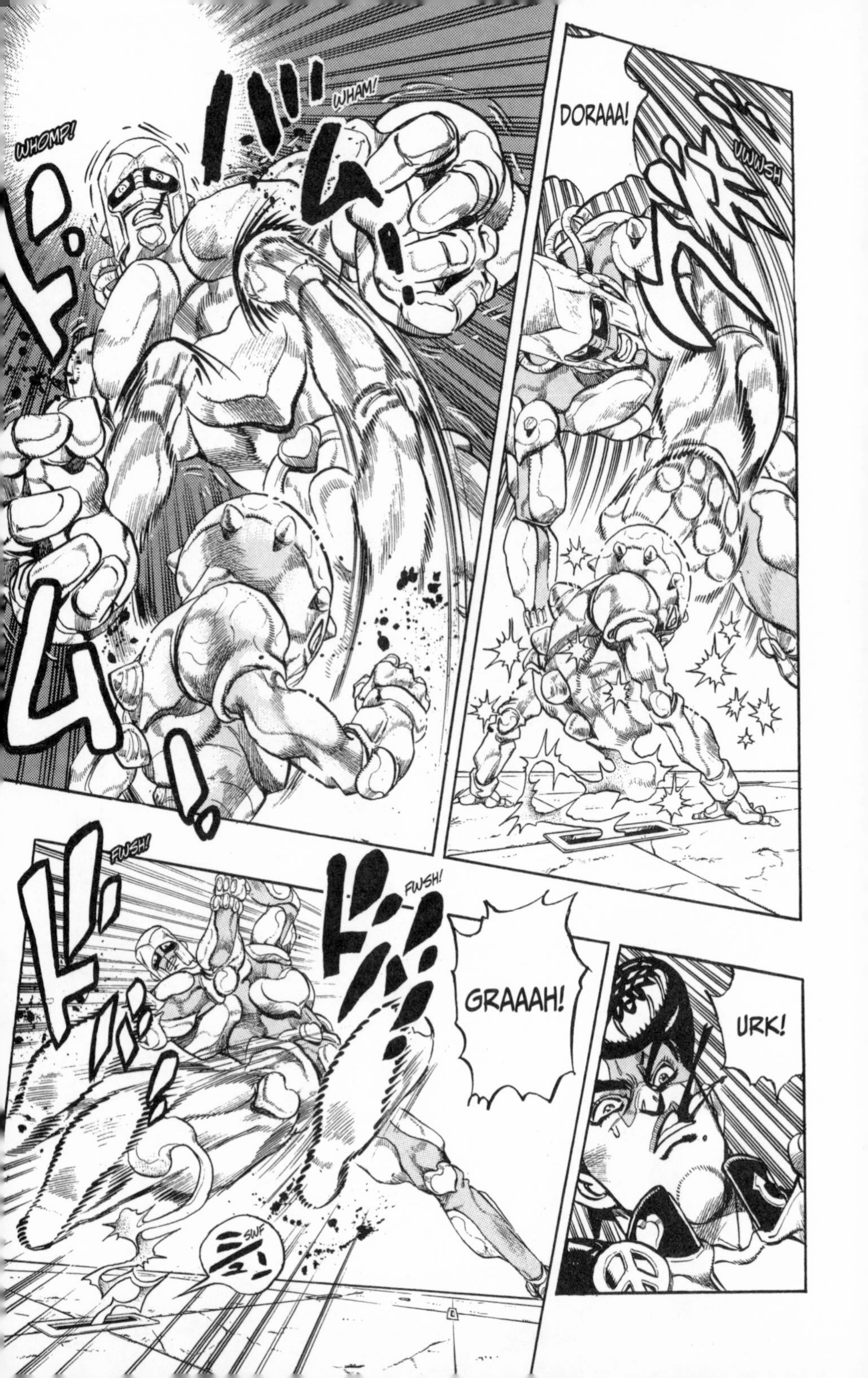
DORAAA!
UWNSH
WHAM!
WHOMP!
URK!
GRAAAH!
FWSH!
FWSH!
SWF

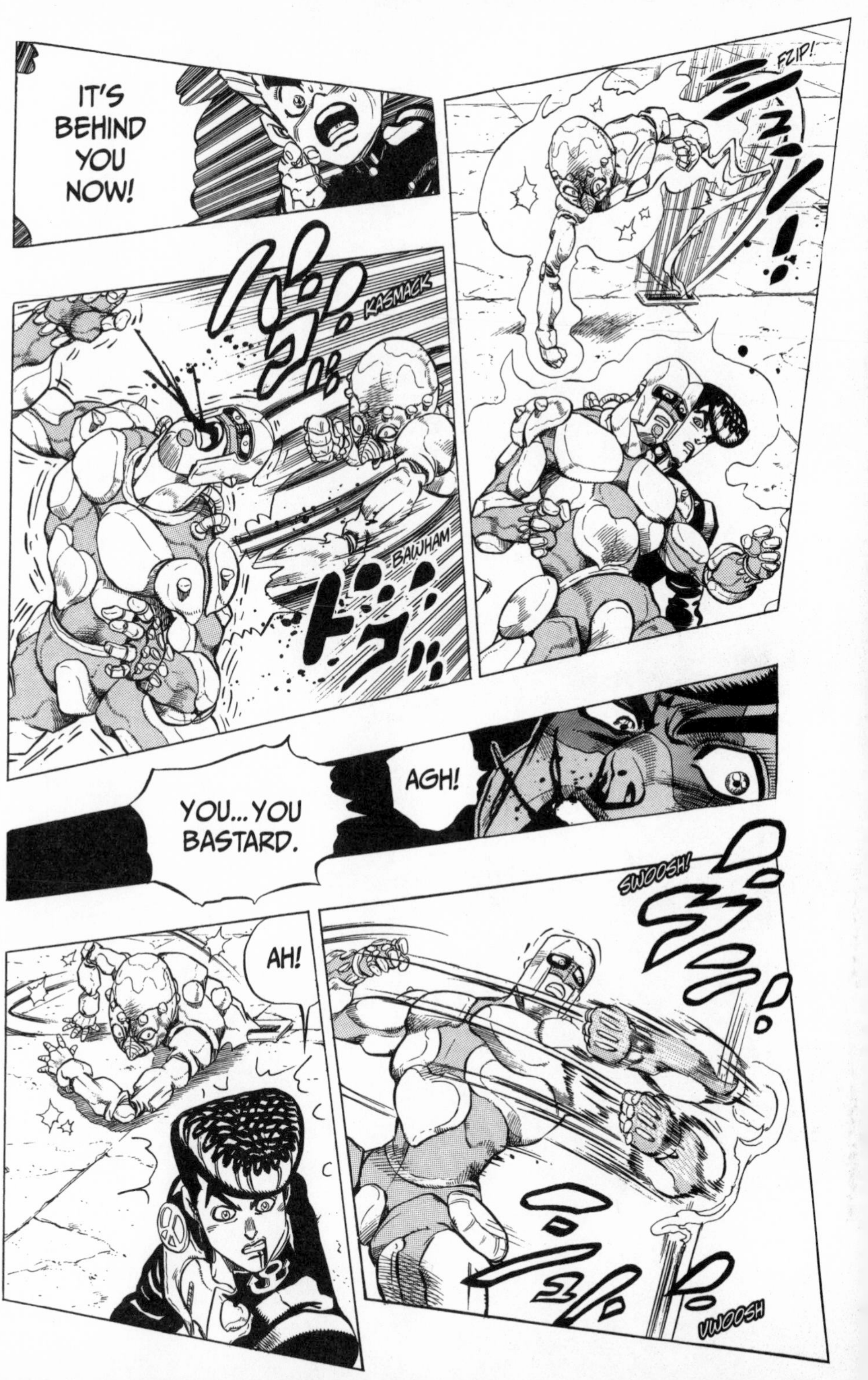
FZIP!
IT'S BEHIND YOU NOW!
KASMACK
BAWHAM
AGH!
YOU...YOU BASTARD.
SWOOSH!
VWOOSH
AH!

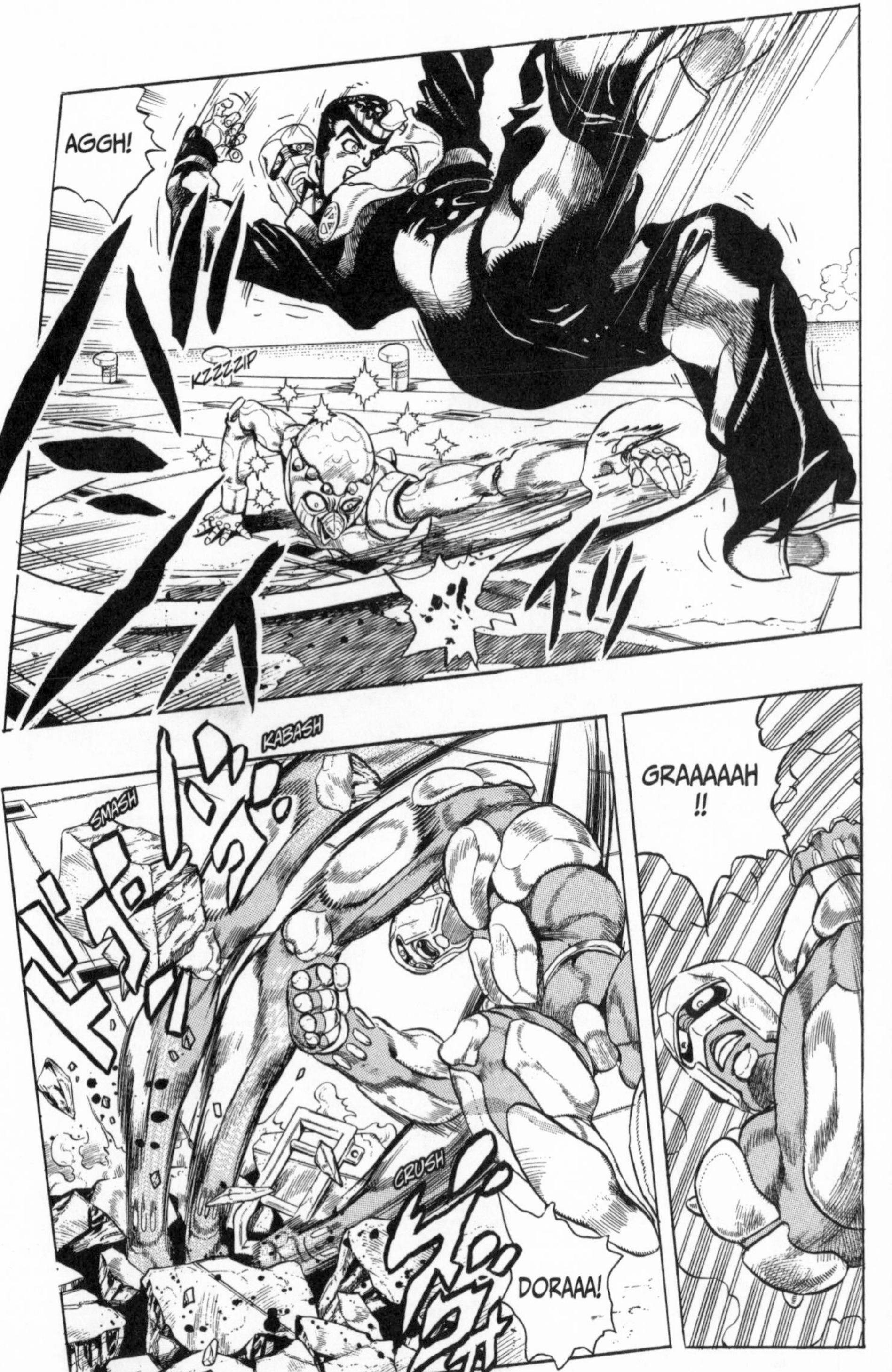
AGGH!
KZZZZIP
GRAAAAAH !!
KABASH
SMASH
CRUSH
DORAAA!

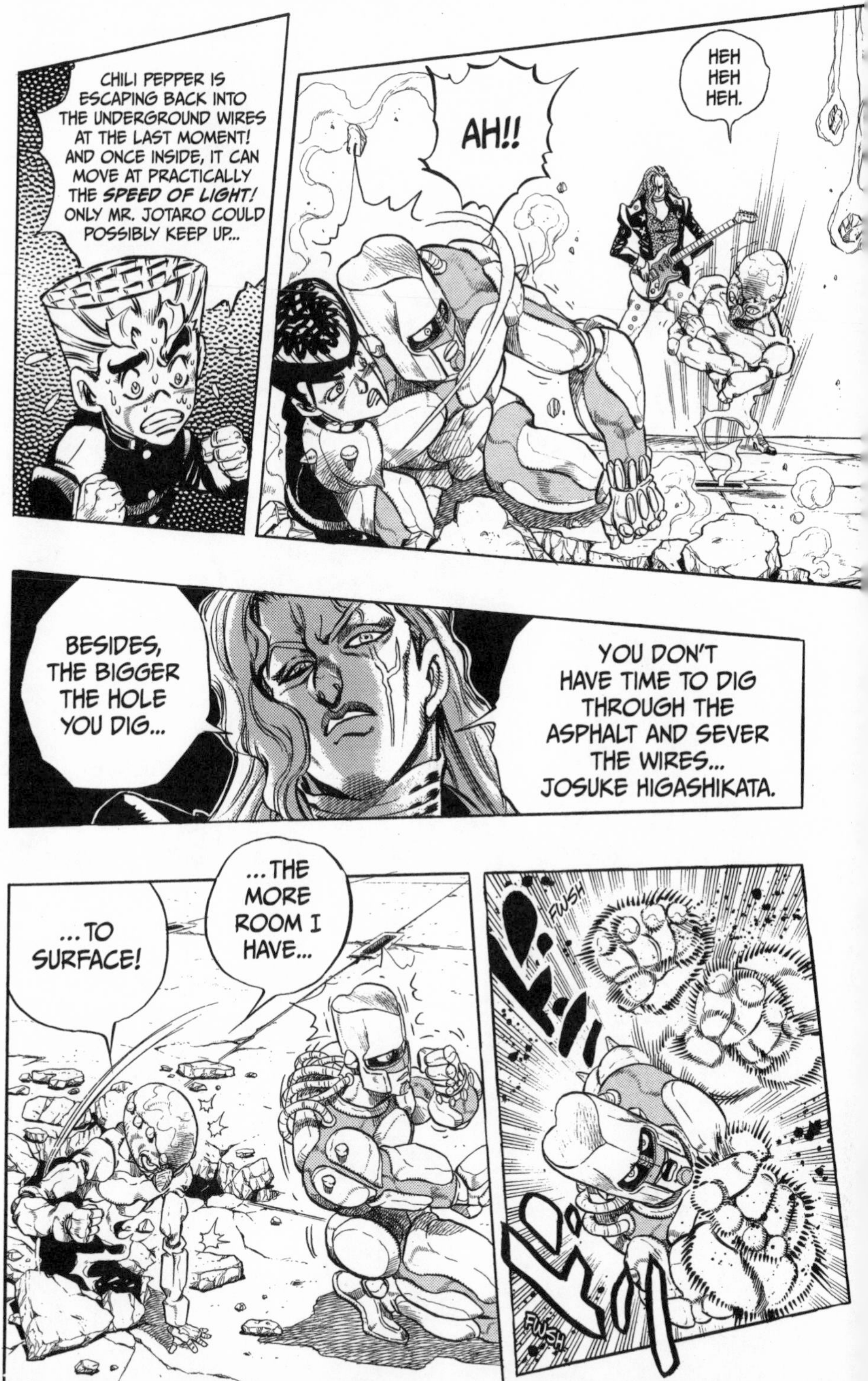
HEH HEH HEH.
AH!!
CHILI PEPPER IS ESCAPING BACK INTO THE UNDERGROUND WIRES AT THE LAST MOMENT! AND ONCE INSIDE, IT CAN MOVE AT PRACTICALLY THE ***SPEED OF LIGHT!*** ONLY MR. JOTARO COULD POSSIBLY KEEP UP...
YOU DON'T HAVE TIME TO DIG THROUGH THE ASPHALT AND SEVER THE WIRES... JOSUKE HIGASHIKATA.
BESIDES, THE BIGGER THE HOLE YOU DIG...
FWSH
FWSH
...THE MORE ROOM I HAVE...
...TO SURFACE!

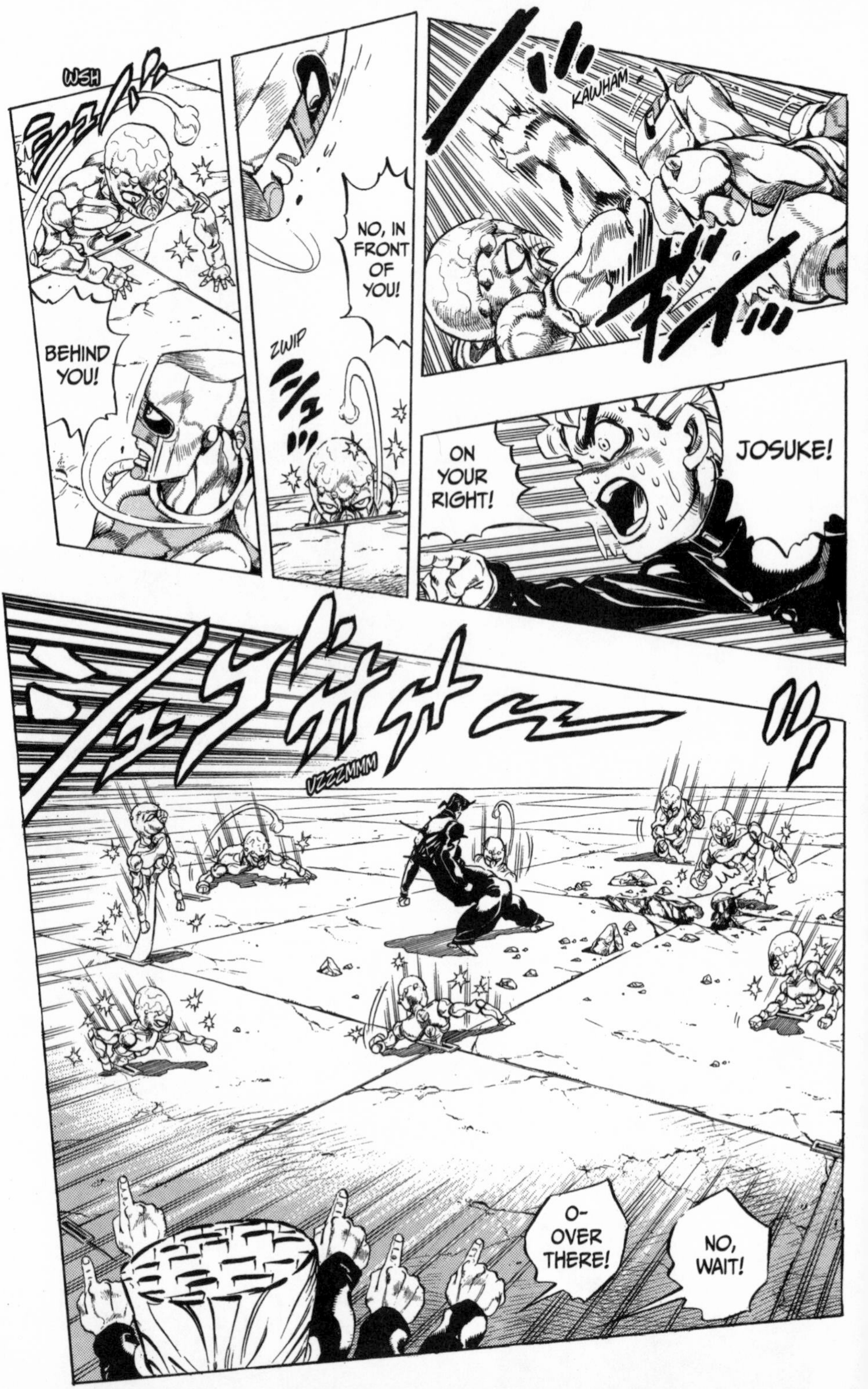
KAWHAM
JOSUKE!
ON YOUR RIGHT!
NO, IN FRONT OF YOU!
ZWIP
WSH
BEHIND YOU!
UZZZMMM
NO, WAIT!
O- OVER THERE!

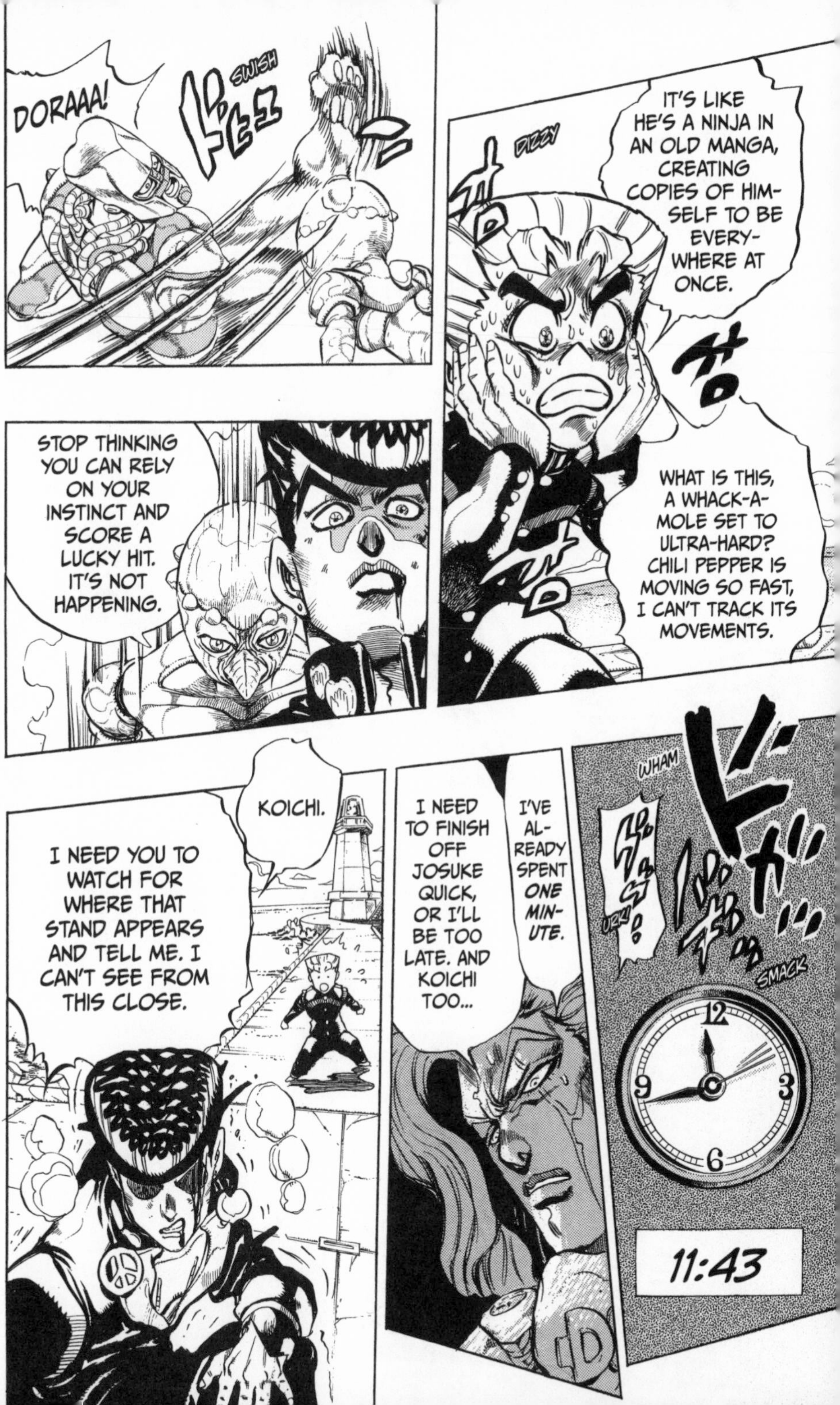
DIZZY
IT'S LIKE HE'S A NINJA IN AN OLD MANGA, CREATING COPIES OF HIM-SELF TO BE EVERY-WHERE AT ONCE.
WHAT IS THIS, A WHACK-A-MOLE SET TO ULTRA-HARD? CHILI PEPPER IS MOVING SO FAST, I CAN'T TRACK ITS MOVEMENTS.
SWISH
DORAAA!
STOP THINKING YOU CAN RELY ON YOUR INSTINCT AND SCORE A LUCKY HIT. IT'S NOT HAPPENING.
WHAM
URK
SMACK
11:43
I'VE AL-READY SPENT ONE MIN-UTE.
I NEED TO FINISH OFF JOSUKE QUICK, OR I'LL BE TOO LATE. AND KOICHI TOO...
KOICHI.
I NEED YOU TO WATCH FOR WHERE THAT STAND APPEARS AND TELL ME. I CAN'T SEE FROM THIS CLOSE.

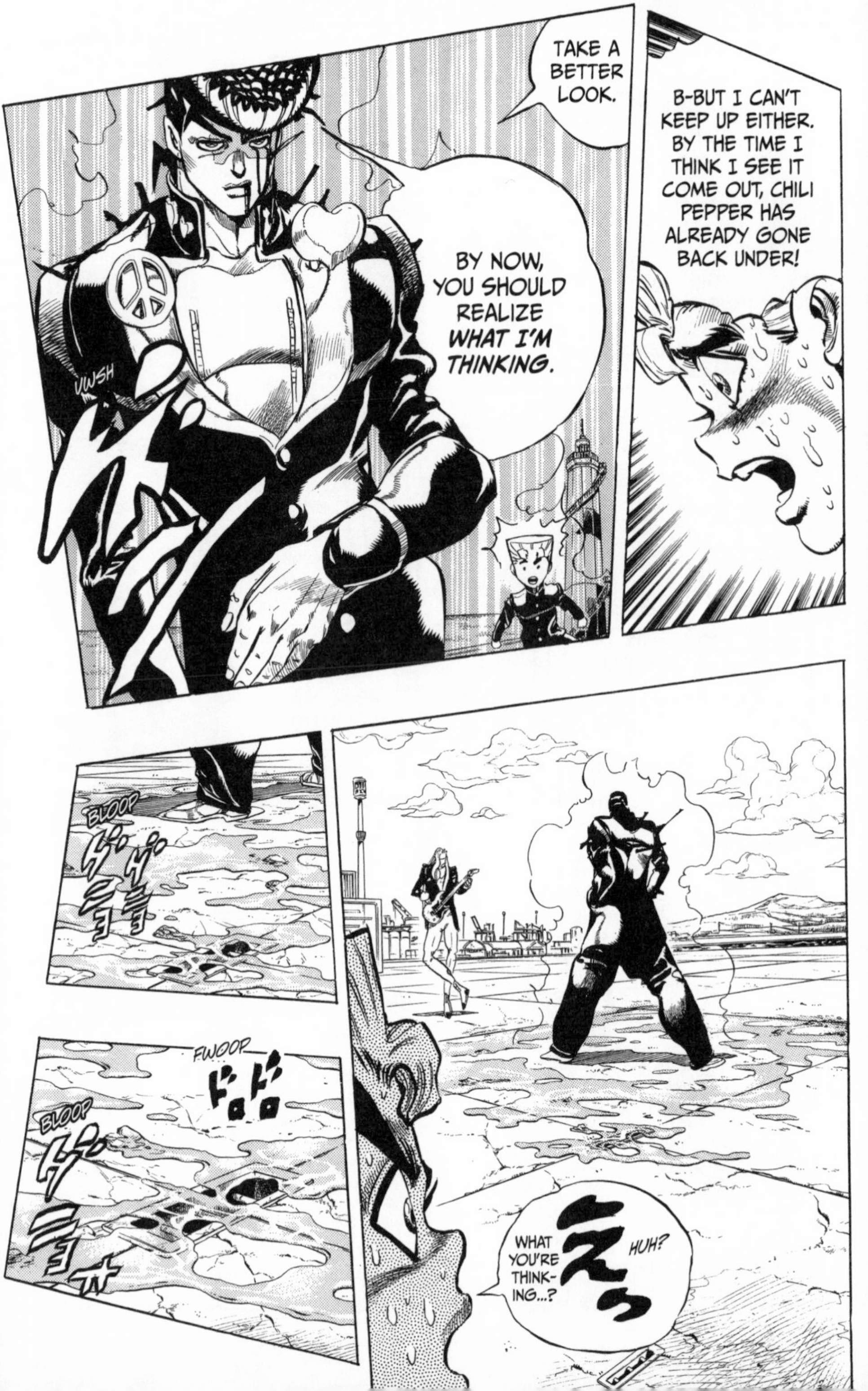
B-BUT I CAN'T KEEP UP EITHER. BY THE TIME I THINK I SEE IT COME OUT, CHILI PEPPER HAS ALREADY GONE BACK UNDER!
TAKE A BETTER LOOK.
BY NOW, YOU SHOULD REALIZE *WHAT I'M THINKING.*
UWSH
WHAT YOU'RE THINK-ING...?
HUH?
BLOOP
FWOOP
BLOOP

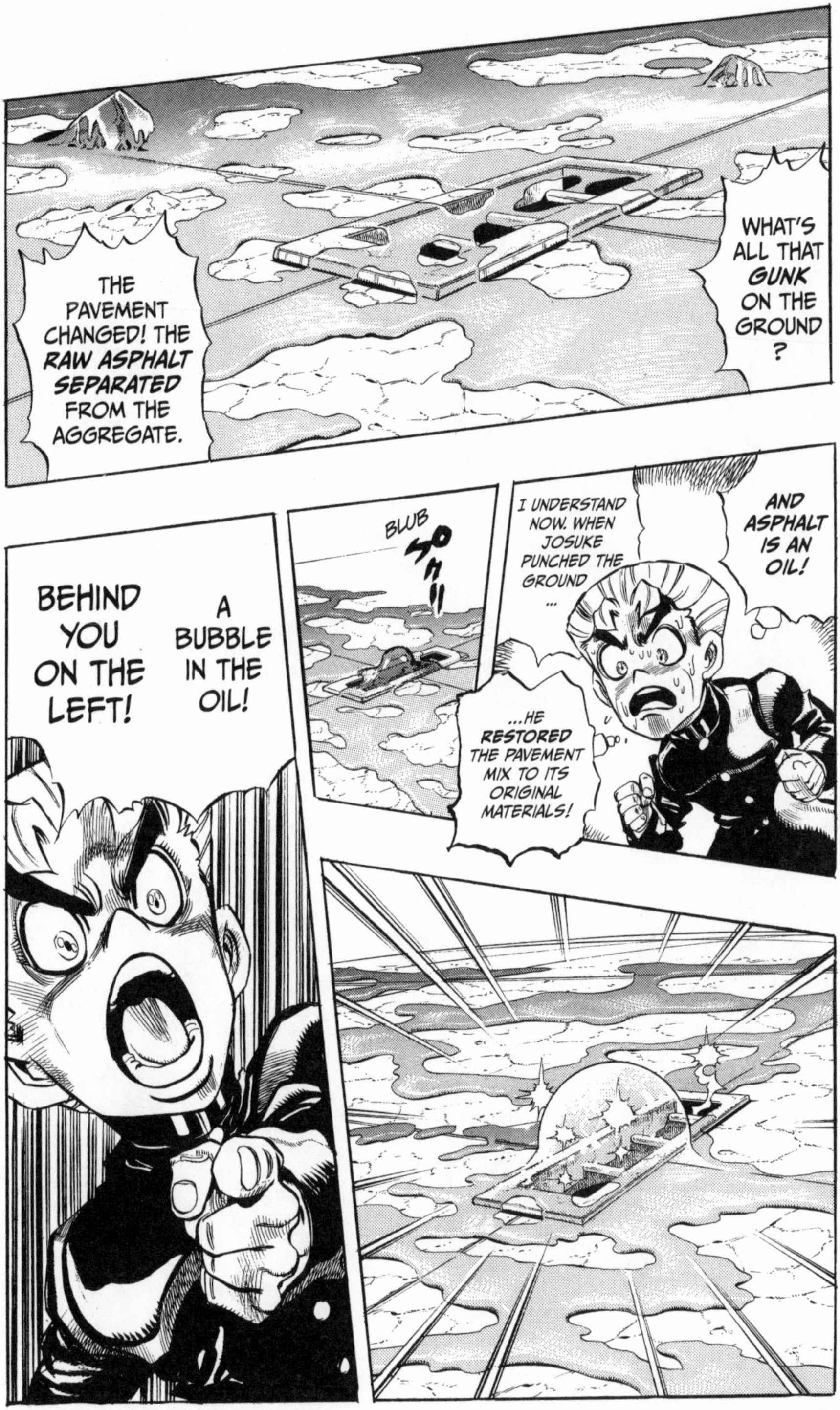
WHAT'S ALL THAT GUNK ON THE GROUND?
THE PAVEMENT CHANGED! THE RAW ASPHALT SEPARATED FROM THE AGGREGATE.
I UNDERSTAND NOW. WHEN JOSUKE PUNCHED THE GROUND...
...HE RESTORED THE PAVEMENT MIX TO ITS ORIGINAL MATERIALS!
AND ASPHALT IS AN OIL!
BLUB
A BUBBLE IN THE OIL!
BEHIND YOU ON THE LEFT!

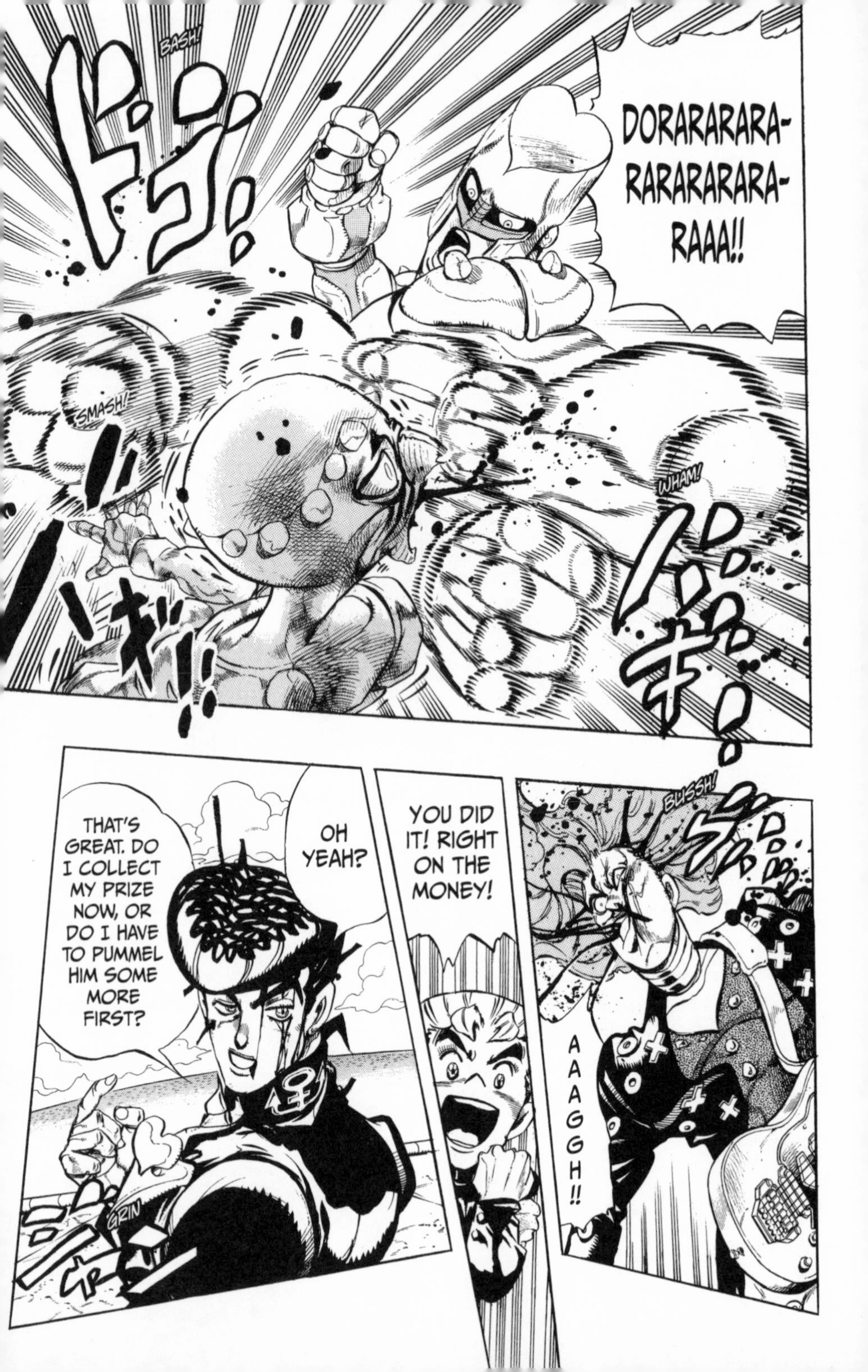
DORARARARA-
RARARARARA-
RAAA!!
BASH!
WHAM!
SMASH!
BUSSH!
AAAAGGH!!
YOU DID IT! RIGHT ON THE MONEY!
OH YEAH?
THAT'S GREAT. DO I COLLECT MY PRIZE NOW, OR DO I HAVE TO PUMMEL HIM SOME MORE FIRST?
GRIN

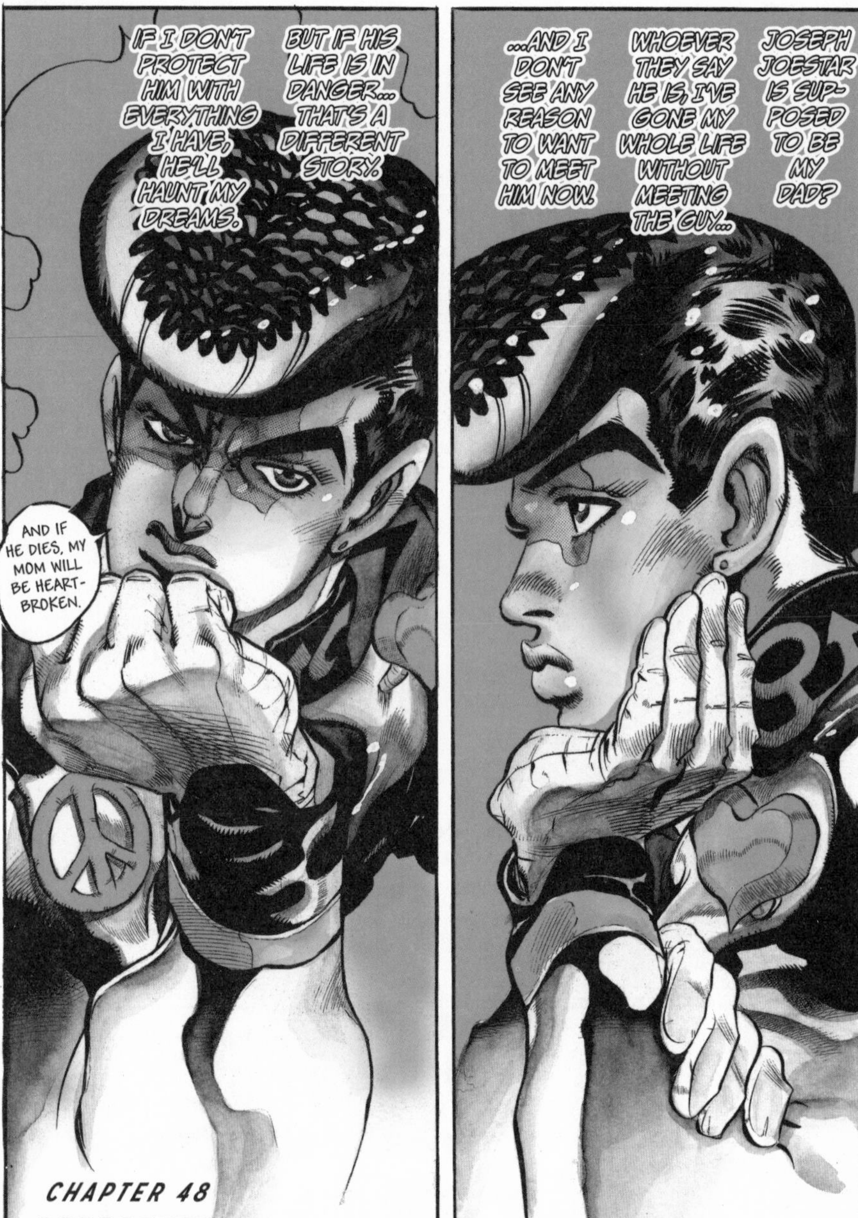
JOSEPH JOESTAR IS SUP-POSED TO BE MY DAD?
WHOEVER THEY SAY HE IS, I'VE GONE MY WHOLE LIFE WITHOUT MEETING THE GUY...
...AND I DON'T SEE ANY REASON TO WANT TO MEET HIM NOW.
BUT IF HIS LIFE IS IN DANGER... THAT'S A DIFFERENT STORY.
IF I DON'T PROTECT HIM WITH EVERYTHING I HAVE, HE'LL HAUNT MY DREAMS.
AND IF HE DIES, MY MOM WILL BE HEART-BROKEN.
CHAPTER 48
CHILI PEPPER, PART 7

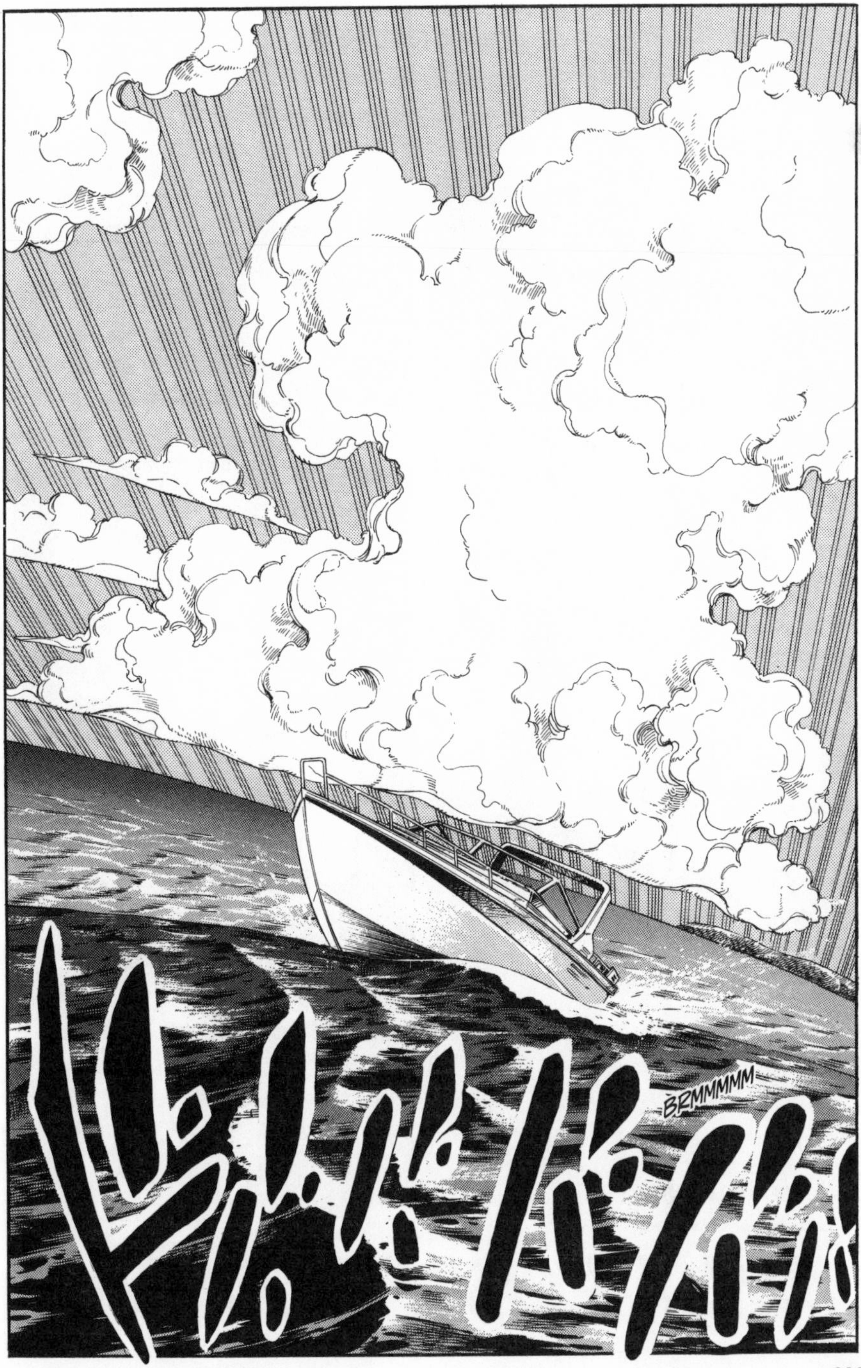
BRMMMMM

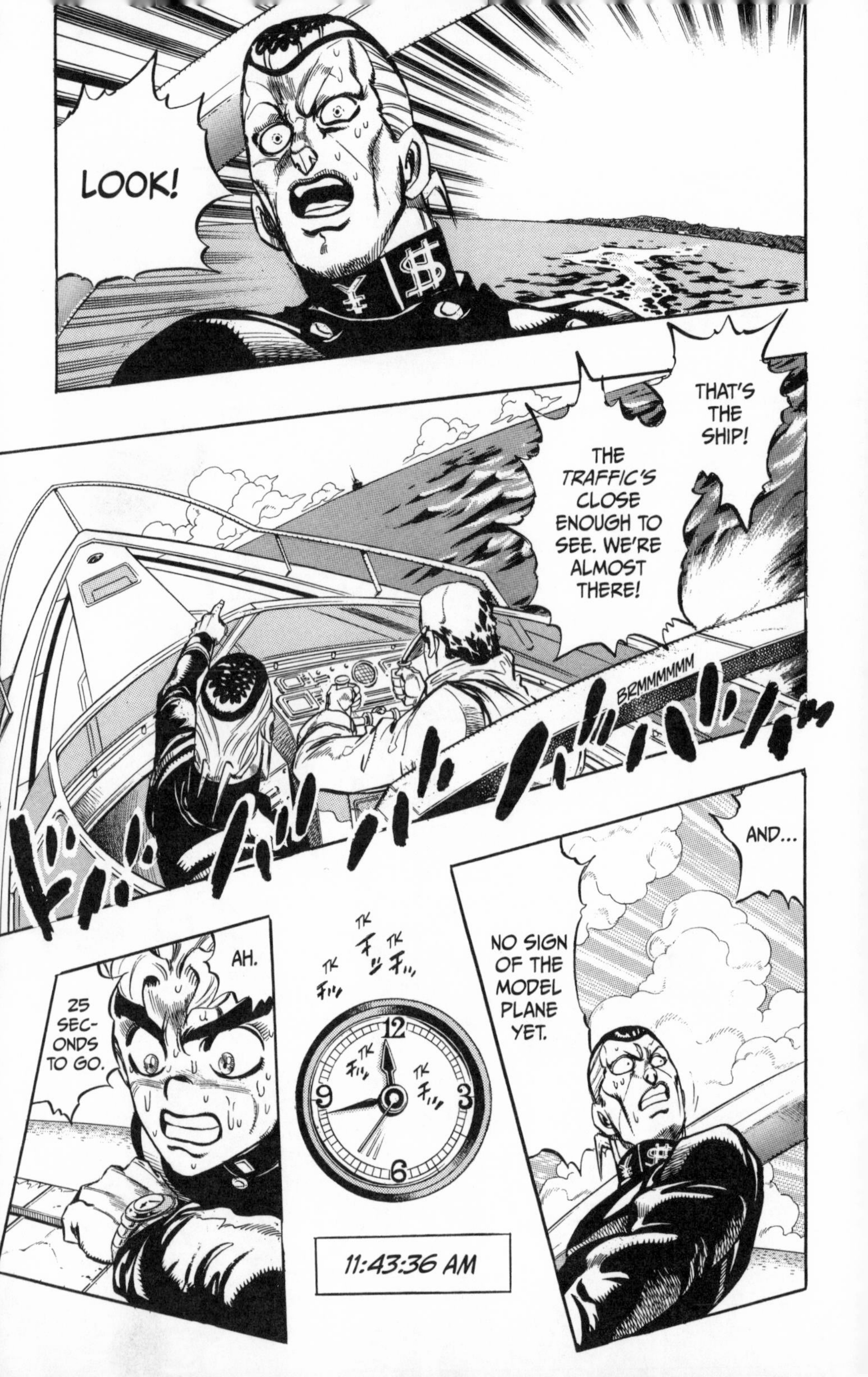
LOOK!
THAT'S THE SHIP!
THE TRAFFIC'S CLOSE ENOUGH TO SEE. WE'RE ALMOST THERE!
BRMMMMMM
AND...
NO SIGN OF THE MODEL PLANE YET.
TK TK TK
TK TK
11:43:36 AM
AH.
25 SECONDS TO GO.

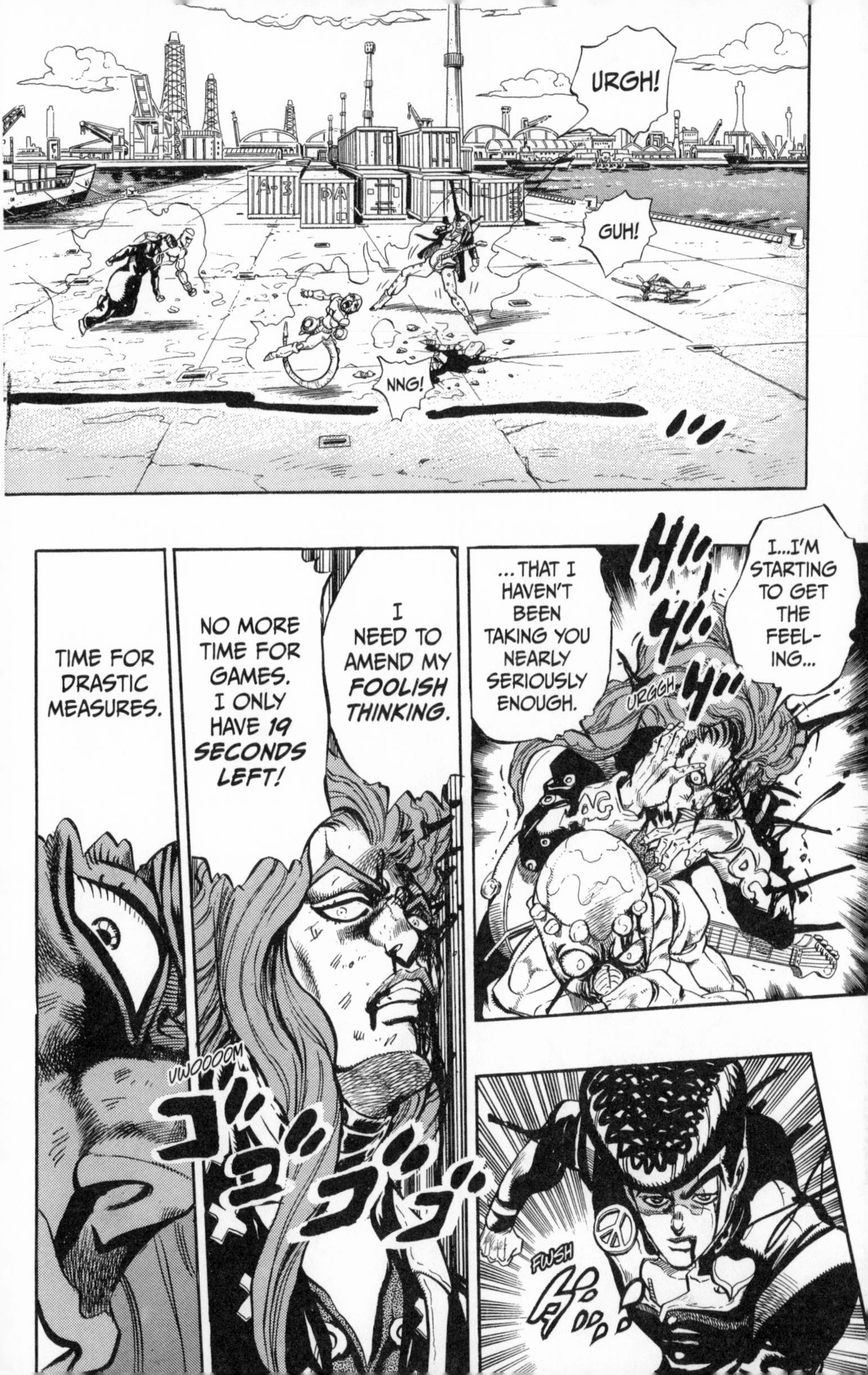
URGH!
GUH!
NNG!
I...I'M STARTING TO GET THE FEEL-ING...
...THAT I HAVEN'T BEEN TAKING YOU NEARLY SERIOUSLY ENOUGH.
URGGH
FWSH
I NEED TO AMEND MY FOOLISH THINKING.
NO MORE TIME FOR GAMES. I ONLY HAVE 19 SECONDS LEFT!
TIME FOR DRASTIC MEASURES.
VWOOOOM

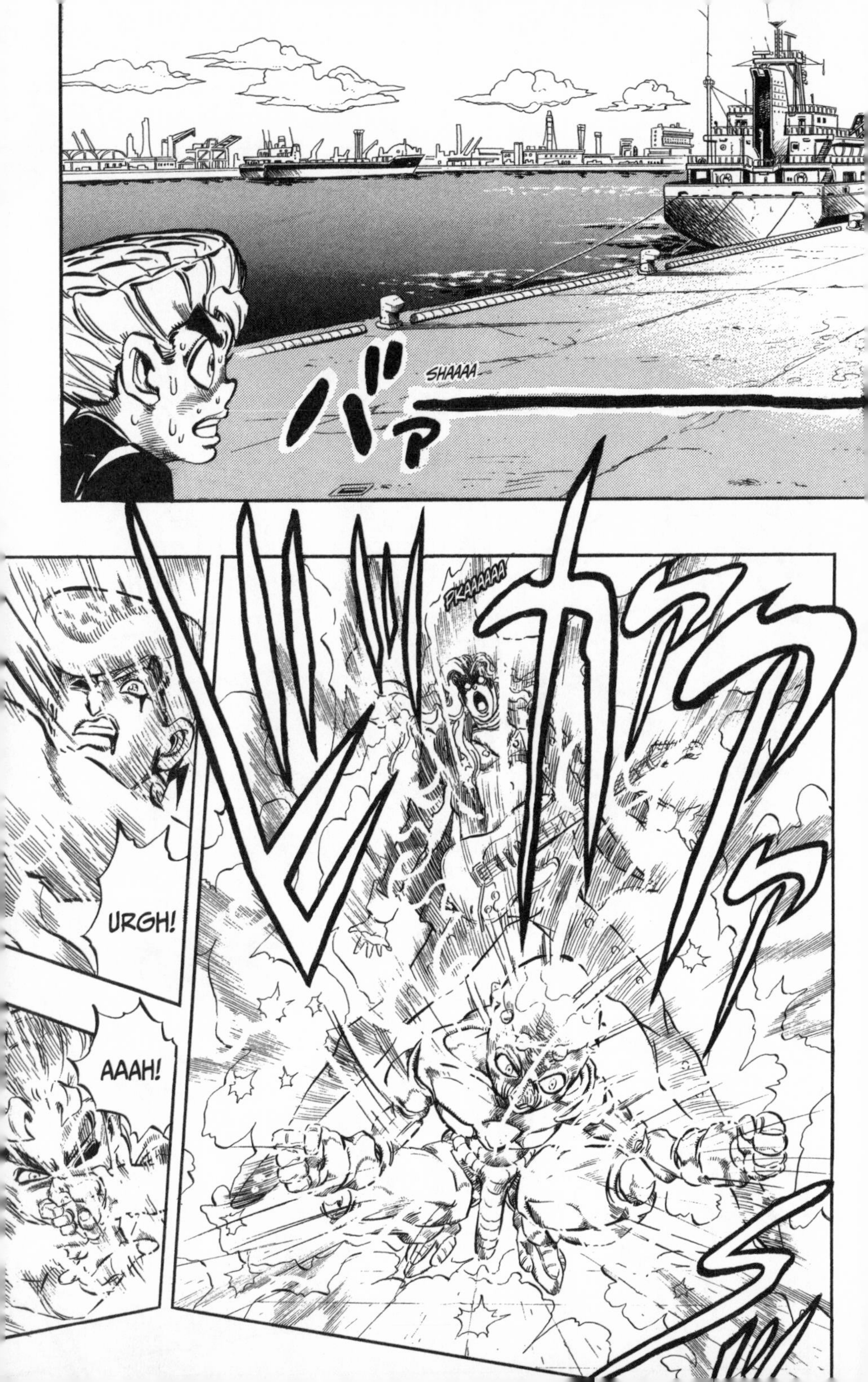
SHAAAA
PIKAAAAAA
URGH!
AAAH!

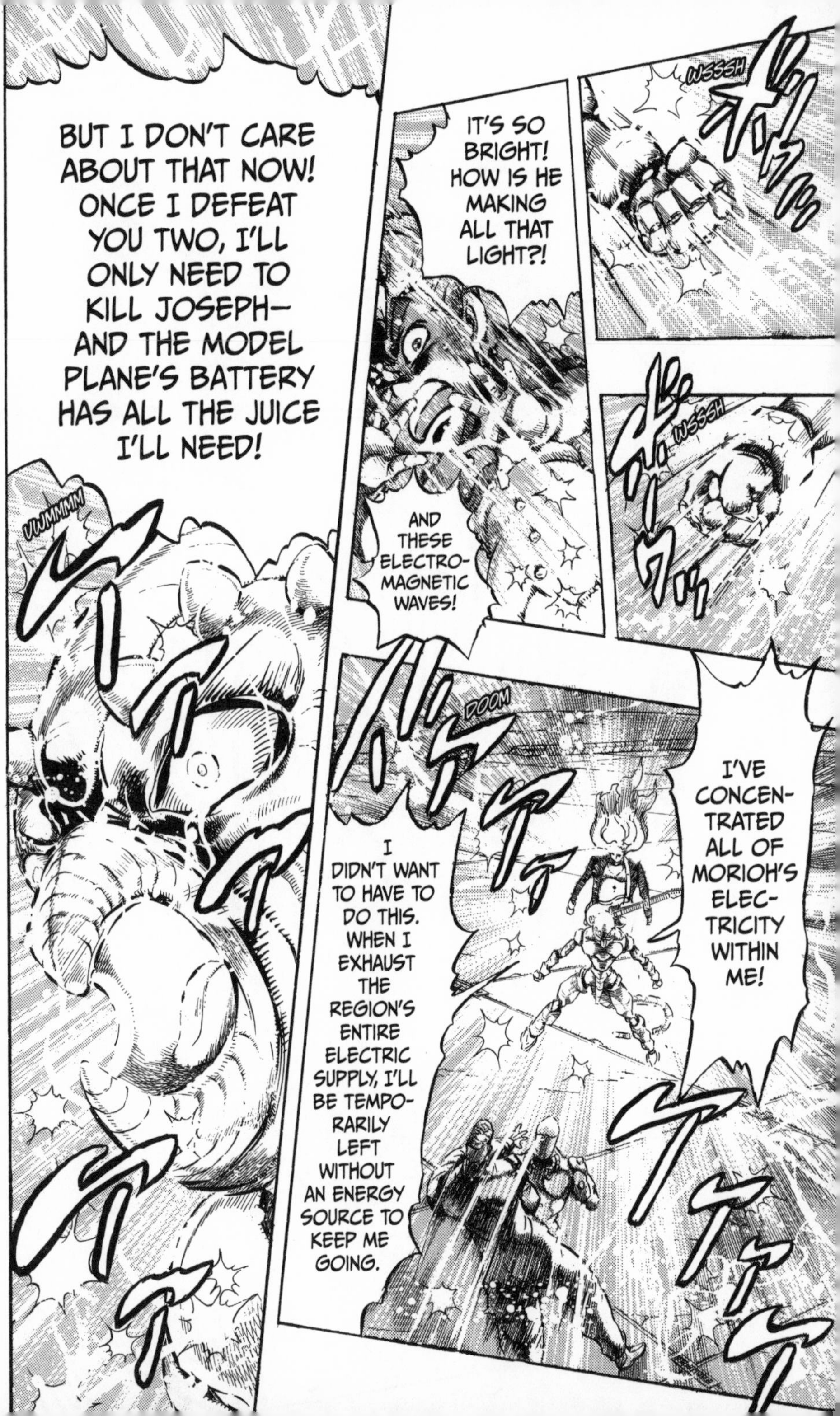
WSSSH
WSSSH
IT'S SO BRIGHT! HOW IS HE MAKING ALL THAT LIGHT?!
AND THESE ELECTRO-MAGNETIC WAVES!
DOOM
I'VE CONCEN-TRATED ALL OF MORIOH'S ELEC-TRICITY WITHIN ME!
I DIDN'T WANT TO HAVE TO DO THIS. WHEN I EXHAUST THE REGION'S ENTIRE ELECTRIC SUPPLY, I'LL BE TEMPO-RARILY LEFT WITHOUT AN ENERGY SOURCE TO KEEP ME GOING.
BUT I DON'T CARE ABOUT THAT NOW! ONCE I DEFEAT YOU TWO, I'LL ONLY NEED TO KILL JOSEPH— AND THE MODEL PLANE'S BATTERY HAS ALL THE JUICE I'LL NEED!
VWMMMM

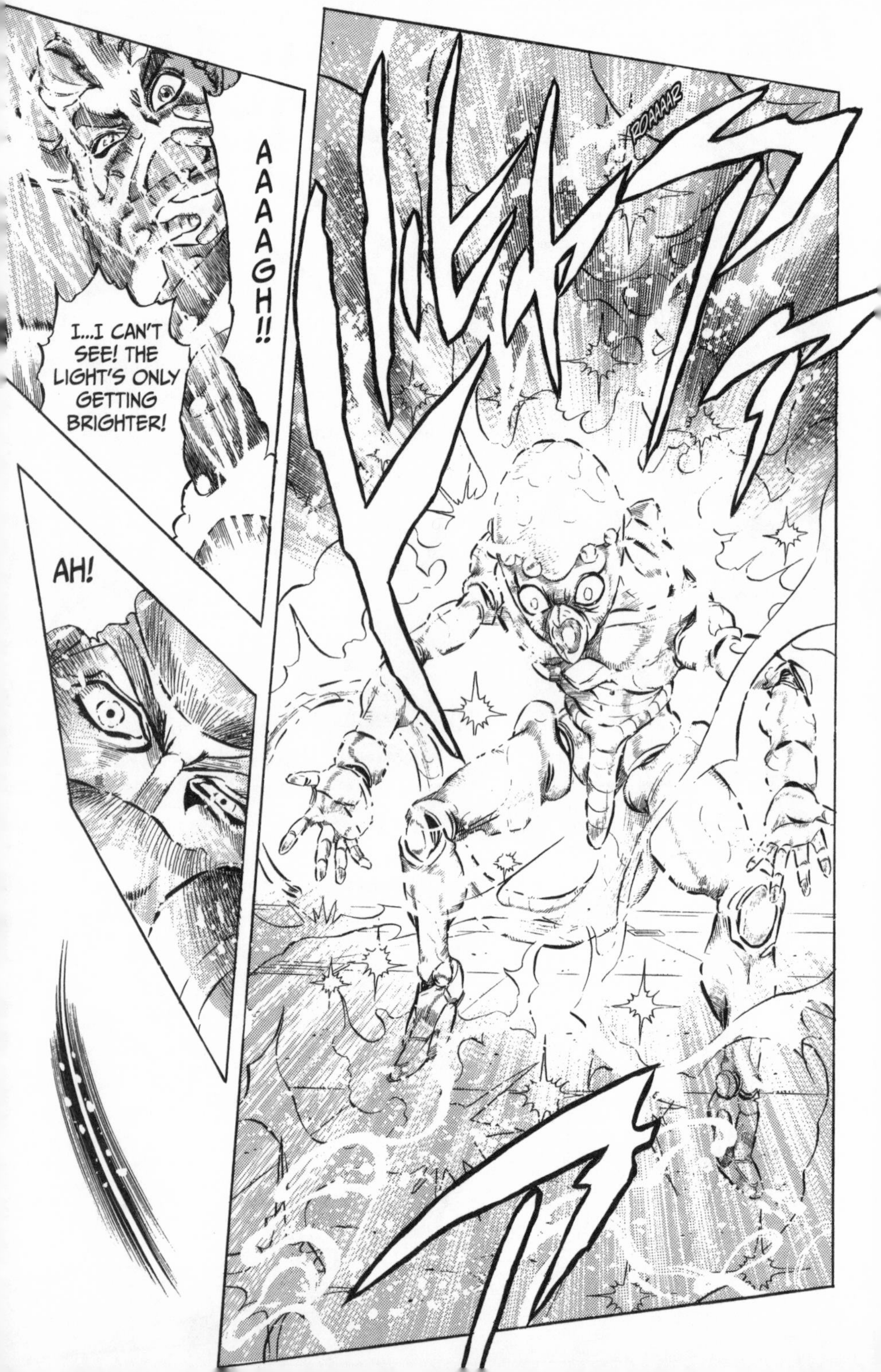
ROAAAAR
AAAAAGH!!
I...I CAN'T SEE! THE LIGHT'S ONLY GETTING BRIGHTER!
AH!

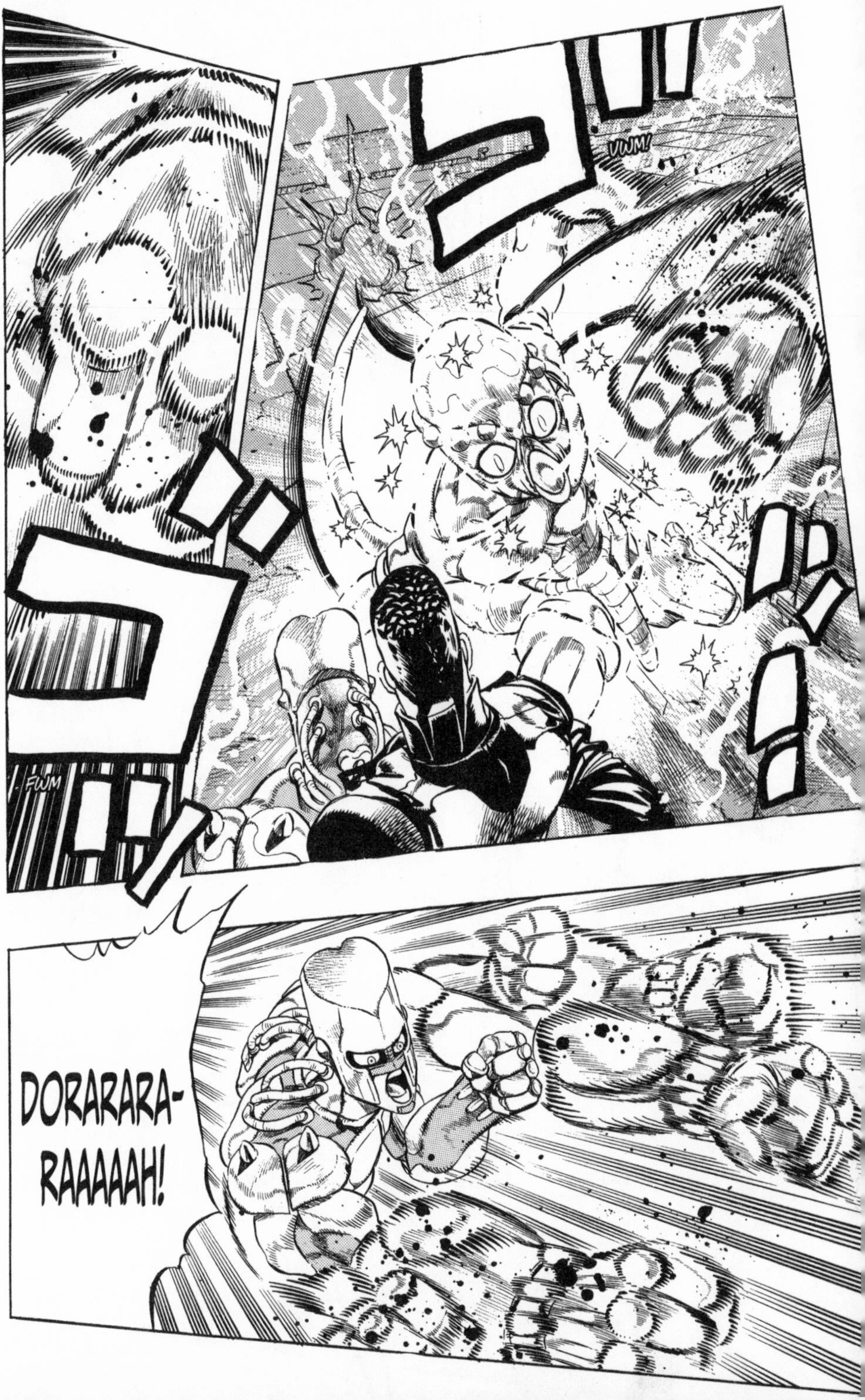
VWM!
FWM
DORARARA-
RAAAAAH!

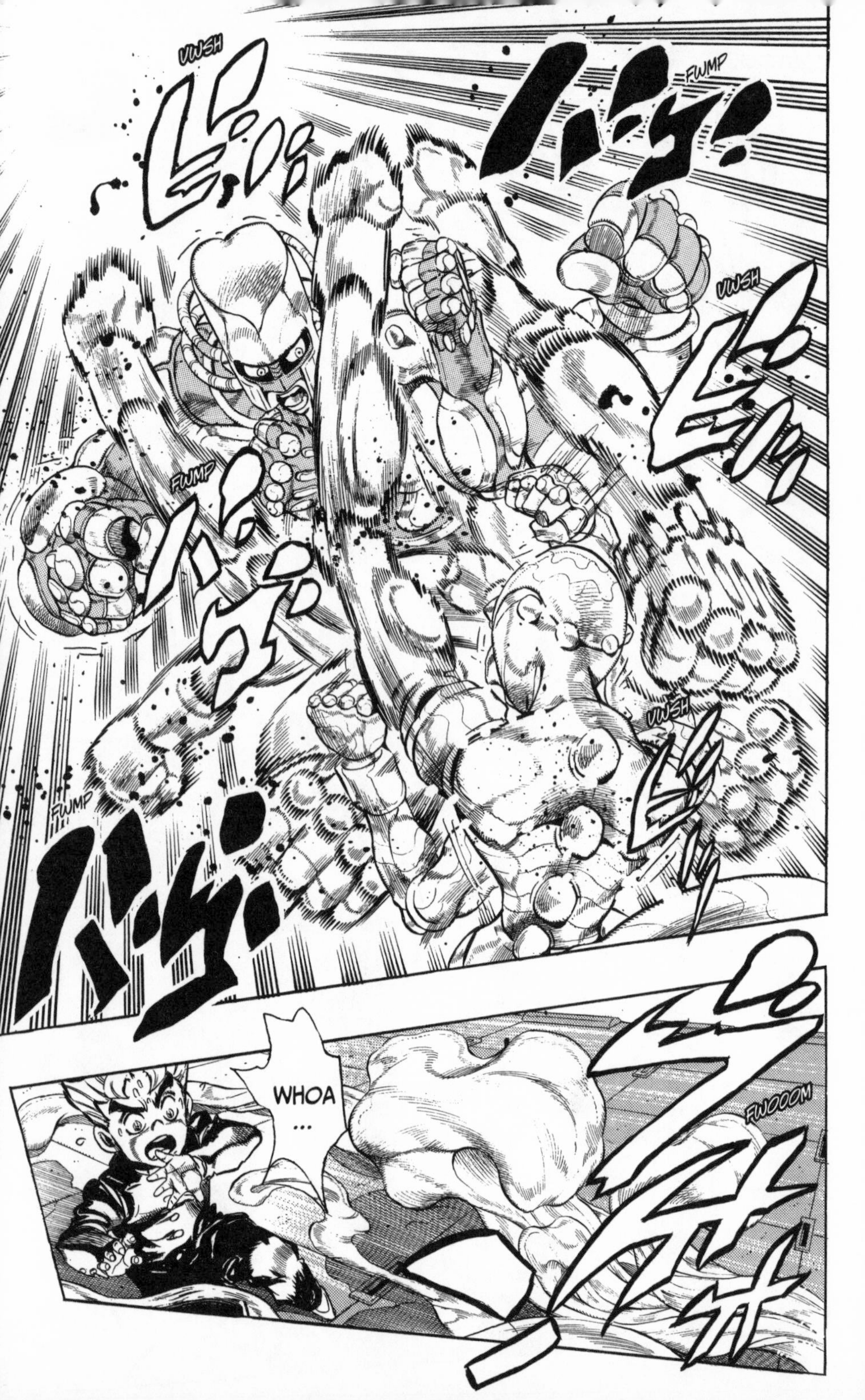
FWUMP
VWSH
VWSH
FWUMP
VWSH
FWUMP
FWOOOM
WHOA ...

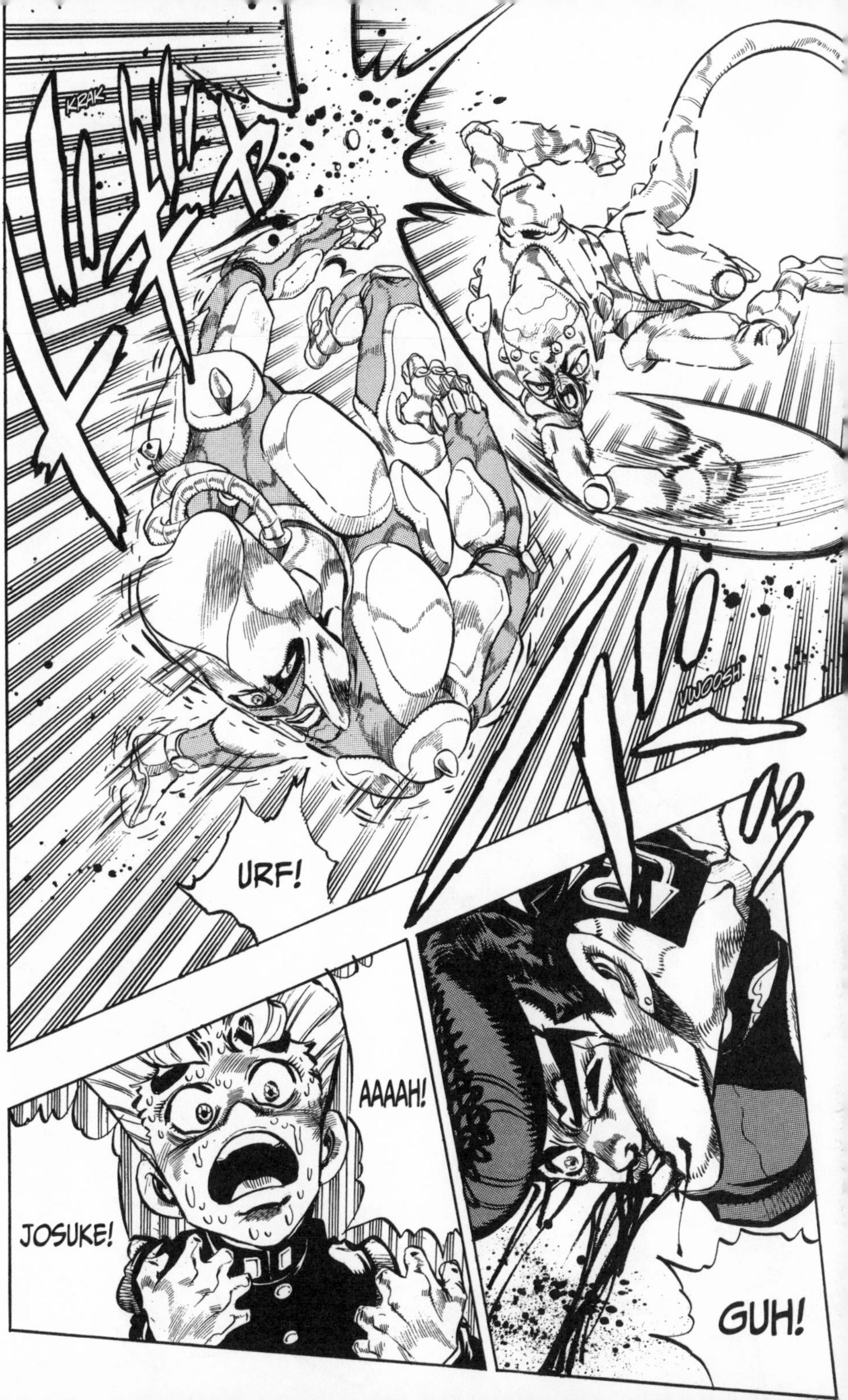
KRAK
VWOOSH
URF!
GUH!
AAAAH!
JOSUKE!

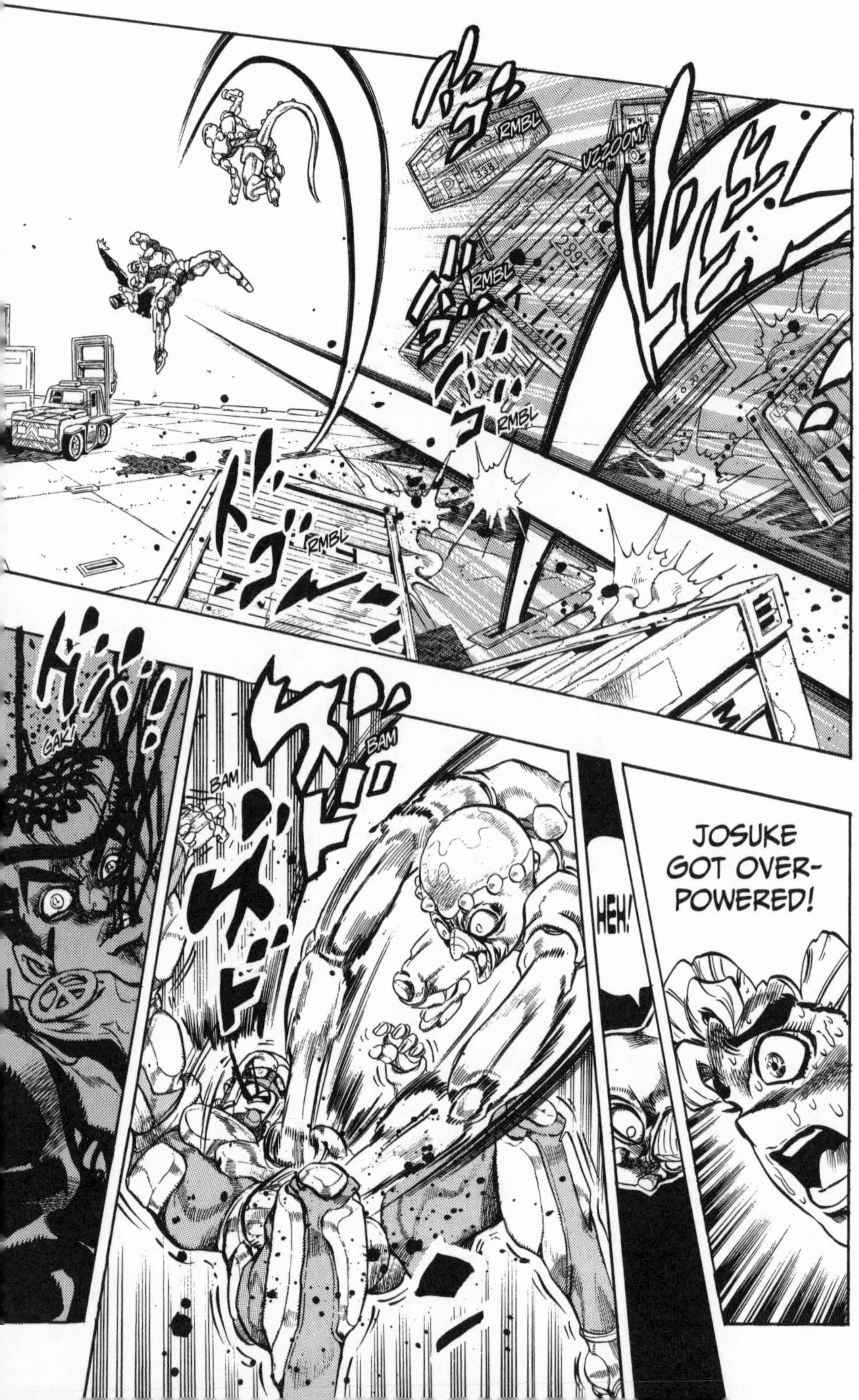
UZZOOM!
RMBL
RMBL
RMBL
RMBL
JOSUKE GOT OVER-POWERED!
HEH!
BAM
BAM
GAK!

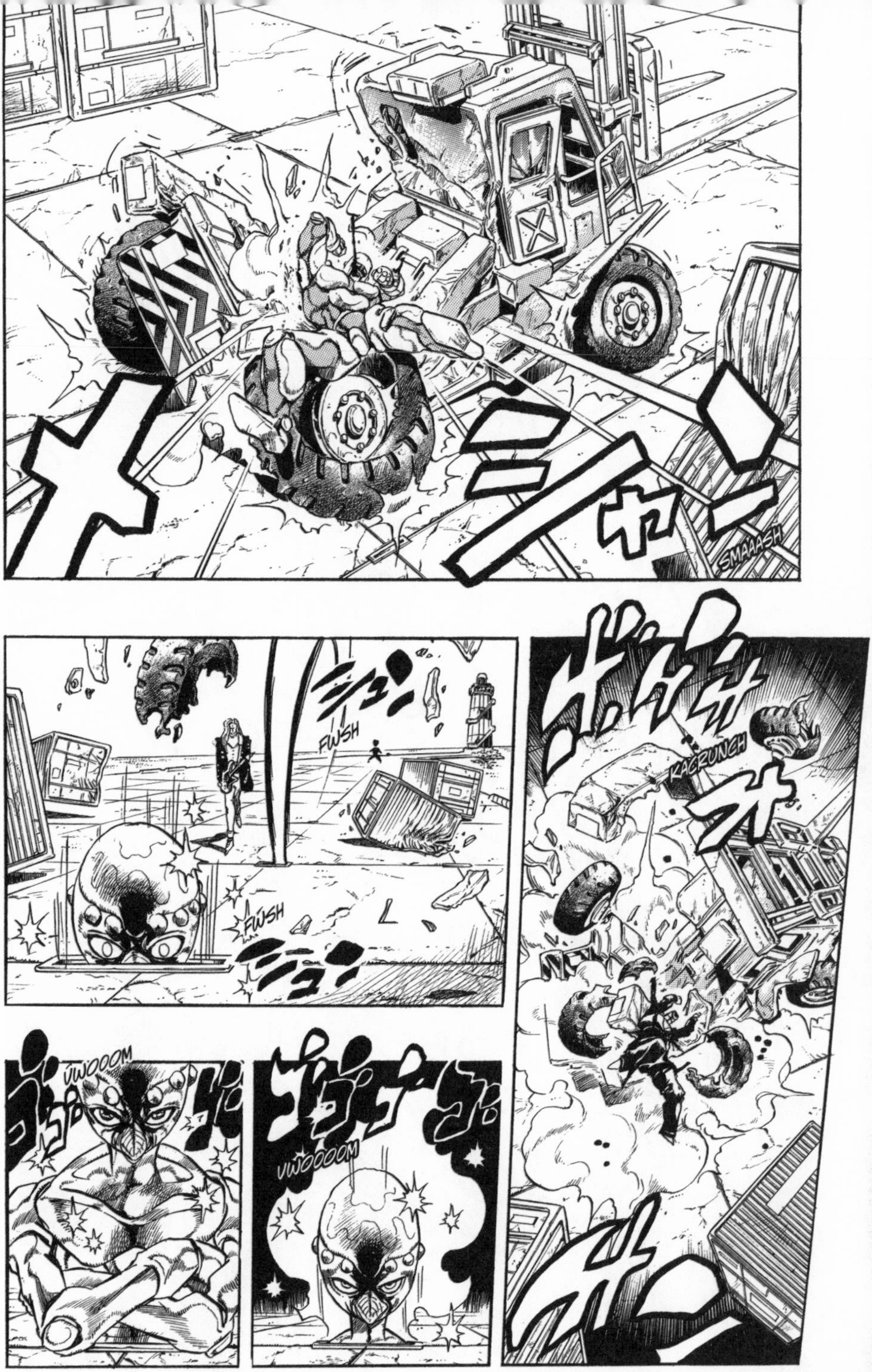
SMAAASH
KAGRUNCH
FWSH
FWSH
VWOOOOM
VWOOOM

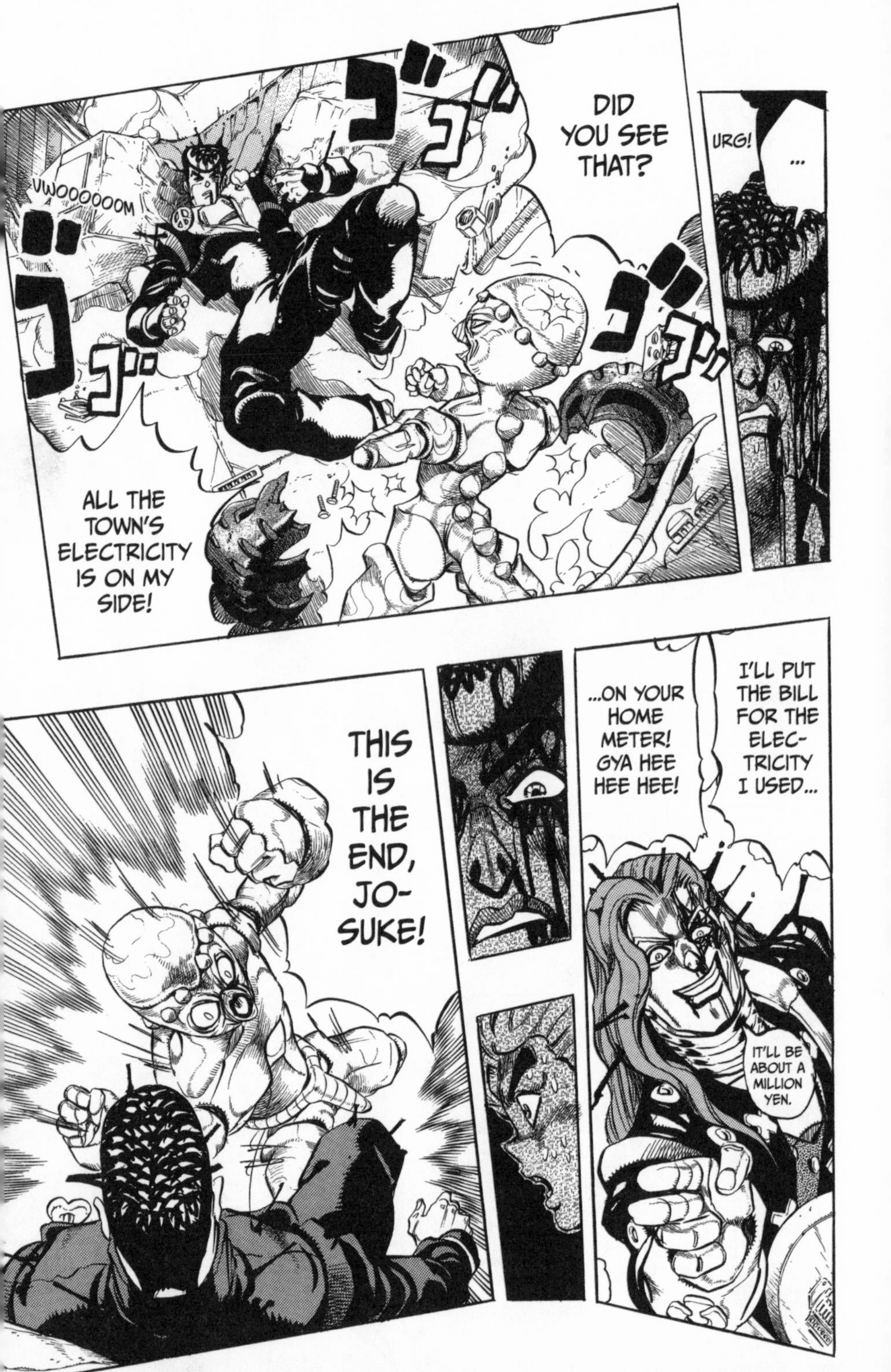
URG!
...
DID YOU SEE THAT?
VWOOOOOOM
ALL THE TOWN'S ELECTRICITY IS ON MY SIDE!
I'LL PUT THE BILL FOR THE ELEC-TRICITY I USED...
...ON YOUR HOME METER! GYA HEE HEE HEE!
IT'LL BE ABOUT A MILLION YEN.
THIS IS THE END, JO-SUKE!

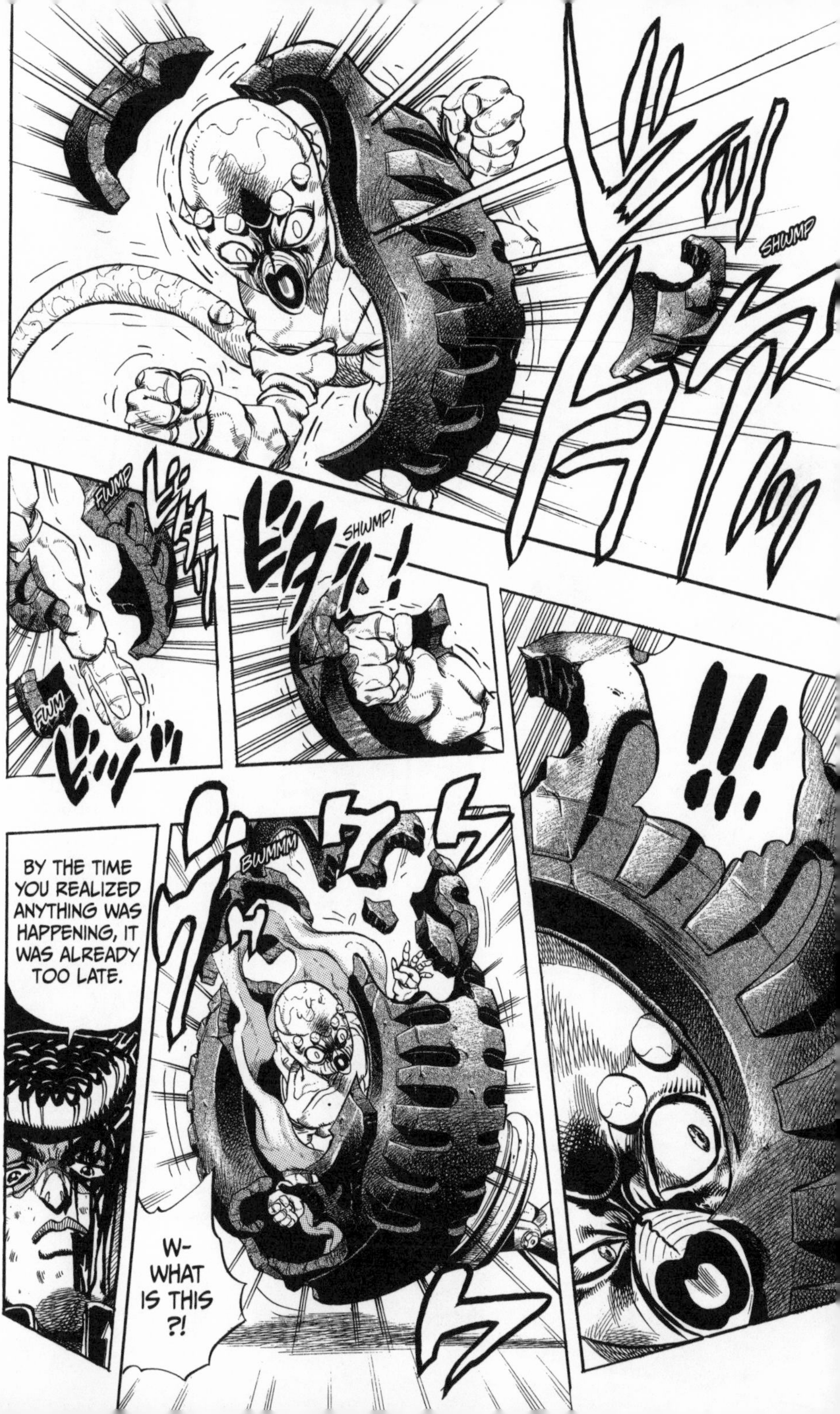
SHWUMP
SHWUMP!
FWUMP
FWM
BWMMM
W- WHAT IS THIS ?!
BY THE TIME YOU REALIZED ANYTHING WAS HAPPENING, IT WAS ALREADY TOO LATE.

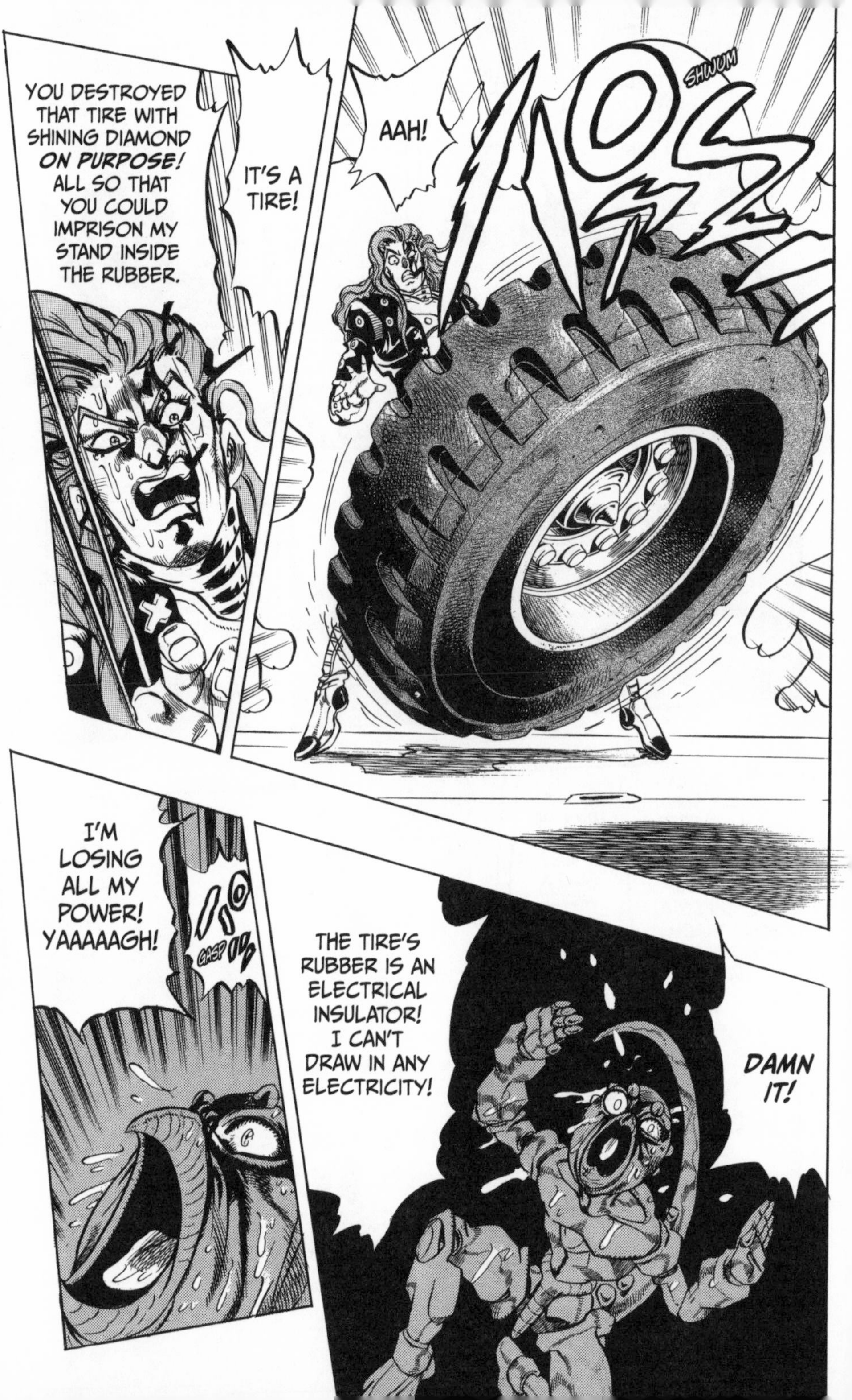
SHWUM
AAH!
IT'S A TIRE!
YOU DESTROYED THAT TIRE WITH SHINING DIAMOND ON PURPOSE! ALL SO THAT YOU COULD IMPRISON MY STAND INSIDE THE RUBBER.
THE TIRE'S RUBBER IS AN ELECTRICAL INSULATOR! I CAN'T DRAW IN ANY ELECTRICITY!
DAMN IT!
I'M LOSING ALL MY POWER! YAAAAAGH!
GASP

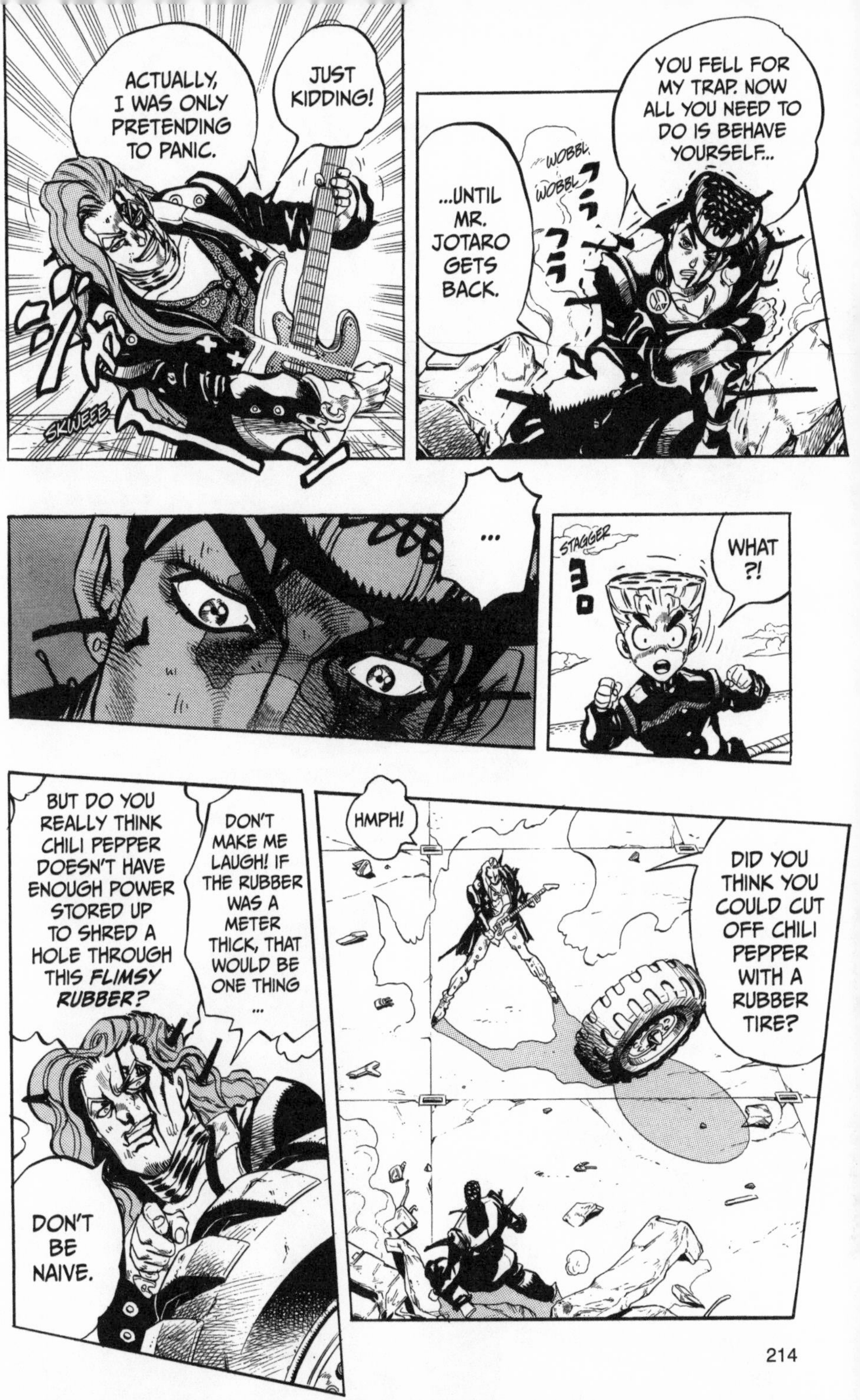
YOU FELL FOR MY TRAP. NOW ALL YOU NEED TO DO IS BEHAVE YOURSELF...
WOBBL WOBBL
...UNTIL MR. JOTARO GETS BACK.
JUST KIDDING!
ACTUALLY, I WAS ONLY PRETENDING TO PANIC.
SKWEEE
STAGGER
WHAT ?!
...
HMPH!
DID YOU THINK YOU COULD CUT OFF CHILI PEPPER WITH A RUBBER TIRE?
DON'T MAKE ME LAUGH! IF THE RUBBER WAS A METER THICK, THAT WOULD BE ONE THING ...
BUT DO YOU REALLY THINK CHILI PEPPER DOESN'T HAVE ENOUGH POWER STORED UP TO SHRED A HOLE THROUGH THIS *FLIMSY RUBBER?*
DON'T BE NAIVE.

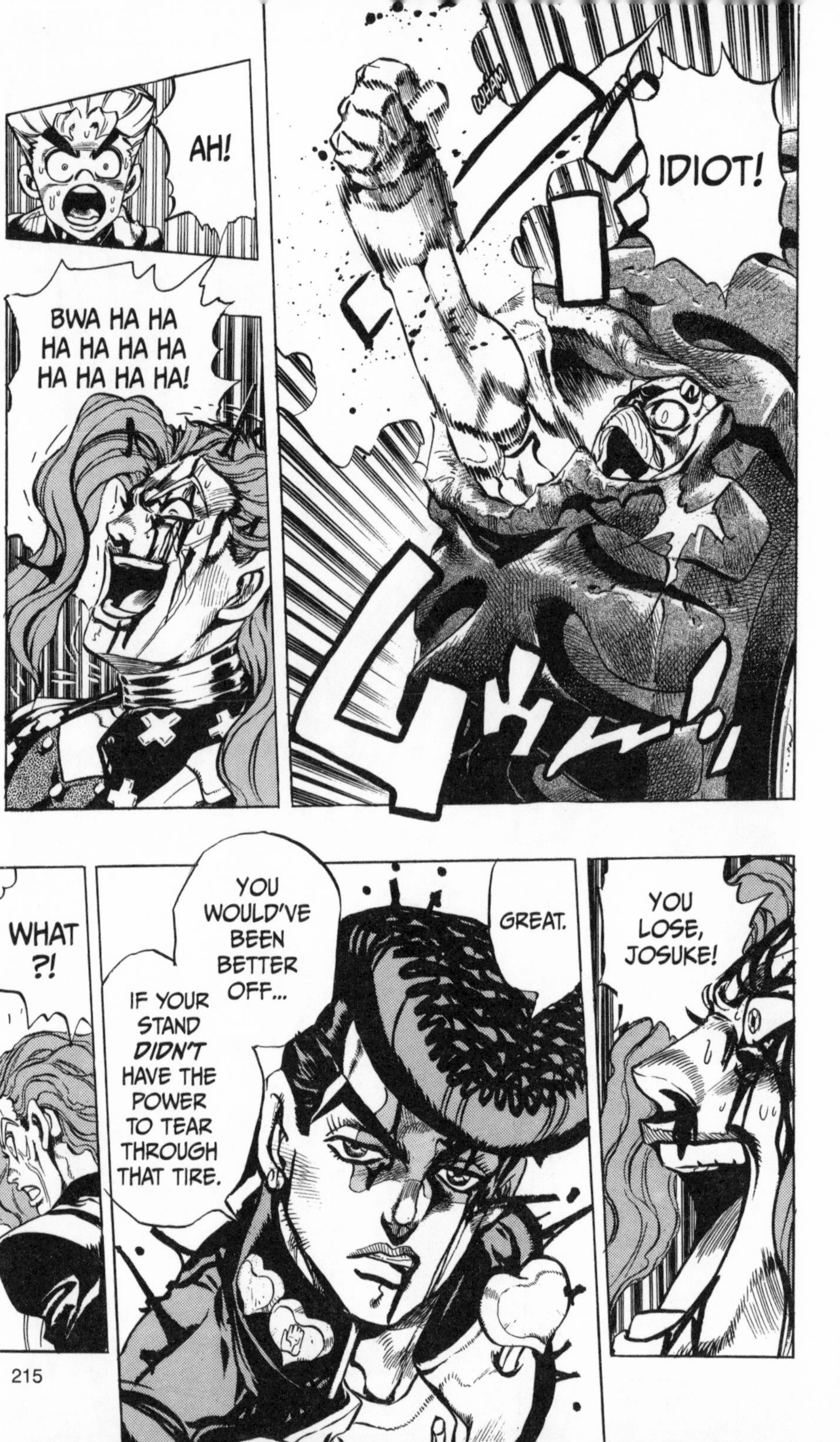
IDIOT!
AH!
BWA HA HA HA HA HA HA HA HA HA HA!
YOU LOSE, JOSUKE!
GREAT.
YOU WOULD'VE BEEN BETTER OFF...
IF YOUR STAND *DIDN'T* HAVE THE POWER TO TEAR THROUGH THAT TIRE.
WHAT?!

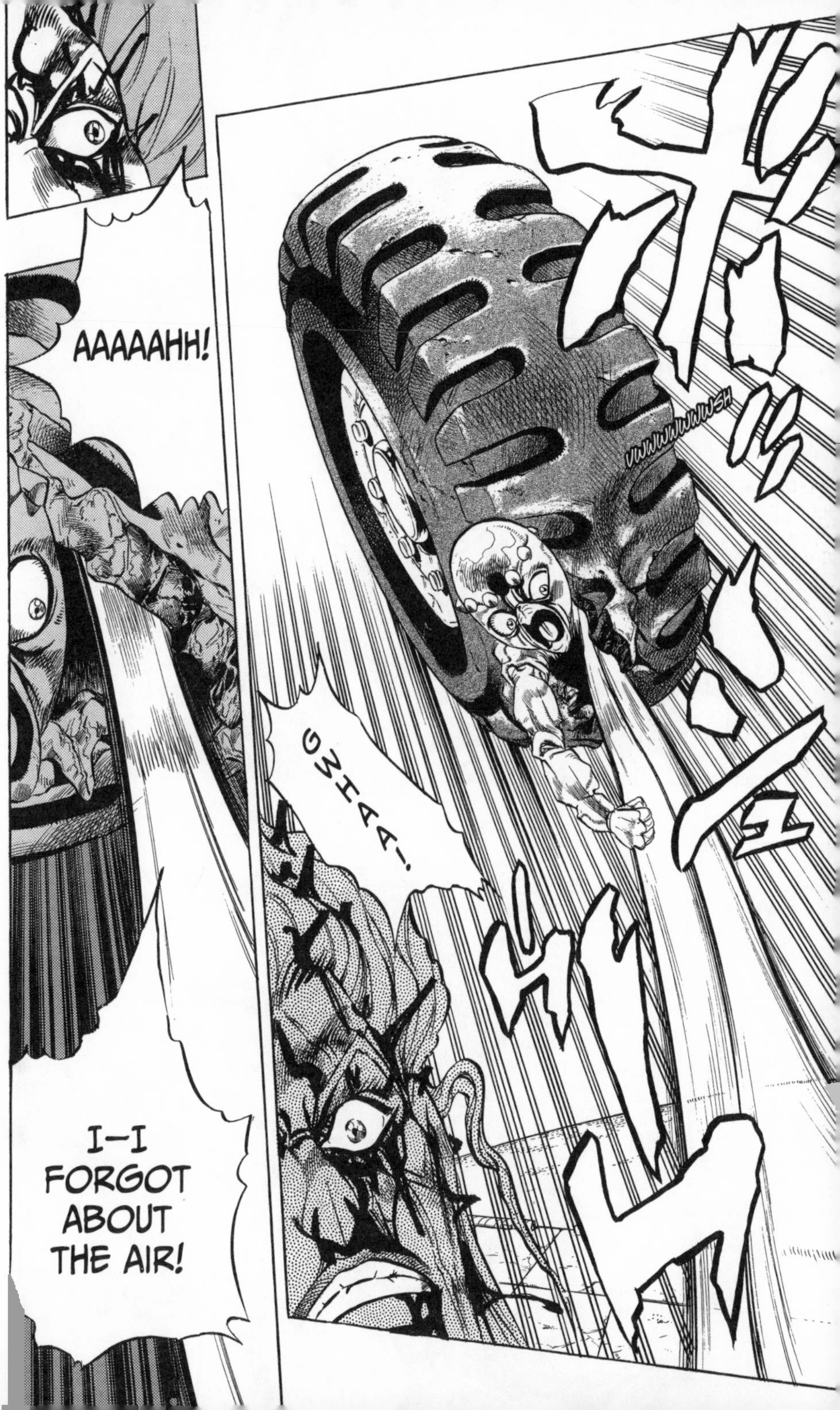
VWWWWWWSH
GWIAA!
AAAAAHH!
I—I FORGOT ABOUT THE AIR!

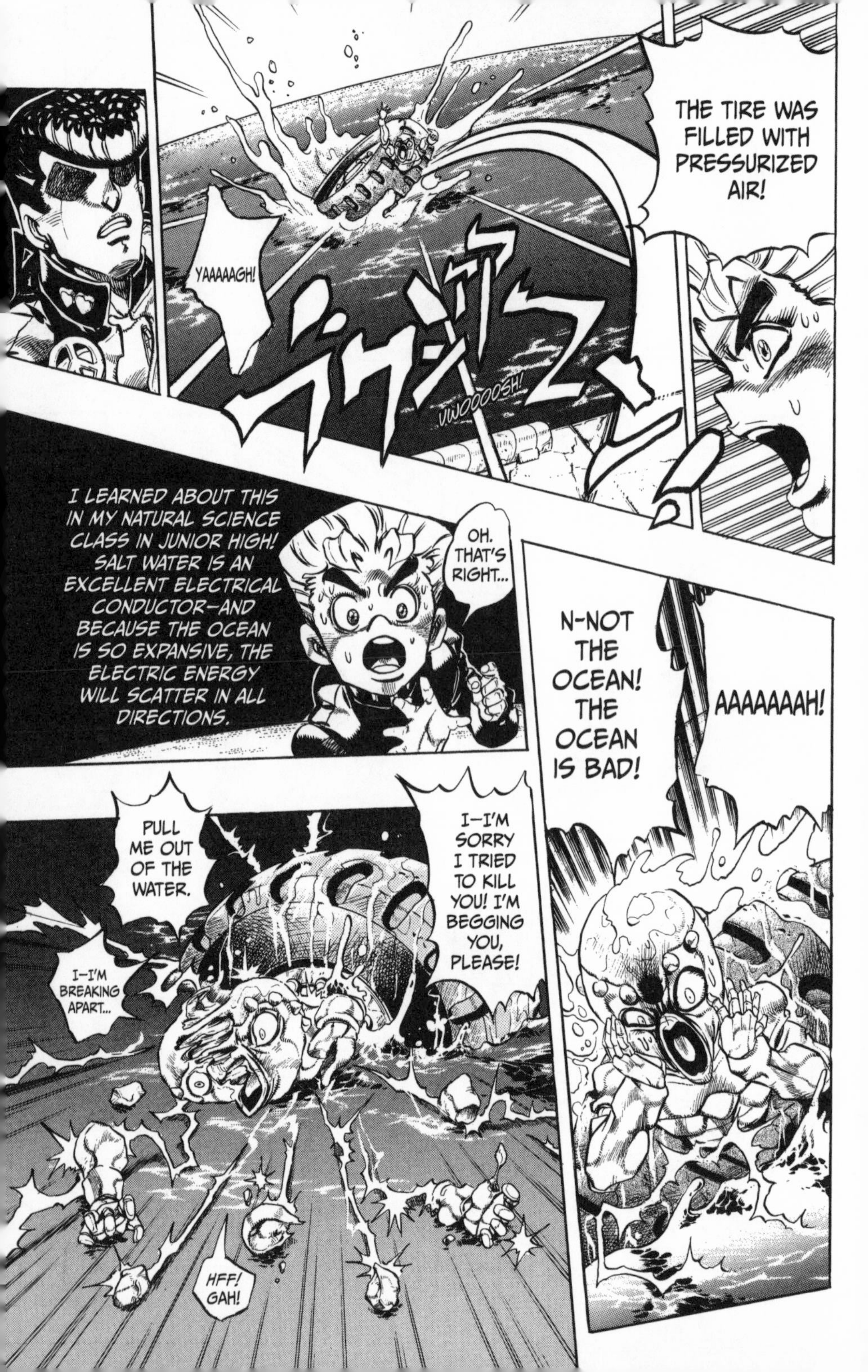
THE TIRE WAS FILLED WITH PRESSURIZED AIR!
YAAAAAGH!
VWOOOOOSH!
AAAAAAAH!
N-NOT THE OCEAN! THE OCEAN IS BAD!
OH. THAT'S RIGHT...
I LEARNED ABOUT THIS IN MY NATURAL SCIENCE CLASS IN JUNIOR HIGH! SALT WATER IS AN EXCELLENT ELECTRICAL CONDUCTOR—AND BECAUSE THE OCEAN IS SO EXPANSIVE, THE ELECTRIC ENERGY WILL SCATTER IN ALL DIRECTIONS.
I—I'M SORRY I TRIED TO KILL YOU! I'M BEGGING YOU, PLEASE!
PULL ME OUT OF THE WATER.
I—I'M BREAKING APART...
HFF! GAH!

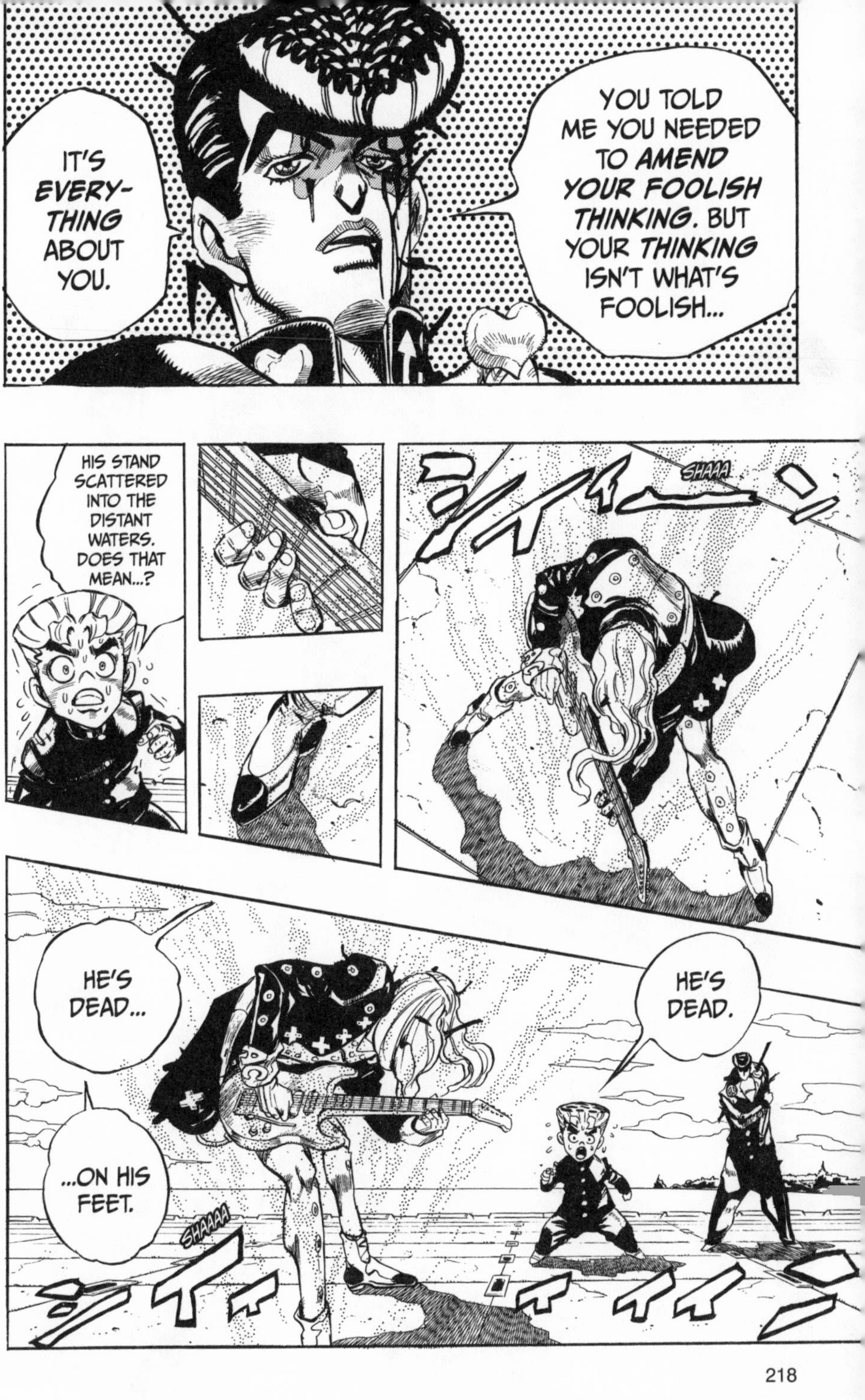
YOU TOLD ME YOU NEEDED TO AMEND YOUR FOOLISH THINKING. BUT YOUR THINKING ISN'T WHAT'S FOOLISH...
IT'S EVERYTHING ABOUT YOU.
SHAAA
HIS STAND SCATTERED INTO THE DISTANT WATERS. DOES THAT MEAN...?
HE'S DEAD.
HE'S DEAD...
...ON HIS FEET.
SHAAAA

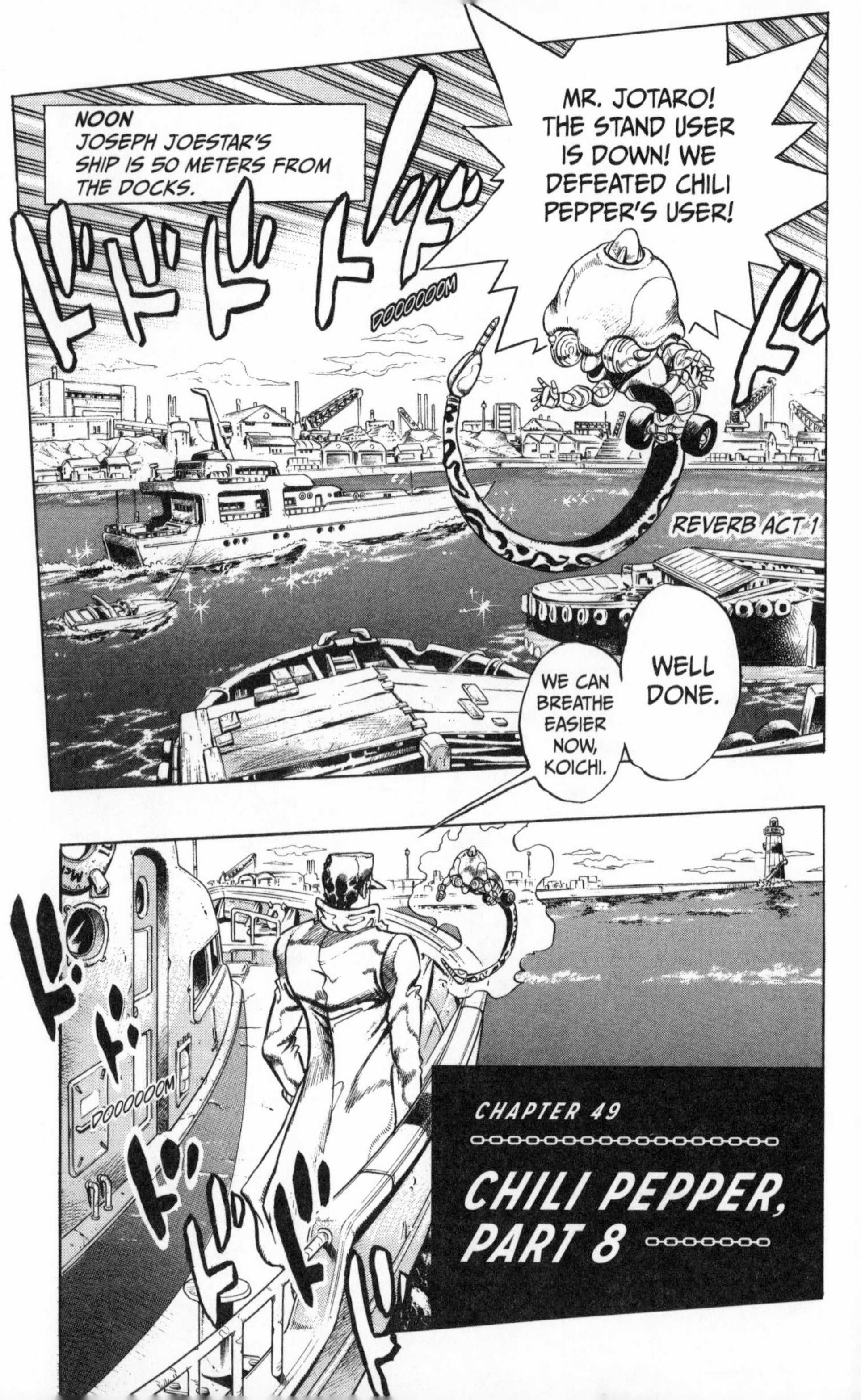
MR. JOTARO! THE STAND USER IS DOWN! WE DEFEATED CHILI PEPPER'S USER!
NOON
JOSEPH JOESTAR'S SHIP IS 50 METERS FROM THE DOCKS.
DOOOOOOM
REVERB ACT 1
WELL DONE.
WE CAN BREATHE EASIER NOW, KOICHI.
CHAPTER 49
CHILI PEPPER, PART 8
DOOOOOOM

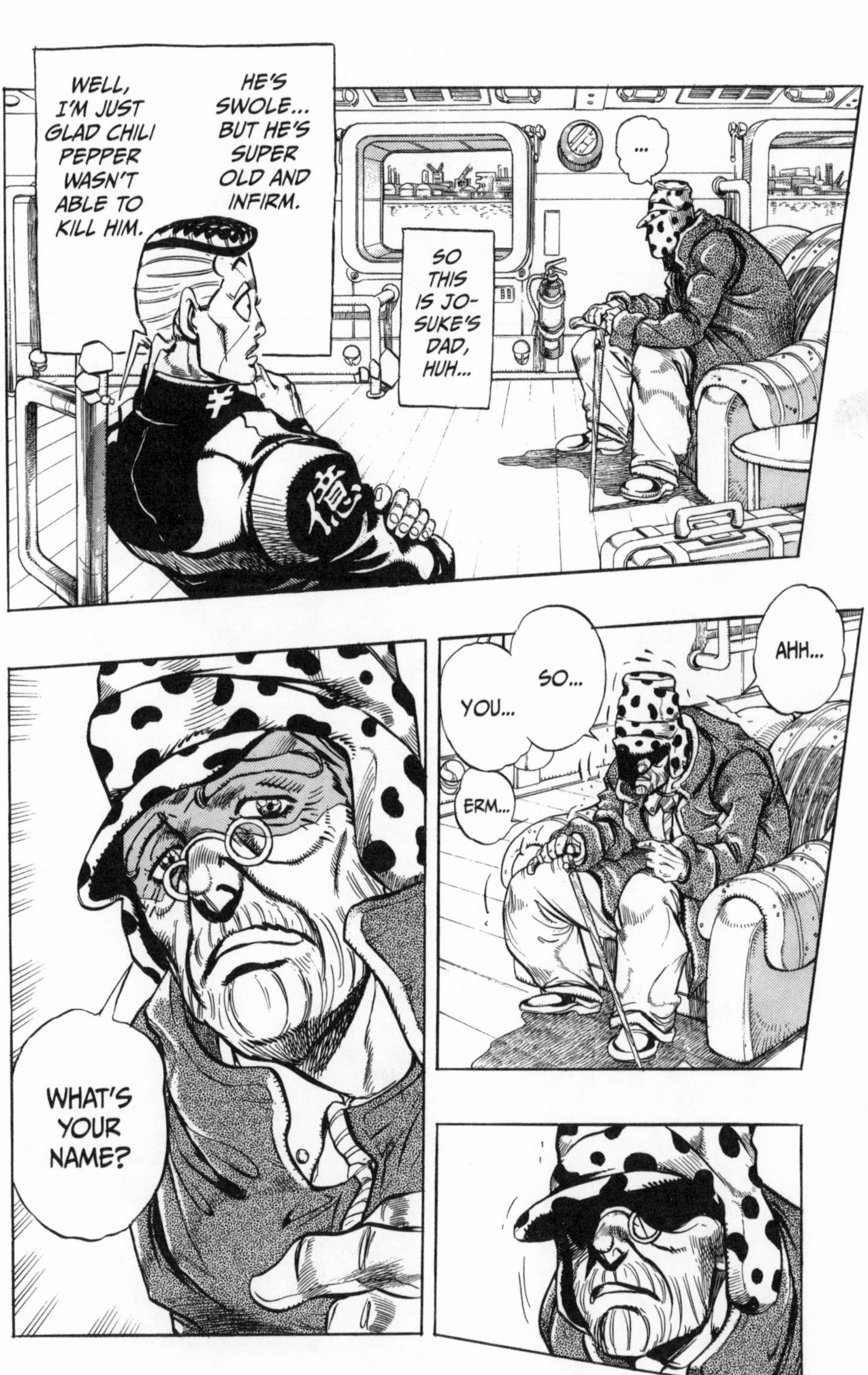
...
SO THIS IS JO-SUKE'S DAD, HUH...
HE'S SWOLE... BUT HE'S SUPER OLD AND INFIRM.
WELL, I'M JUST GLAD CHILI PEPPER WASN'T ABLE TO KILL HIM.
AHH...
SO...
YOU...
ERM...
WHAT'S YOUR NAME?

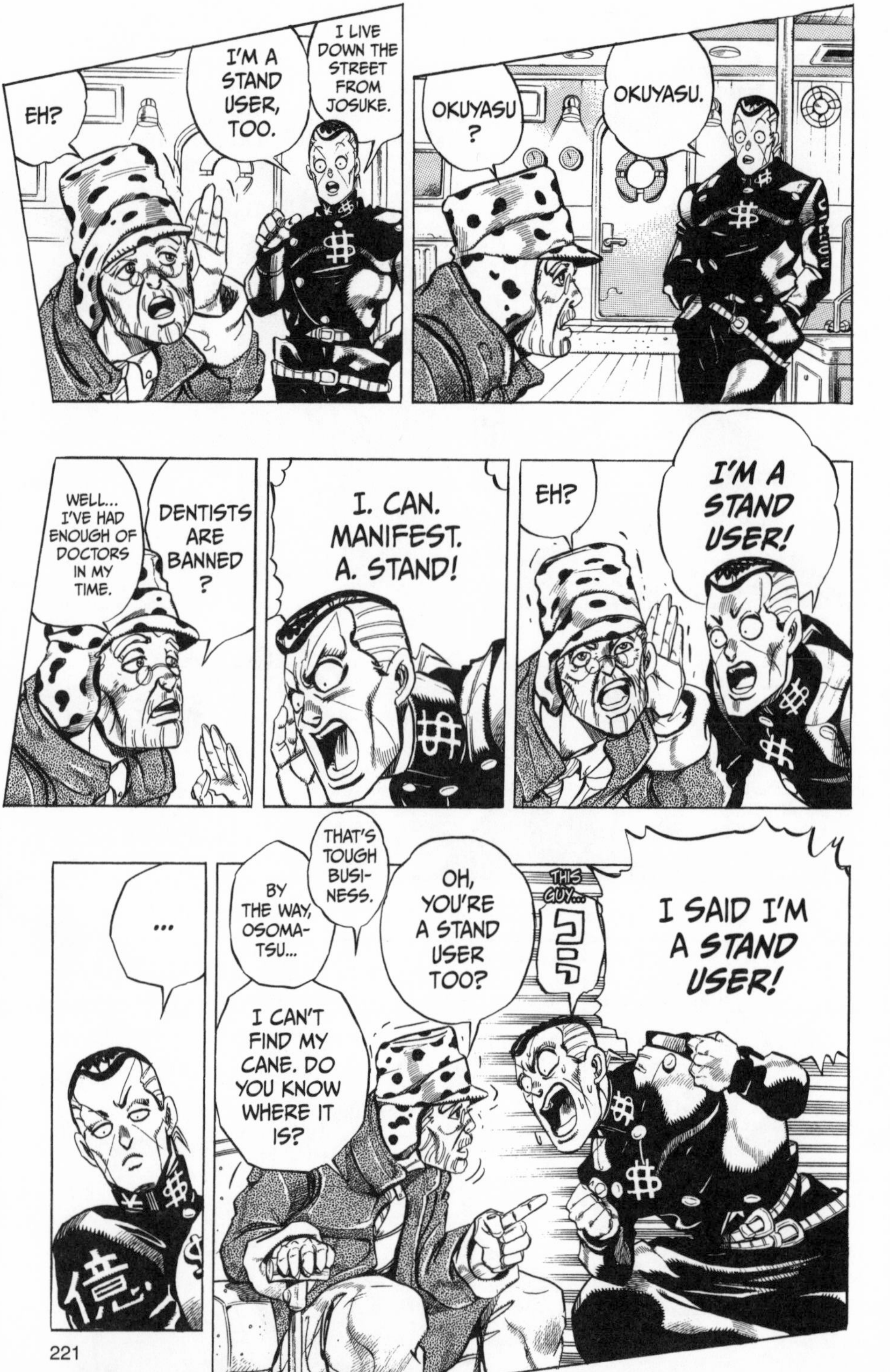
OKUYASU.
OKUYASU ?
I LIVE DOWN THE STREET FROM JOSUKE.
I'M A STAND USER, TOO.
EH?
I'M A STAND USER!
EH?
I. CAN. MANIFEST. A. STAND!
DENTISTS ARE BANNED ?
WELL... I'VE HAD ENOUGH OF DOCTORS IN MY TIME.
I SAID I'M A STAND USER!
THIS GUY...
OH, YOU'RE A STAND USER TOO?
THAT'S TOUGH BUSINESS.
BY THE WAY, OSOMATSU...
I CAN'T FIND MY CANE. DO YOU KNOW WHERE IT IS?
...

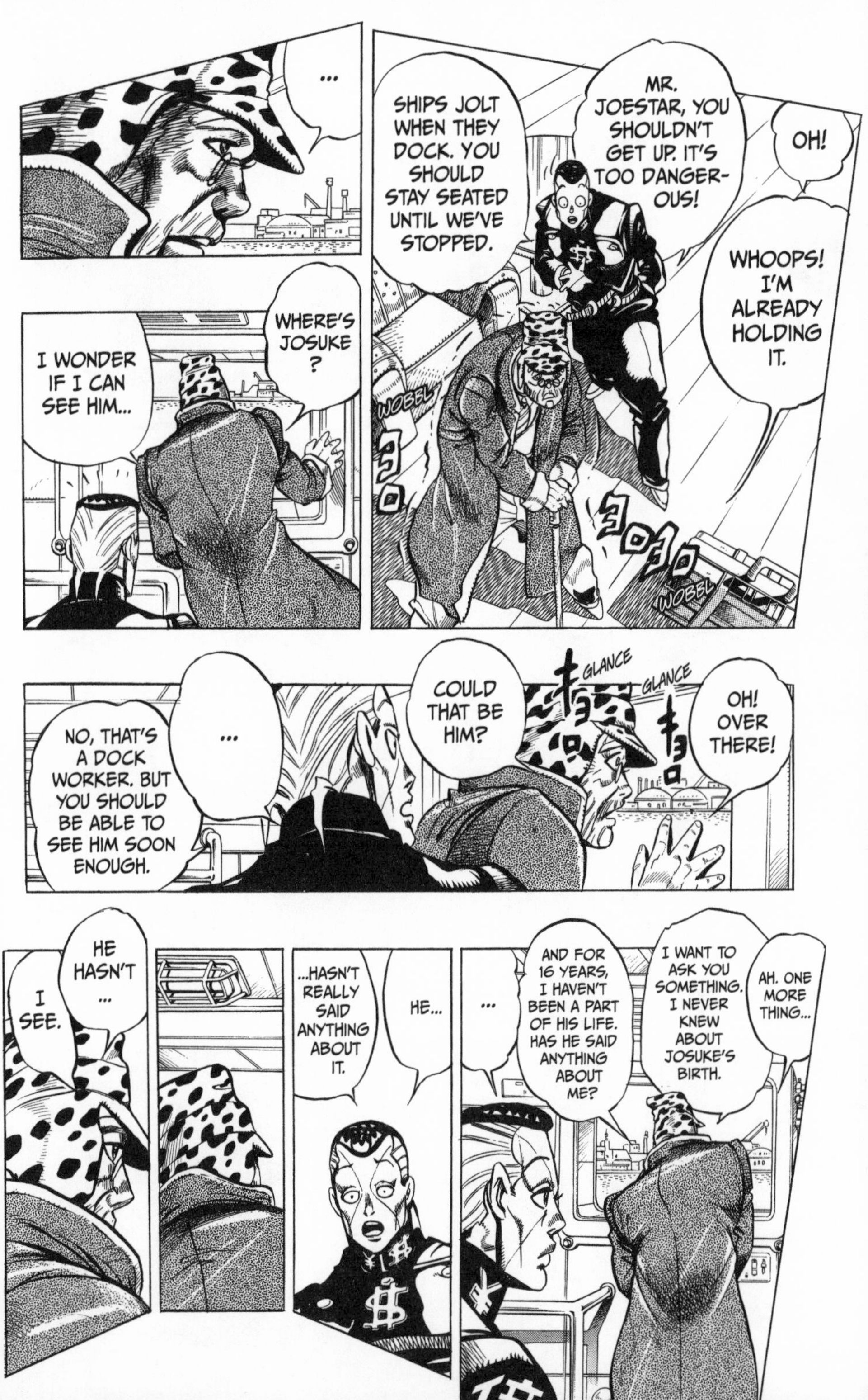
OH!
MR. JOESTAR, YOU SHOULDN'T GET UP. IT'S TOO DANGER-OUS!
SHIPS JOLT WHEN THEY DOCK. YOU SHOULD STAY SEATED UNTIL WE'VE STOPPED.
WHOOPS! I'M ALREADY HOLDING IT.
WOBBL
WOBBL
...
WHERE'S JOSUKE?
I WONDER IF I CAN SEE HIM...
OH! OVER THERE!
GLANCE
GLANCE
COULD THAT BE HIM?
...
NO, THAT'S A DOCK WORKER. BUT YOU SHOULD BE ABLE TO SEE HIM SOON ENOUGH.
AH. ONE MORE THING...
I WANT TO ASK YOU SOMETHING. I NEVER KNEW ABOUT JOSUKE'S BIRTH.
AND FOR 16 YEARS, I HAVEN'T BEEN A PART OF HIS LIFE. HAS HE SAID ANYTHING ABOUT ME?
...
HE...
...HASN'T REALLY SAID ANYTHING ABOUT IT.
HE HASN'T ...
I SEE.

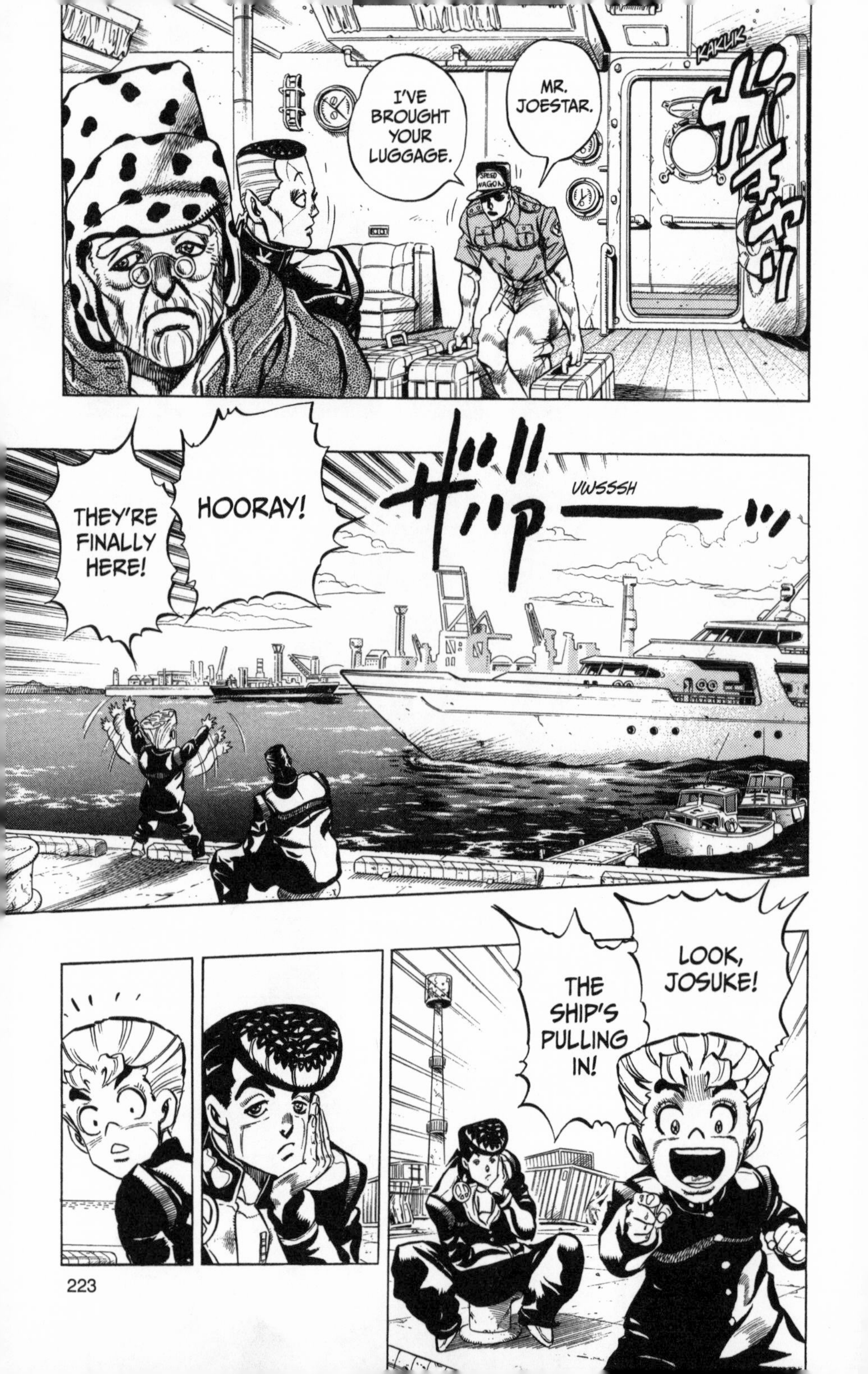
KAKLIK
MR. JOESTAR.
I'VE BROUGHT YOUR LUGGAGE.
UWSSSH
HOORAY!
THEY'RE FINALLY HERE!
LOOK, JOSUKE!
THE SHIP'S PULLING IN!

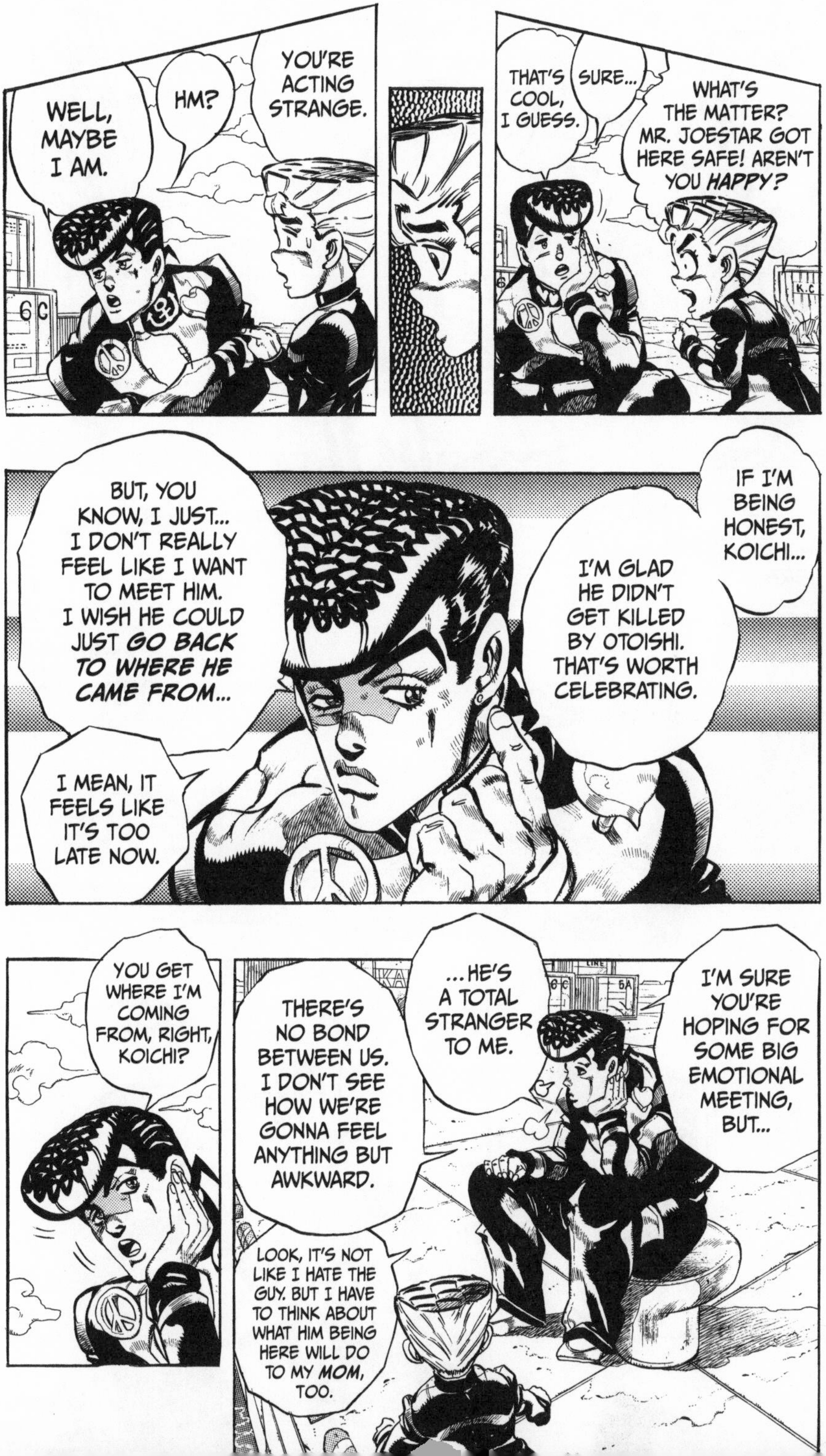
WHAT'S THE MATTER? MR. JOESTAR GOT HERE SAFE! AREN'T YOU *HAPPY?*
SURE...
THAT'S COOL, I GUESS.
YOU'RE ACTING STRANGE.
HM?
WELL, MAYBE I AM.
IF I'M BEING HONEST, KOICHI...
I'M GLAD HE DIDN'T GET KILLED BY OTOISHI. THAT'S WORTH CELEBRATING.
BUT, YOU KNOW, I JUST... I DON'T REALLY FEEL LIKE I WANT TO MEET HIM. I WISH HE COULD JUST *GO BACK TO WHERE HE CAME FROM...*
I MEAN, IT FEELS LIKE IT'S TOO LATE NOW.
I'M SURE YOU'RE HOPING FOR SOME BIG EMOTIONAL MEETING, BUT...
...HE'S A TOTAL STRANGER TO ME.
THERE'S NO BOND BETWEEN US. I DON'T SEE HOW WE'RE GONNA FEEL ANYTHING BUT AWKWARD.
LOOK, IT'S NOT LIKE I HATE THE GUY. BUT I HAVE TO THINK ABOUT WHAT HIM BEING HERE WILL DO TO MY *MOM,* TOO.
YOU GET WHERE I'M COMING FROM, RIGHT, KOICHI?

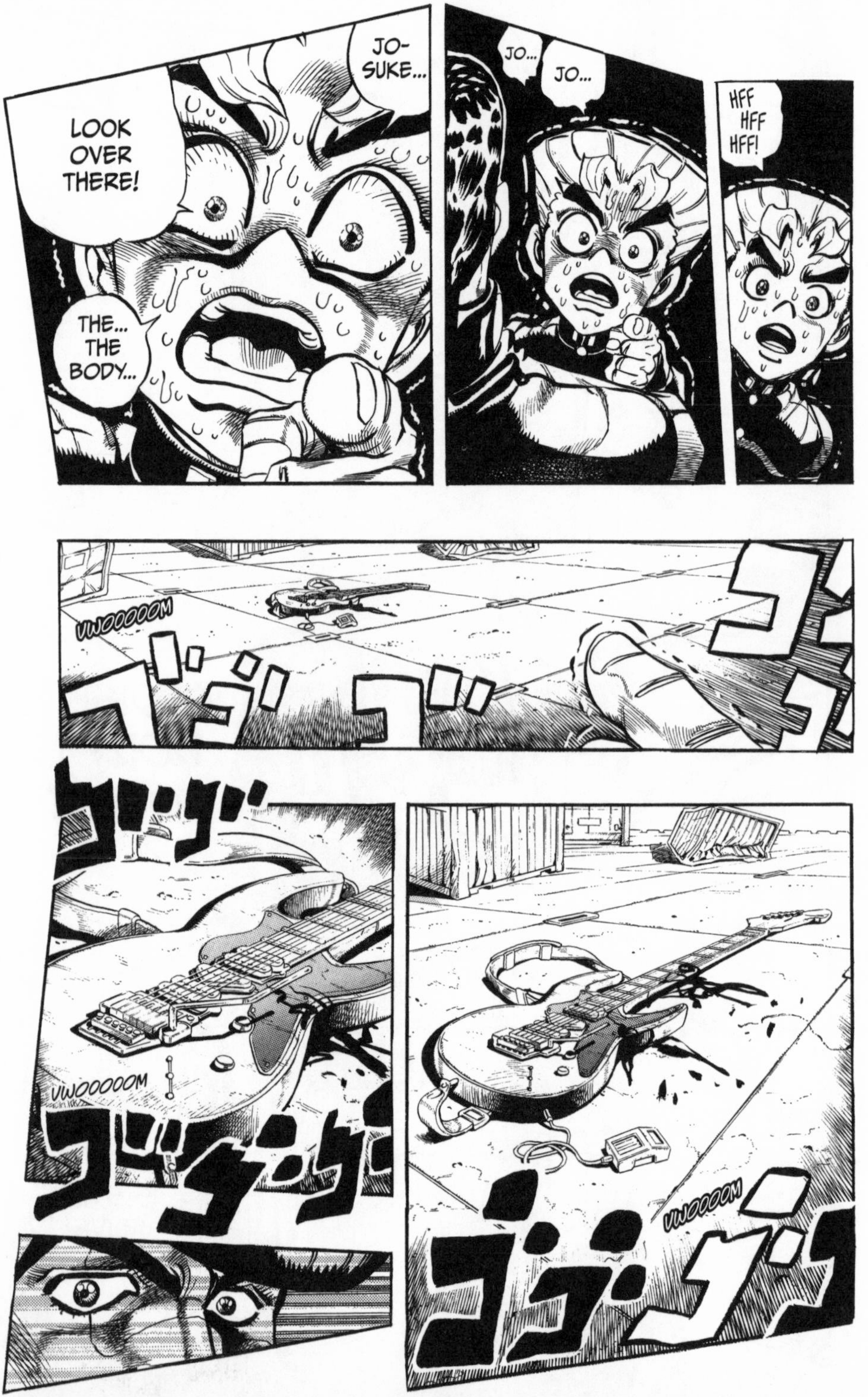
HFF HFF HFF!
JO...
JO...
JO-SUKE...
LOOK OVER THERE!
THE... THE BODY...
VWOOOOOM
VWOOOOM
VWOOOOOM

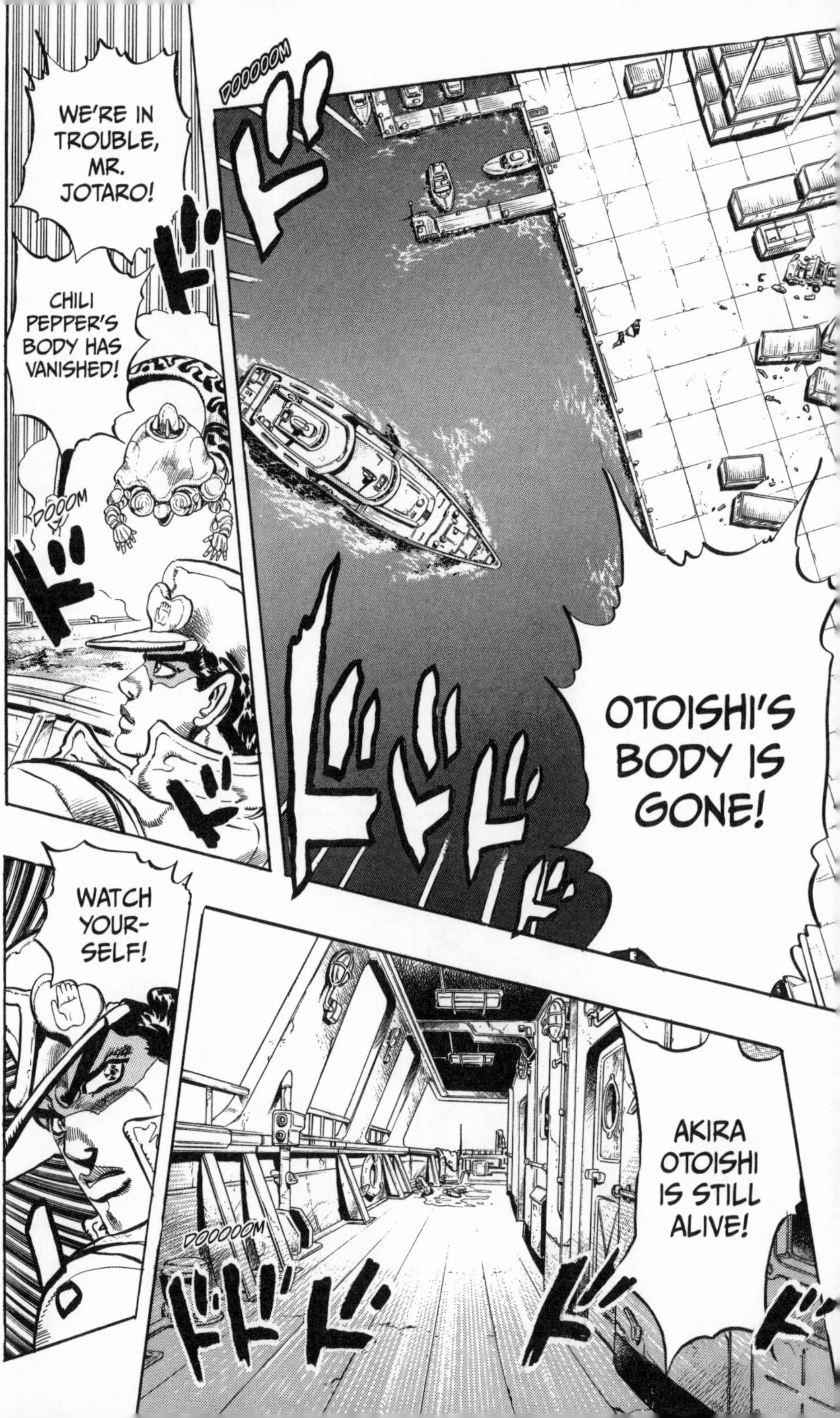
DOOOOOM
OTOISHI'S BODY IS GONE!
WE'RE IN TROUBLE, MR. JOTARO!
CHILI PEPPER'S BODY HAS VANISHED!
DOOOM
AKIRA OTOISHI IS STILL ALIVE!
DOOOOOM
WATCH YOURSELF!

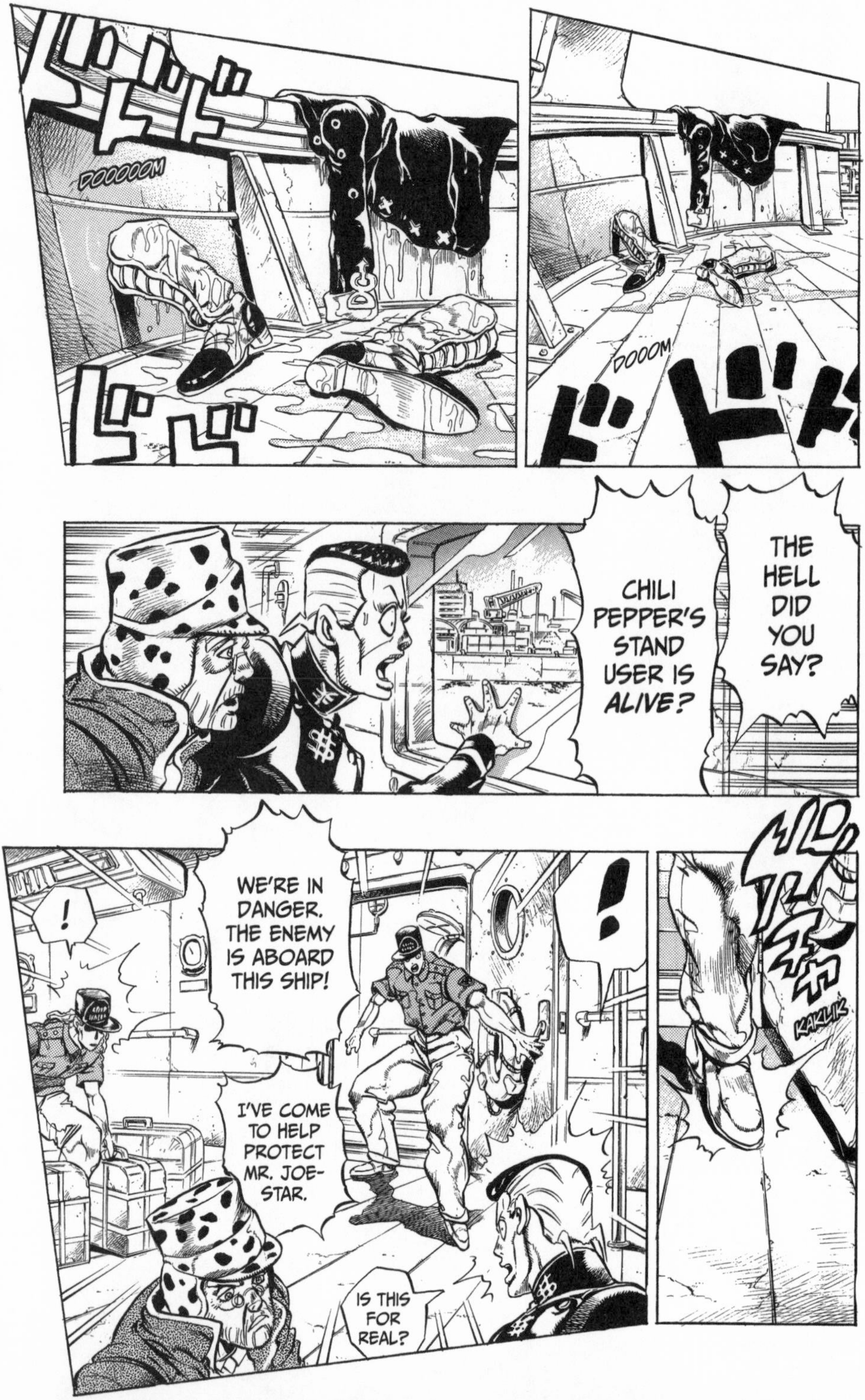
DOOOM
DOOOOOM
THE HELL DID YOU SAY?
CHILI PEPPER'S STAND USER IS ALIVE?
KAKUK
!
WE'RE IN DANGER. THE ENEMY IS ABOARD THIS SHIP!
!
I'VE COME TO HELP PROTECT MR. JOE-STAR.
IS THIS FOR REAL?

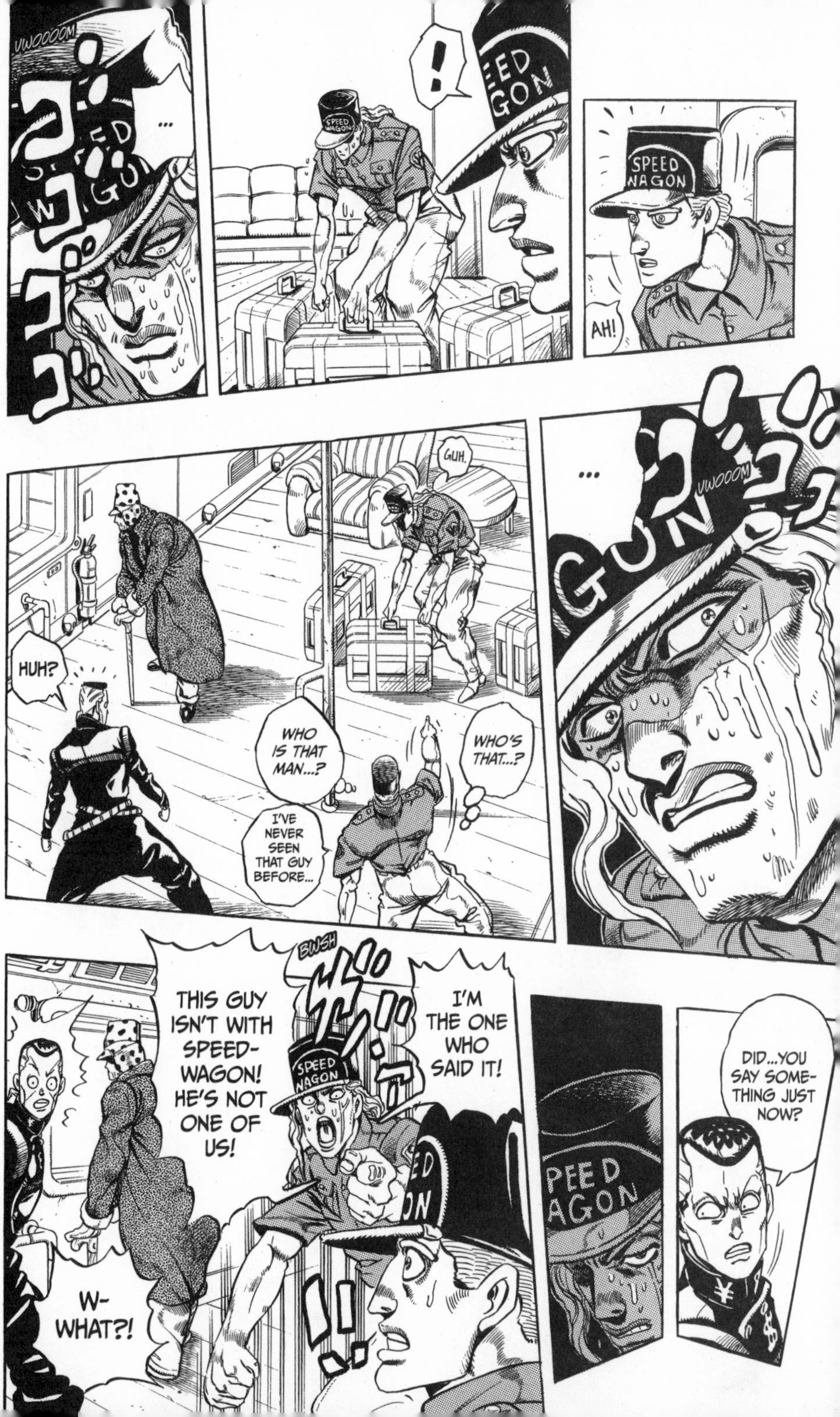
AH!
!
UWOOOOM
...
...
UWOOOM
GUH.
WHO'S THAT...?
WHO IS THAT MAN...?
I'VE NEVER SEEN THAT GUY BEFORE...
HUH?
DID...YOU SAY SOME-THING JUST NOW?
I'M THE ONE WHO SAID IT!
BWSH
THIS GUY ISN'T WITH SPEED-WAGON! HE'S NOT ONE OF US!
W-WHAT?!

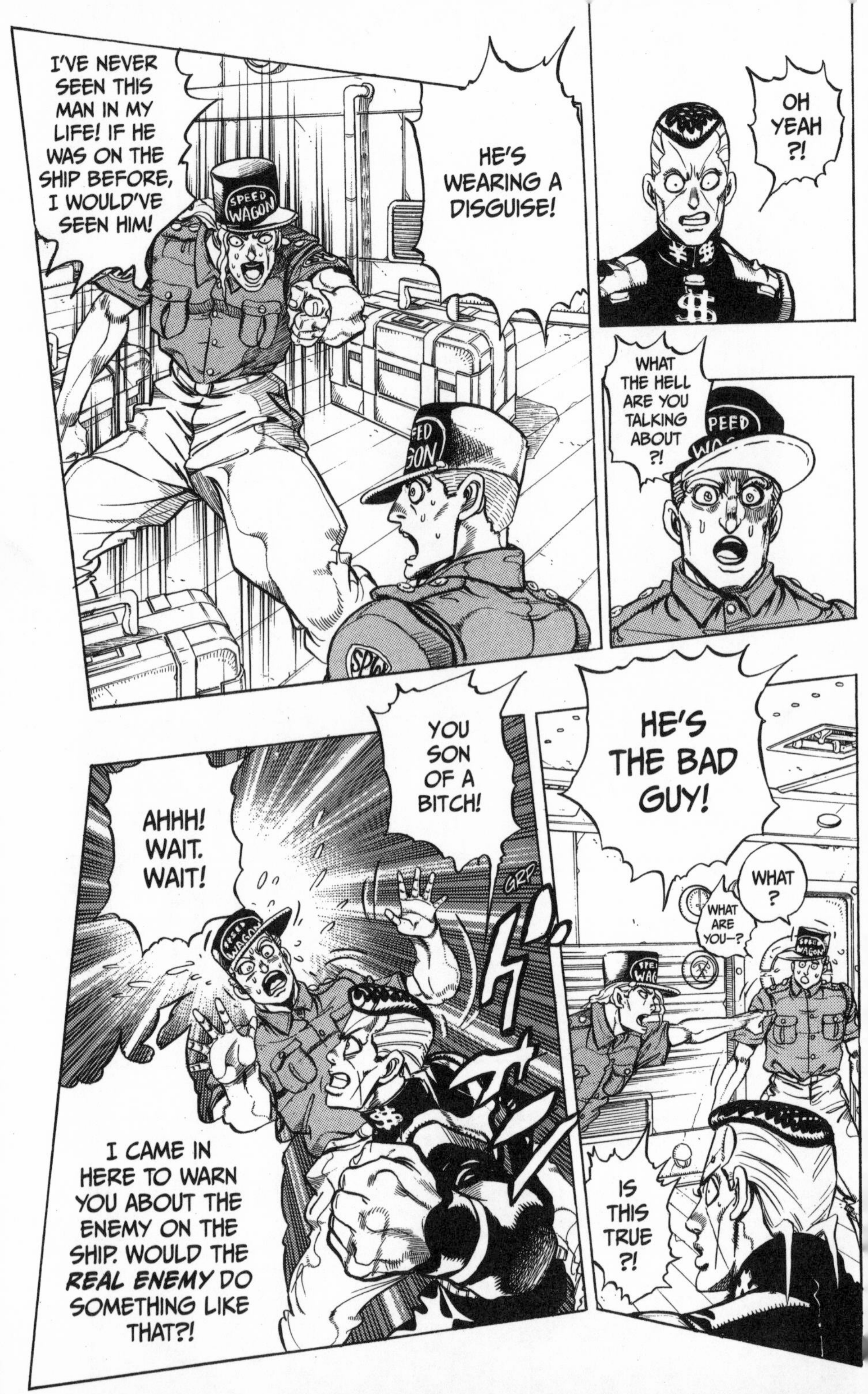
OH YEAH ?!
WHAT THE HELL ARE YOU TALKING ABOUT ?!
I'VE NEVER SEEN THIS MAN IN MY LIFE! IF HE WAS ON THE SHIP BEFORE, I WOULD'VE SEEN HIM!
HE'S WEARING A DISGUISE!
HE'S THE BAD GUY!
WHAT ?
WHAT ARE YOU—?
IS THIS TRUE ?!
YOU SON OF A BITCH!
GRP
AHHH! WAIT. WAIT!
I CAME IN HERE TO WARN YOU ABOUT THE ENEMY ON THE SHIP. WOULD THE *REAL ENEMY* DO SOMETHING LIKE THAT?!

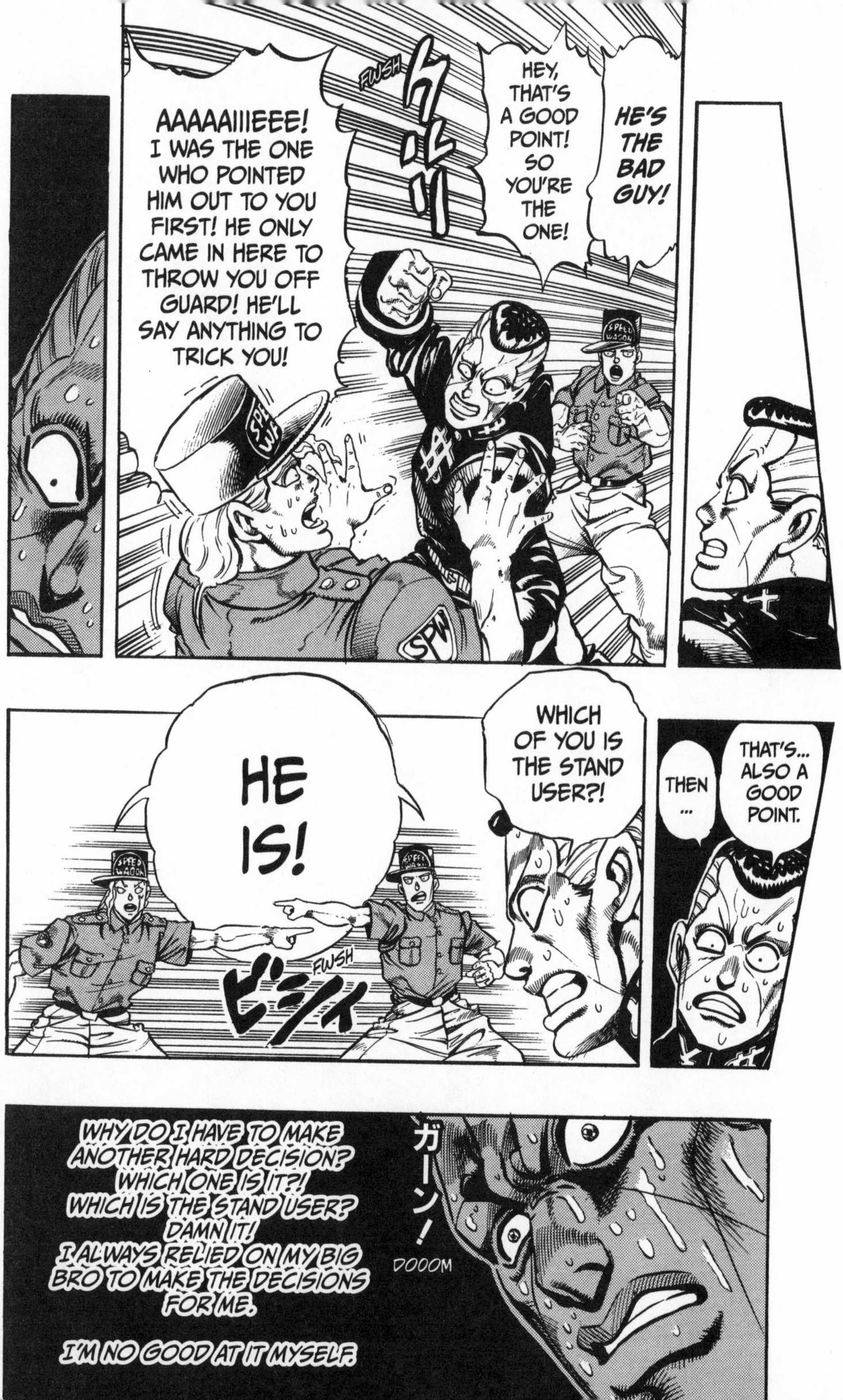
HE'S THE BAD GUY!
HEY, THAT'S A GOOD POINT! SO YOU'RE THE ONE!
FWSH
AAAAAIIIEEE! I WAS THE ONE WHO POINTED HIM OUT TO YOU FIRST! HE ONLY CAME IN HERE TO THROW YOU OFF GUARD! HE'LL SAY ANYTHING TO TRICK YOU!
THAT'S... ALSO A GOOD POINT.
THEN ...
WHICH OF YOU IS THE STAND USER?!
HE IS!
FWSH
ガーン！
DOOOM
WHY DO I HAVE TO MAKE ANOTHER HARD DECISION? WHICH ONE IS IT?! WHICH IS THE STAND USER? DAMN IT! I ALWAYS RELIED ON MY BIG BRO TO MAKE THE DECISIONS FOR ME.
I'M NO GOOD AT IT MYSELF.

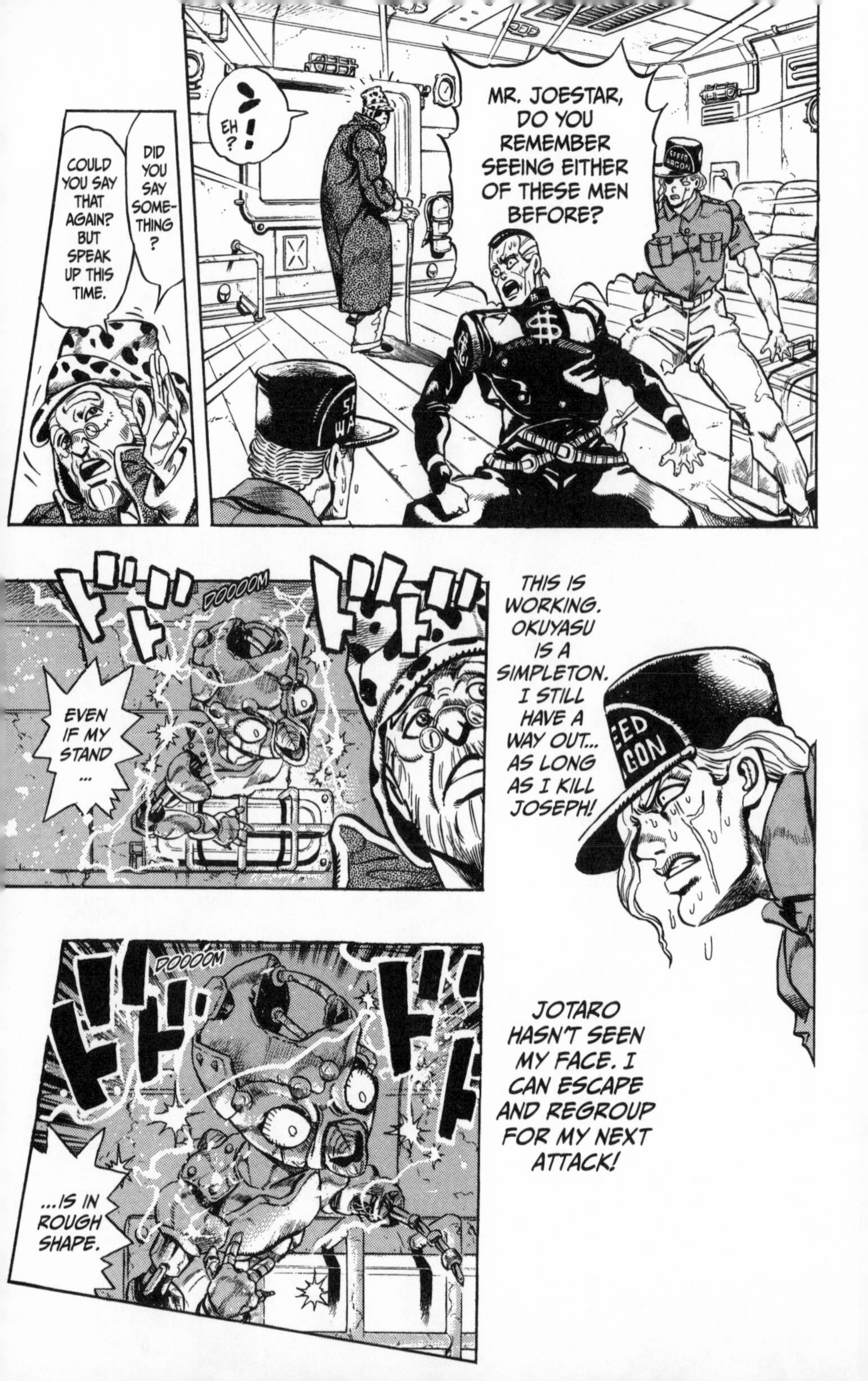
MR. JOESTAR, DO YOU REMEMBER SEEING EITHER OF THESE MEN BEFORE?
EH?
DID YOU SAY SOMETHING?
COULD YOU SAY THAT AGAIN? BUT SPEAK UP THIS TIME.
THIS IS WORKING. OKUYASU IS A SIMPLETON. I STILL HAVE A WAY OUT... AS LONG AS I KILL JOSEPH!
JOTARO HASN'T SEEN MY FACE. I CAN ESCAPE AND REGROUP FOR MY NEXT ATTACK!
DOOOOM
EVEN IF MY STAND ...
DOOOOM
...IS IN ROUGH SHAPE.

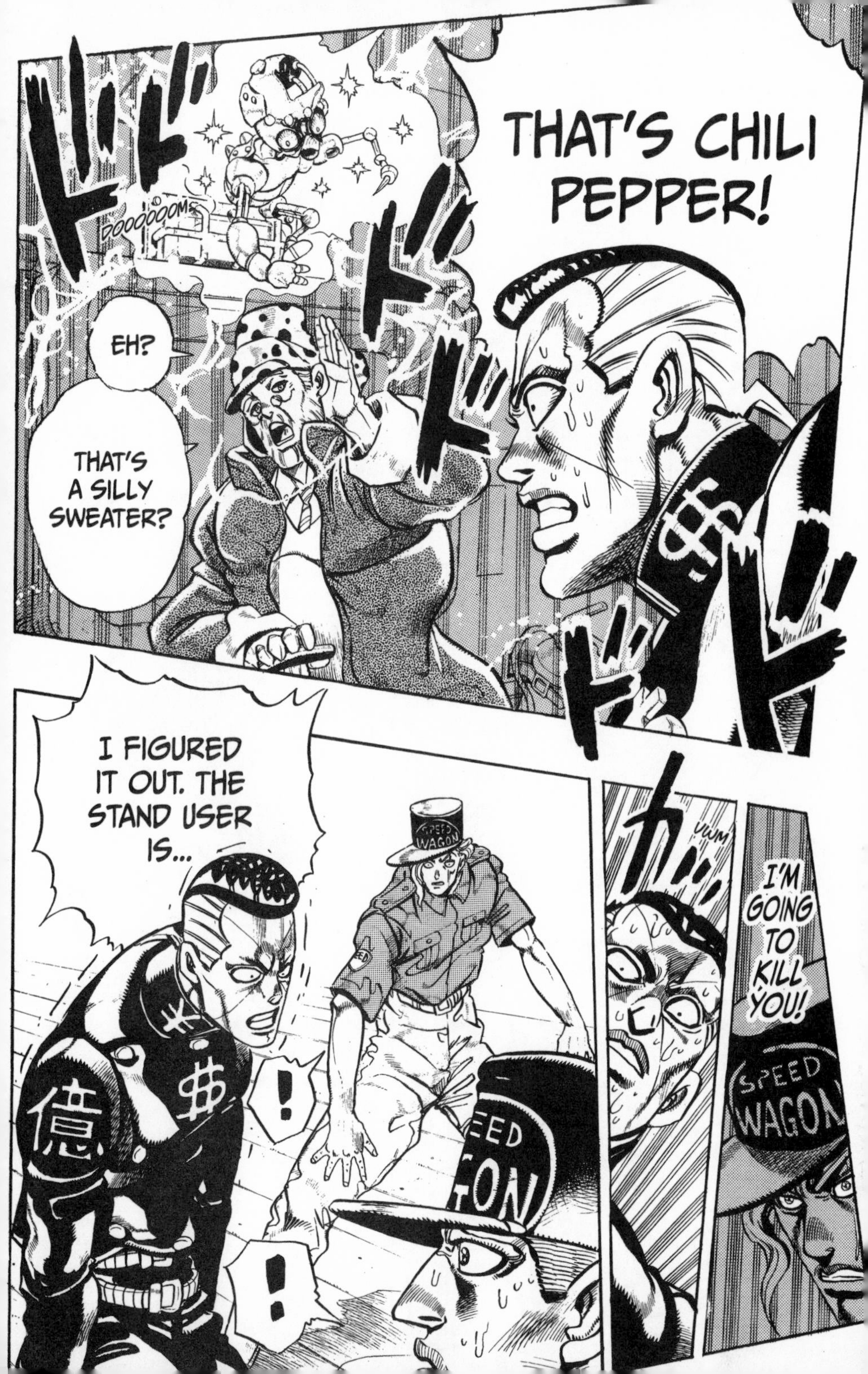
THAT'S CHILI PEPPER!
DOOOOOOOMS
EH?
THAT'S A SILLY SWEATER?
VUM
I'M GOING TO KILL YOU!
I FIGURED IT OUT. THE STAND USER IS...
!
!

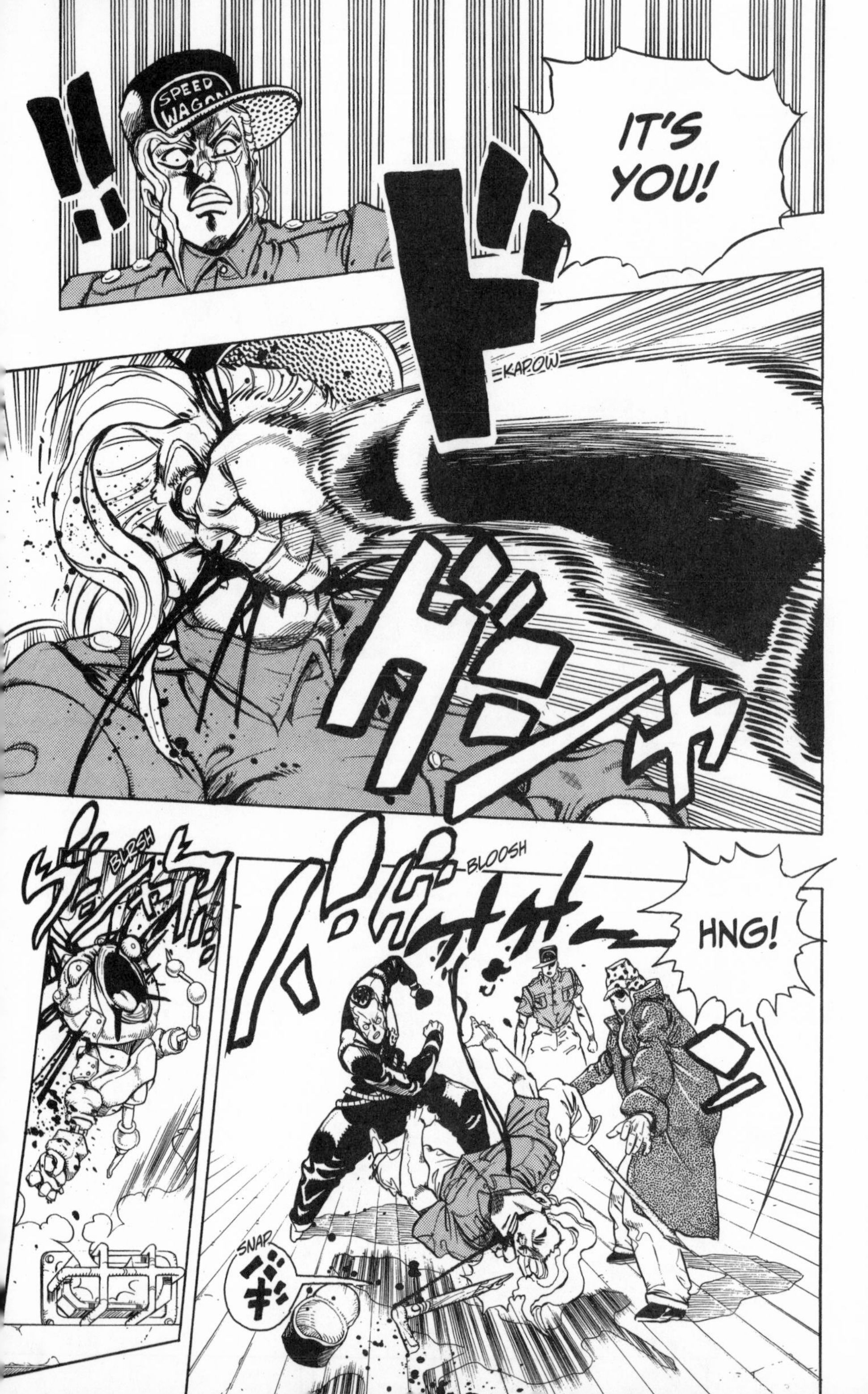
IT'S YOU!
KAPOW
BLOOSH
HNG!
SNAP
BLRSH

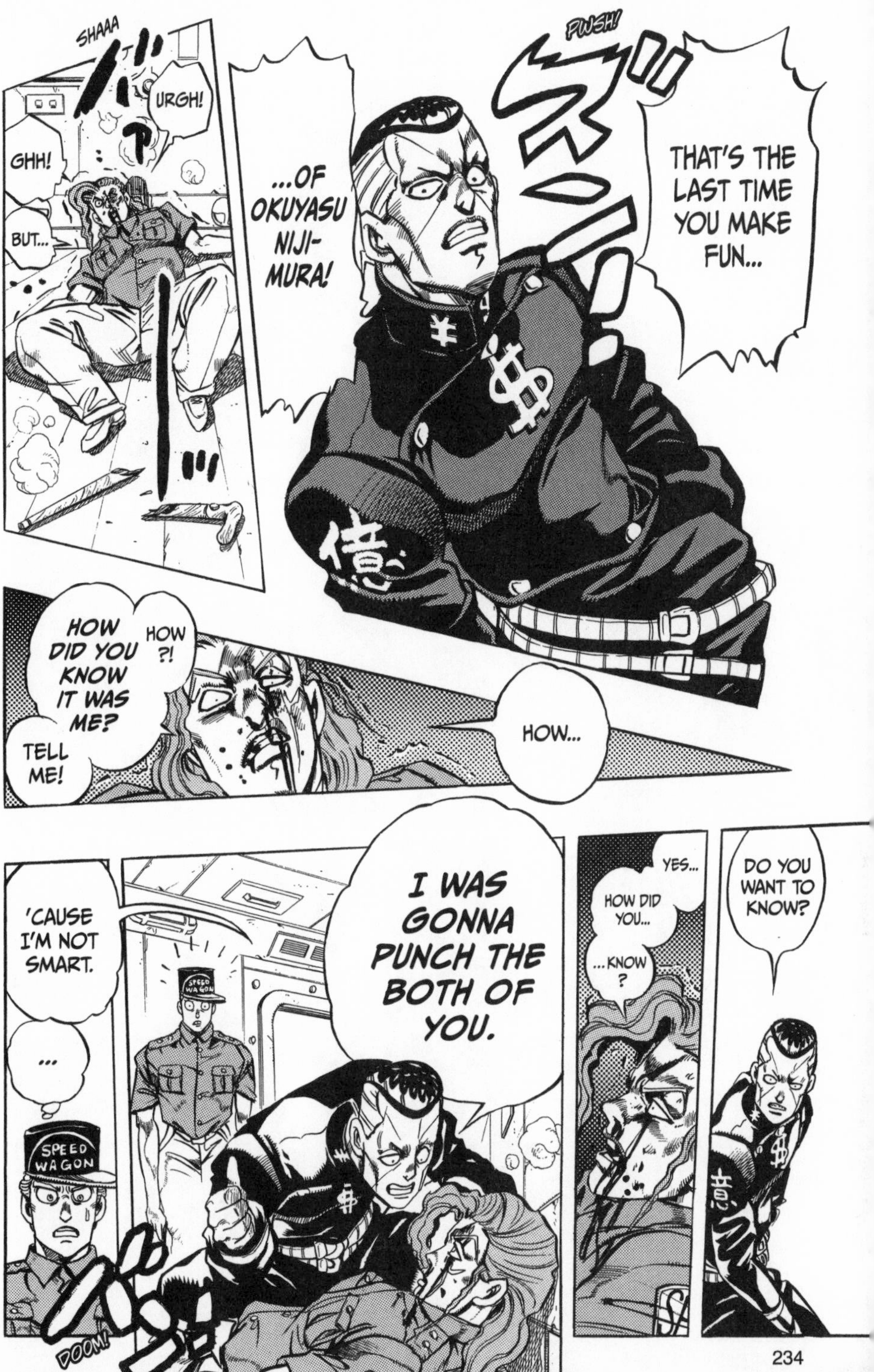

PWSH!
THAT'S THE LAST TIME YOU MAKE FUN...
...OF OKUYASU NIJI-MURA!
SHAAA
URGH!
GHH!
BUT...
HOW...
HOW ?!
HOW DID YOU KNOW IT WAS ME?
TELL ME!
DO YOU WANT TO KNOW?
YES...
HOW DID YOU...
...KNOW ?
I WAS GONNA PUNCH THE BOTH OF YOU.
'CAUSE I'M NOT SMART.
...
DOOM!

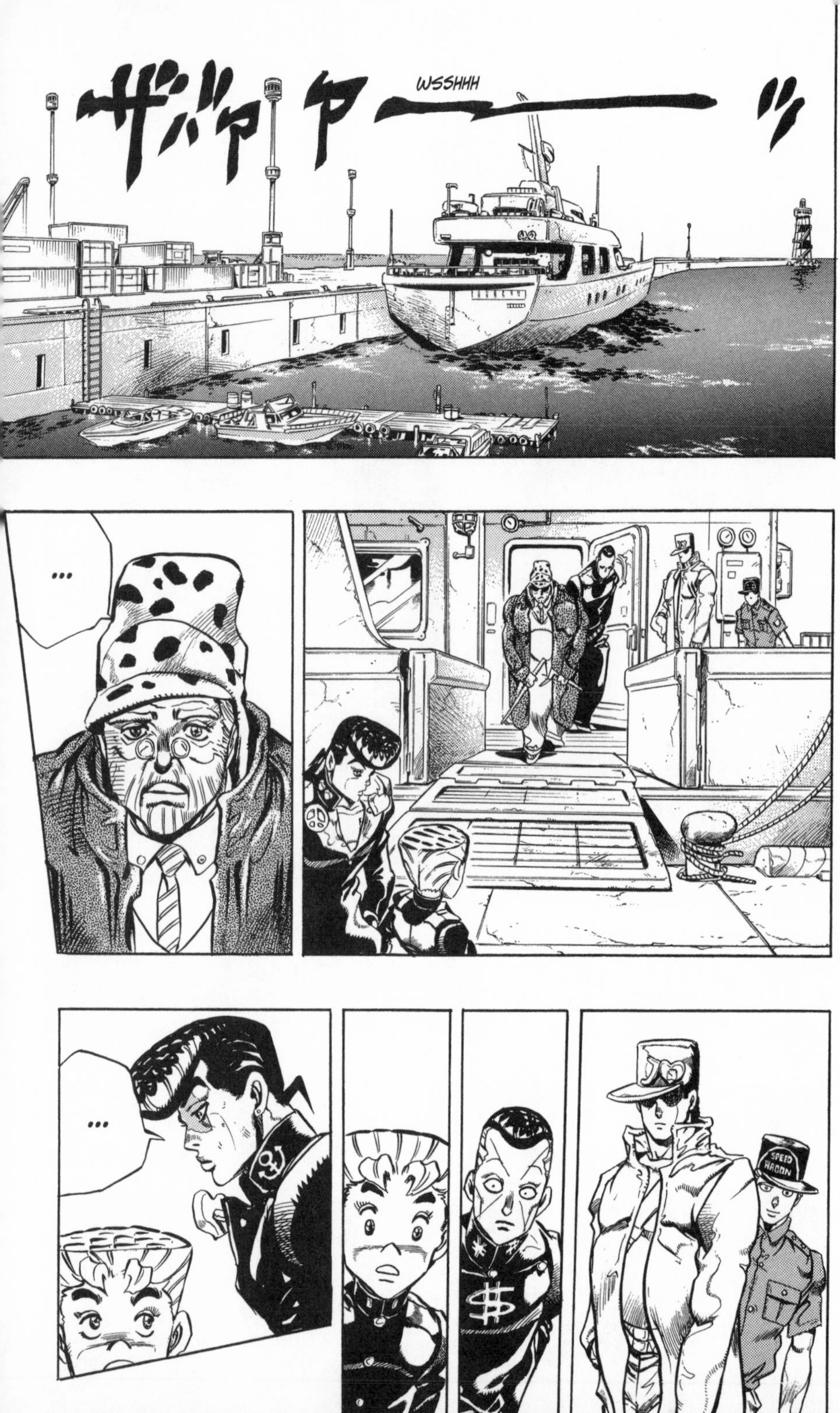
ザバァーーッ
WSSHHH
...
SPEED WAGON
...

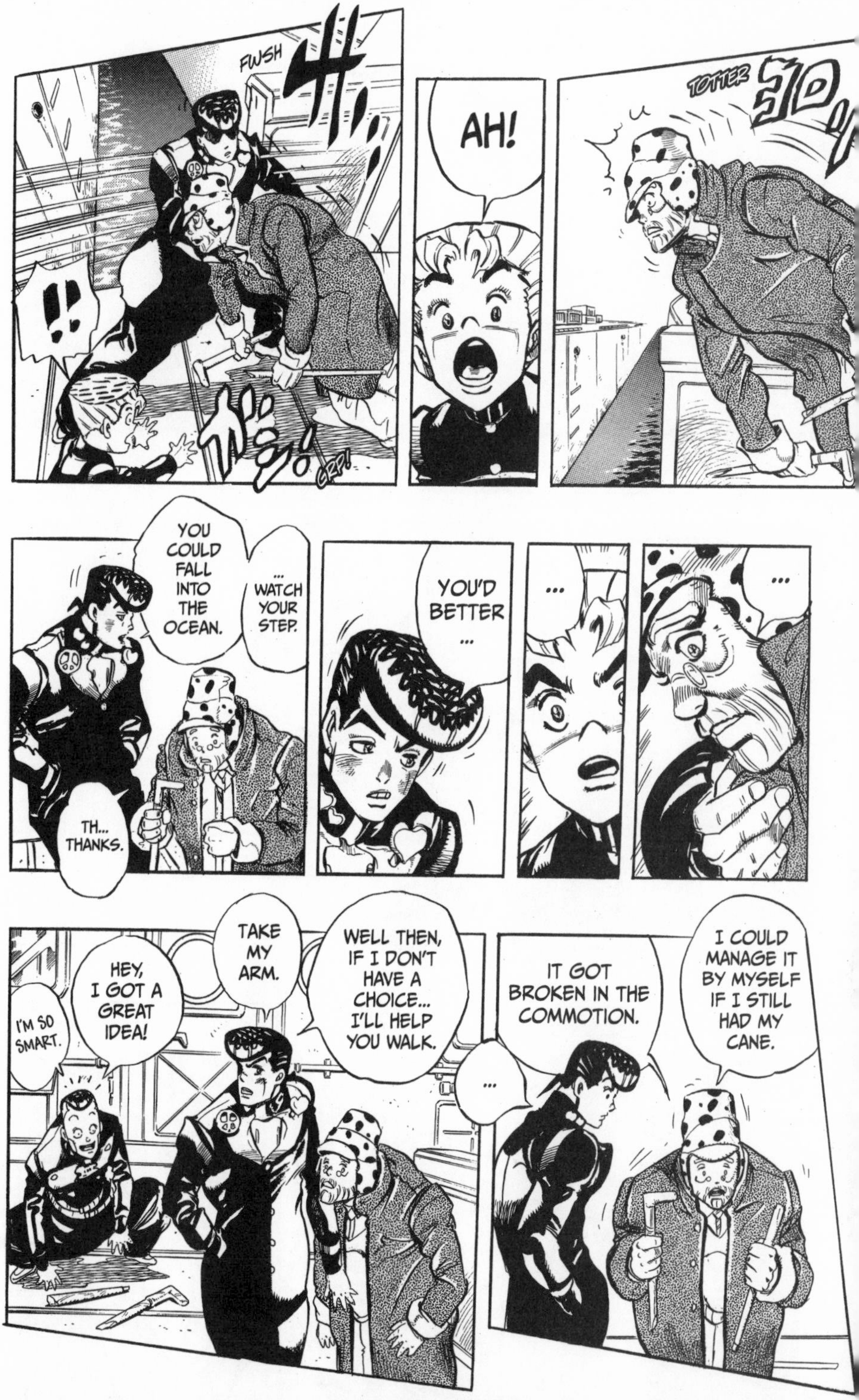
TOTTER
AH!
FWSH
!!
GRIP
...
...
YOU'D BETTER ...
... WATCH YOUR STEP.
YOU COULD FALL INTO THE OCEAN.
TH... THANKS.
I COULD MANAGE IT BY MYSELF IF I STILL HAD MY CANE.
IT GOT BROKEN IN THE COMMOTION.
...
WELL THEN, IF I DON'T HAVE A CHOICE... I'LL HELP YOU WALK.
TAKE MY ARM.
HEY, I GOT A GREAT IDEA!
I'M SO SMART.

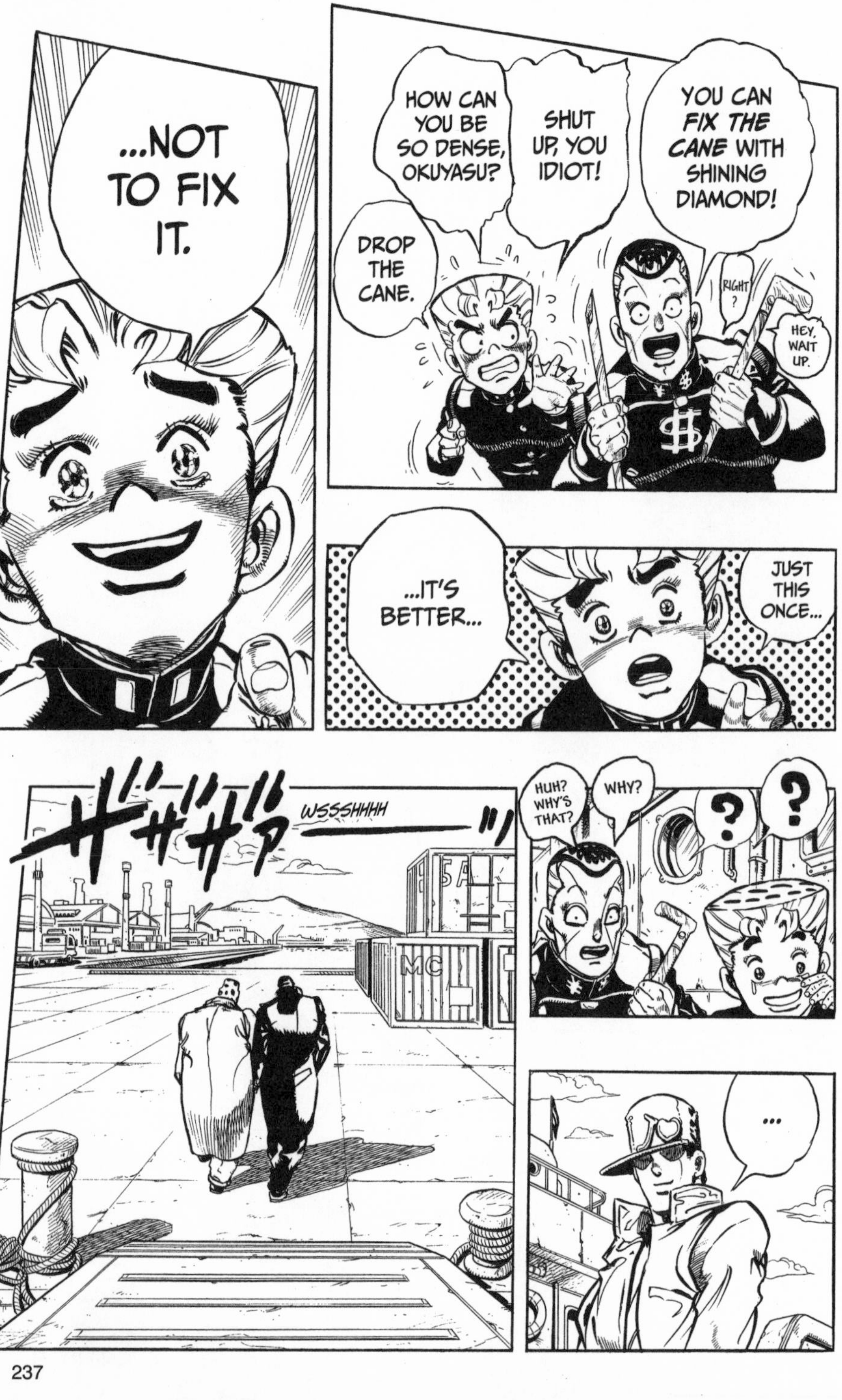
YOU CAN FIX THE CANE WITH SHINING DIAMOND!
SHUT UP, YOU IDIOT!
HOW CAN YOU BE SO DENSE, OKUYASU?
RIGHT?
HEY, WAIT UP.
DROP THE CANE.
JUST THIS ONCE...
...IT'S BETTER...
...NOT TO FIX IT.
?
?
WHY?
HUH? WHY'S THAT?
...
ザザザァ
WSSSHHHH

RED HOT CHILI PEPPER

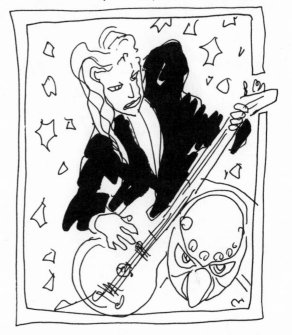

CHAPTER 50

WE PICKED UP SOMETHING CRAZY!, PART 1

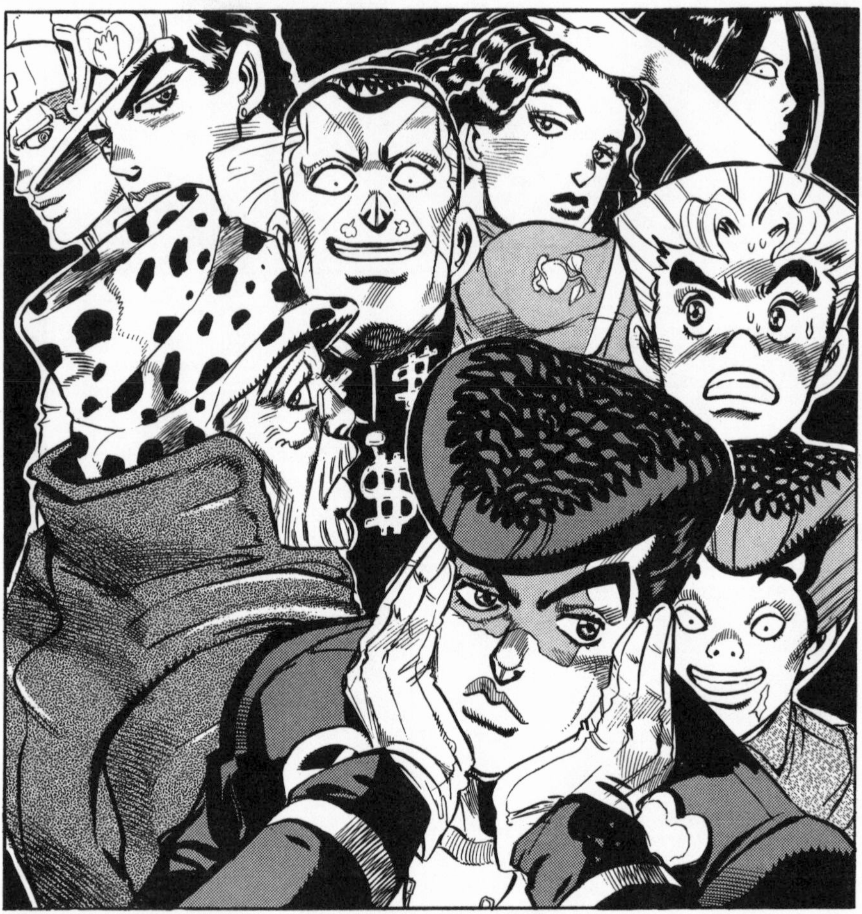

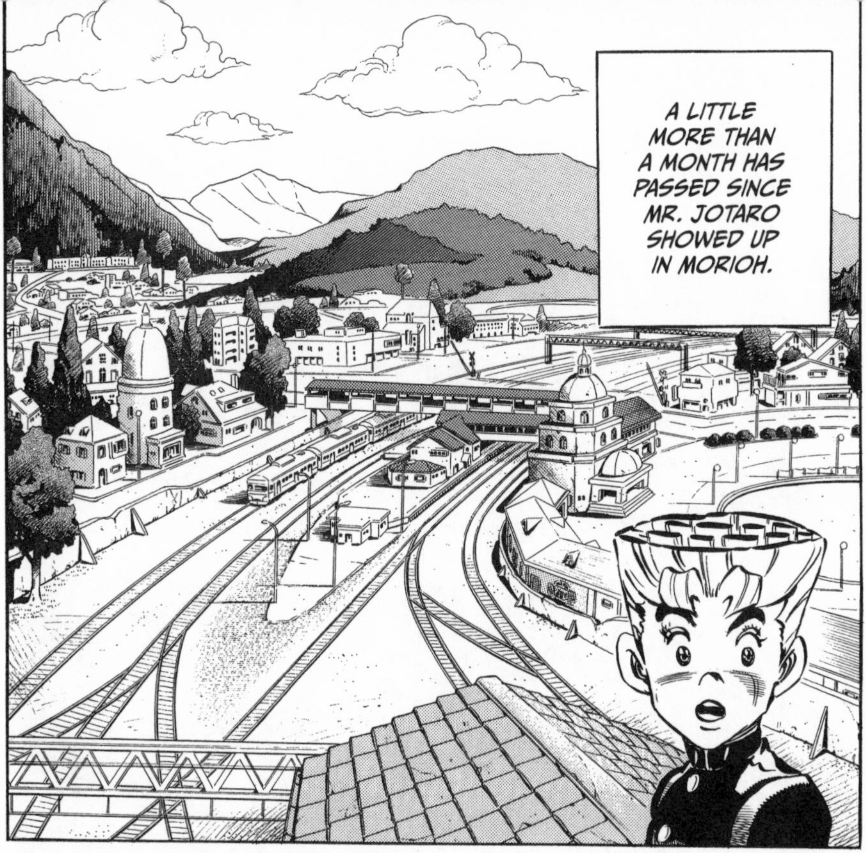
A LITTLE MORE THAN A MONTH HAS PASSED SINCE MR. JOTARO SHOWED UP IN MORIOH.

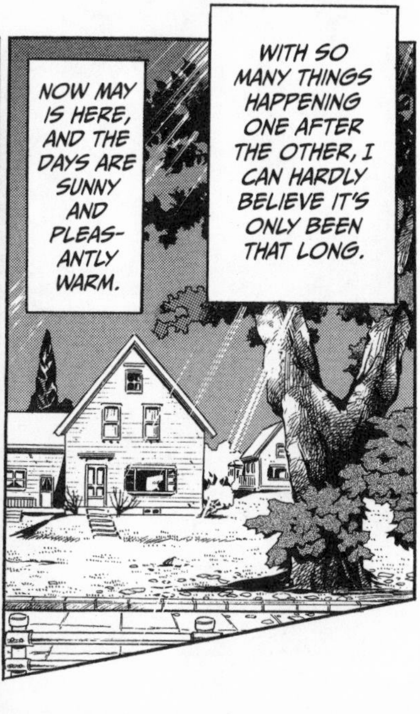
WITH SO MANY THINGS HAPPENING ONE AFTER THE OTHER, I CAN HARDLY BELIEVE IT'S ONLY BEEN THAT LONG.
NOW MAY IS HERE, AND THE DAYS ARE SUNNY AND PLEAS-ANTLY WARM.

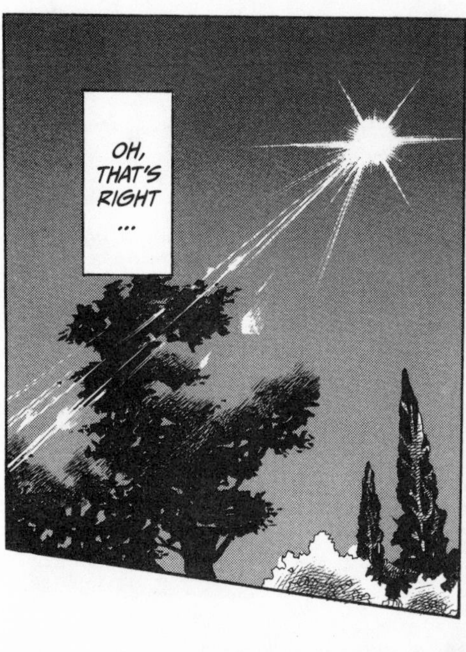
OH, THAT'S RIGHT ...

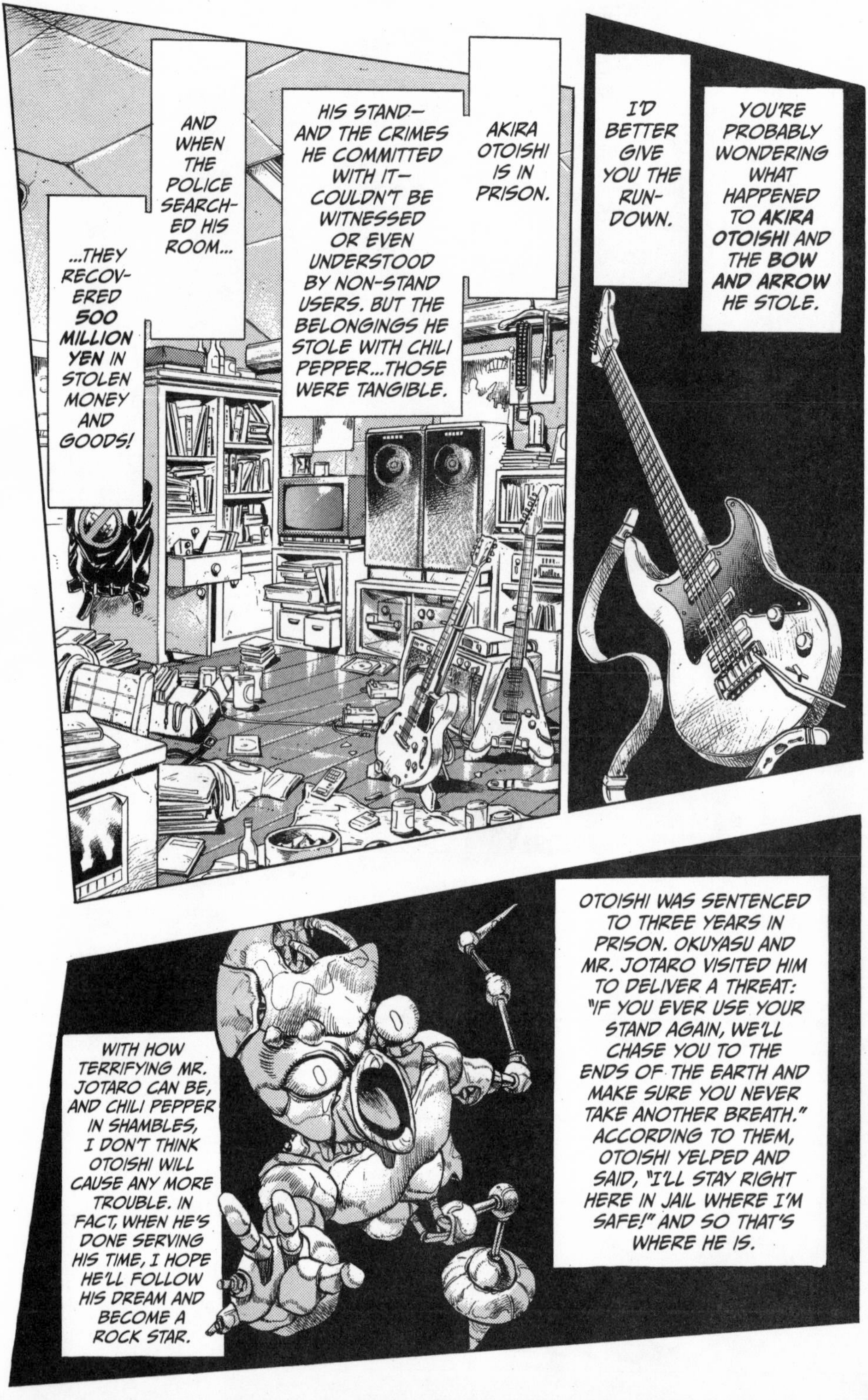
YOU'RE PROBABLY WONDERING WHAT HAPPENED TO **AKIRA OTOISHI** AND THE **BOW AND ARROW** HE STOLE.
I'D BETTER GIVE YOU THE RUN-DOWN.
AKIRA OTOISHI IS IN PRISON.
HIS STAND—AND THE CRIMES HE COMMITTED WITH IT—COULDN'T BE WITNESSED OR EVEN UNDERSTOOD BY NON-STAND USERS. BUT THE BELONGINGS HE STOLE WITH CHILI PEPPER...THOSE WERE TANGIBLE.
AND WHEN THE POLICE SEARCHED HIS ROOM...
...THEY RECOVERED **500 MILLION YEN** IN STOLEN MONEY AND GOODS!
OTOISHI WAS SENTENCED TO THREE YEARS IN PRISON. OKUYASU AND MR. JOTARO VISITED HIM TO DELIVER A THREAT: "IF YOU EVER USE YOUR STAND AGAIN, WE'LL CHASE YOU TO THE ENDS OF THE EARTH AND MAKE SURE YOU NEVER TAKE ANOTHER BREATH." ACCORDING TO THEM, OTOISHI YELPED AND SAID, "I'LL STAY RIGHT HERE IN JAIL WHERE I'M SAFE!" AND SO THAT'S WHERE HE IS.
WITH HOW TERRIFYING MR. JOTARO CAN BE, AND CHILI PEPPER IN SHAMBLES, I DON'T THINK OTOISHI WILL CAUSE ANY MORE TROUBLE. IN FACT, WHEN HE'S DONE SERVING HIS TIME, I HOPE HE'LL FOLLOW HIS DREAM AND BECOME A ROCK STAR.

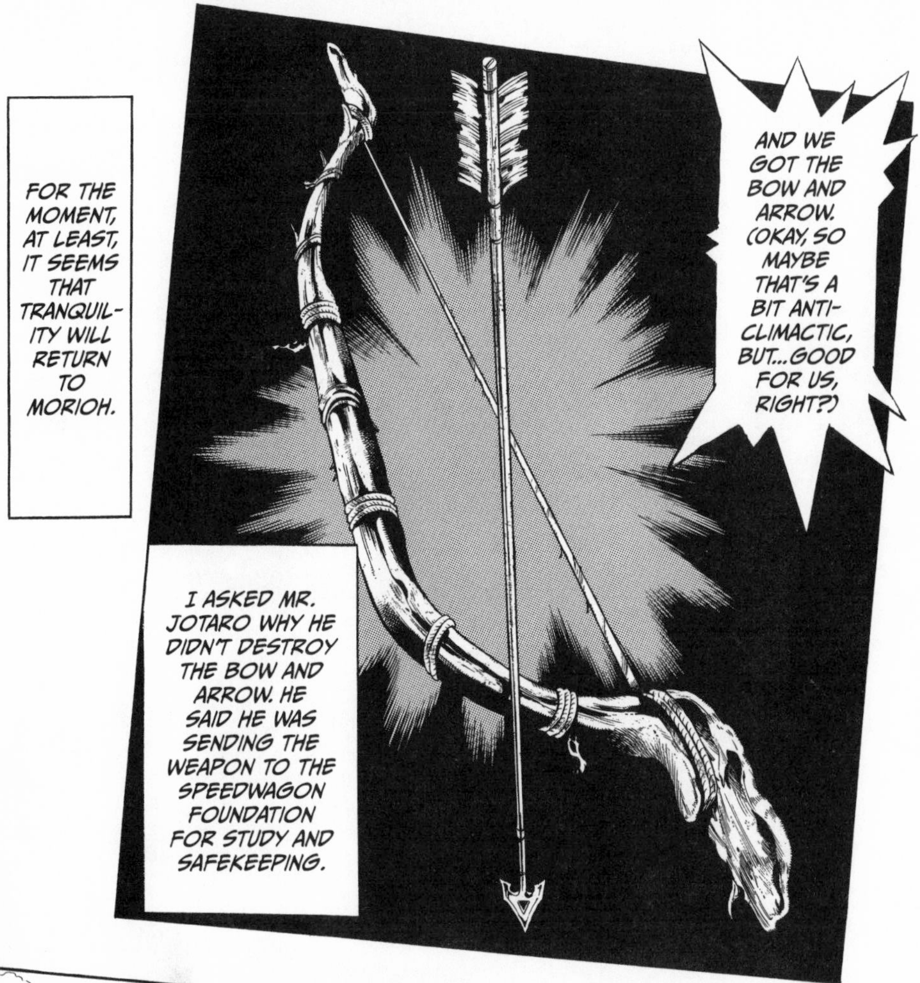
AND WE GOT THE BOW AND ARROW. (OKAY, SO MAYBE THAT'S A BIT ANTI-CLIMACTIC, BUT...GOOD FOR US, RIGHT?)
FOR THE MOMENT, AT LEAST, IT SEEMS THAT TRANQUIL-ITY WILL RETURN TO MORIOH.
I ASKED MR. JOTARO WHY HE DIDN'T DESTROY THE BOW AND ARROW. HE SAID HE WAS SENDING THE WEAPON TO THE SPEEDWAGON FOUNDATION FOR STUDY AND SAFEKEEPING.
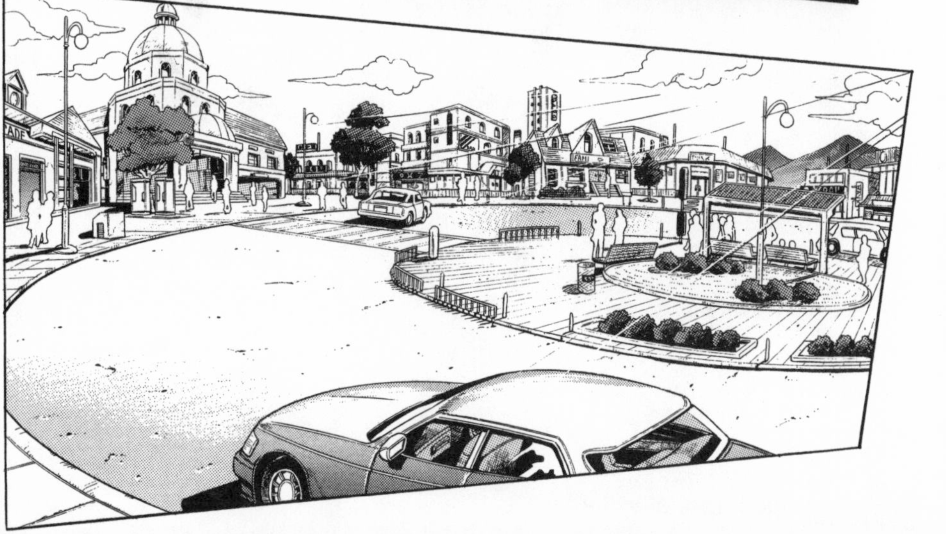

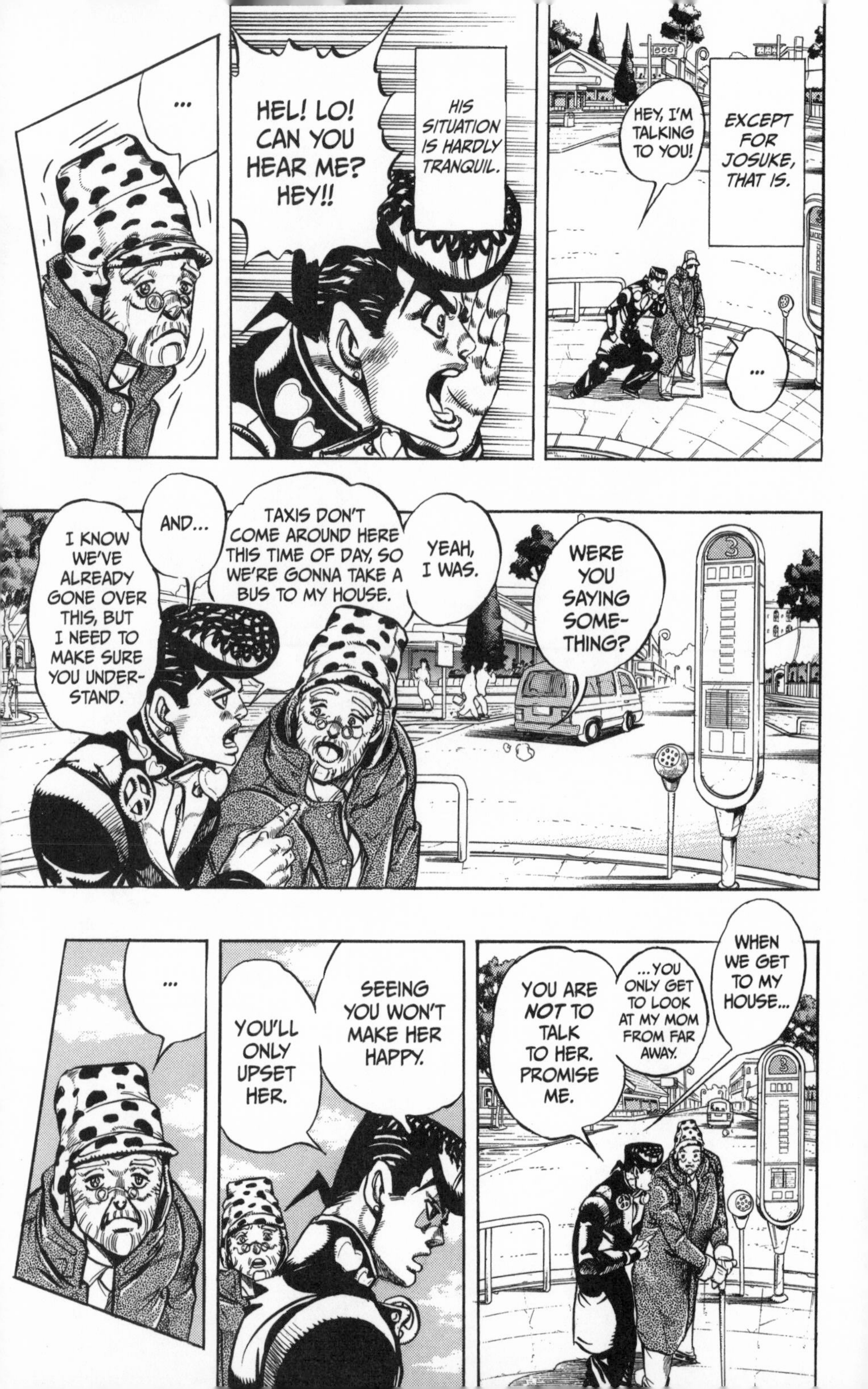
EXCEPT FOR JOSUKE, THAT IS.
HEY, I'M TALKING TO YOU!
...
HIS SITUATION IS HARDLY TRANQUIL.
HEL! LO! CAN YOU HEAR ME? HEY!!
...
WERE YOU SAYING SOME-THING?
YEAH, I WAS.
TAXIS DON'T COME AROUND HERE THIS TIME OF DAY, SO WE'RE GONNA TAKE A BUS TO MY HOUSE.
AND...
I KNOW WE'VE ALREADY GONE OVER THIS, BUT I NEED TO MAKE SURE YOU UNDER-STAND.
WHEN WE GET TO MY HOUSE...
...YOU ONLY GET TO LOOK AT MY MOM FROM FAR AWAY.
YOU ARE *NOT* TO TALK TO HER. PROMISE ME.
SEEING YOU WON'T MAKE HER HAPPY.
YOU'LL ONLY UPSET HER.
...

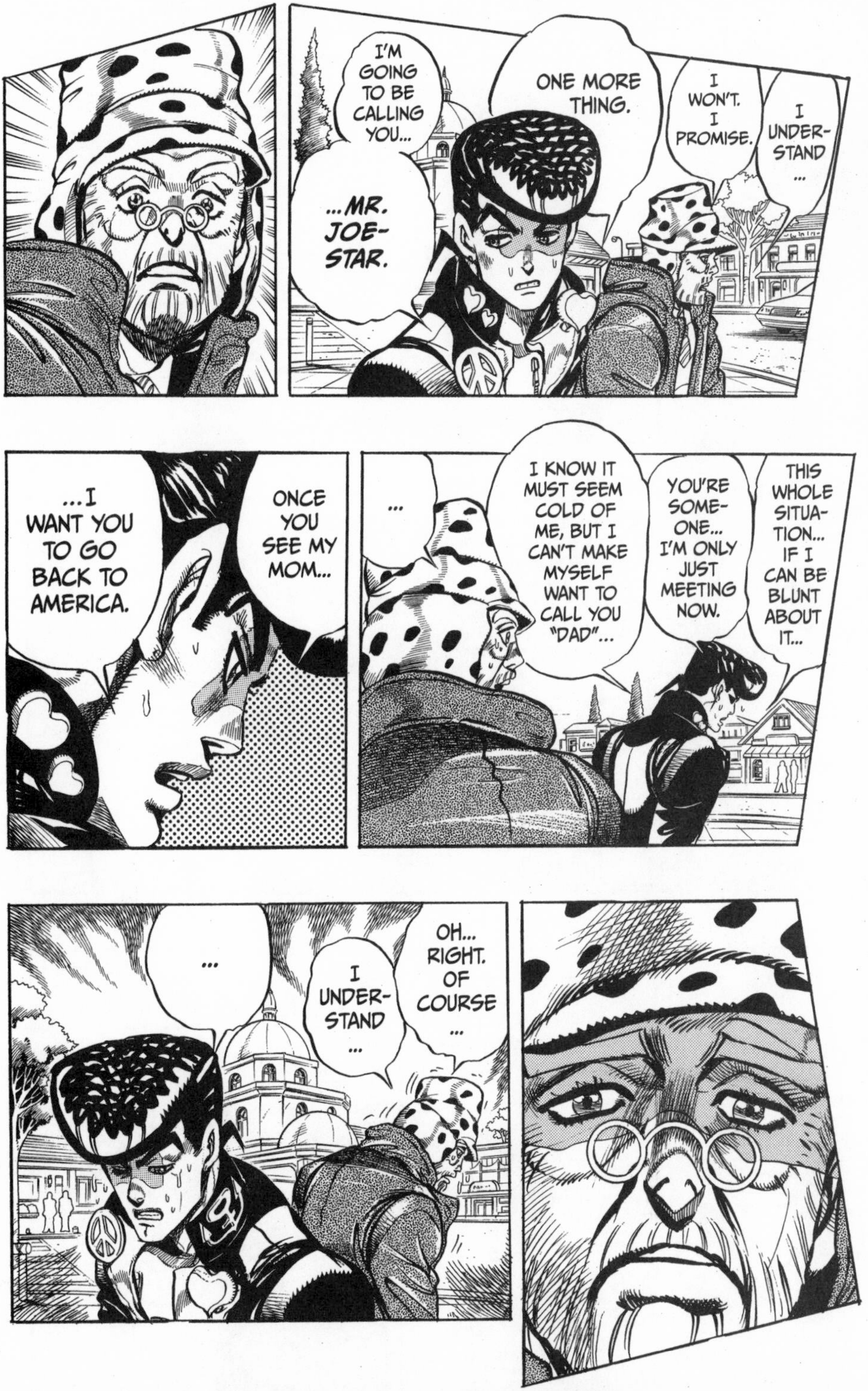
I UNDERSTAND...
I WON'T. I PROMISE.
ONE MORE THING.
I'M GOING TO BE CALLING YOU...
...MR. JOESTAR.
THIS WHOLE SITUATION... IF I CAN BE BLUNT ABOUT IT...
YOU'RE SOMEONE... I'M ONLY JUST MEETING NOW.
I KNOW IT MUST SEEM COLD OF ME, BUT I CAN'T MAKE MYSELF WANT TO CALL YOU "DAD"...
...
ONCE YOU SEE MY MOM...
...I WANT YOU TO GO BACK TO AMERICA.
OH... RIGHT. OF COURSE...
I UNDERSTAND...
...

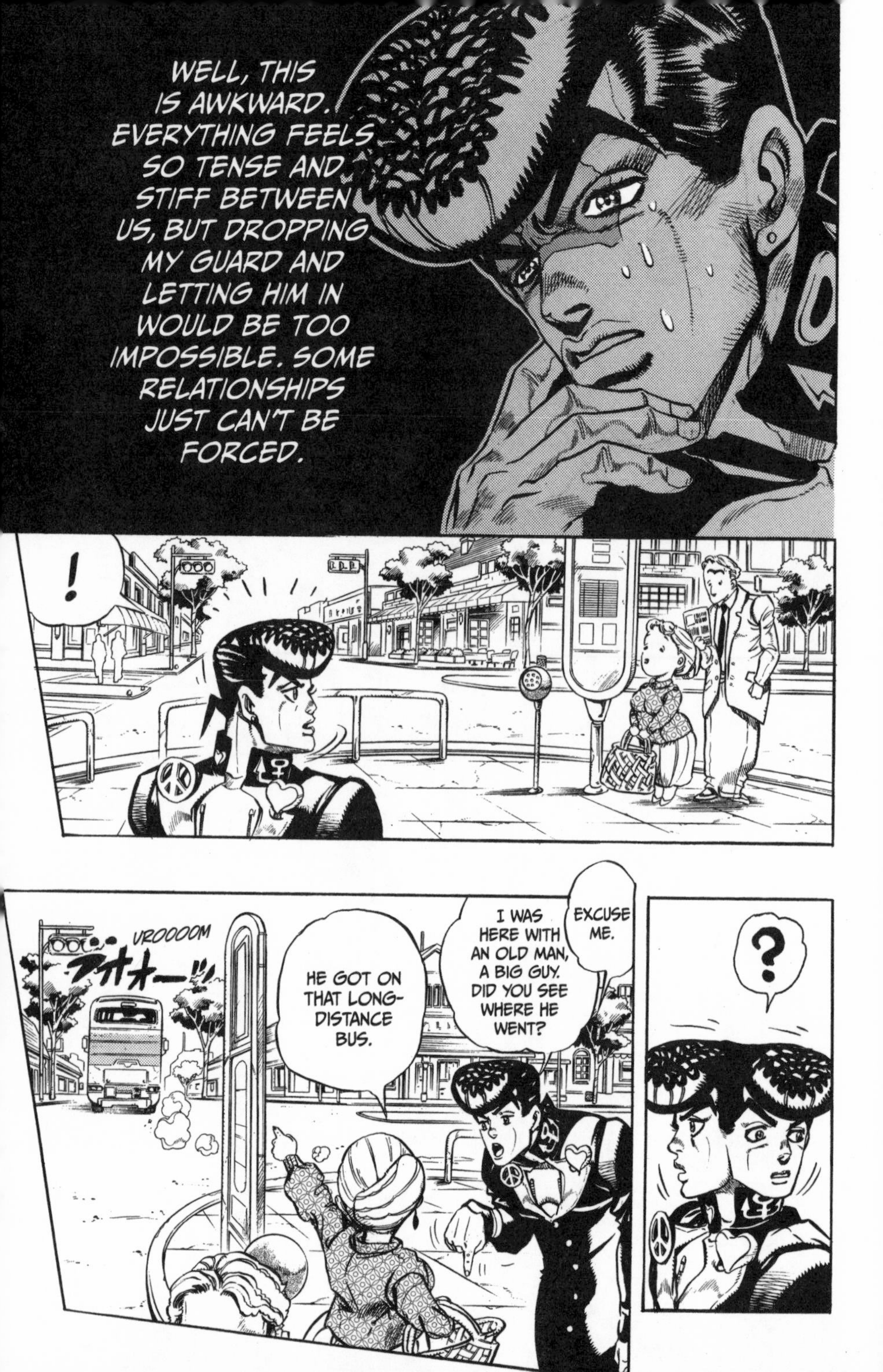
WELL, THIS IS AWKWARD. EVERYTHING FEELS SO TENSE AND STIFF BETWEEN US, BUT DROPPING MY GUARD AND LETTING HIM IN WOULD BE TOO IMPOSSIBLE. SOME RELATIONSHIPS JUST CAN'T BE FORCED.
!
?
EXCUSE ME.
I WAS HERE WITH AN OLD MAN, A BIG GUY. DID YOU SEE WHERE HE WENT?
HE GOT ON THAT LONG-DISTANCE BUS.
VROOOOM
ブオオー!!

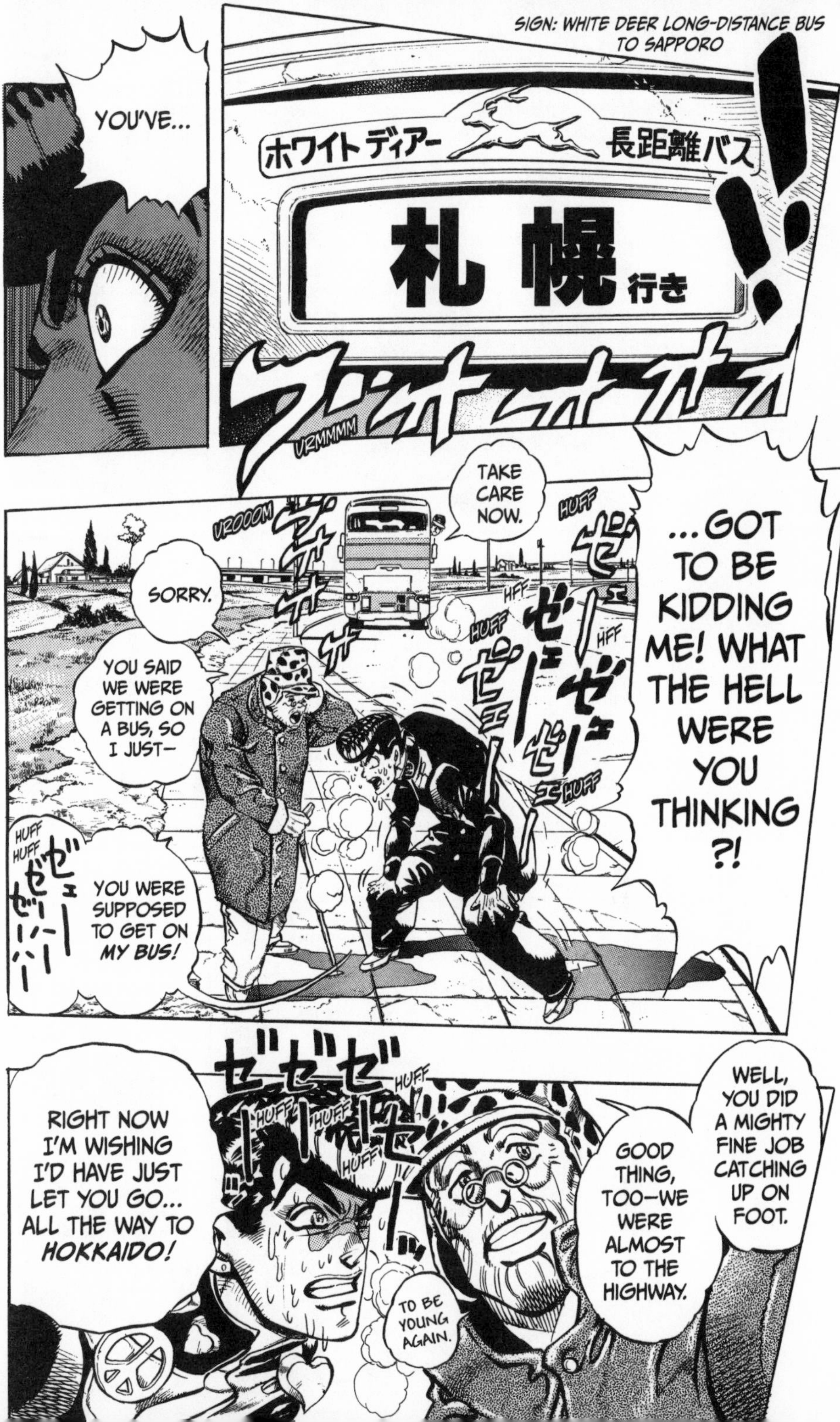
SIGN: WHITE DEER LONG-DISTANCE BUS TO SAPPORO
ホワイト ディアー 長距離バス
札幌行き
URMMMM
YOU'VE...
...GOT TO BE KIDDING ME! WHAT THE HELL WERE YOU THINKING?!
HUFF
HFF
HUFF
HFF
HUFF
TAKE CARE NOW.
VROOOM
SORRY.
YOU SAID WE WERE GETTING ON A BUS, SO I JUST—
HUFF HUFF
YOU WERE SUPPOSED TO GET ON MY BUS!
WELL, YOU DID A MIGHTY FINE JOB CATCHING UP ON FOOT.
GOOD THING, TOO—WE WERE ALMOST TO THE HIGHWAY.
TO BE YOUNG AGAIN.
HUFF
HUFF
HUFF
HUFF
RIGHT NOW I'M WISHING I'D HAVE JUST LET YOU GO... ALL THE WAY TO HOKKAIDO!

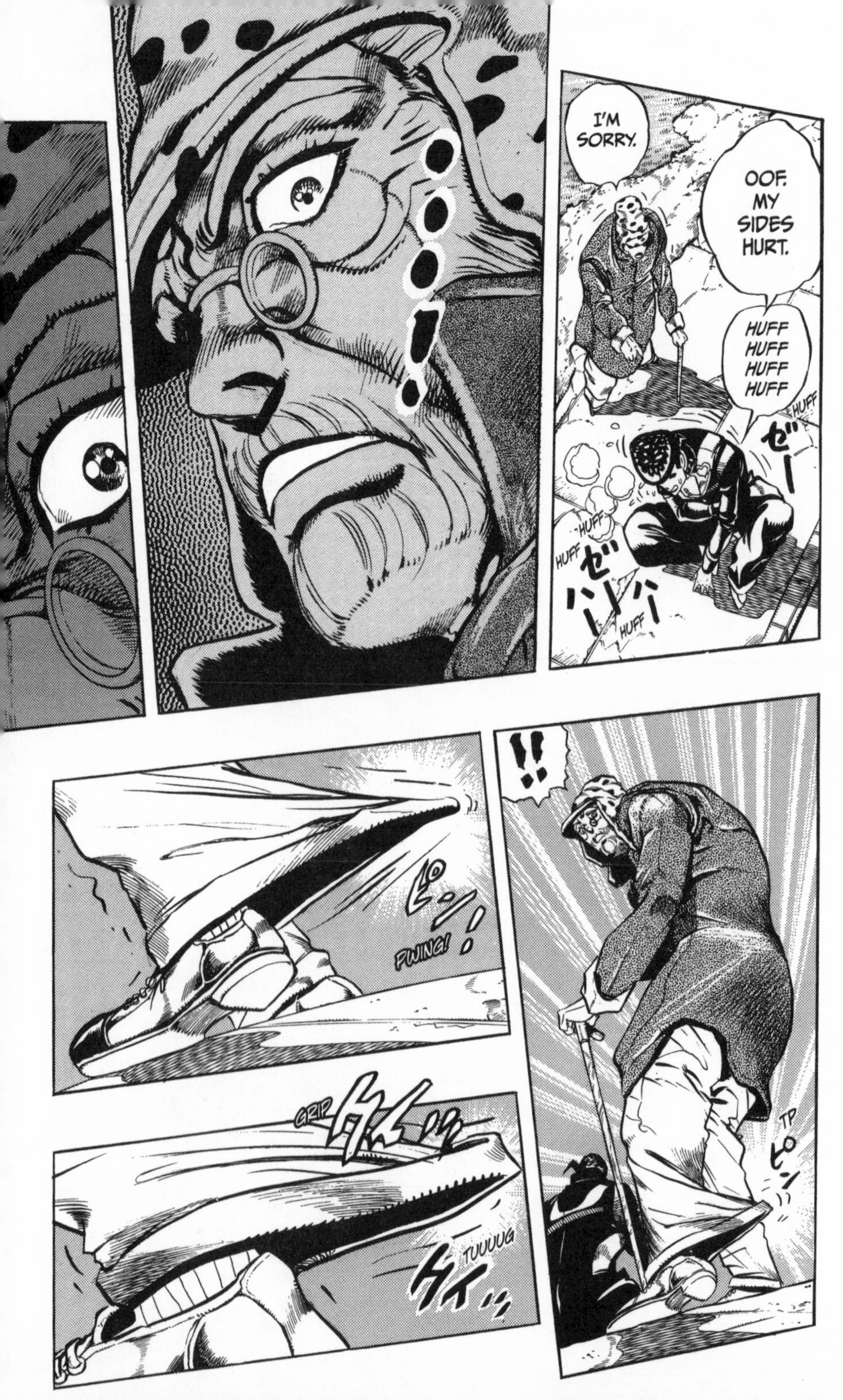
OOF. MY SIDES HURT.
I'M SORRY.
HUFF HUFF HUFF HUFF
HUFF
HUFF
HUFF
HUFF
!!
TP
PWING!
GRIP
TUUUUG

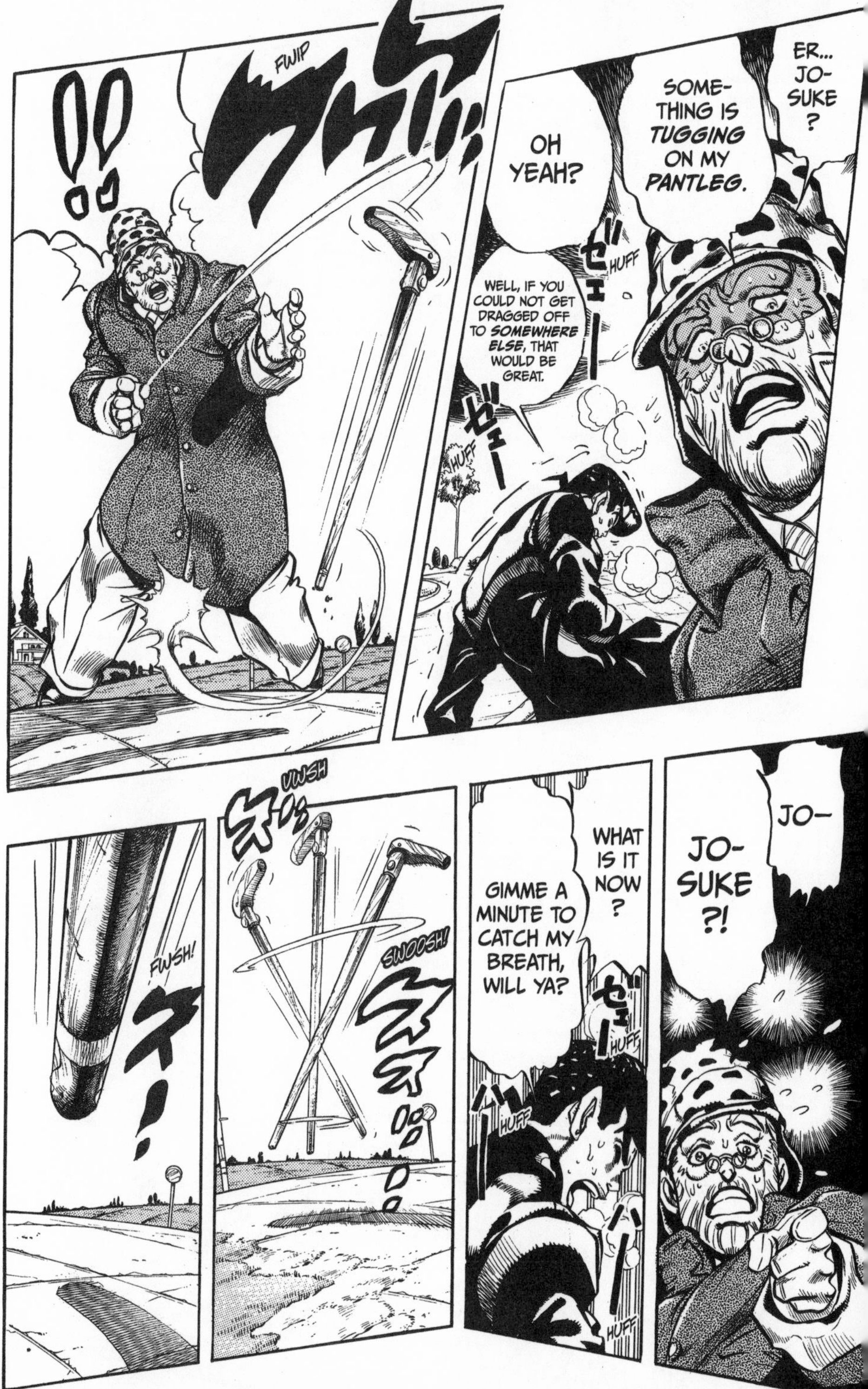

ER... JO-SUKE?
SOME-THING IS TUGGING ON MY PANTLEG.
OH YEAH?
HUFF
WELL, IF YOU COULD NOT GET DRAGGED OFF TO SOMEWHERE ELSE, THAT WOULD BE GREAT.
HUFF
FWIP
JO—
JO-SUKE?!
WHAT IS IT NOW?
GIMME A MINUTE TO CATCH MY BREATH, WILL YA?
HUFF
HUFF
HUFF
VWSH
SWOOSH!
FWSH!

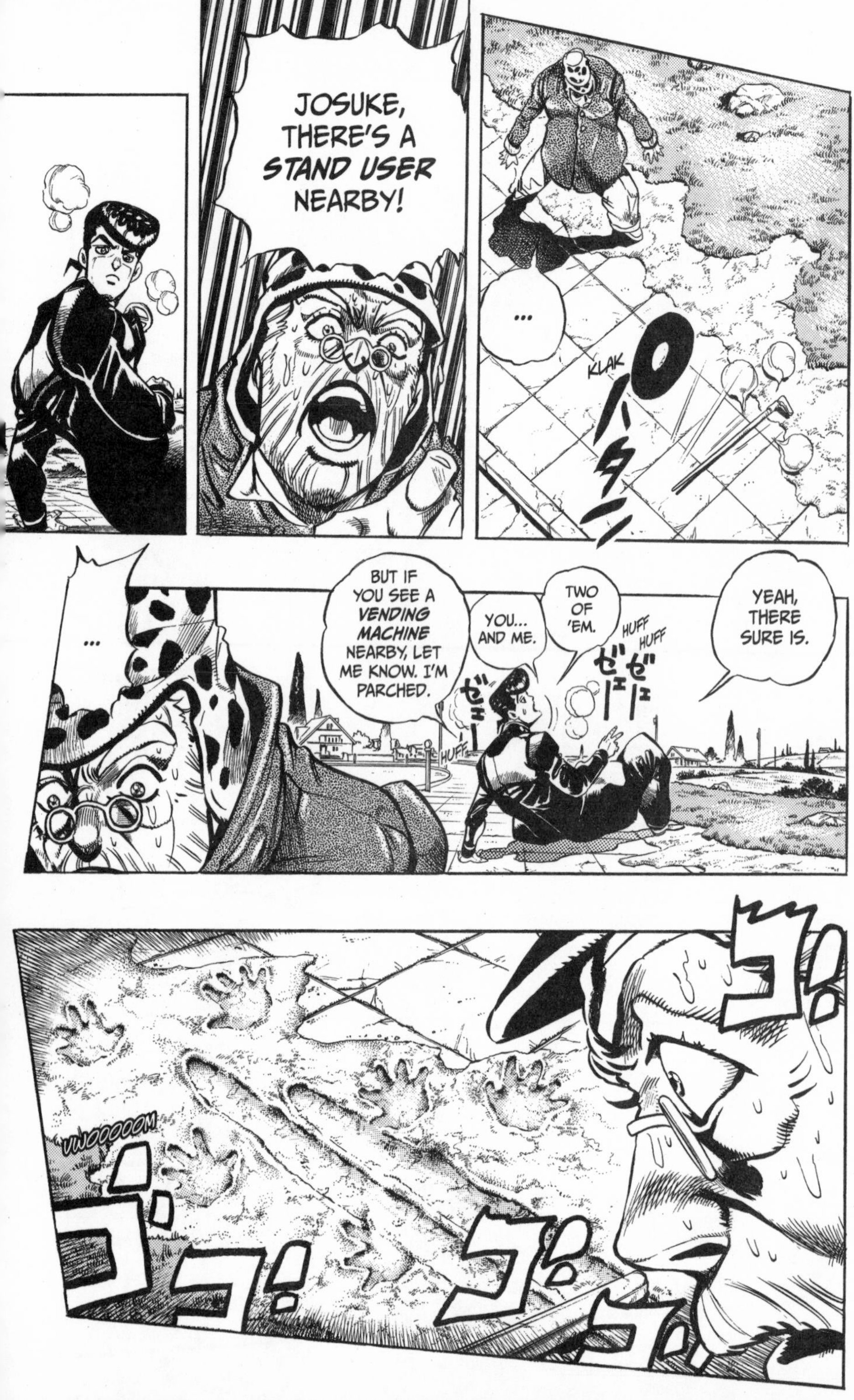

...
KLAK
パタン
JOSUKE, THERE'S A STAND USER NEARBY!
YEAH, THERE SURE IS.
HUFF HUFF
ゼェゼェ
TWO OF 'EM.
YOU... AND ME.
BUT IF YOU SEE A VENDING MACHINE NEARBY, LET ME KNOW. I'M PARCHED.
HUFF
ゼェー
...
ゴ!
ゴ
ゴ!
ゴ
VWOOOOOM
ゴ!

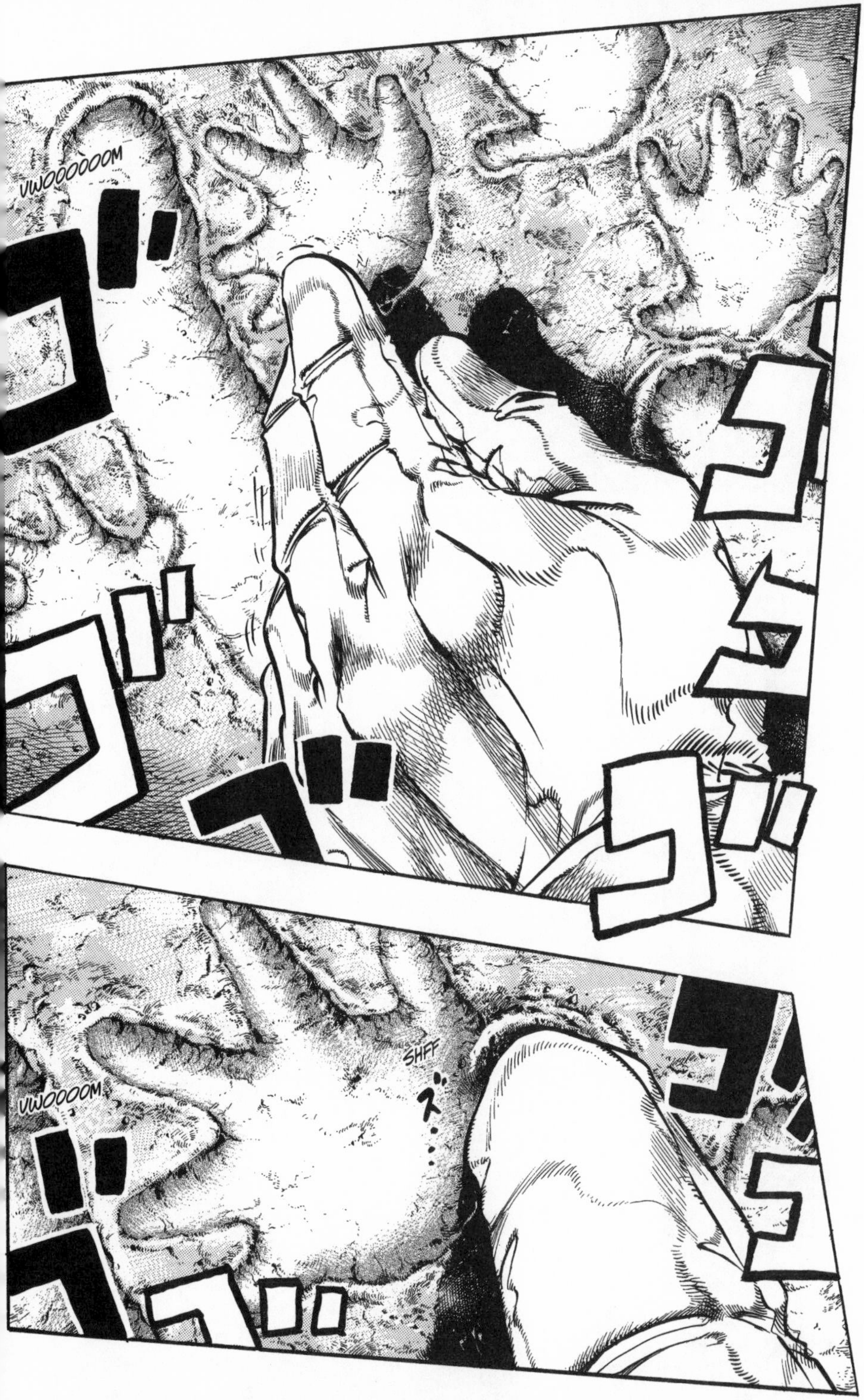
VWOOOOOOOM
ゴゴゴゴゴ
SHFF
ズ…
VWOOOOM
ゴゴゴ

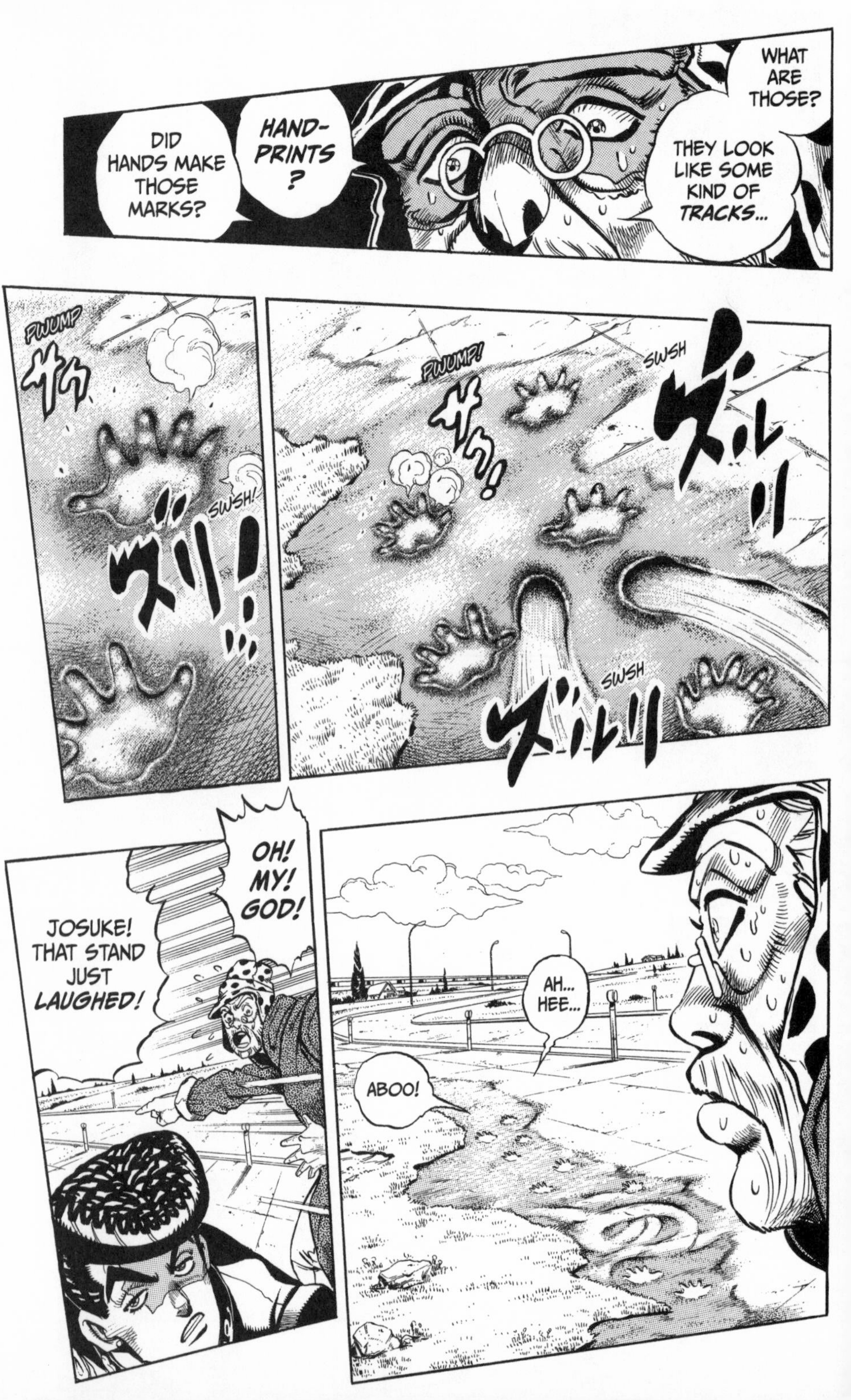
WHAT ARE THOSE?
THEY LOOK LIKE SOME KIND OF TRACKS...
HAND-PRINTS?
DID HANDS MAKE THOSE MARKS?
SWSH
PWUMP!
SWSH
PWUMP
SWSH!
AH... HEE...
ABOO!
OH! MY! GOD!
JOSUKE! THAT STAND JUST LAUGHED!

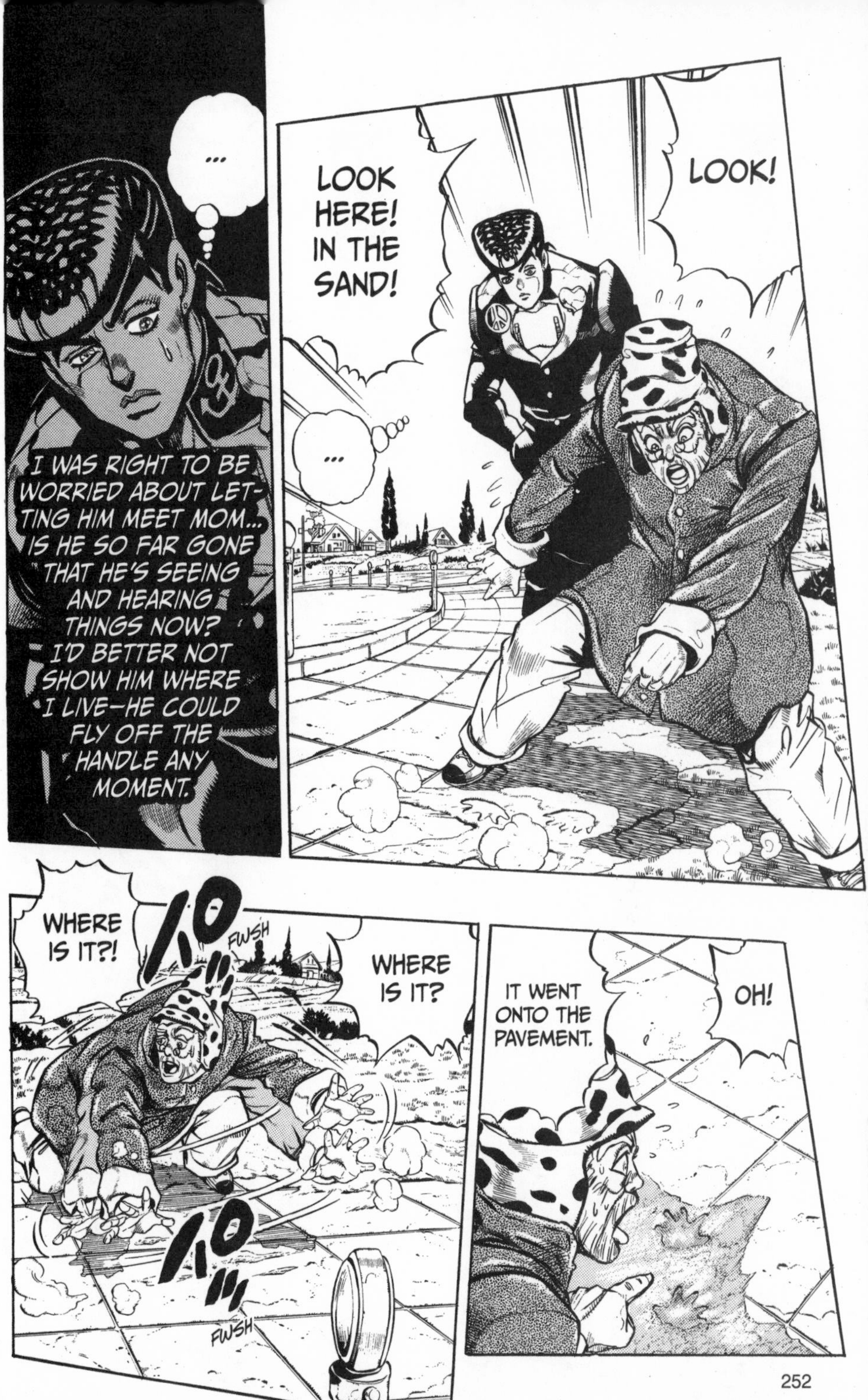
LOOK!
LOOK HERE! IN THE SAND!
...
...
I WAS RIGHT TO BE WORRIED ABOUT LETTING HIM MEET MOM... IS HE SO FAR GONE THAT HE'S SEEING AND HEARING THINGS NOW? I'D BETTER NOT SHOW HIM WHERE I LIVE—HE COULD FLY OFF THE HANDLE ANY MOMENT.
OH!
IT WENT ONTO THE PAVEMENT.
WHERE IS IT?
WHERE IS IT?!
FWSH
FWSH

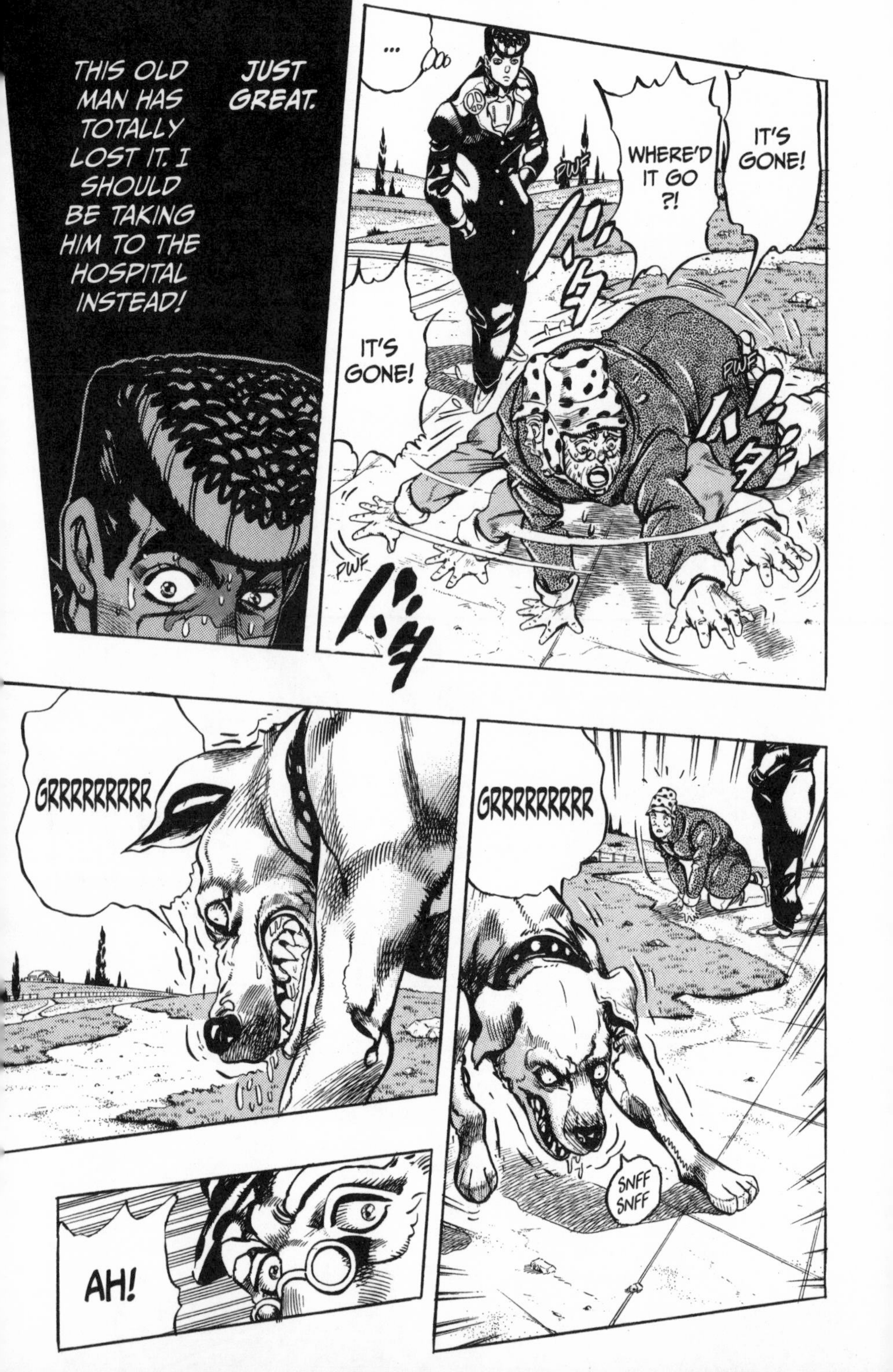

IT'S GONE!
WHERE'D IT GO ?!
...
PWF
IT'S GONE!
PWF
PWF
JUST GREAT.
THIS OLD MAN HAS TOTALLY LOST IT. I SHOULD BE TAKING HIM TO THE HOSPITAL INSTEAD!
GRRRRRRRR
SNFF SNFF
GRRRRRRRR
AH!

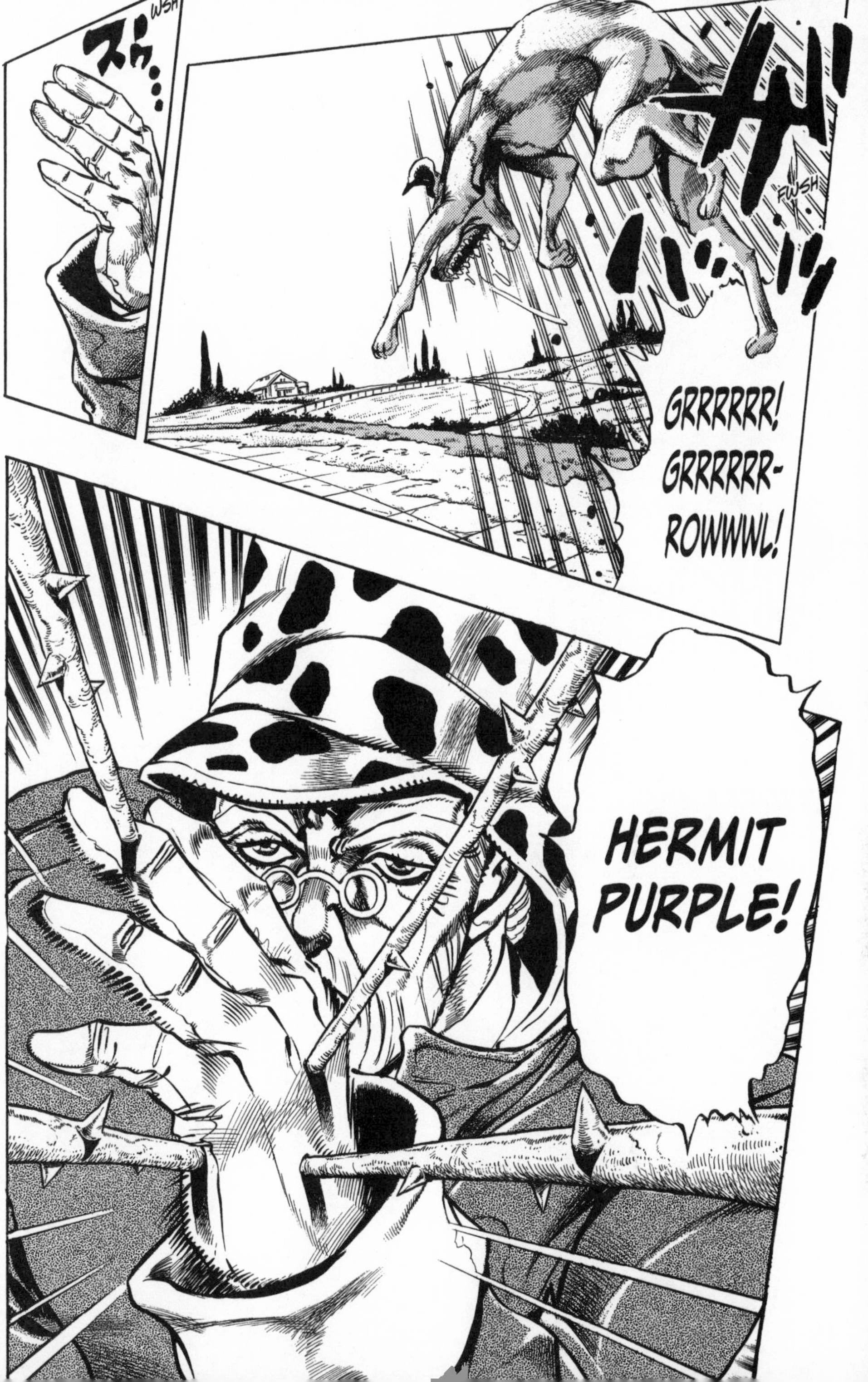
FWSH
GRRRRRR!
GRRRRRR-
ROWWWL!
ズゥ…
WSH
HERMIT
PURPLE!

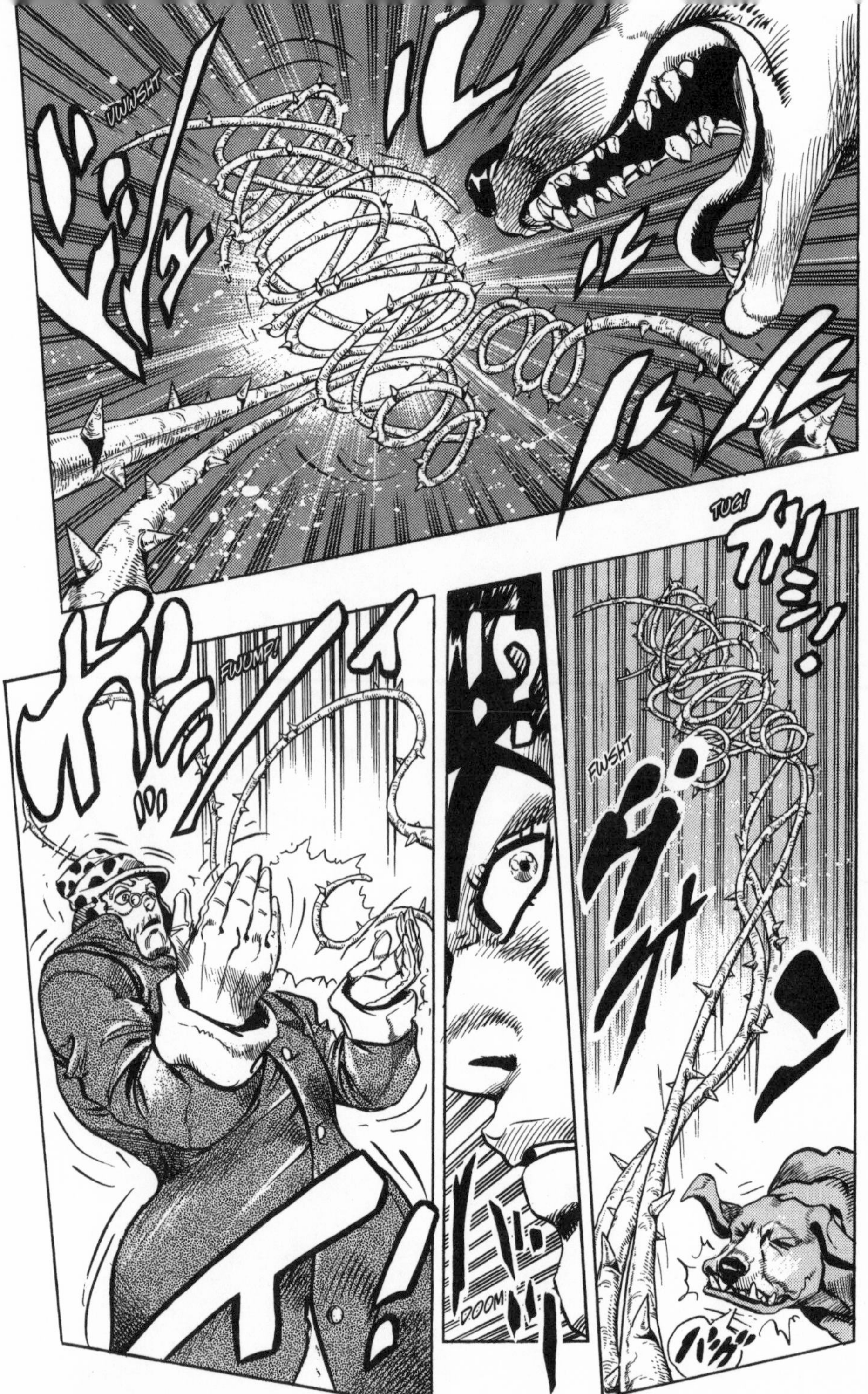
VWWSHT
TUG!
FWSHT
DOOM
FWUMP!

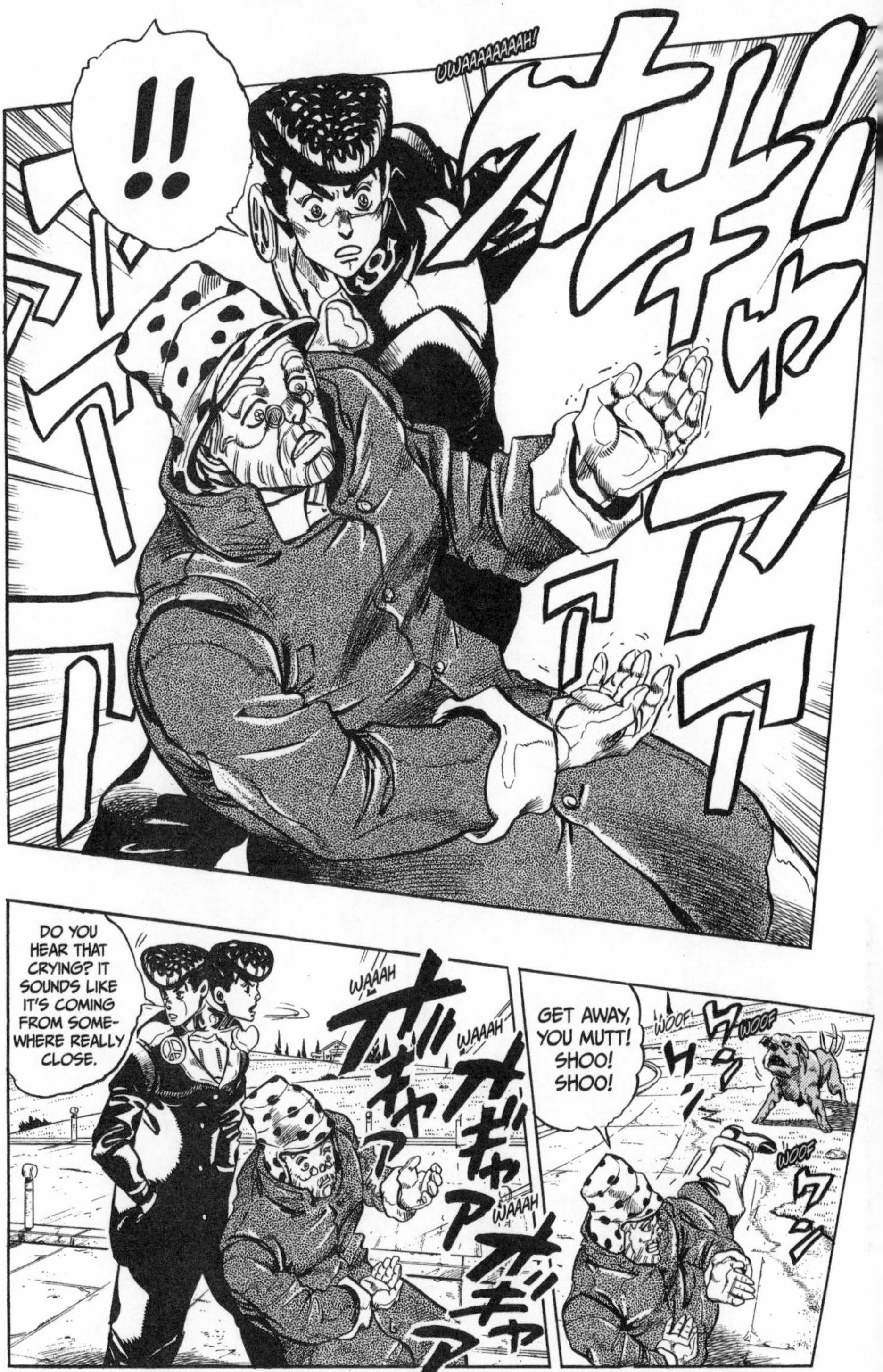
UWAAAAAAAAH!
!!
GET AWAY, YOU MUTT! SHOO! SHOO!
WOOF
WOOF
WOOF
DO YOU HEAR THAT CRYING? IT SOUNDS LIKE IT'S COMING FROM SOME-WHERE REALLY CLOSE.
WAAAH
WAAAH
WAAAH

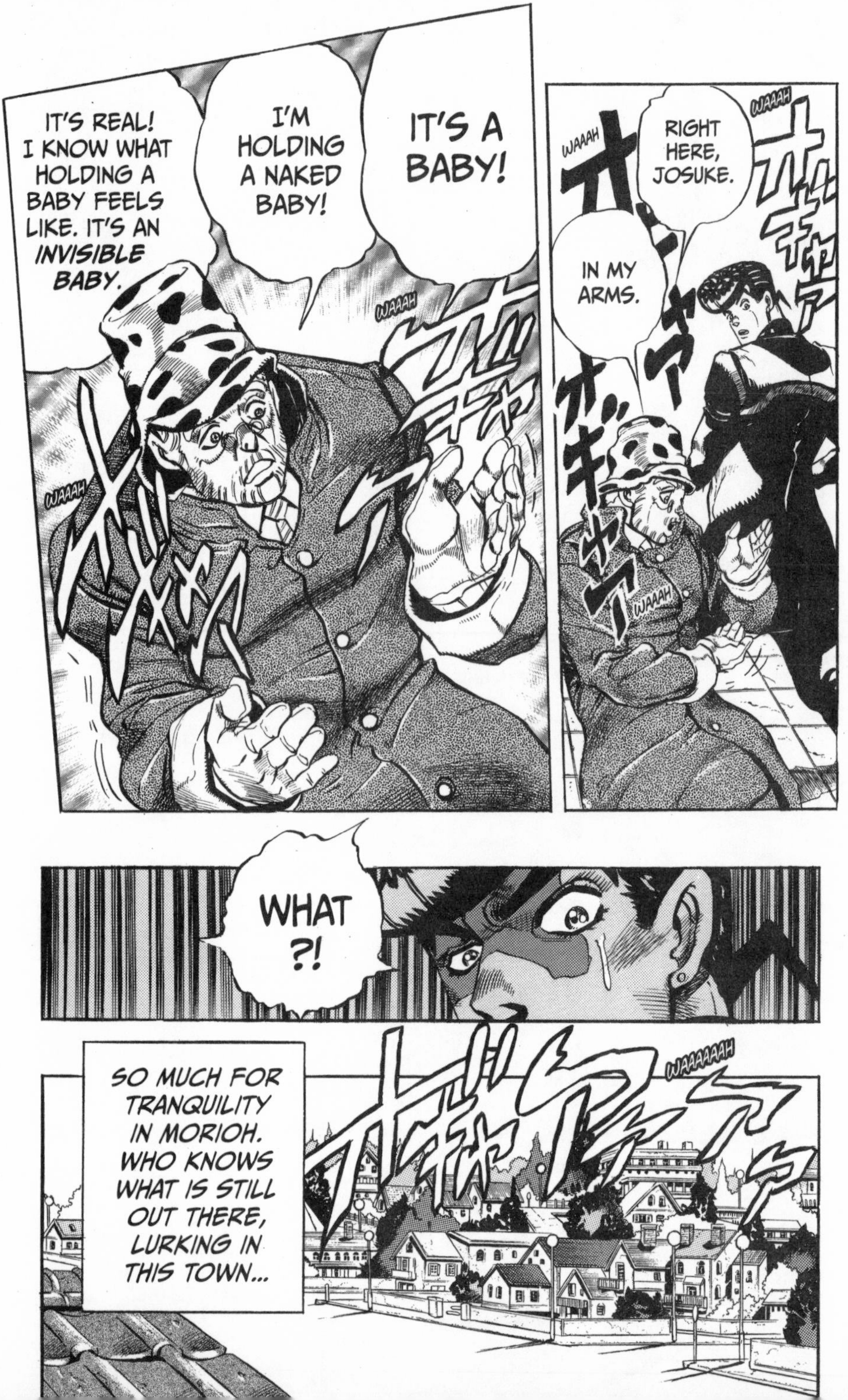
WAAAH
RIGHT HERE, JOSUKE.
WAAAH
IN MY ARMS.
WAAAH
IT'S A BABY!
I'M HOLDING A NAKED BABY!
IT'S REAL! I KNOW WHAT HOLDING A BABY FEELS LIKE. IT'S AN INVISIBLE BABY.
WAAAH
WAAAH
WHAT ?!
WAAAAAAH
SO MUCH FOR TRANQUILITY IN MORIOH. WHO KNOWS WHAT IS STILL OUT THERE, LURKING IN THIS TOWN...

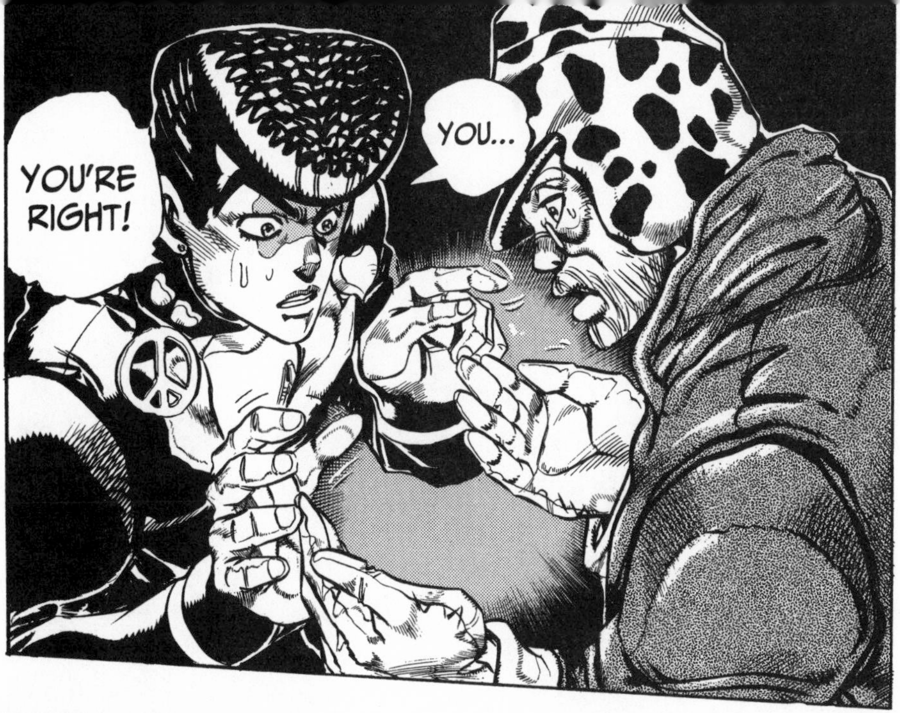
YOU...
YOU'RE RIGHT!

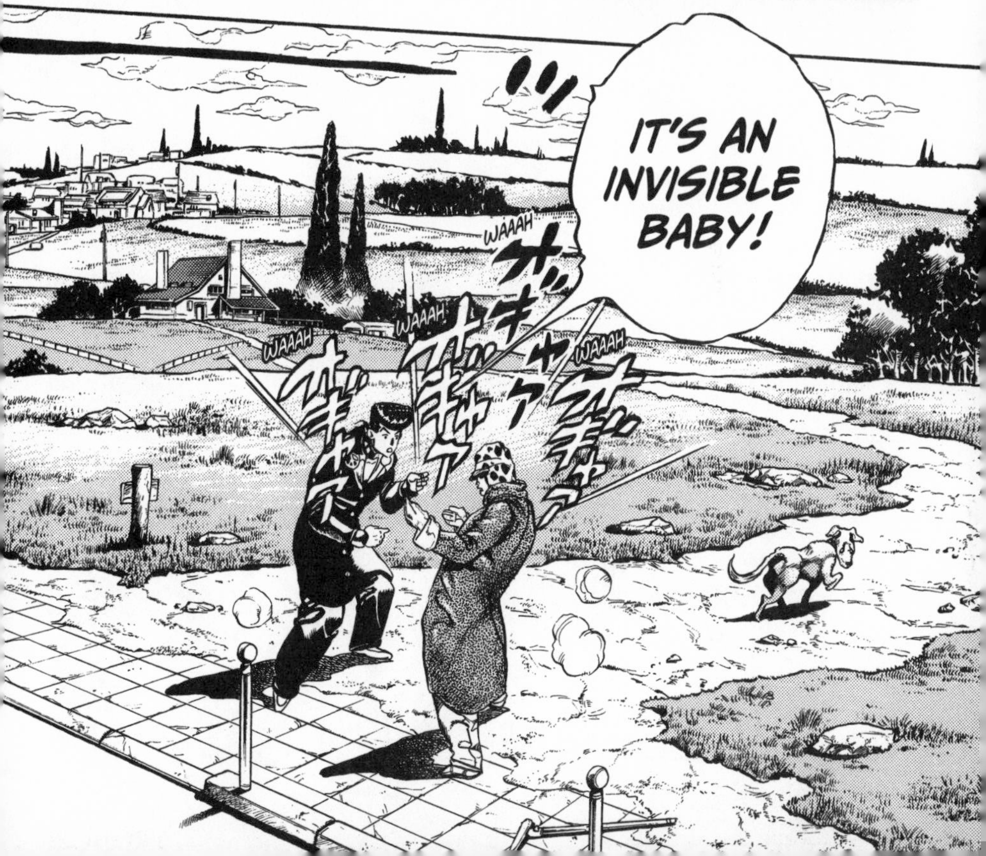
IT'S AN INVISIBLE BABY!
WAAAH
WAAAH
WAAAH
WAAAH

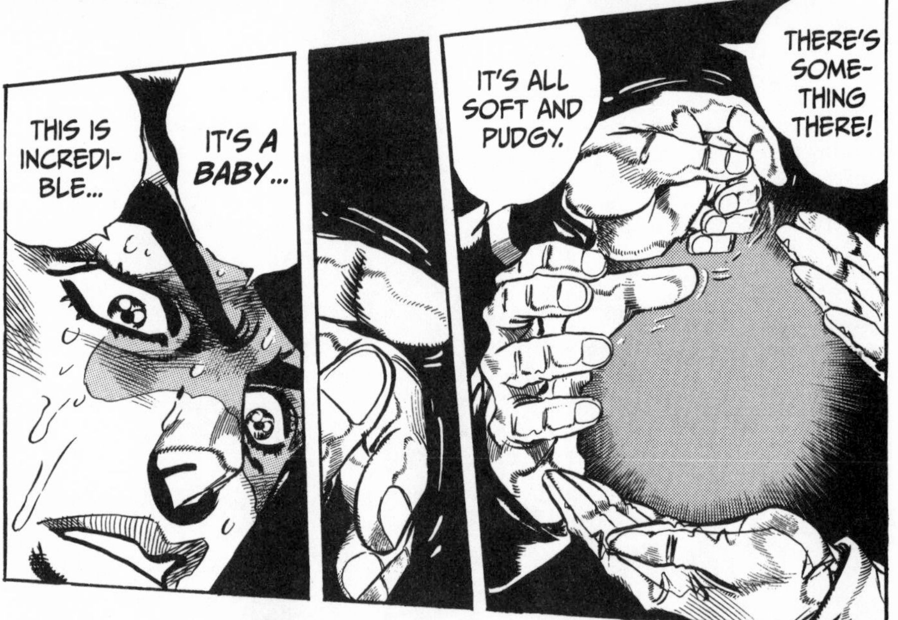
THERE'S SOME-THING THERE!
IT'S ALL SOFT AND PUDGY.
IT'S A BABY...
THIS IS INCREDI-BLE...

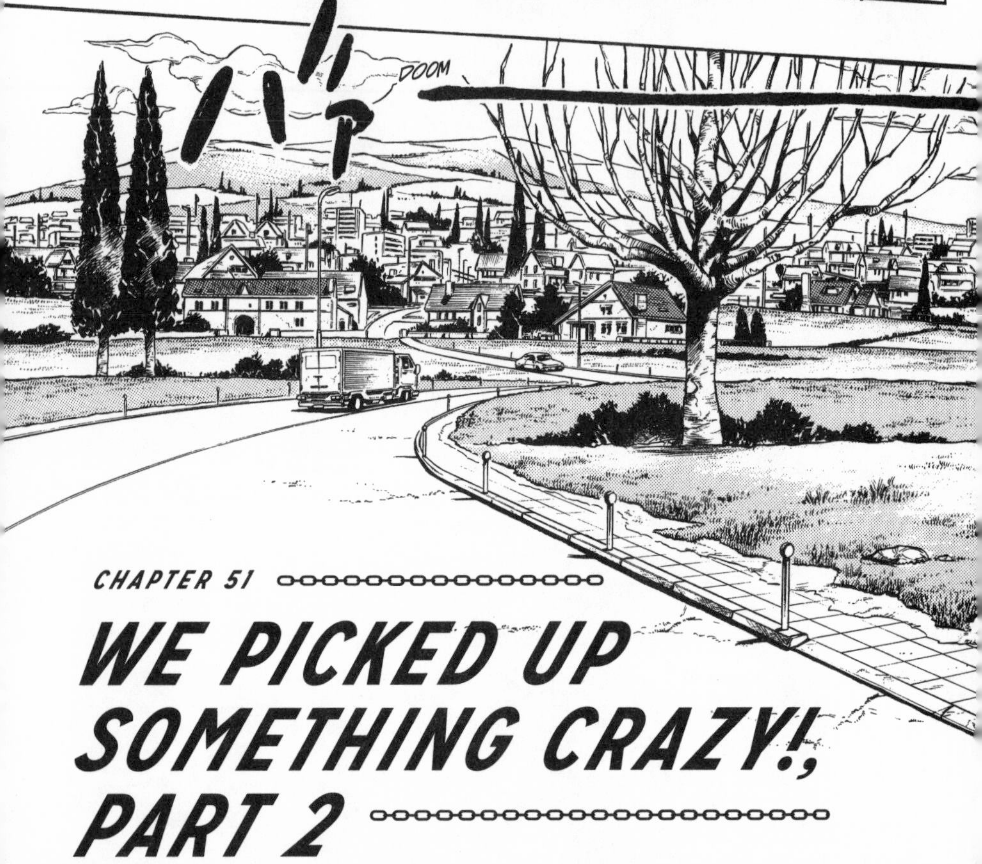
DOOM

CHAPTER 51

WE PICKED UP SOMETHING CRAZY!, PART 2

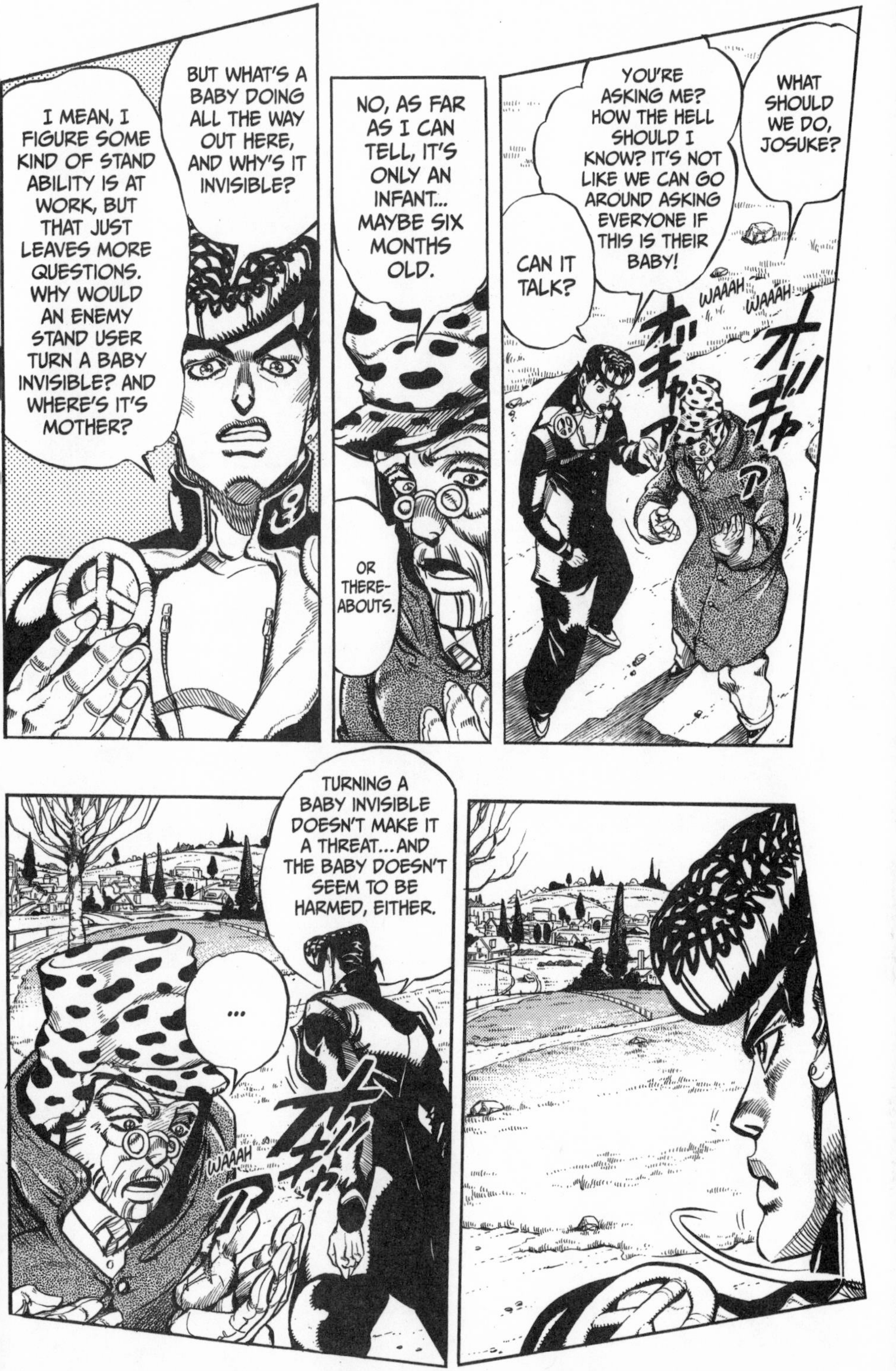
WHAT SHOULD WE DO, JOSUKE?
YOU'RE ASKING ME? HOW THE HELL SHOULD I KNOW? IT'S NOT LIKE WE CAN GO AROUND ASKING EVERYONE IF THIS IS THEIR BABY!
WAAAH WAAAH
CAN IT TALK?
NO, AS FAR AS I CAN TELL, IT'S ONLY AN INFANT... MAYBE SIX MONTHS OLD.
OR THERE-ABOUTS.
BUT WHAT'S A BABY DOING ALL THE WAY OUT HERE, AND WHY'S IT INVISIBLE?
I MEAN, I FIGURE SOME KIND OF STAND ABILITY IS AT WORK, BUT THAT JUST LEAVES MORE QUESTIONS. WHY WOULD AN ENEMY STAND USER TURN A BABY INVISIBLE? AND WHERE'S IT'S MOTHER?
TURNING A BABY INVISIBLE DOESN'T MAKE IT A THREAT...AND THE BABY DOESN'T SEEM TO BE HARMED, EITHER.
...
WAAAH

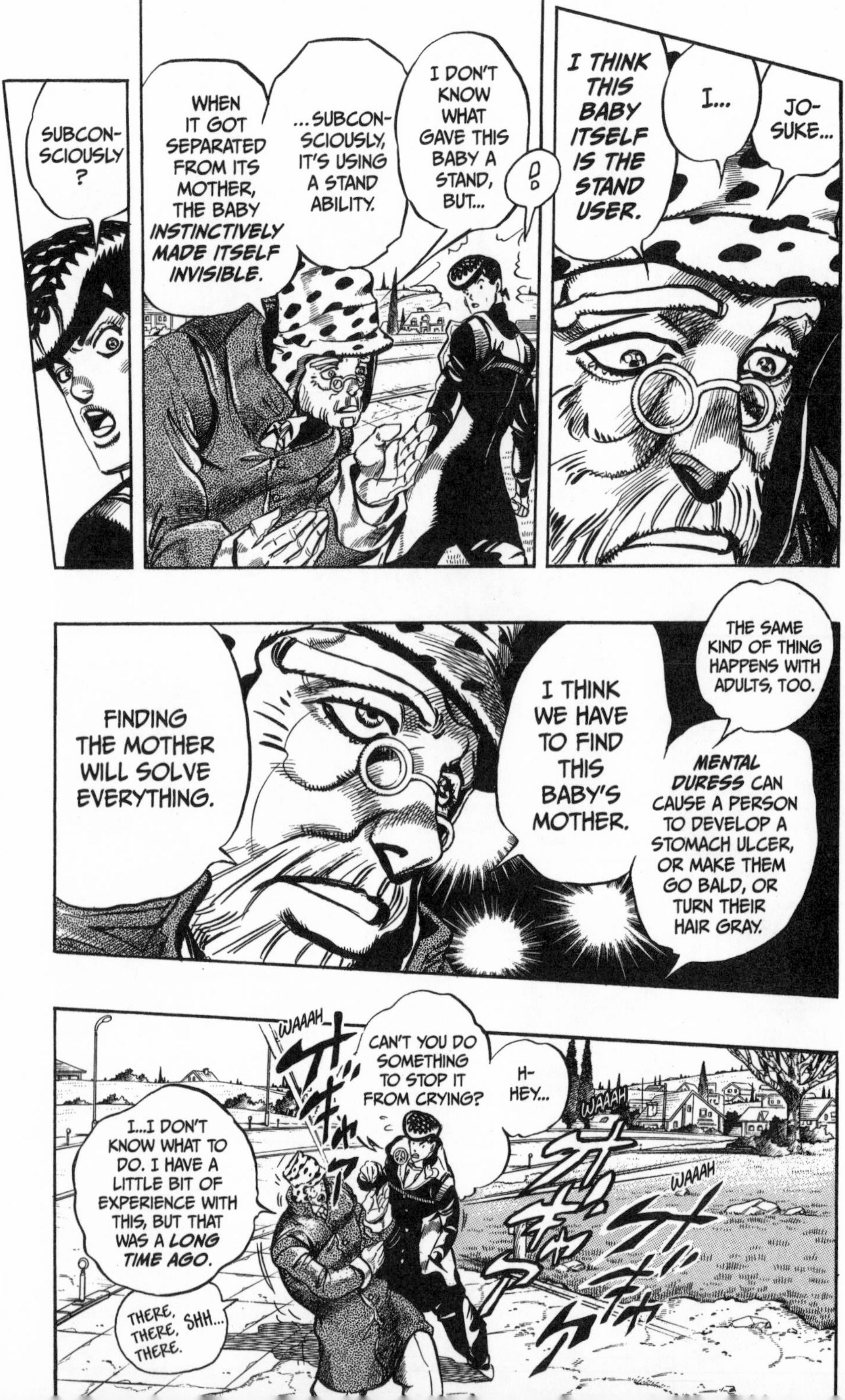
JO-SUKE...
I...
I THINK THIS BABY ITSELF IS THE STAND USER.
I DON'T KNOW WHAT GAVE THIS BABY A STAND, BUT...
...SUBCONSCIOUSLY, IT'S USING A STAND ABILITY.
WHEN IT GOT SEPARATED FROM ITS MOTHER, THE BABY INSTINCTIVELY MADE ITSELF INVISIBLE.
SUBCONSCIOUSLY?
THE SAME KIND OF THING HAPPENS WITH ADULTS, TOO.
MENTAL DURESS CAN CAUSE A PERSON TO DEVELOP A STOMACH ULCER, OR MAKE THEM GO BALD, OR TURN THEIR HAIR GRAY.
I THINK WE HAVE TO FIND THIS BABY'S MOTHER.
FINDING THE MOTHER WILL SOLVE EVERYTHING.
WAAAH
H-HEY...
CAN'T YOU DO SOMETHING TO STOP IT FROM CRYING?
WAAAH
WAAAH
I...I DON'T KNOW WHAT TO DO. I HAVE A LITTLE BIT OF EXPERIENCE WITH THIS, BUT THAT WAS A LONG TIME AGO.
THERE, THERE, SHH... THERE.

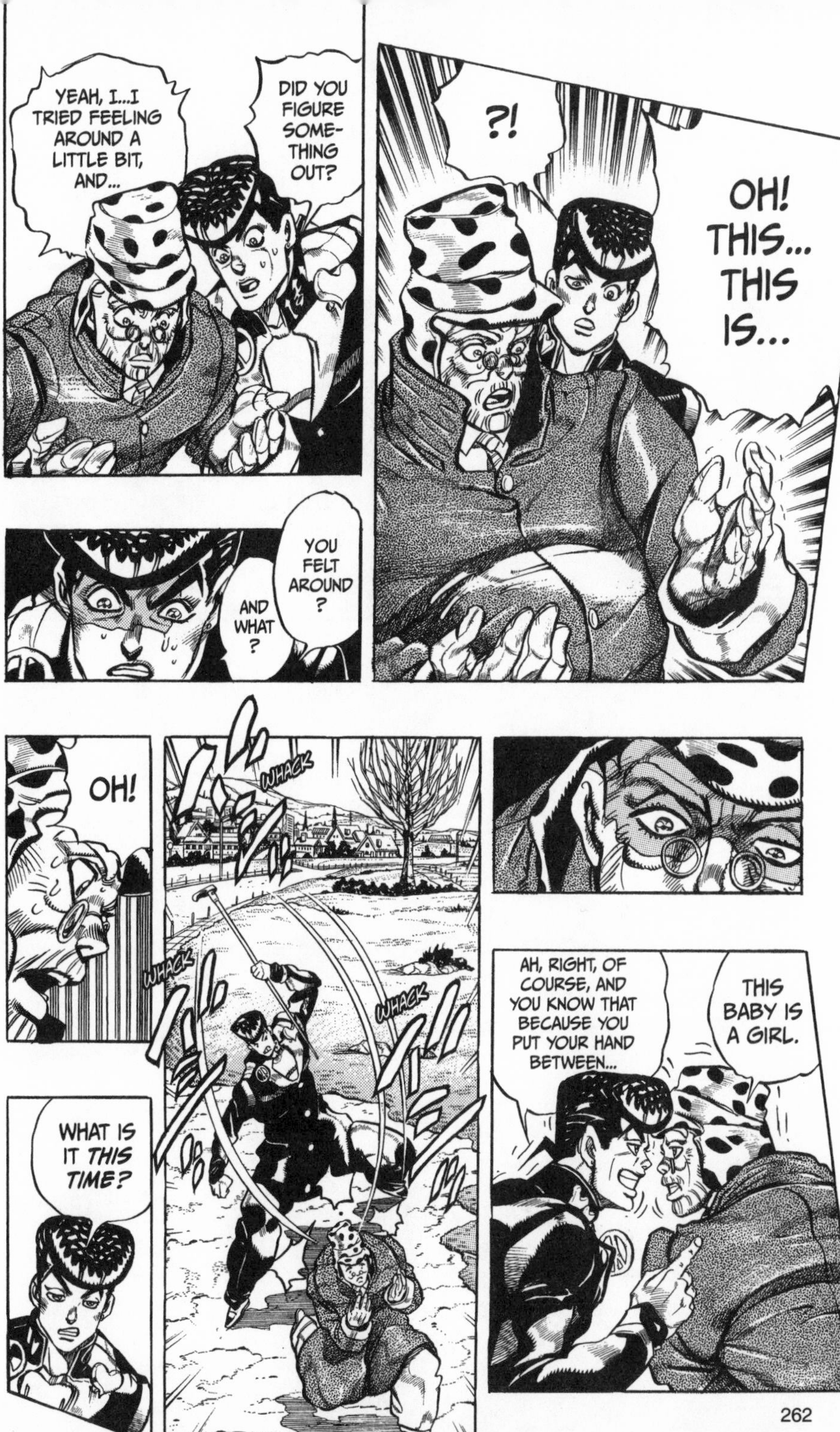
?!
OH! THIS... THIS IS...
DID YOU FIGURE SOME- THING OUT?
YEAH, I...I TRIED FEELING AROUND A LITTLE BIT, AND...
YOU FELT AROUND?
AND WHAT?
THIS BABY IS A GIRL.
AH, RIGHT, OF COURSE, AND YOU KNOW THAT BECAUSE YOU PUT YOUR HAND BETWEEN...
WHACK
WHACK
WHACK
OH!
WHAT IS IT *THIS TIME*?

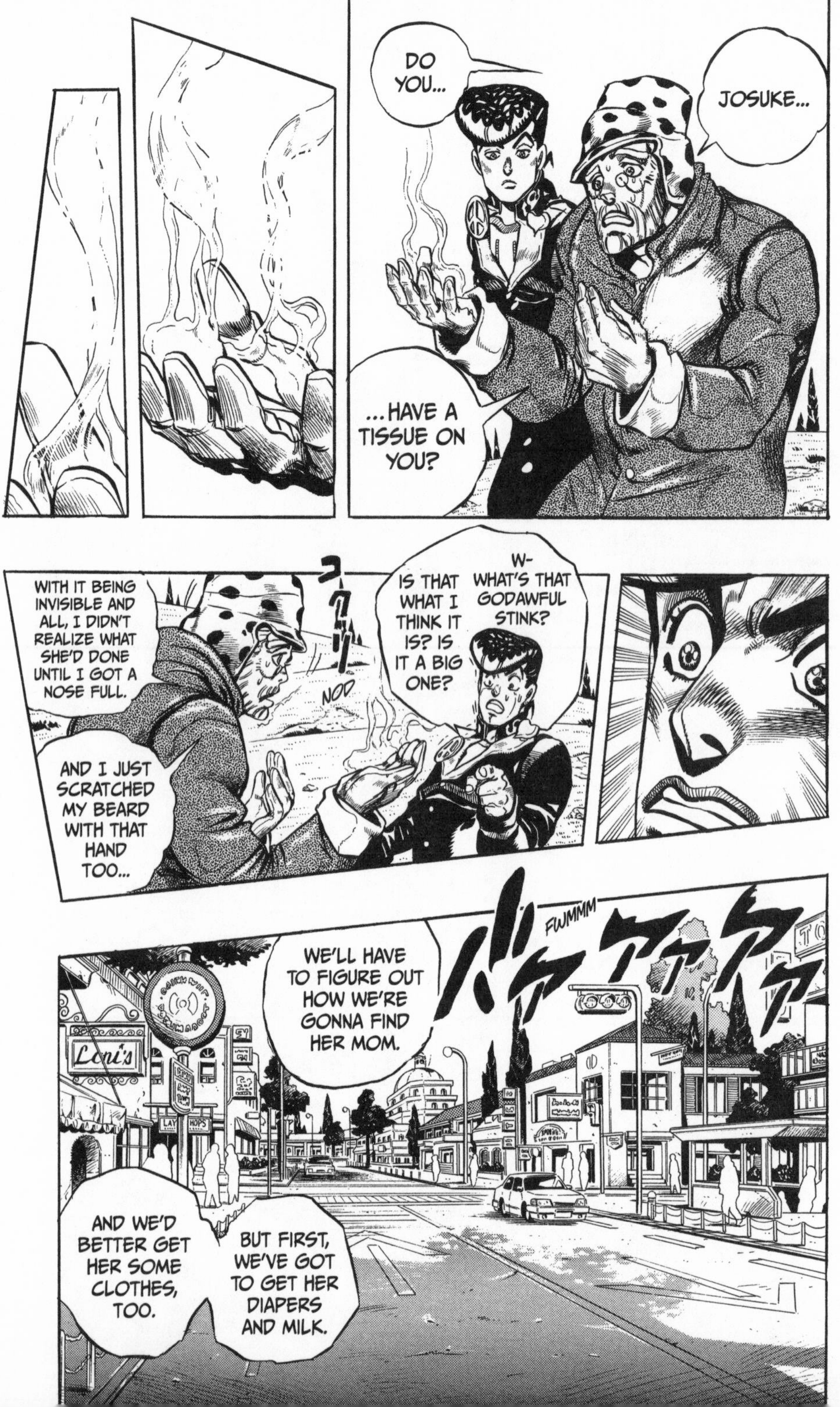
JOSUKE...
DO YOU...
...HAVE A TISSUE ON YOU?
W- WHAT'S THAT GODAWFUL STINK?
IS THAT WHAT I THINK IT IS? IS IT A BIG ONE?
NOD
WITH IT BEING INVISIBLE AND ALL, I DIDN'T REALIZE WHAT SHE'D DONE UNTIL I GOT A NOSE FULL.
AND I JUST SCRATCHED MY BEARD WITH THAT HAND TOO...
FWUMMM
WE'LL HAVE TO FIGURE OUT HOW WE'RE GONNA FIND HER MOM.
Loni's
BUT FIRST, WE'VE GOT TO GET HER DIAPERS AND MILK.
AND WE'D BETTER GET HER SOME CLOTHES, TOO.

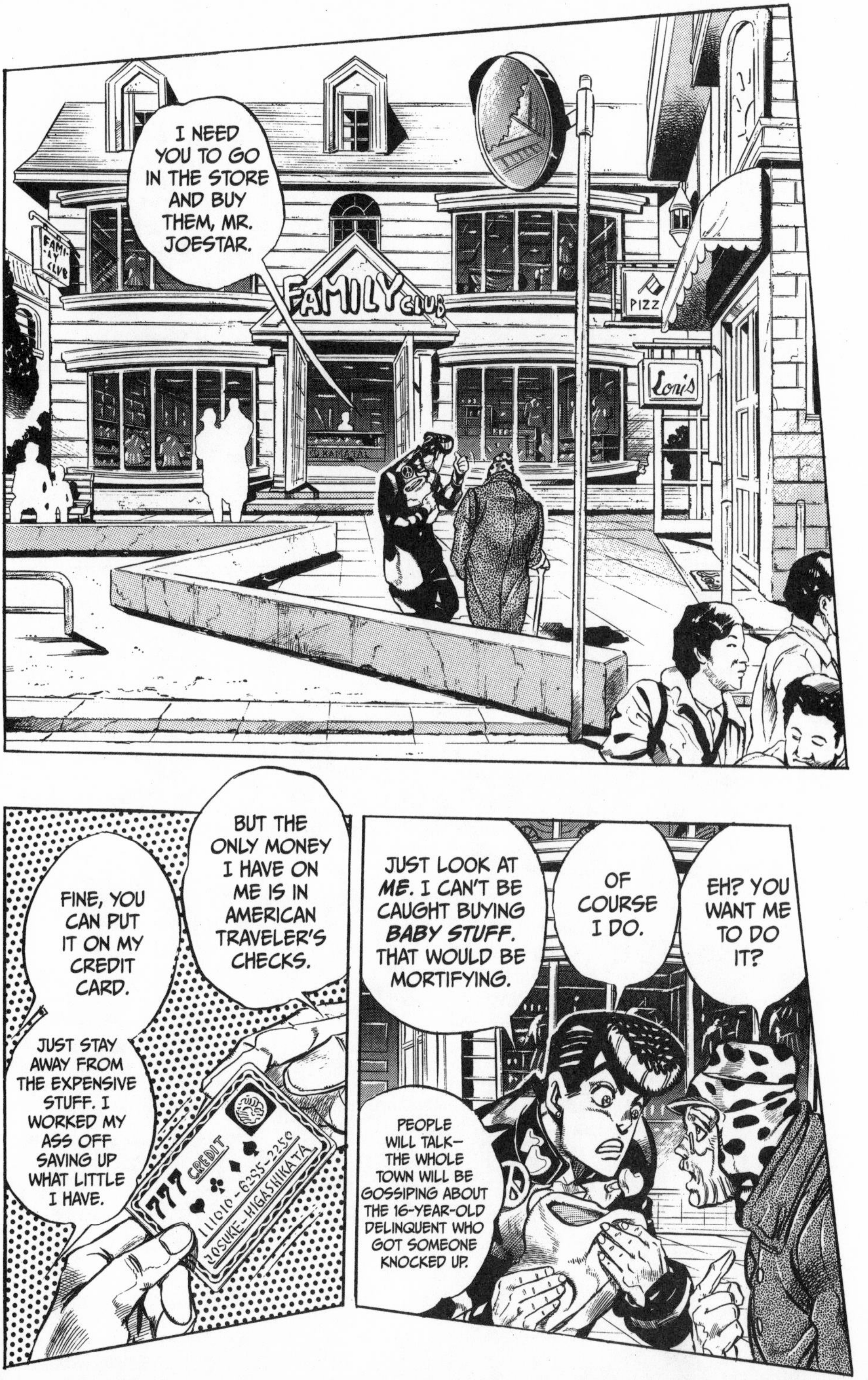
I NEED YOU TO GO IN THE STORE AND BUY THEM, MR. JOESTAR.
FAMILY CLUB
EH? YOU WANT ME TO DO IT?
OF COURSE I DO.
JUST LOOK AT *ME*. I CAN'T BE CAUGHT BUYING ***BABY STUFF***. THAT WOULD BE MORTIFYING.
PEOPLE WILL TALK— THE WHOLE TOWN WILL BE GOSSIPING ABOUT THE 16-YEAR-OLD DELINQUENT WHO GOT SOMEONE KNOCKED UP.
BUT THE ONLY MONEY I HAVE ON ME IS IN AMERICAN TRAVELER'S CHECKS.
FINE, YOU CAN PUT IT ON MY CREDIT CARD.
JUST STAY AWAY FROM THE EXPENSIVE STUFF. I WORKED MY ASS OFF SAVING UP WHAT LITTLE I HAVE.
777 CREDIT
JOSUKE-HIGASHIKATA

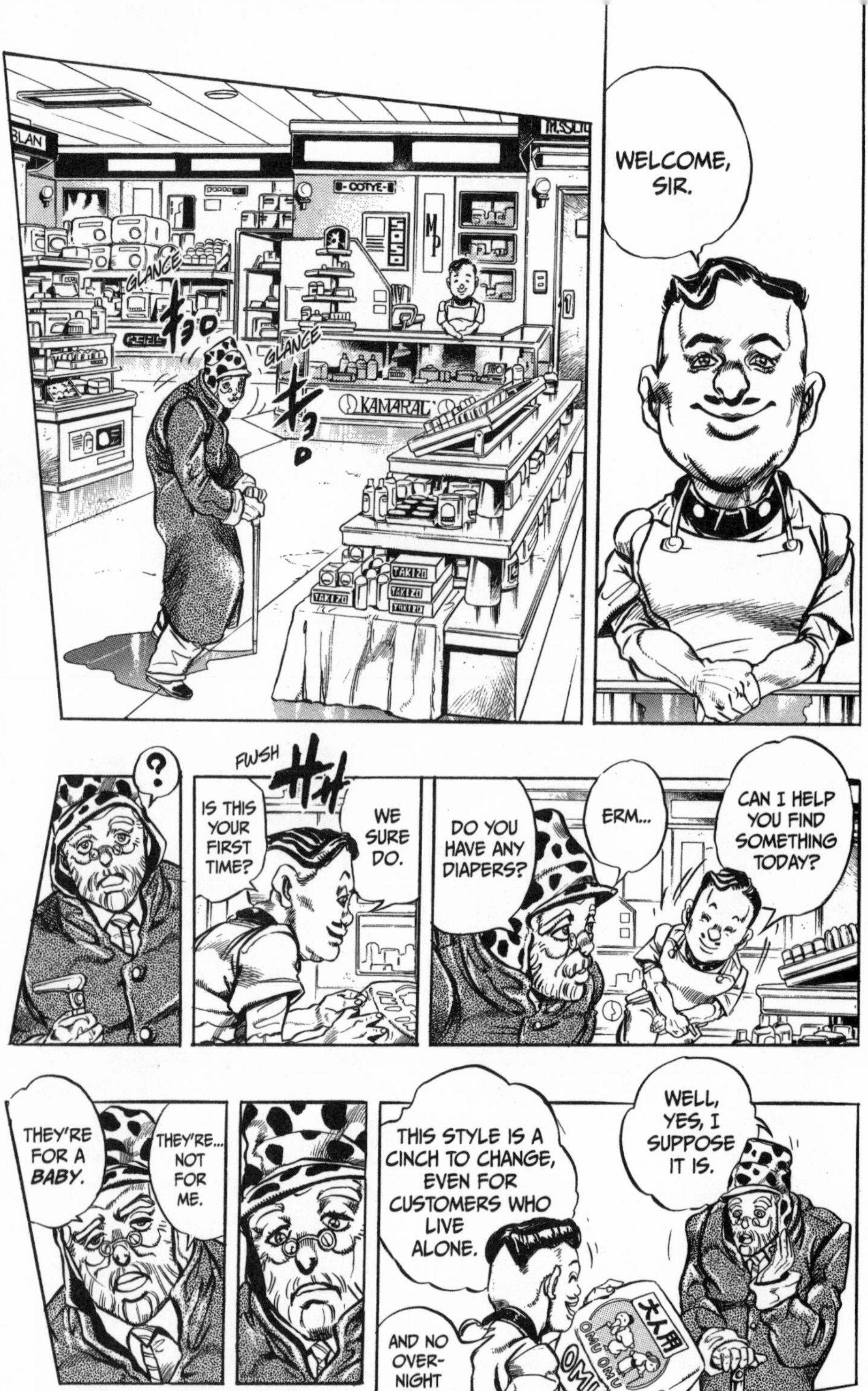
WELCOME, SIR.
GLANCE
GLANCE
BLAN
COTYE
KAMARAC
TAKIZO
CAN I HELP YOU FIND SOMETHING TODAY?
ERM...
DO YOU HAVE ANY DIAPERS?
WE SURE DO.
IS THIS YOUR FIRST TIME?
FWSH
?
WELL, YES, I SUPPOSE IT IS.
THIS STYLE IS A CINCH TO CHANGE, EVEN FOR CUSTOMERS WHO LIVE ALONE.
AND NO OVER-NIGHT LEAKS, EITHER.
大人用
OMU OMU
OMU
THEY'RE... NOT FOR ME.
THEY'RE FOR A BABY.

PACKAGING: ADULT DIAPERS

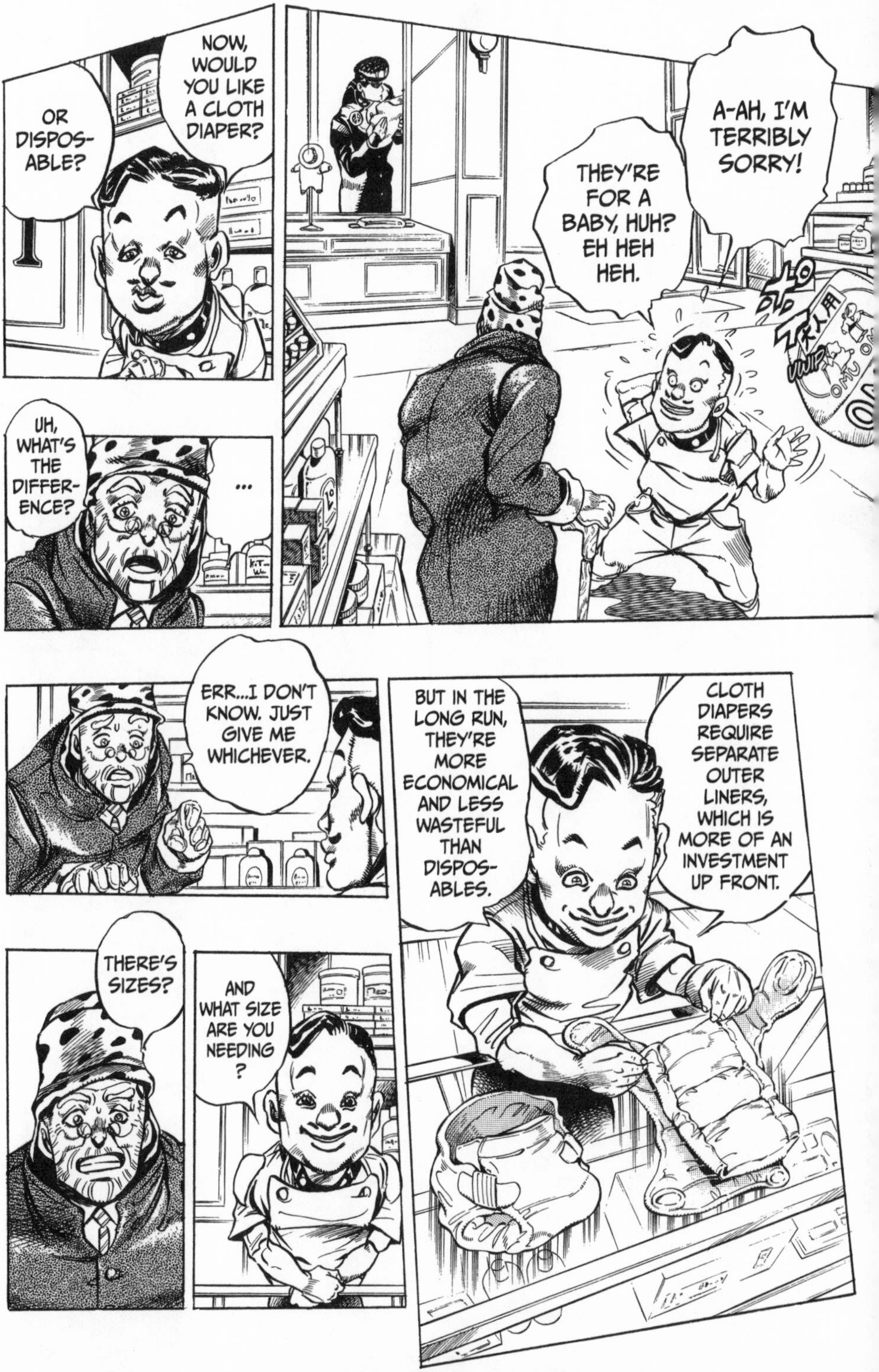
A-AH, I'M TERRIBLY SORRY!
THEY'RE FOR A BABY, HUH? EH HEH HEH.
FWIP
NOW, WOULD YOU LIKE A CLOTH DIAPER?
OR DISPOS-ABLE?
...
UH, WHAT'S THE DIFFER-ENCE?
CLOTH DIAPERS REQUIRE SEPARATE OUTER LINERS, WHICH IS MORE OF AN INVESTMENT UP FRONT.
BUT IN THE LONG RUN, THEY'RE MORE ECONOMICAL AND LESS WASTEFUL THAN DISPOS-ABLES.
ERR...I DON'T KNOW. JUST GIVE ME WHICHEVER.
AND WHAT SIZE ARE YOU NEEDING?
THERE'S SIZES?

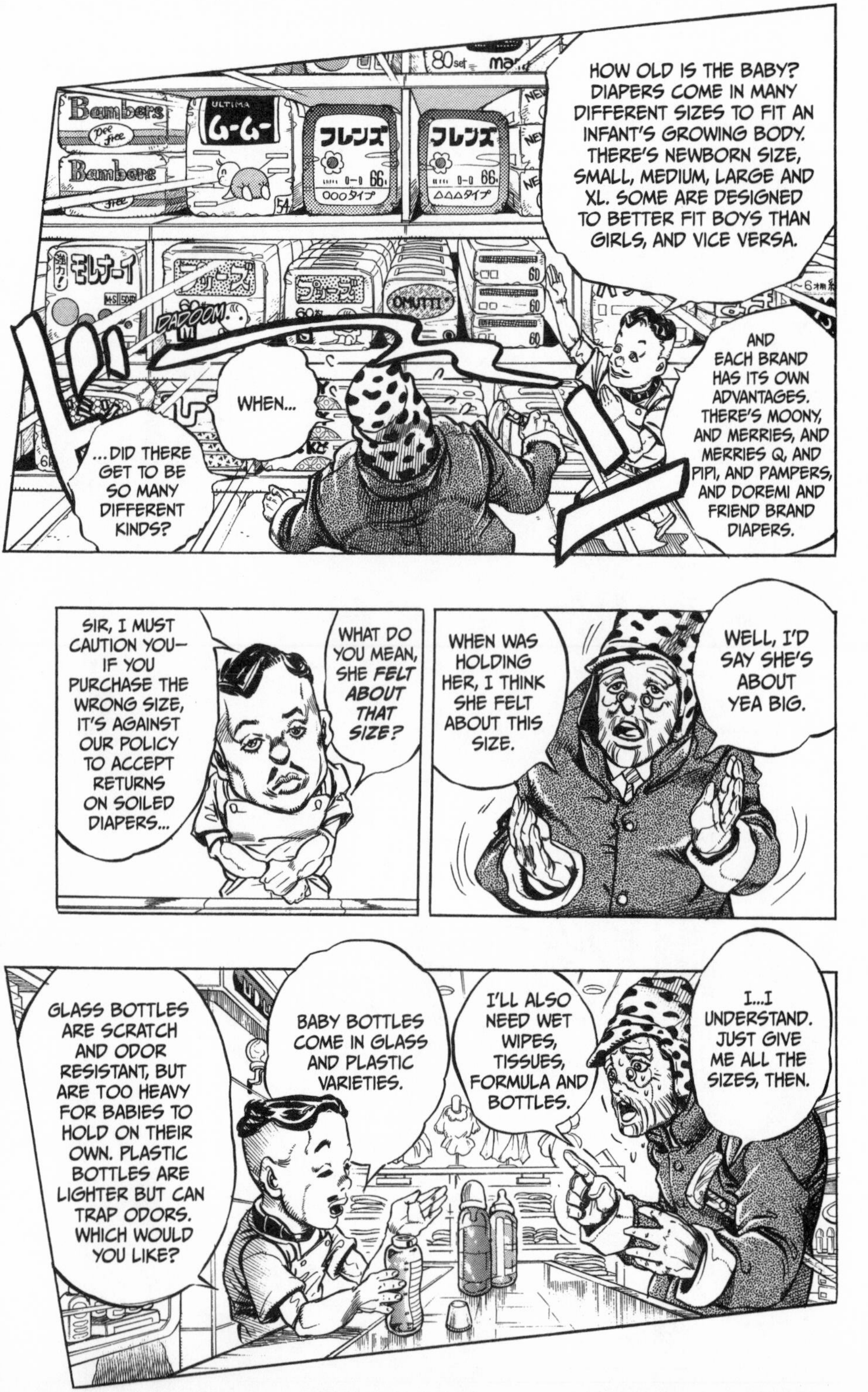
HOW OLD IS THE BABY? DIAPERS COME IN MANY DIFFERENT SIZES TO FIT AN INFANT'S GROWING BODY. THERE'S NEWBORN SIZE, SMALL, MEDIUM, LARGE AND XL. SOME ARE DESIGNED TO BETTER FIT BOYS THAN GIRLS, AND VICE VERSA.
AND EACH BRAND HAS ITS OWN ADVANTAGES. THERE'S MOONY, AND MERRIES, AND MERRIES Q, AND PIPI, AND PAMPERS, AND DOREMI AND FRIEND BRAND DIAPERS.
DADOOM
WHEN...
...DID THERE GET TO BE SO MANY DIFFERENT KINDS?
WELL, I'D SAY SHE'S ABOUT YEA BIG.
WHEN WAS HOLDING HER, I THINK SHE FELT ABOUT THIS SIZE.
WHAT DO YOU MEAN, SHE *FELT ABOUT THAT SIZE?*
SIR, I MUST CAUTION YOU—IF YOU PURCHASE THE WRONG SIZE, IT'S AGAINST OUR POLICY TO ACCEPT RETURNS ON SOILED DIAPERS...
I...I UNDERSTAND. JUST GIVE ME ALL THE SIZES, THEN.
I'LL ALSO NEED WET WIPES, TISSUES, FORMULA AND BOTTLES.
BABY BOTTLES COME IN GLASS AND PLASTIC VARIETIES.
GLASS BOTTLES ARE SCRATCH AND ODOR RESISTANT, BUT ARE TOO HEAVY FOR BABIES TO HOLD ON THEIR OWN. PLASTIC BOTTLES ARE LIGHTER BUT CAN TRAP ODORS. WHICH WOULD YOU LIKE?

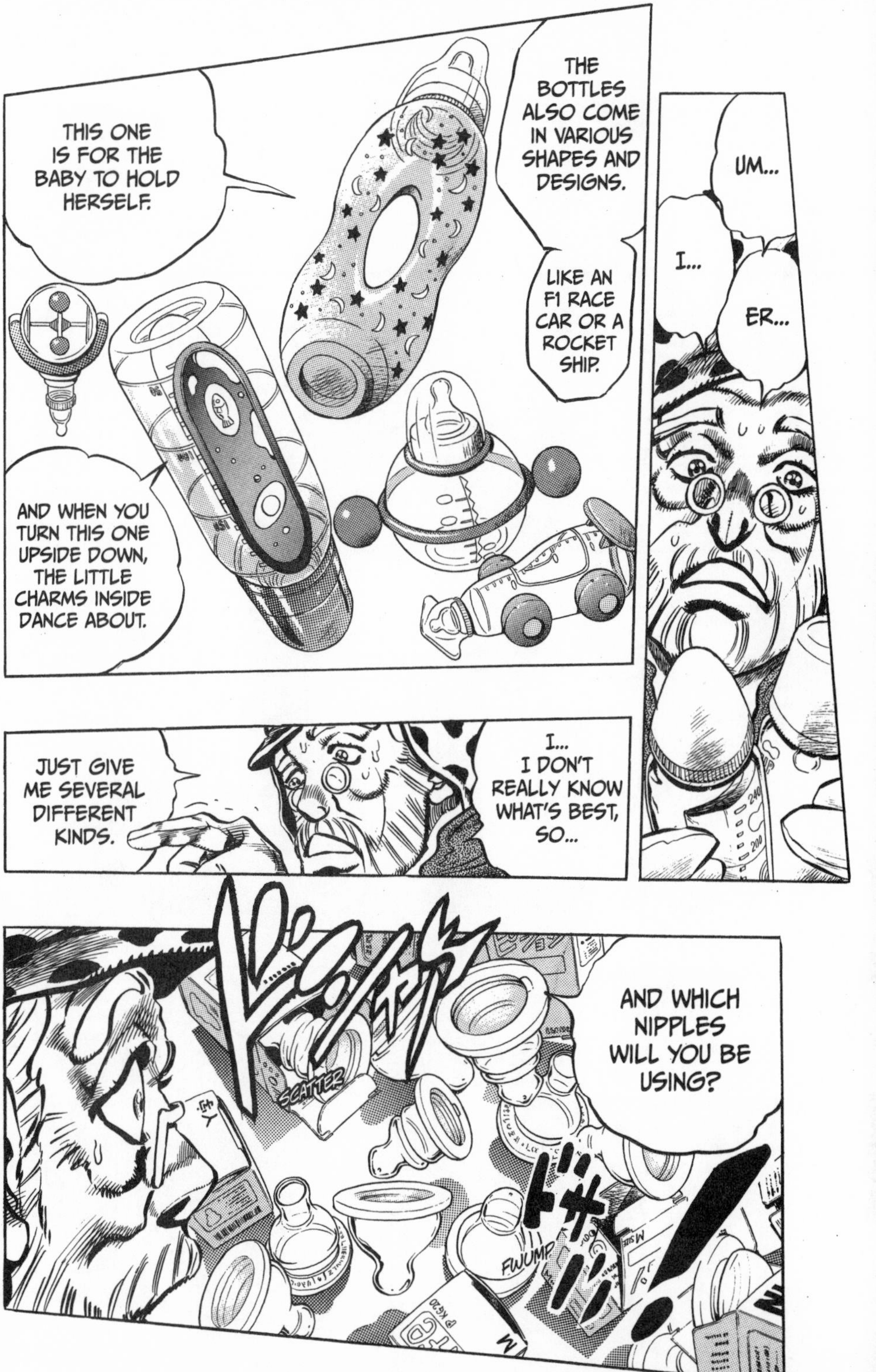
UM...
I...
ER...
THE BOTTLES ALSO COME IN VARIOUS SHAPES AND DESIGNS.
LIKE AN F1 RACE CAR OR A ROCKET SHIP.
THIS ONE IS FOR THE BABY TO HOLD HERSELF.
AND WHEN YOU TURN THIS ONE UPSIDE DOWN, THE LITTLE CHARMS INSIDE DANCE ABOUT.
I... I DON'T REALLY KNOW WHAT'S BEST, SO...
JUST GIVE ME SEVERAL DIFFERENT KINDS.
AND WHICH NIPPLES WILL YOU BE USING?
SCATTER
FWUMP

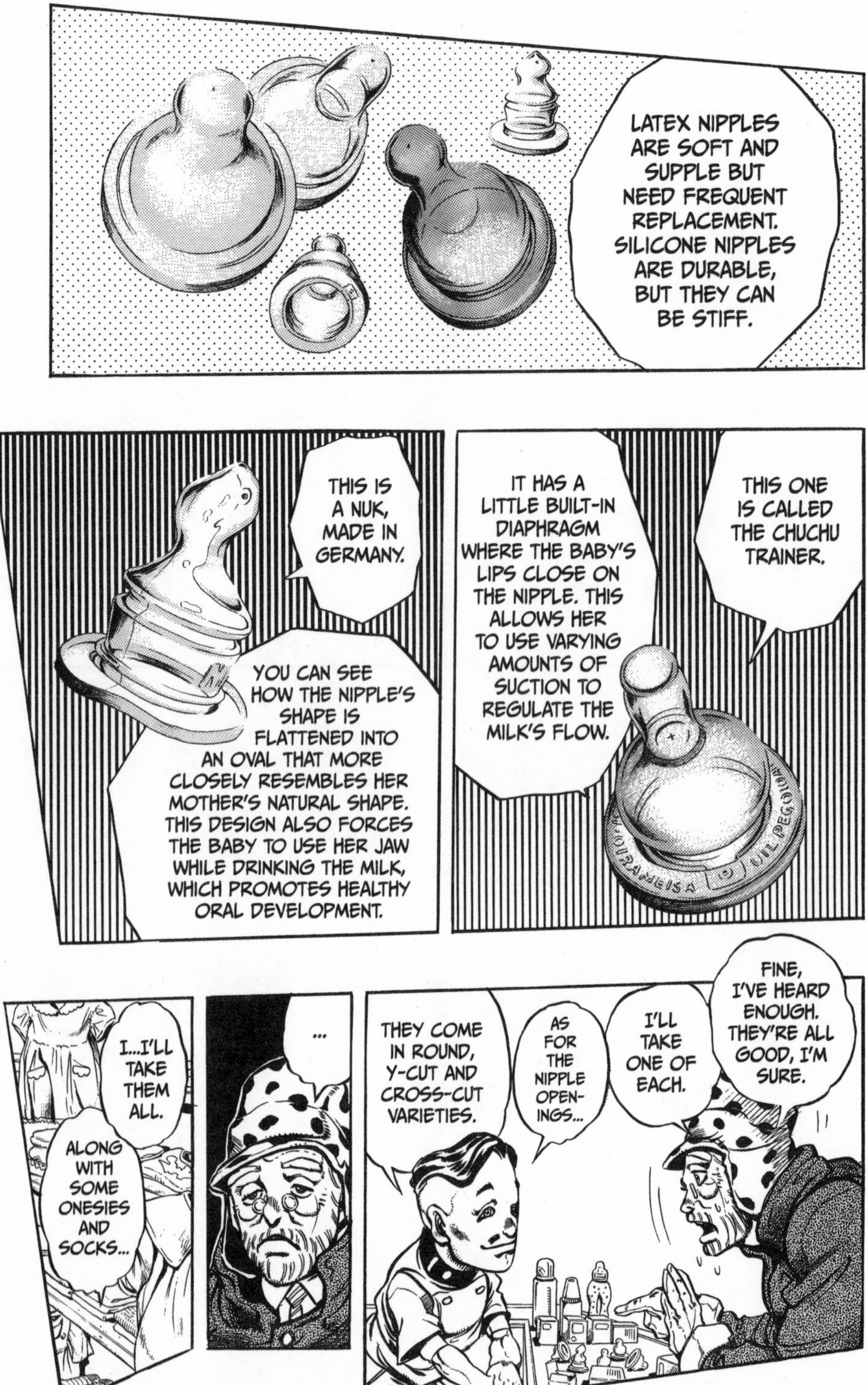
LATEX NIPPLES ARE SOFT AND SUPPLE BUT NEED FREQUENT REPLACEMENT. SILICONE NIPPLES ARE DURABLE, BUT THEY CAN BE STIFF.
THIS ONE IS CALLED THE CHUCHU TRAINER.
IT HAS A LITTLE BUILT-IN DIAPHRAGM WHERE THE BABY'S LIPS CLOSE ON THE NIPPLE. THIS ALLOWS HER TO USE VARYING AMOUNTS OF SUCTION TO REGULATE THE MILK'S FLOW.
THIS IS A NUK, MADE IN GERMANY.
YOU CAN SEE HOW THE NIPPLE'S SHAPE IS FLATTENED INTO AN OVAL THAT MORE CLOSELY RESEMBLES HER MOTHER'S NATURAL SHAPE. THIS DESIGN ALSO FORCES THE BABY TO USE HER JAW WHILE DRINKING THE MILK, WHICH PROMOTES HEALTHY ORAL DEVELOPMENT.
FINE, I'VE HEARD ENOUGH. THEY'RE ALL GOOD, I'M SURE.
I'LL TAKE ONE OF EACH.
AS FOR THE NIPPLE OPEN-INGS...
THEY COME IN ROUND, Y-CUT AND CROSS-CUT VARIETIES.
...
I...I'LL TAKE THEM ALL.
ALONG WITH SOME ONESIES AND SOCKS...

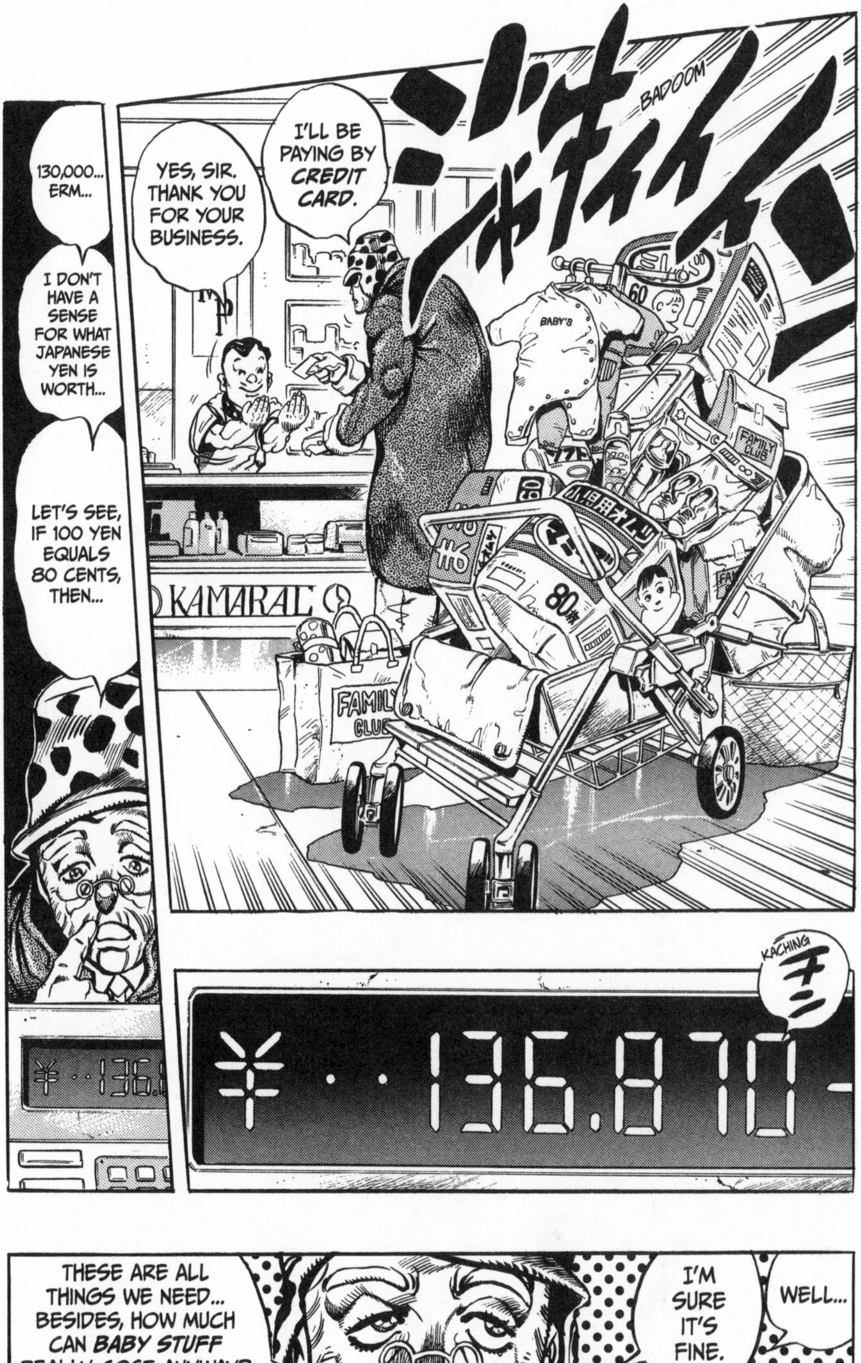
BADOOM
I'LL BE PAYING BY *CREDIT CARD*.
YES, SIR. THANK YOU FOR YOUR BUSINESS.
BABY'S
FAMILY CLUB
KAMARAL
FAMILY CLUB
KACHING
¥··136.870-
130,000... ERM...
I DON'T HAVE A SENSE FOR WHAT JAPANESE YEN IS WORTH...
LET'S SEE, IF 100 YEN EQUALS 80 CENTS, THEN...
WELL...
I'M SURE IT'S FINE.
THESE ARE ALL THINGS WE NEED... BESIDES, HOW MUCH CAN *BABY STUFF* REALLY COST, ANYWAY? SURELY HARDLY ANYTHING AT ALL.

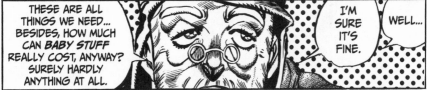

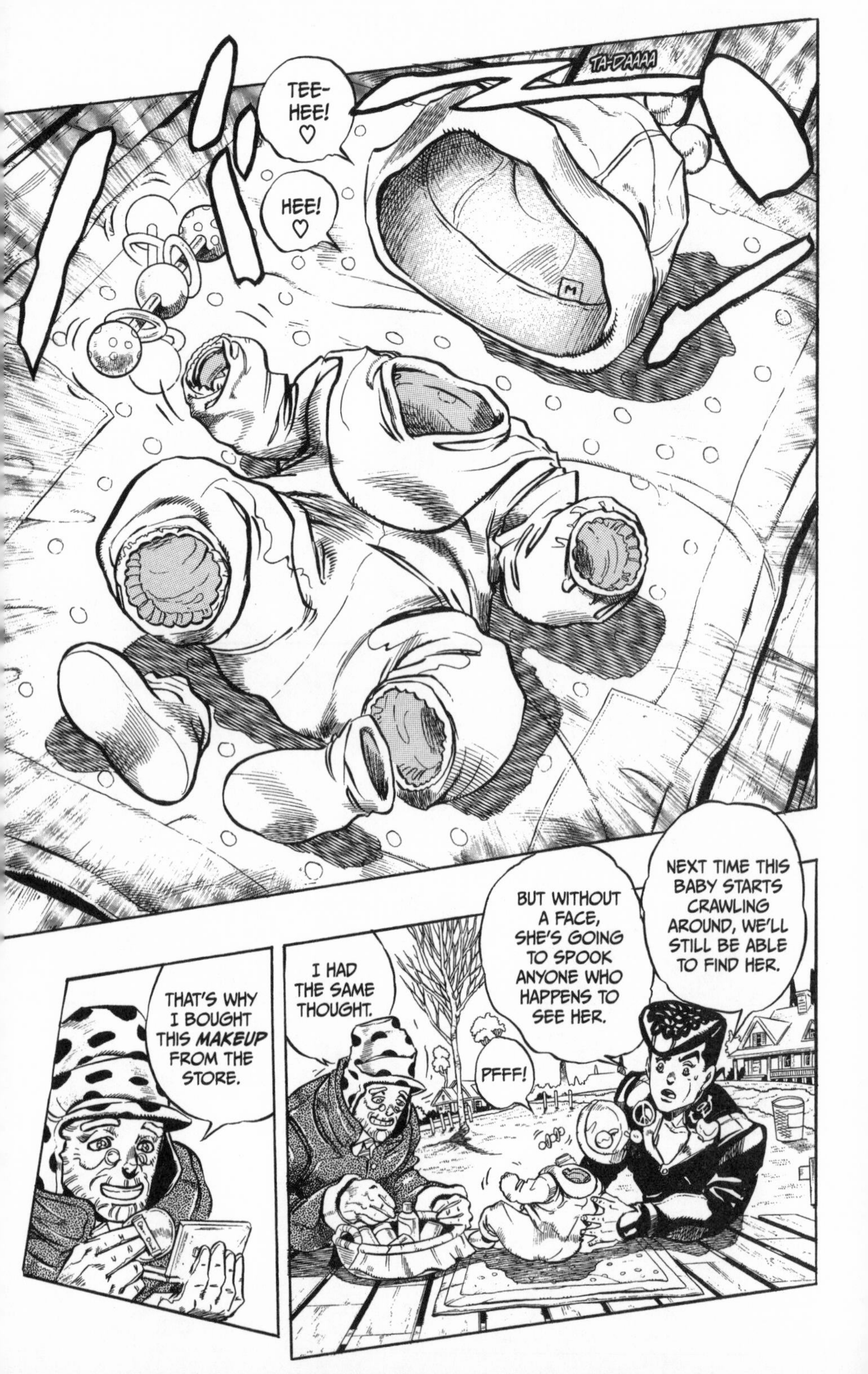
TA-DAAAA
TEE-HEE! ♡
HEE! ♡
NEXT TIME THIS BABY STARTS CRAWLING AROUND, WE'LL STILL BE ABLE TO FIND HER.
BUT WITHOUT A FACE, SHE'S GOING TO SPOOK ANYONE WHO HAPPENS TO SEE HER.
PFFF!
I HAD THE SAME THOUGHT.
THAT'S WHY I BOUGHT THIS *MAKEUP* FROM THE STORE.

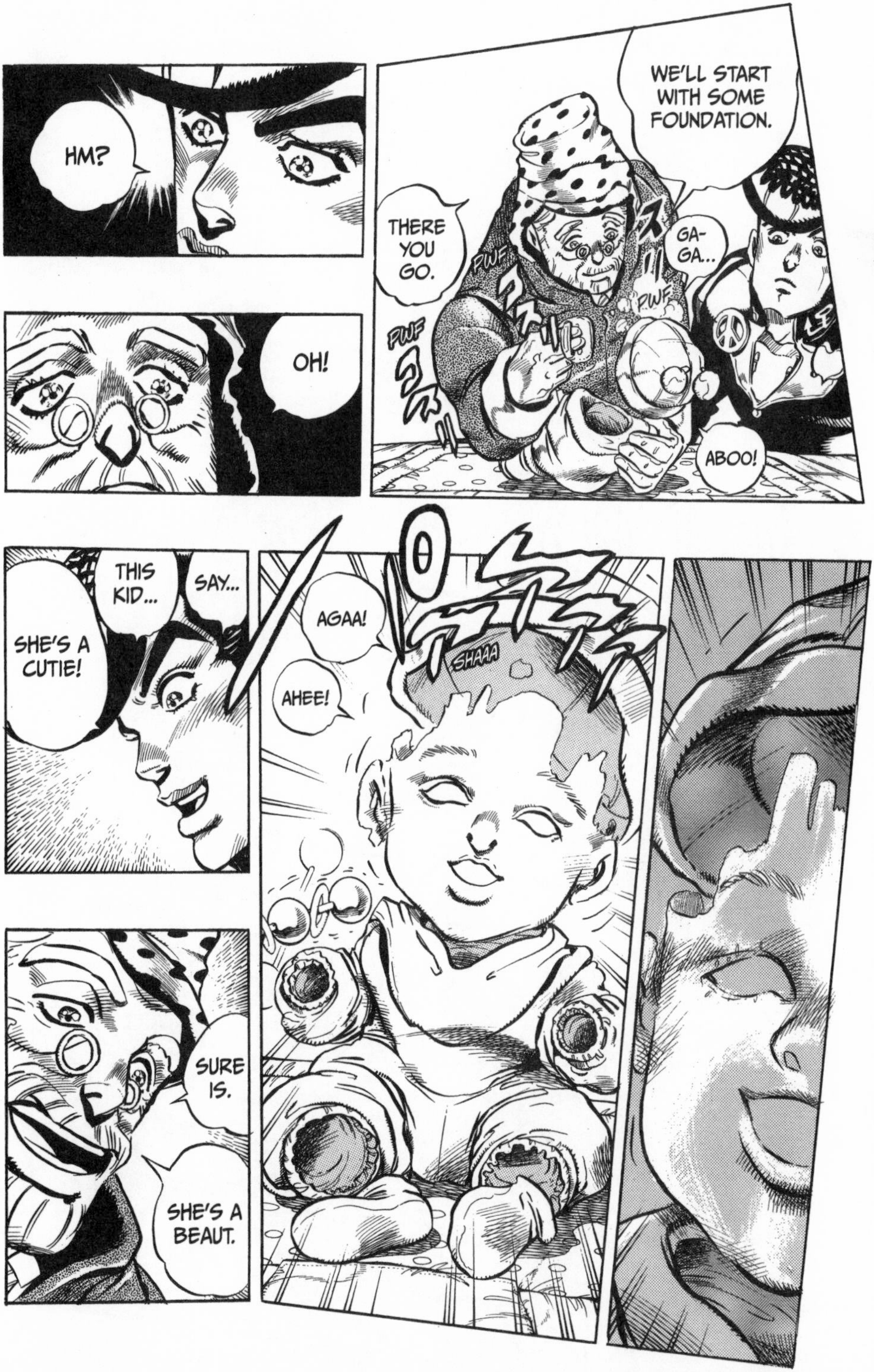
WE'LL START WITH SOME FOUNDATION.
GA-GA...
PWF
THERE YOU GO.
PWF
PWF
ABOO!
HM?
OH!
AGAA!
SHAAA
AHEE!
SAY...
THIS KID...
SHE'S A CUTIE!
SURE IS.
SHE'S A BEAUT.

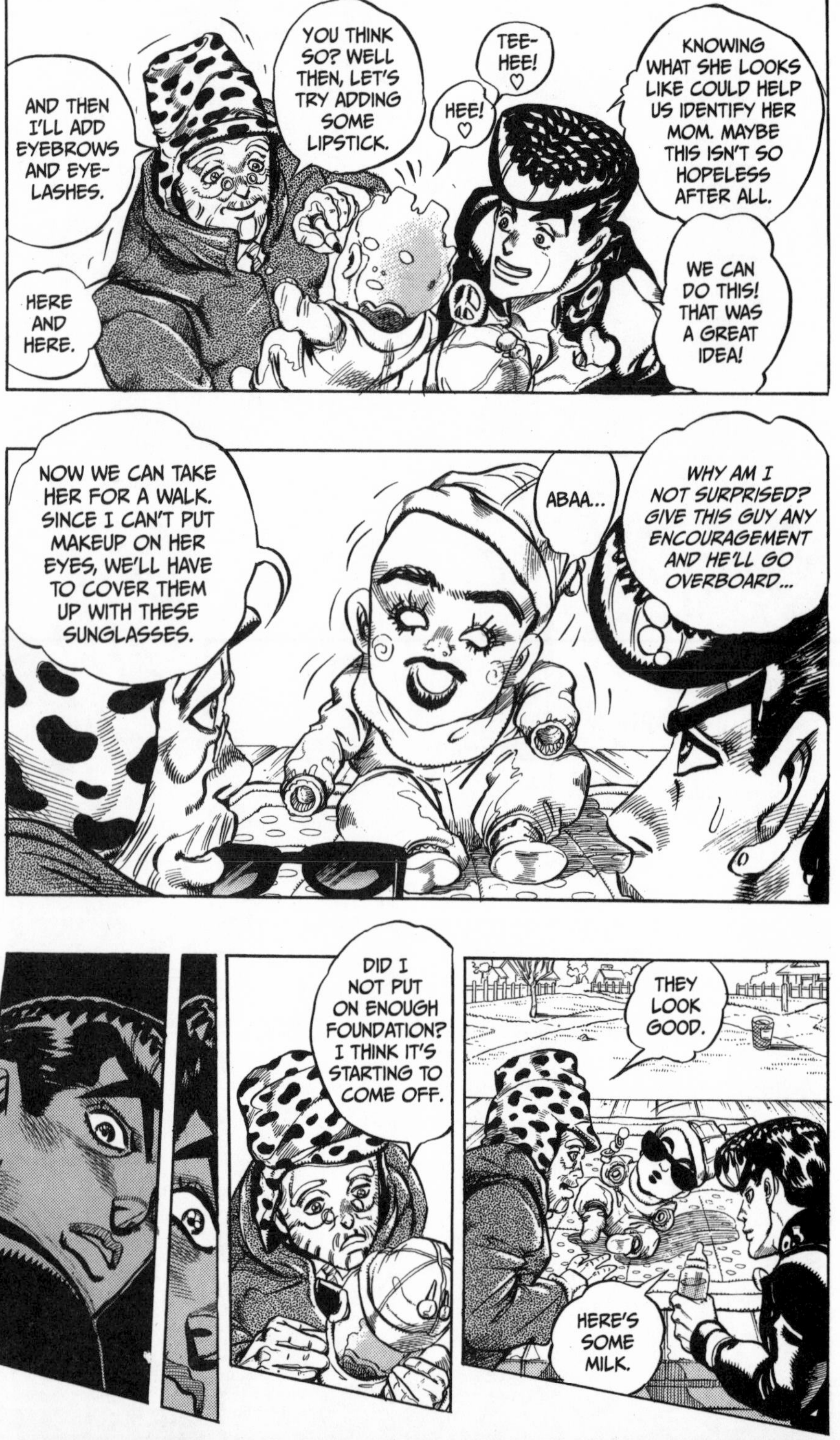
KNOWING WHAT SHE LOOKS LIKE COULD HELP US IDENTIFY HER MOM. MAYBE THIS ISN'T SO HOPELESS AFTER ALL.
WE CAN DO THIS! THAT WAS A GREAT IDEA!
TEE-HEE! ♡
HEE! ♡
YOU THINK SO? WELL THEN, LET'S TRY ADDING SOME LIPSTICK.
AND THEN I'LL ADD EYEBROWS AND EYE-LASHES.
HERE AND HERE.
WHY AM I NOT SURPRISED? GIVE THIS GUY ANY ENCOURAGEMENT AND HE'LL GO OVERBOARD...
ABAA...
NOW WE CAN TAKE HER FOR A WALK. SINCE I CAN'T PUT MAKEUP ON HER EYES, WE'LL HAVE TO COVER THEM UP WITH THESE SUNGLASSES.
THEY LOOK GOOD.
HERE'S SOME MILK.
DID I NOT PUT ON ENOUGH FOUNDATION? I THINK IT'S STARTING TO COME OFF.

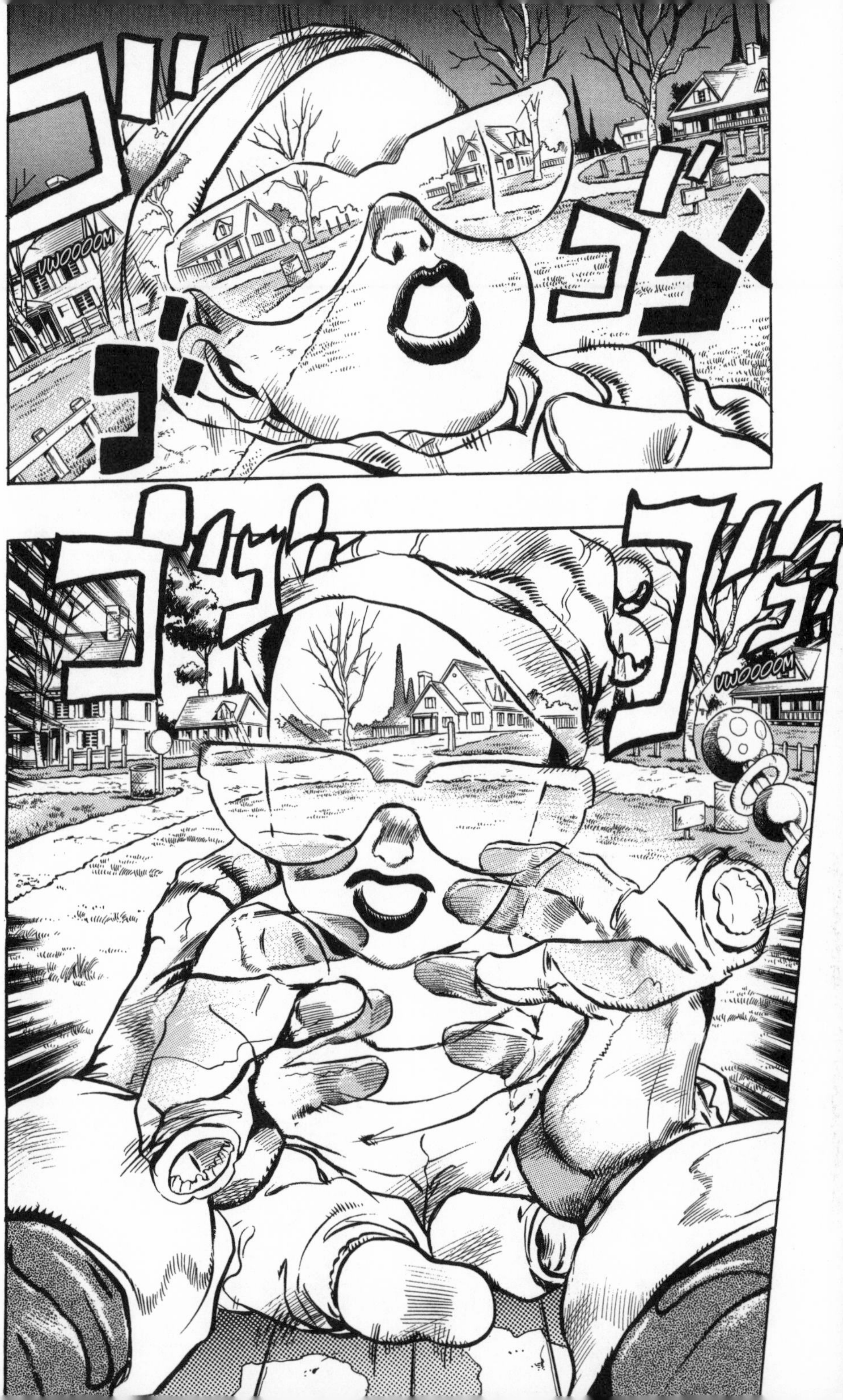
ゴゴ
ゴゴ
VWOOOOM
ゴゴ
VWOOOOM
ゴゴ

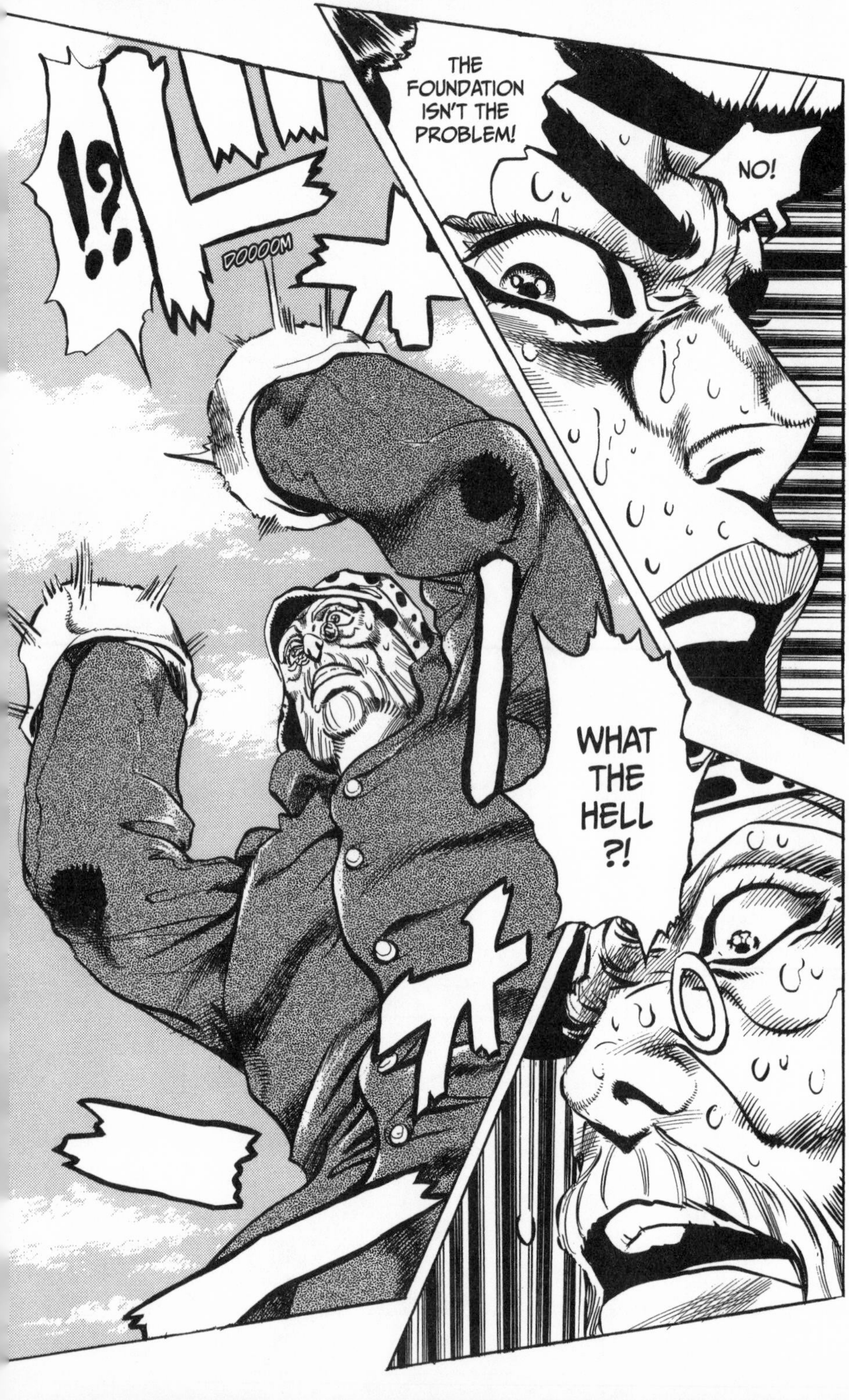
NO!
THE FOUNDATION ISN'T THE PROBLEM!
WHAT THE HELL ?!
!?
DOOOOM

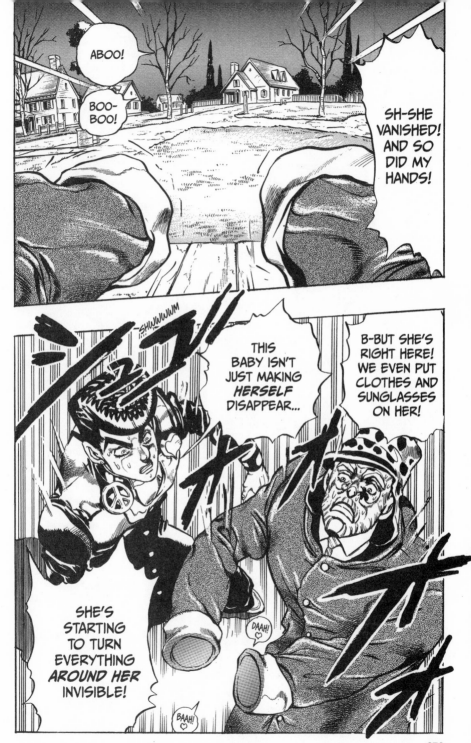

SH-SHE VANISHED! AND SO DID MY HANDS!
ABOO!
BOO-BOO!
B-BUT SHE'S RIGHT HERE! WE EVEN PUT CLOTHES AND SUNGLASSES ON HER!
THIS BABY ISN'T JUST MAKING HERSELF DISAPPEAR...
SHWWWWM
SHE'S STARTING TO TURN EVERYTHING AROUND HER INVISIBLE!
DAAH! ♡
BAAH! ♡

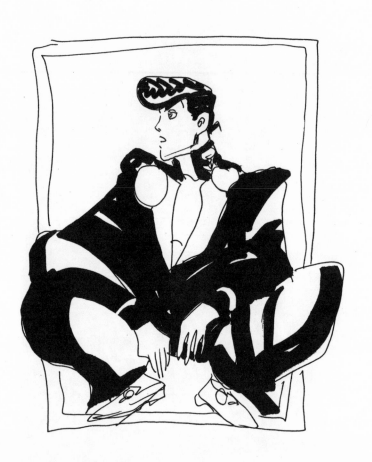

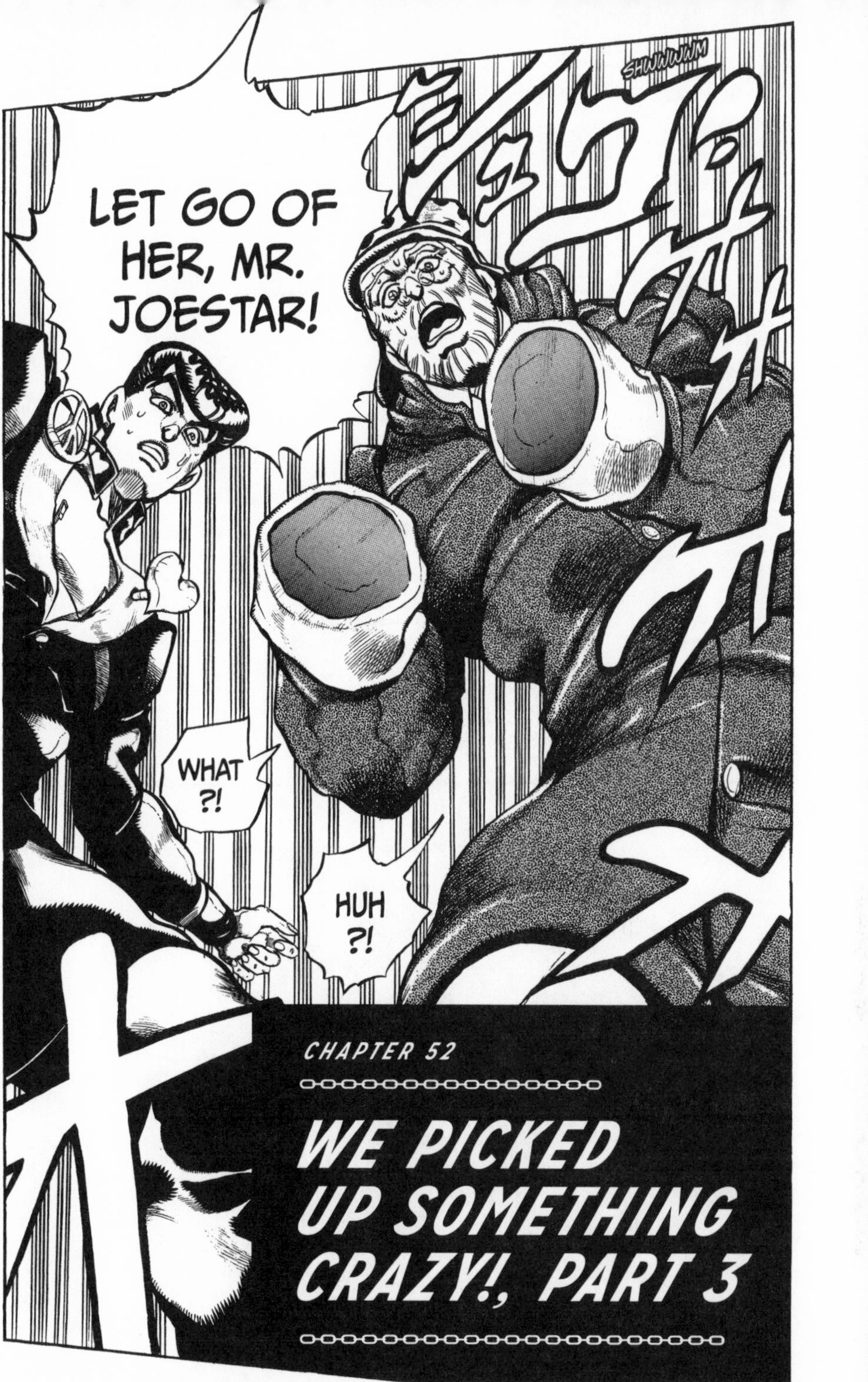
SHWWWWM
LET GO OF HER, MR. JOESTAR!
WHAT ?!
HUH ?!
CHAPTER 52
WE PICKED UP SOMETHING CRAZY!, PART 3

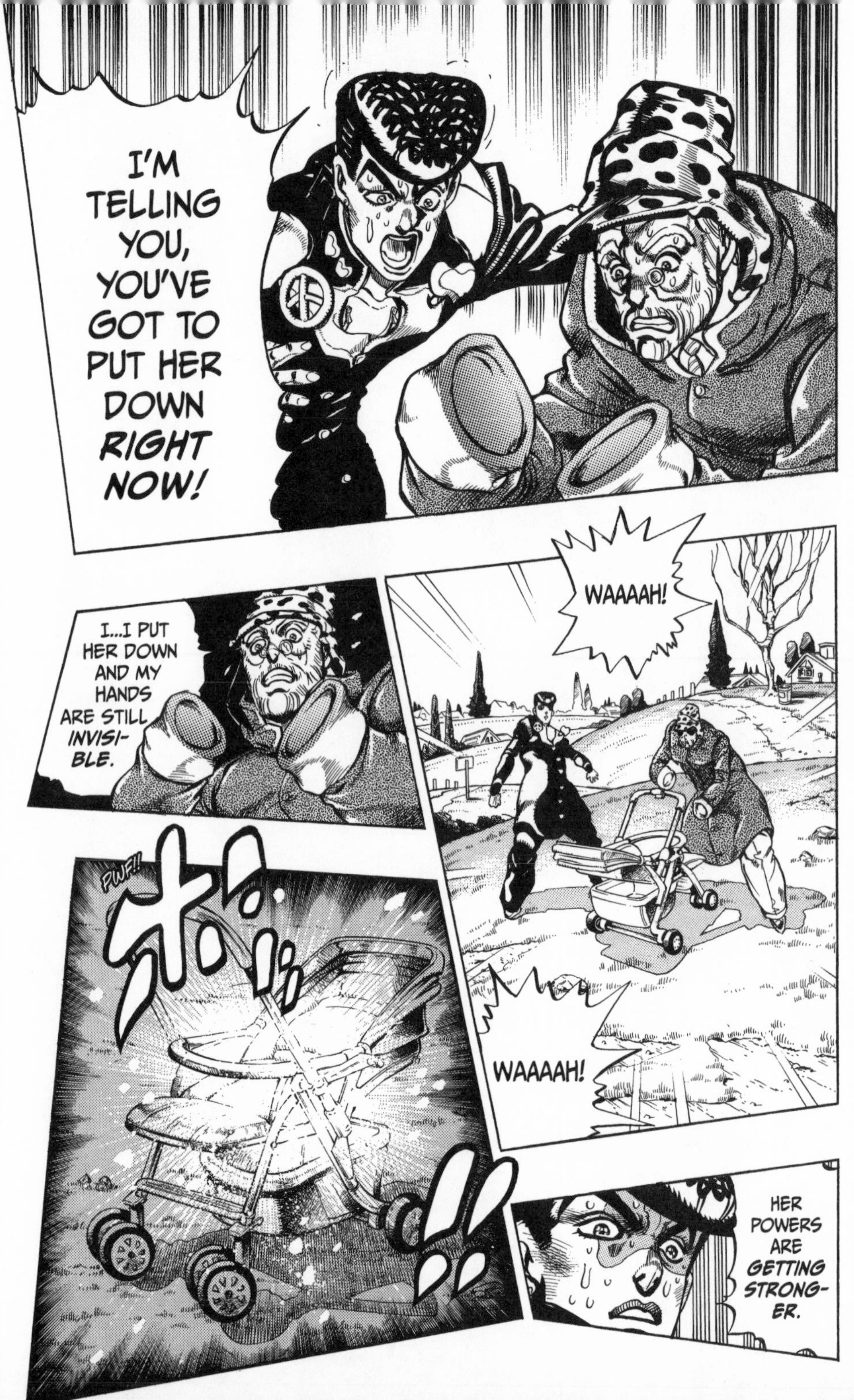

I'M TELLING YOU, YOU'VE GOT TO PUT HER DOWN RIGHT NOW!
WAAAAH!
WAAAAH!
I...I PUT HER DOWN AND MY HANDS ARE STILL INVISI-BLE.
PWF!!
HER POWERS ARE GETTING STRONGER.

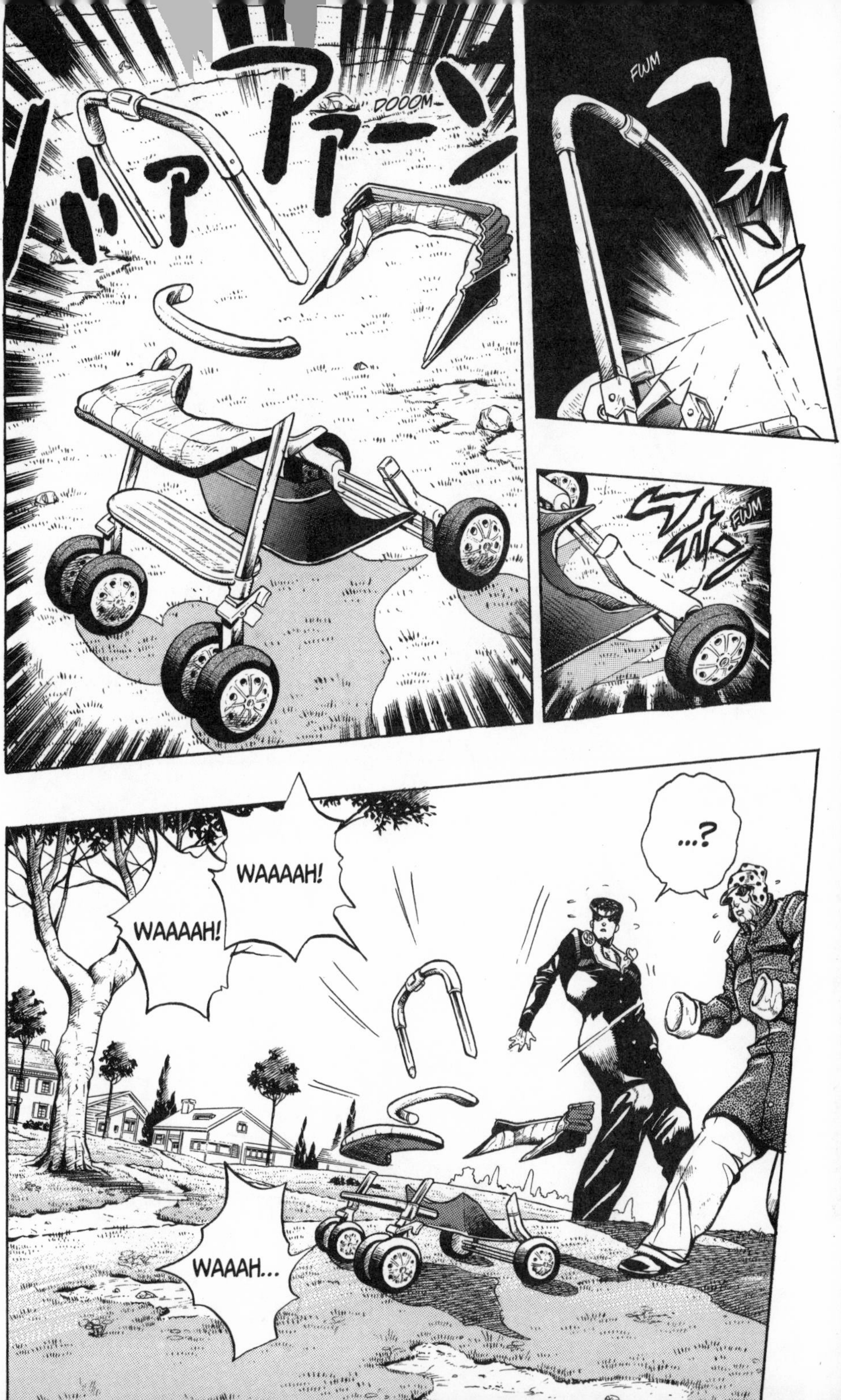
FWM
FWM
DOOOM
...?
WAAAAH!
WAAAAH!
WAAAH...

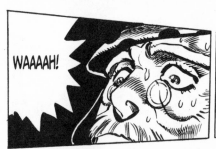

WAAAAH!

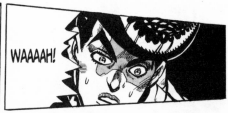

WAAAAH!

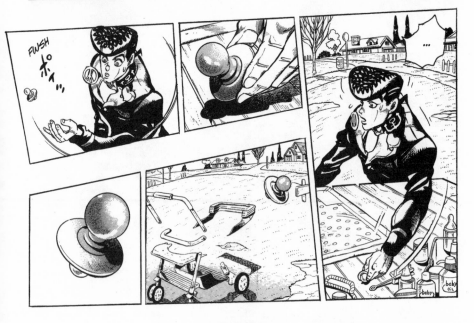

FWSH
ポイッ

...

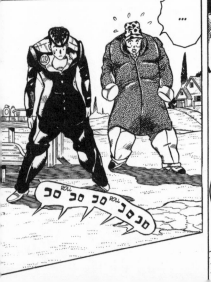

...

ロロ ROLL ロロ ロロ ROLL ロロロ

FLOK
ポクン

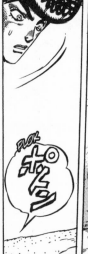

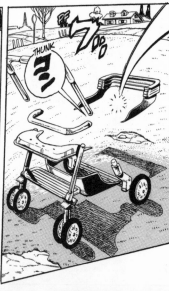

THUNK
コン

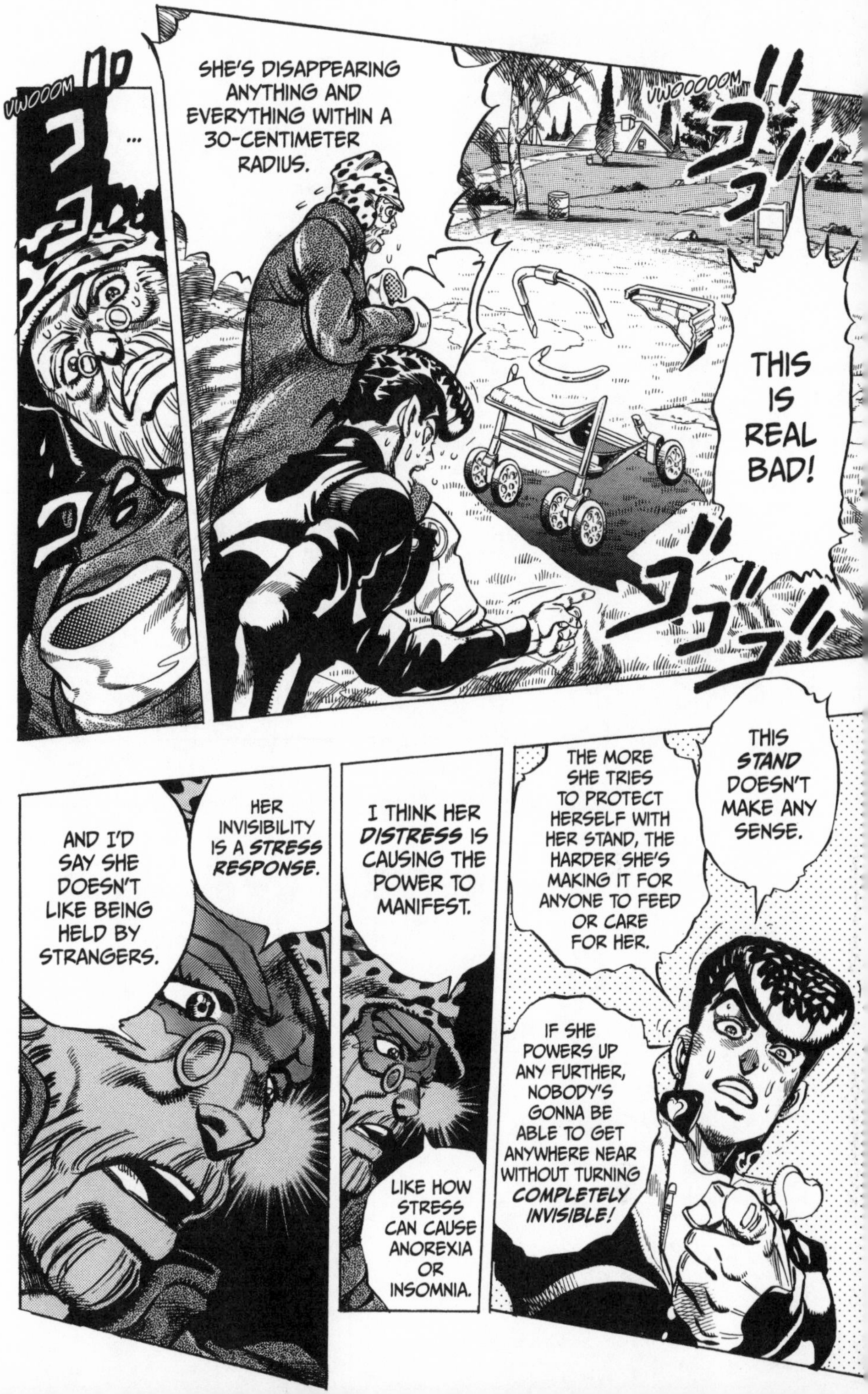
VWOOOOOM
THIS IS REAL BAD!
SHE'S DISAPPEARING ANYTHING AND EVERYTHING WITHIN A 30-CENTIMETER RADIUS.
VWOOOM
...
THIS STAND DOESN'T MAKE ANY SENSE.
THE MORE SHE TRIES TO PROTECT HERSELF WITH HER STAND, THE HARDER SHE'S MAKING IT FOR ANYONE TO FEED OR CARE FOR HER.
IF SHE POWERS UP ANY FURTHER, NOBODY'S GONNA BE ABLE TO GET ANYWHERE NEAR WITHOUT TURNING COMPLETELY INVISIBLE!
I THINK HER DISTRESS IS CAUSING THE POWER TO MANIFEST.
LIKE HOW STRESS CAN CAUSE ANOREXIA OR INSOMNIA.
HER INVISIBILITY IS A STRESS RESPONSE.
AND I'D SAY SHE DOESN'T LIKE BEING HELD BY STRANGERS.

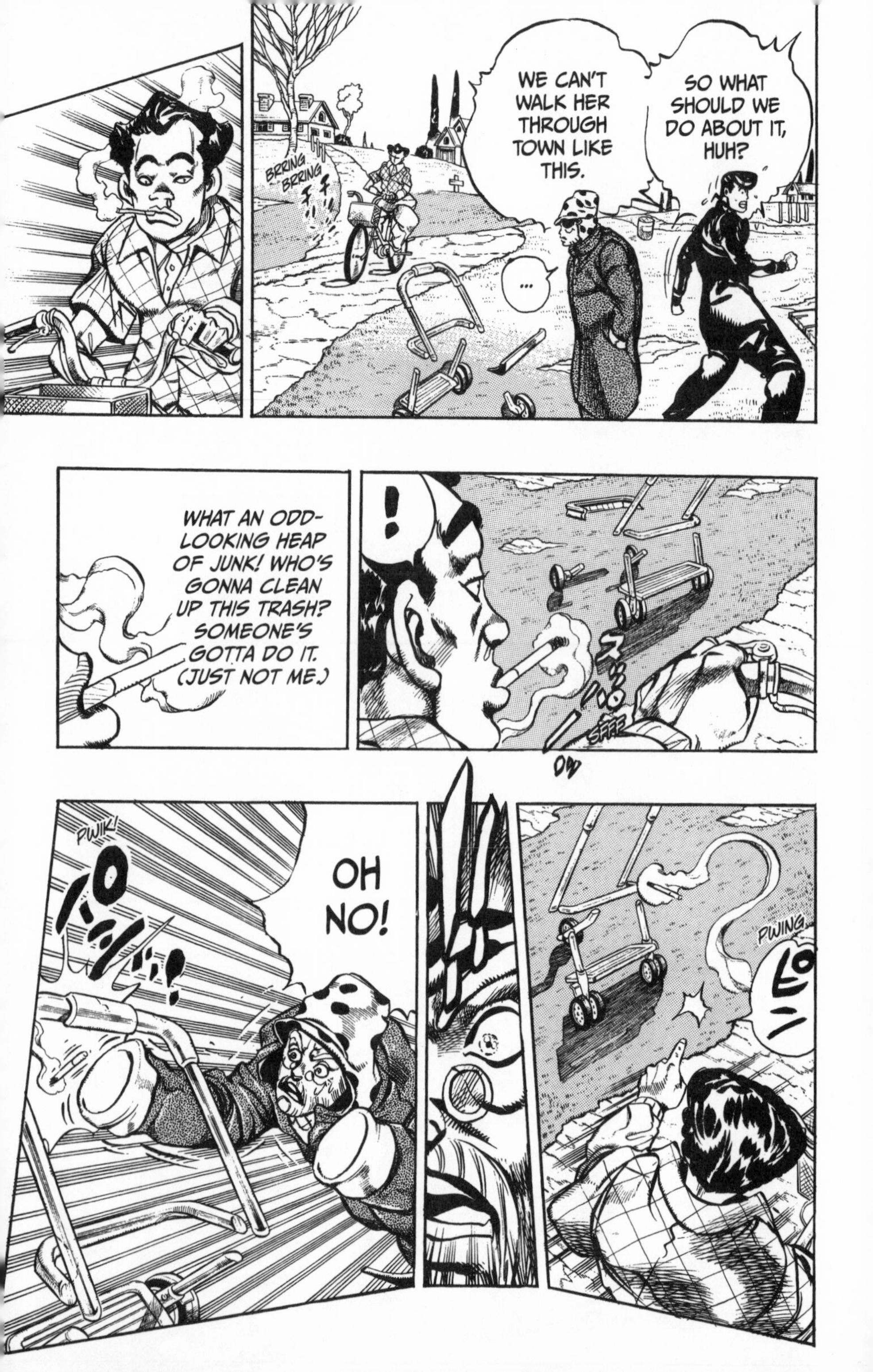

SO WHAT SHOULD WE DO ABOUT IT, HUH?
WE CAN'T WALK HER THROUGH TOWN LIKE THIS.
BRRING BRRING
...
!
WHAT AN ODD-LOOKING HEAP OF JUNK! WHO'S GONNA CLEAN UP THIS TRASH? SOMEONE'S GOTTA DO IT. (JUST NOT ME.)
PWING
PWIK!
OH NO!

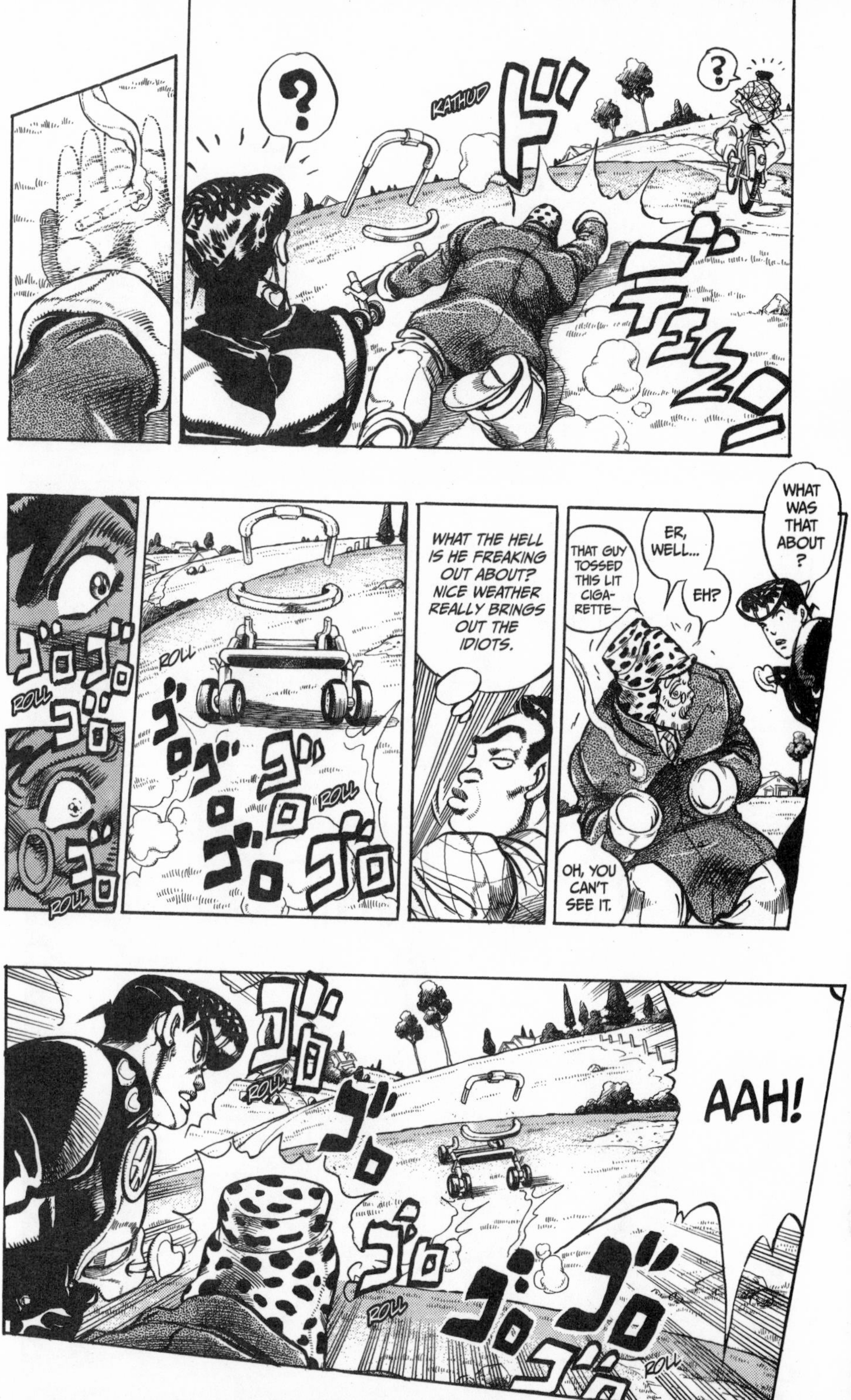
?
KATHUD
?
WHAT WAS THAT ABOUT?
ER, WELL...
EH?
THAT GUY TOSSED THIS LIT CIGA-RETTE—
OH, YOU CAN'T SEE IT.
WHAT THE HELL IS HE FREAKING OUT ABOUT? NICE WEATHER REALLY BRINGS OUT THE IDIOTS.
ROLL
ROLL
ROLL
ROLL
ROLL
AAH!
ROLL
ROLL
ROLL

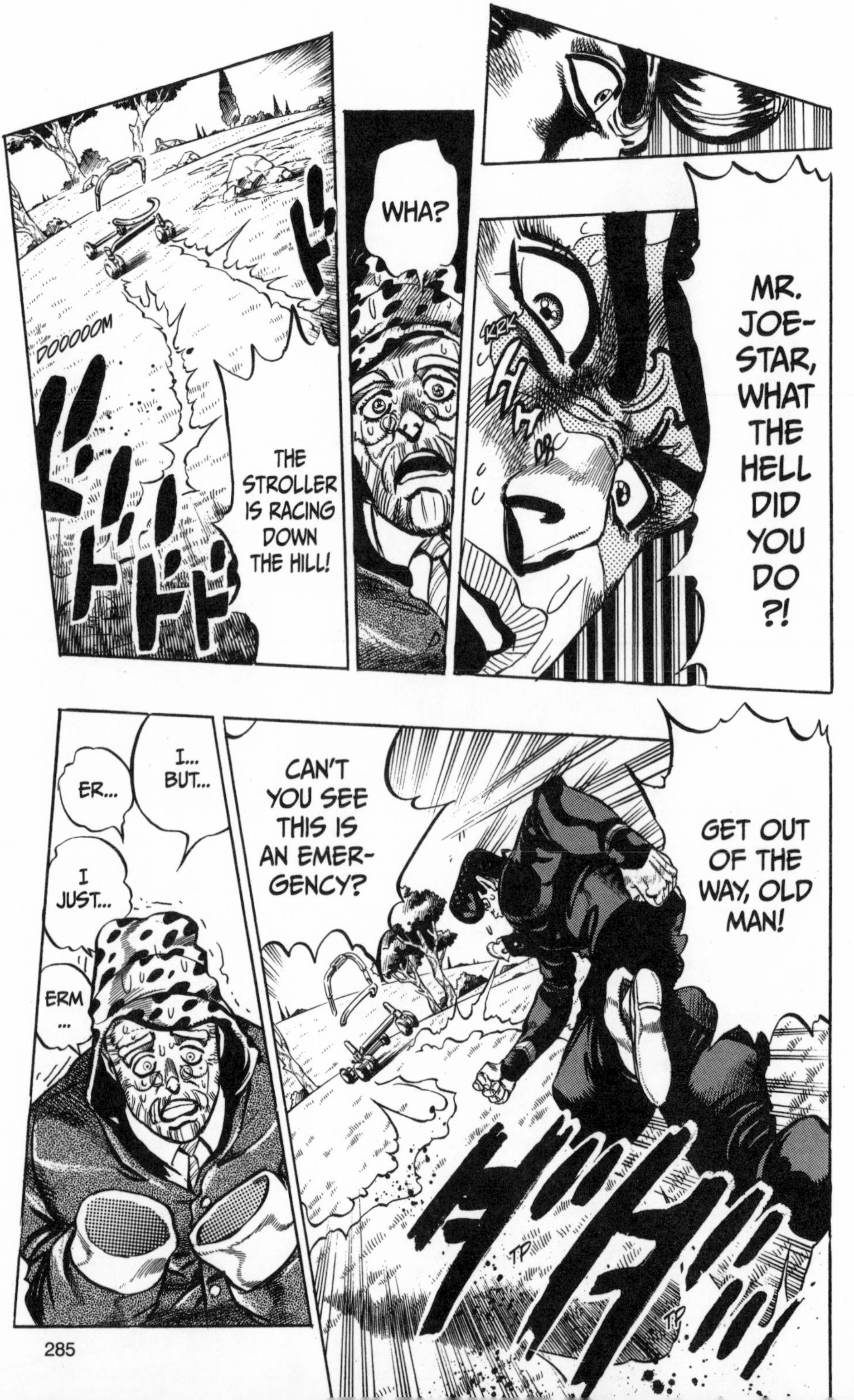
MR. JOE-STAR, WHAT THE HELL DID YOU DO?!
KRK
WHA?
THE STROLLER IS RACING DOWN THE HILL!
DOOOOOM
GET OUT OF THE WAY, OLD MAN!
CAN'T YOU SEE THIS IS AN EMERGENCY?
TP
TP
I... BUT...
ER...
I JUST...
ERM ...

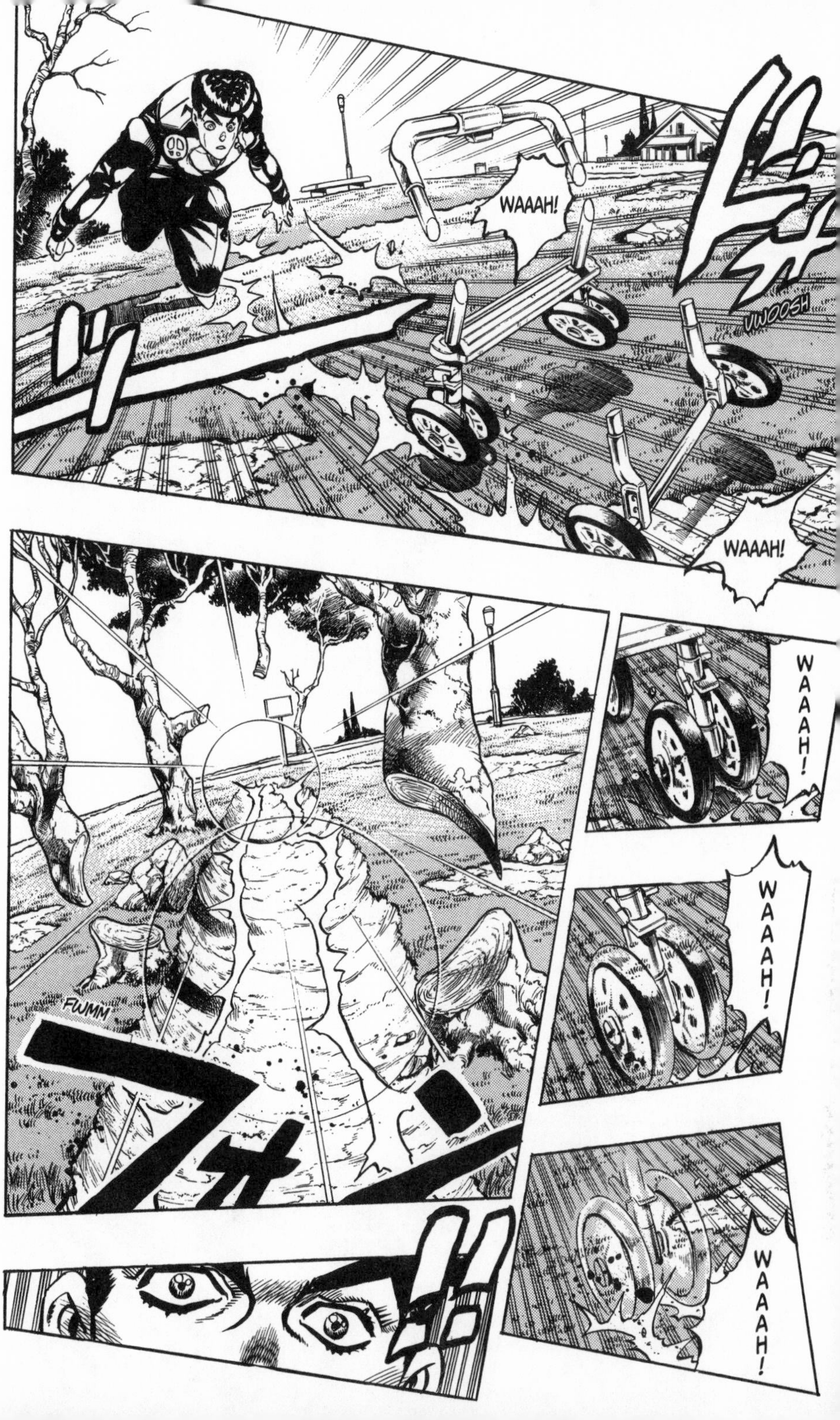
WAAAH!
UWOOSH
WAAAH!
WAAAAH!
WAAAAH!
WAAAAH!
FWMM

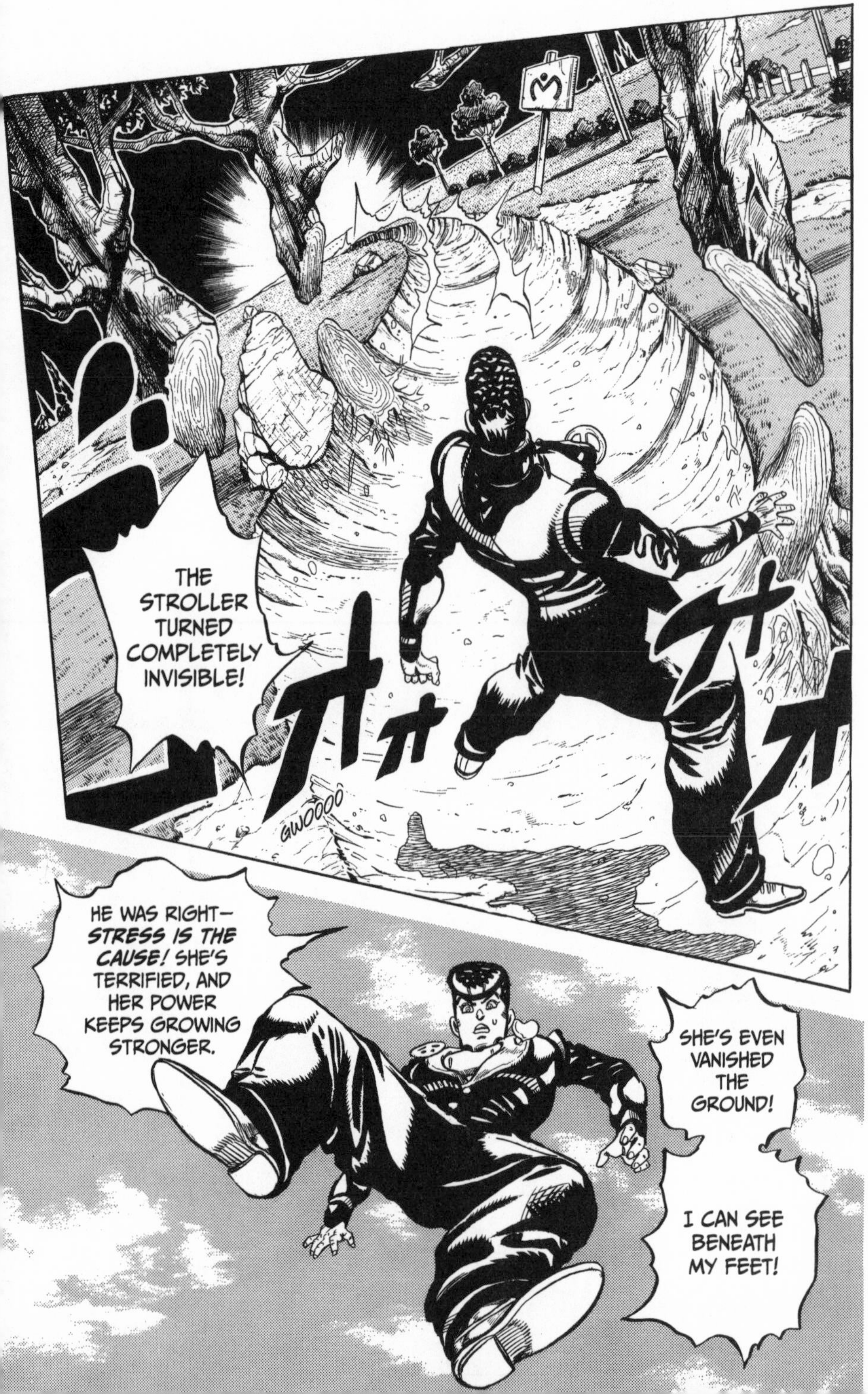
THE STROLLER TURNED COMPLETELY INVISIBLE!
GWOOOO
SHE'S EVEN VANISHED THE GROUND!
I CAN SEE BENEATH MY FEET!
HE WAS RIGHT—*STRESS IS THE CAUSE!* SHE'S TERRIFIED, AND HER POWER KEEPS GROWING STRONGER.

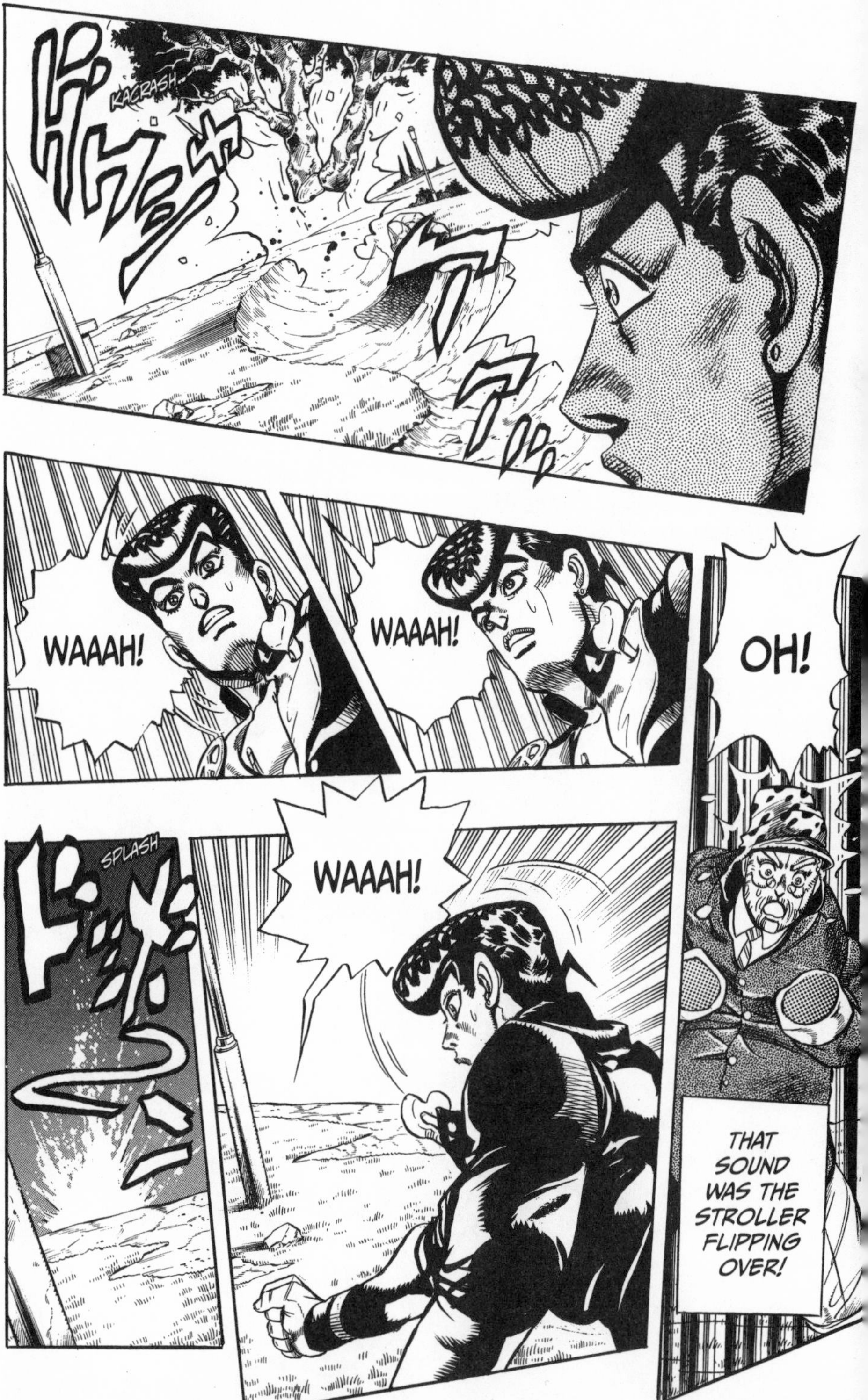
KACRASH
OH!
THAT SOUND WAS THE STROLLER FLIPPING OVER!
WAAAH!
WAAAH!
WAAAH!
SPLASH

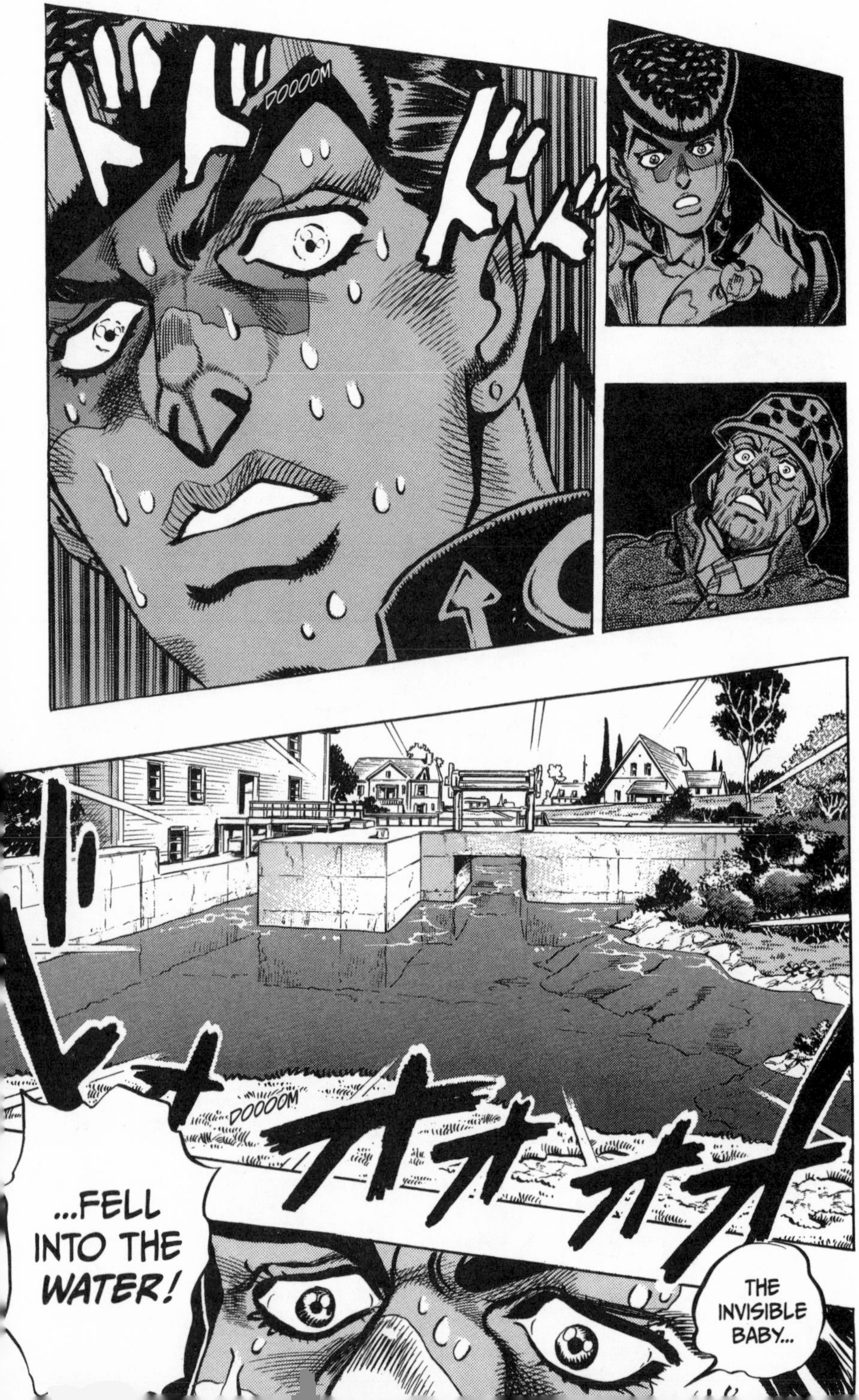
DOOOOM
DOOOOM
THE INVISIBLE BABY...
...FELL INTO THE WATER!

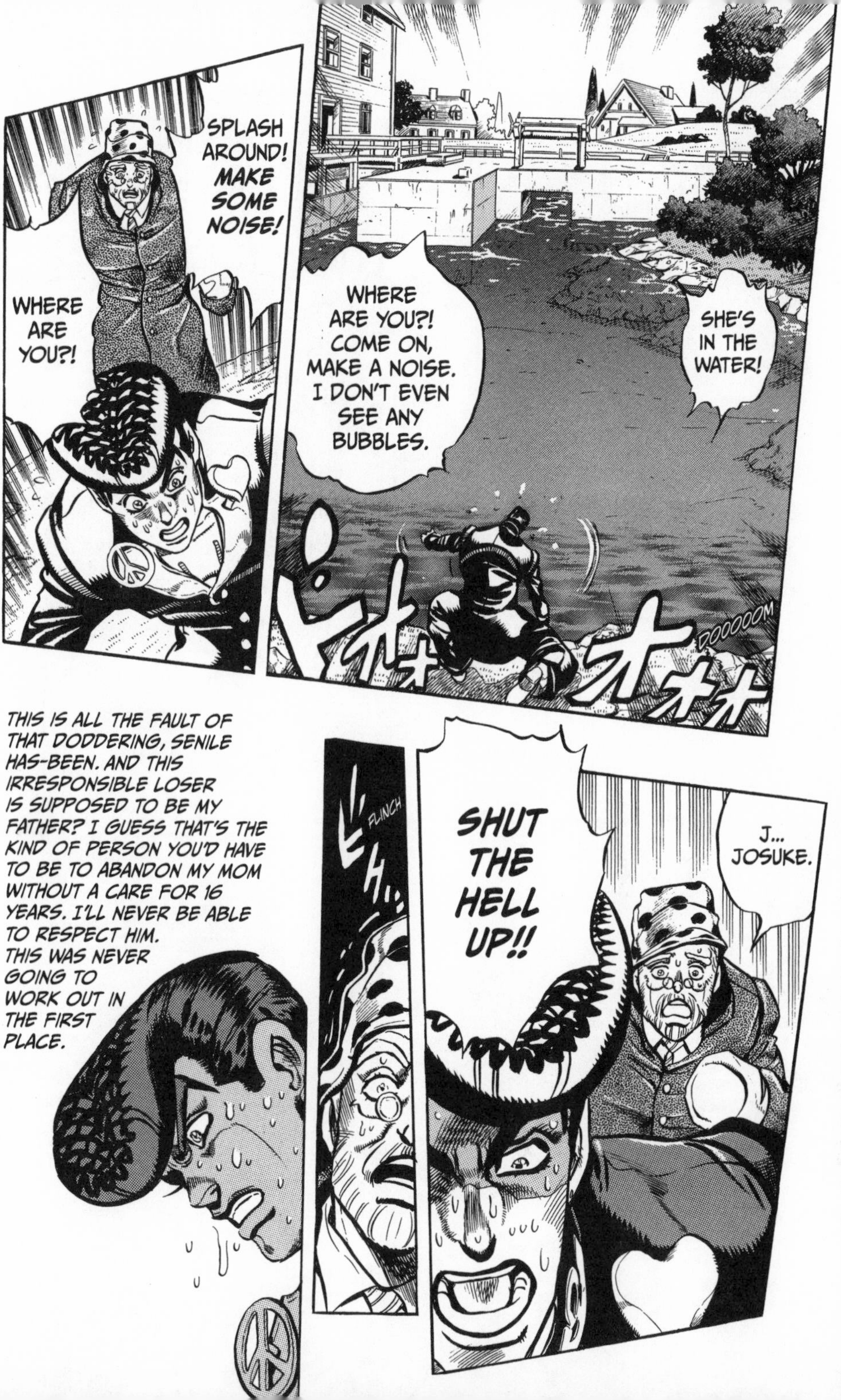
SHE'S IN THE WATER!
WHERE ARE YOU?! COME ON, MAKE A NOISE. I DON'T EVEN SEE ANY BUBBLES.
DOOOOOM
SPLASH AROUND! MAKE SOME NOISE!
WHERE ARE YOU?!
J... JOSUKE.
SHUT THE HELL UP!!
FLINCH
THIS IS ALL THE FAULT OF THAT DODDERING, SENILE HAS-BEEN. AND THIS IRRESPONSIBLE LOSER IS SUPPOSED TO BE MY FATHER? I GUESS THAT'S THE KIND OF PERSON YOU'D HAVE TO BE TO ABANDON MY MOM WITHOUT A CARE FOR 16 YEARS. I'LL NEVER BE ABLE TO RESPECT HIM. THIS WAS NEVER GOING TO WORK OUT IN THE FIRST PLACE.

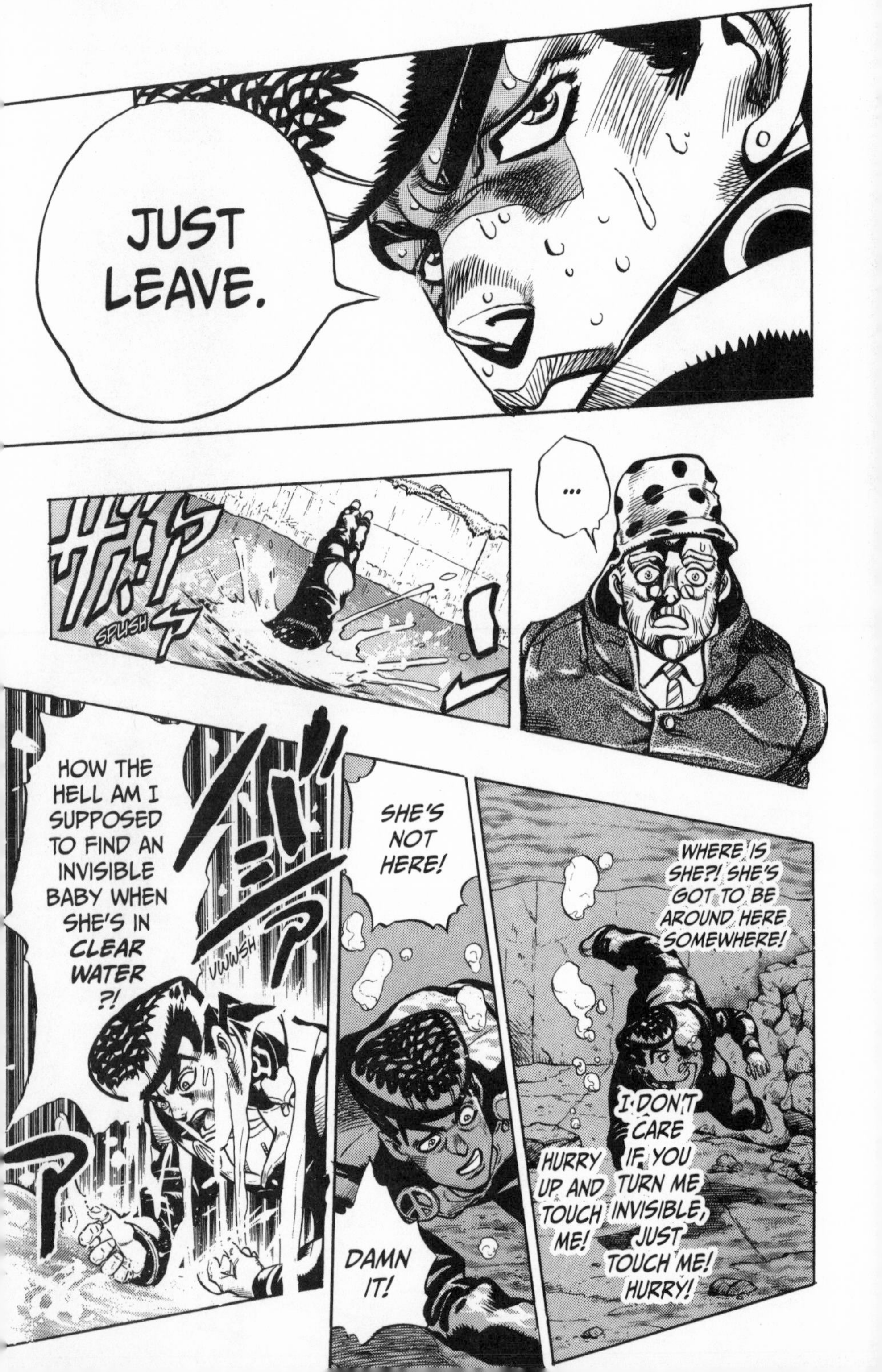
JUST LEAVE.
...
SPLISH
WHERE IS SHE?! SHE'S GOT TO BE AROUND HERE SOMEWHERE!
I DON'T CARE IF YOU TURN ME INVISIBLE, JUST TOUCH ME! HURRY!
HURRY UP AND TOUCH ME!
SHE'S NOT HERE!
DAMN IT!
HOW THE HELL AM I SUPPOSED TO FIND AN INVISIBLE BABY WHEN SHE'S IN CLEAR WATER?!
VWWSH

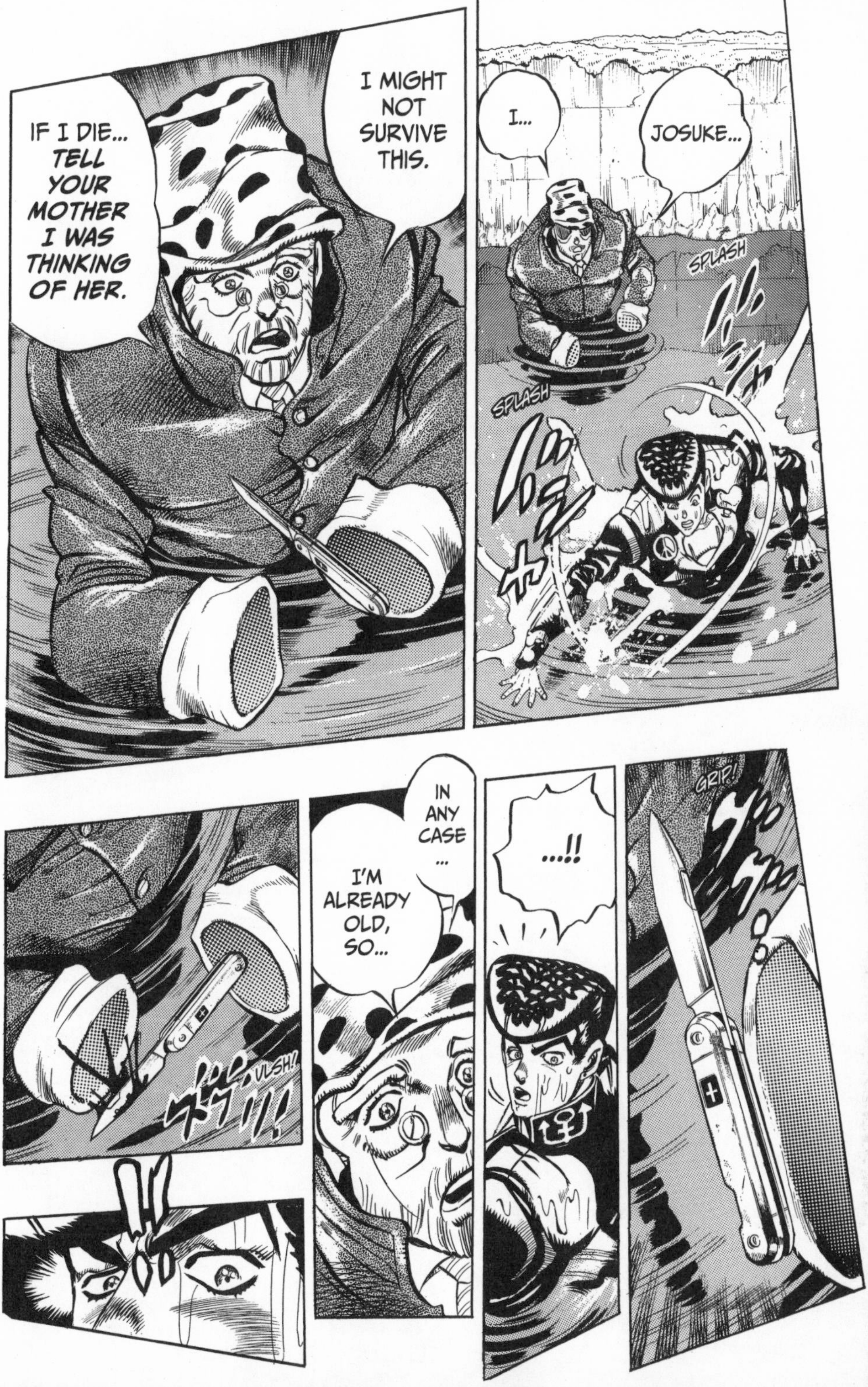
JOSUKE...
I...
SPLASH
SPLASH
I MIGHT NOT SURVIVE THIS.
IF I DIE... TELL YOUR MOTHER I WAS THINKING OF HER.
GRIP!
...!!
IN ANY CASE ...
I'M ALREADY OLD, SO...
VLSH!

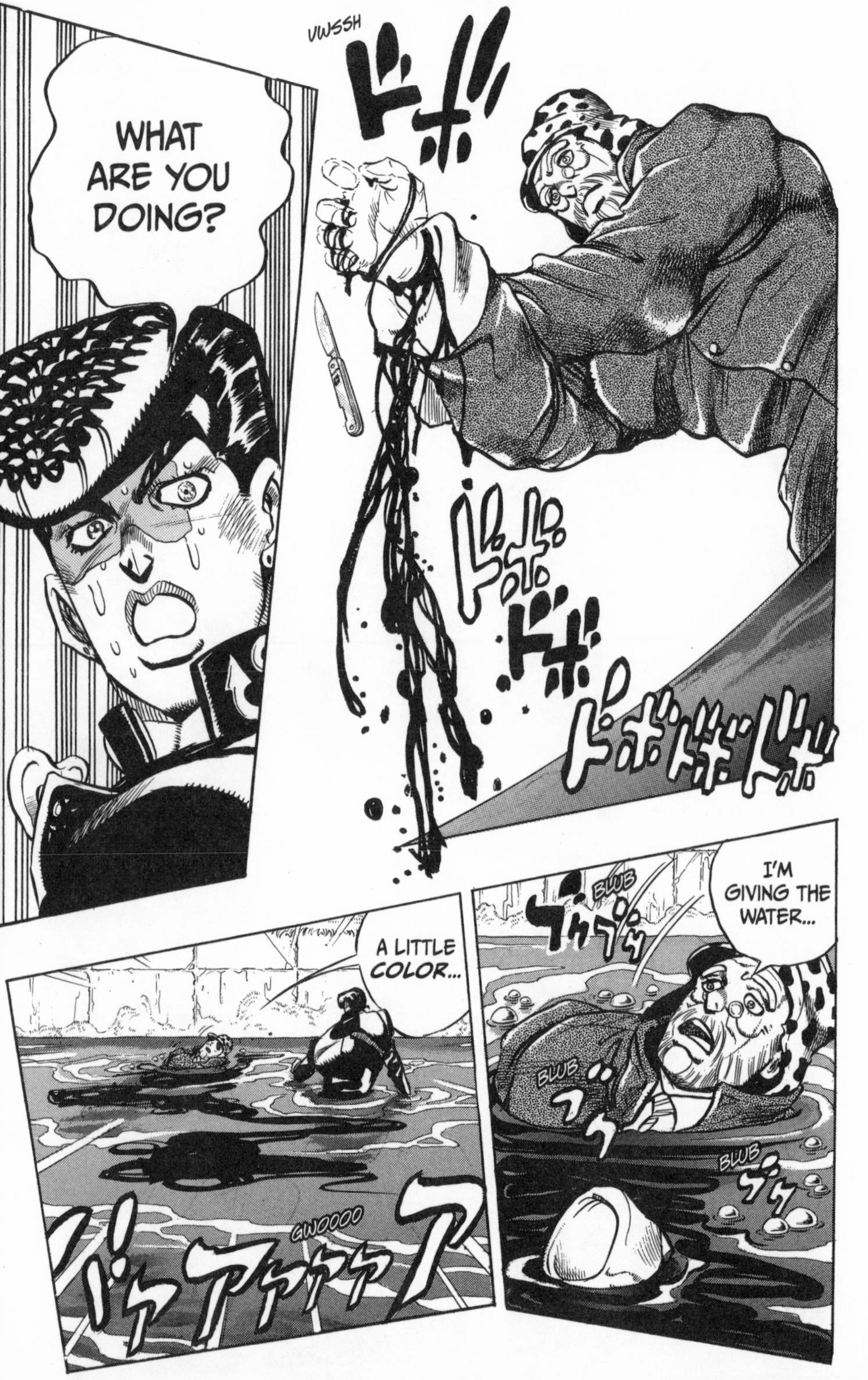
VWSSH
WHAT ARE YOU DOING?
I'M GIVING THE WATER...
BLUB
BLUB
BLUB
A LITTLE COLOR...
GWOOOO

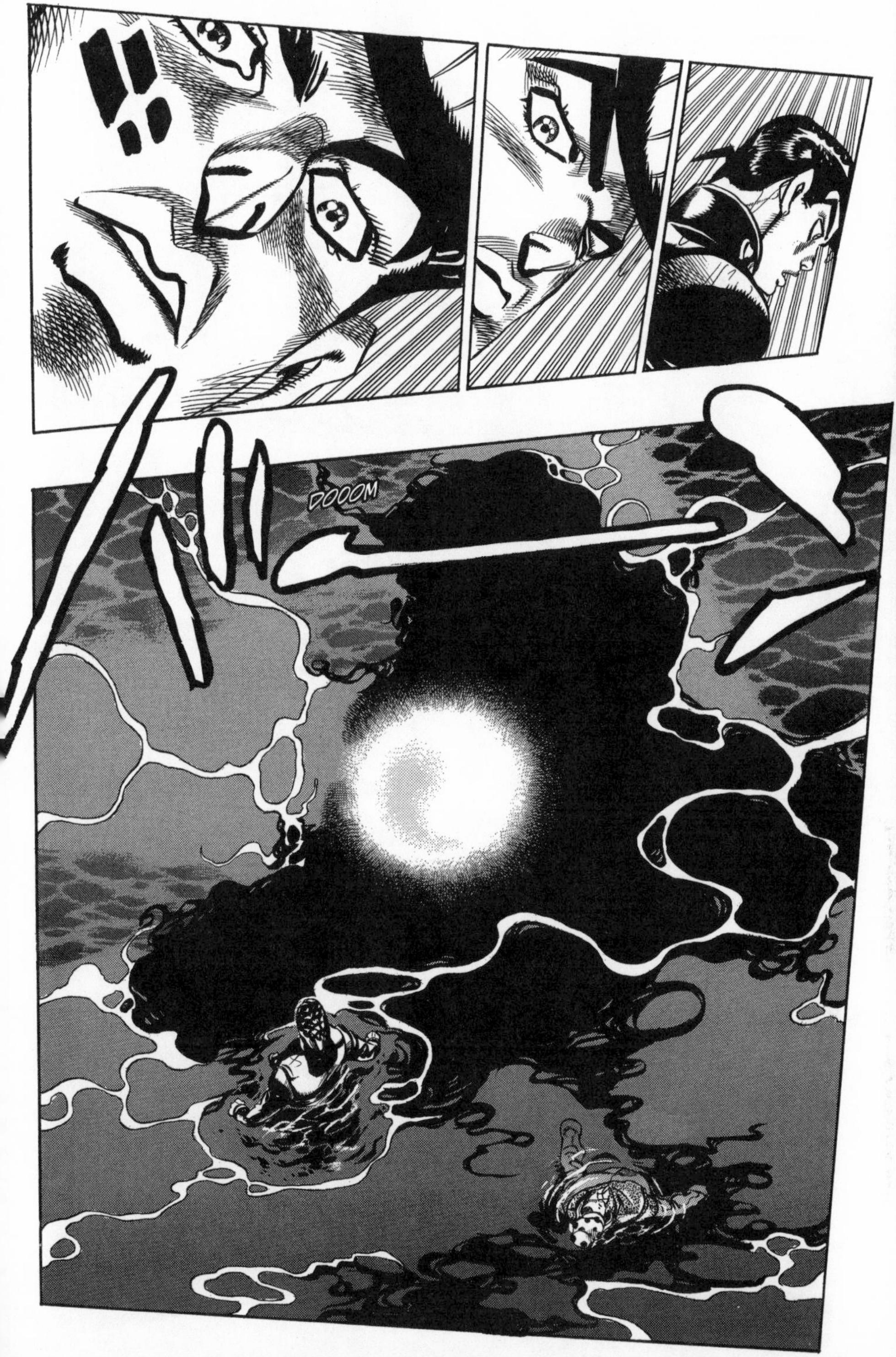
DOOOM

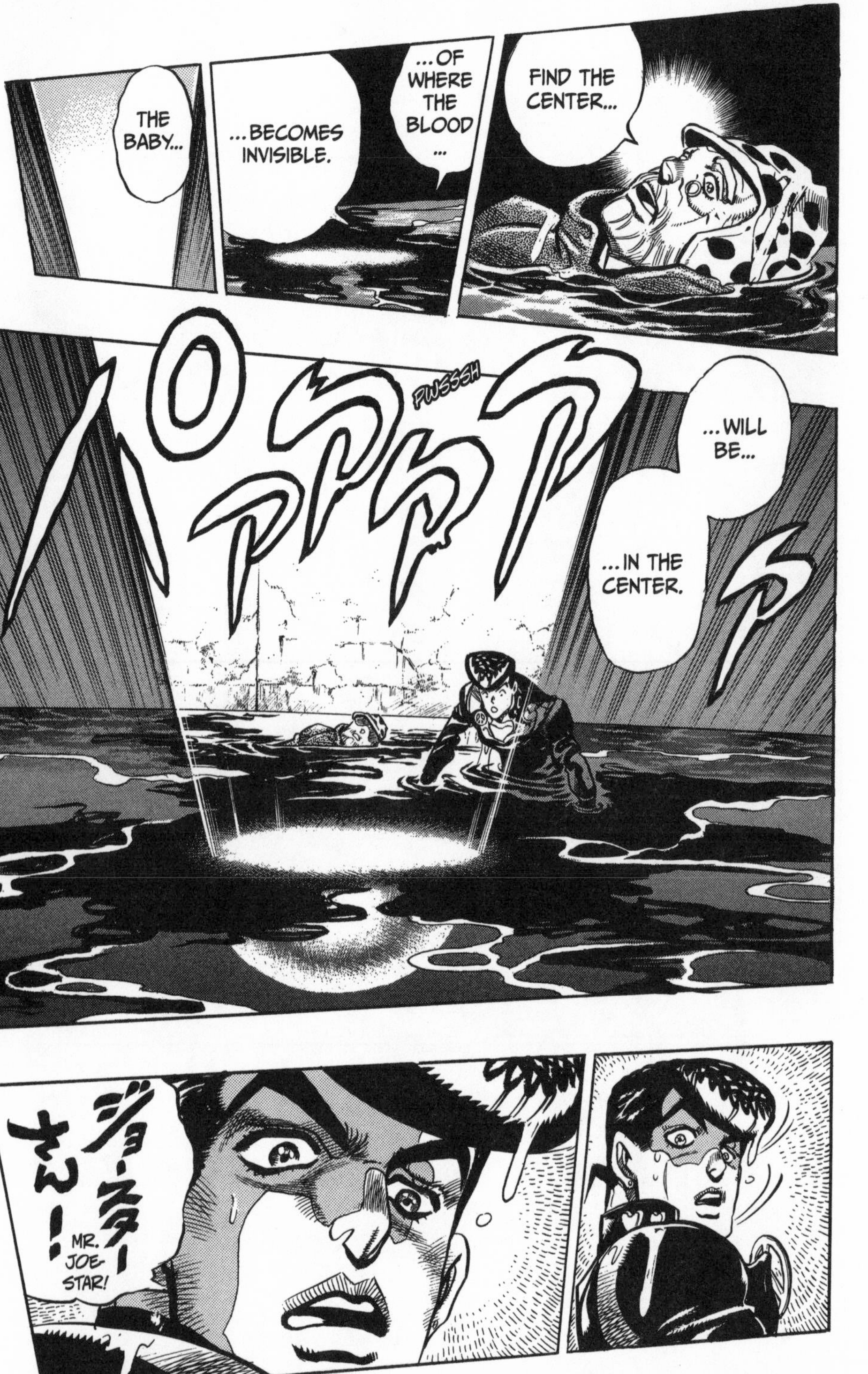
FIND THE CENTER...
...OF WHERE THE BLOOD ...
...BECOMES INVISIBLE.
THE BABY...
...WILL BE...
...IN THE CENTER.
PWSSSH
ジョースターさん!
MR. JOE-STAR!

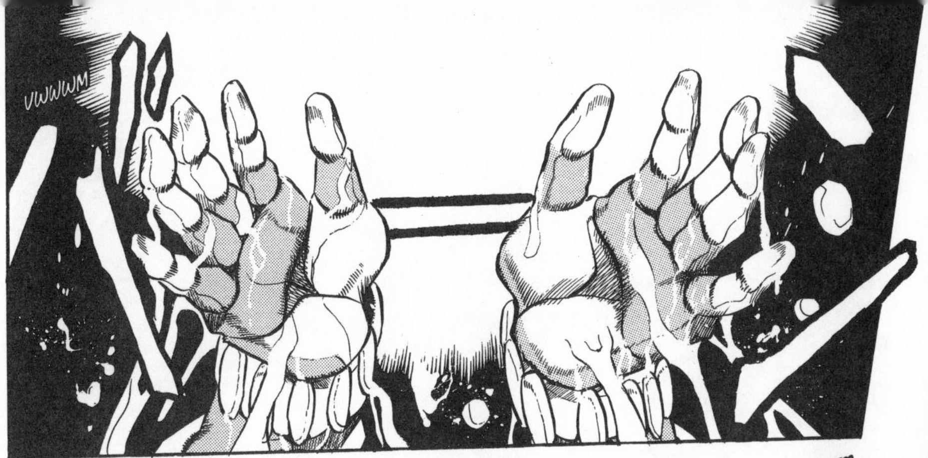
VWWWM

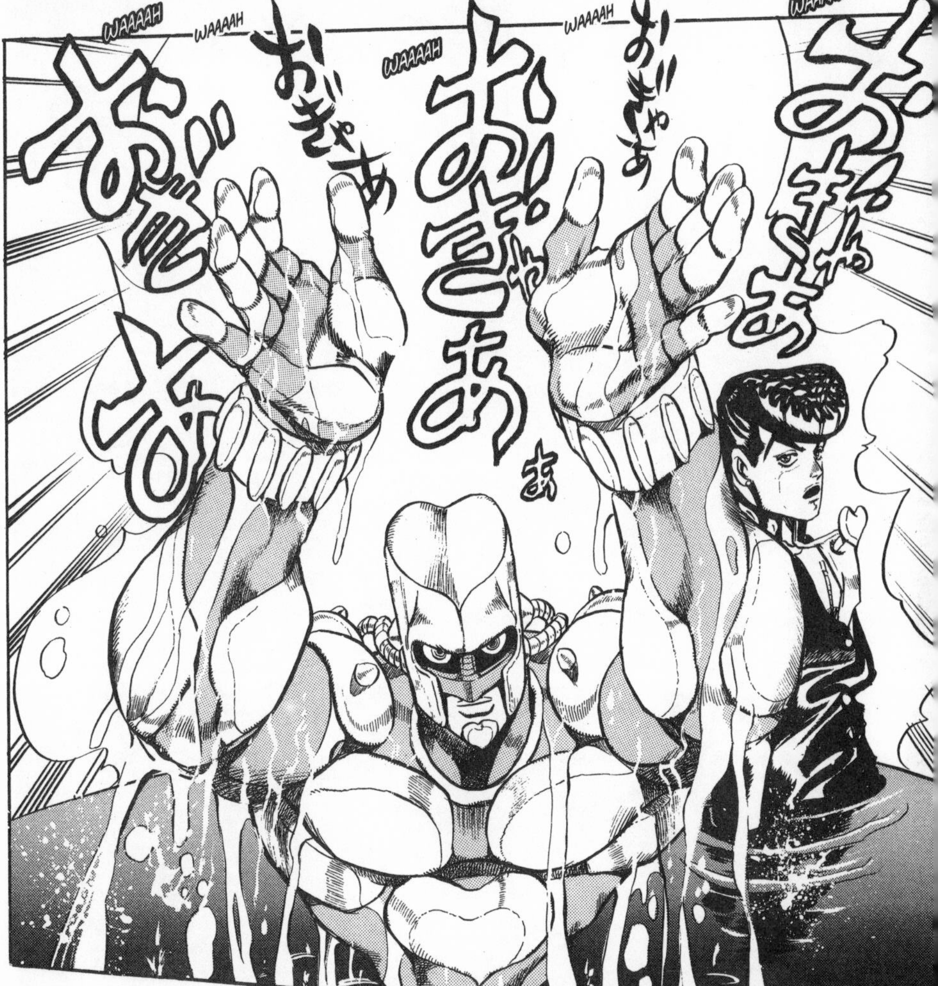
WAAAAH
おぎゃあ
おぎゃあ
WAAAAH
おぎゃあぁ
WAAAAH
おぎゃあ
WAAAAH
WAAAAH
おぎゃあ

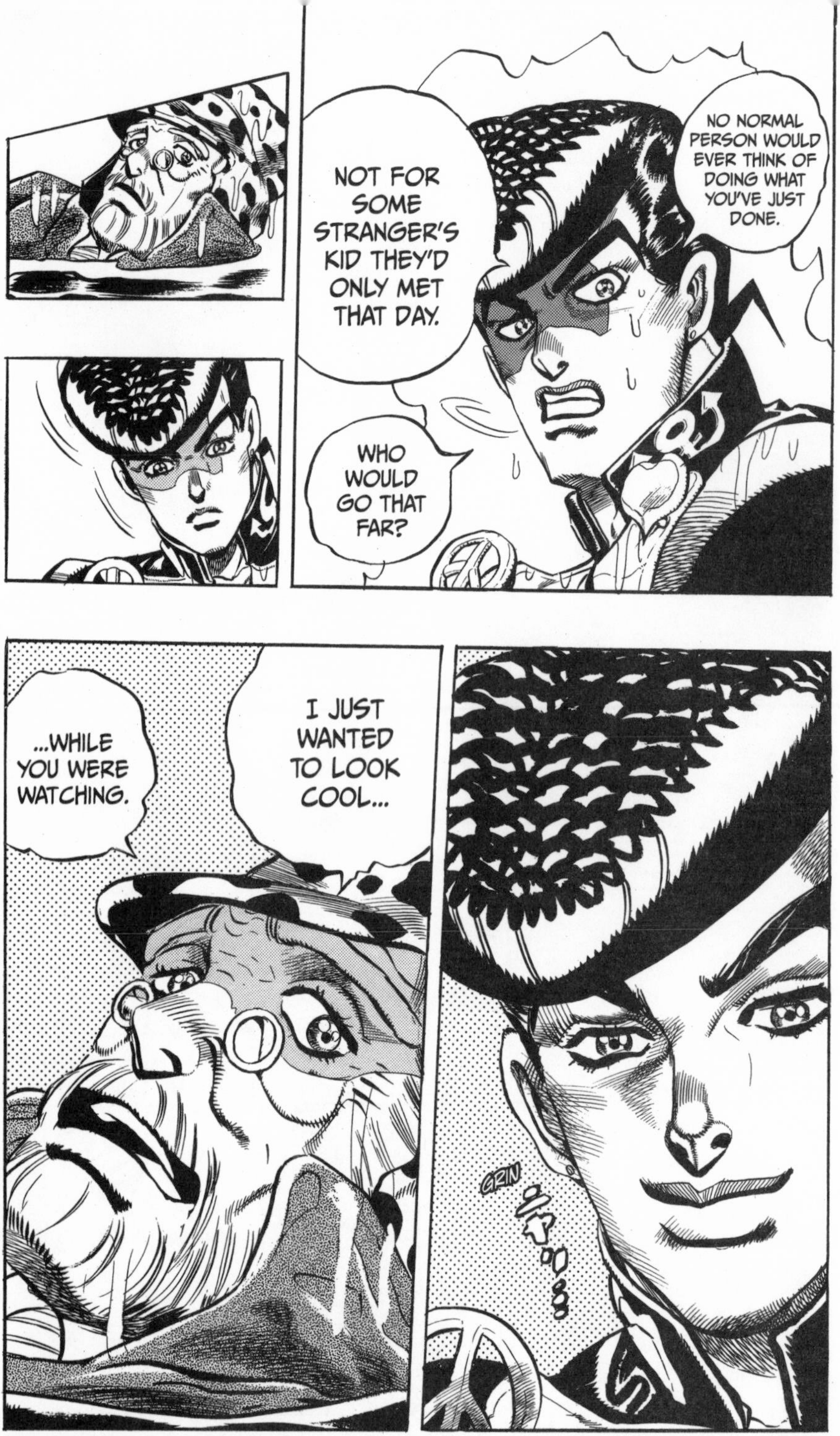
NO NORMAL PERSON WOULD EVER THINK OF DOING WHAT YOU'VE JUST DONE.
NOT FOR SOME STRANGER'S KID THEY'D ONLY MET THAT DAY.
WHO WOULD GO THAT FAR?
GRIN
I JUST WANTED TO LOOK COOL...
...WHILE YOU WERE WATCHING.

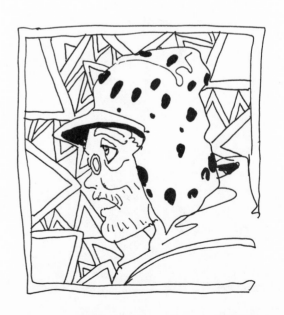

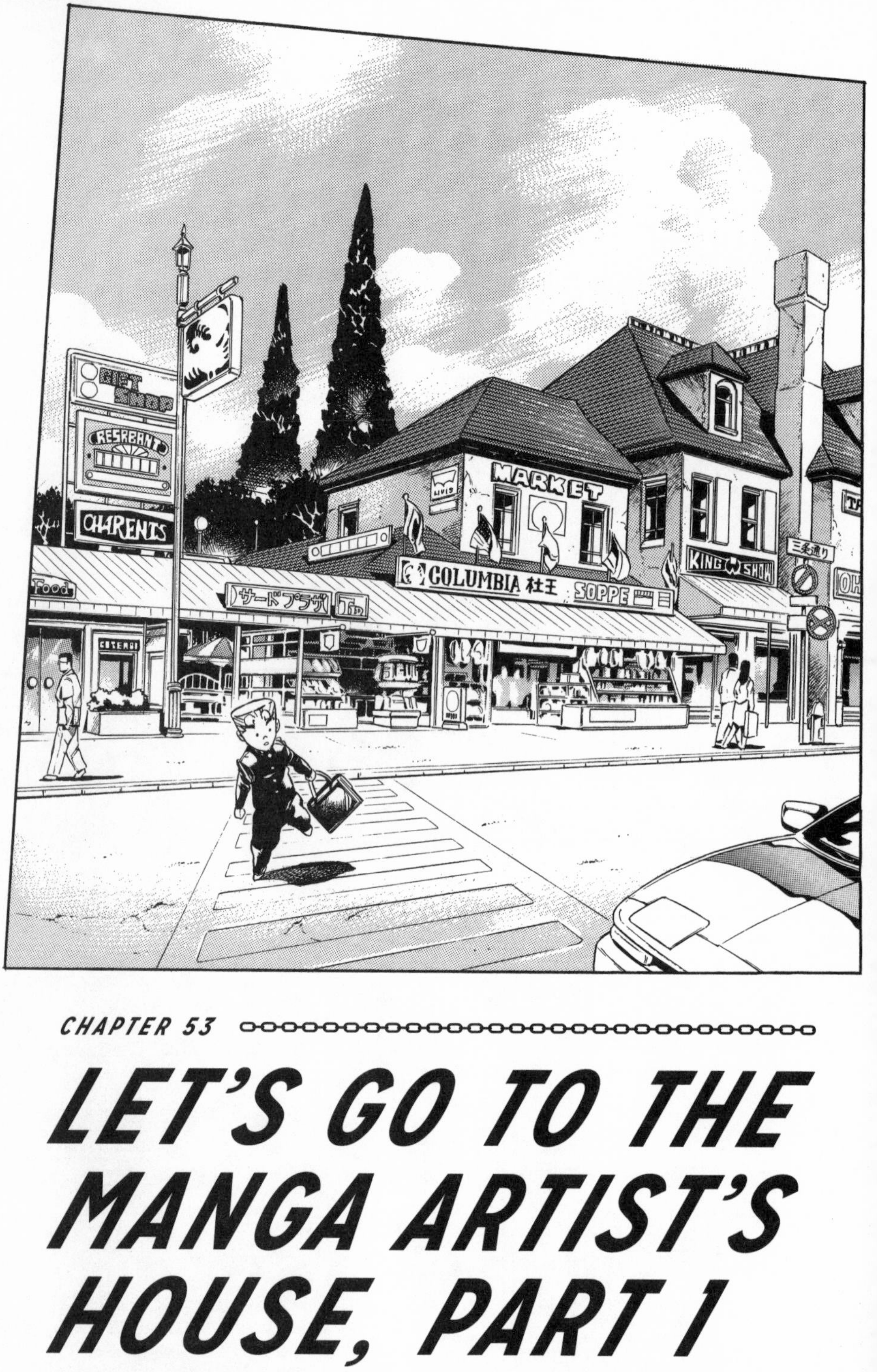
RESRBANT
CHARENTS
Food
サードプラザ
MARKET
COLUMBIA 杜王
SOPPE
KING SHOW
三条通り

CHAPTER 53

LET'S GO TO THE MANGA ARTIST'S HOUSE, PART 1

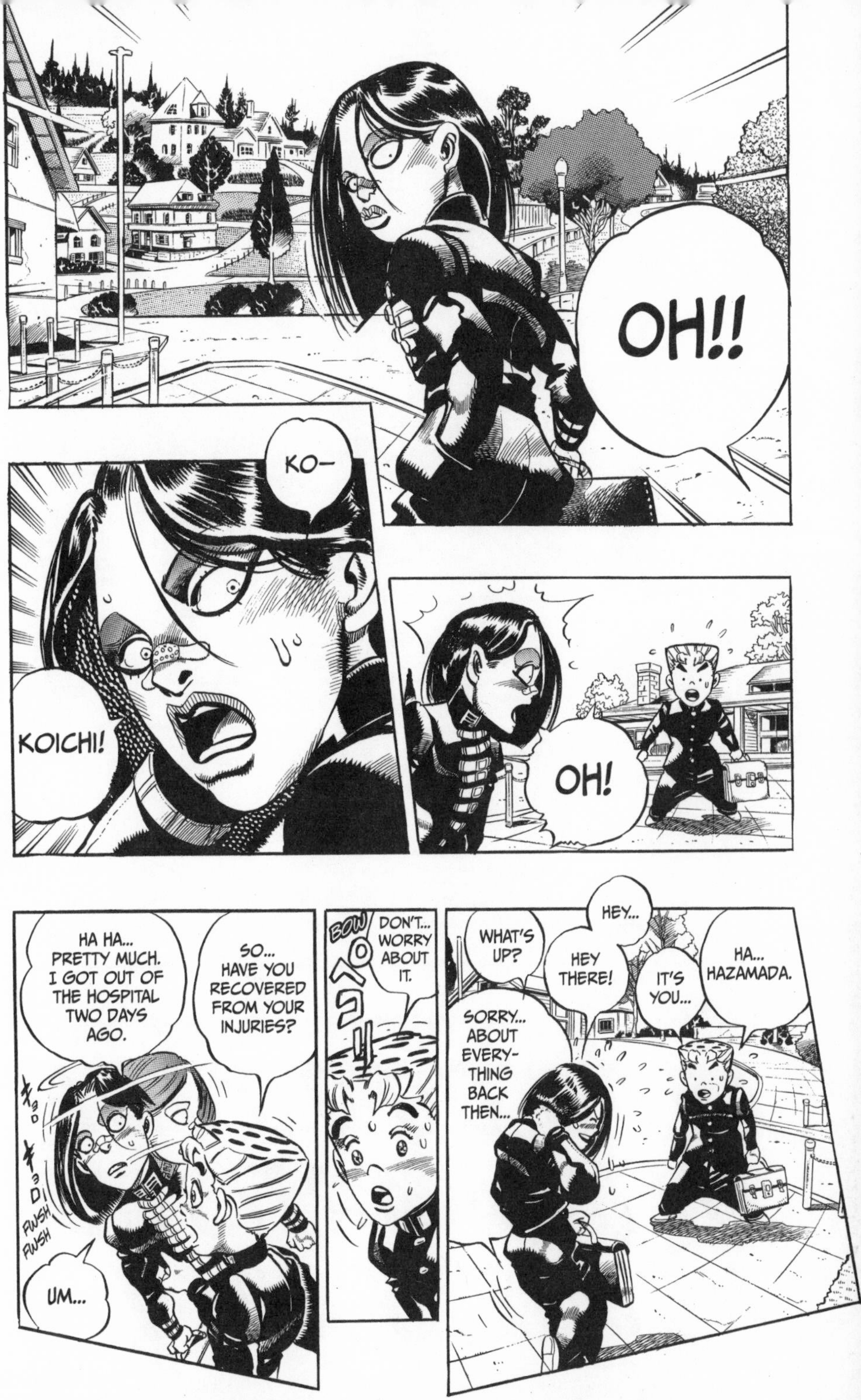
OH!!
OH!
KO-
KOICHI!
HA... HAZAMADA.
IT'S YOU...
HEY...
HEY THERE!
WHAT'S UP?
SORRY... ABOUT EVERY-THING BACK THEN...
BOW
DON'T... WORRY ABOUT IT.
SO... HAVE YOU RECOVERED FROM YOUR INJURIES?
HA HA... PRETTY MUCH. I GOT OUT OF THE HOSPITAL TWO DAYS AGO.
FWSH FWSH
UM...

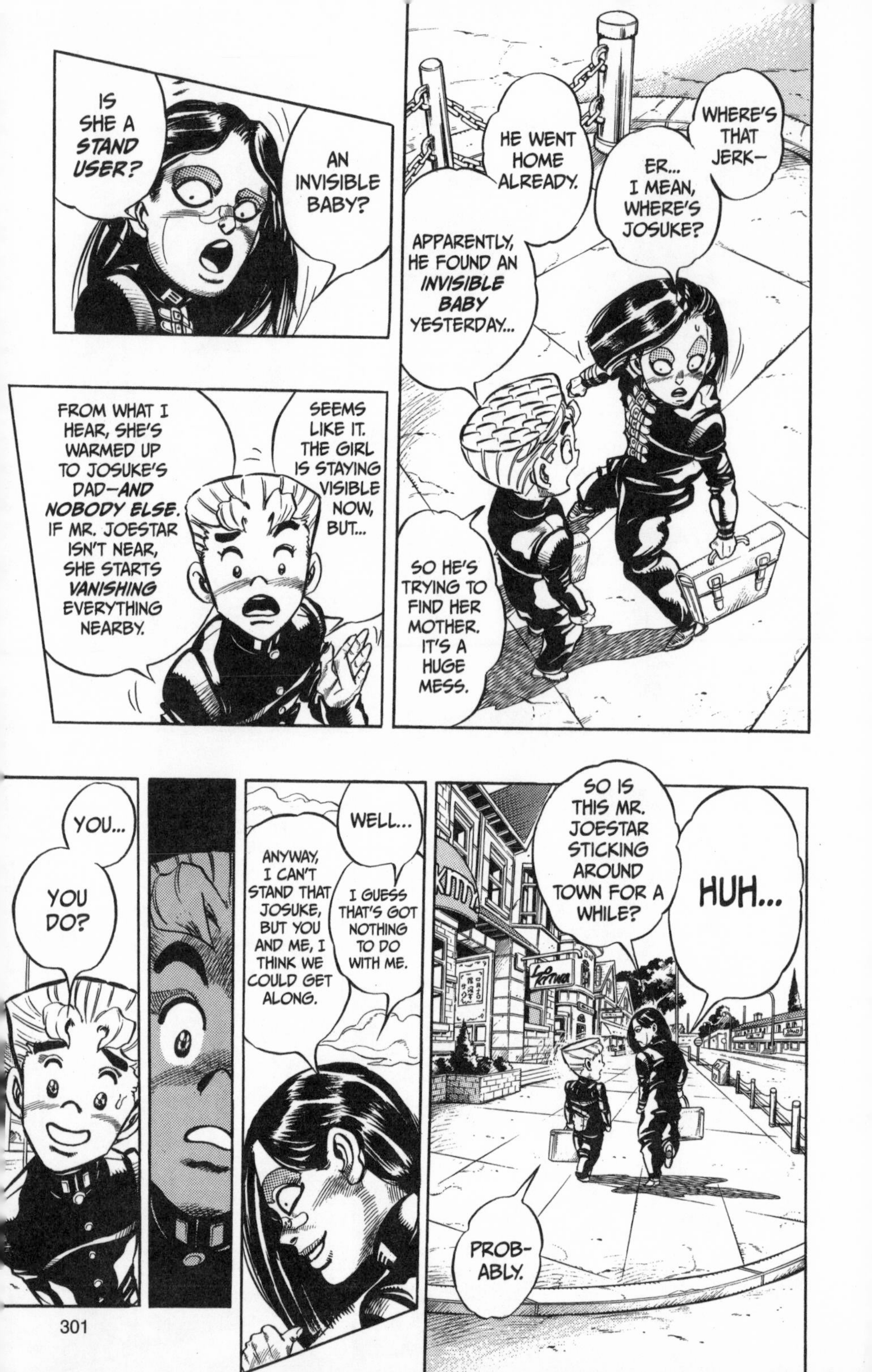
WHERE'S THAT JERK—
ER... I MEAN, WHERE'S JOSUKE?
HE WENT HOME ALREADY.
APPARENTLY, HE FOUND AN INVISIBLE BABY YESTERDAY...
SO HE'S TRYING TO FIND HER MOTHER. IT'S A HUGE MESS.
AN INVISIBLE BABY?
IS SHE A STAND USER?
SEEMS LIKE IT. THE GIRL IS STAYING VISIBLE NOW, BUT...
FROM WHAT I HEAR, SHE'S WARMED UP TO JOSUKE'S DAD—AND NOBODY ELSE. IF MR. JOESTAR ISN'T NEAR, SHE STARTS VANISHING EVERYTHING NEARBY.
HUH...
SO IS THIS MR. JOESTAR STICKING AROUND TOWN FOR A WHILE?
PROB-ABLY.
WELL...
I GUESS THAT'S GOT NOTHING TO DO WITH ME.
ANYWAY, I CAN'T STAND THAT JOSUKE, BUT YOU AND ME, I THINK WE COULD GET ALONG.
YOU...
YOU DO?

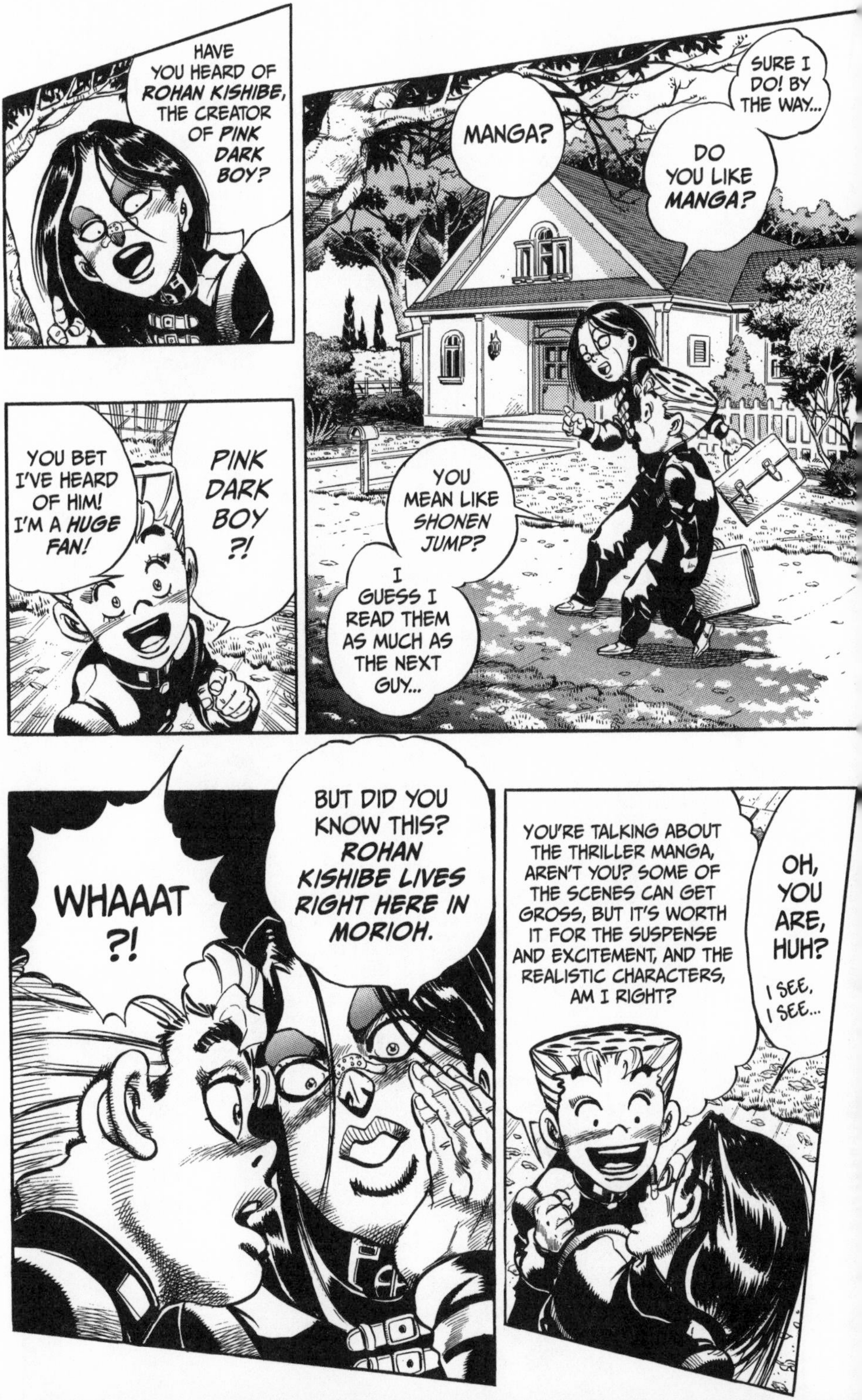
SURE I DO! BY THE WAY...
DO YOU LIKE MANGA?
MANGA?
YOU MEAN LIKE SHONEN JUMP?
I GUESS I READ THEM AS MUCH AS THE NEXT GUY...
HAVE YOU HEARD OF ROHAN KISHIBE, THE CREATOR OF PINK DARK BOY?
PINK DARK BOY ?!
YOU BET I'VE HEARD OF HIM! I'M A HUGE FAN!
OH, YOU ARE, HUH?
I SEE, I SEE...
YOU'RE TALKING ABOUT THE THRILLER MANGA, AREN'T YOU? SOME OF THE SCENES CAN GET GROSS, BUT IT'S WORTH IT FOR THE SUSPENSE AND EXCITEMENT, AND THE REALISTIC CHARACTERS, AM I RIGHT?
BUT DID YOU KNOW THIS? ROHAN KISHIBE LIVES RIGHT HERE IN MORIOH.
WHAAAT ?!

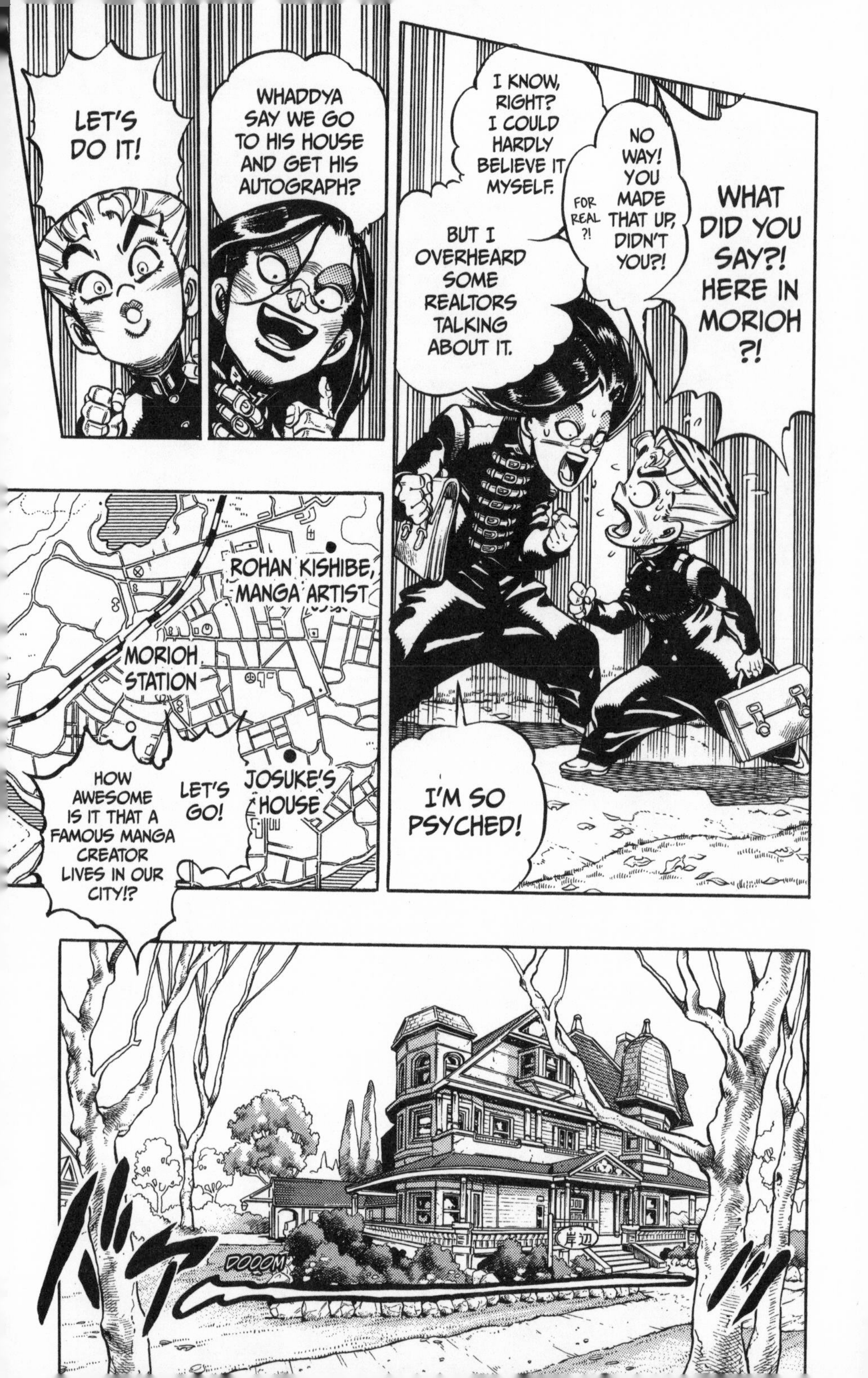
WHAT DID YOU SAY?! HERE IN MORIOH?!
NO WAY! YOU MADE THAT UP, DIDN'T YOU?!
FOR REAL?!
I KNOW, RIGHT? I COULD HARDLY BELIEVE IT MYSELF.
BUT I OVERHEARD SOME REALTORS TALKING ABOUT IT.
I'M SO PSYCHED!
WHADDYA SAY WE GO TO HIS HOUSE AND GET HIS AUTOGRAPH?
LET'S DO IT!
ROHAN KISHIBE, MANGA ARTIST
MORIOH STATION
JOSUKE'S HOUSE
LET'S GO!
HOW AWESOME IS IT THAT A FAMOUS MANGA CREATOR LIVES IN OUR CITY!?
岸辺
DOOOM

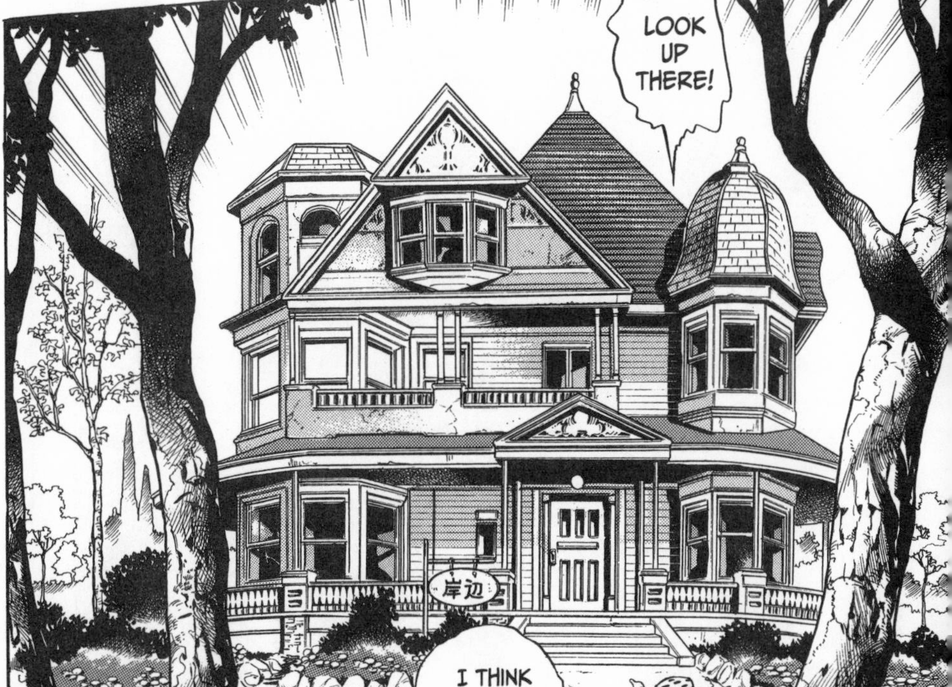
LOOK UP THERE!
岸辺
I THINK THAT MUST BE HIS *STUDIO!*
THE LIGHTS ARE ON.

SIGN: KISHIBE

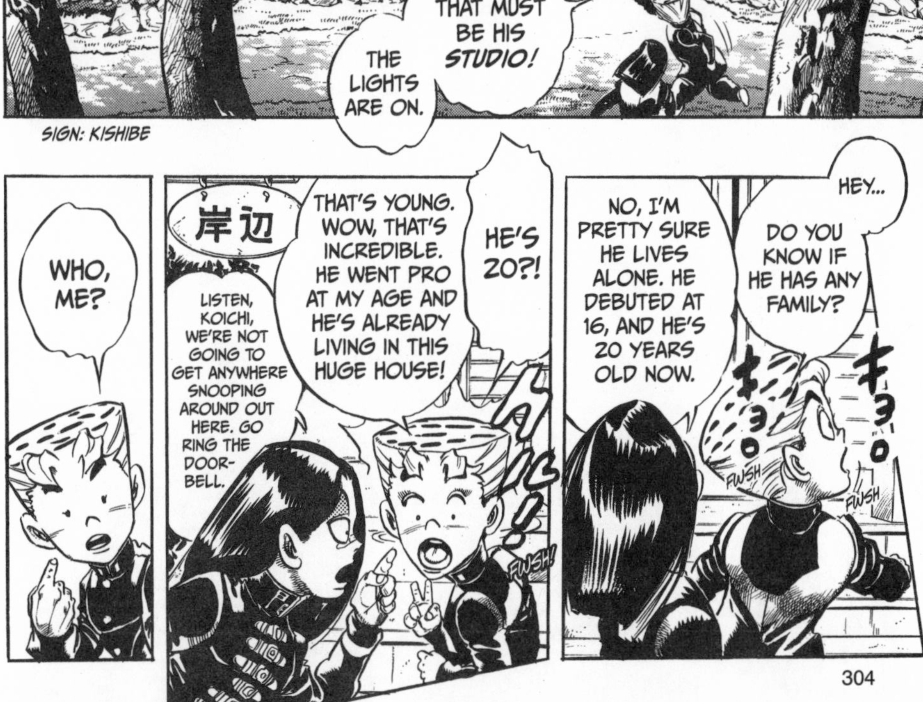
HEY...
DO YOU KNOW IF HE HAS ANY FAMILY?
FWSH
FWSH
NO, I'M PRETTY SURE HE LIVES ALONE. HE DEBUTED AT 16, AND HE'S 20 YEARS OLD NOW.
岸辺
HE'S 20?!
THAT'S YOUNG. WOW, THAT'S INCREDIBLE. HE WENT PRO AT MY AGE AND HE'S ALREADY LIVING IN THIS HUGE HOUSE!
FWSH!
LISTEN, KOICHI, WE'RE NOT GOING TO GET ANYWHERE SNOOPING AROUND OUT HERE. GO RING THE DOOR-BELL.
WHO, ME?

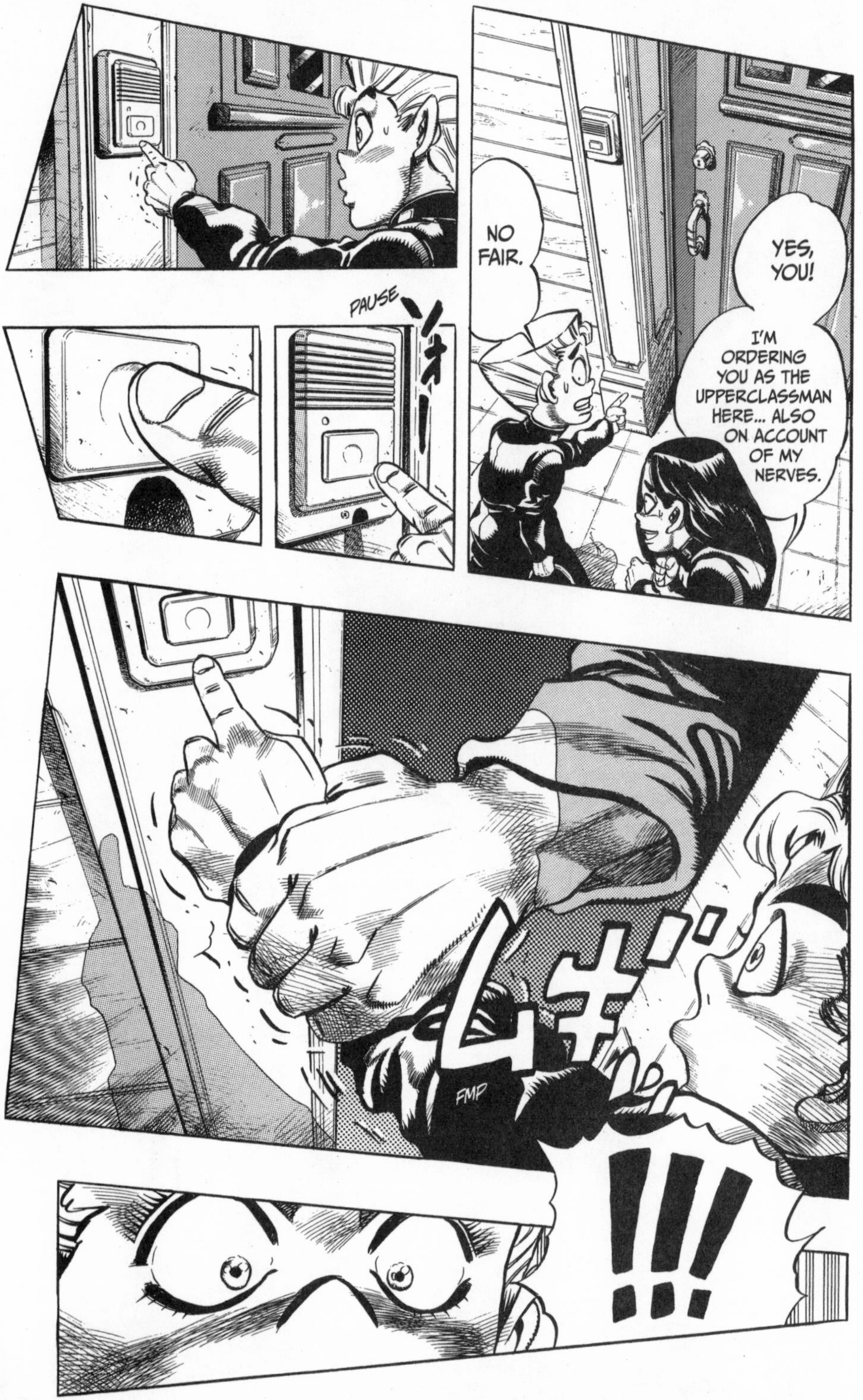
YES, YOU!
I'M ORDERING YOU AS THE UPPERCLASSMAN HERE... ALSO ON ACCOUNT OF MY NERVES.
NO FAIR.
PAUSE
FMP
!!!

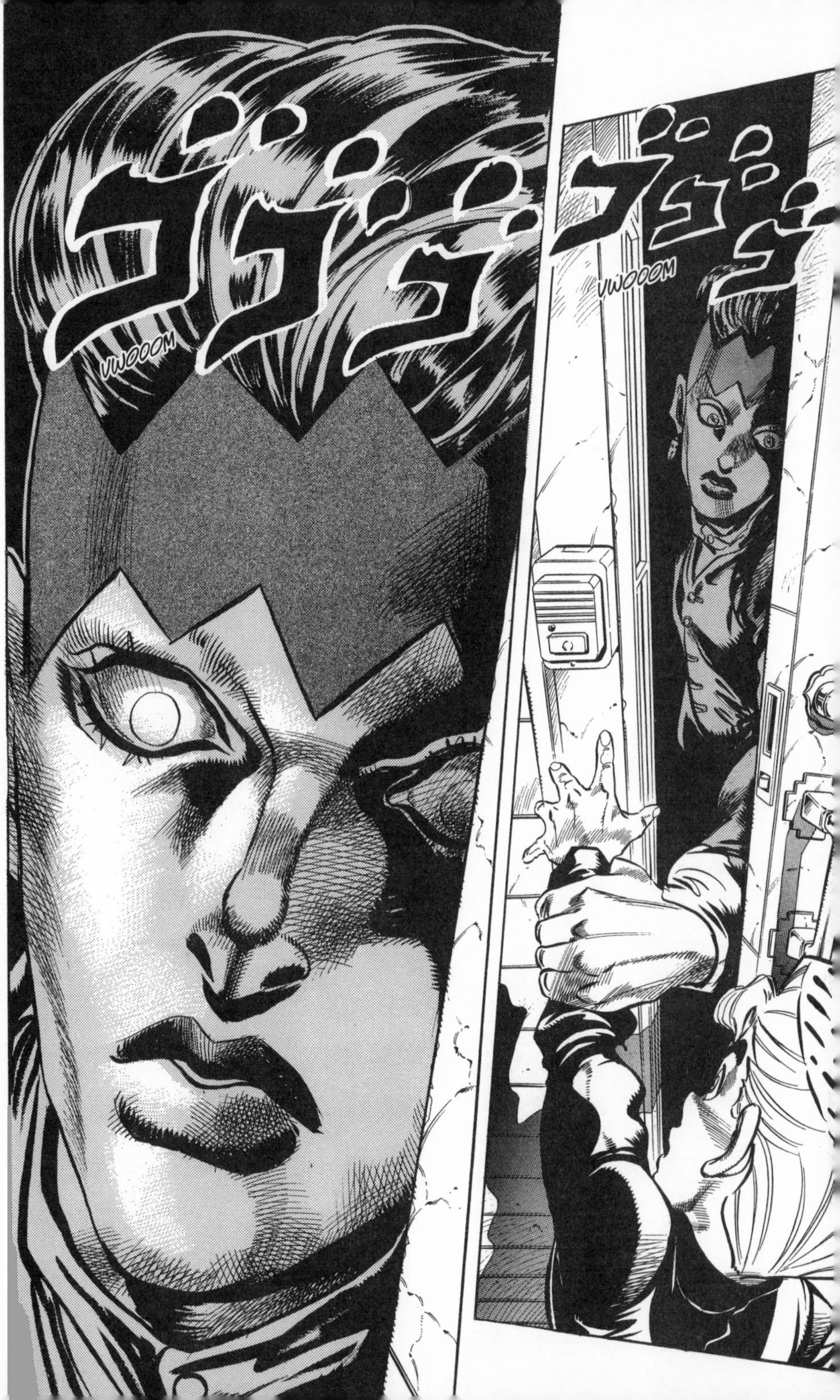
VWOOOM
VWOOOM

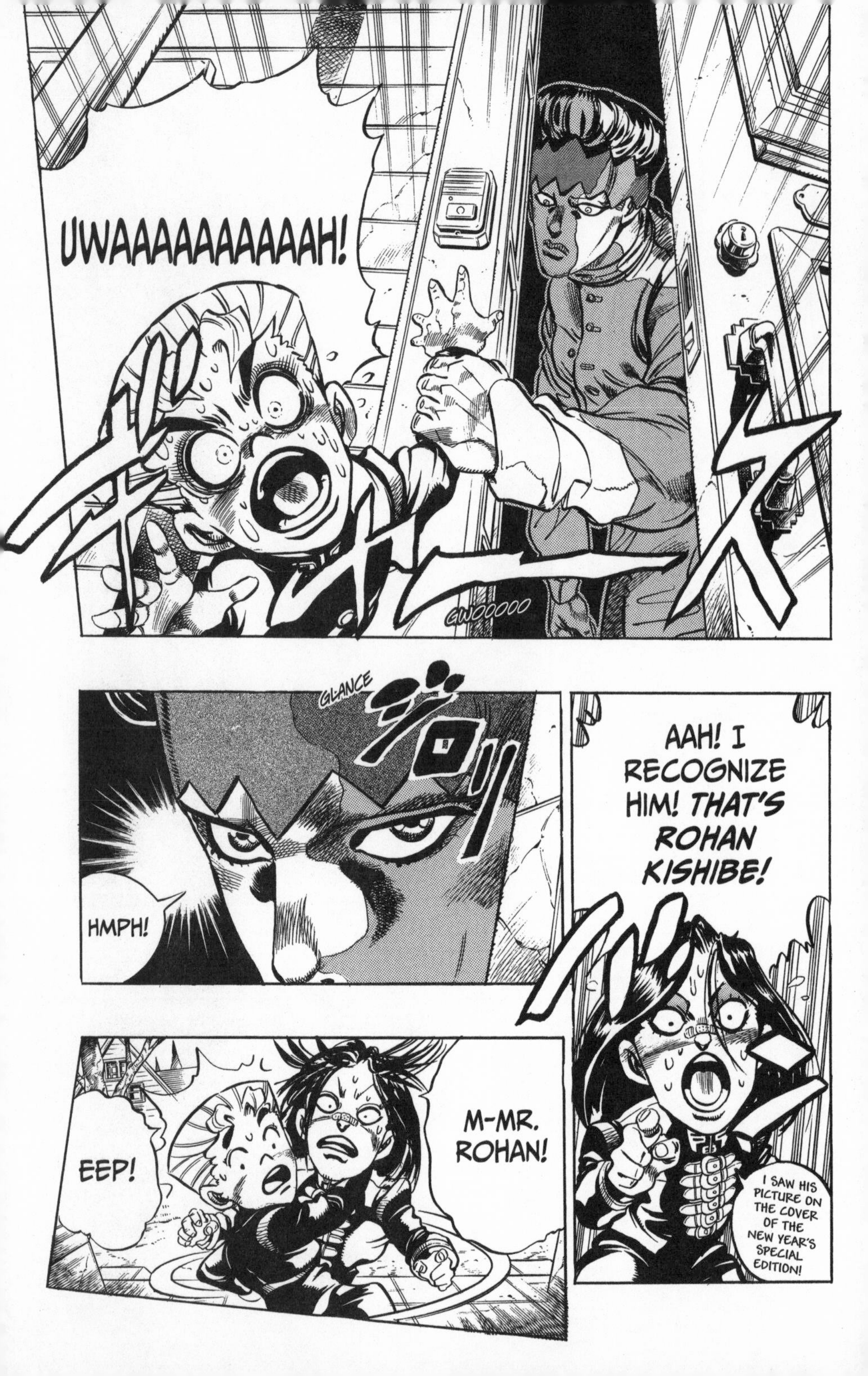
UWAAAAAAAAAAH!
GWOOOOO
AAH! I RECOGNIZE HIM! THAT'S ROHAN KISHIBE!
I SAW HIS PICTURE ON THE COVER OF THE NEW YEAR'S SPECIAL EDITION!
GLANCE
HMPH!
M-MR. ROHAN!
EEP!

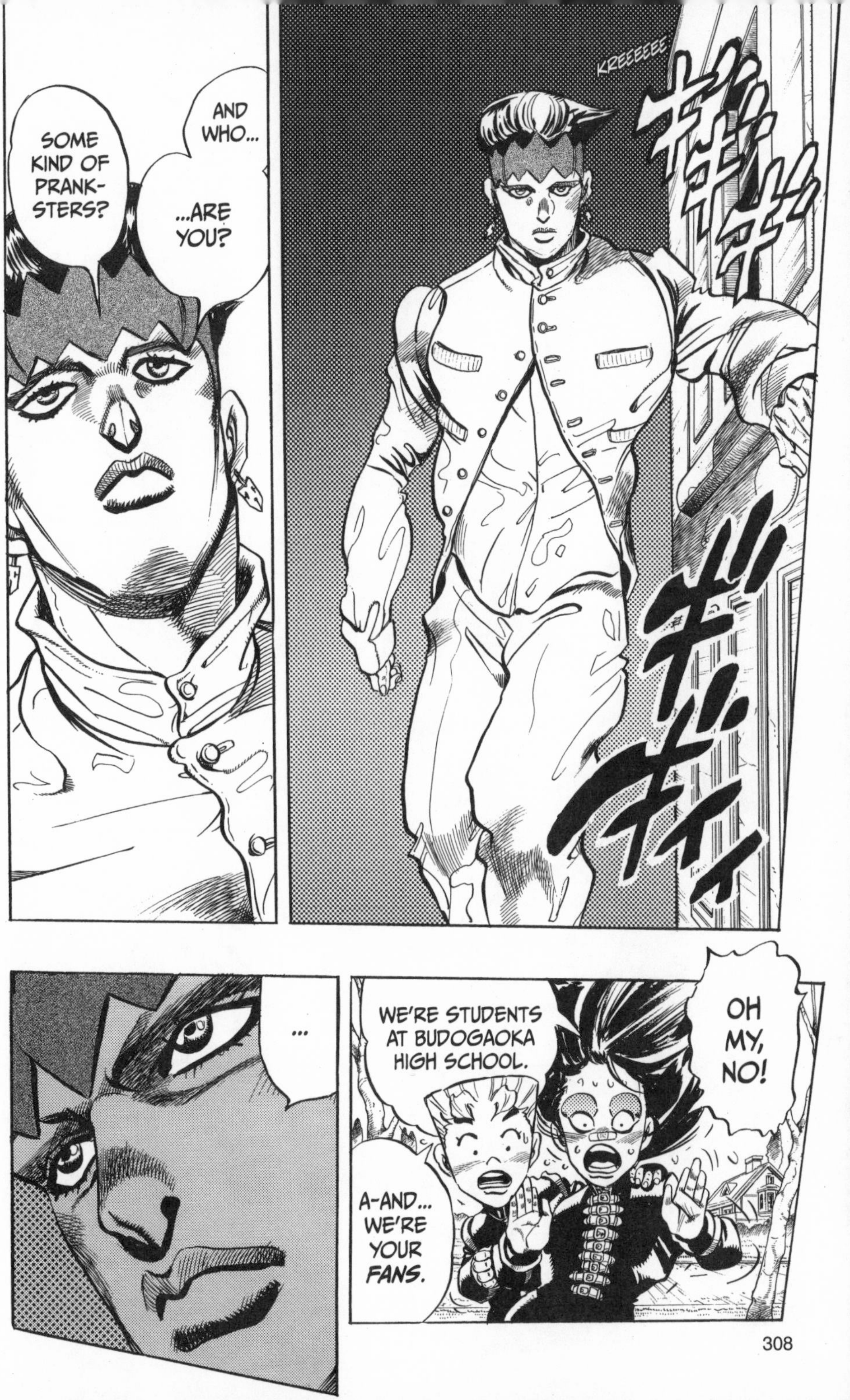
KREEEEEE
AND WHO...
...ARE YOU?
SOME KIND OF PRANK-STERS?
OH MY, NO!
WE'RE STUDENTS AT BUDOGAOKA HIGH SCHOOL.
A-AND... WE'RE YOUR *FANS*.
...

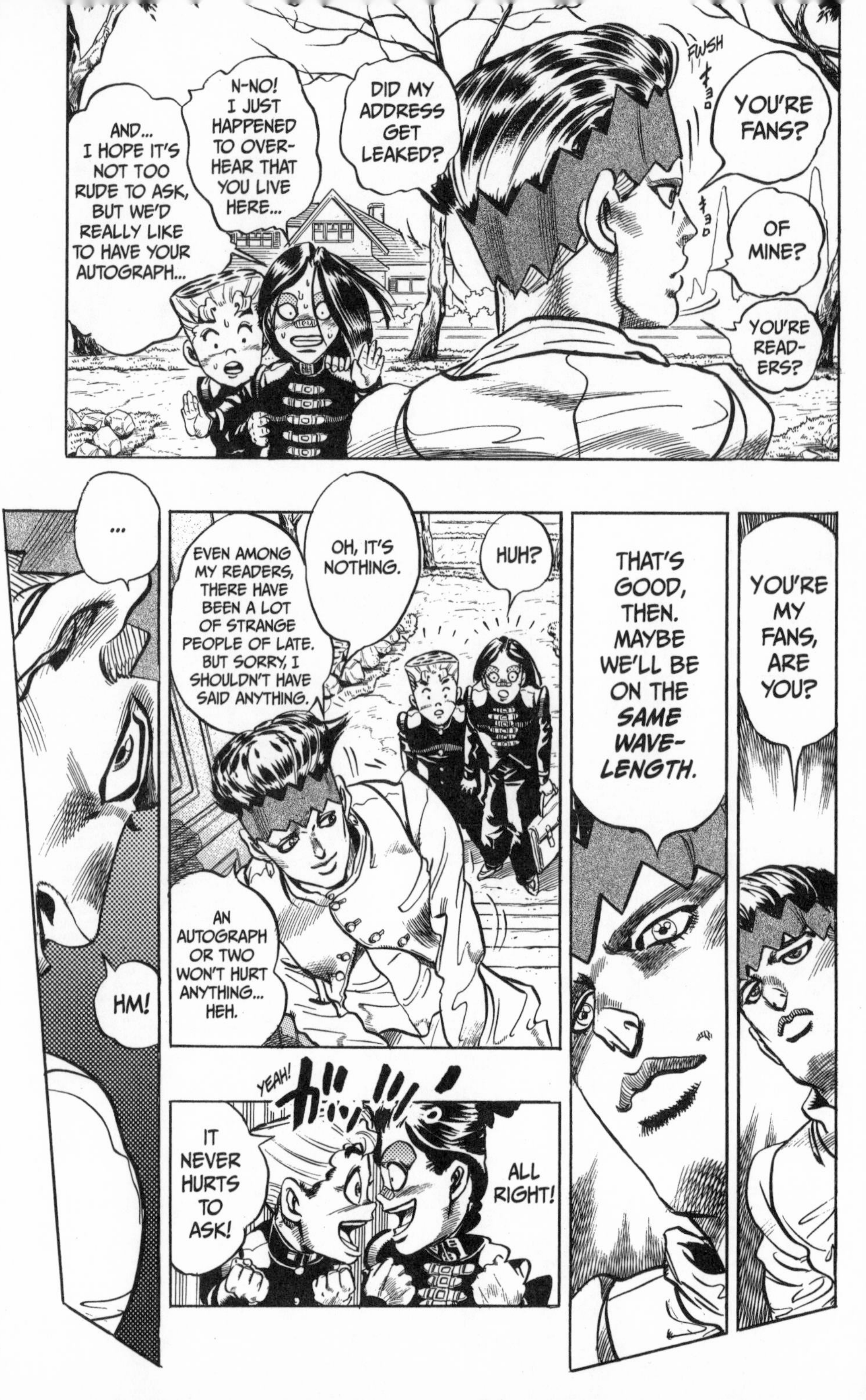
FWSH
YOU'RE FANS?
OF MINE?
YOU'RE READERS?
DID MY ADDRESS GET LEAKED?
N-NO! I JUST HAPPENED TO OVER-HEAR THAT YOU LIVE HERE...
AND... I HOPE IT'S NOT TOO RUDE TO ASK, BUT WE'D REALLY LIKE TO HAVE YOUR AUTOGRAPH...
YOU'RE MY FANS, ARE YOU?
THAT'S GOOD, THEN. MAYBE WE'LL BE ON THE *SAME WAVE-LENGTH.*
HUH?
OH, IT'S NOTHING.
EVEN AMONG MY READERS, THERE HAVE BEEN A LOT OF STRANGE PEOPLE OF LATE. BUT SORRY, I SHOULDN'T HAVE SAID ANYTHING.
AN AUTOGRAPH OR TWO WON'T HURT ANYTHING... HEH.
YEAH!
ALL RIGHT!
IT NEVER HURTS TO ASK!
...
HM!

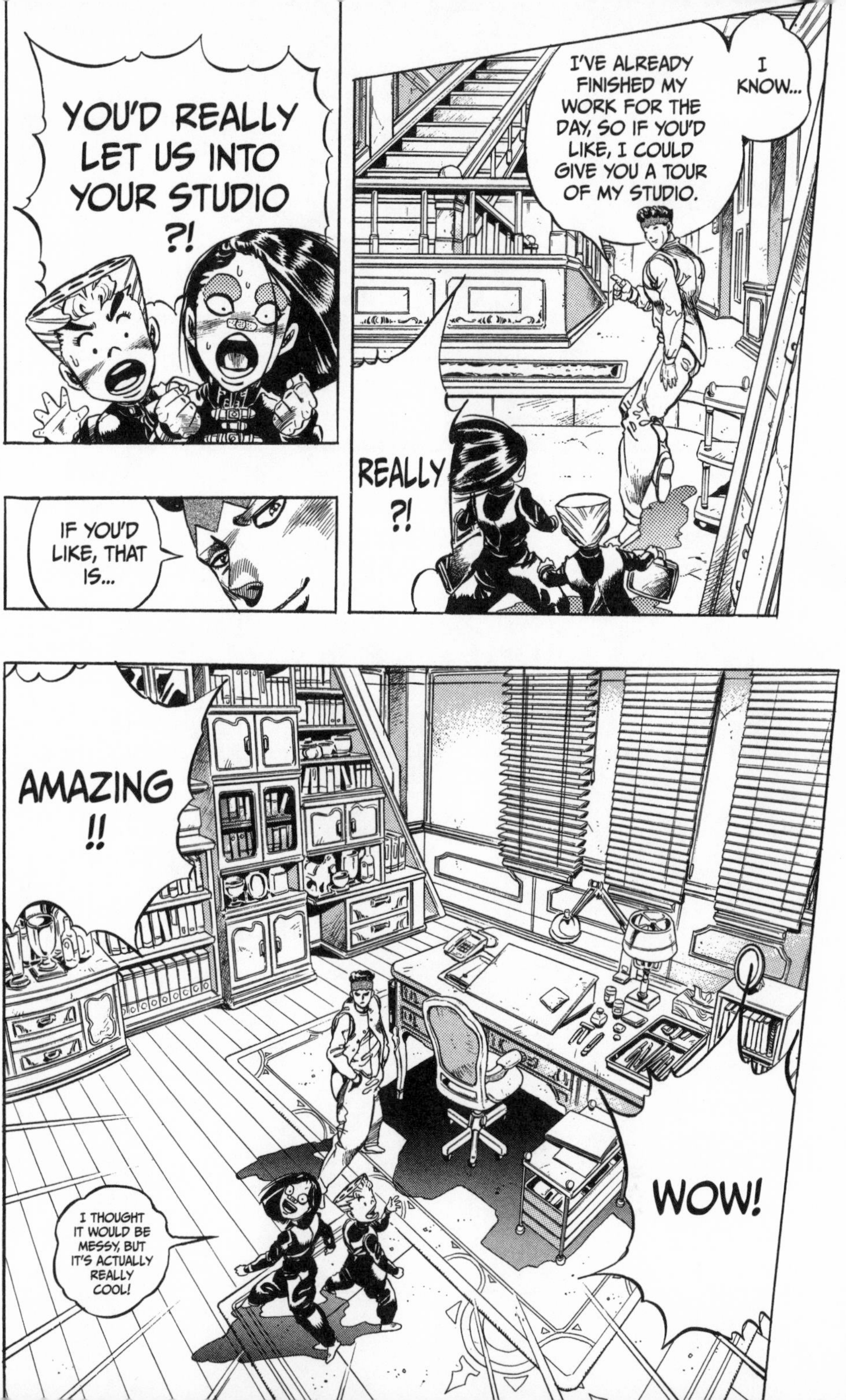
I KNOW...
I'VE ALREADY FINISHED MY WORK FOR THE DAY, SO IF YOU'D LIKE, I COULD GIVE YOU A TOUR OF MY STUDIO.
REALLY ?!
YOU'D REALLY LET US INTO YOUR STUDIO ?!
IF YOU'D LIKE, THAT IS...
AMAZING !!
WOW!
I THOUGHT IT WOULD BE MESSY, BUT IT'S ACTUALLY REALLY COOL!

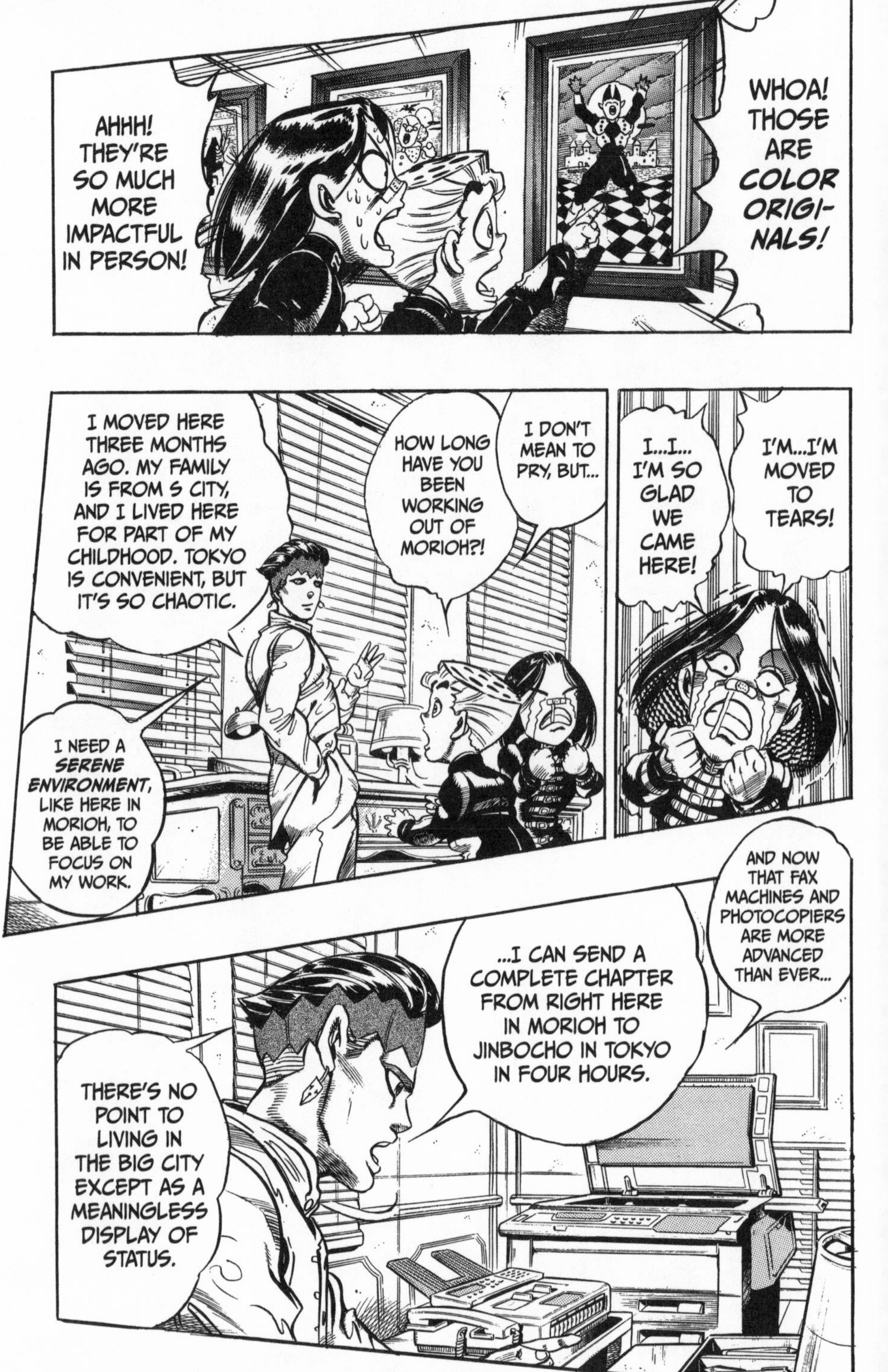
WHOA! THOSE ARE COLOR ORIGI-NALS!
AHHH! THEY'RE SO MUCH MORE IMPACTFUL IN PERSON!
I'M...I'M MOVED TO TEARS!
I...I... I'M SO GLAD WE CAME HERE!
I DON'T MEAN TO PRY, BUT...
HOW LONG HAVE YOU BEEN WORKING OUT OF MORIOH?!
I MOVED HERE THREE MONTHS AGO. MY FAMILY IS FROM S CITY, AND I LIVED HERE FOR PART OF MY CHILDHOOD. TOKYO IS CONVENIENT, BUT IT'S SO CHAOTIC.
I NEED A *SERENE ENVIRONMENT*, LIKE HERE IN MORIOH, TO BE ABLE TO FOCUS ON MY WORK.
AND NOW THAT FAX MACHINES AND PHOTOCOPIERS ARE MORE ADVANCED THAN EVER...
...I CAN SEND A COMPLETE CHAPTER FROM RIGHT HERE IN MORIOH TO JINBOCHO IN TOKYO IN FOUR HOURS.
THERE'S NO POINT TO LIVING IN THE BIG CITY EXCEPT AS A MEANINGLESS DISPLAY OF STATUS.

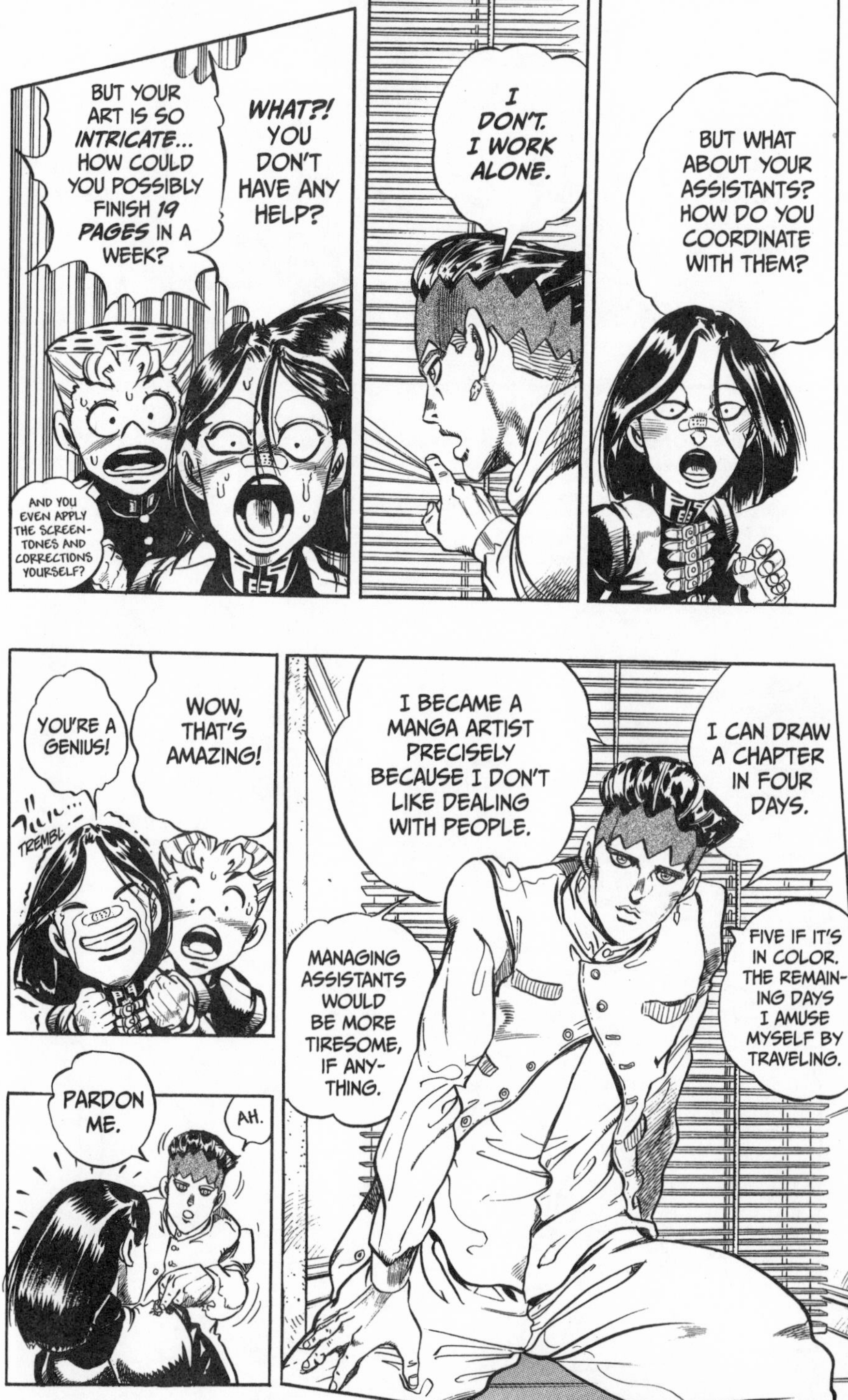
BUT WHAT ABOUT YOUR ASSISTANTS? HOW DO YOU COORDINATE WITH THEM?
I DON'T. I WORK ALONE.
WHAT?! YOU DON'T HAVE ANY HELP?
BUT YOUR ART IS SO INTRICATE... HOW COULD YOU POSSIBLY FINISH 19 PAGES IN A WEEK?
AND YOU EVEN APPLY THE SCREEN-TONES AND CORRECTIONS YOURSELF?
I CAN DRAW A CHAPTER IN FOUR DAYS.
I BECAME A MANGA ARTIST PRECISELY BECAUSE I DON'T LIKE DEALING WITH PEOPLE.
FIVE IF IT'S IN COLOR. THE REMAIN-ING DAYS I AMUSE MYSELF BY TRAVELING.
MANAGING ASSISTANTS WOULD BE MORE TIRESOME, IF ANY-THING.
WOW, THAT'S AMAZING!
YOU'RE A GENIUS!
TREMBL
AH.
PARDON ME.

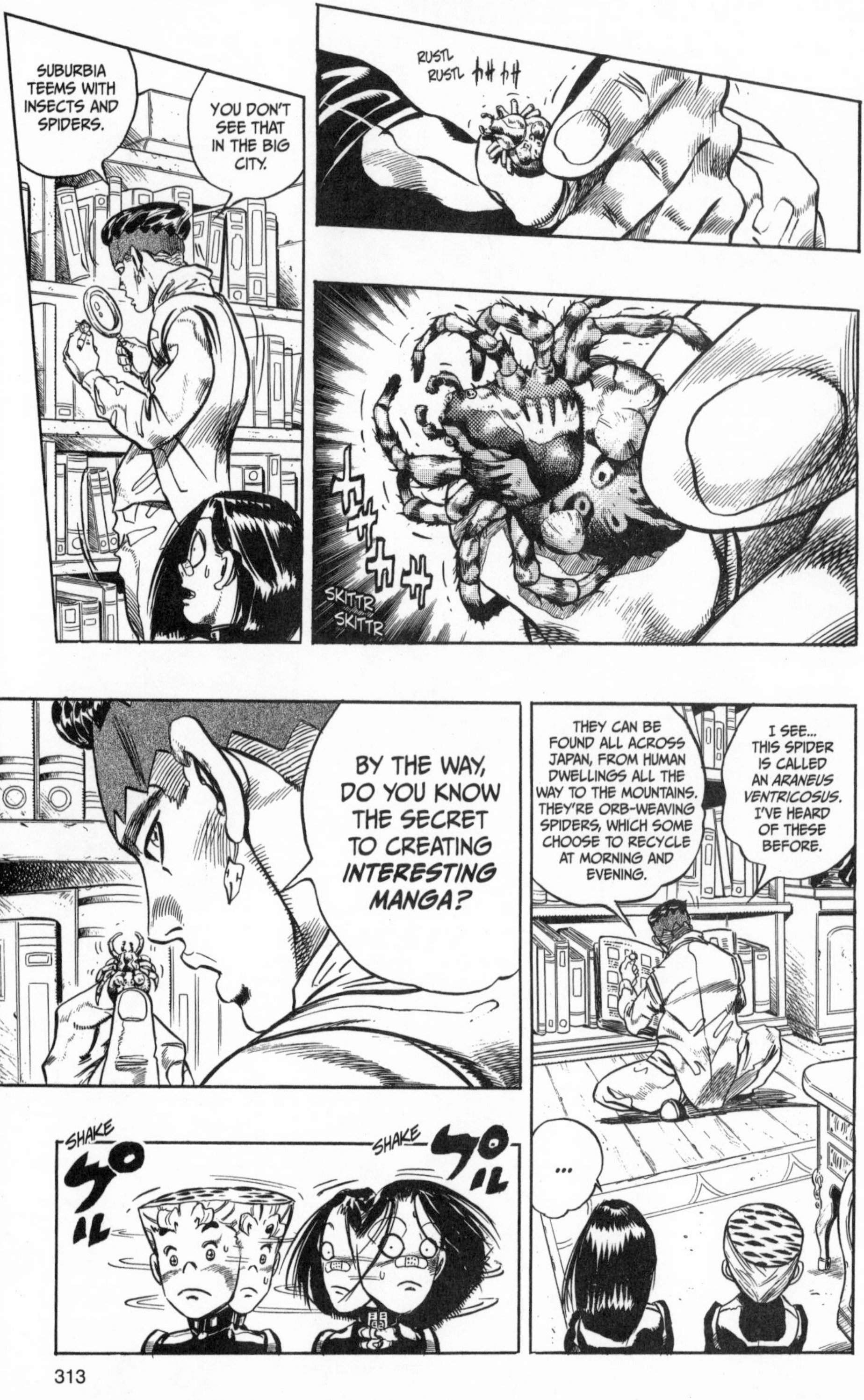
RUSTL
RUSTL
SKITTR
SKITTR
SUBURBIA TEEMS WITH INSECTS AND SPIDERS.
YOU DON'T SEE THAT IN THE BIG CITY.
I SEE... THIS SPIDER IS CALLED AN *ARANEUS VENTRICOSUS.* I'VE HEARD OF THESE BEFORE.
THEY CAN BE FOUND ALL ACROSS JAPAN, FROM HUMAN DWELLINGS ALL THE WAY TO THE MOUNTAINS. THEY'RE ORB-WEAVING SPIDERS, WHICH SOME CHOOSE TO RECYCLE AT MORNING AND EVENING.
...
BY THE WAY, DO YOU KNOW THE SECRET TO CREATING *INTERESTING MANGA?*
SHAKE
SHAKE

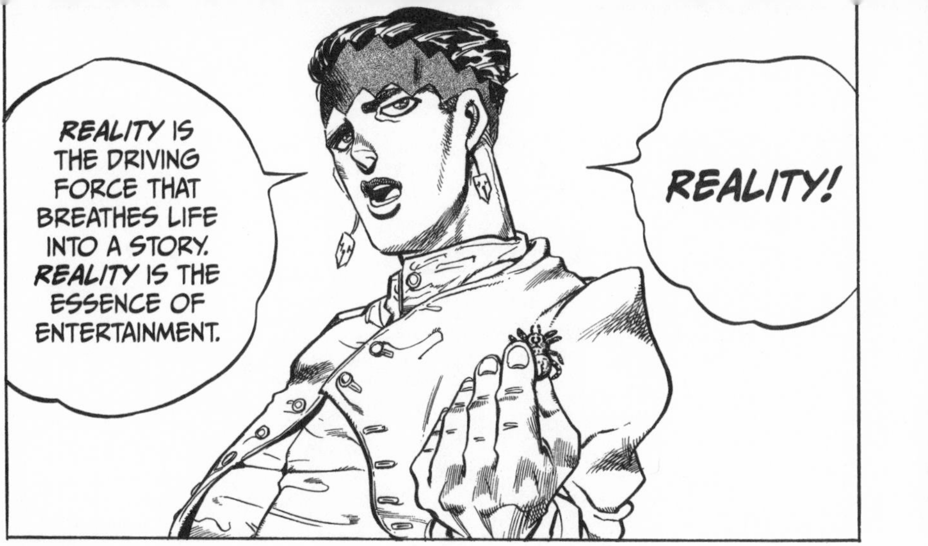
REALITY!
REALITY IS THE DRIVING FORCE THAT BREATHES LIFE INTO A STORY. REALITY IS THE ESSENCE OF ENTERTAINMENT.

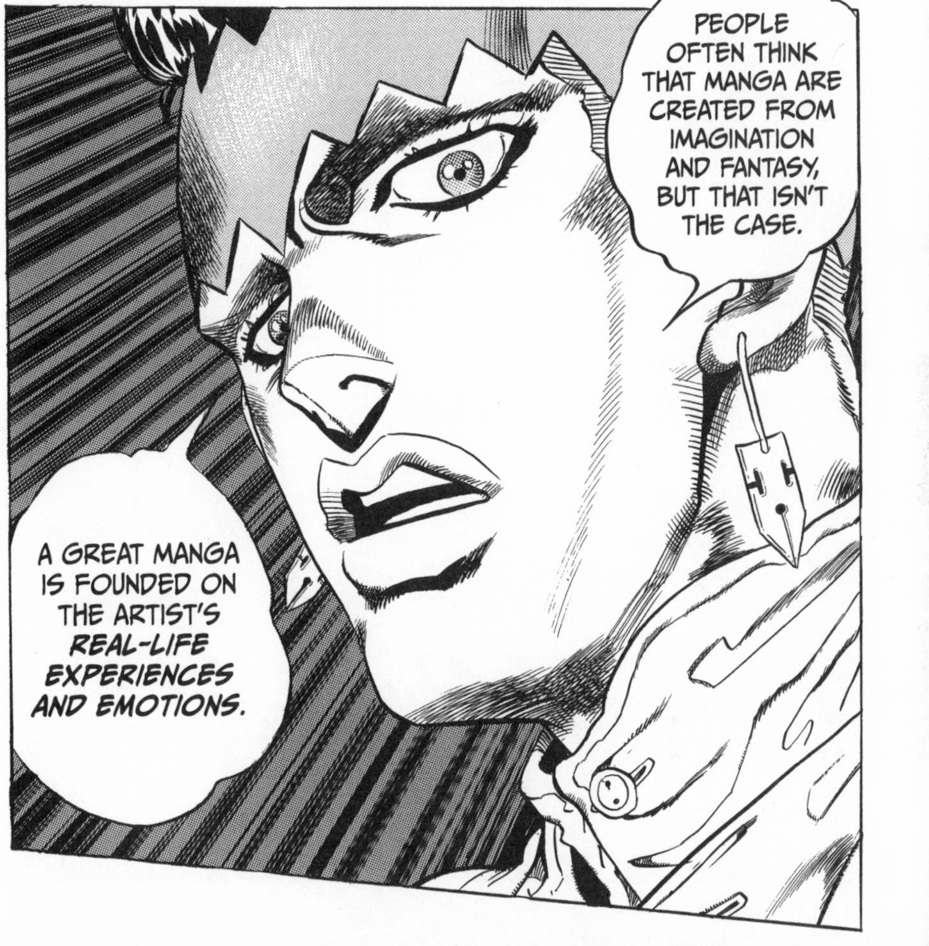
PEOPLE OFTEN THINK THAT MANGA ARE CREATED FROM IMAGINATION AND FANTASY, BUT THAT ISN'T THE CASE.
A GREAT MANGA IS FOUNDED ON THE ARTIST'S REAL-LIFE EXPERIENCES AND EMOTIONS.

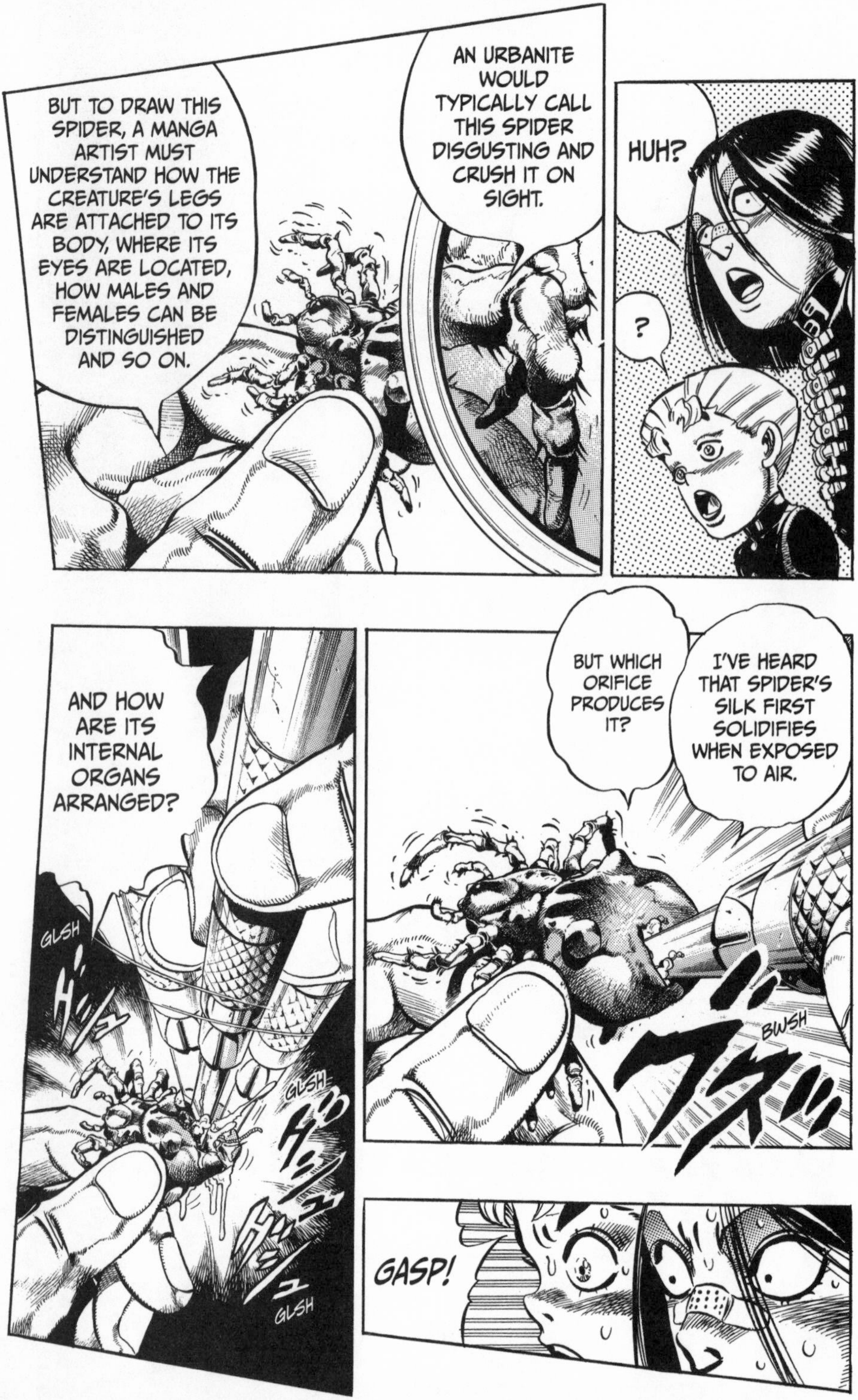
HUH?
?
AN URBANITE WOULD TYPICALLY CALL THIS SPIDER DISGUSTING AND CRUSH IT ON SIGHT.
BUT TO DRAW THIS SPIDER, A MANGA ARTIST MUST UNDERSTAND HOW THE CREATURE'S LEGS ARE ATTACHED TO ITS BODY, WHERE ITS EYES ARE LOCATED, HOW MALES AND FEMALES CAN BE DISTINGUISHED AND SO ON.
I'VE HEARD THAT SPIDER'S SILK FIRST SOLIDIFIES WHEN EXPOSED TO AIR.
BUT WHICH ORIFICE PRODUCES IT?
BWSH
GASP!
AND HOW ARE ITS INTERNAL ORGANS ARRANGED?
GLSH
GLSH
GLSH

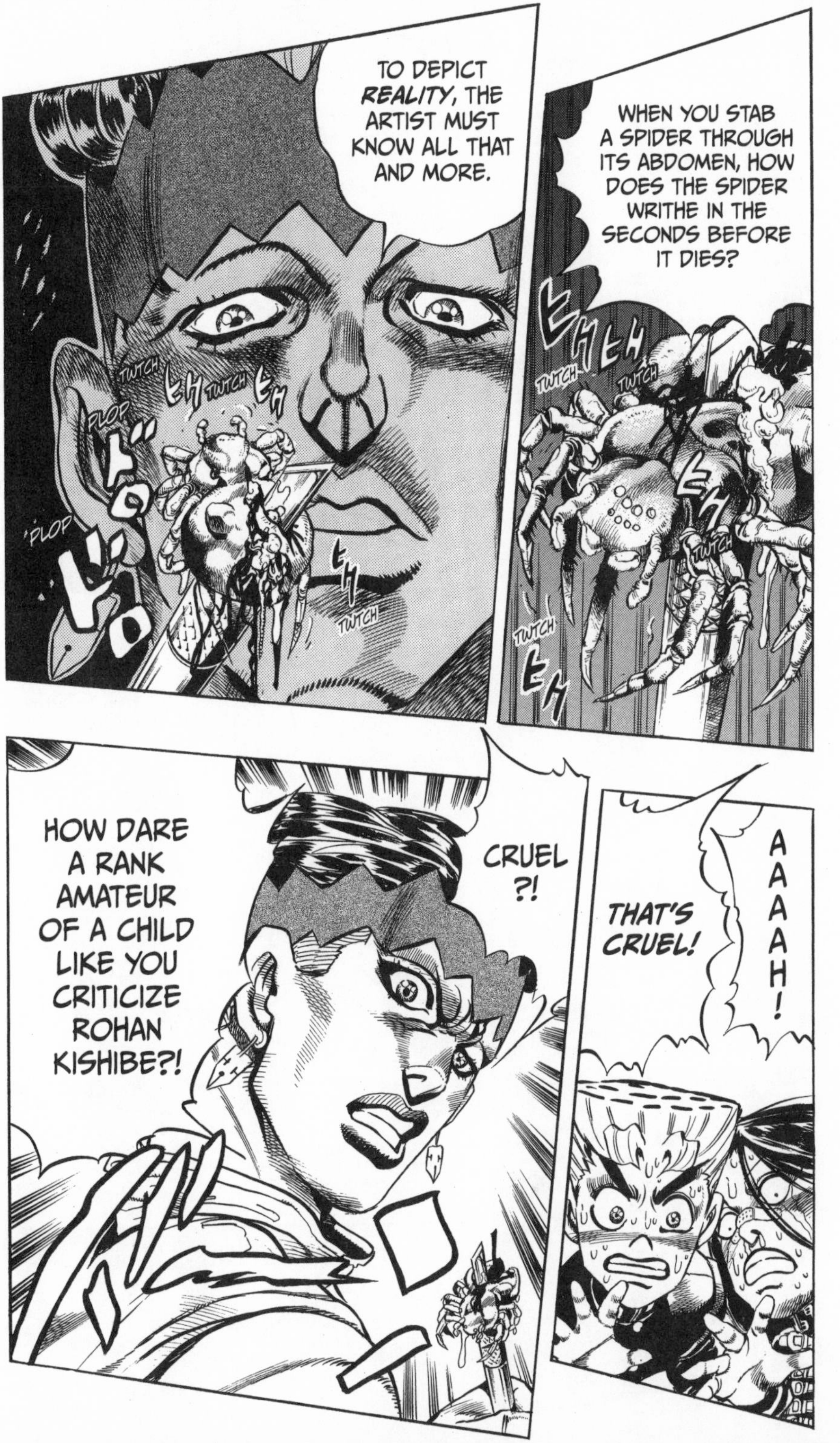
WHEN YOU STAB A SPIDER THROUGH ITS ABDOMEN, HOW DOES THE SPIDER WRITHE IN THE SECONDS BEFORE IT DIES?
TWITCH
TWITCH
TWITCH
TWITCH
TO DEPICT *REALITY*, THE ARTIST MUST KNOW ALL THAT AND MORE.
TWITCH
TWITCH
PLOP
PLOP
TWITCH
AAAAAH!
THAT'S CRUEL!
CRUEL?!
HOW DARE A RANK AMATEUR OF A CHILD LIKE YOU CRITICIZE ROHAN KISHIBE?!

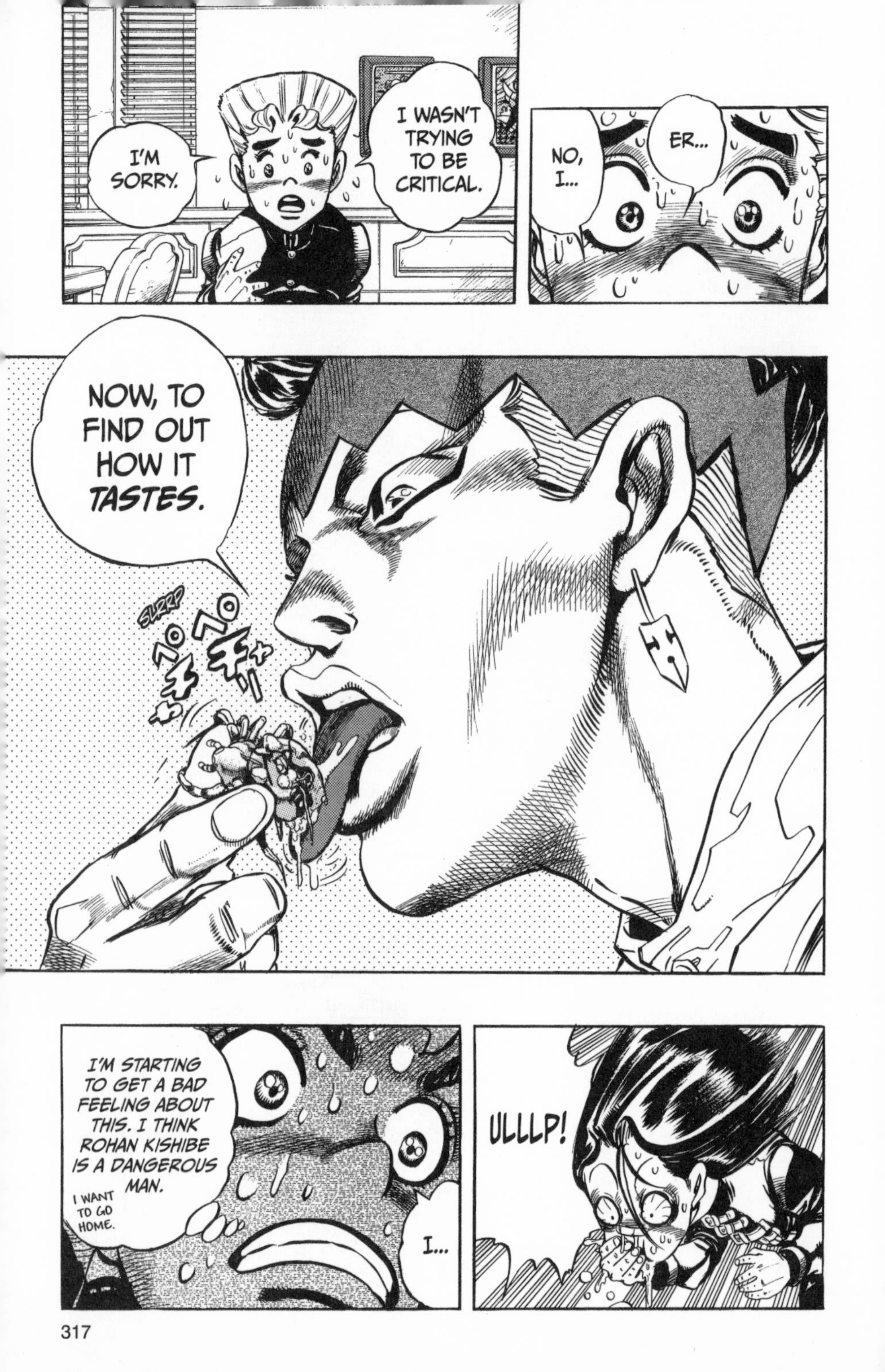
ER...
NO, I...
I WASN'T TRYING TO BE CRITICAL.
I'M SORRY.
NOW, TO FIND OUT HOW IT *TASTES.*
SLRRP
ULLLP!
I'M STARTING TO GET A BAD FEELING ABOUT THIS. I THINK ROHAN KISHIBE IS A DANGEROUS MAN.
I WANT TO GO HOME.
I...

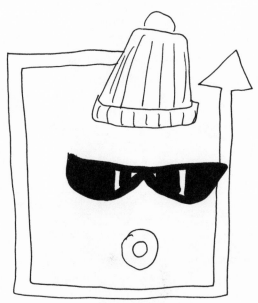

STAND NAME:
ACHTUNG BABY

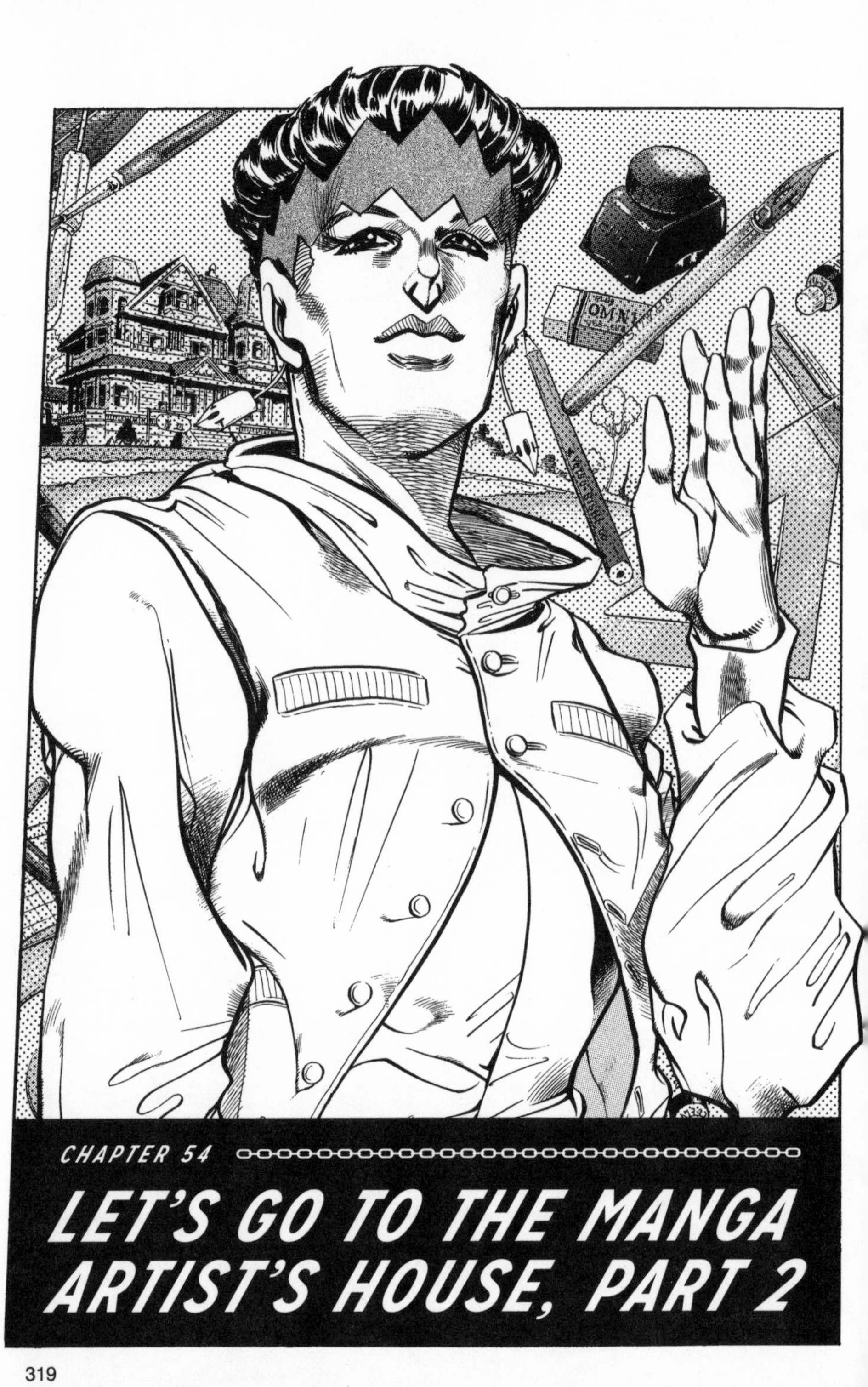
OMNI

CHAPTER 54

LET'S GO TO THE MANGA ARTIST'S HOUSE, PART 2

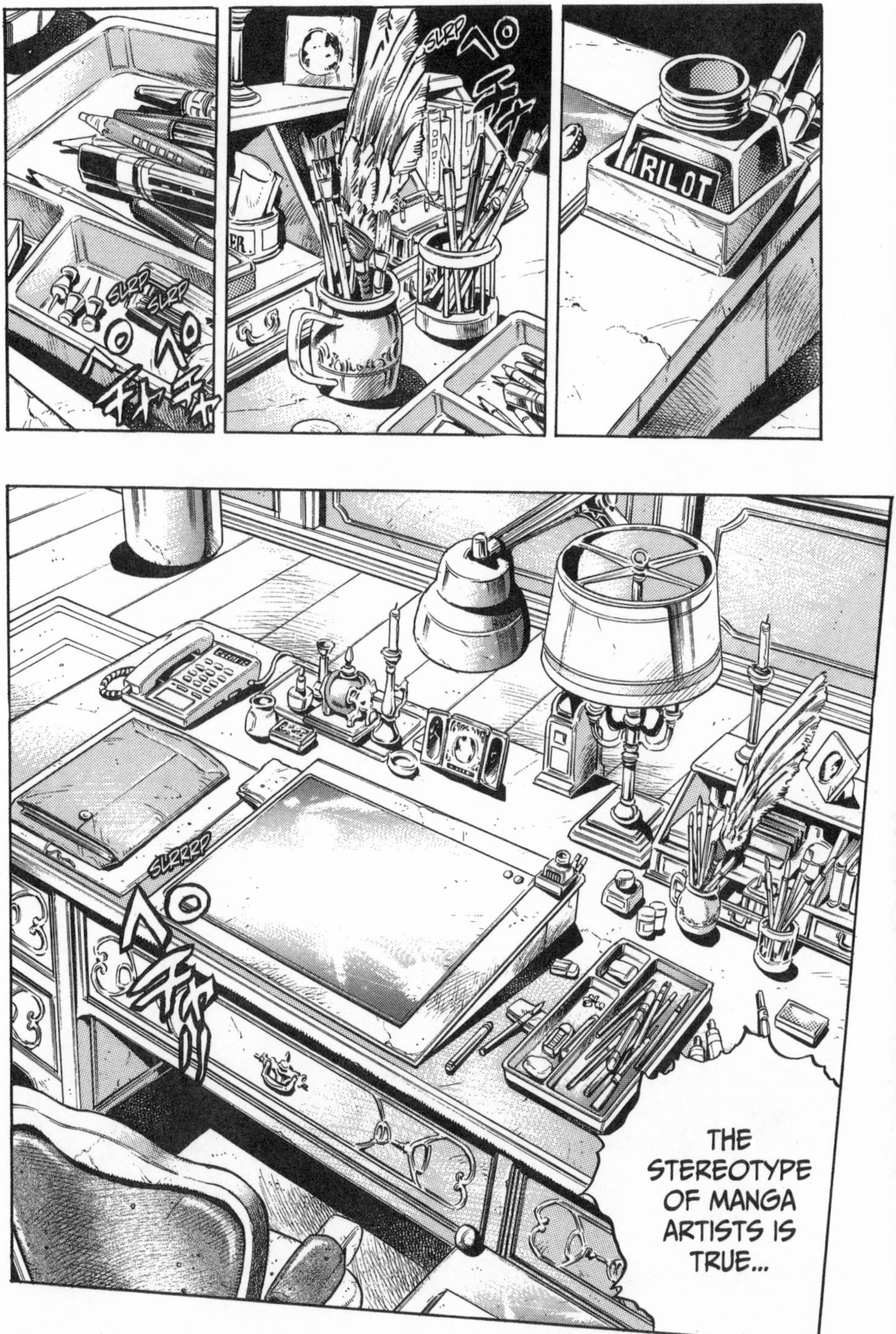
RILOT
SLRP
SLRP
SLRP
SLRRRP
THE STEREOTYPE OF MANGA ARTISTS IS TRUE...

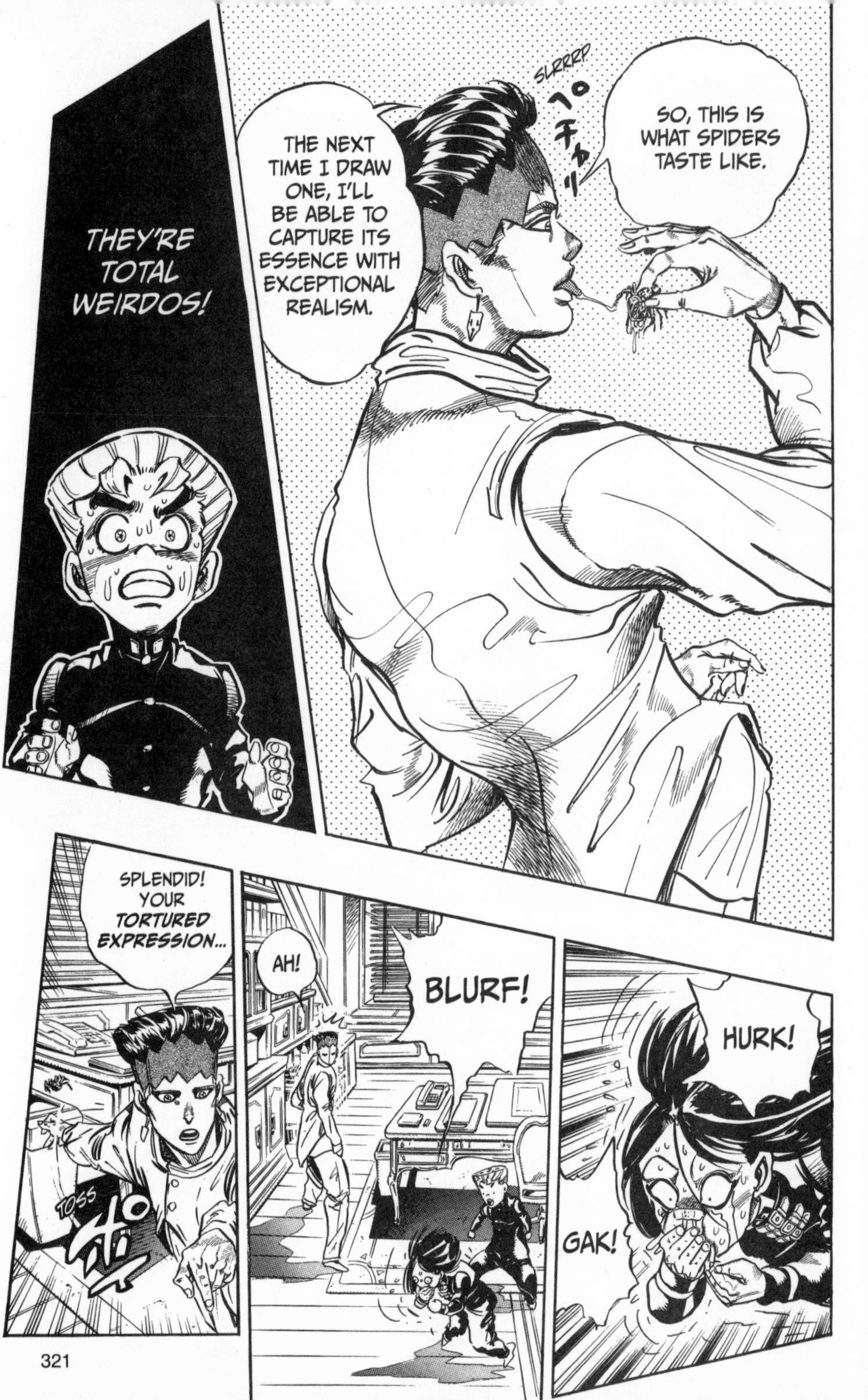
SLRRRP
SO, THIS IS WHAT SPIDERS TASTE LIKE.
THE NEXT TIME I DRAW ONE, I'LL BE ABLE TO CAPTURE ITS ESSENCE WITH EXCEPTIONAL REALISM.
THEY'RE TOTAL WEIRDOS!
HURK!
GAK!
AH!
BLURF!
SPLENDID! YOUR TORTURED EXPRESSION...
TOSS

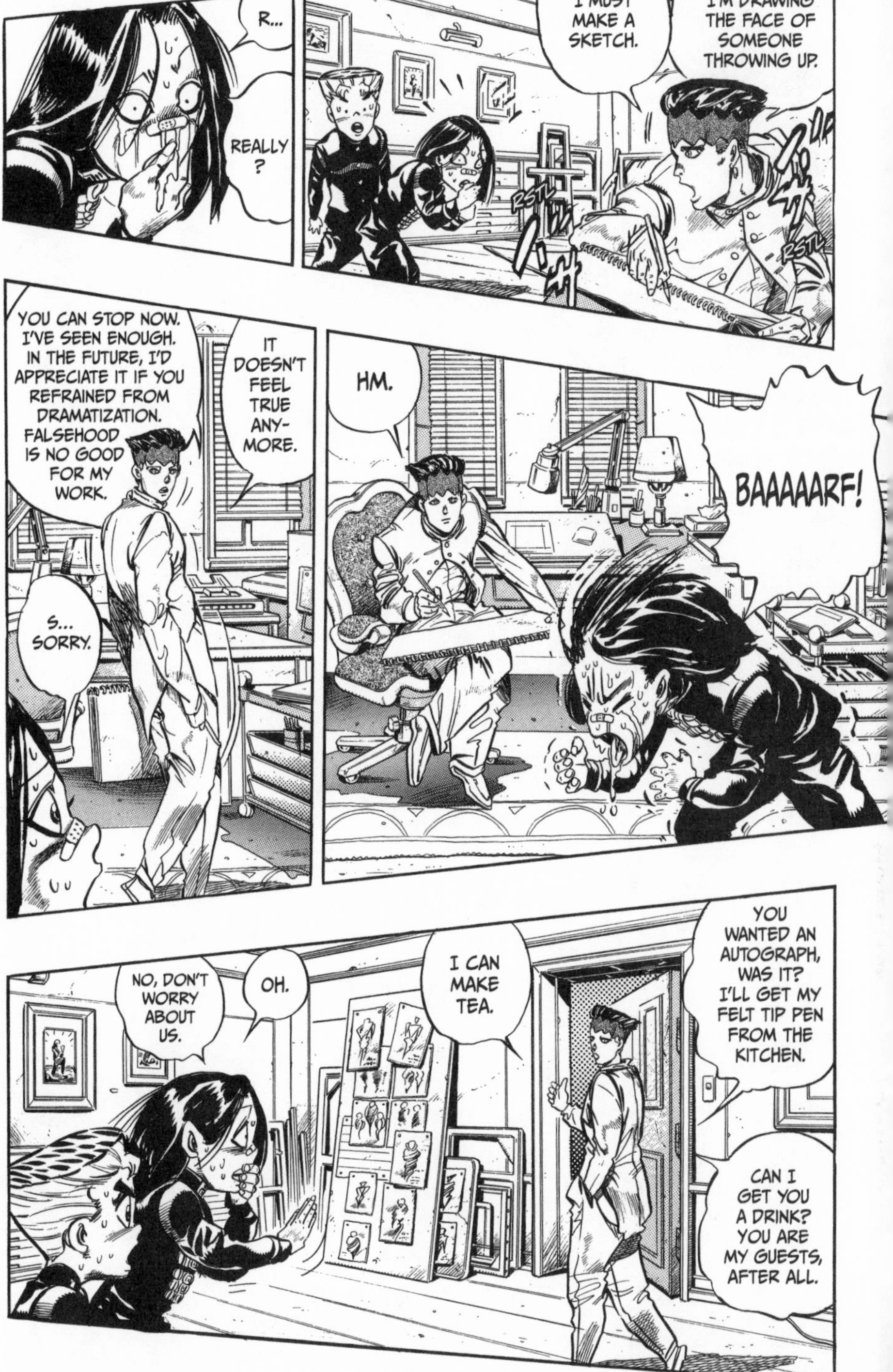
I CAN USE THAT WHEN I'M DRAWING THE FACE OF SOMEONE THROWING UP.
I MUST MAKE A SKETCH.
RSTL
RSTL
R...
REALLY?
BAAAAARF!
HM.
IT DOESN'T FEEL TRUE ANYMORE.
YOU CAN STOP NOW. I'VE SEEN ENOUGH. IN THE FUTURE, I'D APPRECIATE IT IF YOU REFRAINED FROM DRAMATIZATION. FALSEHOOD IS NO GOOD FOR MY WORK.
S... SORRY.
YOU WANTED AN AUTOGRAPH, WAS IT? I'LL GET MY FELT TIP PEN FROM THE KITCHEN.
CAN I GET YOU A DRINK? YOU ARE MY GUESTS, AFTER ALL.
I CAN MAKE TEA.
OH.
NO, DON'T WORRY ABOUT US.

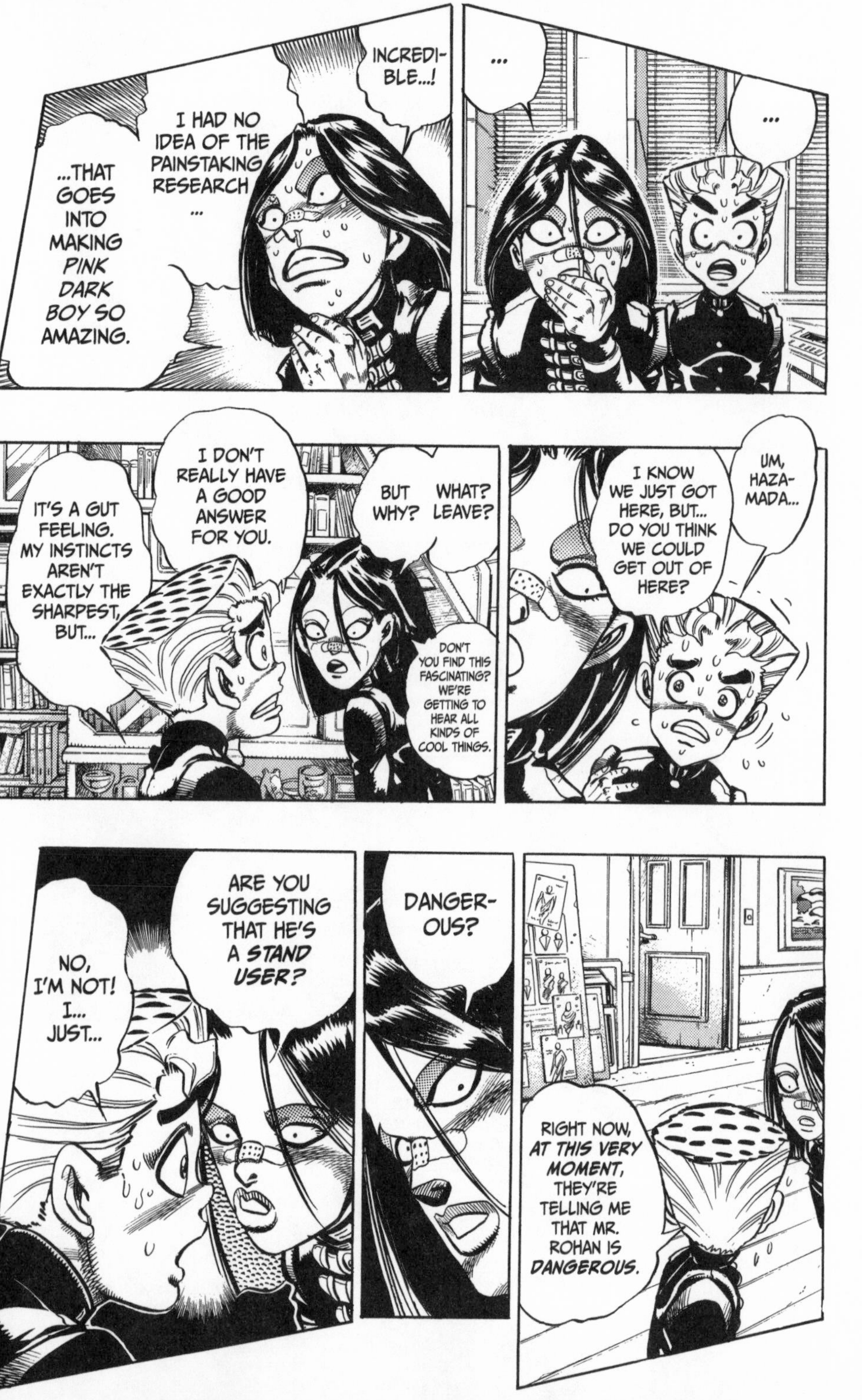
...
...
INCREDIBLE...!
I HAD NO IDEA OF THE PAINSTAKING RESEARCH ...
...THAT GOES INTO MAKING *PINK DARK BOY* SO AMAZING.
UM, HAZAMADA...
I KNOW WE JUST GOT HERE, BUT... DO YOU THINK WE COULD GET OUT OF HERE?
WHAT? LEAVE?
BUT WHY?
I DON'T REALLY HAVE A GOOD ANSWER FOR YOU.
IT'S A GUT FEELING. MY INSTINCTS AREN'T EXACTLY THE SHARPEST, BUT...
DON'T YOU FIND THIS FASCINATING? WE'RE GETTING TO HEAR ALL KINDS OF COOL THINGS.
RIGHT NOW, *AT THIS VERY MOMENT*, THEY'RE TELLING ME THAT MR. ROHAN IS *DANGEROUS*.
DANGEROUS?
ARE YOU SUGGESTING THAT HE'S A *STAND USER?*
NO, I'M NOT! I... JUST...

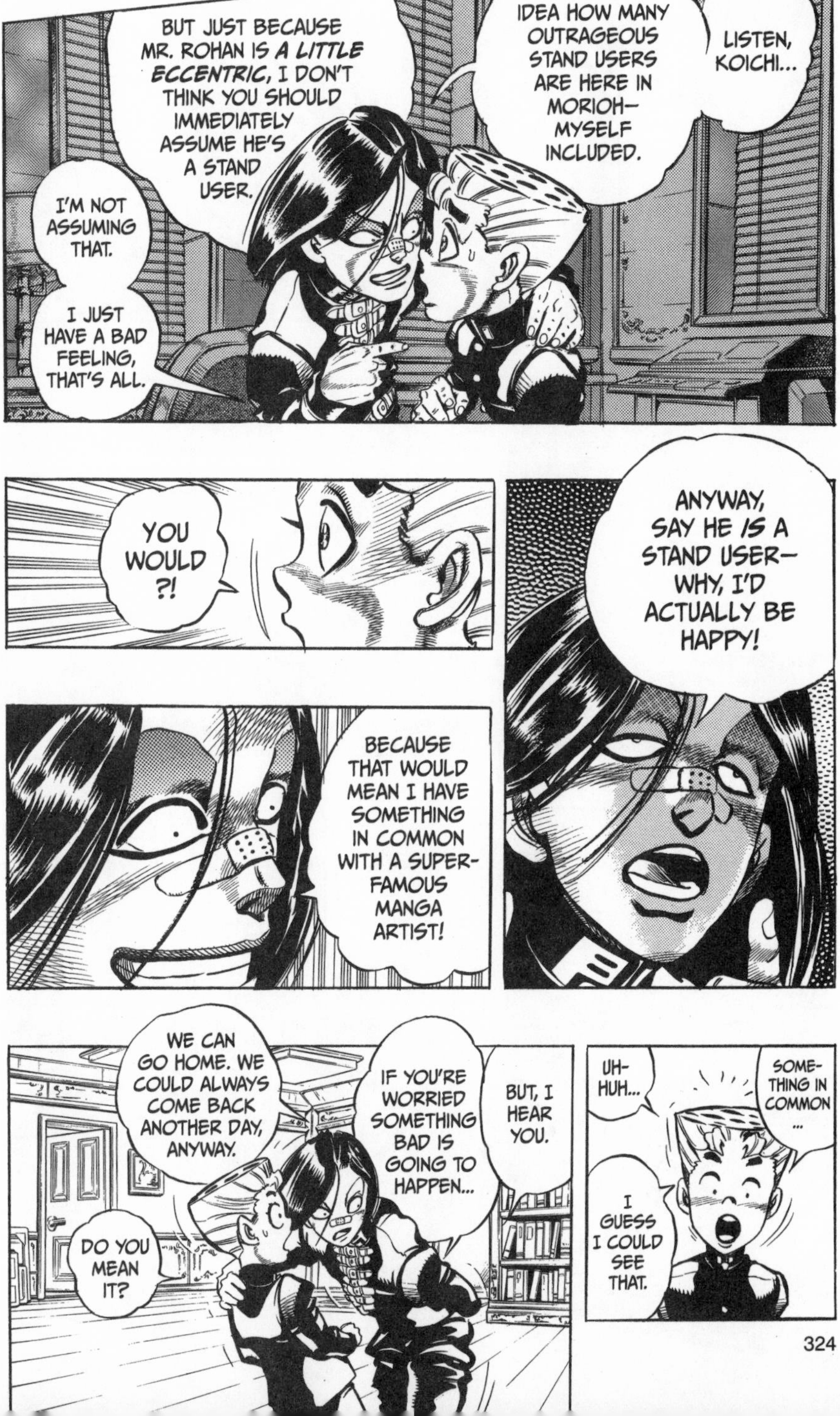
LISTEN, KOICHI...
I HAVE NO IDEA HOW MANY OUTRAGEOUS STAND USERS ARE HERE IN MORIOH—MYSELF INCLUDED.
BUT JUST BECAUSE MR. ROHAN IS A LITTLE ECCENTRIC, I DON'T THINK YOU SHOULD IMMEDIATELY ASSUME HE'S A STAND USER.
I'M NOT ASSUMING THAT.
I JUST HAVE A BAD FEELING, THAT'S ALL.
ANYWAY, SAY HE IS A STAND USER—WHY, I'D ACTUALLY BE HAPPY!
YOU WOULD?!
BECAUSE THAT WOULD MEAN I HAVE SOMETHING IN COMMON WITH A SUPER-FAMOUS MANGA ARTIST!
SOMETHING IN COMMON...
UH-HUH...
I GUESS I COULD SEE THAT.
BUT, I HEAR YOU.
IF YOU'RE WORRIED SOMETHING BAD IS GOING TO HAPPEN...
WE CAN GO HOME. WE COULD ALWAYS COME BACK ANOTHER DAY, ANYWAY.
DO YOU MEAN IT?

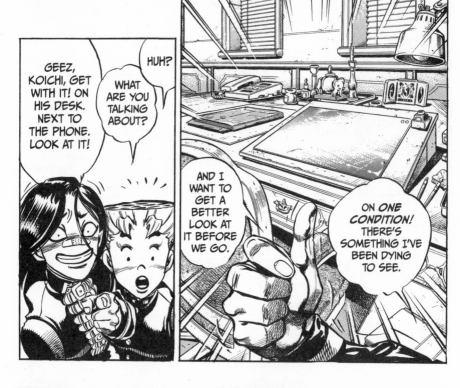

ON *ONE CONDITION!* THERE'S SOMETHING I'VE BEEN DYING TO SEE.
AND I WANT TO GET A BETTER LOOK AT IT BEFORE WE GO.
HUH?
WHAT ARE YOU TALKING ABOUT?
GEEZ, KOICHI, GET WITH IT! ON HIS DESK. NEXT TO THE PHONE. LOOK AT IT!

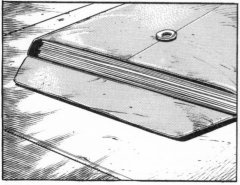

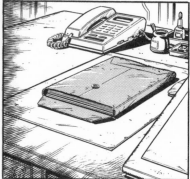

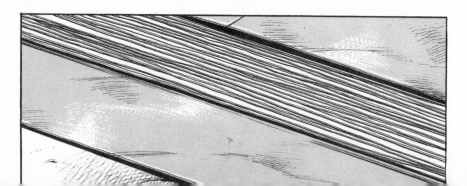

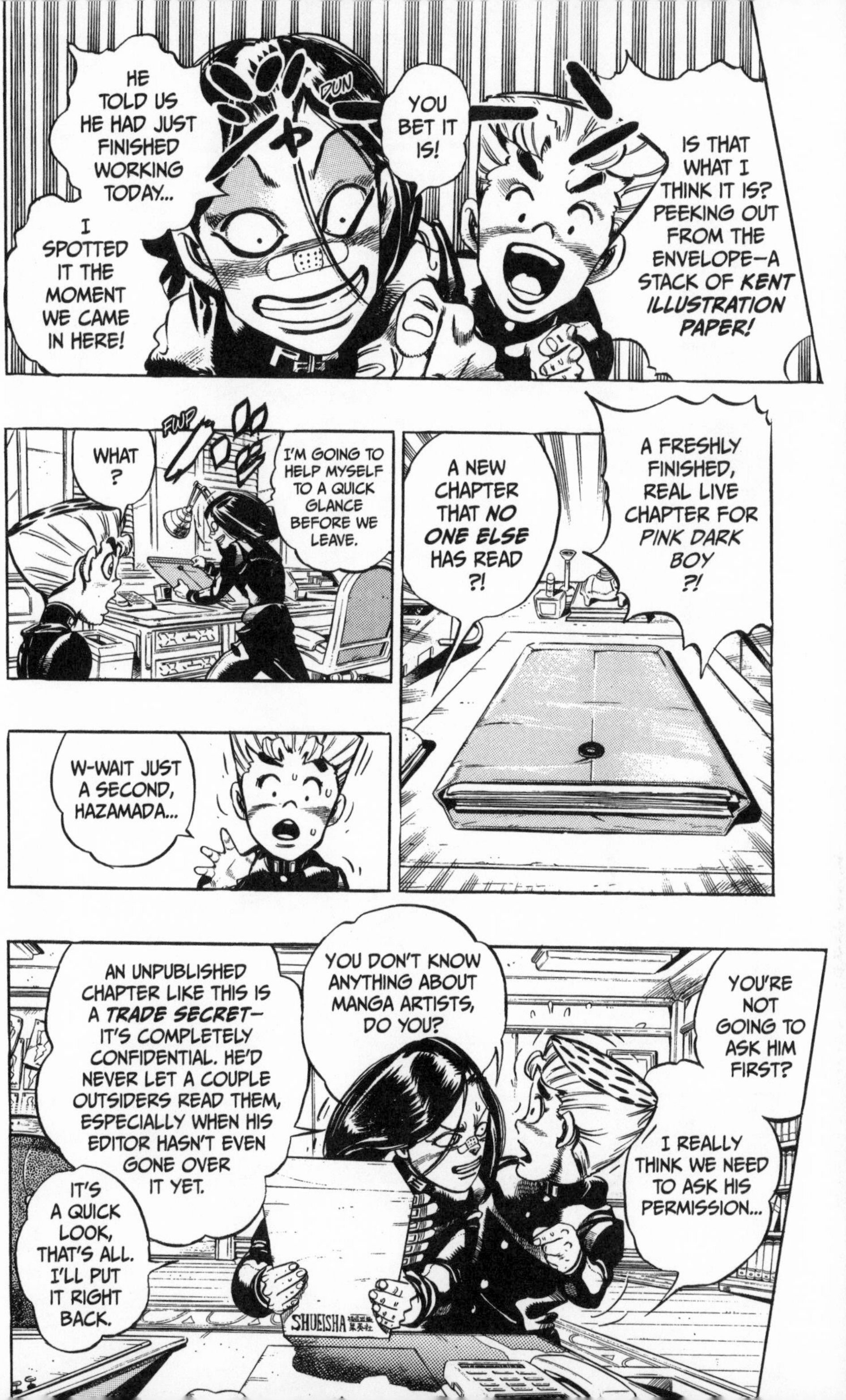
IS THAT WHAT I THINK IT IS? PEEKING OUT FROM THE ENVELOPE—A STACK OF *KENT ILLUSTRATION PAPER!*
YOU BET IT IS!
DUN
HE TOLD US HE HAD JUST FINISHED WORKING TODAY...
I SPOTTED IT THE MOMENT WE CAME IN HERE!
A FRESHLY FINISHED, REAL LIVE CHAPTER FOR *PINK DARK BOY* ?!
A NEW CHAPTER THAT *NO ONE ELSE* HAS READ ?!
I'M GOING TO HELP MYSELF TO A QUICK GLANCE BEFORE WE LEAVE.
FWP
WHAT ?
W-WAIT JUST A SECOND, HAZAMADA...
YOU'RE NOT GOING TO ASK HIM FIRST?
YOU DON'T KNOW ANYTHING ABOUT MANGA ARTISTS, DO YOU?
AN UNPUBLISHED CHAPTER LIKE THIS IS A *TRADE SECRET*—IT'S COMPLETELY CONFIDENTIAL. HE'D NEVER LET A COUPLE OUTSIDERS READ THEM, ESPECIALLY WHEN HIS EDITOR HASN'T EVEN GONE OVER IT YET.
I REALLY THINK WE NEED TO ASK HIS PERMISSION...
IT'S A QUICK LOOK, THAT'S ALL. I'LL PUT IT RIGHT BACK.
SHUEISHA

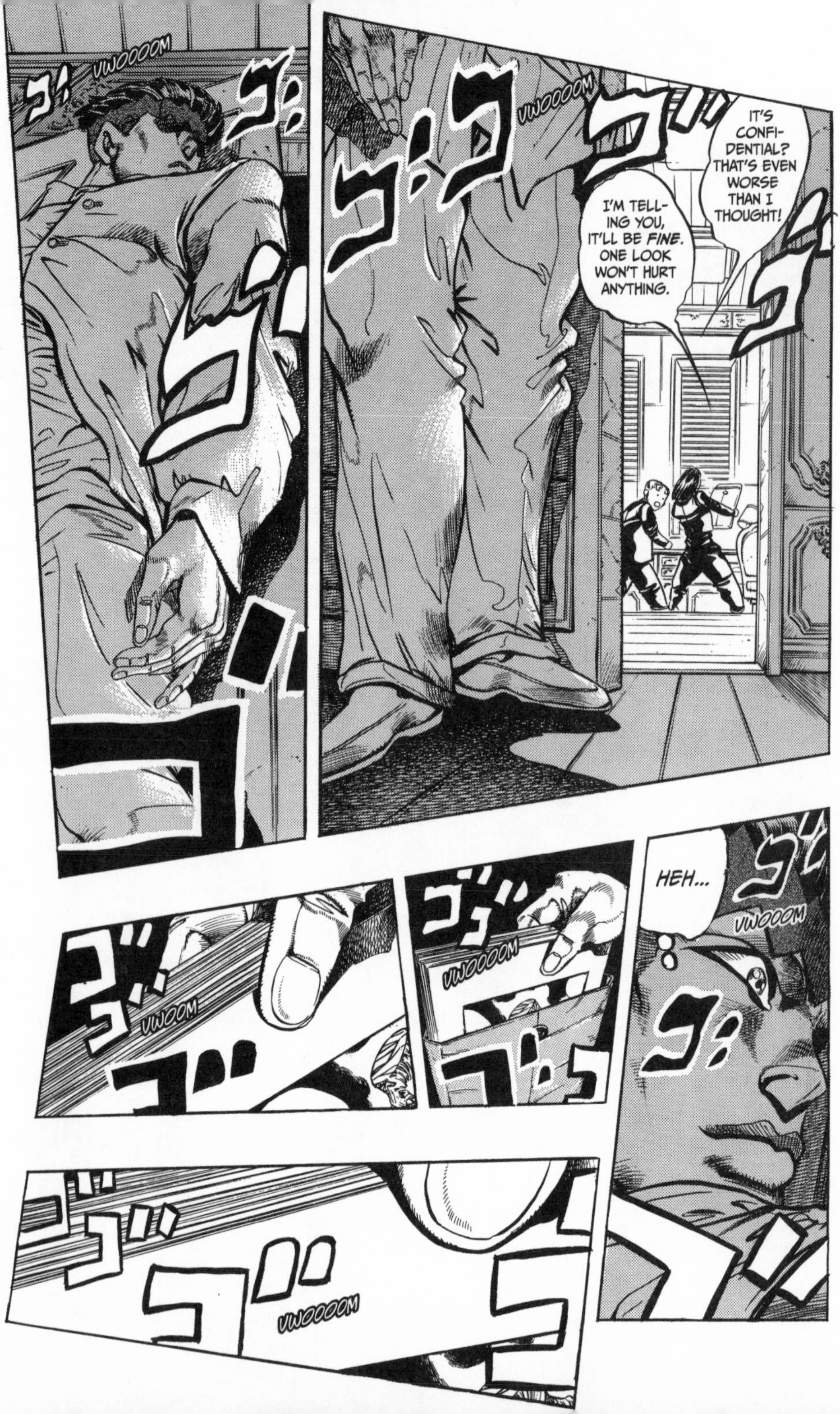
VWOOOOM
IT'S CONFIDENTIAL? THAT'S EVEN WORSE THAN I THOUGHT!
I'M TELLING YOU, IT'LL BE *FINE*. ONE LOOK WON'T HURT ANYTHING.
VWOOOOM
HEH...
VWOOOM
VWOOOOM
VWOOM
VWOOOOM

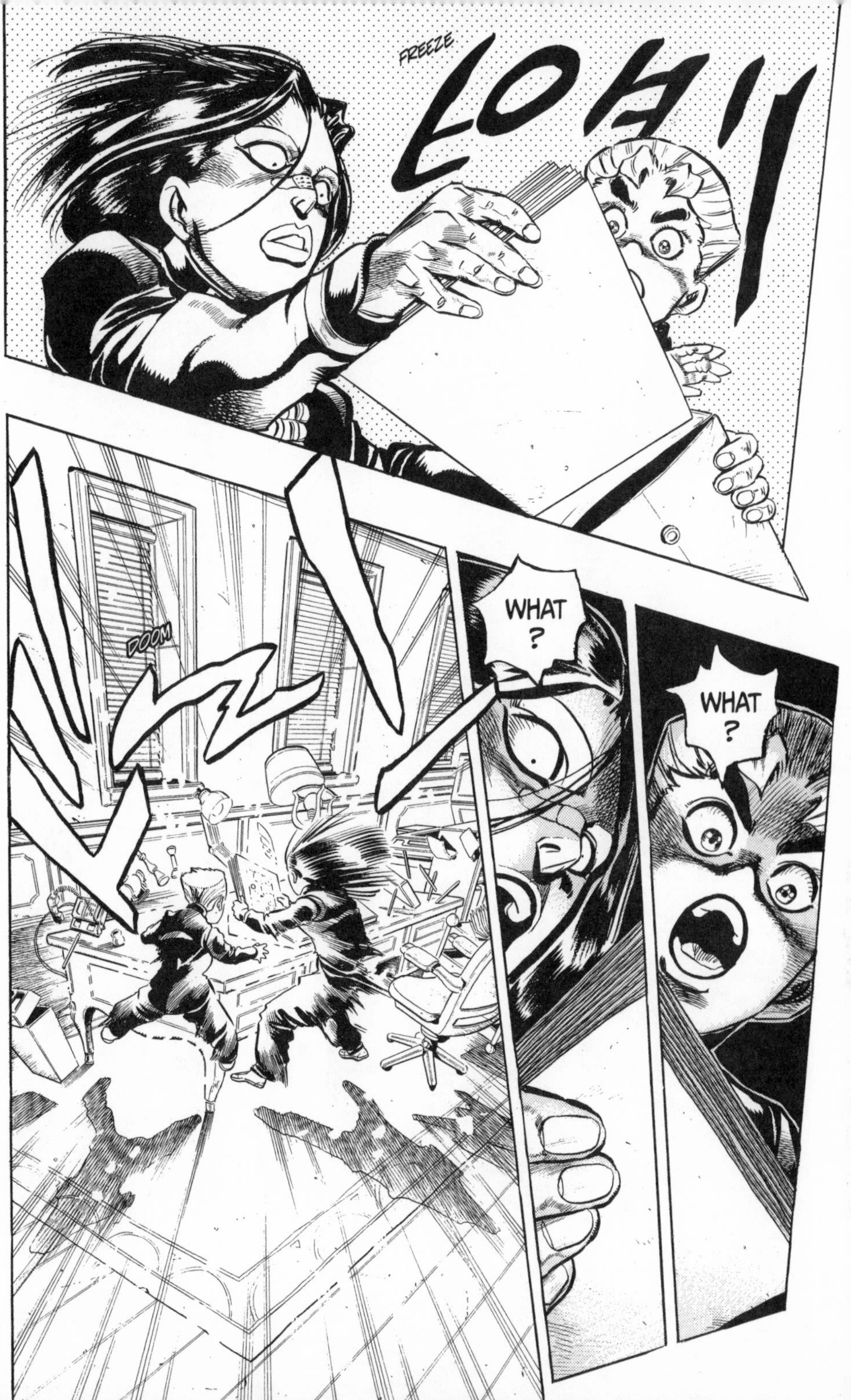
FREEZE
WHAT ?
WHAT ?
DOOM

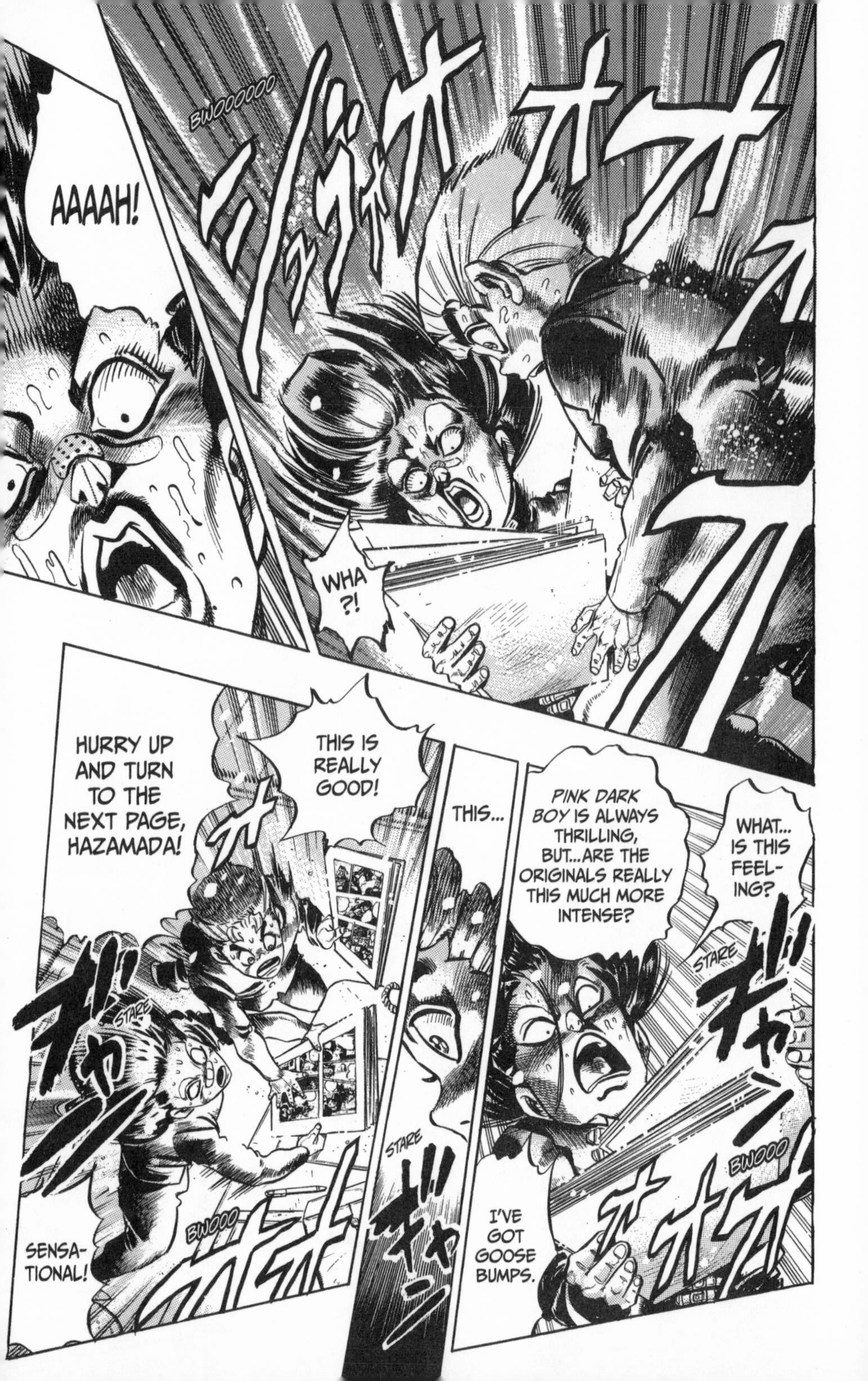
BWOOOOOOO
WHA ?!
AAAAH!
WHAT... IS THIS FEEL-ING?
STARE
PINK DARK BOY IS ALWAYS THRILLING, BUT...ARE THE ORIGINALS REALLY THIS MUCH MORE INTENSE?
BWOOO
I'VE GOT GOOSE BUMPS.
THIS...
STARE
THIS IS REALLY GOOD!
HURRY UP AND TURN TO THE NEXT PAGE, HAZAMADA!
STARE
BWOOO
SENSA-TIONAL!

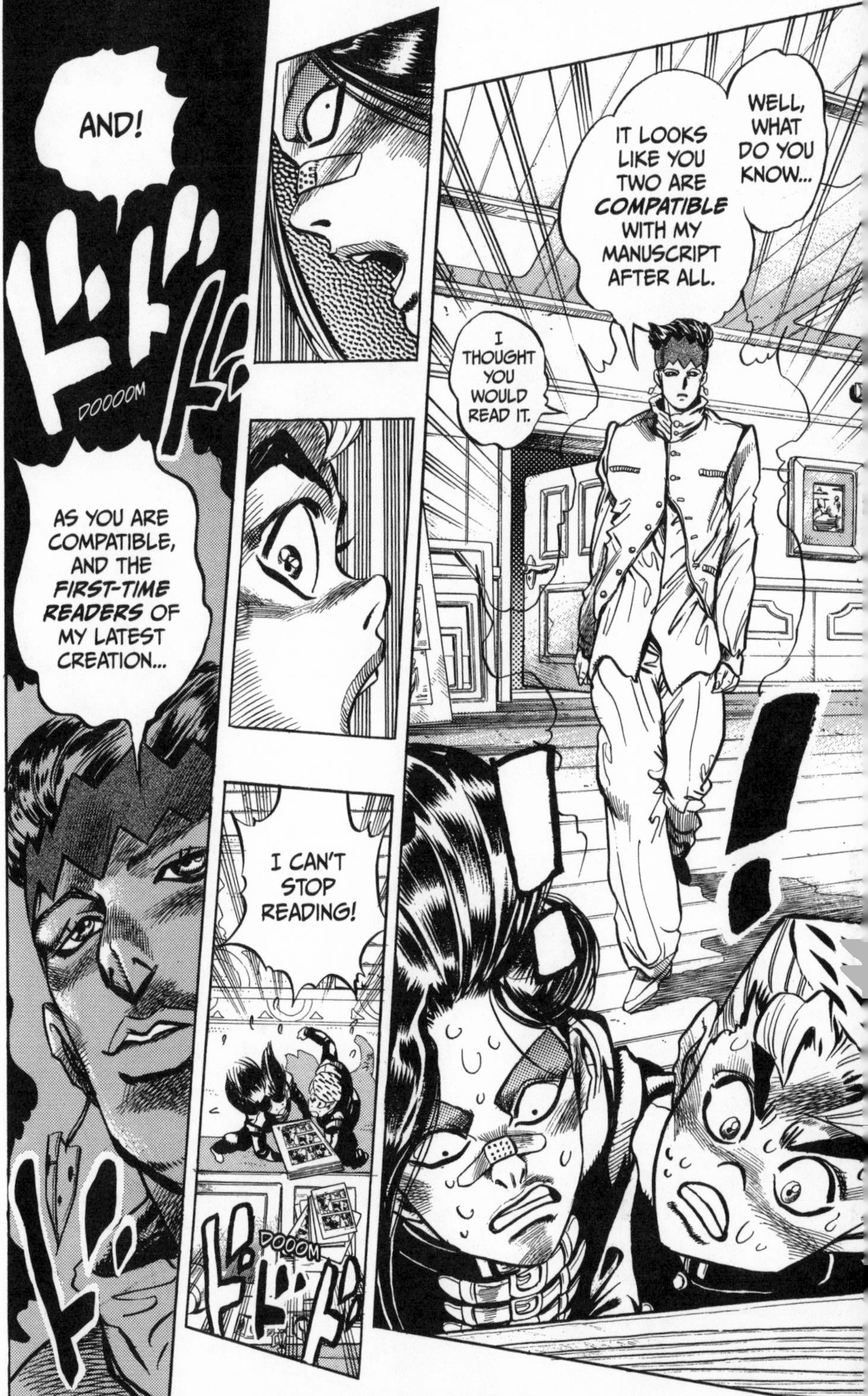
WELL, WHAT DO YOU KNOW...
IT LOOKS LIKE YOU TWO ARE COMPATIBLE WITH MY MANUSCRIPT AFTER ALL.
I THOUGHT YOU WOULD READ IT.
I CAN'T STOP READING!
DOOOM
AND!
DOOOOM
AS YOU ARE COMPATIBLE, AND THE FIRST-TIME READERS OF MY LATEST CREATION...

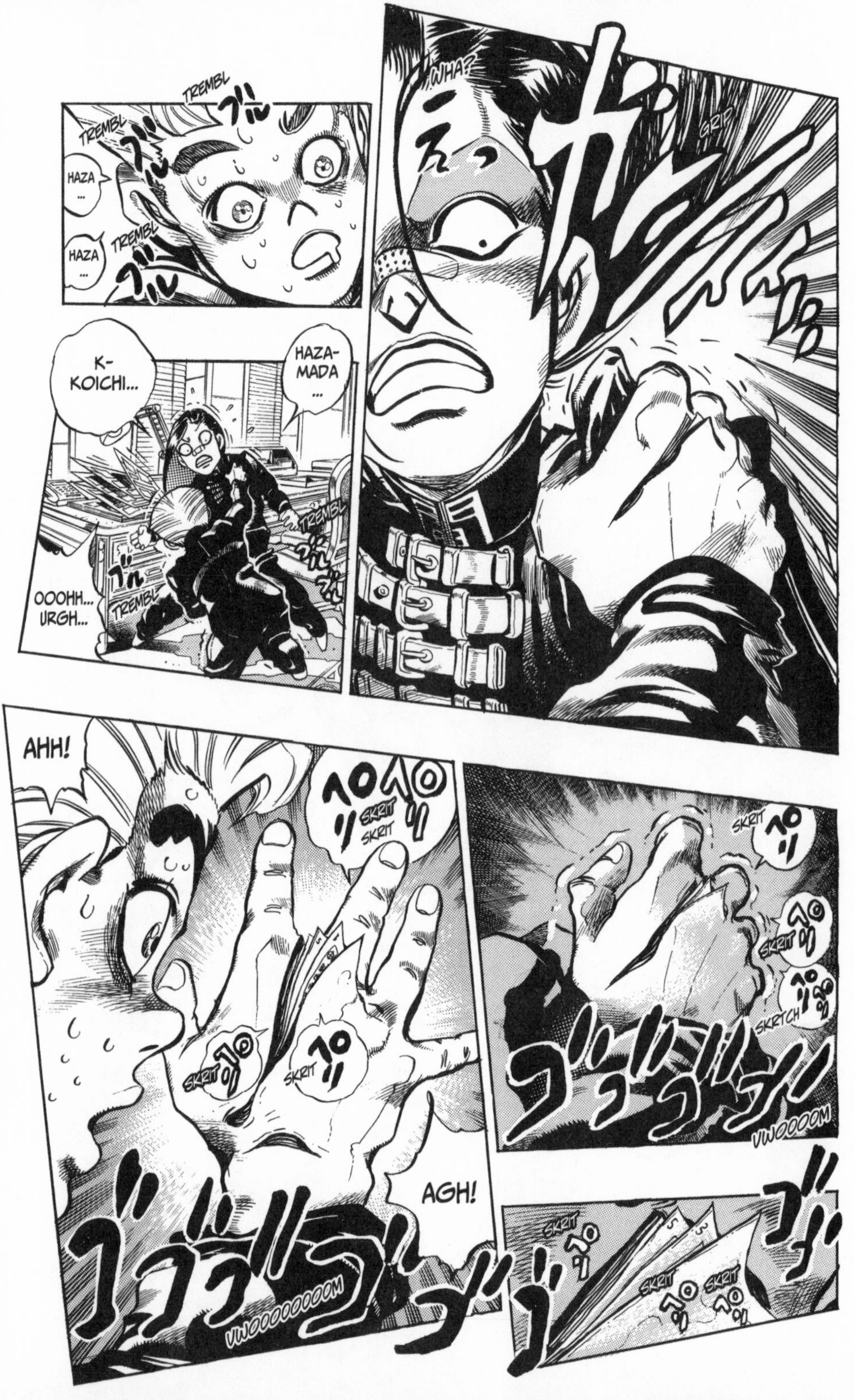
WHA?
GRIP
TREMBL
TREMBL
HAZA...
TREMBL
HAZA...
HAZAMADA...
K-KOICHI...
TREMBL
TREMBL
OOOHH... URGH...
SKRIT
SKRIT
SKRTCH
VWOOOOM
SKRIT
SKRIT
SKRIT
AHH!
SKRIT SKRIT
SKRIT
SKRIT
AGH!
VWOOOOOOOOM

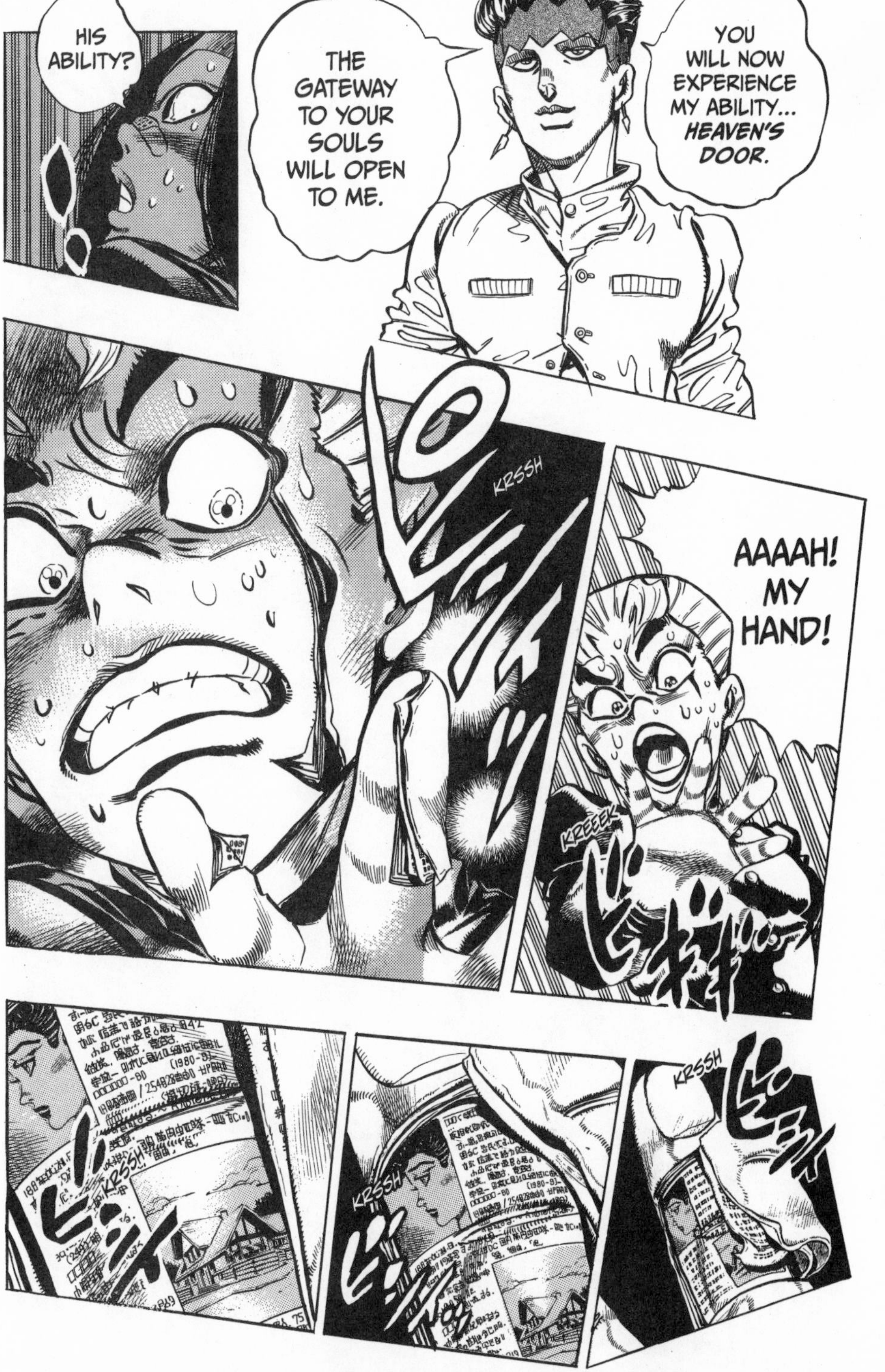
YOU WILL NOW EXPERIENCE MY ABILITY... HEAVEN'S DOOR.
THE GATEWAY TO YOUR SOULS WILL OPEN TO ME.
HIS ABILITY?
AAAAH! MY HAND!
KREEEK
KRSSH
KRSSH
KRSSH
KRSSH

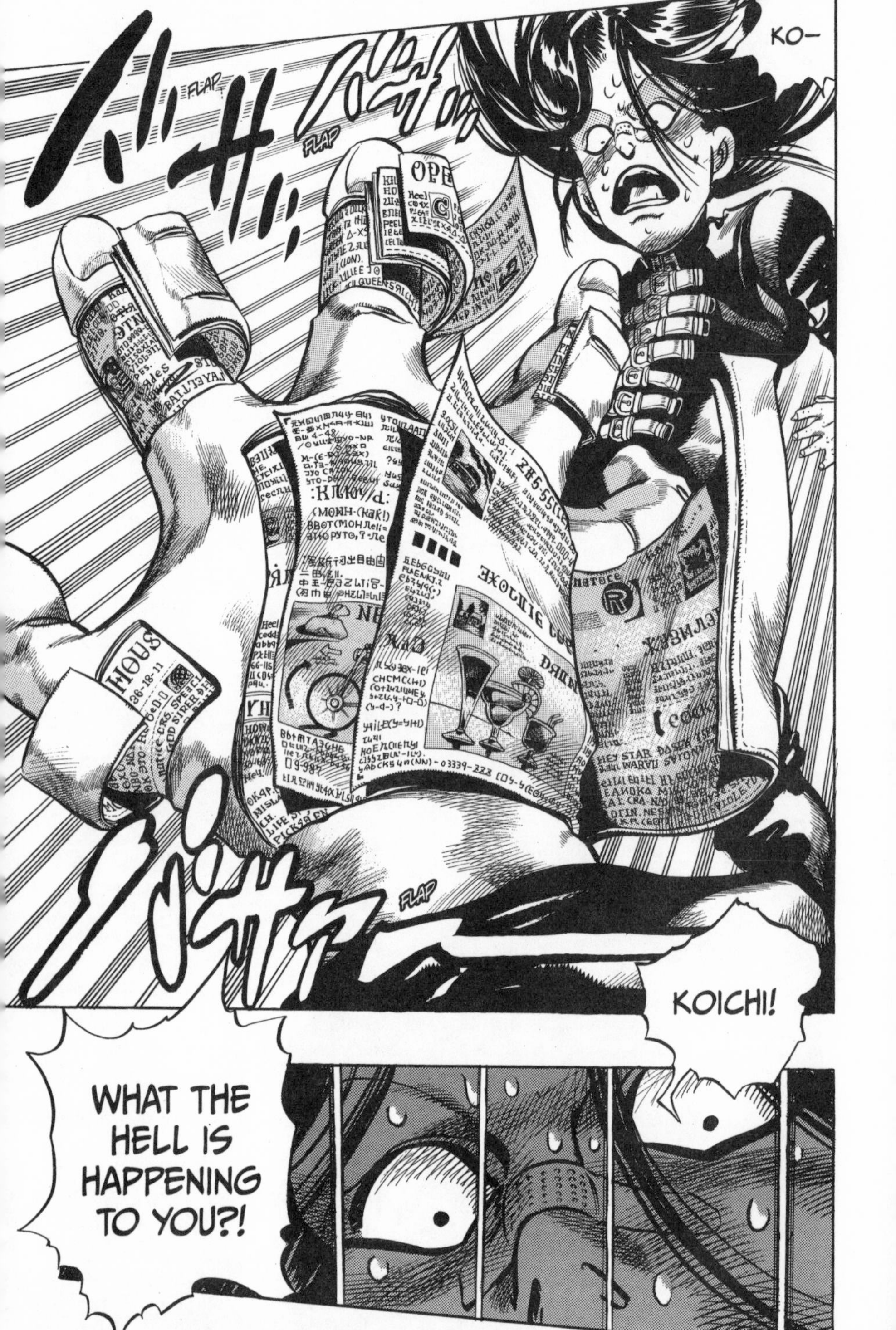
KO-
FLAP
FLAP
FLAP
KOICHI!
WHAT THE HELL IS HAPPENING TO YOU?!

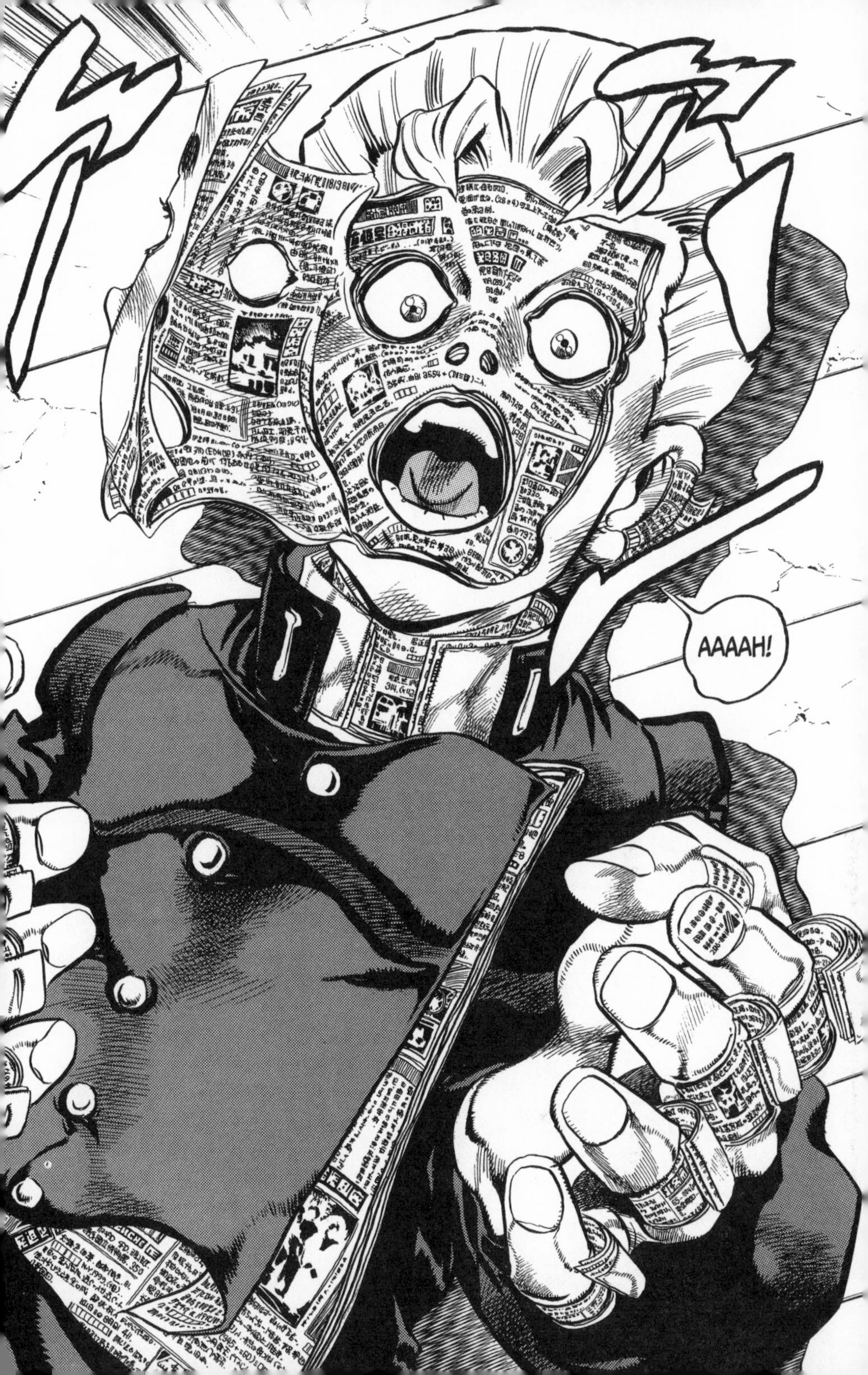
AAAAH!

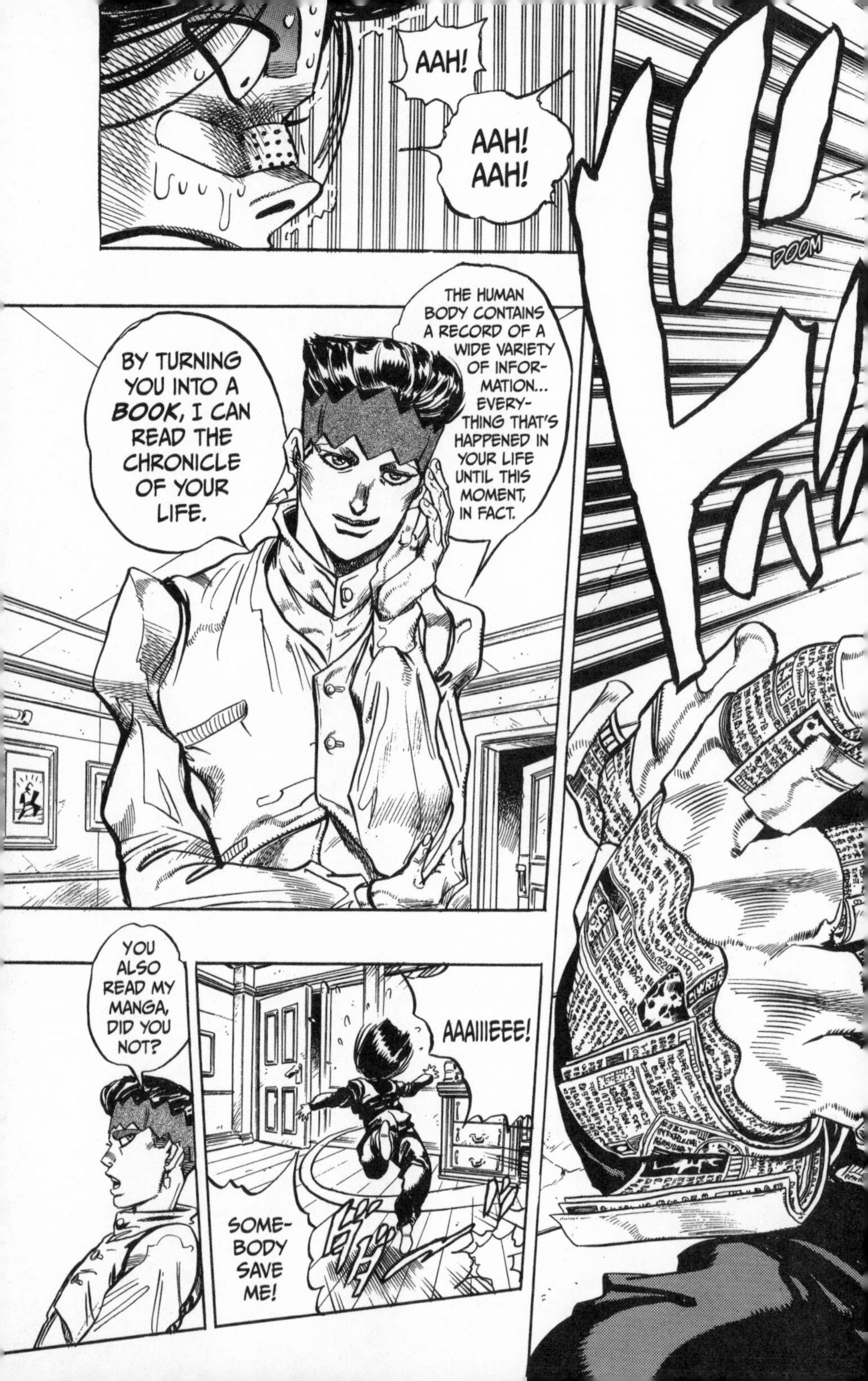
DOOM
AAH!
AAH! AAH!
THE HUMAN BODY CONTAINS A RECORD OF A WIDE VARIETY OF INFORMATION... EVERYTHING THAT'S HAPPENED IN YOUR LIFE UNTIL THIS MOMENT, IN FACT.
BY TURNING YOU INTO A *BOOK*, I CAN READ THE CHRONICLE OF YOUR LIFE.
AAAIIIEEE!
SOMEBODY SAVE ME!
YOU ALSO READ MY MANGA, DID YOU NOT?

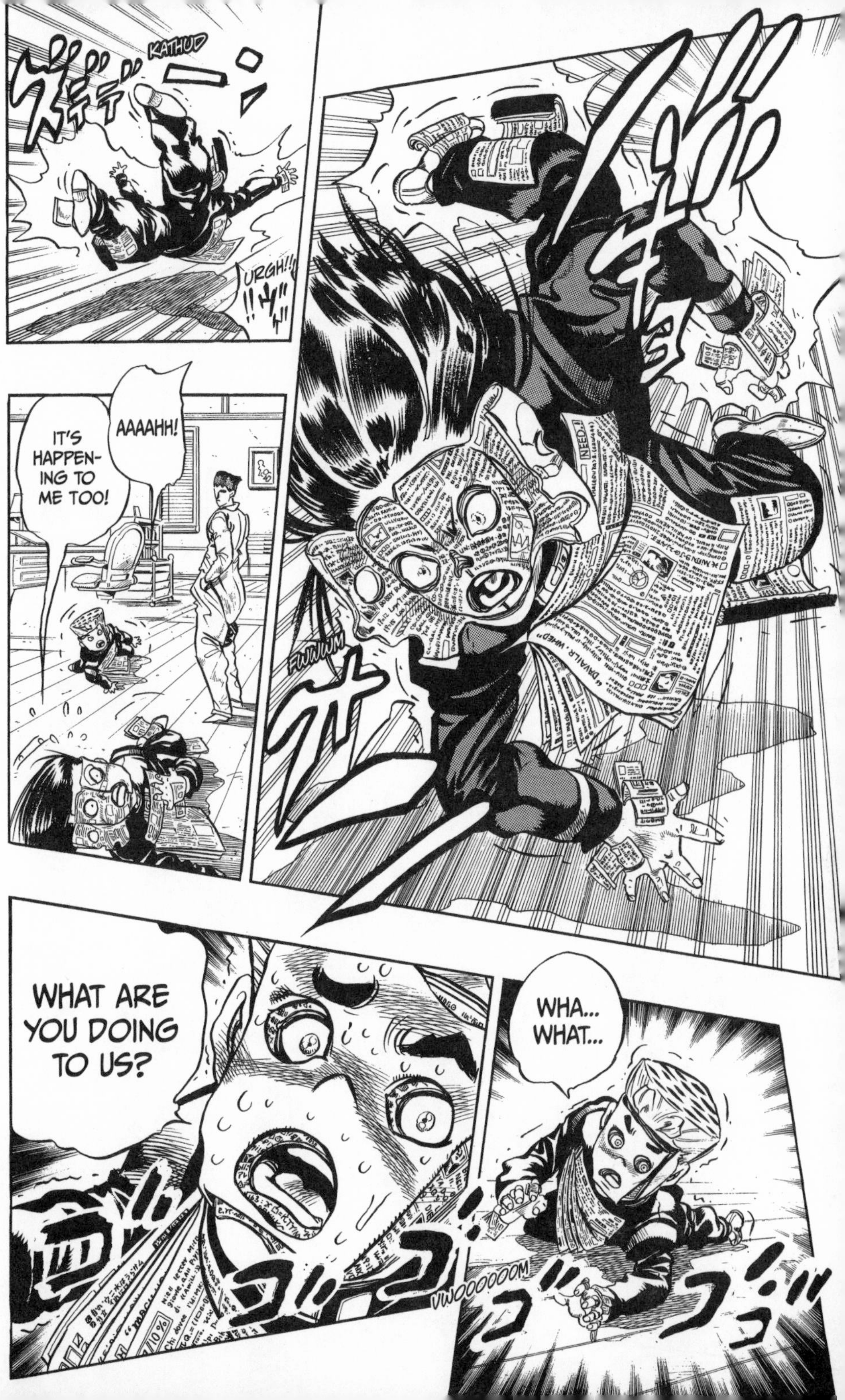
FWUUUM
KATHUD
URGH!!
AAAAHH!
IT'S HAPPENING TO ME TOO!
WHA... WHAT...
VWOOOOOOM
WHAT ARE YOU DOING TO US?

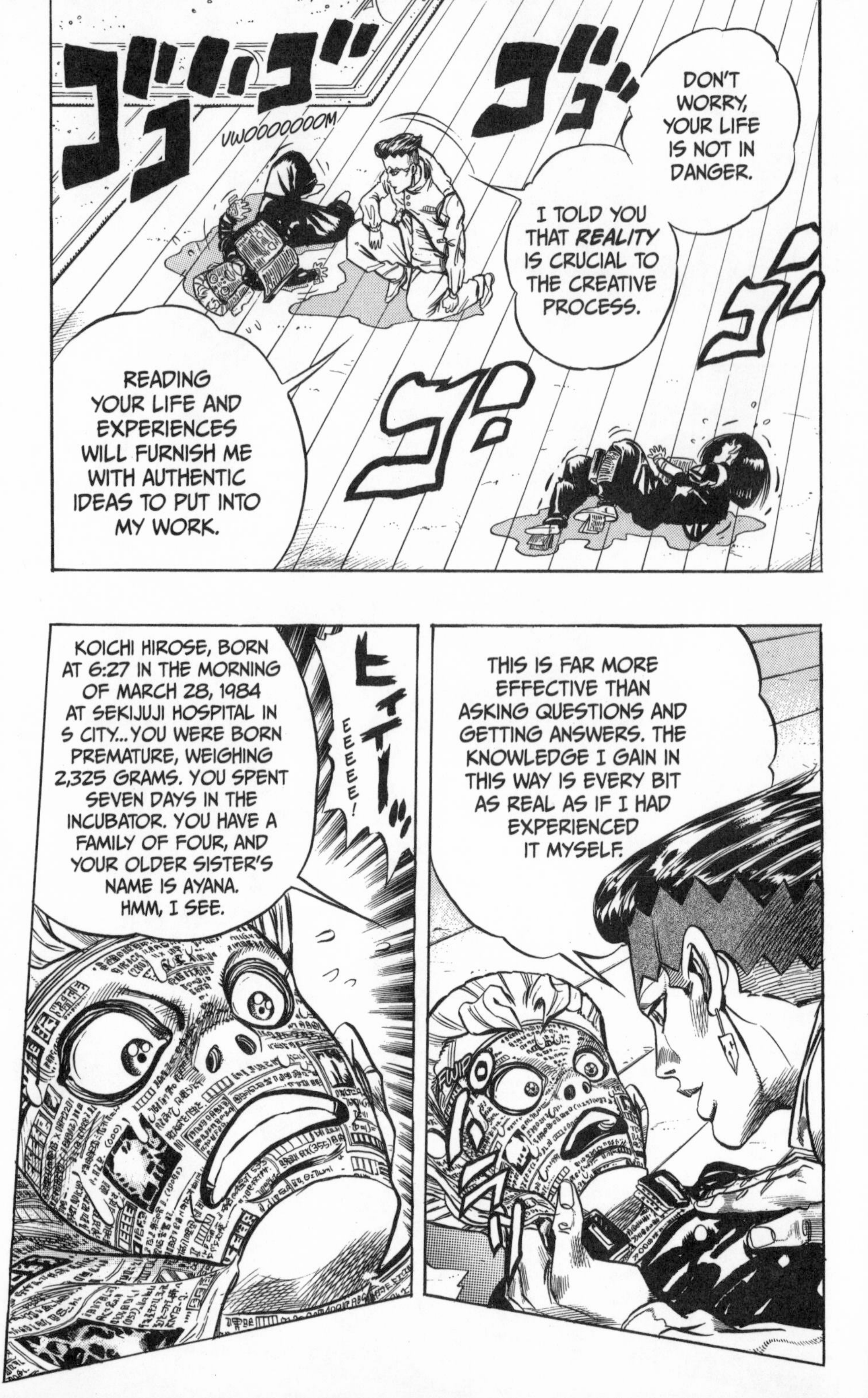
DON'T WORRY, YOUR LIFE IS NOT IN DANGER.
I TOLD YOU THAT *REALITY* IS CRUCIAL TO THE CREATIVE PROCESS.
ゴゴ
ゴゴゴ
VWOOOOOOOM
READING YOUR LIFE AND EXPERIENCES WILL FURNISH ME WITH AUTHENTIC IDEAS TO PUT INTO MY WORK.
THIS IS FAR MORE EFFECTIVE THAN ASKING QUESTIONS AND GETTING ANSWERS. THE KNOWLEDGE I GAIN IN THIS WAY IS EVERY BIT AS REAL AS IF I HAD EXPERIENCED IT MYSELF.
ヒィィィ
EEEEE!
KOICHI HIROSE, BORN AT 6:27 IN THE MORNING OF MARCH 28, 1984 AT SEKIJUJI HOSPITAL IN S CITY...YOU WERE BORN PREMATURE, WEIGHING 2,325 GRAMS. YOU SPENT SEVEN DAYS IN THE INCUBATOR. YOU HAVE A FAMILY OF FOUR, AND YOUR OLDER SISTER'S NAME IS AYANA. HMM, I SEE.

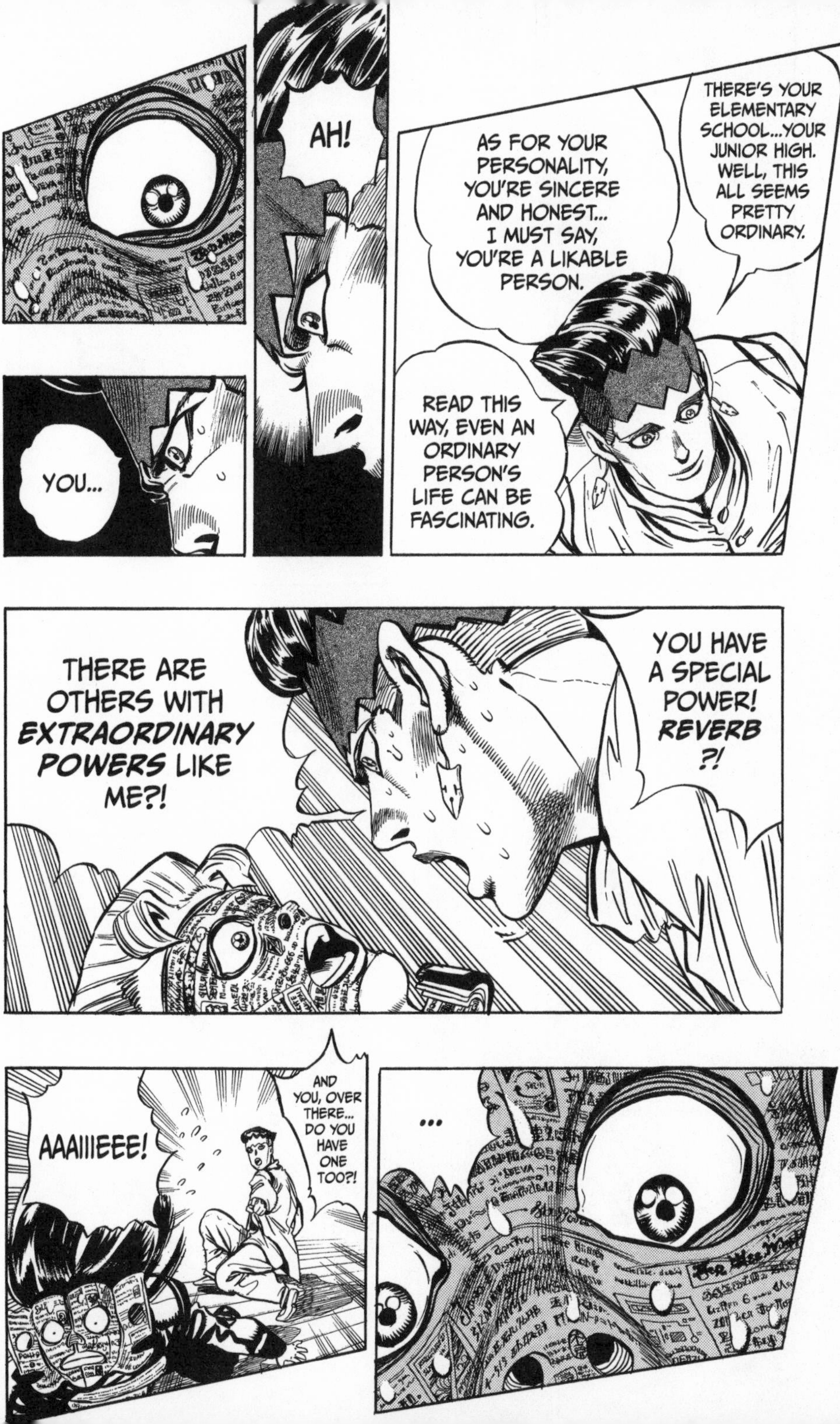
THERE'S YOUR ELEMENTARY SCHOOL...YOUR JUNIOR HIGH. WELL, THIS ALL SEEMS PRETTY ORDINARY.
AS FOR YOUR PERSONALITY, YOU'RE SINCERE AND HONEST... I MUST SAY, YOU'RE A LIKABLE PERSON.
READ THIS WAY, EVEN AN ORDINARY PERSON'S LIFE CAN BE FASCINATING.
AH!
YOU...
YOU HAVE A SPECIAL POWER! REVERB ?!
THERE ARE OTHERS WITH EXTRAORDINARY POWERS LIKE ME?!
...
AND YOU, OVER THERE... DO YOU HAVE ONE TOO?!
AAAIIIEEE!

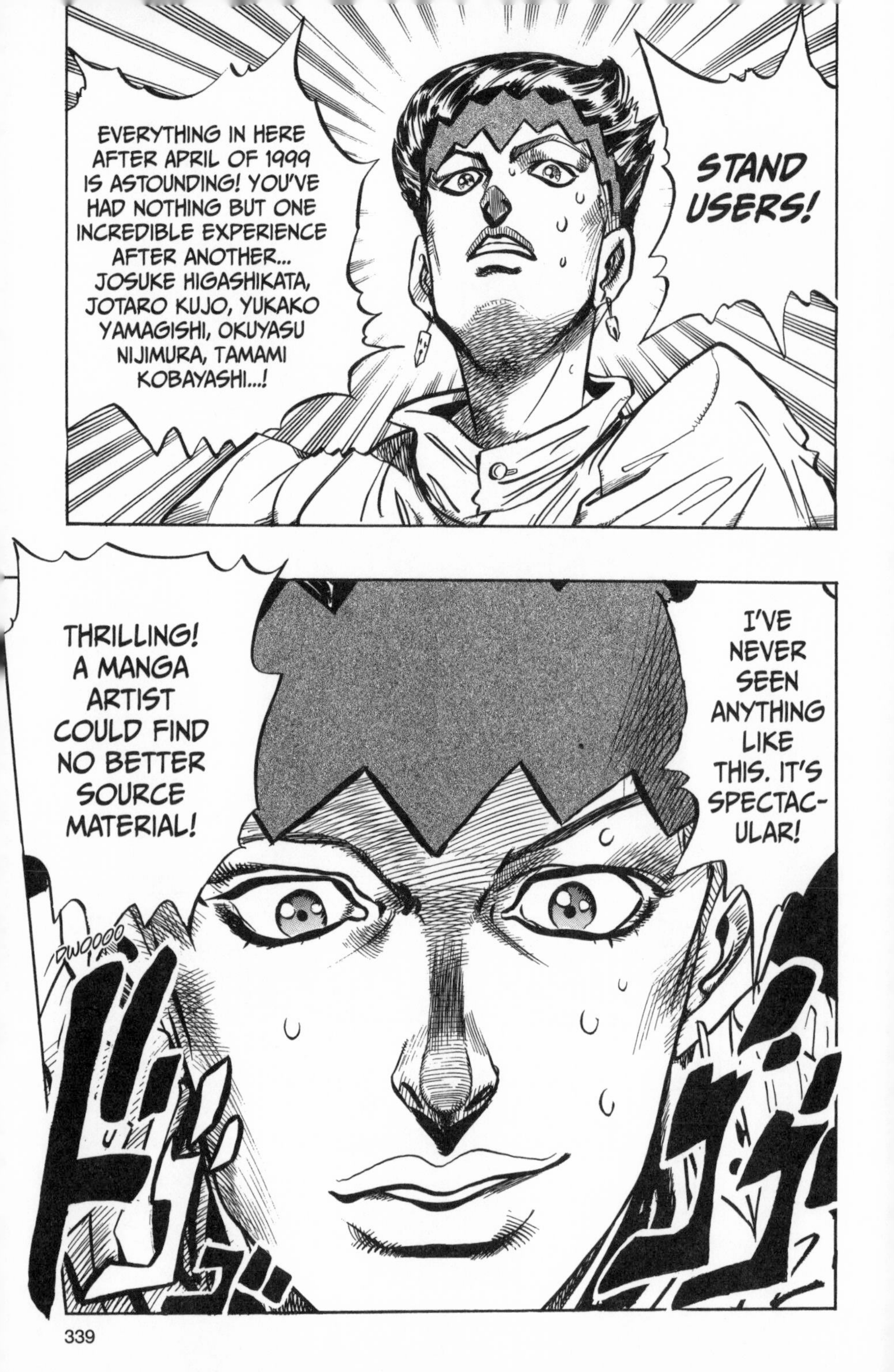
EVERYTHING IN HERE AFTER APRIL OF 1999 IS ASTOUNDING! YOU'VE HAD NOTHING BUT ONE INCREDIBLE EXPERIENCE AFTER ANOTHER... JOSUKE HIGASHIKATA, JOTARO KUJO, YUKAKO YAMAGISHI, OKUYASU NIJIMURA, TAMAMI KOBAYASHI...!
STAND USERS!
I'VE NEVER SEEN ANYTHING LIKE THIS. IT'S SPECTAC-ULAR!
THRILLING! A MANGA ARTIST COULD FIND NO BETTER SOURCE MATERIAL!
DWOOOO

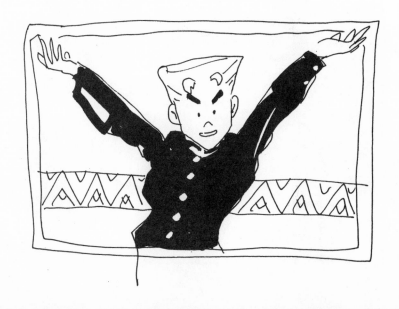

CHAPTER 55

LET'S GO TO THE MANGA ARTIST'S HOUSE, PART 3

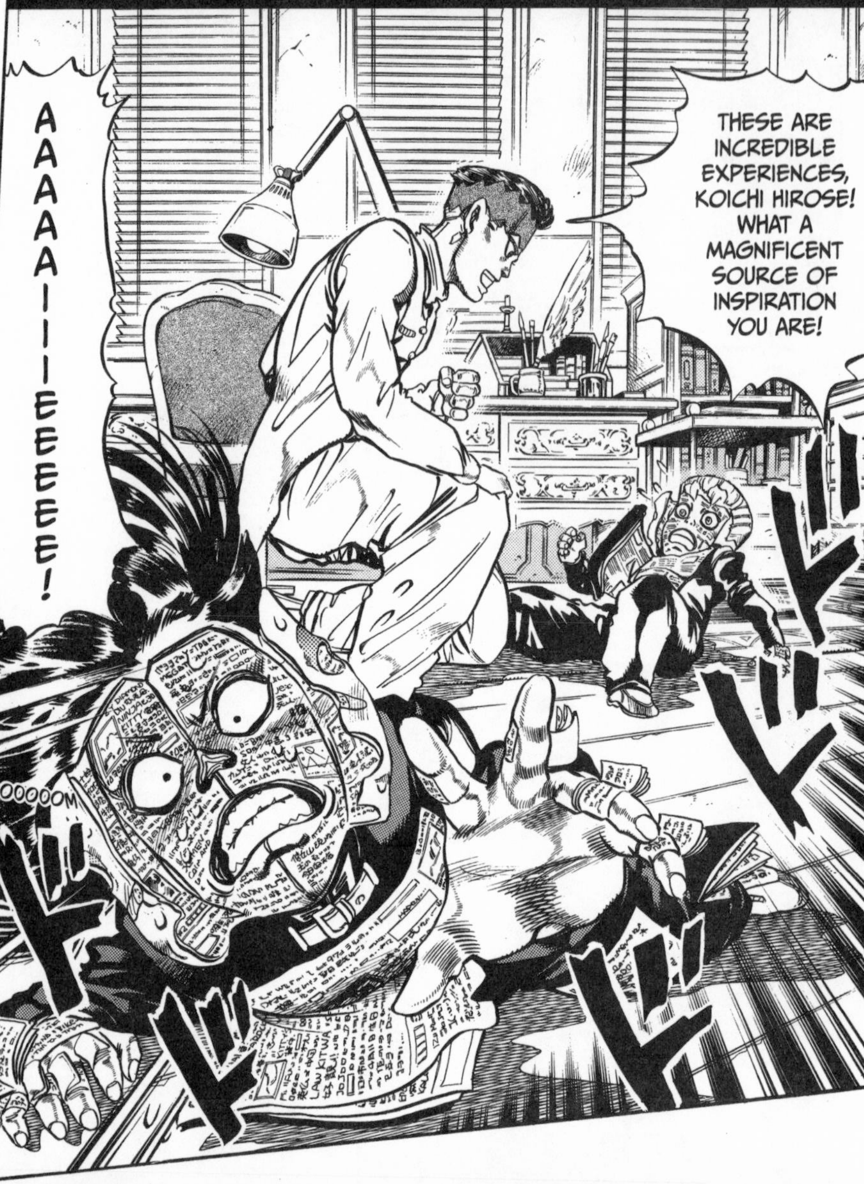
THESE ARE INCREDIBLE EXPERIENCES, KOICHI HIROSE! WHAT A MAGNIFICENT SOURCE OF INSPIRATION YOU ARE!
AAAAAAIIIIEEEEEE!
DOOOOOM

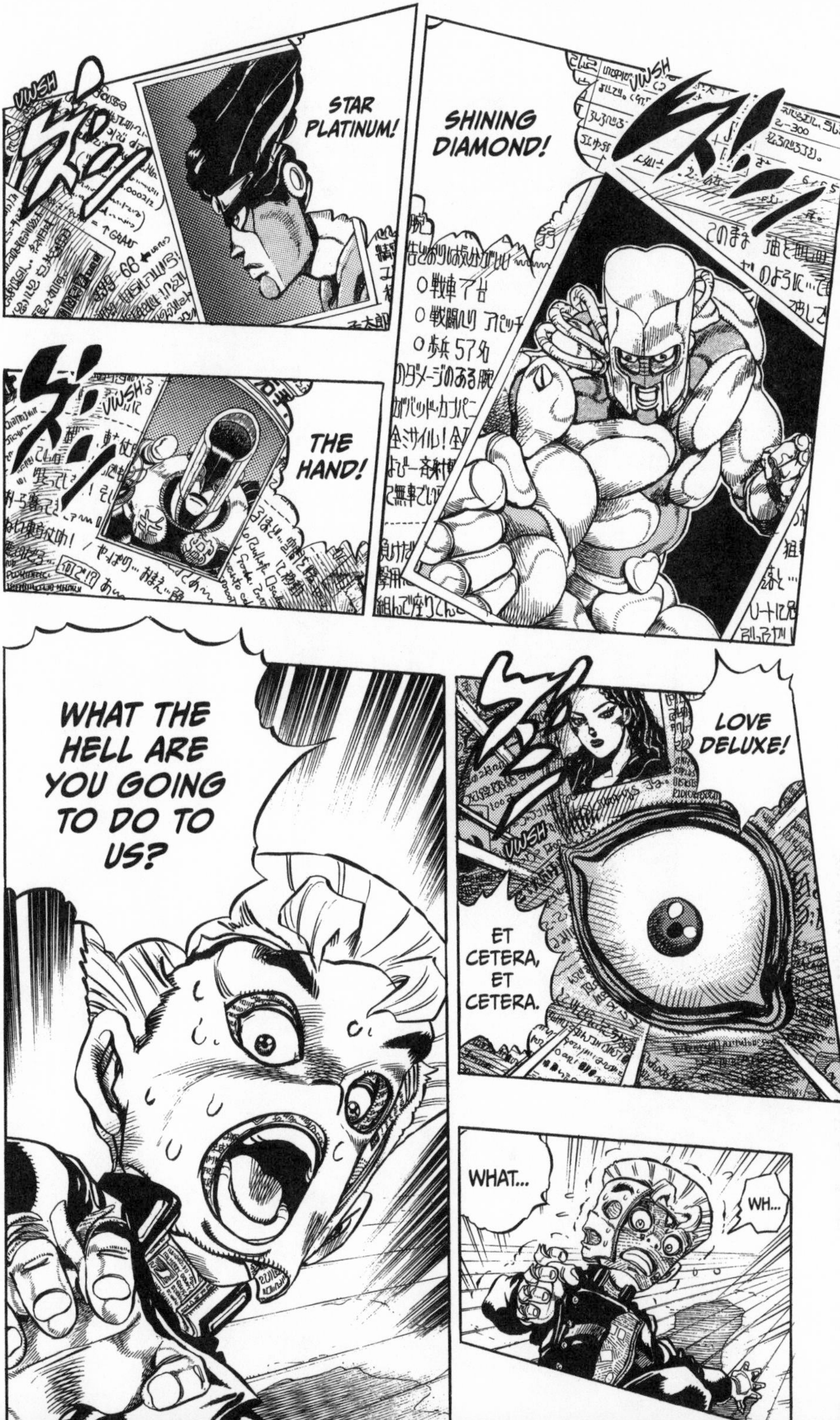
VWSH
SHINING DIAMOND!
VWSH
STAR PLATINUM!
VWSH
THE HAND!
LOVE DELUXE!
VWSH
ET CETERA, ET CETERA.
WHAT...
WH...
WHAT THE HELL ARE YOU GOING TO DO TO US?

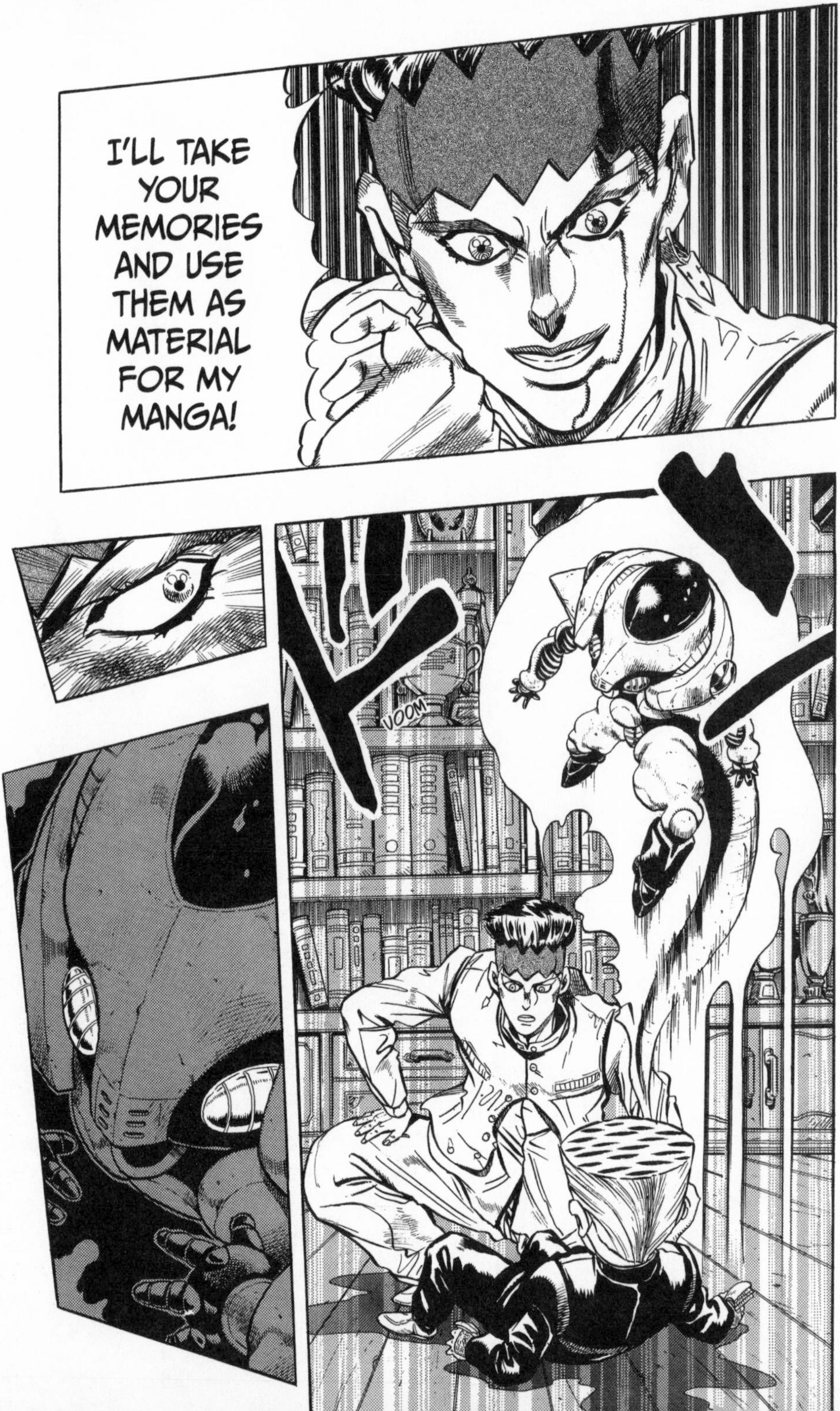
I'LL TAKE YOUR MEMORIES AND USE THEM AS MATERIAL FOR MY MANGA!
VOOM

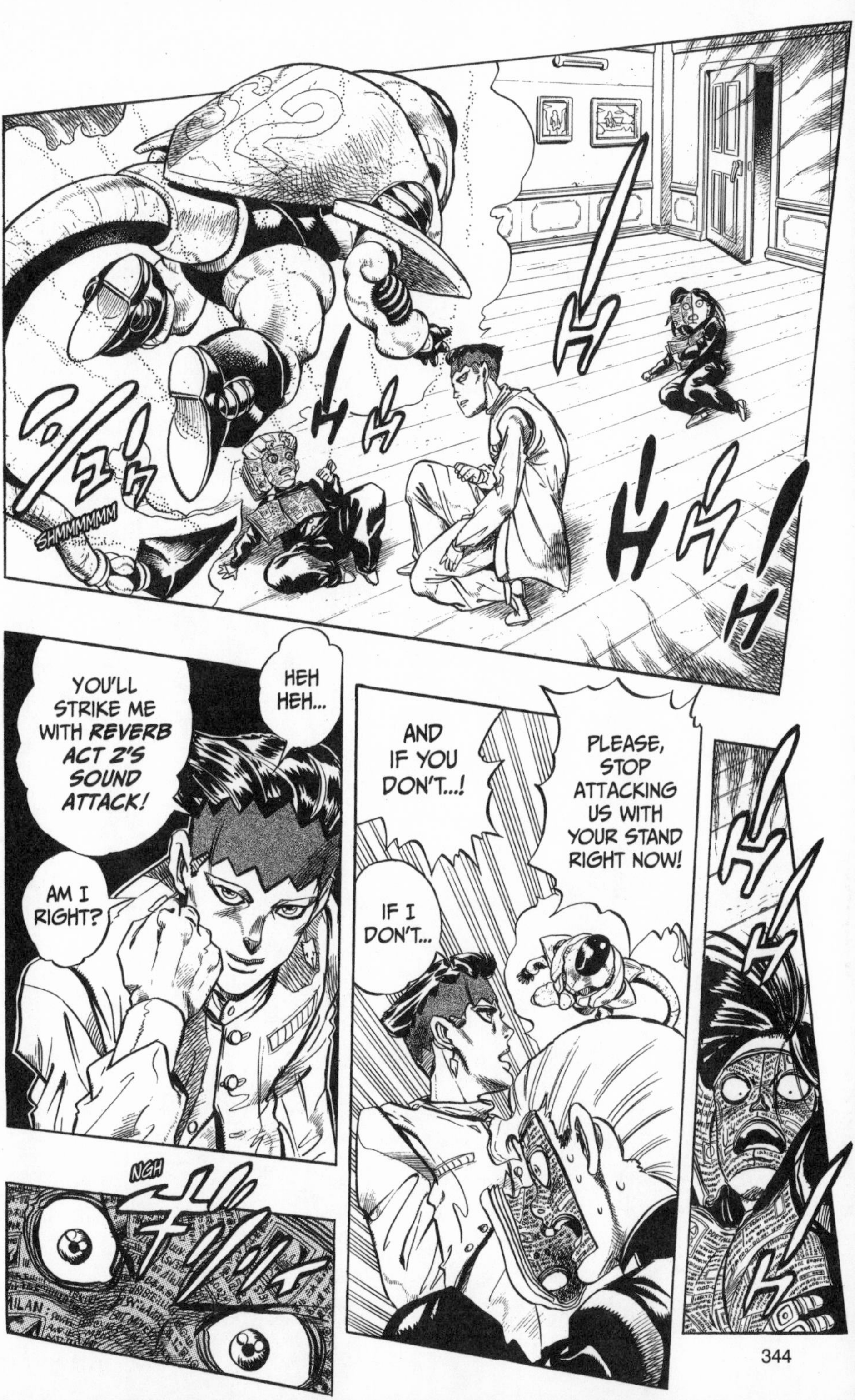
SHMMMMMM
PLEASE, STOP ATTACKING US WITH YOUR STAND RIGHT NOW!
AND IF YOU DON'T...!
IF I DON'T...
HEH HEH...
YOU'LL STRIKE ME WITH *REVERB ACT 2'S* SOUND ATTACK!
AM I RIGHT?
NGH

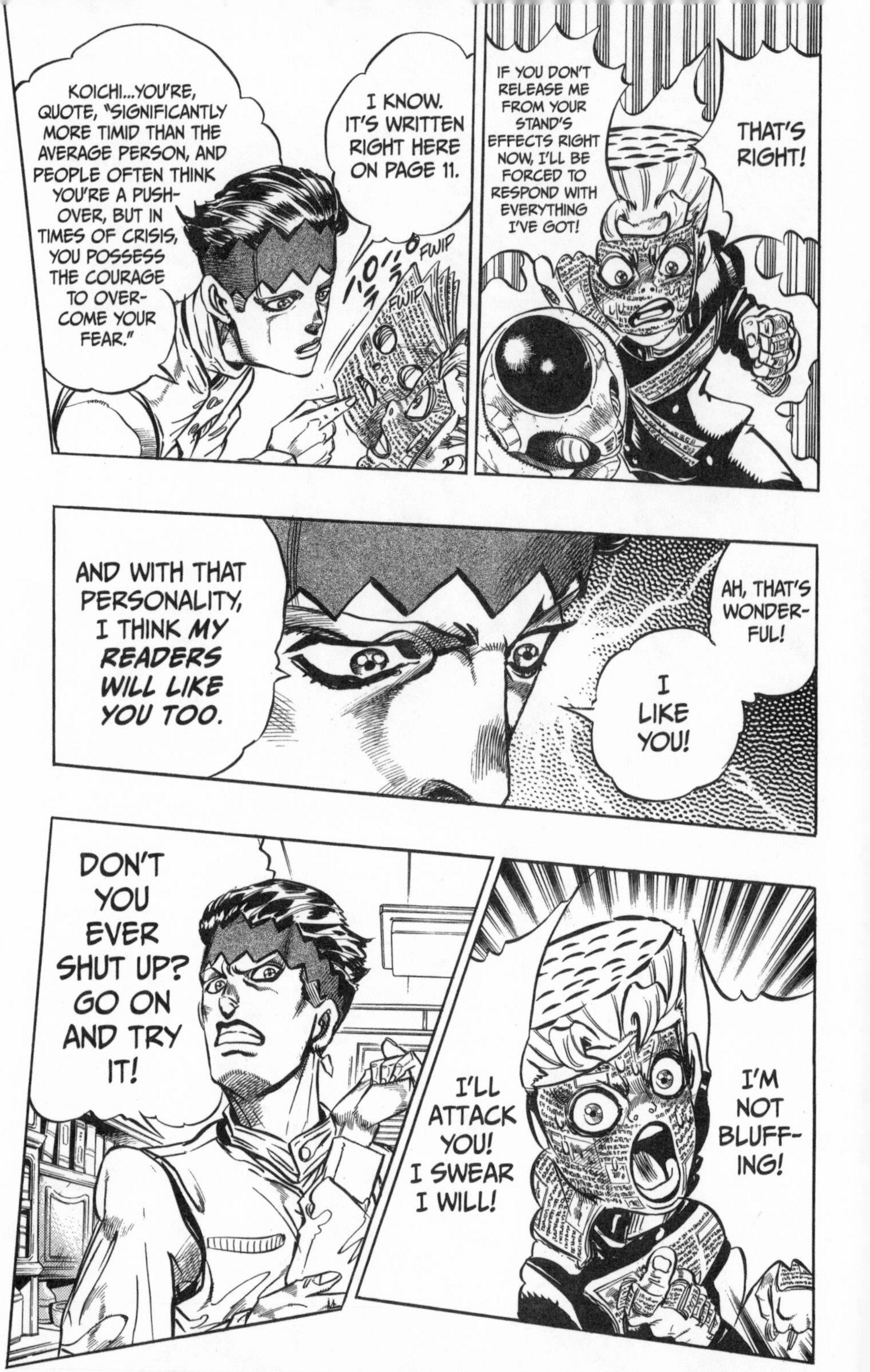
THAT'S RIGHT!
IF YOU DON'T RELEASE ME FROM YOUR STAND'S EFFECTS RIGHT NOW, I'LL BE FORCED TO RESPOND WITH EVERYTHING I'VE GOT!
I KNOW. IT'S WRITTEN RIGHT HERE ON PAGE 11.
FWIP
FWIP
KOICHI...YOU'RE, QUOTE, "SIGNIFICANTLY MORE TIMID THAN THE AVERAGE PERSON, AND PEOPLE OFTEN THINK YOU'RE A PUSH-OVER, BUT IN TIMES OF CRISIS, YOU POSSESS THE COURAGE TO OVER-COME YOUR FEAR."
AH, THAT'S WONDER-FUL!
I LIKE YOU!
AND WITH THAT PERSONALITY, I THINK *MY READERS WILL LIKE YOU TOO.*
I'M NOT BLUFF-ING!
I'LL ATTACK YOU! I SWEAR I WILL!
DON'T YOU EVER SHUT UP? GO ON AND TRY IT!

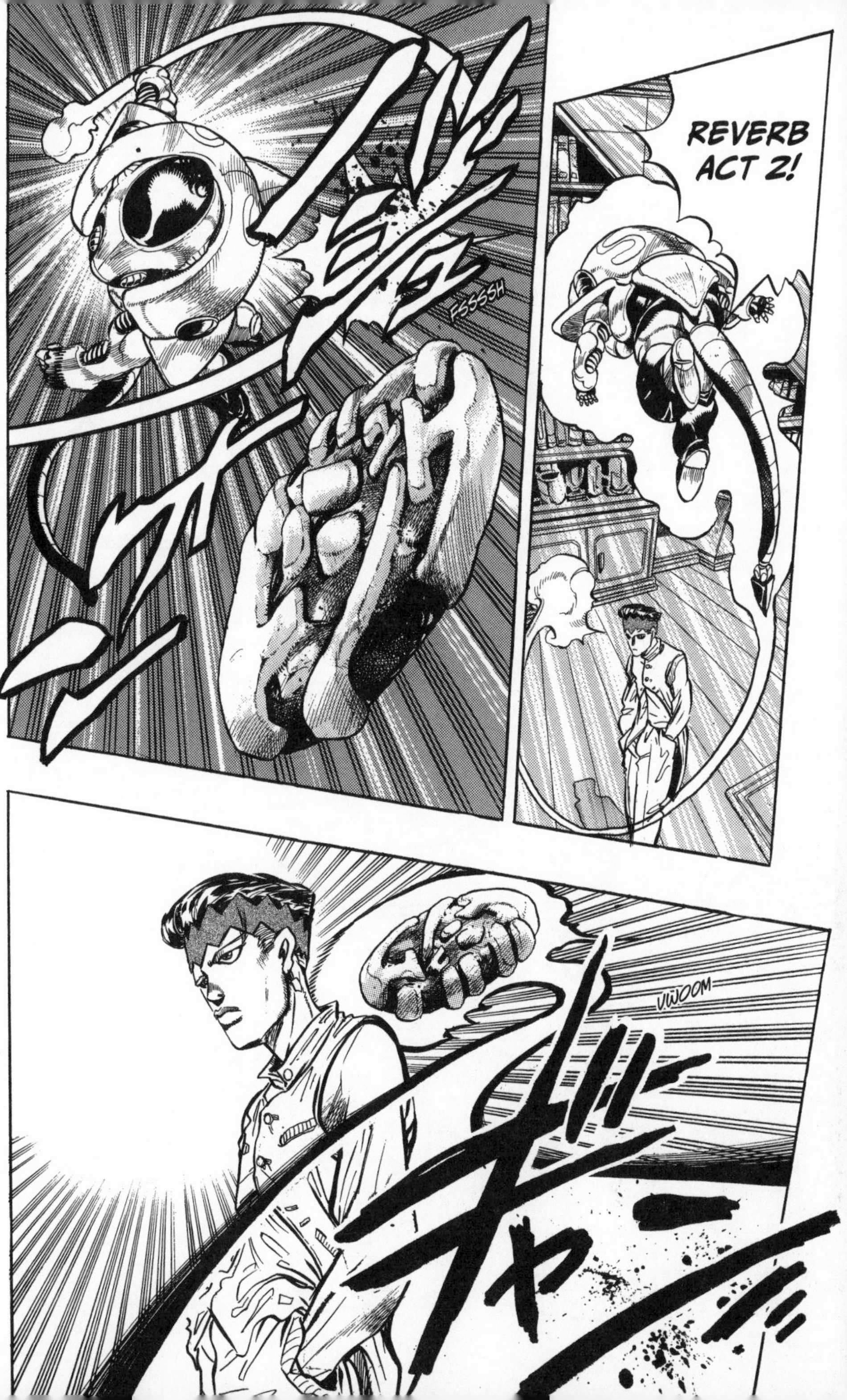
REVERB ACT 2!
FSSSSH
VWOOM

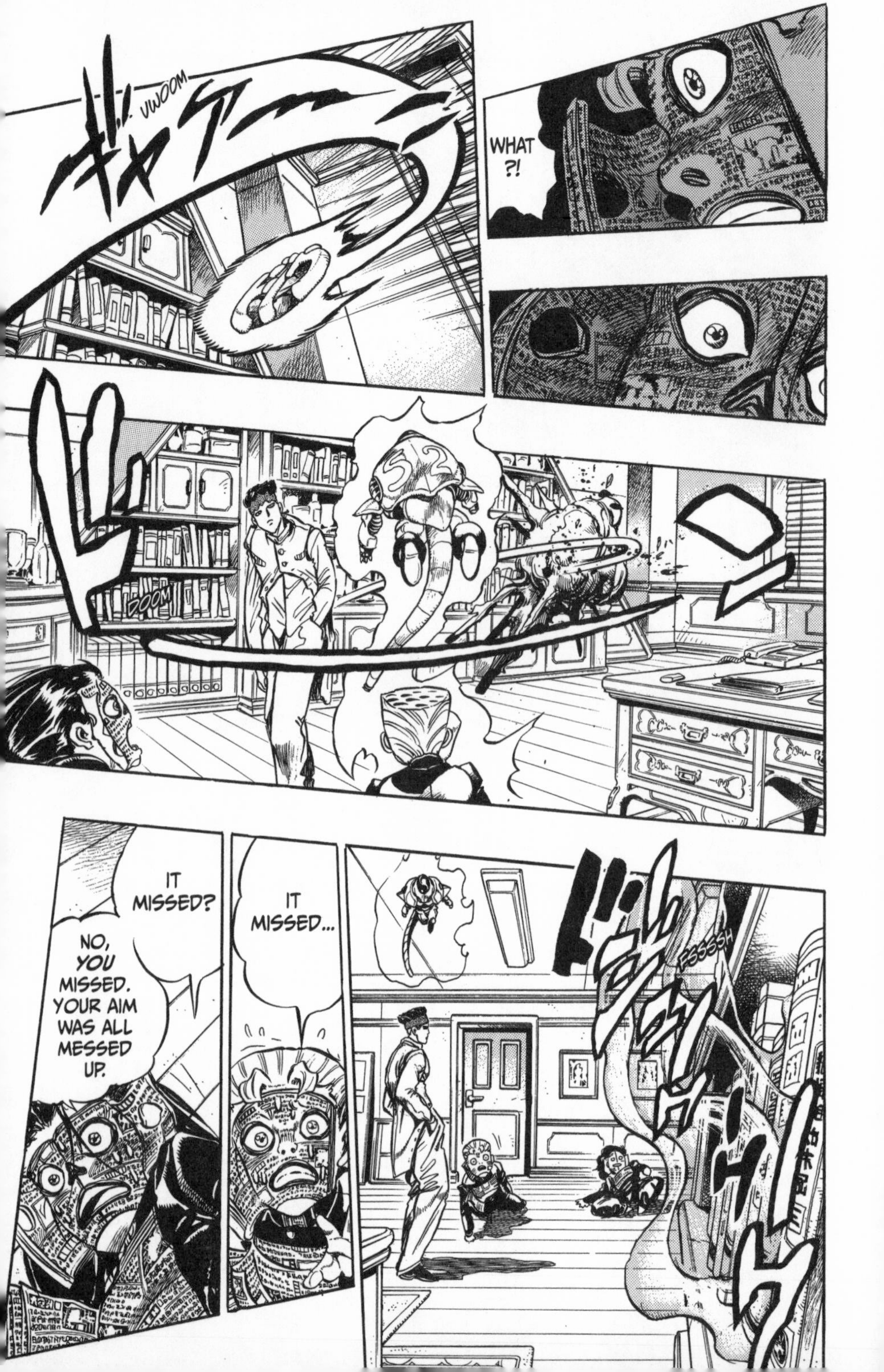
WHAT ?!
VWOOM
DOOM
PSSSSH
IT MISSED...
IT MISSED?
NO, *YOU* MISSED. YOUR AIM WAS ALL MESSED UP.

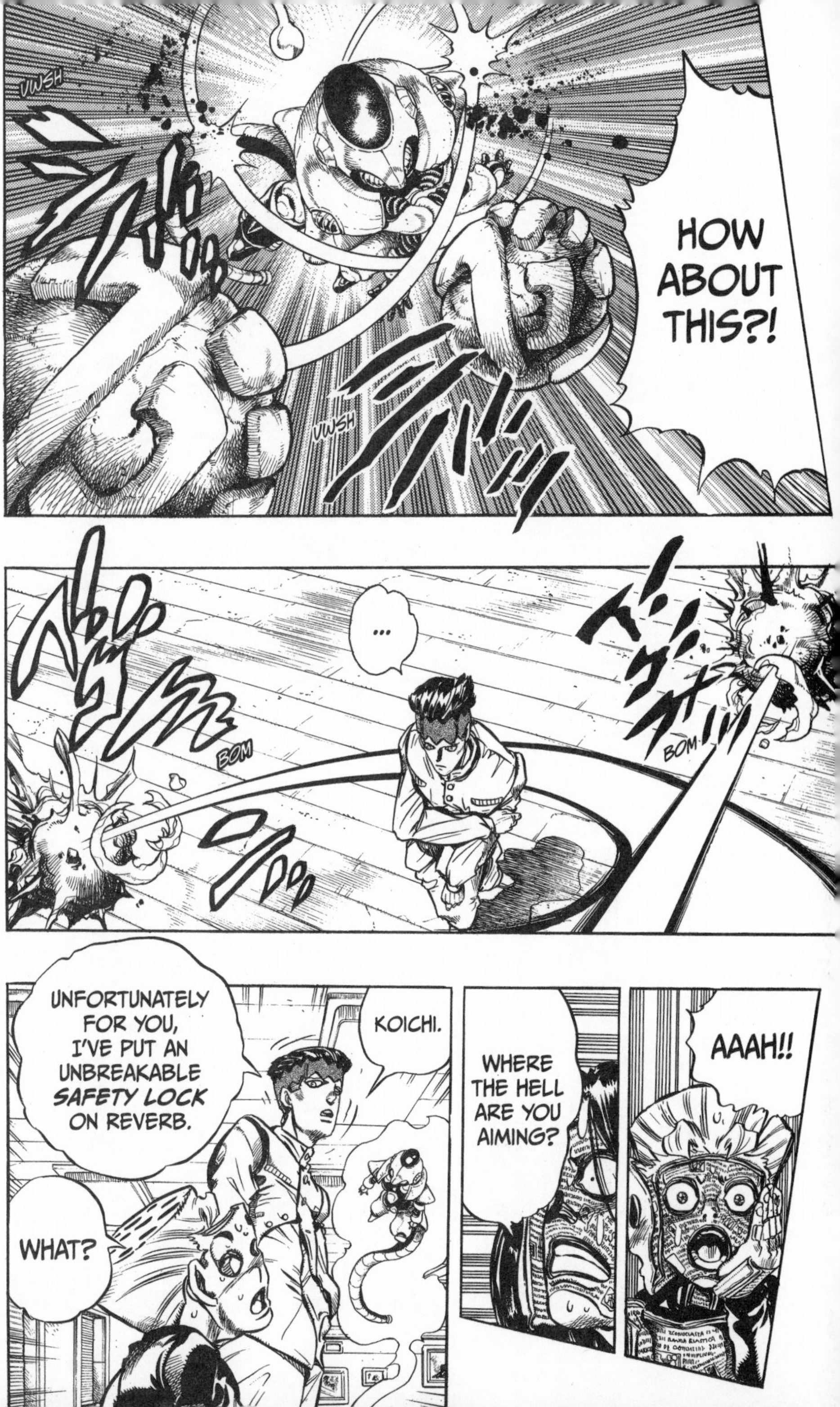

VWSH
HOW ABOUT THIS?!
VWSH
BOM
...
BOM
AAAH!!
WHERE THE HELL ARE YOU AIMING?
KOICHI.
UNFORTUNATELY FOR YOU, I'VE PUT AN UNBREAKABLE *SAFETY LOCK* ON REVERB.
WHAT?

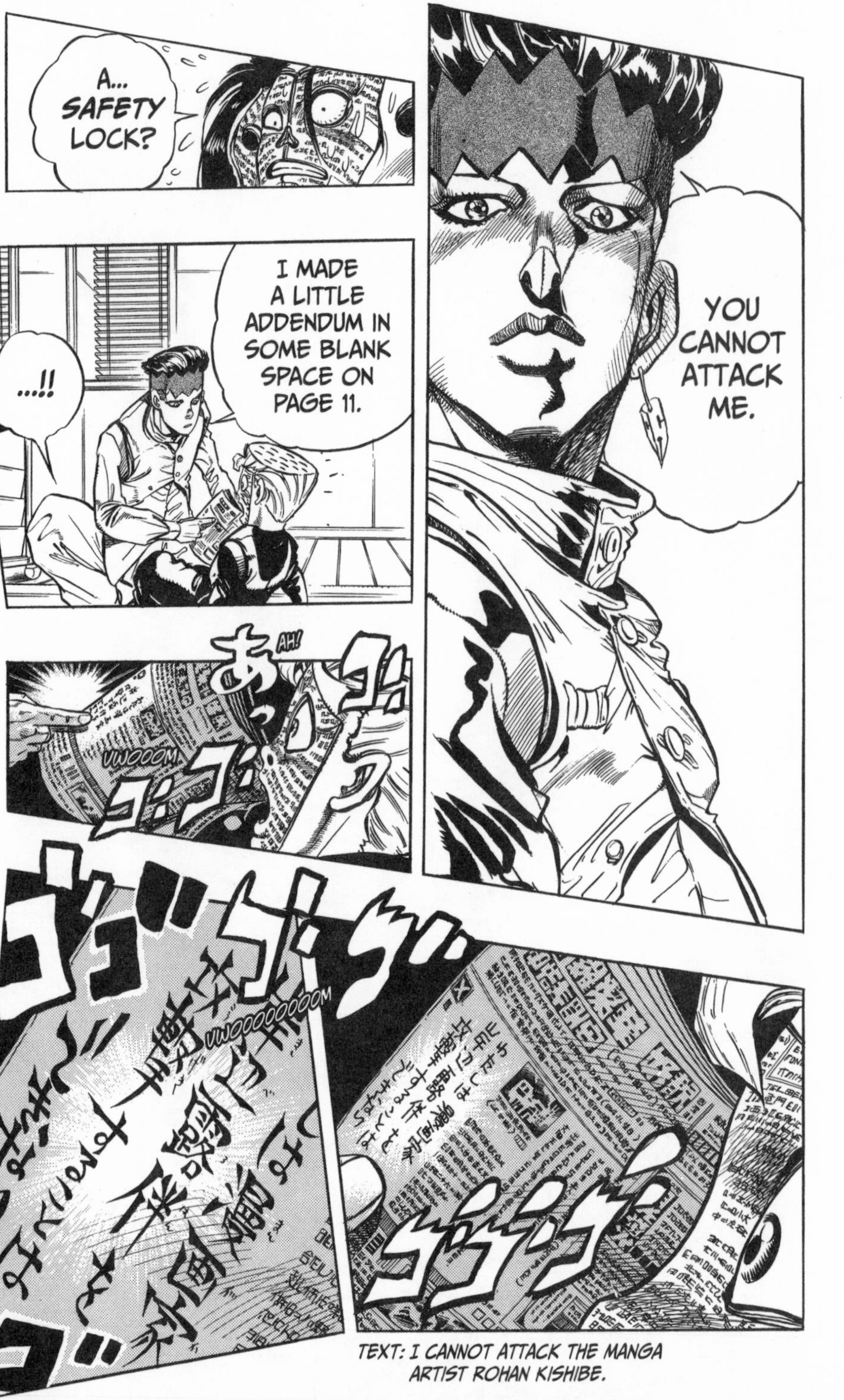
YOU CANNOT ATTACK ME.
A... SAFETY LOCK?
I MADE A LITTLE ADDENDUM IN SOME BLANK SPACE ON PAGE 11.
...!!
AH!
VWOOOM
UWOOOOOOOOOM
TEXT: I CANNOT ATTACK THE MANGA ARTIST ROHAN KISHIBE.

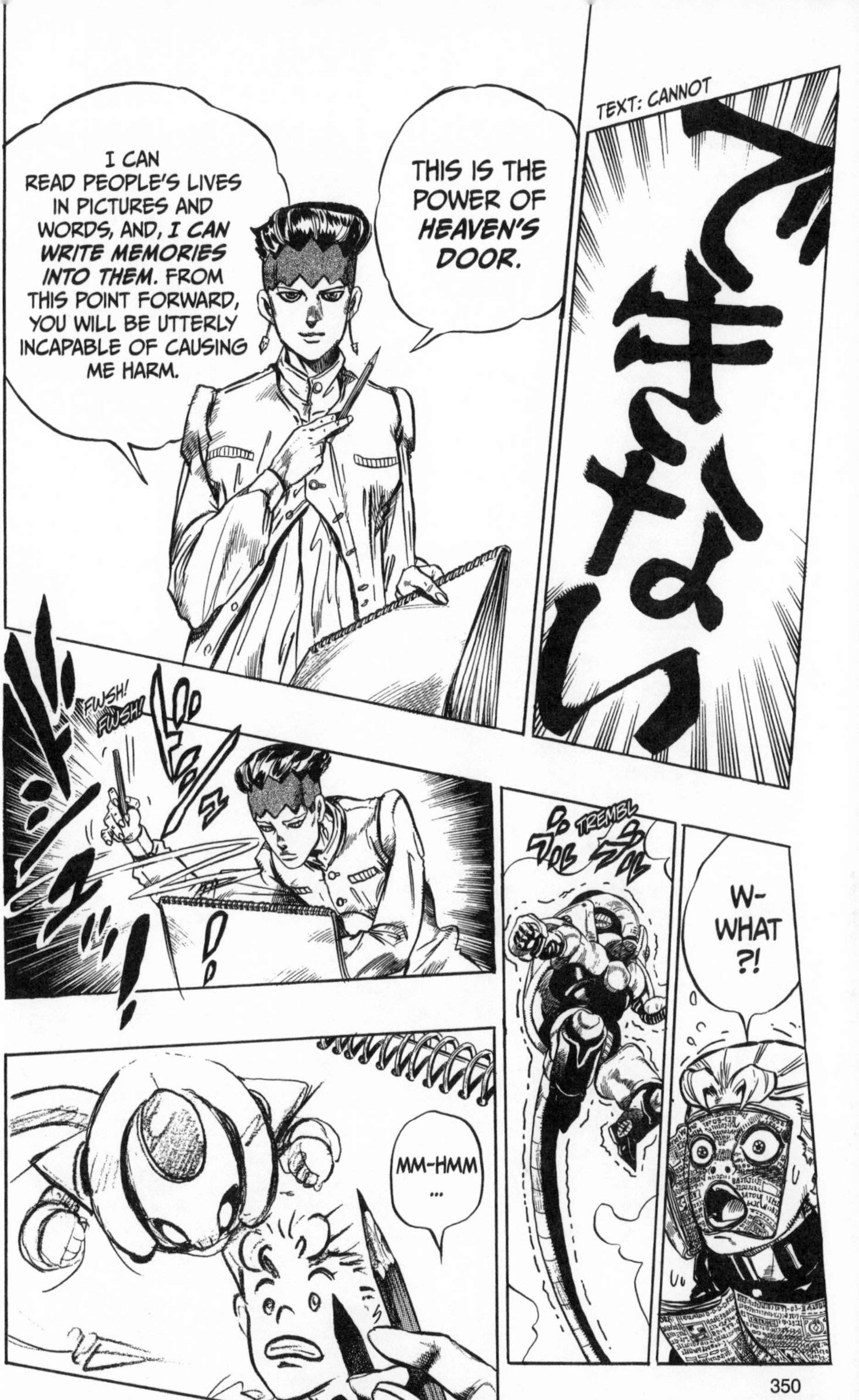

TEXT: CANNOT
できない
THIS IS THE POWER OF *HEAVEN'S DOOR.*
I CAN READ PEOPLE'S LIVES IN PICTURES AND WORDS, AND, *I CAN WRITE MEMORIES INTO THEM.* FROM THIS POINT FORWARD, YOU WILL BE UTTERLY INCAPABLE OF CAUSING ME HARM.
W-WHAT?!
TREMBL
FWSH! FWSH!
MM-HMM...

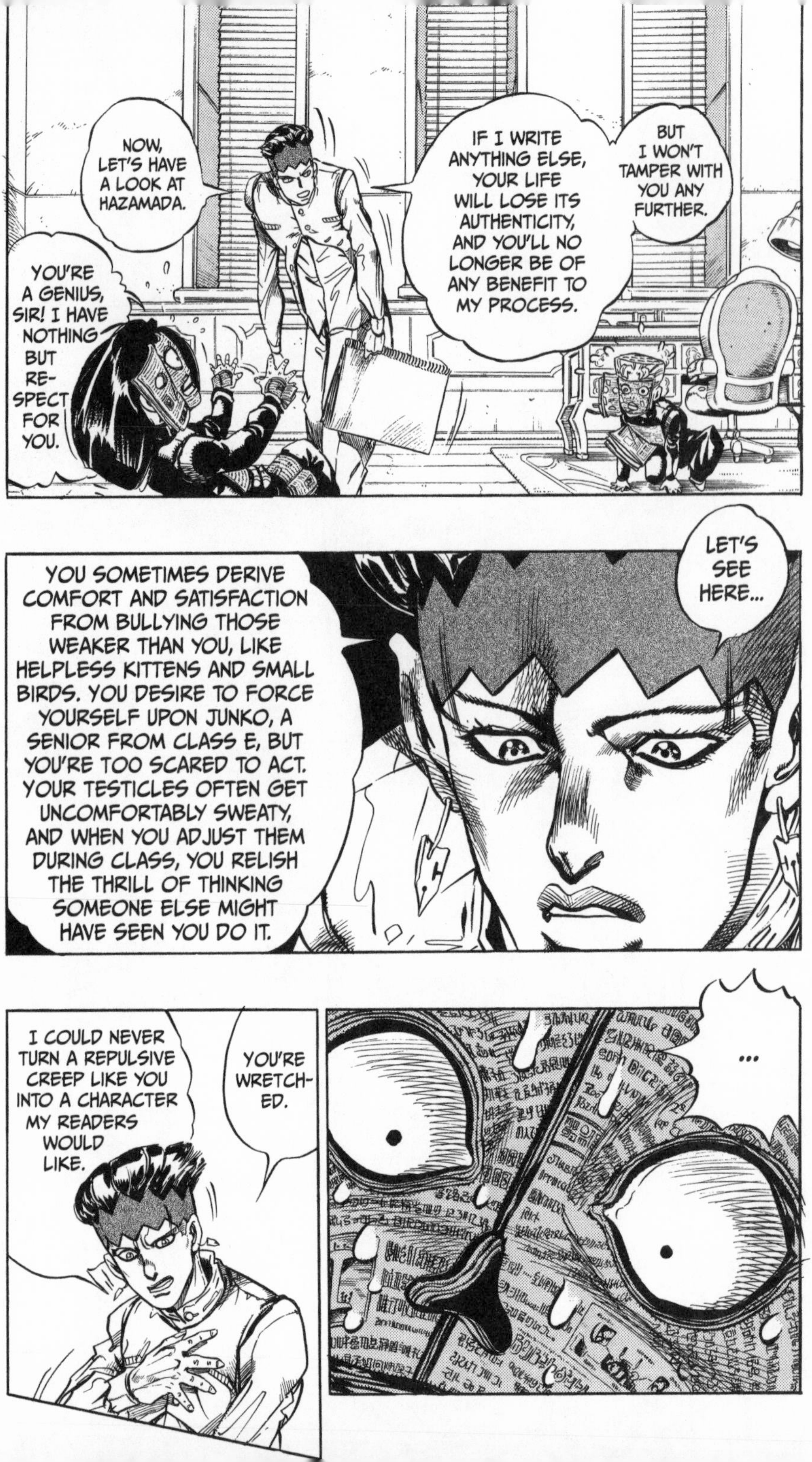
BUT I WON'T TAMPER WITH YOU ANY FURTHER.
IF I WRITE ANYTHING ELSE, YOUR LIFE WILL LOSE ITS AUTHENTICITY, AND YOU'LL NO LONGER BE OF ANY BENEFIT TO MY PROCESS.
NOW, LET'S HAVE A LOOK AT HAZAMADA.
YOU'RE A GENIUS, SIR! I HAVE NOTHING BUT RE-SPECT FOR YOU.
LET'S SEE HERE...
YOU SOMETIMES DERIVE COMFORT AND SATISFACTION FROM BULLYING THOSE WEAKER THAN YOU, LIKE HELPLESS KITTENS AND SMALL BIRDS. YOU DESIRE TO FORCE YOURSELF UPON JUNKO, A SENIOR FROM CLASS E, BUT YOU'RE TOO SCARED TO ACT. YOUR TESTICLES OFTEN GET UNCOMFORTABLY SWEATY, AND WHEN YOU ADJUST THEM DURING CLASS, YOU RELISH THE THRILL OF THINKING SOMEONE ELSE MIGHT HAVE SEEN YOU DO IT.
...
YOU'RE WRETCH-ED.
I COULD NEVER TURN A REPULSIVE CREEP LIKE YOU INTO A CHARACTER MY READERS WOULD LIKE.

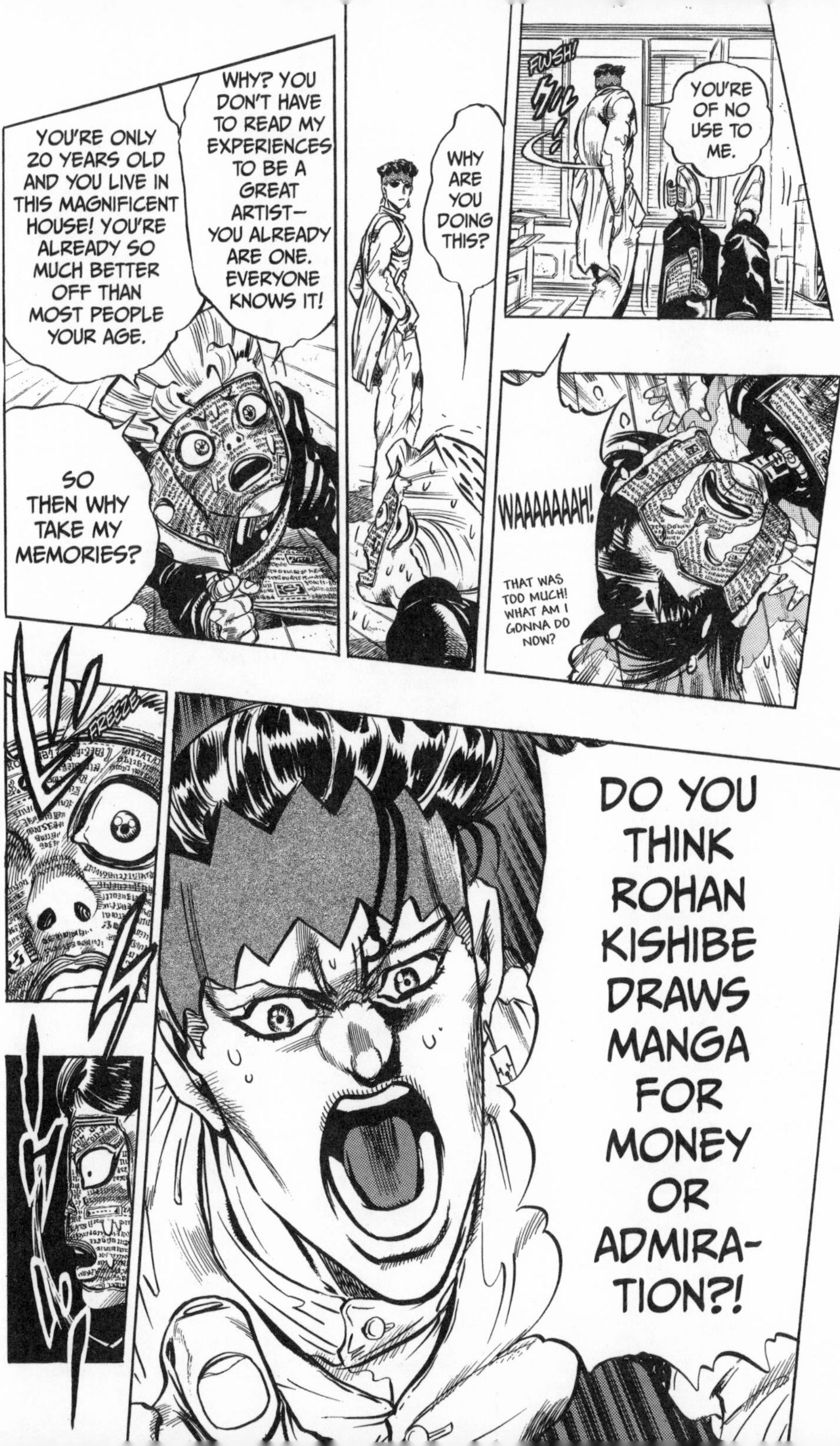
FWSH!
YOU'RE OF NO USE TO ME.
WAAAAAAAH!
THAT WAS TOO MUCH! WHAT AM I GONNA DO NOW?
WHY ARE YOU DOING THIS?
WHY? YOU DON'T HAVE TO READ MY EXPERIENCES TO BE A GREAT ARTIST— YOU ALREADY ARE ONE. EVERYONE KNOWS IT!
YOU'RE ONLY 20 YEARS OLD AND YOU LIVE IN THIS MAGNIFICENT HOUSE! YOU'RE ALREADY SO MUCH BETTER OFF THAN MOST PEOPLE YOUR AGE.
SO THEN WHY TAKE MY MEMORIES?
DO YOU THINK ROHAN KISHIBE DRAWS MANGA FOR MONEY OR ADMIRA-TION?!
FREEZE

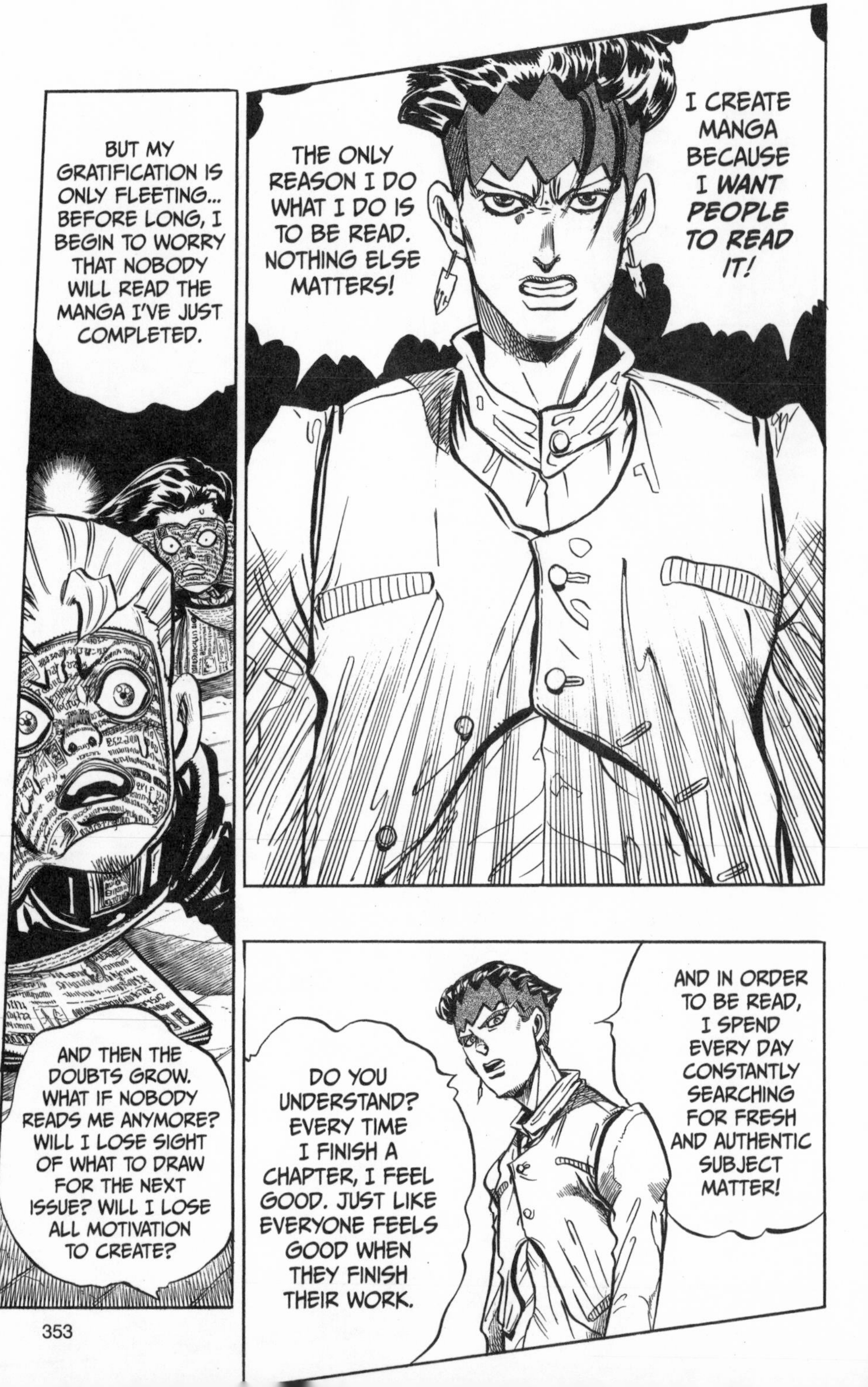
I CREATE MANGA BECAUSE I WANT PEOPLE TO READ IT!
THE ONLY REASON I DO WHAT I DO IS TO BE READ. NOTHING ELSE MATTERS!
AND IN ORDER TO BE READ, I SPEND EVERY DAY CONSTANTLY SEARCHING FOR FRESH AND AUTHENTIC SUBJECT MATTER!
DO YOU UNDERSTAND? EVERY TIME I FINISH A CHAPTER, I FEEL GOOD. JUST LIKE EVERYONE FEELS GOOD WHEN THEY FINISH THEIR WORK.
BUT MY GRATIFICATION IS ONLY FLEETING... BEFORE LONG, I BEGIN TO WORRY THAT NOBODY WILL READ THE MANGA I'VE JUST COMPLETED.
AND THEN THE DOUBTS GROW. WHAT IF NOBODY READS ME ANYMORE? WILL I LOSE SIGHT OF WHAT TO DRAW FOR THE NEXT ISSUE? WILL I LOSE ALL MOTIVATION TO CREATE?

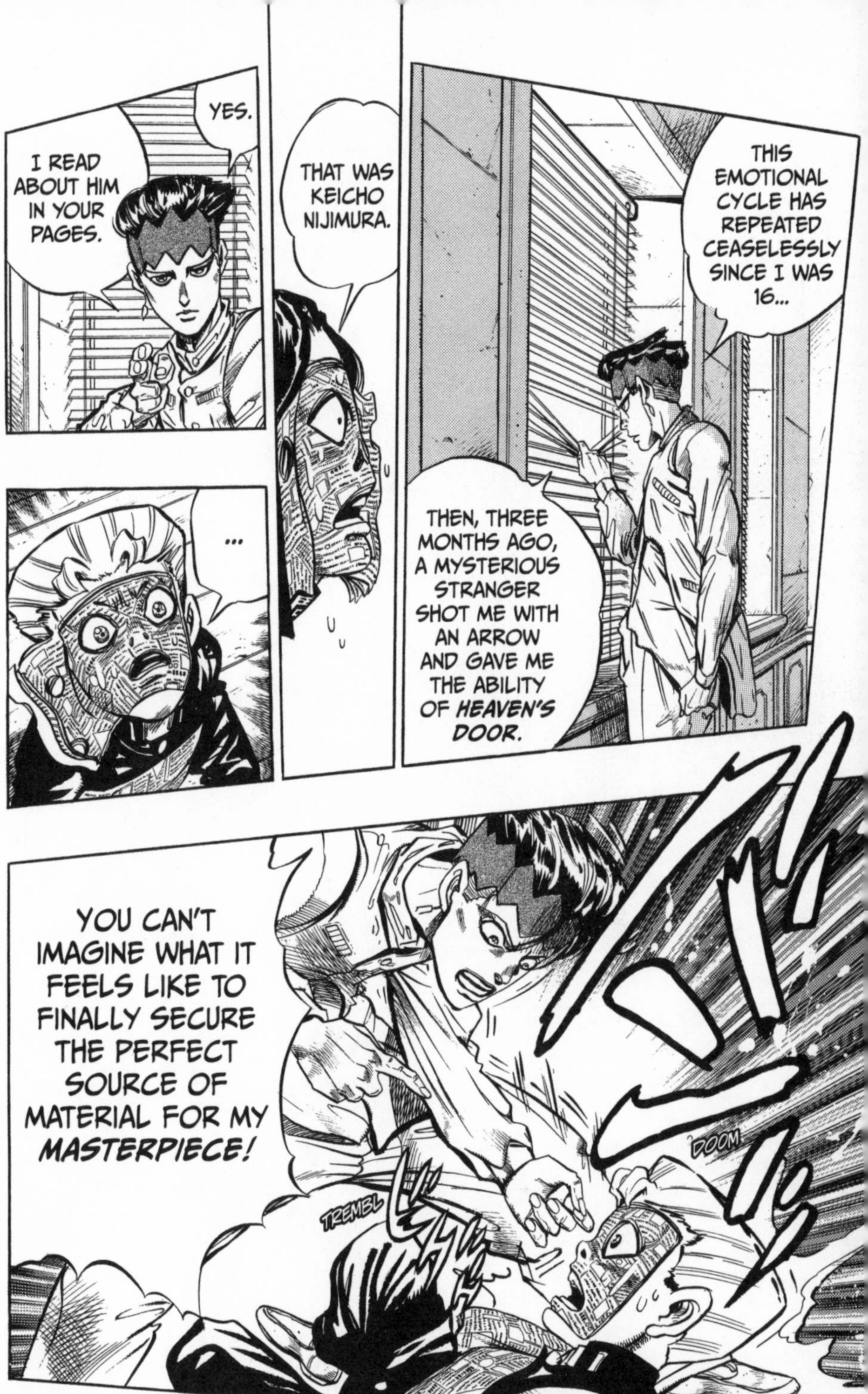
THIS EMOTIONAL CYCLE HAS REPEATED CEASELESSLY SINCE I WAS 16...
THEN, THREE MONTHS AGO, A MYSTERIOUS STRANGER SHOT ME WITH AN ARROW AND GAVE ME THE ABILITY OF *HEAVEN'S DOOR*.
THAT WAS KEICHO NIJIMURA.
YES.
I READ ABOUT HIM IN YOUR PAGES.
...
YOU CAN'T IMAGINE WHAT IT FEELS LIKE TO FINALLY SECURE THE PERFECT SOURCE OF MATERIAL FOR MY *MASTERPIECE!*
DOOM
TREMBL

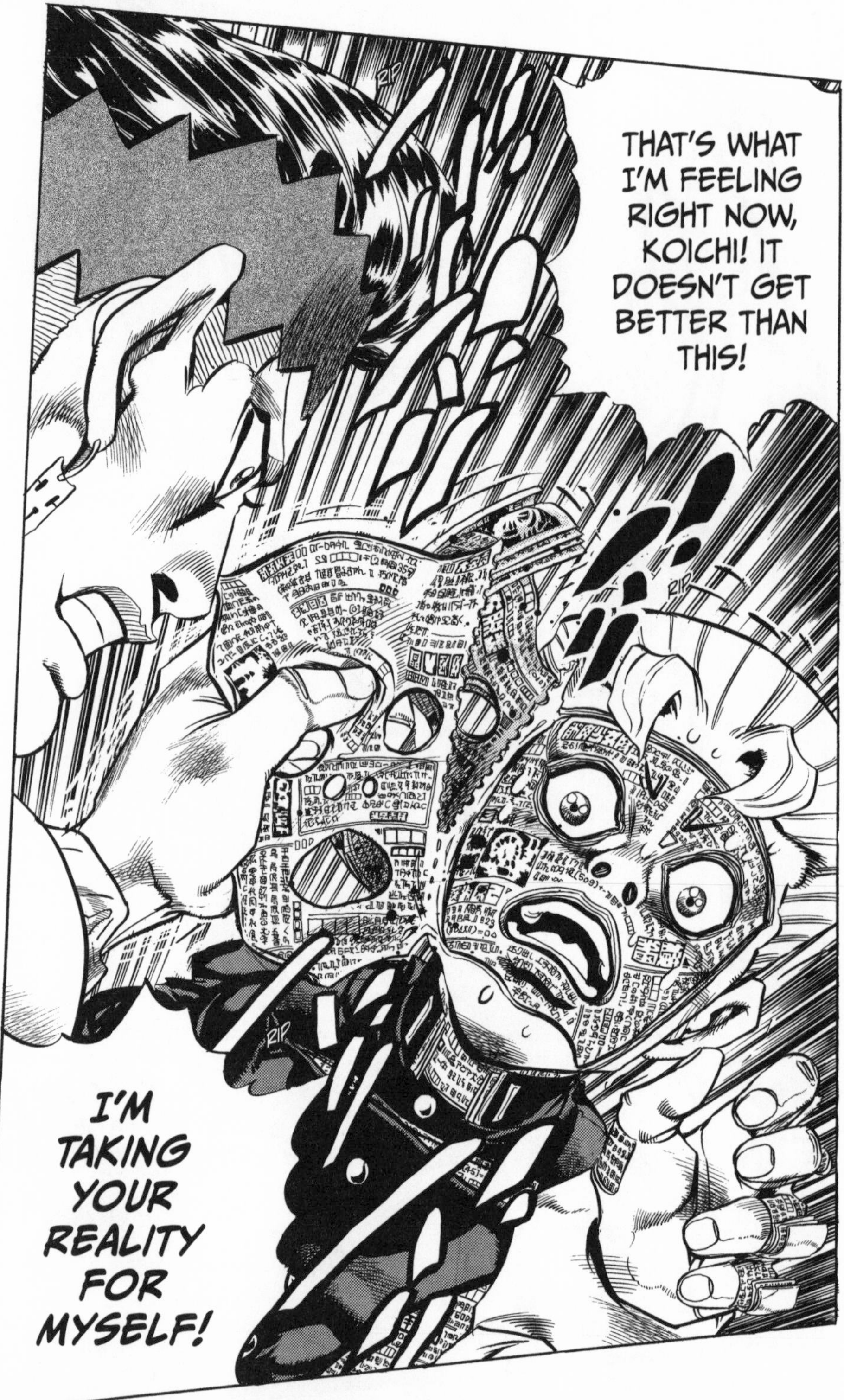
THAT'S WHAT I'M FEELING RIGHT NOW, KOICHI! IT DOESN'T GET BETTER THAN THIS!
I'M TAKING YOUR REALITY FOR MYSELF!

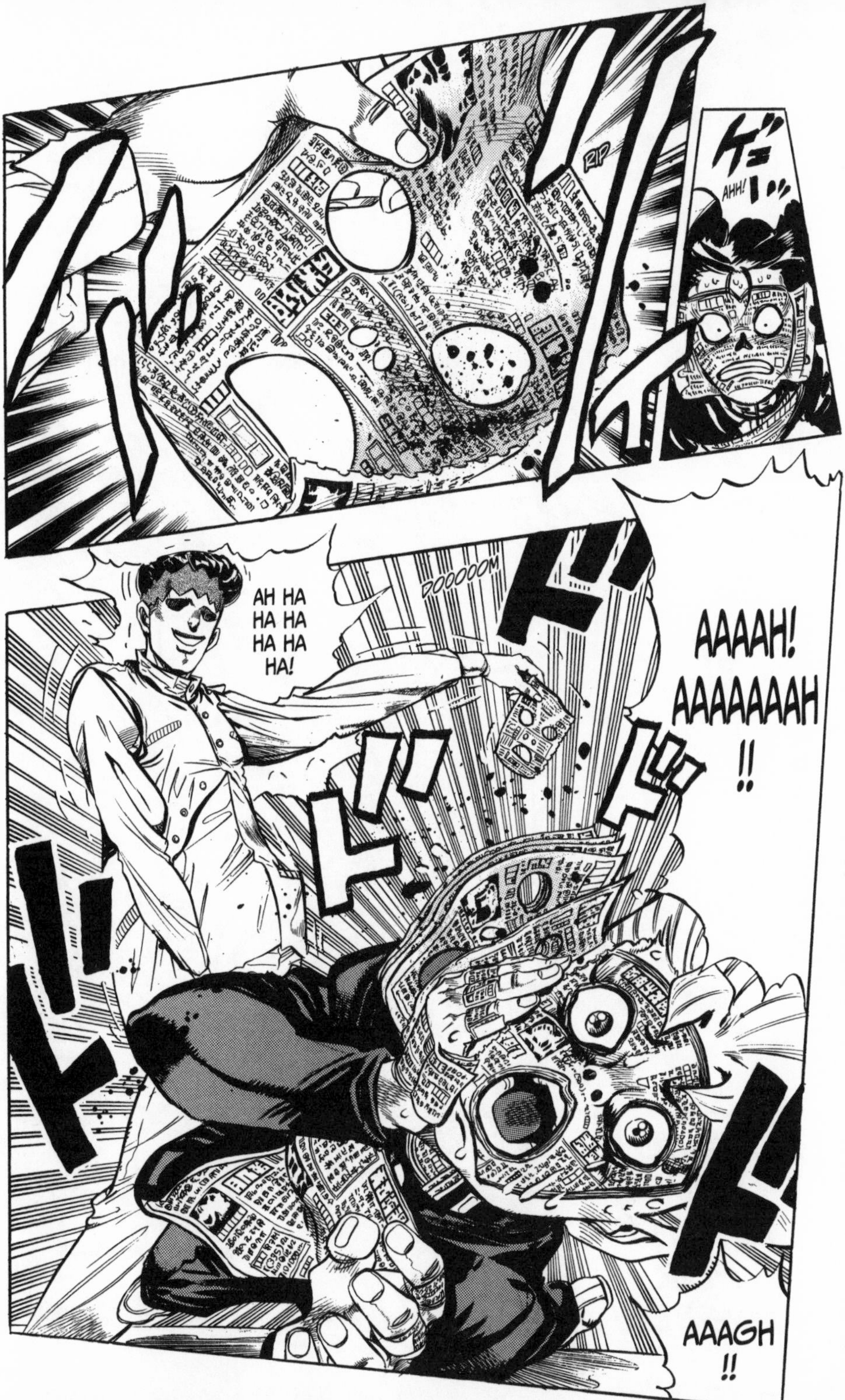
AHH!
RIP
AAAAH! AAAAAAAH !!
DOOOOOM
AH HA HA HA HA HA HA!
AAAGH !!

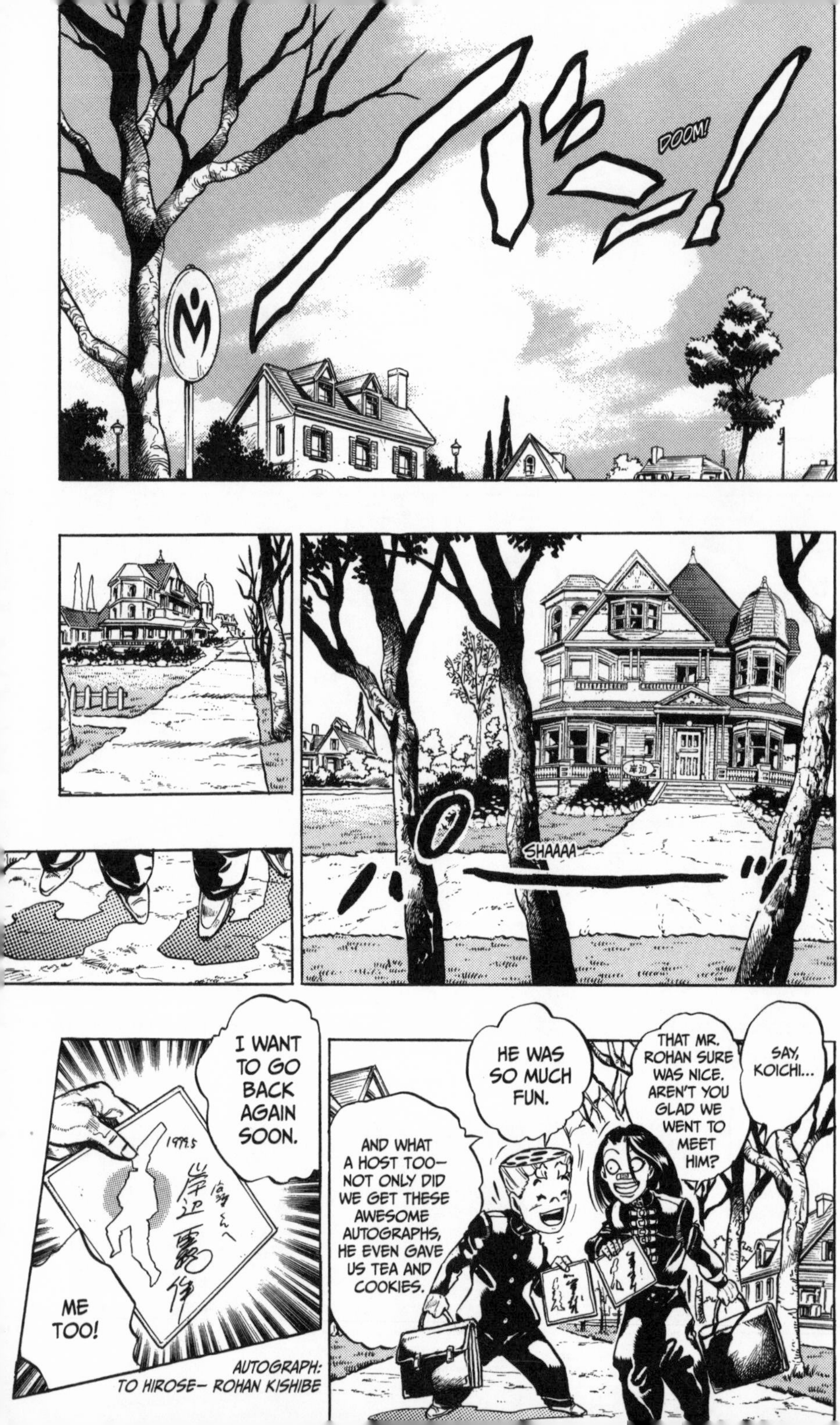
DOOM!
SHAAAA
SAY, KOICHI...
THAT MR. ROHAN SURE WAS NICE. AREN'T YOU GLAD WE WENT TO MEET HIM?
HE WAS SO MUCH FUN.
AND WHAT A HOST TOO—NOT ONLY DID WE GET THESE AWESOME AUTOGRAPHS, HE EVEN GAVE US TEA AND COOKIES.
I WANT TO GO BACK AGAIN SOON.
ME TOO!
AUTOGRAPH: TO HIROSE— ROHAN KISHIBE

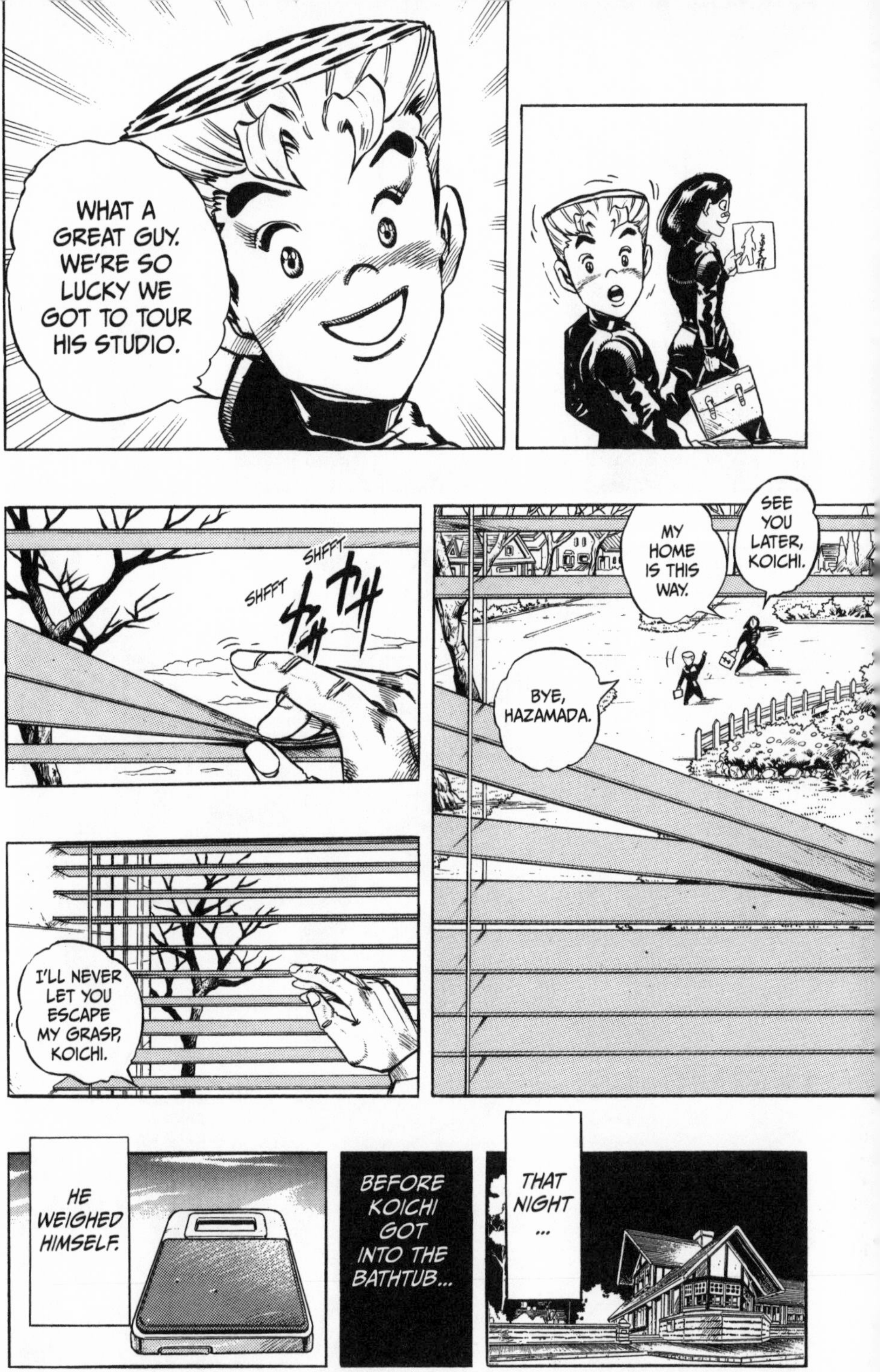
WHAT A GREAT GUY. WE'RE SO LUCKY WE GOT TO TOUR HIS STUDIO.
SEE YOU LATER, KOICHI.
MY HOME IS THIS WAY.
BYE, HAZAMADA.
SHFFT
SHFFT
I'LL NEVER LET YOU ESCAPE MY GRASP, KOICHI.
THAT NIGHT ...
BEFORE KOICHI GOT INTO THE BATHTUB...
HE WEIGHED HIMSELF.

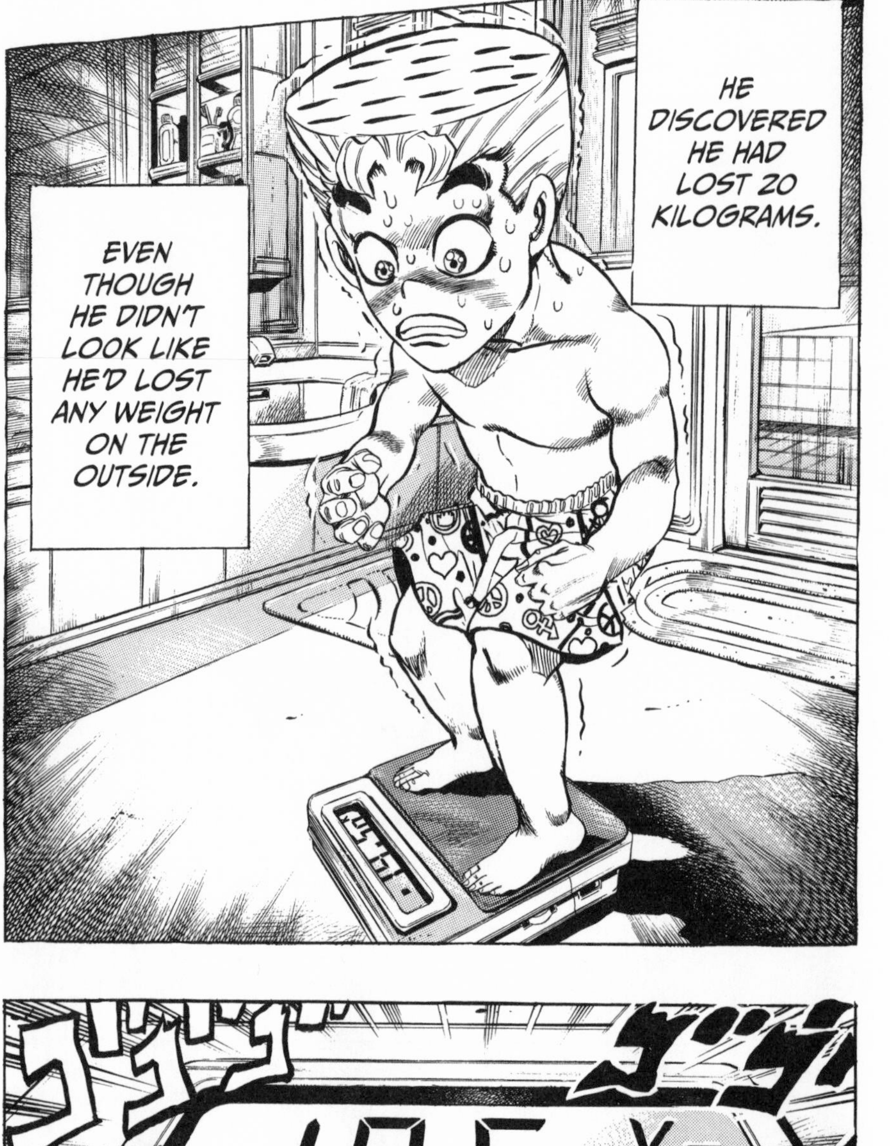
HE DISCOVERED HE HAD LOST 20 KILOGRAMS.
EVEN THOUGH HE DIDN'T LOOK LIKE HE'D LOST ANY WEIGHT ON THE OUTSIDE.
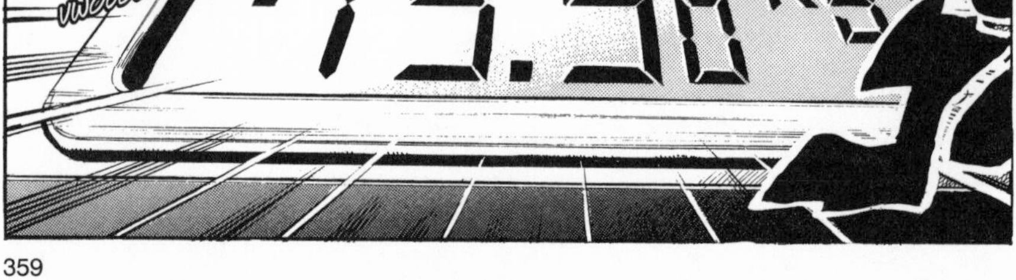
VWOOOOOOM

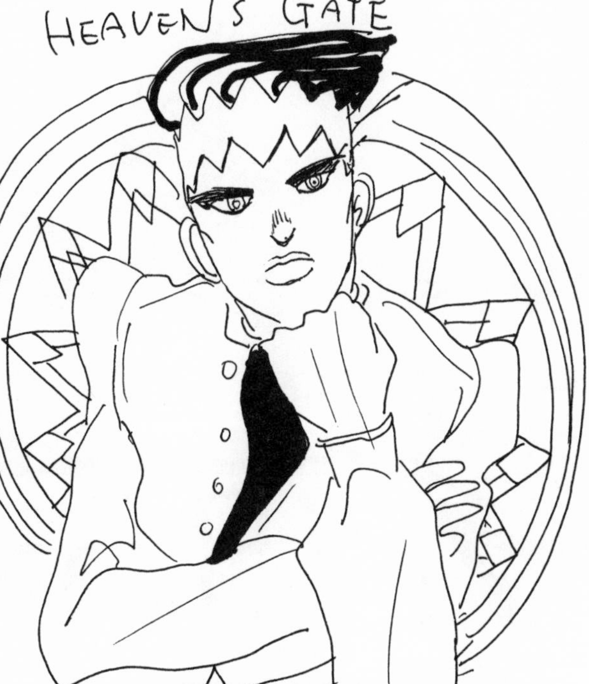
HEAVEN'S GATE

CHAPTER 56 ★ LET'S GO TO THE MANGA ARTIST'S HOUSE, PART 4

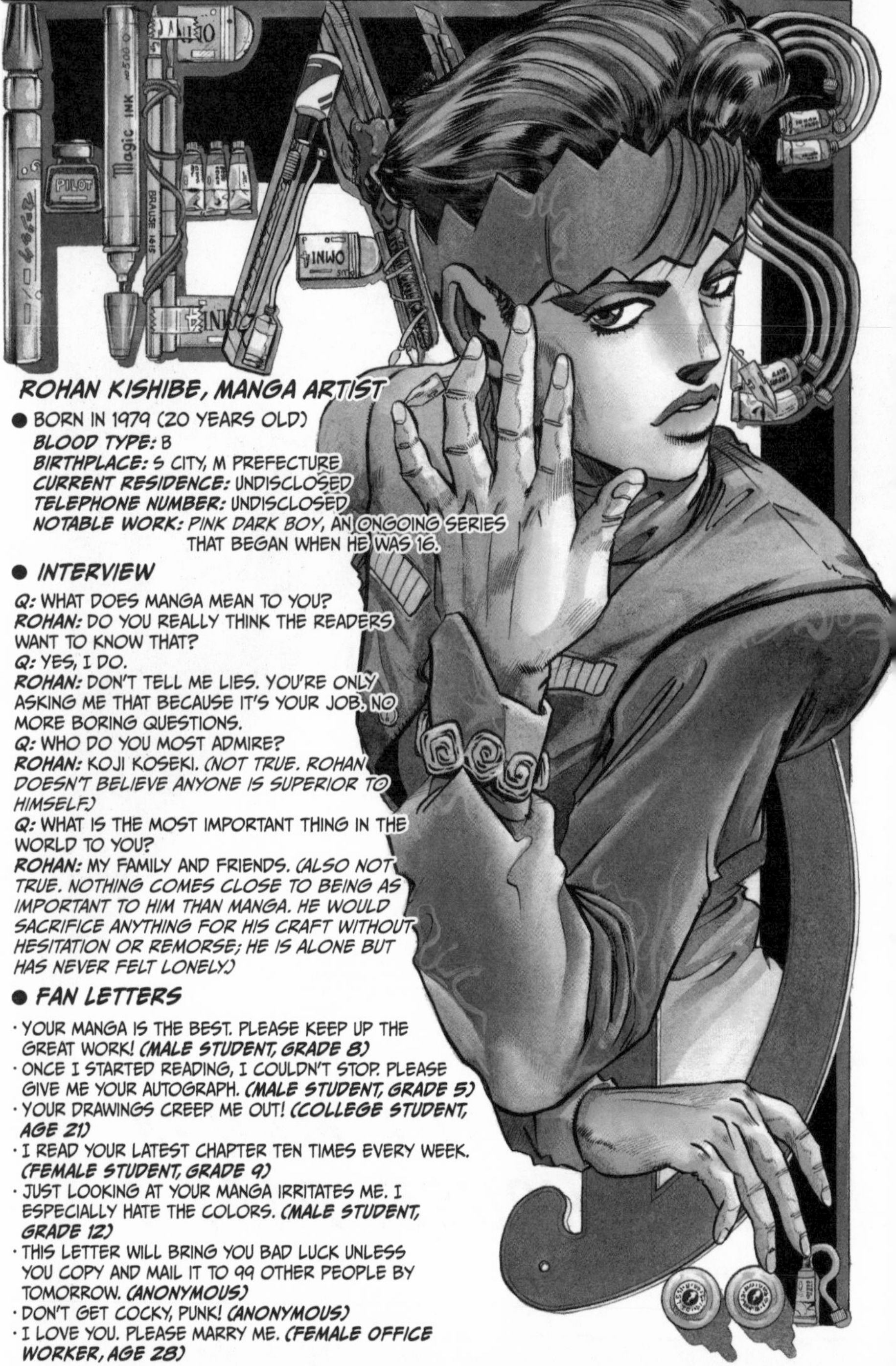
PILOT
Magic INK
BRAUSE 1615

ROHAN KISHIBE, MANGA ARTIST

- BORN IN 1979 (20 YEARS OLD)
  BLOOD TYPE: B
  BIRTHPLACE: S CITY, M PREFECTURE
  CURRENT RESIDENCE: UNDISCLOSED
  TELEPHONE NUMBER: UNDISCLOSED
  NOTABLE WORK: *PINK DARK BOY*, AN ONGOING SERIES THAT BEGAN WHEN HE WAS 16.

● INTERVIEW

Q: WHAT DOES MANGA MEAN TO YOU?
ROHAN: DO YOU REALLY THINK THE READERS WANT TO KNOW THAT?
Q: YES, I DO.
ROHAN: DON'T TELL ME LIES. YOU'RE ONLY ASKING ME THAT BECAUSE IT'S YOUR JOB. NO MORE BORING QUESTIONS.
Q: WHO DO YOU MOST ADMIRE?
ROHAN: KOJI KOSEKI. *(NOT TRUE. ROHAN DOESN'T BELIEVE ANYONE IS SUPERIOR TO HIMSELF.)*
Q: WHAT IS THE MOST IMPORTANT THING IN THE WORLD TO YOU?
ROHAN: MY FAMILY AND FRIENDS. *(ALSO NOT TRUE. NOTHING COMES CLOSE TO BEING AS IMPORTANT TO HIM THAN MANGA. HE WOULD SACRIFICE ANYTHING FOR HIS CRAFT WITHOUT HESITATION OR REMORSE; HE IS ALONE BUT HAS NEVER FELT LONELY.)*

● FAN LETTERS

- YOUR MANGA IS THE BEST. PLEASE KEEP UP THE GREAT WORK! ***(MALE STUDENT, GRADE 8)***
- ONCE I STARTED READING, I COULDN'T STOP. PLEASE GIVE ME YOUR AUTOGRAPH. ***(MALE STUDENT, GRADE 5)***
- YOUR DRAWINGS CREEP ME OUT! ***(COLLEGE STUDENT, AGE 21)***
- I READ YOUR LATEST CHAPTER TEN TIMES EVERY WEEK. ***(FEMALE STUDENT, GRADE 9)***
- JUST LOOKING AT YOUR MANGA IRRITATES ME. I ESPECIALLY HATE THE COLORS. ***(MALE STUDENT, GRADE 12)***
- THIS LETTER WILL BRING YOU BAD LUCK UNLESS YOU COPY AND MAIL IT TO 99 OTHER PEOPLE BY TOMORROW. ***(ANONYMOUS)***
- DON'T GET COCKY, PUNK! ***(ANONYMOUS)***
- I LOVE YOU. PLEASE MARRY ME. ***(FEMALE OFFICE WORKER, AGE 28)***

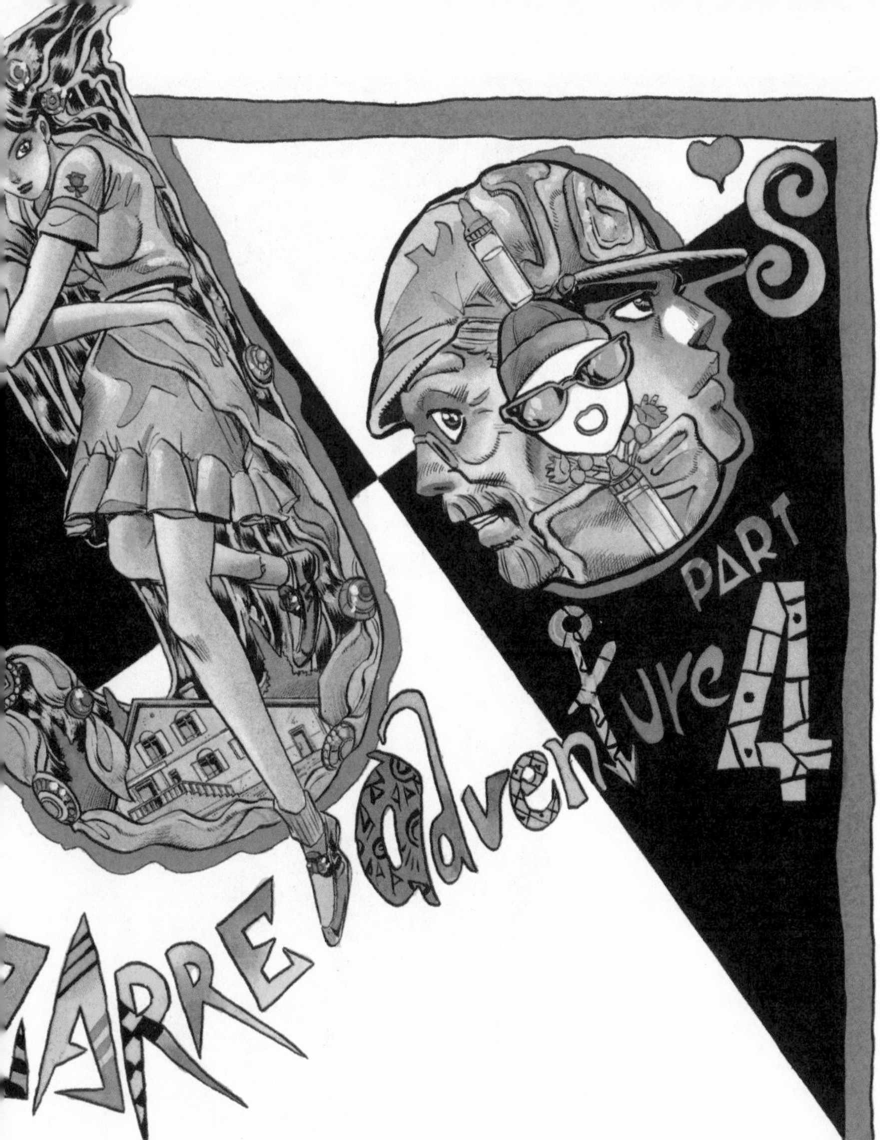
adventure
PART 4

CHAPTER 56

LET'S GO TO THE MANGA ARTIST'S HOUSE, PART 4

H. ARAKI

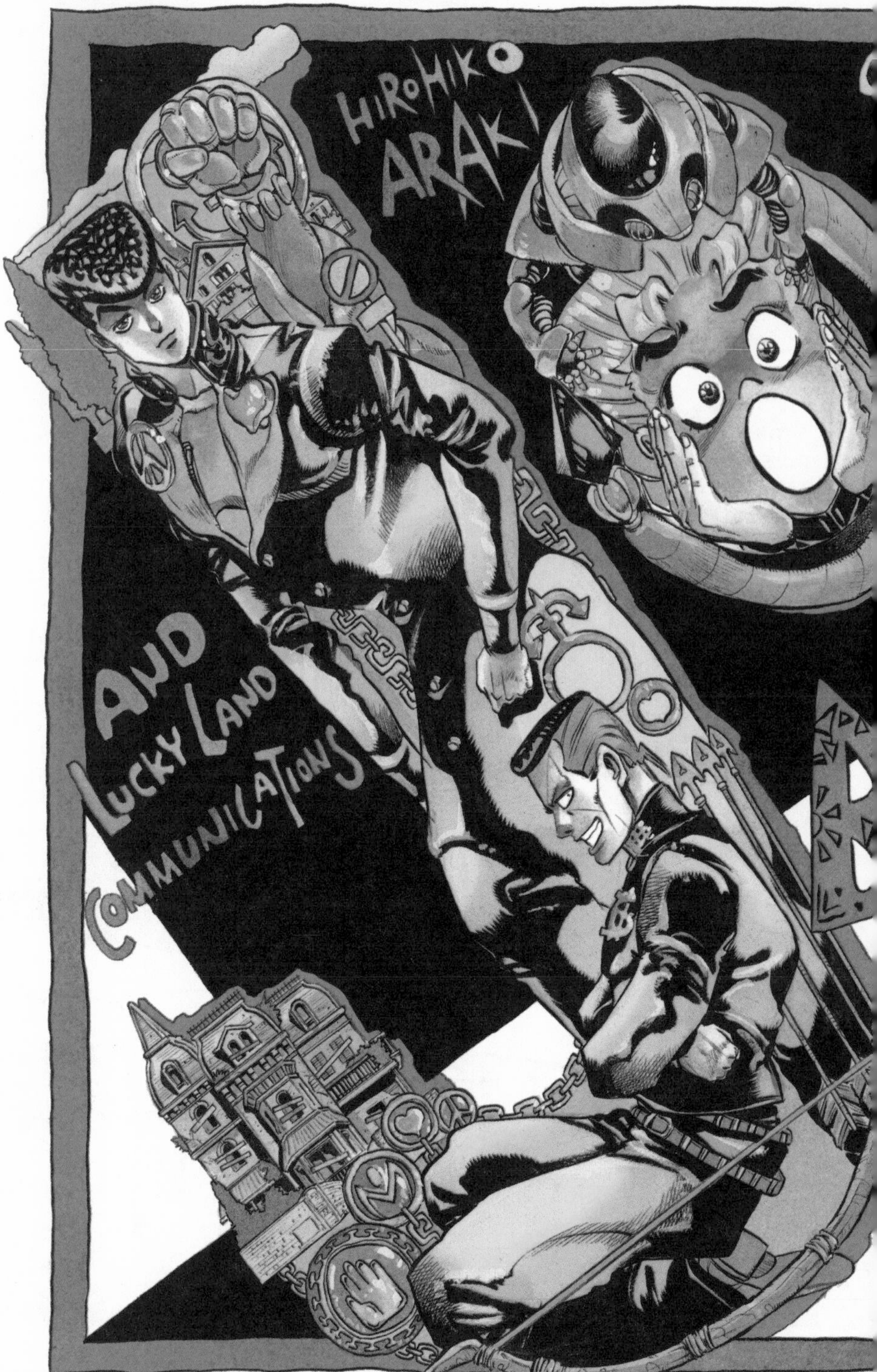
HIROHIKO ARAKI
AND LUCKY LAND COMMUNICATIONS

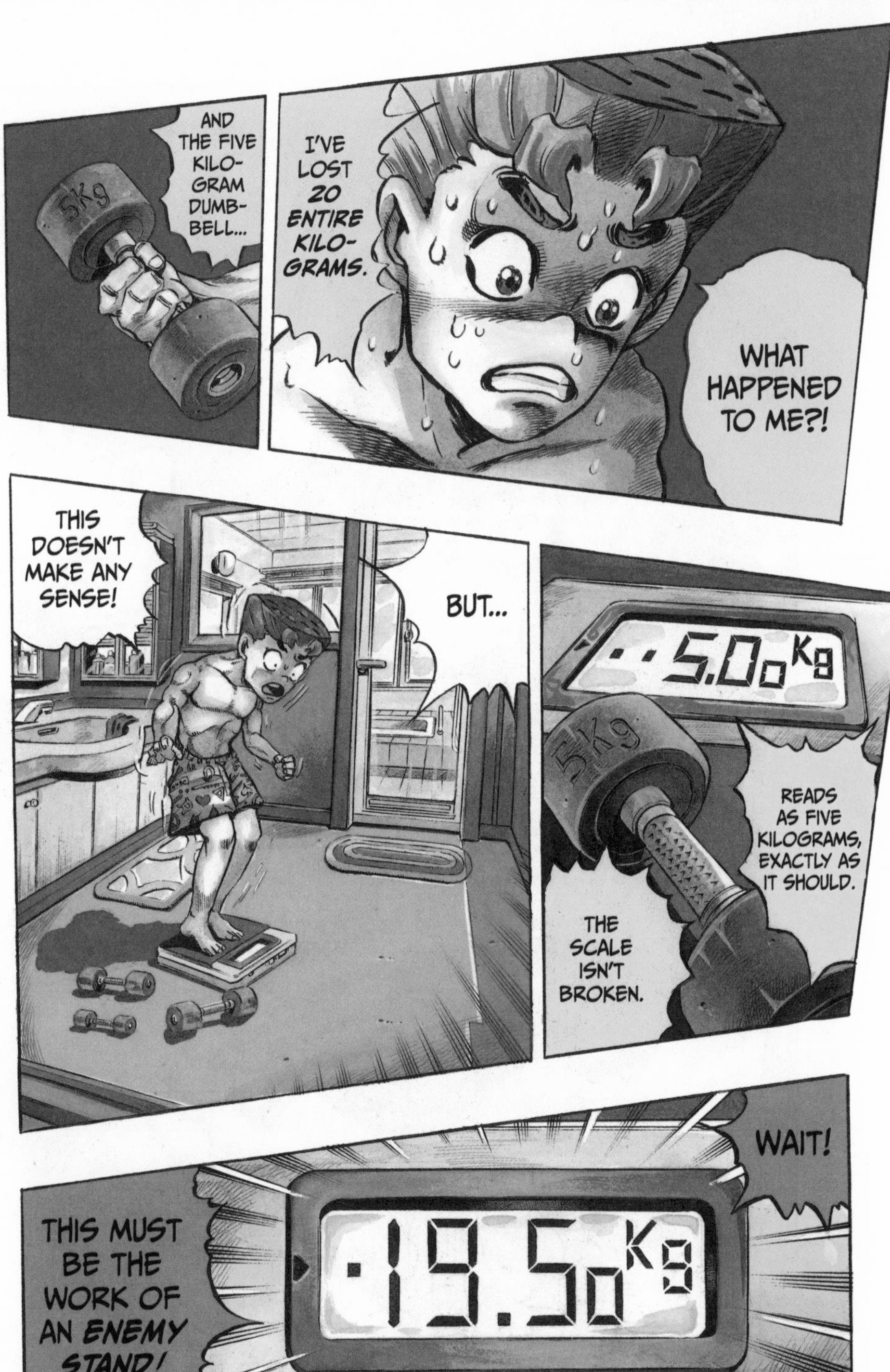
I'VE LOST 20 ENTIRE KILOGRAMS.
WHAT HAPPENED TO ME?!
AND THE FIVE KILOGRAM DUMBBELL...
5Kg
5.00Kg
5Kg
READS AS FIVE KILOGRAMS, EXACTLY AS IT SHOULD.
THE SCALE ISN'T BROKEN.
THIS DOESN'T MAKE ANY SENSE!
BUT...
WAIT!
19.50Kg
THIS MUST BE THE WORK OF AN *ENEMY STAND!*

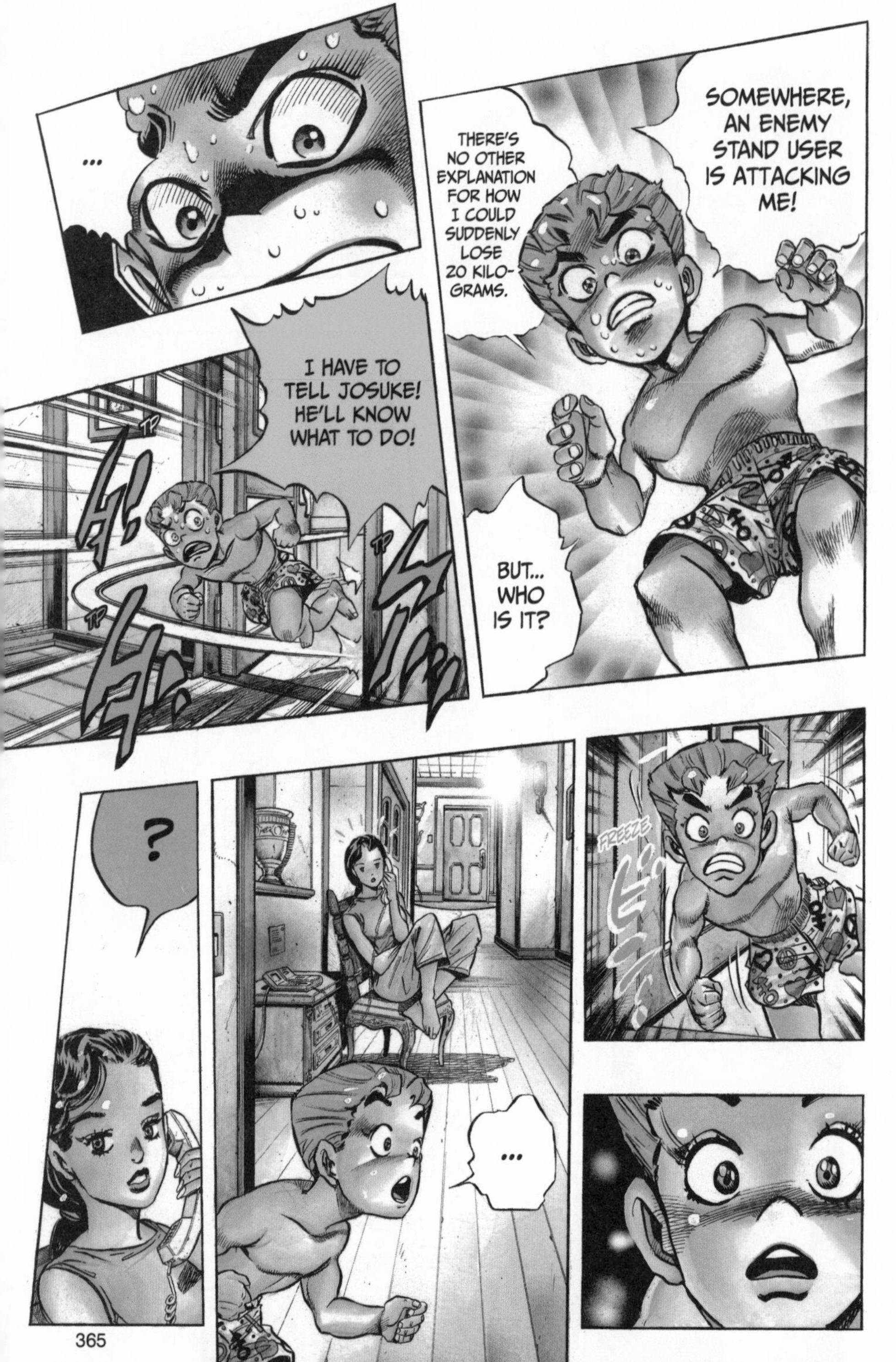
SOMEWHERE, AN ENEMY STAND USER IS ATTACKING ME!
THERE'S NO OTHER EXPLANATION FOR HOW I COULD SUDDENLY LOSE 20 KILOGRAMS.
BUT... WHO IS IT?
...
I HAVE TO TELL JOSUKE! HE'LL KNOW WHAT TO DO!
FREEZE
...
?

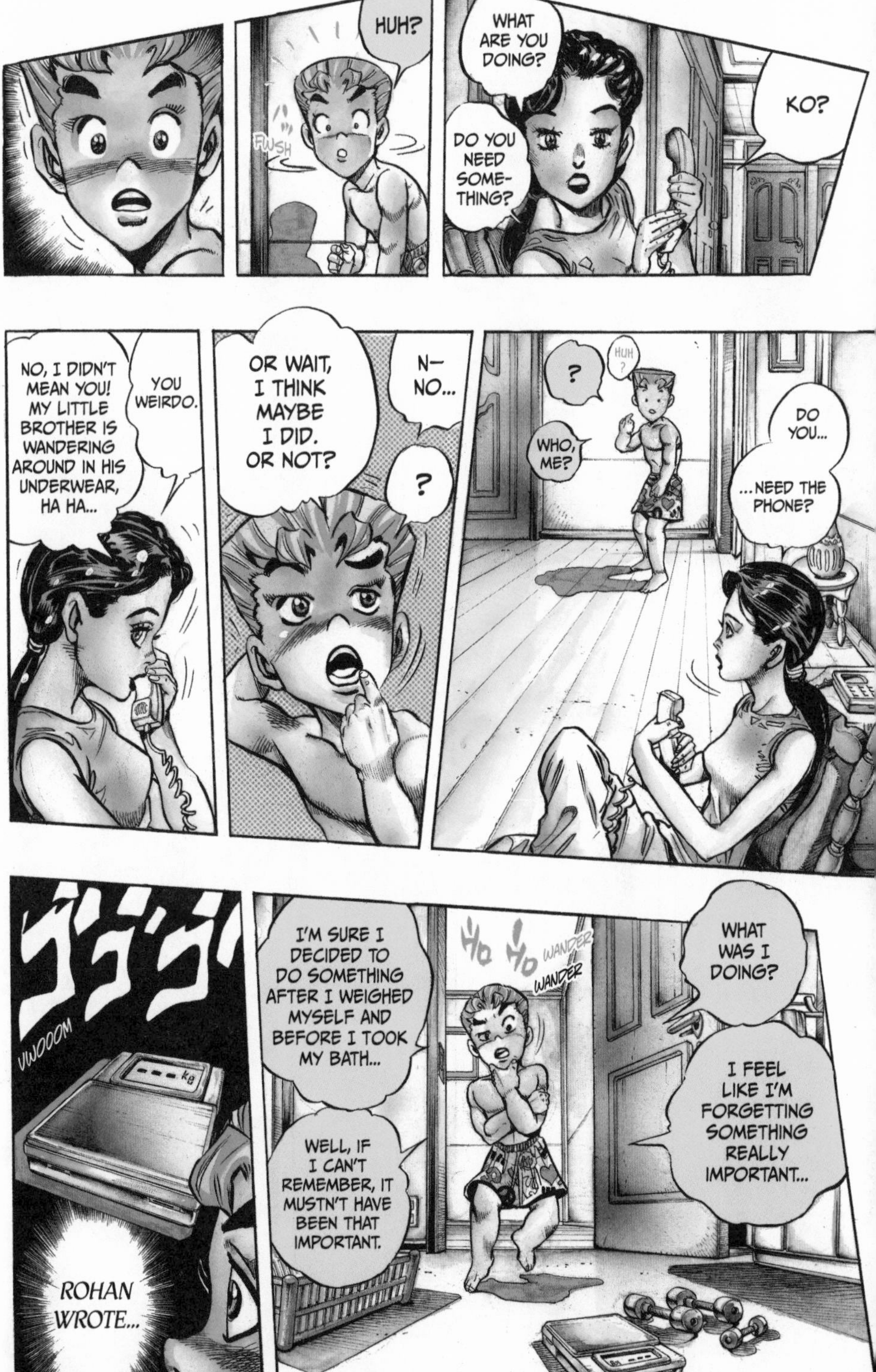
KO?
WHAT ARE YOU DOING?
DO YOU NEED SOME-THING?
HUH?
FWSH
DO YOU...
...NEED THE PHONE?
HUH ?
?
WHO, ME?
N— NO...
OR WAIT, I THINK MAYBE I DID. OR NOT?
?
YOU WEIRDO.
NO, I DIDN'T MEAN YOU! MY LITTLE BROTHER IS WANDERING AROUND IN HIS UNDERWEAR, HA HA...
WHAT WAS I DOING?
I FEEL LIKE I'M FORGETTING SOMETHING REALLY IMPORTANT...
WANDER
WANDER
HO HO
I'M SURE I DECIDED TO DO SOMETHING AFTER I WEIGHED MYSELF AND BEFORE I TOOK MY BATH...
WELL, IF I CAN'T REMEMBER, IT MUSTN'T HAVE BEEN THAT IMPORTANT.
ゴゴゴ
VWOOOM
--- kg
ROHAN WROTE...

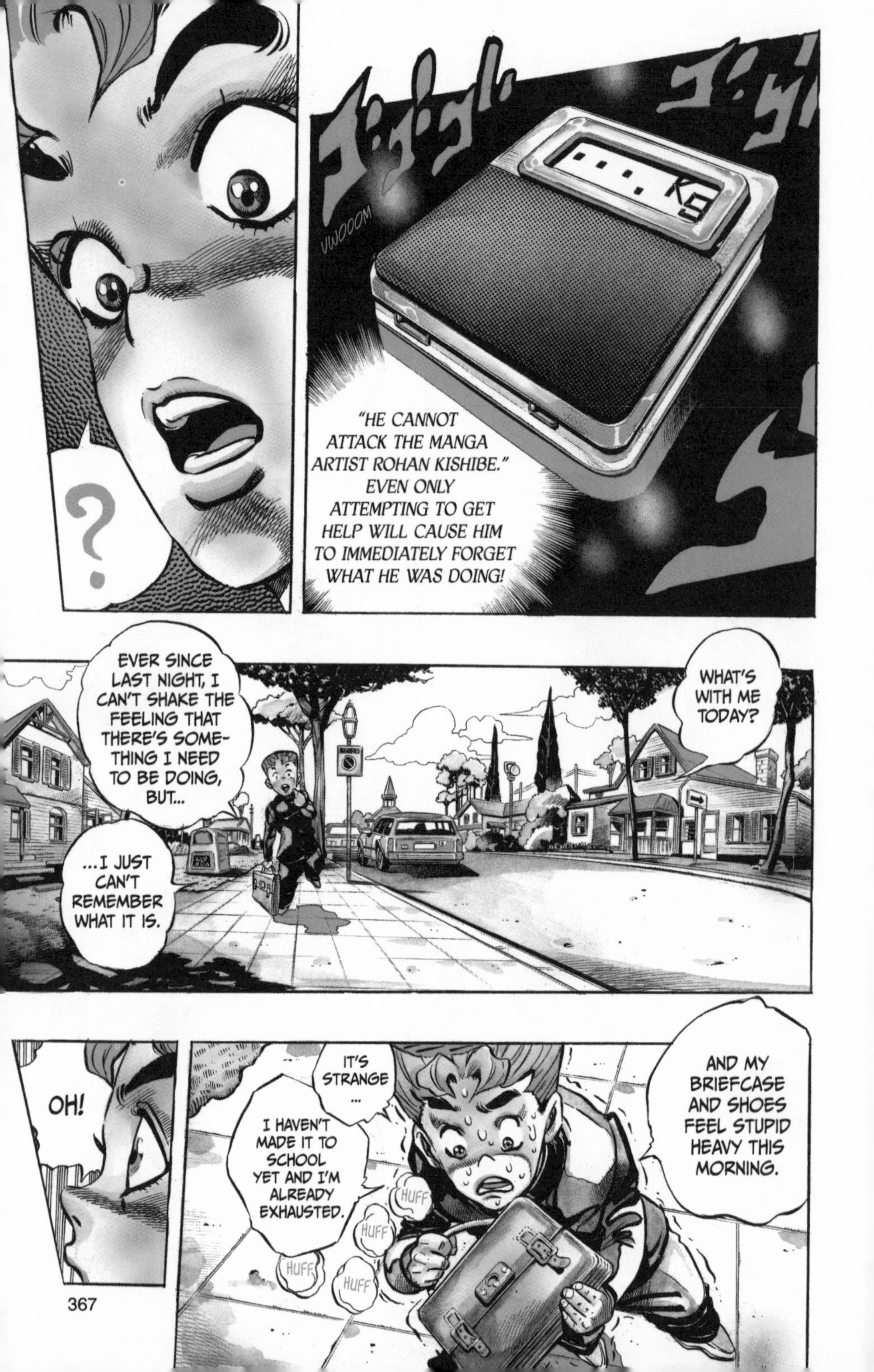
VWOOOM
...Kg
"HE CANNOT ATTACK THE MANGA ARTIST ROHAN KISHIBE." EVEN ONLY ATTEMPTING TO GET HELP WILL CAUSE HIM TO IMMEDIATELY FORGET WHAT HE WAS DOING!
?
WHAT'S WITH ME TODAY?
EVER SINCE LAST NIGHT, I CAN'T SHAKE THE FEELING THAT THERE'S SOME-THING I NEED TO BE DOING, BUT...
...I JUST CAN'T REMEMBER WHAT IT IS.
AND MY BRIEFCASE AND SHOES FEEL STUPID HEAVY THIS MORNING.
IT'S STRANGE...
I HAVEN'T MADE IT TO SCHOOL YET AND I'M ALREADY EXHAUSTED.
HUFF
HUFF
HUFF
HUFF
OH!

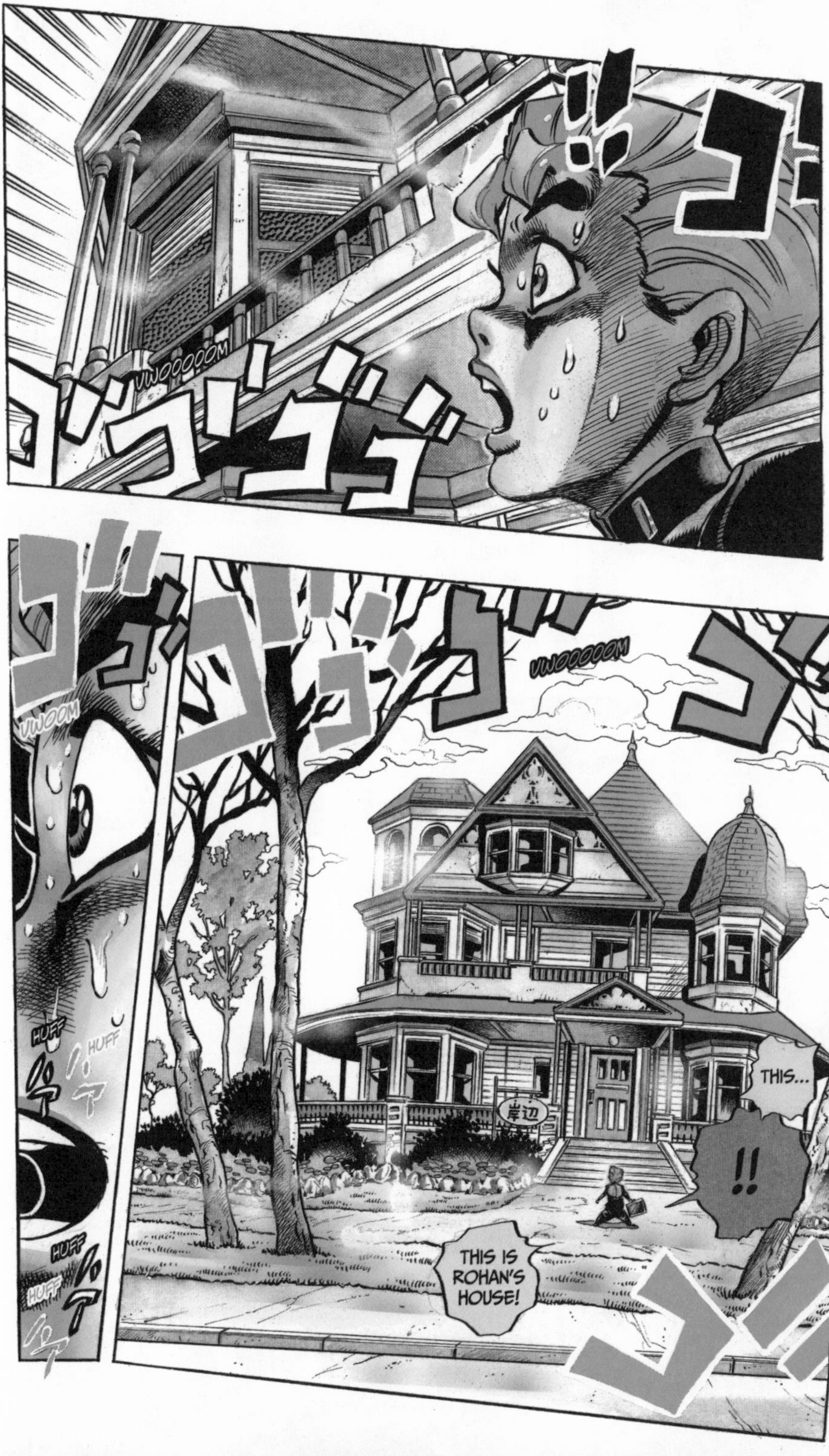
UWOOOOOM
UWOOOOOM
THIS...
!!
THIS IS ROHAN'S HOUSE!
UWOOM
HUFF
HUFF
HUFF
HUFF

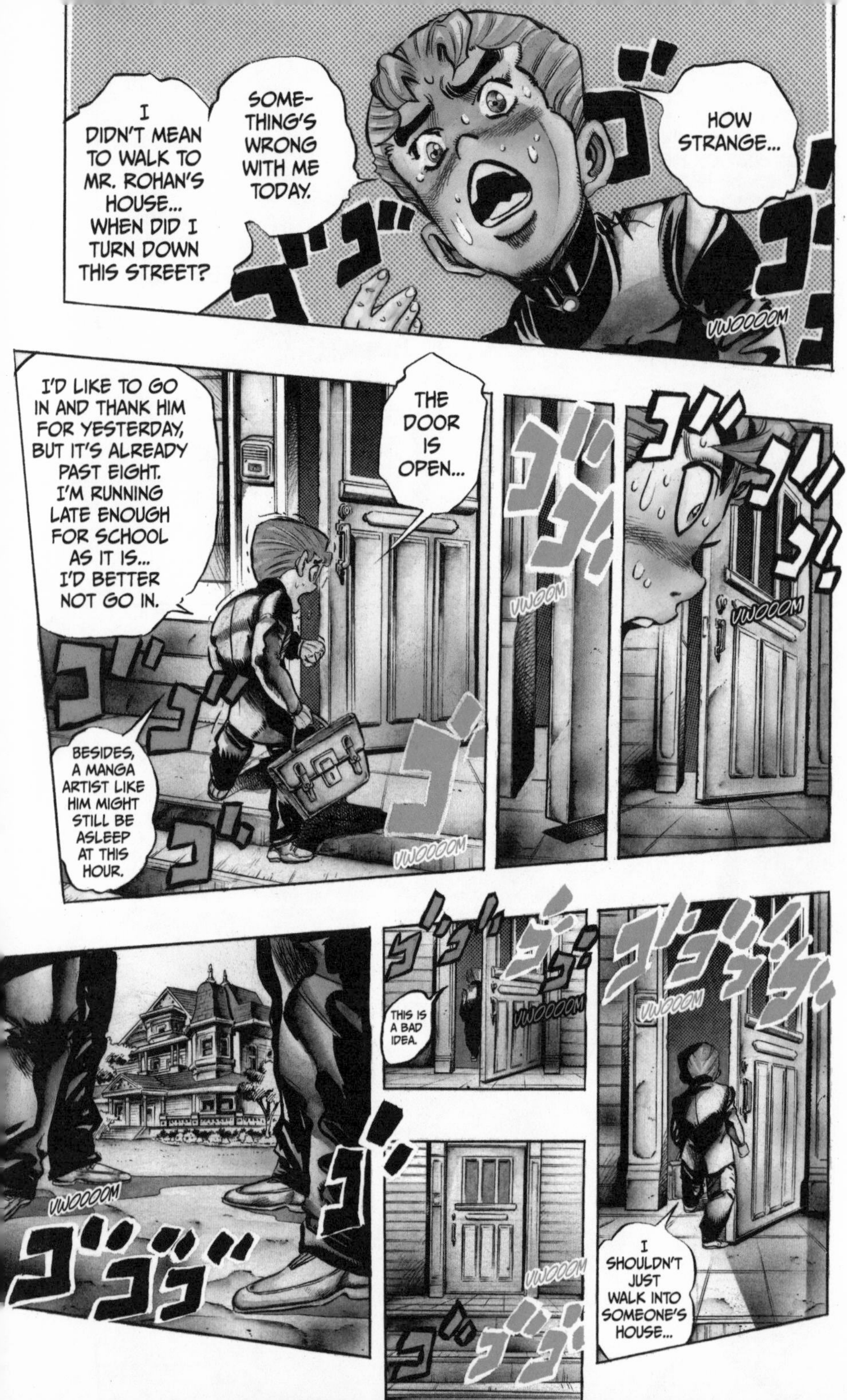
HOW STRANGE...
SOMETHING'S WRONG WITH ME TODAY.
I DIDN'T MEAN TO WALK TO MR. ROHAN'S HOUSE... WHEN DID I TURN DOWN THIS STREET?
VWOOOOM
VWOOOM
VWOOM
THE DOOR IS OPEN...
I'D LIKE TO GO IN AND THANK HIM FOR YESTERDAY, BUT IT'S ALREADY PAST EIGHT. I'M RUNNING LATE ENOUGH FOR SCHOOL AS IT IS... I'D BETTER NOT GO IN.
BESIDES, A MANGA ARTIST LIKE HIM MIGHT STILL BE ASLEEP AT THIS HOUR.
VWOOOOM
VWOOOM
I SHOULDN'T JUST WALK INTO SOMEONE'S HOUSE...
THIS IS A BAD IDEA.
VWOOOOM
VWOOOM
VWOOOOM

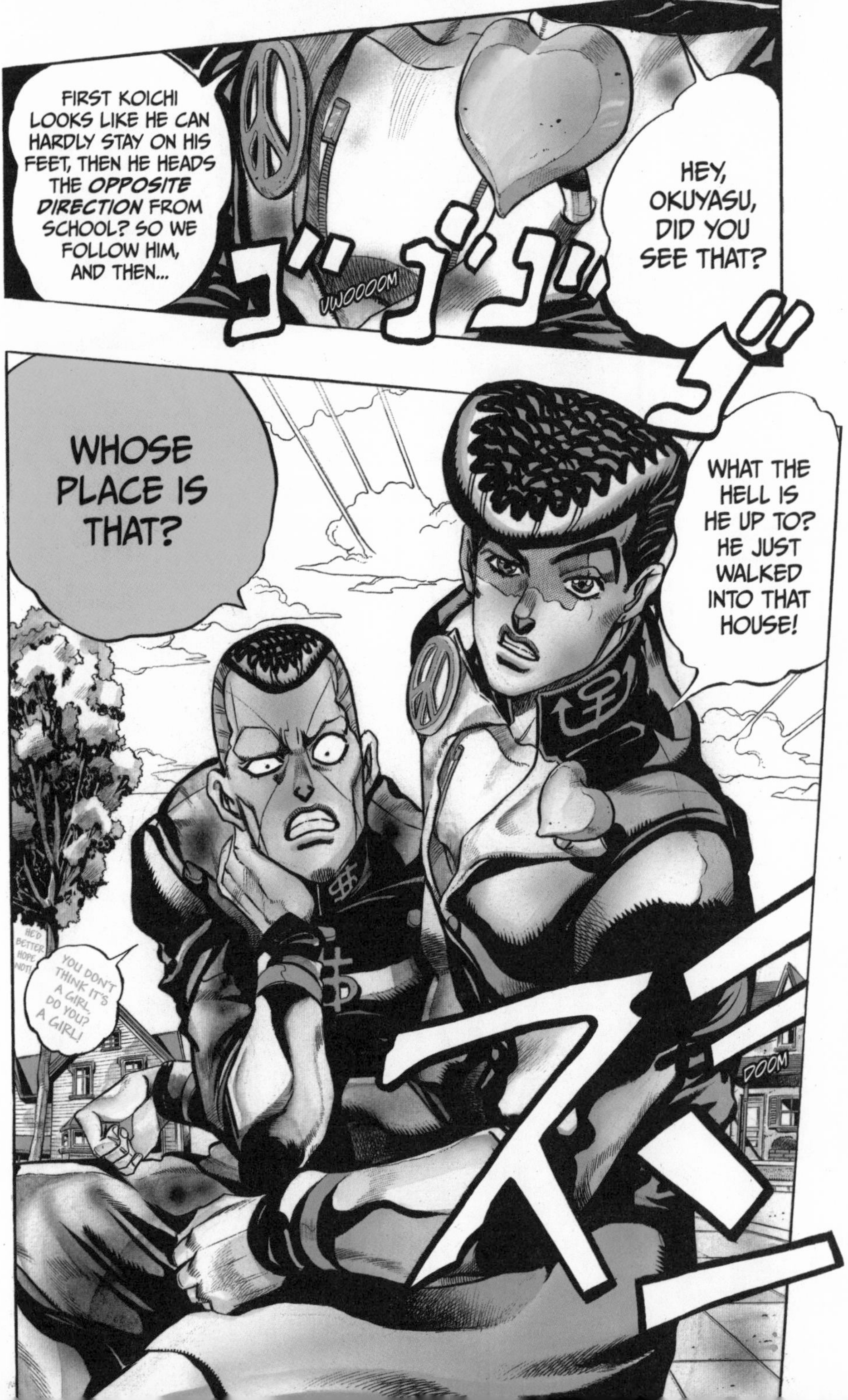
HEY, OKUYASU, DID YOU SEE THAT?
FIRST KOICHI LOOKS LIKE HE CAN HARDLY STAY ON HIS FEET, THEN HE HEADS THE *OPPOSITE DIRECTION* FROM SCHOOL? SO WE FOLLOW HIM, AND THEN...
UWOOOOM
WHAT THE HELL IS HE UP TO? HE JUST WALKED INTO THAT HOUSE!
WHOSE PLACE IS THAT?
DOOM
YOU DON'T THINK IT'S A GIRL, DO YOU? A GIRL!
HE'D BETTER HOPE NOT!

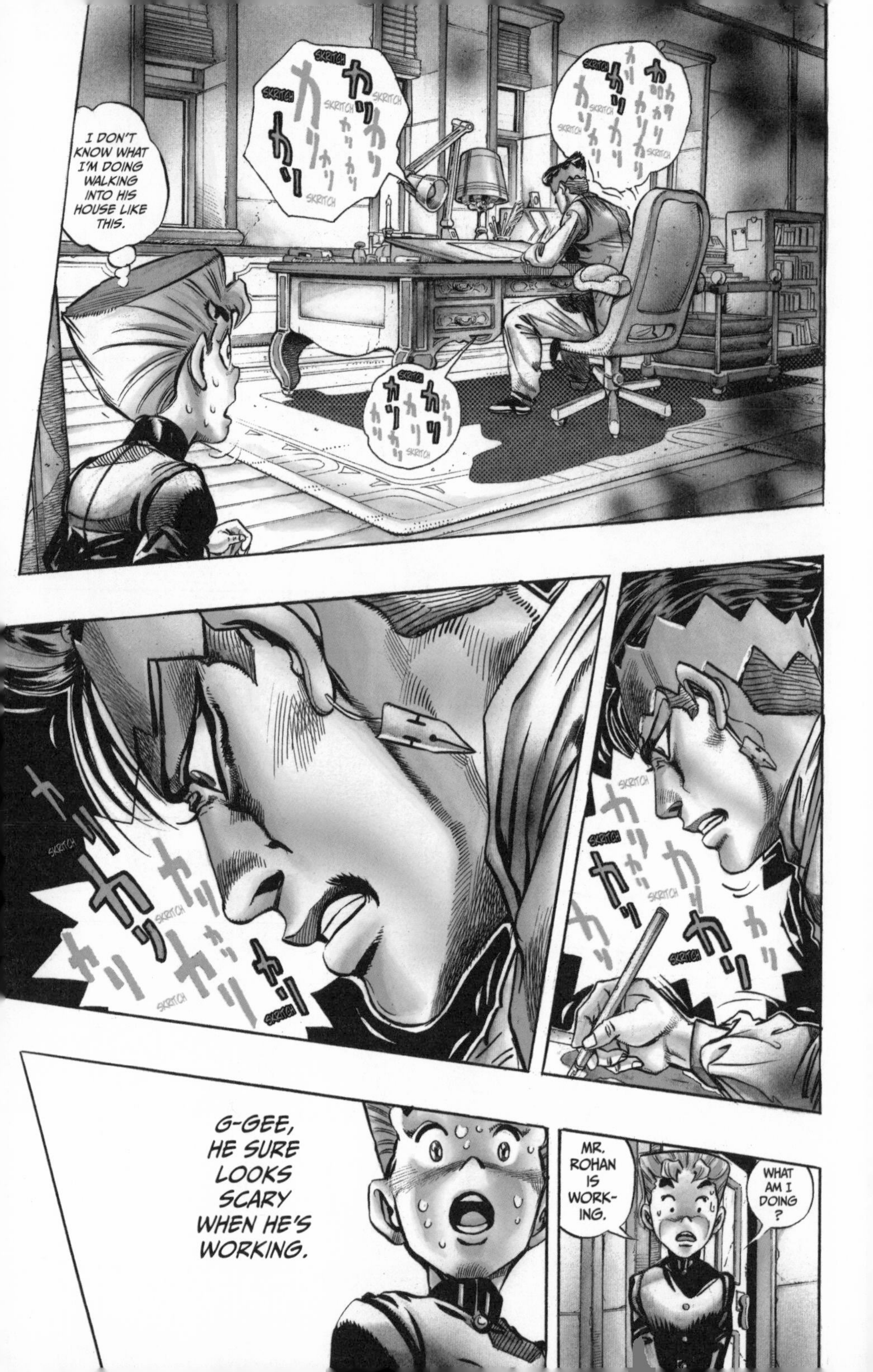
SKRITCH
SKRITCH
SKRITCH
I DON'T KNOW WHAT I'M DOING WALKING INTO HIS HOUSE LIKE THIS.
SKRITCH
SKRITCH
SKRITCH
SKRITCH
SKRITCH
SKRITCH
SKRITCH
SKRITCH
SKRITCH
SKRITCH
SKRITCH
SKRITCH
SKRITCH
SKRITCH
WHAT AM I DOING?
MR. ROHAN IS WORK-ING.
G-GEE, HE SURE LOOKS SCARY WHEN HE'S WORKING.

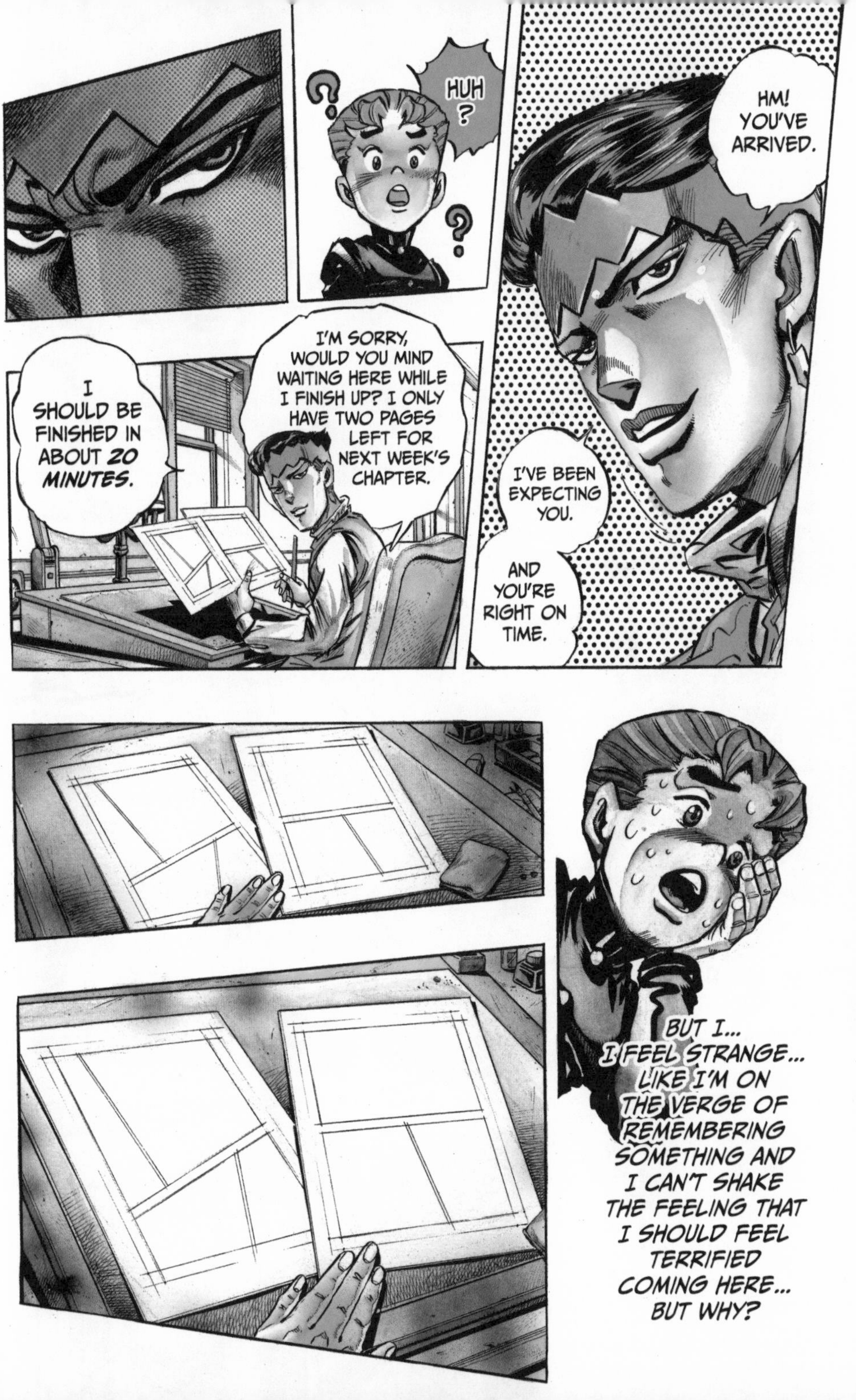
HM! YOU'VE ARRIVED.
I'VE BEEN EXPECTING YOU.
AND YOU'RE RIGHT ON TIME.
HUH?
I'M SORRY, WOULD YOU MIND WAITING HERE WHILE I FINISH UP? I ONLY HAVE TWO PAGES LEFT FOR NEXT WEEK'S CHAPTER.
I SHOULD BE FINISHED IN ABOUT 20 MINUTES.
BUT I... I FEEL STRANGE... LIKE I'M ON THE VERGE OF REMEMBERING SOMETHING AND I CAN'T SHAKE THE FEELING THAT I SHOULD FEEL TERRIFIED COMING HERE... BUT WHY?

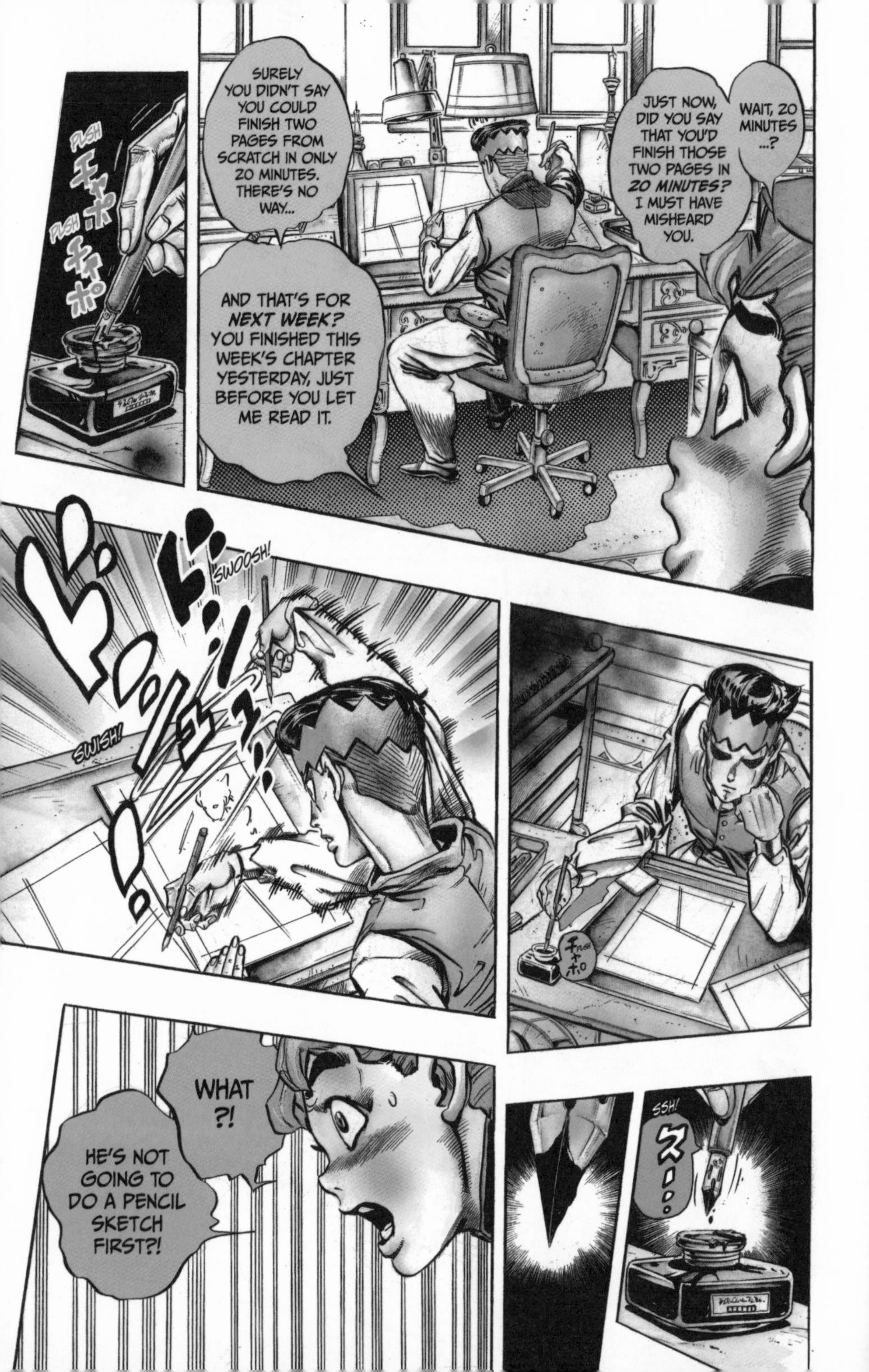
WAIT, 20 MINUTES ...?
JUST NOW, DID YOU SAY THAT YOU'D FINISH THOSE TWO PAGES IN *20 MINUTES?* I MUST HAVE MISHEARD YOU.
SURELY YOU DIDN'T SAY YOU COULD FINISH TWO PAGES FROM SCRATCH IN ONLY 20 MINUTES. THERE'S NO WAY...
AND THAT'S FOR *NEXT WEEK?* YOU FINISHED THIS WEEK'S CHAPTER YESTERDAY, JUST BEFORE YOU LET ME READ IT.
PUSH
PUSH
PUSH
SWOOSH!
SWISH!
SSH!
WHAT?!
HE'S NOT GOING TO DO A PENCIL SKETCH FIRST?!

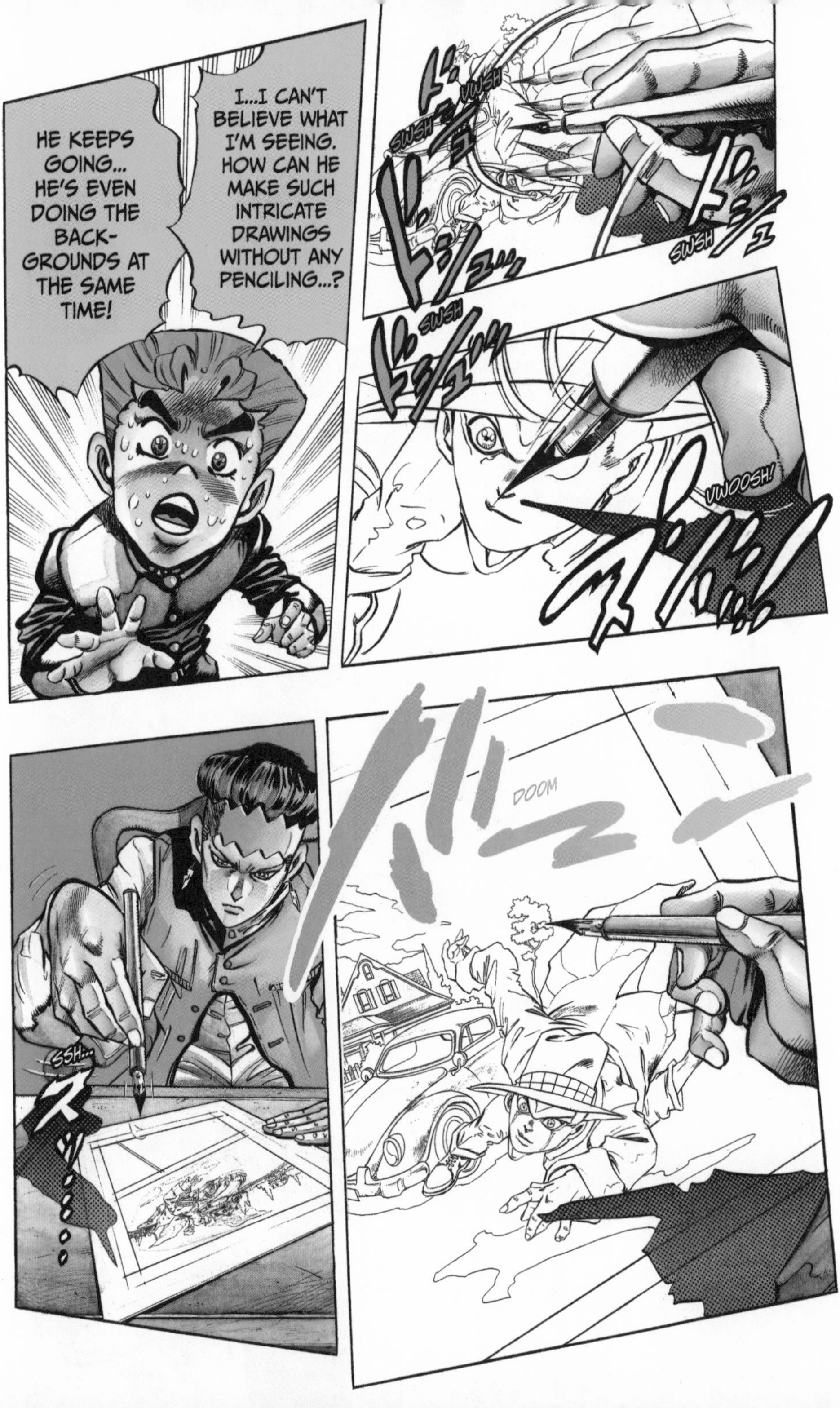
VWSH
SWSH
SWSH
SWSH
VWOOSH!
I...I CAN'T BELIEVE WHAT I'M SEEING. HOW CAN HE MAKE SUCH INTRICATE DRAWINGS WITHOUT ANY PENCILING...?
HE KEEPS GOING... HE'S EVEN DOING THE BACK-GROUNDS AT THE SAME TIME!
DOOM
SSH...

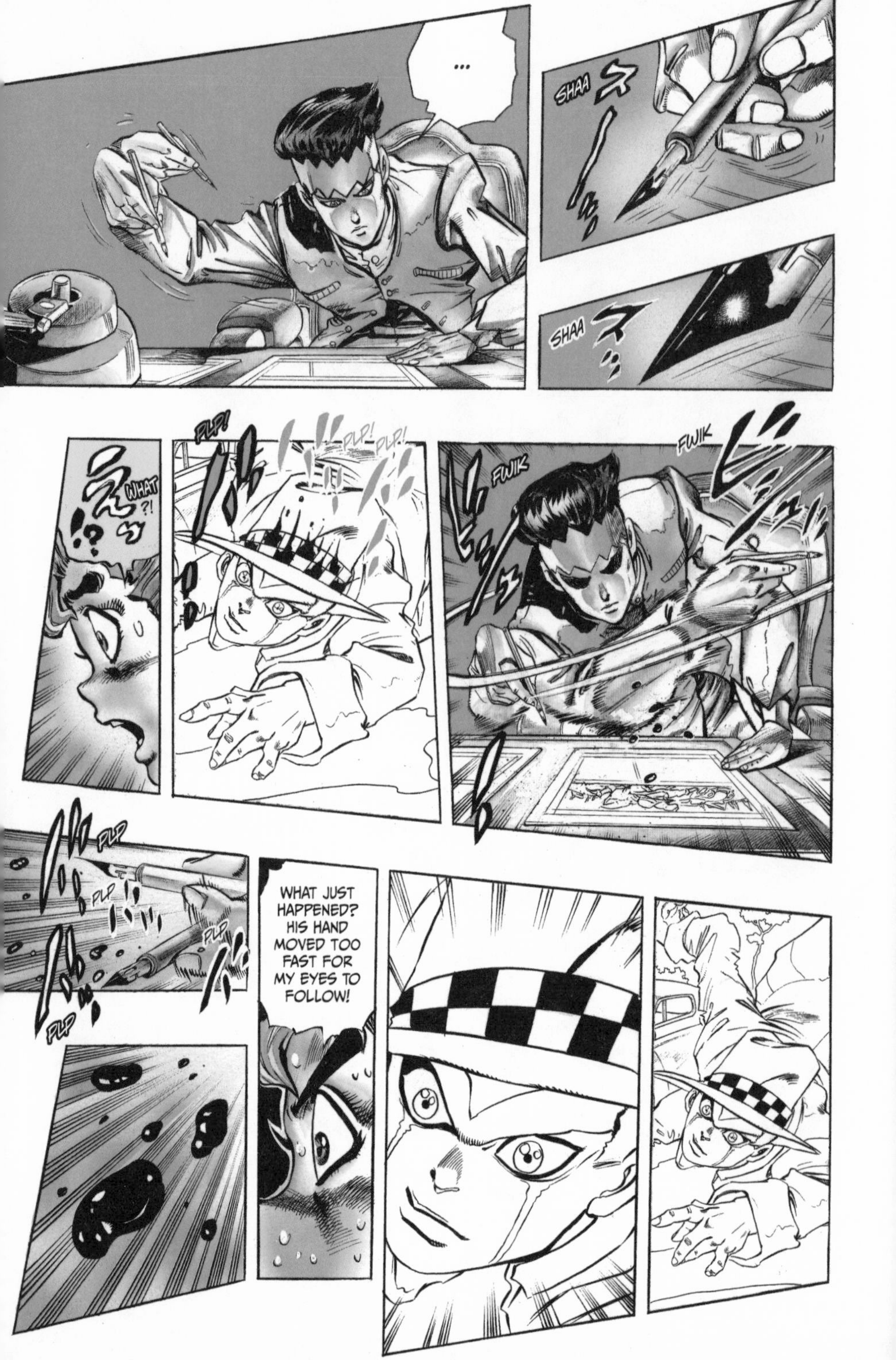
SHAA
SHAA
...
FWIK
FWIK
PLP!
PLP!
PLP!
WHAT ?!
WHAT JUST HAPPENED? HIS HAND MOVED TOO FAST FOR MY EYES TO FOLLOW!
PLP
PLP
PLP
PLP

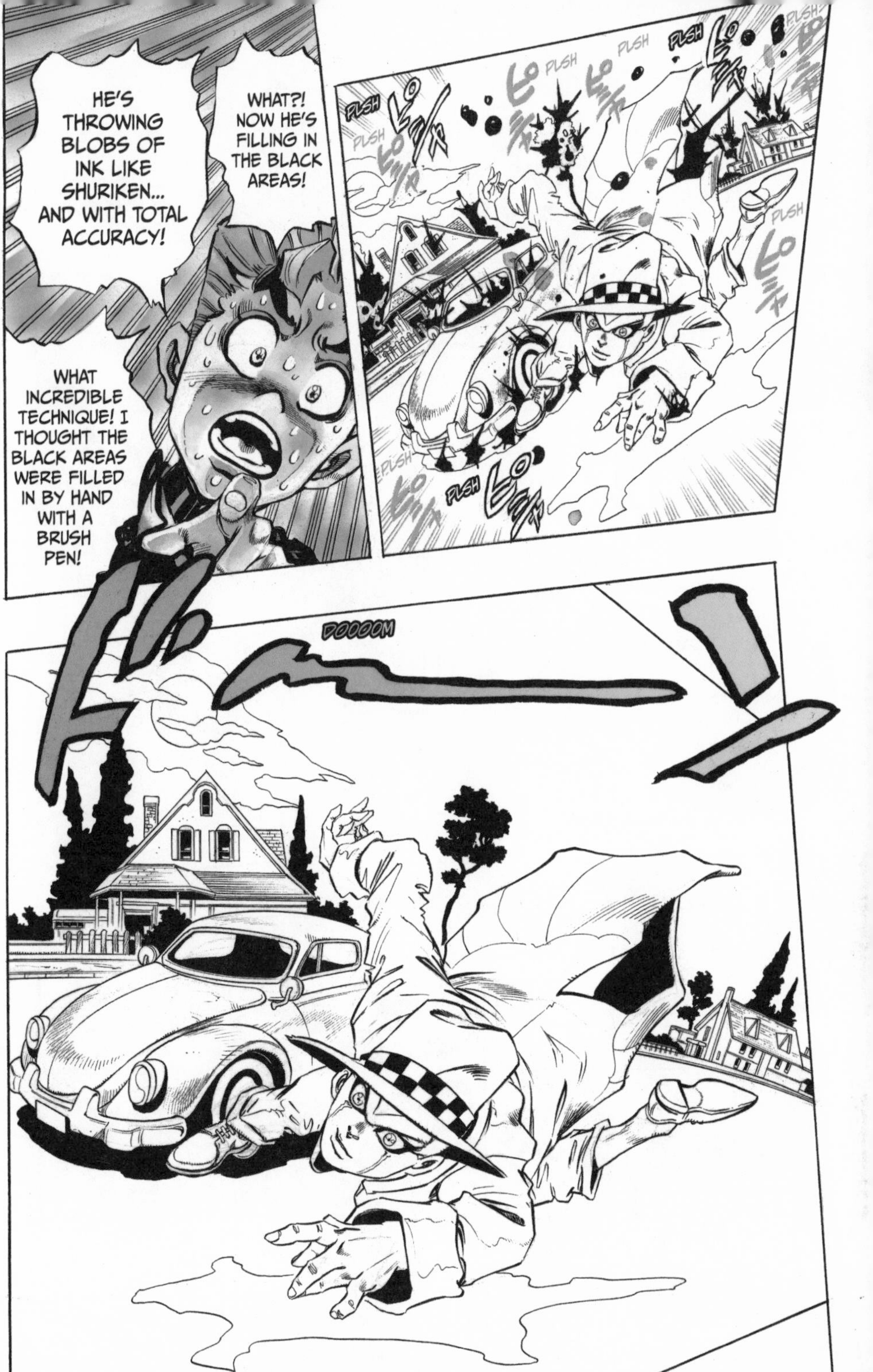
PLSH
PLSH
PLSH
PLSH
PLSH
PLSH
PLSH
PLSH
PLSH
WHAT?! NOW HE'S FILLING IN THE BLACK AREAS!
HE'S THROWING BLOBS OF INK LIKE SHURIKEN... AND WITH TOTAL ACCURACY!
WHAT INCREDIBLE TECHNIQUE! I THOUGHT THE BLACK AREAS WERE FILLED IN BY HAND WITH A BRUSH PEN!
DOOOOM

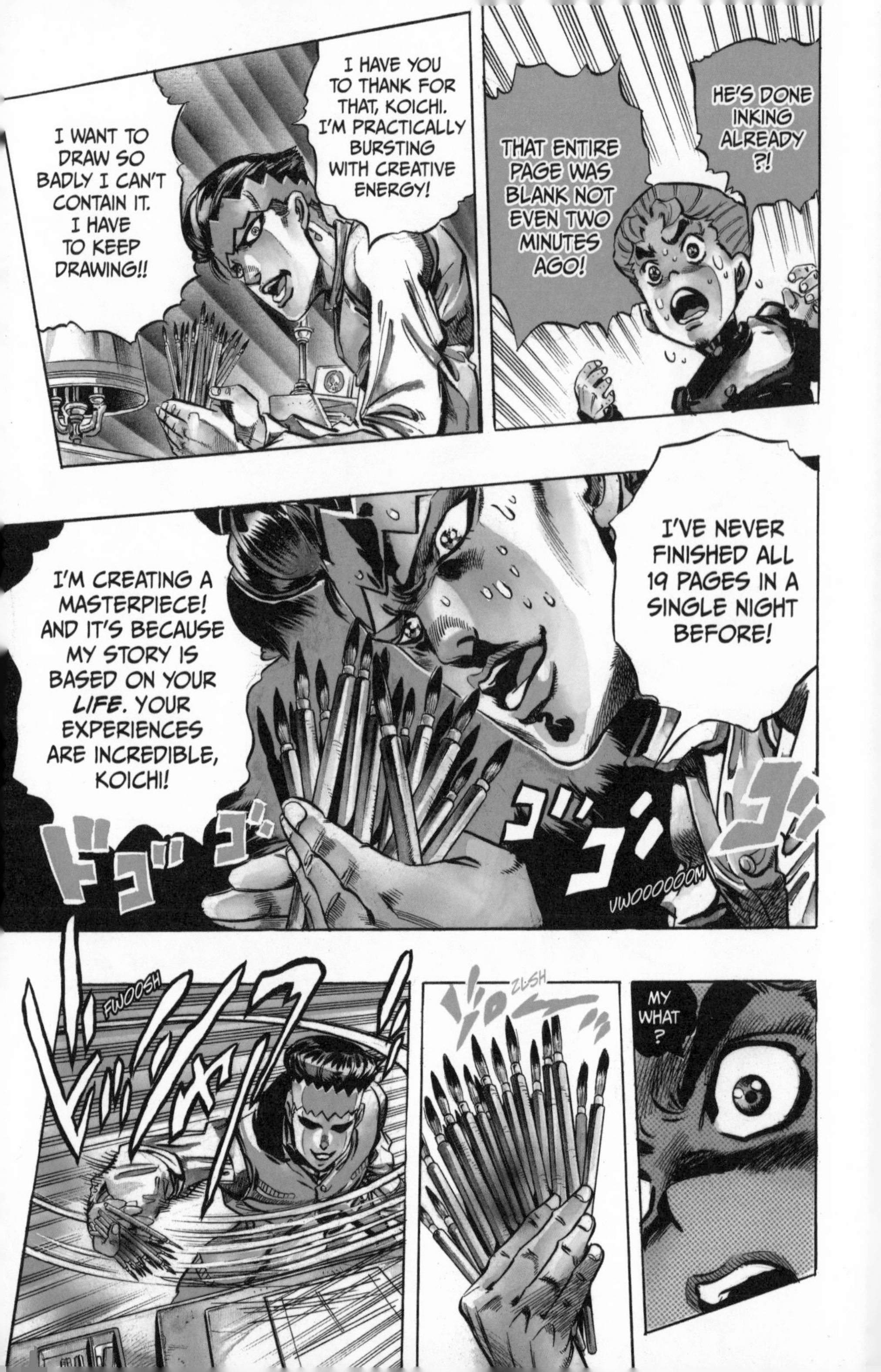
HE'S DONE INKING ALREADY ?!
THAT ENTIRE PAGE WAS BLANK NOT EVEN TWO MINUTES AGO!
I HAVE YOU TO THANK FOR THAT, KOICHI. I'M PRACTICALLY BURSTING WITH CREATIVE ENERGY!
I WANT TO DRAW SO BADLY I CAN'T CONTAIN IT. I HAVE TO KEEP DRAWING!!
I'VE NEVER FINISHED ALL 19 PAGES IN A SINGLE NIGHT BEFORE!
I'M CREATING A MASTERPIECE! AND IT'S BECAUSE MY STORY IS BASED ON YOUR *LIFE*. YOUR EXPERIENCES ARE INCREDIBLE, KOICHI!
VWOOOOOOM
MY WHAT ?
ZLISH
FWOOSH

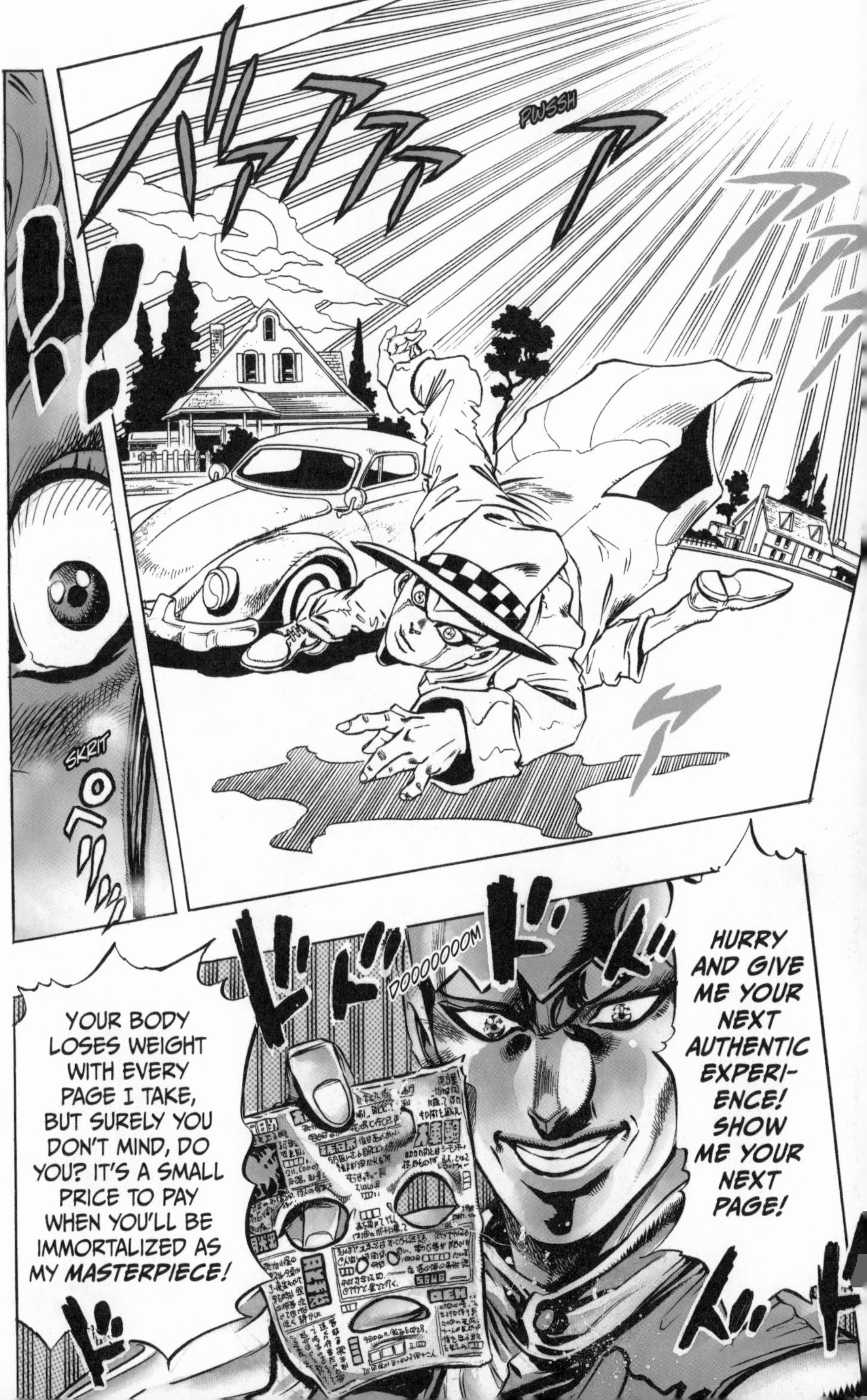
PWSSH
SKRIT
HURRY AND GIVE ME YOUR NEXT AUTHENTIC EXPERI-ENCE! SHOW ME YOUR NEXT PAGE!
DOOOOOOOOM
YOUR BODY LOSES WEIGHT WITH EVERY PAGE I TAKE, BUT SURELY YOU DON'T MIND, DO YOU? IT'S A SMALL PRICE TO PAY WHEN YOU'LL BE IMMORTALIZED AS MY *MASTERPIECE*!

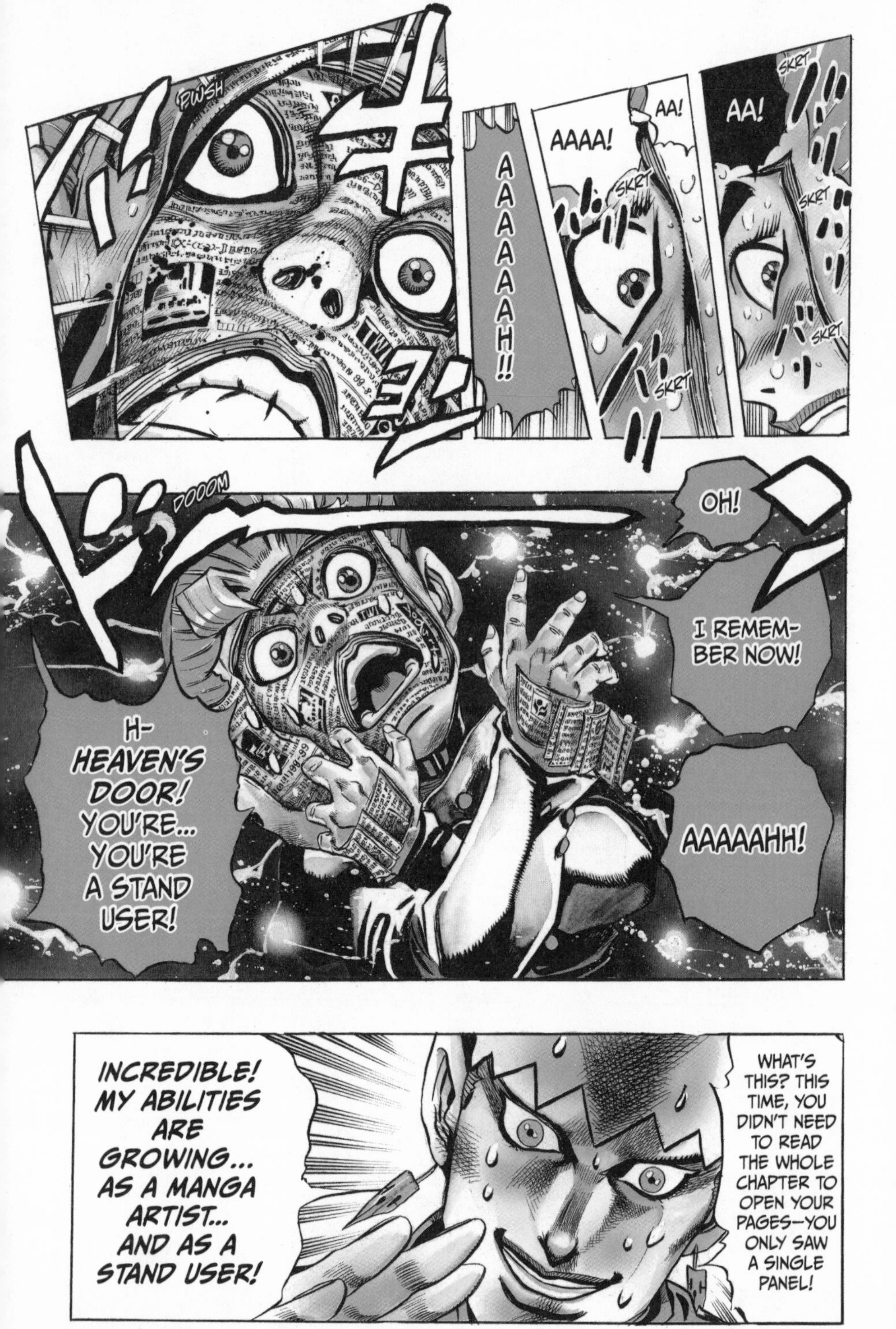
SKRT
AA!
SKRT
SKRT
AA!
AAAA!
SKRT
SKRT
AAAAAAAH!!
PWSH
DOOOM
OH!
I REMEM-
BER NOW!
AAAAAHH!
H-
HEAVEN'S
DOOR!
YOU'RE...
YOU'RE
A STAND
USER!
WHAT'S THIS? THIS TIME, YOU DIDN'T NEED TO READ THE WHOLE CHAPTER TO OPEN YOUR PAGES—YOU ONLY SAW A SINGLE PANEL!
INCREDIBLE! MY ABILITIES ARE GROWING... AS A MANGA ARTIST... AND AS A STAND USER!

PART 4, VOLUME 3 / END

AUTHOR'S COMMENTS

I've always thought of the Academy Awards as prestigious, but their selections are not always particularly entertaining movies. When Clint Eastwood's *Unforgiven* won Best Picture, I was as happy as if it were my own movie—so happy, in fact, that I couldn't sleep. I chortled in bed, even though Clint Eastwood was no acquaintance of mine, and I gained nothing personally from the prize. Why was I so happy? Fans are strange creatures.

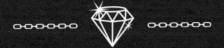

For 60 years, my father thought *yūbin-uke* (mailboxes) were called *yūbin-oke* (mail buckets). Surely across six decades he had many opportunities to realize his mistake, and it's a small miracle that he managed to persist despite the odds. As for myself, I watched the movie *The Day of the Jackal* dozens of times mistakenly thinking its title was *The Eye of the Jackal*, and up until only recently, I thought the manga *Dokaben* was called *Dokabeso*.

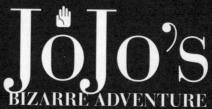

JoJo's

BIZARRE ADVENTURE

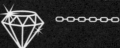

PART 4: DIAMOND IS UNBREAKABLE

VOLUME 3

BY HIROHIKO ARAKI

DELUXE HARDCOVER EDITION

Translation: Nathan A. Collins
Touch-Up Art & Lettering: Mark McMurray
Design: Adam Grano
Editor: David Brothers

Printed in the U.S.A.

Published by VIZ Media, LLC
P.O. Box 77010
San Francisco, CA 94107

10 9 8 7 6 5 4 3 2 1
First printing, November 2019

VIZ MEDIA

SHONEN JUMP

viz.com

shonenjump.com

THIS IS THE LAST PAGE

JoJo's BIZARRE ADVENTURE

has been printed in the original
Japanese format in order to preserve
the orientation of the original artwork.

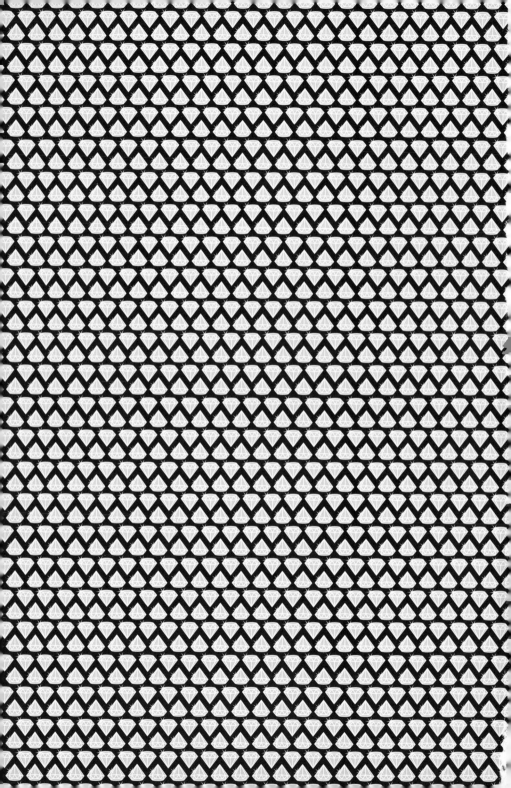

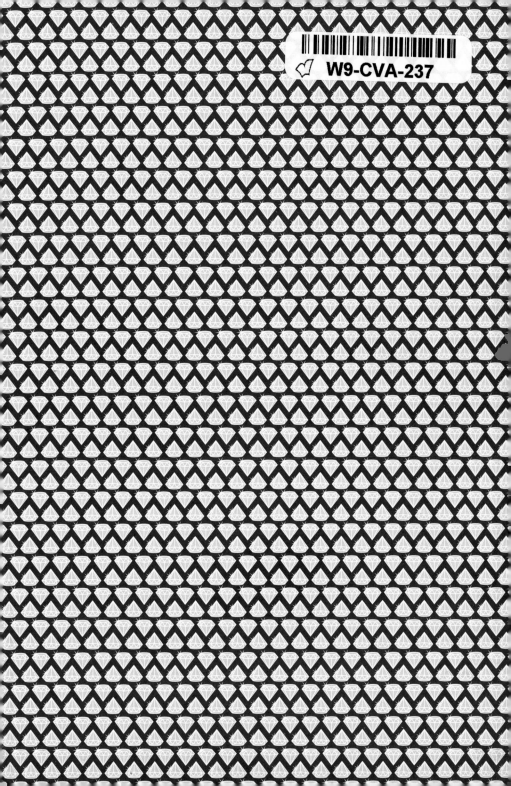